THEOLOGY

MORAL THEOLOGY

By

Rev. Heribert Jone, O.F.M. Cap., J.C.D.

Translated and Adapted to the Laws and Customs of
The United States of America by

Rev. Urban Adelman, O.F.M. Cap., J.C.D.

This edition of MORAL THEOLOGY is revised
in accordance with
THE EIGHTEENTH GERMAN EDITION.

TAN BOOKS AND PUBLISHERS, INC.
Rockford, Illinois 61105

Nihil Obstat: Pius Kaelin, O.F.M. Cap.
                     Censor Deputatus

Imprimi Potest: Giles Staab, O.F.M. Cap.
                     Provincial
                     November 30, 1961

Imprimatur: ✝ John J. Wright, D.D.
                     Bishop of Pittsburgh
                     December 8, 1961

The *Nihil Obstat* and *Imprimatur* are official declarations that a book or pamphlet is free of doctrinal or moral error. No implication is contained therein that those who have granted the *Nihil Obstat* and *Imprimatur* agree with the contents, opinions or statements expressed.

Copyright © 1961 by Ferdinand Schoeningh of Paderborn.

This book was photographically reproduced from the edition published by The Newman Press, Westminster, Maryland in 1962.

Moral Theologie has also been published in French, Italian, Polish, Dutch, Portuguese and Spanish, as well as in the original German.

ISBN: 0-89555-472-0

Library of Congress Catalog Card No.: 92-60957

Printed and bound in the United States of America.

TAN BOOKS AND PUBLISHERS, INC.
P.O. Box 424
Rockford, Illinois 61105
1993

PUBLISHER'S PREFACE

We are very pleased to bring back into print at this time Fr. Heribert Jone's *Moral Theology*. Written specifically as a handbook of moral theology for priests busy in the pastoral life, it serves beautifully also as a general reference for all, as well as a book the informed layman will be fascinated to peruse. The fact that this book went through 18 editions in German, as well as in its English translation, and was translated also into 7 other languages is ample testimony that it was accepted universally throughout the Catholic Church as authoritative and reliable.

The present printing was made from the 1962 edition—the last in English. Some may wonder why we would bring back to print a book of this vintage, since many changes have occurred in Church disciplinary law. The answer is simple: the merits of the book demand it. To the best of our knowledge, there is no other moral theology book in print today quite like it, and whereas certain disciplines have changed in the Church during the intervening 31 years, nonetheless, the general principles of morality—based on Natural Law and Revelation—remain exactly the same, as does the method of application of these principles to specific cases. Some Church disciplines have changed, yes, but most of us know what these are, and therefore the overriding majority of the book remains of vital use.

Jone's *Moral Theology* will surprise most readers with its comprehensiveness and authoritativeness, all in such a small book. Over 2,300 topics are covered in this "small" book, and it is fully indexed besides. Here is a book that is desperately needed today, for it is one that will end confusion on most matters of moral theology and will end as well the imagined need for guesswork and personal opinion on a host of topics that have been clearly settled long since.

May this book circulate far and wide and do all the good it is capable of doing. Especially, may priests everywhere once more consult it in their pastoral work, digest its contents and come to revere and love the divinely inspired morality of the Catholic faith, as yet one more gem of evidence pointing to the divine origin of our holy religion. And may they in turn share the principles contained in this book with their flocks and form them according to the traditional mind of the Church with regard to moral theology.

Thomas A. Nelson
April 28, 1993

PREFACE TO THE FIFTEENTH EDITION

The fact that this book is in its fifteenth edition and has appeared in various languages is evidence that it answers an urgent need. I will preface this edition with an answer to my critics on the purpose of this book.

Besides my work as professor, I have always engaged in a certain amount of pastoral work. Hence, I have learned from experience how important it is that one in the care of souls be able to judge correctly the sinful character of certain actions. A conscientious priest is always aware of the fact that, unless a matter be previously crystal clear to him, he stands in great danger of making a decision in keeping with his sentiments at the moment or according to a subjective opinion. To obviate this danger he generally has recourse to books. Most books, however, are so written that a reference to them is quite time-consuming, which a priest busy in pastoral work can ill afford. It was precisely to meet this situation that I undertook this work in the first place.

Although every action must be weighed subjectively, here are the means by which to judge an action objectively.... By saying that every action must be weighed subjectively, I mean that one must investigate in the first place whether there is a perfectly responsible human act present. Then, as far as merely human laws are concerned, he should inquire if there be an excuse from their observance, and whether or not one might use epikeia. The principles applicable in each individual case cannot be explained repeatedly in any work of Theology. These principles are briefly outlined in the book *First Principles*.

As the priest in pastoral work must have a knowledge of moral questions, so those preparing for the priesthood must learn them, too. Examinations belong to a seminary training, hence, this work should be helpful to students.

In our time, particularly in the areas of Catholic Action, there are those of the laity who—without always being obliged to approach a priest—have occasion to pass judgment on timely issues from a Catholic point of view. These, too, should find this work helpful.

It is understood that in Moral Theology statements are not only made, but substantiated. Reasons are often lacking in this book, else it would develop into such proportions as would defeat its primary purpose.

Moreover, Catholic Moral Theology should also be a study in virtue; but this, too, had to be omitted, since our aim is primarily to supply confessors with knowledge necessary to act as competent judges in the confessional.

I agree with all those who desire that the claims of Moral Theology be ever and always better grounded. Moreover, I am firmly convinced that Catholic Moral Theology should not rest satisfied merely to teach what is forbidden; but should also be a science of perfection.

Finally, it is my ardent desire that there will be many who will not be satisfied merely to criticize negatively and tell us how Theology *should* be written; but who will promote this study by constructive criticism and by writings of their own.

Stuehlingen, Germany   February 2, 1953

THE AUTHOR

TRANSLATOR'S NOTE

This edition is the eighteenth in English. Some editions have undergone more than one printing. The new eighteenth German edition is at hand. Very few additions and changes from the seventeenth have been noted. In only one instance did the author change his opinion. To be able to pray the Office with a companion, he now considers a sufficient reason for commuting one's Office (page 95). Reference to censures "l.s." is omitted from line 31 on page 294. A few decisions of the Holy Office are added. The new regulations concerning Holy Communion for the sick are incorporated in this edition.

State regulations concerning Marriage (698), Ethical Directives in Hospital Procedure (213), etc., remain a unique feature of the English version of this handbook.

What changes the forthcoming Council will necessitate remains to be seen; but in our next edition we hope to include a complete index of the Canons quoted in this work.

In addition to the English, French, Italian, Dutch, Portuguese and Spanish translations, one is being prepared in Arabic — further evidence of the work's popularity.

Pittsburgh, Pa.

Feast of the Annunciation
March 25, 1962

Fr. Urban S. Adelman, O.F.M. Cap.

ANALYTICAL INDEX

Book II. The Commandments

Book III. The Sacraments

Analytical Index

MORAL
THEOLOGY

INTRODUCTION

I. Concept of Moral Theology. Moral theology is the scientific exposition of human conduct so far as it is directed by reason and faith to the attainment of our supernatural final end.

In *contradistinction* to moral theology is ethics or moral philosophy which is based on human reason alone and recognizes only a natural end. Dogmatic theology treats of God, His essence and activity for the salvation of mankind. Ascetical theology is concerned with the attainment of Christian perfection. Mystical theology deals with the higher forms of contemplation and union with God. Pastoral theology is the science of the cure of souls. Finally, Canon Law regulates the external, ecclesiastical life of the members of the church.

2. II. Division of Moral Theology. Moral theology is divided into three parts: The doctrine on first principles, on the commandments and on the Sacraments.

First principles treat of the general conditions and qualities with which every action must be endowed in order that it may contribute to man's supernatural, ultimate end. The doctrine on the commandments has as its object those laws that man must observe to attain his end. The doctrine on the Sacraments treats of the divinely instituted means for reaching man's last end.

Book I

3.   FIRST PRINCIPLES

Man must attain to his last end by personal activity in conformity with the remote (objective) and proximate (subjective) norms of moral action, namely, law and conscience. — These norms are violated by sin; their observance is made easy by the virtues. — Thus the division of the doctrine on first principles is given.

Part I

PERSONAL ACTIVITY

Personal actions, by means of which man attains his supernatural end, must be human, morally good and supernaturally meritorious. — Since supernaturally meritorious acts are treated in dogmatic theology we are not concerned with them here.

Chapter I

HUMAN ACTS

Human acts (actus humani) are those actions that proceed from knowledge and free will (writing).

Human acts are to be distinguished from the *acts of man* (actus hominis), i.e., those acts of human beings that are not dependent upon knowledge and free will (breathing).

4.   *Article I*

Principles of Human Acts

I. The knowledge must embrace:

1. *The action itself.*

The so-called "motus primo primi" are not human acts and consequently have no moral character, e.g., thoughts, imaginations and tendencies which are elicited by the intellectual or volitional faculties of man before he becomes aware of them, e.g., an impulse of anger, aversion, etc.

5. — 2. *The object of the action* with all its proximate circumstances.

An action is human, and, therefore, good or bad, only in so far as its object is known. If one kills another knowing him to be his father, he is guilty of patricide. If he thinks his victim is a stranger he is guilty of homicide. If he believes it is an animal which he may lawfully hunt, he commits no sin at all.

6. — 3. *The possibility* of not acting or of acting otherwise.

Only when this possibility is recognized can there be free consent of the will, without which neither good nor evil deeds are imputable.

II. The free consent of the will may be:

7. — 1. *A perfectly or an imperfectly voluntary act* according as something is willed with full knowledge and full consent or only with imperfect knowledge and imperfect consent.

Thus an imperfectly voluntary act is one performed in semi-wakefulness, partial intoxication or during a violent fit of passion.

8. — 2. *An actually or virtually voluntary act* according as the consent of the will is actually present to the consciousness of the agent or endures only in its effects without his being conscious thereof.

An actually voluntary act is had, e.g., when one is conscious of the fact that he is now baptizing. A virtually voluntary act is had if one, having the intention to baptize, goes to the font, but in the act of baptizing is so distracted that he no longer realizes what he is doing.

The *habitually* and *interpretatively* voluntary acts differ from the foregoing. An habitually voluntary act is one that was at one time an actually voluntary act but, although not revoked, nevertheless does not continue in itself nor in its effect and, therefore, does not influence the resultant action, e.g., the conferring of a Sacrament; but which is nevertheless sufficient, that an effect be produced upon one, e.g., the reception of a Sacrament. — An interpretatively voluntary act is one that never existed, but which would exist if the person acting had the necessary knowledge. It is insufficient even for the reception of a Sacrament.

9. — 3. *A directly or indirectly voluntary act* (voluntarium in se vel in causa) according as something is willed in itself or is not willed in itself, but only permitted because of its inseparable connection with some action or omission.

That likewise is willed "in itself" which is only willed as a means, e.g., the death of the foetus to save the mother.

10.   *Article II*

Imputability of Human Acts

The *imputability* of a human act consists in this that one may be declared the free author of an action and its consequences and may be held responsible for the same.

Since we must positively will the good and avoid the evil, imputability differs according as there is question of a directly or an indirectly voluntary act.

11. — I. **The directly voluntary act** (voluntarium in se) is always imputed to the agent as either good or bad.

12. — II. **An indirectly voluntary act** (voluntarium in causa) is never ascribed to the agent if it concerns a good effect, but in many cases it is imputed to him if the effect is bad.

13. — 1. The *imputability* of a bad effect requires:

a) That the effect be *foreseen* at least in a confused way.

Intoxication is, therefore, not imputed to him who is ignorant of the strength of the wine he takes, or at least does not think of it.

b) That it be *in the power* of the agent to omit the action or at least to render it ineffective.

Therefore, if one has, culpably or not, contracted a bad habit, e.g., of cursing, and makes earnest efforts to rid himself of the habit, the indeliberate acts of cursing which may occur in spite of those efforts, are not attributed to him as sins. — Should such a person make only insufficient efforts to avoid them, he would in this case be guilty of venial sin. — If he makes no effort at all, he would be guilty of a grave sin, not, however, each individual time he curses, but at that moment when, realizing his duty to rid himself of the bad habit, he makes no corresponding effort to do so.

c) That there be an *obligation to omit the action* in order that the effect may not follow.

For further details confer the following number.

If the foregoing conditions required for the imputability of an evil effect are verified the sin is committed at the moment when the cause is posited. One is guilty of sin even if the cause accidentally fails to produce its effect.

14. — 2. *Undertaking an act* that has an *evil effect* is lawful only if the following four conditions are simultaneously verified.

a) The action itself must be *good* or at least morally *indifferent*.

b) A good effect must follow from the action at least *as immediately as* the evil effect.

Hence, this rule is sometimes referred to as the "principle of double effect." Should the good effect only follow by means of the evil effect, then evidently this latter must first be willed as an evil means, which cannot be justified by a good end. (Cf. 42). — Therefore, an unmarried mother may not procure abortion to avoid disgrace. On the other hand it is lawful for a pregnant woman to take medicine which is necessary for her health even though this medicine should cause an abortion. Likewise, one may attend a sick person even though this may cause one sexual temptations.

c) The *intention* must be directed to the good effect exclusively.

If therefore the good effect can be obtained by means that have no evil effect such means must be preferred.

d) There must be a *sufficient reason* to permit the evil effect.

The reason must be in proportion to the malice of the evil effect, to the certainty of its following, to the immediacy with which it will follow and to the gravity of the agent's personal obligation (e.g., piety, contract) to avoid the evil effect, and also to the probability that the evil effect would not follow if the action were omitted, e.g., if the only saloon keeper in town refuses to give a toper drink the latter will not become intoxicated.

15.   *Article III*

Obstacles to Human Acts

An obstacle to human activity is anything that impairs either knowledge or free will. In proportion to the hindrance, imputability may be diminished or it may be wanting altogether.

I. Ignorance. 1. *Concept*. By ignorance is here meant the lack of necessary knowledge.

What is said of ignorance holds also for *error*, which is a false judgment about something; and for *inadvertence* which is had when one knows a thing quite well, but for the moment does not think of it. — False notions about religious or moral matters, as well as prejudices do not in themselves differ from error.

16. — 2. *Division*. Ignorance may be divided into:

a) Ignorance of *law* or of *fact* (juris vel facti) according as the law itself or some fact is not known.

b) Ignorance that is *antecedent, consequent* or *concomitant*.

Ignorance is antecedent if it is not willed and if it precedes the free consent of the will. It matters not whether the ignorance exercises an influence on an action, so that the action would not have taken place if the necessary knowledge had been present (antecedent in the strict sense) or whether it has no such influence on the action, so that the action would have taken place even if there had been no such ignorance (concomitant ignorance).

Consequent ignorance is willed either directly or indirectly, proceeding thus from the free will.

c) Ignorance that is *vincible* or *invincible*.

Ignorance is called vincible if it can be dispelled by moral diligence in keeping with the proximate circumstances of the person and object. If the use of such means is insufficient to remove the ignorance it is called invincible. — According to the greater or lesser degree of negligence of which one is guilty, vincible ignorance may be *simply vincible, crass* or *supine.* If one deliberately wills to remain ignorant, his vincible ignorance is *affected.* (Cf. 425).

17. — 3. *Influence* of ignorance on the will and consequently on moral imputability.

a) Invincible ignorance destroys the voluntariness of an act and also its sinfulness.

If one eats meat on Friday, being firmly convinced that it is Thursday, he does not sin. Hence anxiety regarding actions one did years ago, not knowing their sinful character, is unreasonable.

b) Vincible ignorance (except it be affected) diminishes the voluntariness of an act and its sinfulness.

Unless one's blameworthy negligence is insignificant, his vincible ignorance does not diminish liberty to the extent that a gravely sinful action becomes only venially sinful. — The *gravity* of the sin is determined by the degree of culpable negligence, not by the effects that follow such negligence. The worse these effects are foreseen to be, the greater must be the effort made to avoid them.

18. — **II. Violence. 1.** *Concept.* Violence is force brought to bear upon one against his will by some extrinsic agent.

When *absolute* violence is used the will resists as best it can. *Relative* violence is that which can be overcome by greater opposition, but the extra effort is either not made or sufficient resistance is offered only externally while internal consent is being given.

19. — 2. *Influence* on Imputability.

a) Absolute violence destroys free will. Therefore, whatever is done under its influence is not imputable.

External resistance is necessary if the force can be repelled or if scandal or the danger of consent should result from non-resistance. If one is certain he will not consent he may omit external resistance if this is very difficult or dangerous.

b) *Relative violence* diminishes free will and consequently imputability.

20. — III. Fear. 1. *Concept.* Fear is mental anxiety because of an impending evil.

We are here considering the influence which an evil exercises on the mind. Apart from this an evil often greatly influences the sensitive faculty. (Cf. 23.) The evil may threaten him who fears, or his relatives, friends, etc.

21. — 2. *Division.* Fear may be:

a) *Grave* or *slight* according as to whether one is threatened by a grave evil which one cannot easily escape; or only by a slight one, or even by a great evil which one can easily avoid. (Cf. 723 sqq.)

Fear is absolutely or relatively grave according as it exercises a great influence upon the average person or only upon a particular person, e.g., because of his timidity. — *Reverential fear* consists in this, that a subject fears to oppose someone to whom he is obliged to show reverence. If by this kind of fear one understands the dislike one experiences in offending some respectable person it is only a slight fear. If because of such opposition one must expect vexation, perpetual disfavor, etc., reverential fear may also be grave.

b) *Extrinsic* or *intrinsic* according as its cause is external or internal.

Fear of death because of the imminent danger of shipwreck is extrinsic; fear of death from a disease is intrinsic. — If extrinsic fear is caused by some free agent it will be *just* or *unjust* according as the person causing it is justified in so doing or not.

22. — 3. *Influence* of fear on imputability. Fear does not destroy the voluntary character of our actions; but it usually lessens their guilt as also their merit. They are simply voluntary but also involuntary in a certain regard.

Fear makes one will what otherwise he would not will. If, under the influence of fear, one consents to the good or bad act with resistance, its merits or guilt is thereby lessened. It is to be noted, however, that the obligation of the positive law sometimes ceases on account of great inconvenience. (Cf. 56.) Similarly, laws often invalidate actions that have been posited through great fear or they make such actions rescindable at the instance of him who was influenced by fear. Fear which influences the sensitive appetite may, by this very fact, affect imputability in the same manner as does passion. (Cf. 25.)

23. — IV. Concupiscence. 1. Concept. Concupiscence or passion is a movement of the sensitive appetite which is produced by good or evil as apprehended by the imagination.

24. — 2. *Division.* Concupiscence is:

a) Antecedent when it precedes the action of the will and induces the will to consent.

This takes place, for example, in involuntary movements of hatred, anger and of the sexual appetite.

b) Consequent, if it follows the free determination of the will and is either freely consented to or deliberately aroused.

Concupiscence is deliberately aroused if one consciously fosters motions that arise of their own accord, or if one purposely stimulates his passions, e.g., by reading immoral literature or by reflecting upon injuries received.

25. — 3. *Influence* on Imputability.

a) Antecedent concupiscence always lessens imputability and at times even destroys it entirely according as one is hindered in the use of his reason or completely deprived thereof by passion.

A grave sin may nevertheless be committed even though imputability is lessened. Moreover the passion is generally willed indirectly, either because one exposes himself to danger without adequate reason or because he does not resist his passionate disposition in spite of a clear knowledge of his obligation in that regard. — Practically it is often difficult to determine whether the diminution of imputability is sufficient to excuse one from grave sin or not. In such cases one must leave the judgment to God.

b) *Consequent* passion never lessens imputability, but generally increases it.

The increase of imputability is due to the fact that the sensitive movement is purposely intensified by consequent concupiscence so that the good or evil is willed more intensely.

26. — V. Habit is a facility and a readiness of acting in a certain manner acquired by repeated acts.

Some habits effect an organic change in the human organism (habits of drink, impurity, etc.); others have no such effect.

27. — 1. *Division*. Habits are *natural* or *moral*.

Natural habits are those contracted without advertence to their effects in the moral sphere; or at least they persist against the will. Moral habits are those that are either freely contracted or consciously maintained.

28. — 2. *Influence* on Imputability.

a) Whoever *strives earnestly* to rid himself of a bad habit does not sin in doing the evil deed by force of habit without advertence to its sinful character.

b) Whoever does *not strive earnestly* to break himself of a bad habit, although he adverts to his obligation of so doing, sins *every time* he adverts to this. He does not sin, however, at the moment he acts by force of a neglected habit, if he does so without adverting to the sinful character of his action.

Such a sin is indirectly willed, i.e., voluntary in cause (Cf. 13).

29. — VI. Nervous mental diseases are disorders of the brain and nervous system, involving a sympathetic influence on the mind and will.

Functional diseases are such as manifest themselves by disturbances in the operation of the organs, without apparent pathological change in the organs themselves. — Organic nervous diseases are those in which some pathological affection of the nerve substance itself is noticeable, for instance, in softening of the brain.

30. — 1. *Specific Mental Disturbances.*

a) Neurasthenia is a permanent condition of abnormal irritability of the nervous system, associated with a tendency to premature exhaustion.

Neurasthenics are affected by external stimuli and by internal exhaustion much more intensely than the objective state of things would warrant. Hence they imagine themselves to be afflicted with various kinds of illnesses, although in reality they are bodily sound. Furthermore, their depressed disposition brings on a disturbance in the activity of their will; influenced by a feeling of dissatisfaction, the will loses the power to come to a decision (abulia), or to carry out its decision (anenergia).

31. *b) Hysteria* consists in a pathological irritability by virtue of which psychic experiences can, in a blindly impulsive way, react with abnormal intensity on exterior behavior and on various forms of physical expression.

Hysterics either react with abnormal vehemence, or they do not react at all, or, at most, only mildly, even to the strongest stimuli. Combined with this condition we also find anomalies of the emotional life. — Most striking in hysterics is their affective irritability; uncontrolled outbursts of anger are followed by happy abandon and exuberance of spirit; egotism is strongly developed in them, likewise a mania for attracting attention, and self-assertiveness. Combined with all this there is a strong propensity to lying and stealing, and to moral dissipation. — Extreme caution must always be exercised by the priest in his relations with hysterics.

32. *c) Compulsion phenomena* are psychic factors, which do not admit of normal repression by volitional influences, so that a man may be compelled to think or to act in a certain way.

There are compulsive memory images, **compulsive feelings,** compulsive observations, compulsive fears, **compulsive doubts,** compulsive actions, etc. Under this heading we must also group the various manias, e.g., kleptomania; also all irresistible urges.

33. *b) Hypochondria* is a pathological state arising from depressive common human feelings and organic sensations, combined with exaggerated anxiety concerning the meaning of these phenomena.

Hypochondriacs imagine themselves the victims of every possible disease. They examine their feces for tapeworms, their phlegm for tuberculosis; urinary sediment they take to be kidney stones; their taste buds, cancerous growths; every harmless skin affection is syphilis; an oppressive feeling in the head is an indication of softening of the brain, etc. In the more degenerate forms of hypochondria, the patient makes even more fantastic discoveries: there is a frog in his stomach; he has no bowels or no brains, etc. All this gives rise to a state of anxiety; the patient becomes alarmed, he suffers convulsions and develops a propensity to suicide.

34. *e) Melancholia* is a permanent state of despondency, growing out of the fact that the emotional tone attending all perception assumes a depressive character at the slightest stimulation, while with normal people it becomes so only when the stimulation has reached a certain high degree of intensity.

Morbid melancholia must not be confused with the melancholy temperament. Such patients are incapable of joy, for every fresh impression brings on a pang of sadness. Even words of solace, and especially any attempt to cheer them up, are but as wormwood to their spirit. Add to this that the process of mental presentation is slowed down and becomes impeded. The associative mental power breaks down, memory fails to function properly. — The will encounters resistance from numerous quarters, and finds it hard to make decisions, and even harder to put them into execution. — Sometimes there are neither feelings of pleasure nor pain; complete lack of all mental sensibility manifests itself. Such patients complain of inner desolation, of inability to love those of their own family circle, of incapacity for prayer or contrition. — Their inhibitions can become so great that all bodily activity ceases. — But it may also happen that the feelings of fear and anxiety attendant upon melancholia may impel patients to wander about restlessly, to bite at their nails, to tear at their hair, to sigh and moan and groan, to scream to the point of frenzy. — Then they begin to labor under delusions, for instance, that they are leading a wicked, impious life, or that they have led such a life. Often they become hypochondriacs. They may also be haunted by hallucinations and illusions: they see the devil, they hear threatening voices, etc. They are very prone to suicide; they look upon death either as a liberation from fear and anxiety, or as an expiation for sin. These sudden impulsive ideas assert themselves in their minds so forcibly as to displace all contrary ideas. Usually they are able to conceal their thoughts of suicide. The more advanced melancholics, moreover, are pronounced mental cases.

35. *f) Psychopathic inferiority* is a permanent state of intellectual and moral infirmity.

Though the intelligence rating of some few psychopaths may be surprisingly high, still there will always be some element of eccentricity about them. — But generally their intelligence is decidedly inferior. In their criminal acts such individuals neglect even the most ordinary considerations of prudence and allow others to use them for the most dangerous undertakings. — Besides, their affections cloud their judgment; punishments they deem spite work; juridical decisions are the result of prejudice. For this reason it is so difficult to educate these psychopaths. — And since they lack the power of prolonged concentration, their recollections become indistinct and their memory fails them. Should, however, their fancy be vividly aroused and auto-suggestion ensue, memory illusions will develop, to which they cling tenaciously. Quite often, too, they are guilty of intentional lying. — The will lacks strength and stability; decisions are made on the spur of the moment. — The emotional life suffers even greater disturbance. The affective life may be highly tensioned, manifested, for example, by a very irascible temperament. But they may also evince a blunted affective life, combined with great apathy and absolute inactivity. Cross egotism may be found side by side with tenderness of feeling, scrupulosity with laxity, coarseness with sentimentality, etc. — Most psychopathic patients tend towards moral degeneracy. They do, indeed, have a knowledge of good and evil, but they lack moral sentiments. They scarcely ever experience the emotions of sympathy, of gratitude, of love, of contrition, of courtesy, of propriety; they lack all susceptibility for praise or blame. Their interests are all selfish and limited to sense enjoyment. Hence they show no consideration whatever for their environment or their family, they are devoid of shame and altogether unrestrained and careless.

36. — 2. *Imputability* is destroyed to the extent that certain ideas and fancies so take possession of their mind, that it cannot at all or only with great difficulty give attention to other considerations; consequently, freedom of choice is either altogether impeded or at least greatly diminished.

The *reason* why certain ideas take complete possession of their mind in this way may lie in this, that they are so overpowering as to dislodge all other ideas from consciousness altogether or almost so; or it may be that other ideas do not emerge into consciousness or do so only in a passing, fleeting way.

The feeble-minded person, for instance, who sets fire to a barn, will often think only of the delight that the fire will afford him, but not of the damage or the sinfulness connected with his act. — The morbidly melancholy person often is aware only of his evil forebodings, and suicide seems to him to be the only way out. Ethical objections do not even present themselves for the moment. — Ethical considerations do come to the mind of the unstable, morbidly fickle character at the time of temptation, but often, they are brushed aside by other ideas before they can exercise their influence. — In a man devoid of feeling, a brutal act will scarcely arouse any reaction at all; hence he does not adjudge such acts so bad as they really are. — In the self-assertive and fantastic psychopath anything that subserves the glorification of self or the realization of his own ideas, becomes his sole interest, crowding out all other considerations. — In the morbidly irritable person the affections, e.g., of anger or fear, may become so intense, that only the idea corresponding to the affection may be present in his mind, and this he proceeds to execute without any further deliberation. — The abulic psychopath often does not come to a decision (abulia) or to the execution of a decision (anenergia), because the respective obligation does not sufficiently impress itself upon his consciousness. The reason for this is either that for want of energy the obligation to decide or to act is only dimly emphasized by the emotions, or that feelings of aversion towards doing so have taken complete possession of consciousness.

37. In the individual case it will be very difficult to determine *to what extent* freedom of choice and hence responsibility are nullified. In most instances this must be left to the judgment of God. — The confessor should be very mild in his judgment of these psychopathic penitents. As a rule, however, it will not be in place to assure them outright that under the given circumstances they no longer sin, for in a specific case this could hardly be determined;

moreover, there is also the danger that the penitent might give up all efforts at restraining his evil inclinations. If these penitents have been guilty of an objectively grave sinful action they should ordinarily not be allowed to receive Holy Communion without previous confession. But because a doubt as to the gravity of their sin will usually persist, the confessor may in certain cases more readily presume that opportunity for confession was not present because of a dearth of confessors. (Cf. 504.) — Diseased penitents may, even when clear insight is present, be excused from positive obligations, especially those arising out of the Commandments of the Church. (Cf. 56.)

Compulsion ideas, however (blasphemous thoughts, for instance), and compulsion affects arise entirely independently of the will and persist against the will, and are, therefore, not sinful. This must absolutely be made clear to the penitents if they are accustomed to consider the very presence of such thoughts sinful, even though they indignantly repulse them. Often, too, such penitents will confess that they consented to impure feelings, mistaking the natural pleasurable sensations for consent. — It may sometimes be more difficult to diagnose compulsion, when there is question of matters in which even normal people have inordinate inclinations. In such cases there may be danger of self-deception. However, it is possible that for the moment violent impulses may, with or without previous struggle, overwhelm all rational reflection and impel to blind action; thus the act is performed without, or at least almost without deliberation, and hence, there is no sin at all or at most a venial sin. Actions which are performed with a clear realization that one could also, and indeed should, act otherwise, will be grievously or venially sinful according to the concrete circumstances.

Compulsory representations may be aggravated by the very fact that an attitude of anxiety and fear is developed towards them and that desperate efforts are made to avoid them; for in this wise the attention is concentrated upon them. In such cases the patients do best to disregard such phenomena altogether. Then, too, since examination of conscience and confession but serve to draw detailed attention anew to such thoughts, thus aggravating the temptation, these patients are often excused from making a detailed examination of conscience and a complete confession. (Cf. 568.) It would be best for these patients always to return to the same confessor. If they have agreed to do that, the confessor may allow the first confession to be a detailed manifestation of their whole case. In subsequent confessions, however, he should allow only general accusations, as for instance: "I accuse myself of my sins against faith, against holy purity, etc., in the manner in which I first confessed them to you." If doubt and fear become very intensified, it is only right that these patients be told that in their condition they can hardly commit a mortal sin, although they must, of course, resist their evil inclinations.

If the act corresponding to the compulsion is not evil in itself, but constitutes only an occasion of sin, etc., the compulsion may often be got rid of by performing the act to which the person is impelled. For the purpose of effecting a cure it is perfectly permissible for a patient to expose himself to such an occasion. But since the end does not justify the means, one cannot, even in the interests of a cure, allow these patients to perform actions which are evil in themselves; and this applies also to those patients, who, because of their diseased condition, are no longer fully responsible for their actions. — At times a scrupulous conscience (Cf. 86) is associated with compulsory representations. (Cf. *Nervous Mental Diseases and their Pastoral Treatment*, Schulte-Tschippert. G. Coldwell, London.)

38. Chapter II

MORAL ACTS

I. Concept. A moral act is an act done freely and with advertence to its relation to the norm of morality.

The *ultimate norm* of morality is the eternal law of God determining the essence, acts and ends of all things according to their moral values. The *proximate norm* of morality is the human mind in as far as it recognizes the eternal law and applies it in individual instances (conscience). An act is morally good or morally bad according as it agrees or disagrees with the norm of morality. It is controverted whether there can be morally *indifferent acts* in the concrete.

39. — II. The Principles of morality or the determinants of the moral act are all those elements of human conduct that have a bearing upon the norm of morality, namely, the object, circumstances and end.

That an action be morally good none of these elements may conflict with the norm of morality.

40. — 1. The *object* is the thing with which an action is essentially concerned, e.g., taking another's goods in an act of stealing.

The object of an action may be good, bad or indifferent.

41. — 2. The *circumstances* are those proximate conditions that help to determine the moral nature of a human act; they stand in relation to it as accidents to the substance.

Circumstances may concern the object, the agent, or the action itself, e.g., the theft of a sacred object, ill-treatment of one's mother, long-standing enmity. — Circumstances may make a good action a bad one, a venial sin a mortal sin, or vice versa. They may also add a new goodness or badness to an action.

An external act probably takes its entire moral value from the interior disposition and, therefore, in itself has no influence on the goodness or badness of the action. Accidentally, however, it generally does influence the moral value of an action, since by it the inner act is often repeated, is of longer duration and gains added intensity, and also because the external act may serve to either edify or scandalize others.

42. — 3. The *end* or motive is the reason for which the agent undertakes an act.

If the motive is *morally sinful,* the whole action is bad, no matter whether the end is a unique end or whether other aims are associated with it. — If the end is *venially sinful,* the whole action is venially sinful if the agent has no other end in view. If, however, besides the bad end good ends are also intended, the action is partly good and partly venially sinful, e.g., if one gives alms partly out of charity and partly because of vanity. — *A good motive* imparts additional moral goodness to a good act; but it never takes away the badness from an evil act; therefore, the end does not justify the means.

PART II

43.   ## THE LAW

The supreme objective norm of morality is the *eternal law*, i.e., God's Divine Plan by which all created things are directed from all eternity to one supreme end and aim. God has in time made known His Divine Will through the *natural moral law* and the *positive divine law*. He also makes known His Will mediately through *human laws* which may be enacted by the Church or State.

Chapter I

LAW AND COGNATE CONCEPTS

Customs, precepts and privileges have many things in common with law.

I. A law is a permanent, rational norm for free activity enacted and adequately promulgated by the superior of a public community for the sake of the common welfare.

1. *Common welfare* demands that a law be just, morally good, possible of observance, and necessary for, or at least conducive to the common good.

A law that falls short of these qualifications does not serve the common welfare and, therefore, has no binding force.

44. — 2. *Promulgation* is necessary in order that a law may actually oblige its subjects.

Laws of the *Holy See* are usually promulgated in the *Acta Apostolicae Sedis*. Their obligation begins three months after the publishing date of the issue in which they appear, unless the nature of the matter demands immediate observance, or if it is expressly stated otherwise in the law (C. 9). *Bishops* determine the manner of promulgating episcopal laws, which, unless otherwise specified, oblige from the moment of their promulgation (C. 335).

45. — **II. Custom** or legalized usage is a right which has been introduced with consent of the competent authority by the majority of the members of a public community through their frequent, public, fully deliberate and continued manner of acting.

While that which is enacted by a law is determined by the lawgiver, the object of a custom is specified by the subjects. The binding force of both law and custom derives from the competent authority.

Customs are *divided* into customs in accordance with, contrary to, or in addition to the law (iuxta, contra and praeter legem) according as they interpret, abrogate or create a new law.

A *new obligation* is introduced by custom if a majority of the members of a community frequently posit certain acts with the intention of obliging themselves and if they continue to do so for forty uninterrupted years, provided the custom is reasonable (C. 28). — Concerning the *cessation* of a law by contrary custom, see 77. — Laws are *interpreted* by customs that are in accordance with the law (Cf. 55).

46. — III. A precept is a command or a binding manifestation of the will of a superior issued either in virtue of private authority (father, employer, etc.) or public jurisdiction (pope, bishop, governor, etc.). That a precept issued in the latter instance be not a law it is required that the command be imposed either upon individual persons only or upon the public community merely as a temporary injunction.

Precepts, imposed upon individuals, *cease* upon the death or cessation from office of him who issued them, unless they were imposed before two witnesses or by means of some authentic document (C. 24).

IV. Privileges will be treated separately because of the extensive consideration they require (Cf. 79 sqq.).

47. Chapter II

LEGISLATOR AND SUBJECT

I. The Legislator. 1. God is the *Supreme Lawgiver.*

The natural and the positive divine law have God as their Author. Human legislators both in the Church and State derive their authority from God.

2. The Holy Father is the *ecclesiastical legislator* for the entire Church (C. 218) as also is a General Council in union with him.

Plenary and *Provincial Councils* can legislate for their districts (C. 291), as can also *diocesan bishops* (C. 335, 362) and in like manner Vicars and Prefects Apostolic (C. 294), Abbots and Prelates nullius for theirs (C. 323). For the members of an exempt religious institution the *General Chapter* at least can make laws (C. 501).

48. — 3. According to the form of government, the *civil legislator* may be either the ruler alone, or in conjunction with the representatives, or the latter in conjunction with the president, or simply the representative body (Congress).

If a *usurper* has seized power his decrees oblige in conscience when the previous legal form of government can no longer be restored, or if it is certain that the usurping regime will be permanently established. Apart from either of these contingencies there is an obligation in conscience to observe the laws of the usurper only in so far as obedience is necessary for the maintenance of order or the avoidance of scandal.

49. — **II. Subjects of Law.** 1. The *natural law* obliges all men.

Whoever has not the use of reason does not sin formally by transgressing the moral law because of ignorance; but another sins who induces him to do so. The same holds for an unlettered person who has the use of reason, but is ignorant of the precepts of right reason or conclusions flowing from the first principles. This seldom occurs in regard to the primary or general conclusions, but more often in the case of secondary precepts of the natural law.

50. — 2. The *positive divine law* of the New Testament obliges all men first of all to receive Baptism and thereby become members of the Church.

Having been made a Christian through Baptism, a person is then obliged to observe the other positive laws of the New Testament, but only those that pertain to the reception of the Sacraments.

The ceremonial and judicial laws of the *Mosaic Code* have been abrogated. Its moral enactments that are in harmony with the natural law continue and oblige in virtue of the natural law.

51. — 3. *Ecclesiastical law* obliges all baptized persons who have attained the use of reason and are seven years of age, and also children under seven years of age when the Church explicitly so rules.

Therefore, even the *excommunicated* as well as *heretics* and *schismatics* are obliged by the laws of the Church. Generally, however, they do not sin by transgressing them because of inculpable ignorance.

Some divines believe the Church does not intend to impose upon *heretics* who are in good faith those of her laws that are primarily ordained for personal sanctification (e.g., observance of Holydays and days of fasting and abstinence); but that it is always forbidden to induce them to transgress such laws. Other laws (e.g., matrimonial impediments) enacted for the common good of the Church oblige heretics, unless they are exempt as in C. 1070, 1099.

Children who have the use of reason, but have not completed their seventh year are bound by ecclesiastical law only when this is expressly stated (C. 12), as in canons 859 (Easter Communion) and 906 (annual confession).

Whoever is habitually deprived of the *use of reason* (the insane) is not bound by the laws of the Church; he is bound, however, if the loss of reason is only temporary. Therefore, one may not serve an intoxicated person meat on Friday.

52. *a) General laws* oblige those for whom they are made wherever they may be (C. 13).

If a Catholic is dispensed from a general law of the Church in his home diocese (from fasting or from the observance of a Holyday) he must observe that law when sojourning in or passing through a strange diocese where the law is in force. On the other hand when away from home he may use an indult dispensing from a law in the strange diocese even though such an indult does not obtain in his home diocese (C. 14). The same holds for transients or those who have no place of residence (C. 14). Whoever has observed a general law (e.g., fast and abstinence on Dec. 7) in one place need not observe it again if he passes to another locality

where the law obliges at a later date (because of the transference
of the Feast).

53. *b*) *Particular laws* oblige only those who have a
domicile or quasi-domicile within the respective territory
and only when they actually reside there (C. 13).

When such a resident is absent from his own territory he is
nevertheless obliged by the law of his home diocese if its transgression proves harmful in his own territory or if there is a question of a personal law (C. 14). He must likewise observe the particular laws of the territory where he is visiting if the laws concern the public order or require certain formalities for legal transactions (C. 14). *Transients* or those without a fixed residence are
obliged by the particular laws of the territory where they happen
to be (C. 14).

54. — 4. *Civil laws* oblige the subjects of the respective States.

For the sake of the common welfare, aliens residing in the country are held to the observance of laws that concern property, contracts, and crimes. They must likewise observe police regulations.
Citizens absent from their country are subject to the laws of their
fatherland in things that pertain to their status as citizens, their
office, possessions, and the duties they have back home; not, however, in things concerning public peace or legal formalities. Concerning the clergy confer 409.

55.   Chapter III

INTERPRETATION, OBLIGATION AND
OBSERVANCE OF THE LAW

I. *Interpretation of the Law.*

1. The *interpretation* or explanation of a law may be
authentic, doctrinal or customary.

a) The *authentic interpretation* of a law (C. 17) is given by the
legislator, his successor or someone authorized to do so. Should
such an interpretation be given in the form of a law it has the
binding force of a law. If it merely explains certain terms of the
law that are already obvious in themselves it need not be promul-

gated and has retroactive application. If it clarifies a law in itself doubtful, or extends or restricts the meaning of the words, it must be promulgated and is not retrospective. — If it is given in the form of a *judicial sentence* or a *rescript* for an individual case it has no legal force and obliges only those persons or affects those things for which it is given.

b) The *doctrinal interpretation* of a law is given by jurists. In the first place it takes regard to the proper meaning of terms in their context; if the meaning is doubtful or obscure, it has recourse to parallel legislation, and takes into consideration the purpose and circumstances of the law, and the intention of the legislator (C. 18). — A fundamental rule of jurisprudence is to put as broad as possible an interpretation on the words of a favorable law and to interpret unfavorable laws strictly (e.g., penal laws). (C. 19.)

c) The *customary interpretation* of a law is (next to the authentic) the best interpretation (C. 29), since it obtains the force of a law by custom. It is, therefore, to be preferred to any grammatical or philological explanation of the law.

56. — 2. The *Interpretation* of a law in accordance with the **mind of the legislator** (epikeia or equity) is the reasonable taking for granted that the lawgiver would not wish to oblige in some particularly difficult case even though the case is obviously covered by the wording of the law.

Equity avoids the Scylla of legalism which cannot see beyond the letter of the law, and the Charybdis of anarchism which repudiates all law, and, by overriding the rigor of the law, judges according to the spirit of the law. Epikeia may not be used if one can readily approach the lawgiver for information. Nor can it be applied to laws that void acts (invalidating laws) or to laws that render persons incapable of undertaking certain legal actions (incapacitating laws). The common welfare requires that certainty be had about the validity of such acts. — There is no question of epikeia or equity in those cases where the lawgiver absolutely could not oblige because, for example, special circumstances make the observance sinful or impossible. (Cf. 69 sqq.)

57. — II. Obligation of the Law. 1. *The existence.* All laws oblige in conscience, but not all oblige in the same manner.

This obtains even if the legislator is an atheist and does not believe in a conscience.

a) *Most laws* impose an obligation in conscience to perform or omit a certain action.

b) *Purely penal laws* impose an obligation in conscience to accept the penalties incurred for their violation, but not to omit or perform the actions prescribed by the laws. Wherefore, purely penal laws, as far as the performance or omission of an action goes, have no supernatural sanction (e.g., for a grave transgression, the punishment of hell). In many cases, however, one cannot prescind from the supernatural sanction. In other cases, according to many authors, it is left to the discretion of the lawgiver to determine whether or not his enactments are purely penal. Some ecclesiastical laws and the statutes of many Religious Institutes are purely penal in character. Whether state laws are penal or not depends (so far as the common welfare does not require a supernatural sanction) on the free will of the civil legislator. Hence, much will depend upon whether or not the lawgiver follows modern trends in regard to supernatural sanctions in his legislative philosophy. Even though one does not sin by transgressing a purely penal law, it might readily happen that disobedience will offend against some virtue, e.g., charity or veracity.

c) *Invalidating and incapacitating laws* often oblige in conscience namely, when they declare certain legal actions invalid which by nature are valid, or declare certain persons incapable of positing certain actions who are really capable of doing so. Sometimes, however, they do not forbid the contrary act, but only declare it void either when posited or only after a judicial sentence. Such an action must be held void in conscience. Frequently such laws merely bar legal assistance in the prosecution of some claim.

d) *Laws based on the presumption* of a common danger always oblige, even though in particular cases the danger is absent (C. 21), e.g., the law regarding the reading of forbidden books. — Laws based on the presumption of a definite fact, do not oblige in conscience if the fact is falsely presumed. Thus, if one is sentenced to make restitution for causing unjust damage, he is not bound to observe the sentence if it is certain he had no part in causing the damage; if compelled to do so he is justified in resorting to secret compensation.

58. — 2. *The Gravity.* Laws always oblige under venial sin in unimportant matters. In grave matters they oblige under mortal sin, unless the lawgiver wills that they bind only under venial sin.

Cf. 97 as to what constitutes a grave matter.

59. — 3. *The Extent.* Since one must observe the law, he also has the duty:

a) To acquire a *knowledge of the law.*

A cleric must, therefore, read the official diocesan publication to learn the ordinances of his bishop.

b) To use the *ordinary means* which are absolutely necessary for the observance of the law.

Hence, a priest must have a breviary, and take it with him on a journey.

60. *c)* To remove or anticipate *obstacles* which make the law (proximately) impossible of observance.

α) If the time for the observance of a law is *at hand,* it is forbidden to render oneself incapable of its observance, unless there is a correspondingly good reason for doing so. The gravity of the reason must be in proportion to the importance of the law, the nearness of the time for its fulfillment, and the frequency of the law's non-observance by putting such an obstacle in the way of its fulfillment. — One may not take a trip on Saturday afternoon merely for pleasure if doing so makes attendance at Mass the next day impossible (Cf. 198).

β) If the time for observing the law is still *remote* such an obstacle may be placed in the way of its observance. One may, therefore, take a pleasure trip even if Sunday Mass is thereby rendered impossible, provided he leaves before Saturday or Sunday morning.

γ) One may never do anything *with the intention* of rendering the observance of the law impossible. Hence, it is sinful to work merely to be excused from the obligation of fasting.

There is no obligation to remain *subject* to the law. Thus, it is not forbidden on a day of abstinence to go to a locality where a dispensation from the law has been granted and there eat meat.

61. *d)* To avoid the *danger of transgression.*

The greater and more proximate the danger and the weightier the law, the greater is the duty of avoiding the danger. Cf. also 607.

62. — III. The Observance of the Law. 1. *The manner of fulfillment.*

a) Negative or prohibiting laws are observed by the mere fact that one forbears doing the thing proscribed.

Whoever has the intention of not omitting the forbidden act sins in thought.

b) Affirmative laws or those that prescribe an action are observed according to the following distinction:

α) Laws that require a certain matter to be done are satisfied if the thing required is done.

Whoever is obliged to pay a debt or tax is freed from his obligation as soon as he pays the required amount, even though at the time of payment he is completely irresponsible and does not know what he is doing. The obligation is fulfilled also when (e.g., in a forced sale) one's debt is paid against his will. A debt may also be paid by someone other than the debtor if one may presume this to be agreeable to the debtor.

β) Laws that call for a personal service require that he who is obliged by the law must observe it with knowledge and free will.

One cannot, therefore, fulfill his Sunday obligation by proxy. Nor is the obligation satisfied if one is asleep throughout the entire Mass.

63. — 2. *The intention to satisfy one's obligation.*

a) If the obligation *exists independently* of the will of the subject, the law will be observed even if in doing the thing prescribed the subject of the law has the intention of not yet observing the law.

Whoever communicates during the Easter time or hears Mass on Sunday, not knowing that it is the paschal season or that it is Sunday, or even if knowing this, intends to fulfill these obligations only later, has, nevertheless, observed the law and satisfied his obligation. However, it is necessary in such a case that he have the intention to pray and to hear Mass.

b) If the obligation *is derived* from the subject's intention to bind himself, even then, the intention to satisfy the obligation is not required. But should one at the time he performs the obligatory act have the intention of *not* satisfying his obligation, the obligation would not be satisfied.

If one vows to say the rosary he fulfills his vow as soon as he says the rosary, even though he does not think of his vow when saying it. But if in saying the rosary he deliberately did not want to fulfill his vow, the vow would thereby not be fulfilled.

64. — 3. *The intention of fulfilling the purpose of the law* is not necessary.

Therefore, if one feasts on the most delicate fish on Friday he observes the law of abstinence, although he practices no mortification which is the purpose of the law. So, too, a stingy man observes the law of fasting, even though he fasts because he is too miserly to buy food.

65. — 4. *The state of grace* is not required unless it belongs to the substance of the work prescribed.

Therefore, one does not observe the precept of the Church to confess and communicate annually if he does so sacrilegiously. One does, however, satisfy his obligation of praying the breviary or of saying his penance if he does so in mortal sin.

66. — 5. *Several obligations* can be fulfilled by one and the same act, unless this be forbidden by him who imposes the obligation.

Should a Holyday of obligation fall on Sunday one's double obligation is satisfied by attending one Mass. Viaticum received during the paschal season satisfies one's Easter duty. If attendance at Mass is imposed as a penance in confession the Sunday Mass generally does not suffice, unless the priest declares otherwise.

67. *The time for the fulfillment of a law.*

a) Several laws may be observed *at the same time* provided the different actions simultaneously undertaken are not mutually exclusive and the one imposing the obligation has not forbidden it.

Therefore, one may say his breviary or the penance received in confession during the Sunday Mass. Whether one may go to confession and hear an obligatory Mass at the same time depends on whether or not the confession is of such a nature that it will permit sufficient attention to the Mass.

b) Generally speaking one cannot observe a law *before the legal time* for its fulfillment.

Sunday obligation is not satisfied by attending Mass on Saturday, nor is the Easter Duty satisfied by receiving the Sacraments before the paschal time. Neither may one say his penance before going to confession.

c) If the time designated for the observance of the law *has commenced,* and one foresees he will later be hindered from observing it, he must do so in advance.

If one foresees the impossibility to communicate after Easter he must comply with his Easter duty on or before the Feast. So, too, if one cannot attend a late Mass on Sunday he must assist at an earlier one.

d) If the legal *time has elapsed* before one has complied with the law, his duty ceases if the lawgiver intended that with the passing of time the obligation also cease (tempus ad finiendam obligationem). He would still have to observe the law if the time limit was assigned to urge the fulfillment of the obligation (tempus ad urgendam obligationem).

He who misses Mass on Sunday, eats meat on Friday, omits his breviary, etc., sins, but need not make up these omissions. — But if one does not communicate during the Easter time he not only sins, but is still bound to make his Easter.

68.   Chaper IV

CESSATION OF OBLIGATION

Although the law continues in force, its obligation ceases to bind in case of ignorance, impossibility, dispensation, or privilege. — Besides, the obligation ceases if one leaves the territory where the laws obtain, laws being territorial (Cf. 60). Since this latter point presents no difficulty it does not call for further treatment.

I. Ignorance, if invincible, excuses from formal **sin,** even though there is a material violation of the law.

Ignorance also excuses from the penalty, but not from the effects of voiding or incapacitating laws (C. 16, Cf. 673). *Vincible ignorance* does not excuse from sin. (Cf. 17), and often not from the penalty (Cf. 425).

69. — II. Impossibility. 1. *Physical impossibility* excuses from the observance of any and every law (Cf. also 87).

2. *Moral impossibility.*

a) Negative or prohibiting natural laws never cease to oblige in case of moral impossibility.

Such laws forbid actions that are intrinsically evil. Therefore, idolatry, blasphemy, onanism, perjury, etc., are not allowed even to save one's life.

b) All other laws cease to oblige when it is morally impossible to observe them.

This includes the affirmative natural laws, some divine positive laws and all human laws. — Therefore, one is not obliged to give his life to save the life of his neighbor, to make an integral confession at great risk of health, nor to fast in spite of hard work. — The more important a law is, the greater is the inconvenience required to excuse one from it. Divine laws oblige more strictly than human laws; prohibiting, are stricter than affirmative laws.

Exceptions or cases where laws do oblige at great inconvenience: α) if the transgression is in contempt of God, religion or the Church; β) if the common good is at stake; γ) if a freely chosen position imposes certain heroic sacrifices; δ) if another person would otherwise be placed in extreme spiritual need.

3. *Partial impossibility* excuses totally from the observance of the law if the obligation is indivisible.

An obligation is divisible if that part of it which one can observe is sufficient to attain the end of the law. — Thus, if one vows to make a pilgrimage but finds he cannot reach the shrine, he need not even begin the pilgrimage; whereas, he who cannot recite the entire divine office must recite whatever part of it he can. — If one is certain that he cannot observe the whole law, and doubts whether he can observe it partially, he is, as a rule, not obliged to anything, since he would otherwise be plagued unceasingly by doubts.

70. — 4. In a ***conflict of obligations*** the higher one takes precedence.

Duties conflict when two laws apparently oblige simultaneously and only one can be observed. As a matter of fact only the more important one actually obliges. Thus, the natural law takes precedence over the positive law. Among the laws of nature a law that prohibits precedes a law that commands. Divine positive law takes precedence over human legislation; the law of a superior society must be preferred to the law of a society which is subordinate to it in purpose and function. — Therefore, e.g., whoever must care for a dangerously ill person and cannot at the same time attend Sunday Mass, is not obliged to hear Mass. — If two duties conflict and one cannot in any way determine which of the two is the more important, he does not sin no matter which obligation he fulfills (Cf. 89).

71. — III. Dispensation 1. *Concept*. A dispensation is a relaxation of the obligation of a law in a special case granted by competent authority (C. 80).

Dispensation differs α) from a privilege (Cf. 79). — β) from a permission by which one is not freed from the observance of a law, but actually observes the law insofar as he obtains the legally required consent of authority to do something, e.g., a religious obtains permission from his superior to go on a journey. — γ) from an interpretation which declares that the law does not oblige in a certain instance since in this case there is no exemption from an obligation, but merely a declaration to the effect that none existed from the beginning.

A dispensation is always *granted* by an act of the will of a competent superior, since only in this manner can the obligation be lifted. This act of the will need not necessarily be expressed by outward signs. Because of the necessity of this act a dispensation (unlike a permission) cannot be presumed, e.g., by presupposing that, "if the superior knew of this, he would grant a dispensation."

72. — 2. The *author* of a dispensation must have jurisdiction since the obligation imposed by law is removed.

Therefore, a superioress cannot grant a dispensation; but she may grant a permission or even declare that the law does not oblige in certain instances. Such an interpretation in a favorable sense may also be given by one who is not a superior, e.g., a doctor may declare a sick person incapable of fasting.

The following individuals can grant a dispensation: the lawgiver, his successor, his superior, or anyone whom any of these three may delegate (C. 80). They may dispense not only their own subjects, but anyone within their jurisdiction. If the dispensation concerns a recurring obligation, e.g., fasting or abstinence, the dispensation continues even after the strangers have again left the territory.

Whoever has general faculties to dispense *may also dispense himself*, except when the power to dispense is to be exercised only in the Sacrament of Penance (Cf. also 392).

73. — 3. A *sufficient reason* is required for the lawgiver, his successor, or superior to dispense lawfully; others require such a reason to dispense validly.

For an exception to this rule confer 680. — The reason must be in proportion to the gravity of the law. It need not be so great, however, as would be required to excuse one from the observance of the law. — In a doubt as to whether one's reason is sufficient or not he may ask for a dispensation and his superior may validly and lawfully grant it (C. 84). *If one doubts* whether a dispensation is necessary at all, it is recommended that he consult his superior, although there is generally no obligation to do so, unless there is question of the validity of a Sacrament, e.g., marriage when in doubt about the existence (dubium facti) of an impediment. — If the dispensation is very necessary for the subject, the superior is obliged in charity to grant it. Should the dispensation not be granted in such instances, the subject may not act contrary to the law unless already excused by moral impossibility (Cf. 69).

74. — 4. The ***interpretation*** of a dispensation must generally be made so that its wording be understood in the strict sense (C. 85).

An *exception* to this rule obtains if the dispensation is given motu proprio or in the interest of the common good or if the dispensation is already contained in the legal enactments.

Faculties to grant dispensations are to be broadly interpreted if they are general faculties, since they are a favor granted to him who dispenses. Thus, if a confessor is given faculties to dispense in the internal forum, he may use his faculties also outside the Sacrament of Confession. The faculty to dispense in a particular case must be interpreted strictly (C. 85). Together with the faculties to dispense are granted all other powers without which the faculties cannot be exercised (Cc. 200, 66).

75. — 5. The ***cessation*** of a dispensation may take place (C. 86) by:

a) Revocation on the part of the competent superior.

The lawgiver always revokes a dispensation validly. Whoever is delegated to dispense may revoke a dispensation for a sufficient reason, if he has received the power to do so. This is the case with those who have general faculties to dispense.

b) The *death* of him who granted the dispensation, but only in the rare cases in which he has expressly so determined.

Thus, a dispensation ceases if granted with such clauses as "ad beneplacitum nostrum," "donec voluero," not, however, if the clause reads "ad beneplacitum Sedis," or "donec revocavero."

c) Renunciation on the part of the one dispensed, if accepted by the competent superior.

He is competent to accept a renunciation who dispenses in virtue of his own power and he who has received general faculties to dispense. Failure to use a dispensation is not a sign of renunciation. Whoever is duly dispensed from fasting may still use his dispensation even after observing the fast for a long time.

If John receives a dispensation to marry Anna, but marries Bertha instead, he may still marry Anna after the death of Bertha without a new dispensation.

d) The *complete cessation of the principal reason* for the dispensation in the case of recurring obligations.

Thus, one dispensed from fasting by reason of illness, must fast as soon as he recovers his health. If one doubts whether or not the reason for his dispensation has ceased he may continue to use the dispensation.

Should the dispensation have an indivisible effect it does not expire with the cessation of the principal cause for which it was granted. Therefore, if one has received a marriage dispensation "ad legitimandam prolem" he may use the dispensation even if the child dies before the marriage, provided, however it is still living at the moment the dispensation is granted (Cf. 680).

e) *Leaving the territory,* if the dispensation is territorial, not if it is a personal dispensation.

Members of a diocese where a dispensation from the law of abstinence is granted on certain days, may not use this dispensation in other dioceses where no such dispensation exists.

IV. Privilege. Cf. 79 sqq.

76. Chapter V

THE CESSATION OF LAWS

A law ceases in consequence of a new law, a legitimate custom or through the cessation of its purpose.

I. A new law abrogates a former law if it expressly states this, or if it is directly contrary to the old law or if it regulates anew the entire subject matter of the old law (C. 22).

In case of doubt the revocation of an earlier law may not be presumed, but as far as possible the later law must be harmonized with it (C. 23). — If the new law is only partially contrary to the old, then the old law is repealed only in part. A general law revokes special laws only when this is explicitly stated (C. 22). —

The Code revokes: all contrary legislation, whether general or particular, unless the opposite is explicitly mentioned concerning particular laws; all former penalties which were not incorporated in the Code; all the general disciplinary legislation of the Church which is not contained either in the Code itself or in approved liturgical books (C. 6). — A new law also revokes existing *legal customs;* but a general law does not revoke a particular custom unless it expressly says so. So, too, a law revokes a centenary or immemorial custom only when this is explicitly stated (C. 30). Abstracting from a few exceptions, the Code revokes all contrary customs even though they be particular, century old or immemorial. Centenary or immemorial customs contrary to the law may be tolerated if the Code has not reprobated them and the Ordinaries believe they cannot prudently be abolished (C. 5).

77. — II. Custom revokes a law of the Church only if it is reasonable and has enjoyed forty years of uninterrupted observance. If the law forbids contrary customs in the future, only a centenary or immemorial custom can revoke the law (C. 27).

A custom expressly reprobated by law is unreasonable (C. 27). — A new custom may also revoke an existing legal custom (C. 30).

78. — III. The purpose of a law may cease for all people or only for individual persons; likewise, a law's observance may become useless or even harmful.

1. A law ceases automatically if it becomes *universally useless.*

Such a law loses an essential characteristic; it no longer serves the common good (Cf. 43).

2. If a law becomes *harmful for an individual,* it ceases to oblige him if its observance becomes morally impossible, or if the said person may use epikeia.

Concerning moral impossibility and its restrictions, confer 69; epikeia, confer 56.

3. If a law becomes *useless for an individual* he is still obliged to observe it according to the much more common opinion.

The common welfare would otherwise suffer because many would imagine the law to be useless for them. — If, however, in an individual case the law is manifestly useless and non-compliance gives no scandal, one may follow the milder opinion and claim exemption. But even this latter exception would not apply in the case of legislation passed to avert a common danger (C. 21), as, for example, the Church's laws on the prohibition of books.

79. Chapter VI

PRIVILEGES

I. Concept. A privilege is a right granting to individuals or individual classes of persons a favor not due to them by law.

A privilege is like a *law* in this that it is a permanent norm and it obliges others not to hinder the privileged person in the use of his special right. It differs from a law in that it may also be granted to a private person, whereas a law can only be passed for a community.

A privilege differs from a *dispensation* by reason of its permanent character, dispensations usually being granted for special cases. A dispensation is, furthermore, always against the law, while a privilege may be beside the law (Cf. 80). In a privilege against the law the privileged person is no longer a subject of the law, whereas one dispensed remains subject to the law, but is only freed from its observance.

80 —II. Division. Privileges may be:

a) Beside or *against* the law (præter vel contra ius).

The latter derogates from the law, not the former, e.g., a privilege against the law is freedom from choir duty; a privilege beside the law is the faculty to dispense. Habitual faculties granted perpetually or for a definite period of time or for a certain number of cases, are considered privileges beside the law (C. 66).

b) Personal or *real,* according as the immediate subject is a person or a thing.

"Thing" here may mean a church, convent, diocese, state or dignity, etc.

c) Favorable or *odious.*

Favorable privileges are a burden to no one, e.g., the faculty to absolve from reserved cases. An odious privilege, although it benefits individuals, curtails the rights of others or places a burden upon them, e.g., the privilege of a private oratory through which public services are prejudiced.

81. — III. Interpretation of Privileges. Odious privileges must be interpreted strictly; favorable ones, broadly.

Even privileges that infringe upon the rights of others must be so interpreted that the privileged person will actually be deemed receiving a favor (C. 68).

82. — IV. Privileges are acquired by direct grant, communication, legitimate custom or by prescription.

83. — V. Use of Privileges. 1. In itself there is *no obligation* to use a privilege which has been granted one for his personal advantage. For special reasons, however, one may be obliged to use his privilege (C. 69).

Therefore, one who has the privilege of a private oratory need not use his privilege, and, according to some authors, even if he could not otherwise hear Mass on Sunday. — Reasons that make the use of a privilege obligatory are: a command on the part of a competent superior, avoidance of scandal, charity and justice. Thus a confessor, having begun to hear a confession, is obliged to use his privilege to absolve from reserved cases by virtue of an implicit contract.

2. The use of a privilege *is obligatory* if it is granted in the interest of the common welfare, since one may not injure the common good.

Therefore, clerics must prudently use the privileges of their state (Cf. 409 sqq.); and religious, their privilege of exemption.

84. — VI. Cessation of Privileges. A privilege ceases by:

1. *Revocation* on the part of a competent superior (C. 71, 60). Revocation may take place by:

a) A *law*.

A general law to the contrary revokes privileges granted by the Code. Other privileges are not revoked by law, unless the law expressly states otherwise, or unless the law is passed by the superior of the grantor of the privilege.

b) *A special act* (i.e., of revocation) on the part of a competent superior.

In this case the privilege remains until the revocation is made known to the grantee.

2. The **death** of the grantor or his loss of office terminates privileges granted with the clause "ad beneplacitum nostrum" or an equivalent phrase (C. 73).

An equivalent clause would be "durante meo munere," but not the expression "donec revocavero."

3. **Renunciation** of the grantee which is accepted by the competent superior (C. 72).

Privileges granted for one's personal advantage may be renounced by private individuals, others may not.

Non-use or *contrary use* of a privilege does not contain a renunciation. In such manner those privileges only are lost that are prejudicial to others, provided there is either a legitimate prescription against them or the non-use is equivalent to a tacit renunciation (C. 76). — A privilege is not automatically lost by *abuse,* but a person misusing his privilege should be deprived of it (C. 78).

4. The **death** of the privileged person (C. 74) or the complete *destruction* of the thing or place with which the privilege is connected (C. 75).

A moral person becomes extinct when a competent superior suppresses it or if it has ceased to exist for a hundred years (C. 102). Local privileges revive if the place destroyed is rebuilt within fifty years (C. 75).

5. A **change of circumstances:** viz., if, according to the judgment of the superior, the privilege becomes harmful or its use unlawful (C. 77).

6. The *expiration of the period of time* or the exhaustion of the number of cases for which it is granted (C. 77).

If no definite period of time is indicated a privilege is presumed to be perpetual (C. 70). Even after the time has elapsed or the number of cases has been exhausted acts of jurisdiction of the internal forum exercised through inadvertence are valid (C. 77, 207).

Part III

CONSCIENCE

85.   Chapter I

CONCEPT AND DIVISION

I. Concept. Conscience in the proper sense of the term is a judgment of the practical reason on the moral goodness or sinfulness of an action.

Conscience becomes the proximate norm of moral conduct by applying the law to a concrete case.

II. Division. 1. *Antecedent* and *consequent* conscience are so called according as the judgment is passed before an action is performed or only thereafter.

In the *antecedent* conscience there is present the realization of obligation and imputability in relation to the norm of morality; the *consequent* conscience is accompanied by the sentiment of tranquility or remorse.

2. *Right* or *erroneous* is one's conscience according as the verdict of reason agrees or disagrees with objective truth.

An erroneous conscience is either culpable or inculpable, vincible or invincible.

3. *Certain, doubtful, probable* and *perplexed* conscience.

A *certain* conscience passes judgment without fear of error. For moral certainty it suffices that all reasonable fear be excluded. In reality, however, an absolutely certain conscience can still be erroneous.

The *doubtful* conscience suspends its judgment. — The doubt may either concern a fact (dubium facti) or the lawfulness of an act and the existence of the law (dubium juris). — A speculative doubt concerns the nature of an action and its moral character in general. A practical doubt concerns the lawfulness of an individual action about to be performed. Practical certainty is compatible with speculative doubt.

The *probable* conscience passes judgment for weighty reasons, but with a reasonable fear of erring. Relative to the degree of probability, we distinguish probable, more probable and most probable opinions.

The *perplexed* conscience is one which, when confronted with two alternative precepts, fears sin in complying with either of them.

86. — 4. *Tender, lax* and *scrupulous* conscience.

This distinction concerns principally a permanent disposition of conscience.

The *tender* conscience forms an objectively correct judgment with comparative facility even in finer distinctions between good and evil.

The *lax* conscience, on insufficient grounds, judges a thing to be lawful which is sinful, or something to be a venial sin which is actually a mortal sin.

The *scrupulous* conscience, prompted by purely imaginary reasons, is in constant dread of sin where there is none, or of mortal sin where there is only venial sin. The basic factor in a scrupulous conscience is not so much error as fear. The anxieties are not really rational in character, hence they do not really enter into the judgment of conscience. There is question here rather of representations of the fantasy, of sentient judgment, of impulses and movements of the sensitive appetite or emotions.

The following are *symptoms* of a scrupulous conscience: examination of conscience over petty, often ridiculous matters, restless rumination, scrutinizing all possible circumstances that accompanied an action or could have done so, frequent change of judgment, indecision, fear of possible sin in all things, consultation of different confessors, the fear of not being properly understood

by them, clinging to one's own opinion in the face of their decisions. — Sometimes it is not easy to recognize the scrupulous
conscience. Especially with regard to himself, a person should not
trust his own judgment, but accept the verdict of his confessor.
A person may sometimes be scrupulous in some things and lax
in others.

The *causes* of scrupulosity are: disorders in health, congenital
morbid conditions of the organism (abnormal irritability, anemia,
manic-depressive impulses or pressure on the brain), vivid fantasy,
predominance of sentiment over reason, precocious ingenuity, excessive introspection, lack of judgment; sometimes also secret pride
that justifies itself against every reproach or endeavors to acquire
certainty to the exclusion of all doubt, even unreasonable doubt;
finally, a lack of confidence in divine mercy. Scrupulous people
are often to blame for aggravating their condition by not consistently using the prescribed remedies.

Remedies for scrupulosity are: prayer and trust in God; unconditional, trustful obedience to one's spiritual director; formation of general rules of moral conduct and faithful adherence to
them, even at the risk of making an occasional mistake; avoiding
idleness; removal of the causes of scrupulosity, especially the
organic disturbances.

87.   Chapter II

THE BINDING FORCE OF CONSCIENCE

I. A certain conscience must always be obeyed
when it commands or forbids.

This holds for both the right and the erroneous conscience. —
Therefore, if one lies to help a neighbor out of a difficulty, convinced that to do so is an act of charity, he actually does perform
a laudable act of fraternal charity; and should he act contrary to
his erroneous conscience he would sin. Whoever thinks that today is a day of abstinence and eats meat sins, although, as a
matter of fact, it is not a day of abstinence. But he who acts contrary to a certain, though erroneous, conscience does not incur the
penalties that are ipso facto incurred by a transgression of the law.
Thus, one who strikes a layman thinking him to be a priest,
commits, indeed, a sacrilege, but does not incur excommunication.
That which is *unavoidable* cannot be sinful, even though one falsely
believes it to be a grave sin. Thus, a prisoner who cannot attend

Mass on Sunday does not sin even though he thinks he has sinned mortally.

A certain conscience *may always be followed* when it permits something. Therefore, if one eats meat on Friday in the belief that it is Thursday, he does not sin.

88. — II. In a practical doubt about the lawfulness of an action one may never act.

For the difference between a practical and a speculative doubt confer 85. — A hunter, doubting whether that which he is aiming at be an animal or a man, is guilty of homicide if he kills, even though it turns out that he slew an animal. — Evidently one need not bother about unreasonable doubts. Thus, if in spite of using all prescribed precautions, one kills another while driving an automobile, he has not sinned even though he often thought he might kill some one while driving.

That which is said of a practical doubt applies also to the practically *probable conscience*.

89. — III. With a perplexed conscience one must do that which seems to him the lesser evil. If both alternatives seem equally sinful, he may do as he pleases.

The *reason* is that impossibility precludes sin. (Cf. 69). The supposition is, however, that the action will not brook delay without great harm, and that no means are at hand to form a right conscience.

90. — IV. A lax conscience may generally not be followed without grave sin if one thereby transgresses a law that obliges gravely.

The reason is that such a conscience must generally be considered as culpably erroneous. Such a person must pay more attention to doubts that occur to him than others need to do, and he may not so readily disregard them as mere scruples. — In exceptional cases the laxist may be excused from grave sin, namely, if he is unaware of the state of his conscience and does not recognize, even in a general way, the malice of an action or his duty to make further investigation.

91. — V. One may act contrary to a **scrupulous**

conscience without sinning, even if the action be undertaken with great fear of committing sin.

The scrupulous conscience is nothing else but a state of fear. — The principle laid down holds even if the scrupulous person at the moment of acting does not think of his fear as a mere scruple. It suffices that he be habitually aware that he may do anything which he does not know for certain to be a mortal sin. A scrupulous person *may* do anything he sees conscientious people do, even though it be against his conviction. He need not use more than average carefulness when acting. If he cannot apply the directions given him and cannot seek advice, he may do as he chooses, provided there is no question of doing what is evidently and certainly sinful. A scrupulous person, by reason of great harm that he may do to himself, may be excused from many positive duties, e.g., fraternal correction, confessional integrity. If impure thoughts arise by his looking at innocent objects or persons, he may look attentively at such things and becomingly at such persons, and pay no attention to the resulting emotions. If the scruple concerns the fulfillment of a duty (breviary, penance, vow, etc.) he may presume that he has adquately fulfilled his obligation. If the scruple concerns the sufficiency of his contrition he may decide in his own favor. He need not confess sins committed before his last confession, unless he can swear that he certainly sinned gravely, and that he certainly has not yet confessed the sin. Even in this latter instance there may be circumstances that will excuse him from an integral confession. The same holds for doubts about the validity of previous confessions. — Scrupulous persons who mistake their feeling of anxiety for remorse of conscience should be informed that the cause of this anxiety is the nerves and not some sin of which they may be guilty.

There is even a *duty* to act contrary to scruples, for one might otherwise sin by pride, self-will and disobedience, or because one's health or one's business might thereby suffer. If the scrupulous person is of a good will, he will not readily sin grievously in an individual case. Because of the disadvantages mentioned the confessor should not permit more than one complete manifestation of the scruples or one general confession. Even this single manifestation of the state of his conscience must be forbidden if the scrupulous person had shortly before discussed matters with a different confessor and will evidently not remain long with the present one.

92. Chapter III

THE FORMATION OF A PRACTICALLY CERTAIN CONSCIENCE

One must try to form a practically certain conscience, since it is never lawful to act with a practical doubt about the lawfulness of an action (Cf. 88).

I. A direct solution to doubts of conscience in matters of frequent occurrence and lesser importance can usually be obtained by reflection, by investigation and by asking counsel.

Such a solution is necessary as long as there is well-founded hope that the doubt can be solved in this wise if a degree of care in keeping with the importance of the matter at hand is employed, provided one does not choose to do the more certain thing in every case.

93. — II. An indirect solution to doubts of conscience, i.e., one made by having recourse to certain principles and moral systems, is necessary if certainty cannot be obtained by the direct method.

In an indirect solution the theoretical doubt about the lawfulness or necessity of an action remains; but certainty is obtained as to what one must or may do here and now.

1. If there is question of the necessary attainment of an end one must choose what is more certain if one cannot dispel the theoretical doubt.

If eternal salvation is at stake one must use those means that will certainly lead to that end. As long as certain means are available one may not employ means that are only probably sufficient. — In administering the Sacraments one must, out of reverence due to the Sacrament, and often out of justice and charity, decide in favor of the opinion that safeguards the validity of the Sacrament. If one cannot have certainly valid matter for the administration of a Sacrament, he may for the sake of a soul's salvation use doubtful matter. — If there is question of the certain right of another or of an injury threatening him, we must follow that opinion according to which the other will certainly

— 43 —

obtain justice or be protected from harm. Thus, a physician may
not use remedies whose effectiveness is doubtful, if certainly effective
remedies are available; a hunter may not shoot when he reasonably doubts whether he will injure a man by doing so.

**94. — 2. If the lawfulness of an action is doubt-
ful** one may follow any opinion that is well-founded,
even if the contrary opinion is more probable.

a) An opinion is *well-founded* if it would induce a
prudent person to give his assent even after he has
considered the reasons to the contrary. The fear that the
opposite may be true need not be excluded.

The reasons for an opinion may be intrinsic or extrinsic according as they rest on insight and understanding or are based on the
authority of others. In this latter instance it is presumed that these
others have an insight into the intrinsic reasons. — Only a good
moralist can pass on intrinsic evidence; whereas, a person of
average education may judge the extrinsic reasons. An unlettered
person should abide by the judgment of a prudent confessor or
pastor. Priests may follow the opinions of recognized moralists, or
even follow Saint Alphonse alone.

In many cases it is relatively easy to determine whether an
opinion that bespeaks freedom from an obligation is well-founded
or not by the application of *reflex principles*. Some of the most
important of these principles are: in doubt do what is generally
done (in dubio judicandum est ex communiter contingentibus);
in doubt decide in favor of the validity of an action already done
(in dubio standum est pro valore actus); no one may be presumed
wicked unless his wickedness has been proved (nemo malus nisi
probetur); in doubt we must interpret, favorable things broadly;
unfavorable things, strictly (favores sunt ampliandi, odiosa res-
tringenda).

b) It is *lawful to follow* such a well-founded opinion:

α) no matter which law is in question.

This holds, be the law human, divine, positive or natural law.
The doubt may be whether the law exists or has ceased to exist,
e.g., because of fulfillment.

β) even if in other cases one has decided in favor of
the contrary opinion.

— 44 —

Therefore, one may in one instance accept an inheritance coming to him from an informal testament, and in another instance he may petition a judicial declaration of the invalidity of such a testament. — *In one and the same matter* one may not, however, follow two contrary opinions, since by doing so one would certainly transgress the law. Thus, if one has accepted the inheritance he must also recognize as valid and, therefore, pay off the legacies contained in an informal testament.

95. Note. *The Various Moral Systems.*

Since the opinion we have just stated (94) is not shared by all moralists we shall merely mention the different moral systems.

a) Absolute tutiorism teaches that in every difference of opinion, one must choose what is certain and thus decide in favor of compliance with the law; and that only full certainty of the opposite frees one from observance of the law.

b) Mitigated tutiorism frees from an obligation if the opinion in favor of liberty is probable in the highest degree (probabilissima).

c) Probabiliorism maintains that only then may one follow the opinion that favors liberty when the reasons for this opinion are certainly more probable than those which favor the law.

d) Aequiprobabilism demands that the opinion favoring freedom be equally or almost equally probable as the opinion favoring the law. Furthermore, one may apply this principle only when the doubt concerns the existence of a law, not in a doubt as to whether an existing law has ceased to bind, or has been fulfilled.

e) Compensationism or the Principle of the Sufficient Reason teaches that when one doubts the lawfulness of an action he must have a sufficiently grave reason to decide in favor of the opinion that is contrary to the law. The graver the law and the more probable are the reasons favoring it, the greater also must be the reasons for exposing oneself to the danger of a material transgression.

f) Probabilism is the system we adopted (94), and according to it any one may follow the opinion that favors liberty as long as he is certain that it is well-founded, even though the contrary opinion be more probable.

g) Laxism permits one to follow the opinion that favors liberty even though it be only slightly or doubtfully probable.

In evaluating these various systems we need only remember

that the systems of absolute tutiorism and laxism have been condemned by the Church. All other systems are tenable.

In practice the confessor should endeavor to freely choose the more perfect thing himself and should likewise advise his penitents to do the better thing. Let him not forget, however, that he has no right to impose his own opinion on his penitents as long as the contrary view is solidly probable (Cf. 605).

Part IV

SIN

96.   Chapter I

SIN IN GENERAL

I. Concept. Sin is the free transgression of a divine law.

Every law is, in a sense, a derivation from the divine law; therefore, the transgression of any law is sinful.

The *requisites* for every sin are: a) the transgression of a law, at least a putative law, b) the knowledge of the transgression; a confused knowledge suffices, c) free consent.

Differing from formal sin just defined is material sin, i.e., the violation of a law without knowledge or consent; God never imputes a material sin as a fault. Before a civil court, however, one is held responsible in some cases (Cf. 347).

97. — **II. Division.** According to their *theological difference* sins may be either mortal or venial.

1. A ***mortal sin*** is the transgression of a divine law in a grievous matter with full knowledge and consent.

a) A *matter* may be *grievous* in itself, or because of circumstances, or on account of its purpose.

Human laws sometimes oblige under venial sin even in important matters (Cf. 58).

With reference to the importance of the matter itself we distinguish between α) *mortal sins ex toto genere suo*, i.e., sins which according to their nature can never be venial (they allow of no lightness of matter), e.g., unbelief, lewd desires. Such sins can be venial only through imperfect attention or partial consent; β) *mortal sins ex genere suo*, i.e., sins whose matter is important in itself, but which in particular cases may be light, thus sins which within the same species may be mortal or venial, as the theft of something valuable or of a trifle; γ) *venial sins ex toto genere suo*, i.e., sins that always remain venial as long as no circumstance is superadded to change the species of the sin, e.g., immoderation in sleep or laughter, etc. These may be mortal sins because of an erroneous conscience.

98. *b) Full knowledge* of the serious nature of a sinful action is present if one is clearly conscious of the fact that the act is mortally sinful.

It *suffices* that one clearly realizes that the act may possibly be a mortal sin. It is likewise enough if the knowledge is had when one makes up his mind to sin mortally, even if in doing the deed one does not think of its sinful character.

Imperfect knowledge, and consequently no mortal sin, is had when actions are performed in semi-wakefulness, partial intoxication or very great distraction. On the influence of passion and mental diseases, confer 23 sqq.

c) Free consent is present if one freely wills an act although he has clearly recognized the gravity of its sinful character.

No sin is committed if one does not will the deed, no matter how clear his knowledge may be. Thus he does not sin who, with the best of will, cannot dispel unchaste or blasphemous thoughts, even though he knows such thoughts are gravely sinful. The same holds for the emotions. The determination to do a deed must not be confused with the pleasure of the sensitive appetite, nor with the compulsory idea "I want to sin."

A sign of imperfect knowledge and consent would be the fact that one does not complete an action when he can easily do so, or the fact that one is so minded that he would rather die than sin mortally.

If after performing an action one adverts to its sinfulness only *in a general way,* without reflecting whether it is a mortal or venial sin, he may presume that he sinned only venially, even though it was a grave matter, provided he has otherwise a tender conscience and does not commit mortal sins. Concerning those with a lax conscience, confer 90.

99. — 2. A *venial sin* is committed if, with either perfect or imperfect knowledge and consent, one transgresses a law which does not oblige seriously; or if, with imperfect knowledge and consent, he violates a law that obliges gravely.

Concerning the obligation of the law, confer 58.

A *venial sin* is also committed if one transgresses an objectively grave law but, due to his invincibly erroneous conscience, thinks it obliges only venially. — A venial sin may become a *mortal sin* on account of an erroneous conscience or scandal, or because of the proximate danger of its leading to mortal sin, or because of formal contempt of the law or by reason of a gravely sinful purpose.

100. — **III. The Specific Distinction of Sins.** As to their species, sins are distinguished according to their specifically different objects (St. Thomas) or the virtues to which they are opposed (Scotus) or the laws they violate (Vasquez).

Practically, these three opinions do not differ, since the virtues differ according to the distinction of their objects; and laws differ in accordance with the different virtues to which they refer.— Infidelity, despair and hatred of God are specifically different sins because they violate specifically different virtues. Specifically different sins are also committed when the same virtue is violated but in different or opposite ways, e.g., a person is injured in his honor or in his possessions; so, too, one sins against liberality either by avarice or by prodigality. *An individual act* that offends against several *virtues* also contains several specifically different malices, thus, self-abuse in one consecrated to God is a sin against chastity and against the virtue of religion. An individual act that violates several *laws* or precepts contains several specifically different sins if the laws were enacted in the interest of different virtues. Thus theft is only one sin even though the thief violates a divine and a human law at one and the same time. If, however, one who has vowed not to eat meat, does so on a day of abstinence, he commits two specifically different sins,   namely, a sin against temperance by disobeying a law of the Church, and a sin against religion by breaking his vow.

In confession one need mention only those species of sins of which he was conscious at the time he sinned. This holds even if he later learns that he objectively committed a greater number of sins than he realized.

101. — IV. The Numerical Distinction of Sins.

The *general rule* is: there are numerically as many different sins as there are *morally* distinct sinful actions. When the acts are only *physically,* and not morally distinct, there is no numerical plurality of sins.

For a numerical distinction of sins it suffices that an individual act virtually contain a plurality of sinful, morally distinct actions, and therefore sins.

102. — 1. *Morally distinct actions,* and therefore, numerically distinct sins are had:

a) In all specifically distinct sins.

Thus, theft and murder are not only specifically, but also numerically distinct sins. If a particular act contains a manifold specific malice, it virtually contains also a plurality of sinful actions, and is equivalent to several numerically distinct sins.

b) When several actions are willed and performed for their own sake. This occurs:

α) In external actions, as often as the acts are complete in themselves according to their nature, or in the case of other external actions, which do not constitute a moral unity either as a part of, or as a means to another action, or as the result of the same outburst of passion.

If one communicates unworthily twice, he sins two times. Similarly, he who commits self-abuse twice, becomes intoxicated twice, etc. — In how far other external acts constitute a moral unity, confer 103.

β) In internal acts, sins are numerically distinct as

often as a sufficient interruption takes place. Such an interruption is always present when one freely discontinues the internal act. Should one discontinue involuntarily, an interruption of longer duration would be required, especially if one has the intention to commit the corresponding external action.

He commits only one sin who cherishes hateful thoughts for any length of time, even though during this time he exchanges a few words with a passing friend, after which he immediately reverts to his thoughts of hate. But if the evil trend of his thoughts is completely broken, because of an interruption of two or three hours and he thereafter resumes his hateful thoughts, he commits two numerically distinct sins. — He who resolves to steal, and then is sorry for his resolution, but later again resolves to steal commits two distinct sins. Such resolutions, however, are not broken by ordinary natural interruptions such as sleeping, eating, and looking after one's business. In general an act of this kind constitutes a longer moral unity the more intensive it is. Thus the resolution to take revenge lasts longer than the decision to read a bad book.

c) *In an individual act that terminates in several objects* that have no moral connection and are not willed or cannot be willed as such.

Therefore, he commits two distinct sins who sets fire to his enemy's house, or resolves to do so, in order to kill him; similarly, he who pays no attention to the Mass while at Church on Sunday in order to rob someone.

103. — 2. *Physically,* but not morally distinct, are actions which constitute only one individual sin. This occurs:

a) When *several acts* terminate in only one object. Thus:

α) If they proceed from one sinful emotion.

Therefore, he who in the same fit of anger strikes his enemy several times or utters several curses, satisfies his obligation of self-accusation by saying: "I struck another," or "I cursed." The same holds in regard to unchaste touches, etc.

Several sins are committed, however, even though the acts proceed from one and the same impulse of passion, if the acts affect morally distinct objects or if according to their nature they are complete in themselves (Confer 102).

β) If several acts serve as means to an end.

Hence, he commits only one sin of murder who to kill his enemy buys a revolver, frequently renews his resolution, goes out in search of his enemy and finally shoots him. — A man commits only one sin of fornication who makes up his mind to sin with an unmarried woman, goes to see her, speaks immodestly with her, touches her impurely, has intercourse, after which he is guilty of other unchaste words and touches, but without the intention of having intercourse again. — He who makes up his mind to steal a hundred dollars from a chest and for this purpose pilfers small sums on different occasions commits one grave sin. He likewise sins once against the law of not reading forbidden literature who reads a forbidden book, even though it takes him several days to do so.

If for any reason at all the *purpose intended fails* of accomplishment, the individual acts performed as a preparation still constitute only one sin. — If the means employed were indifferent in themselves these need not even be mentioned in confession. It is sufficient to say: I had the intention to kill someone. But if the preparatory acts were bad, e.g., impure touches, they would have to be confessed at least in a general way.

104. γ) If they form a part of one individual sinful action.

Whether something constitutes one sinful action or not is determined by the nature of the thing or by the legal requirements. — Thus, although it is a mortal sin to omit only one of the hours of the Divine Office, it is likewise only one mortal sin to omit the whole Office, provided one resolved beforehand not to say his breviary for the day; but two sins would be committed if one begins by intending to omit only Matins, and later in the day resolves not to say the Office at all. He commits several sins who omits his Office for several days, misses Mass on Sunday, and does not observe a prescribed fast. A priest commits only one sin by absolving several persons successively or distributing Holy

Communion to a number of people at one time while in the state of mortal sin. On the theological species of these latter sins see 453.

b)When *one act* terminates in *several objects* of the same species and these objects constitute a moral unity either according to their nature or in the mind of the agent.

Thus, he commits only one sin who cherishes a hatred for several persons or who would like to kill them; likewise he who decides not to fast during the whole of Lent, or who resolves not to say his Divine Office. If he subsequently carries out his resolution by distinct external acts, e.g., on different days, he is guilty of a corresponding number of sins. — Similarly, if one entertains an individual unchaste desire toward several persons; but he would commit several sins if he were to meet these people successively and cherish the unholy desire toward the one and then the other, for in this manner several acts would terminate in several objects. — Furthermore, he sins only once who calumniates an entire family or "all his enemies." Probably, too, if one kills several people by throwing a bomb, or if a thief steals something which belongs to several individuals, provided he looks upon those injured as a unity, and has not the wish to injure the individual persons as such.

In confession such a penitent would have to indicate at least in a general way that his action affected several objects, since the confessor would otherwise conclude that his action concerned only one object, and the penitent would thus commit a venial sin of deceiving his confessor.

105. Chapter II

PARTICULAR SINS

I. Internal sins are such as are consummated by the spiritual faculties, viz., understanding and free will.

These are often called "bad thoughts." The faithful frequently do not classify them according to the following three numbers. — Confession of these sins is necessary in as far as they are recognized as sinful while being committed. The confessor must take care not to confuse penitents by detailed questioning.

106. — 1. *Morose delectation* is deliberate complacency in a sinful object presented by the imagination, but unaccompanied by a desire for it.

The *difference* between morose delectation and merely thinking about what is sinful consists in this that in the first case one takes pleasure in the sinful imagination, whereas in merely thinking of what is sinful one either takes no pleasure at all therein or only in the consciousness of possessing that particular knowledge. Furthermore, morose delectation is always sinful, whereas it may be lawful and even a duty to think of sinful things, e.g., in the case of a doctor or a confessor in procuring necessary information. — Merely thinking of what is sinful is a venial sin if done out of curiosity; it is a mortal sin, however, if without a sufficient reason such thinking becomes a proximate occasion of mortal sin, e.g., taking pleasure in the sin thought of or (in sexual matters) enjoyment of the sexual pleasure that follows such thinking. This latter is not (mental) morose delectation specifically so-called, but rather sexual pleasure (delectatio venerea) the morality of which will be dealt with in the treatise on the sixth commandment (Cf. 222).

Pleasure in regard to the *manner* in which a sin, e.g., a forgery, was committed is in itself not a sin.

a) The *species and gravity* of these sins are determined by the object in which one takes morose pleasure.

If the object is theft, murder or adultery, the delectation is a sin of the same nature. — Morose complacency usually concerns the object in a general way (e.g., ill-gotten goods), and not its particular circumstances (church property). Wherefore, these circumstances as a rule do not impart their specific malice to the sinful pleasure.

b) The *forbidden character* of morose delectation remains even though the object will later become lawful or if it was formerly lawful.

Engaged persons, therefore, may not imagine their future marital relationships as present and take pleasure therein, even though they do so only mentally. The same must be said of the widowed concerning past marital relations. — But it is *no sin* in itself for betrothed persons to think of what is lawful in married life and to desire it. Yet such thoughts are often sinful because they arouse sexual passion, and are not easily confined to the intellect.

107. — 2. *Sinful joy* (gaudium) is the voluntary complacency in an accomplished evil deed, be it done by ourselves or by others.

What is said of this joy applies also to boasting about one's sin, to the sadness because of the omission of a wicked action, and to the sadness regarding the performance of an obligatory good work. — If the good work was not obligatory the sadness is only a venial sin, and this only if the sadness was unreasonable.

a) The *moral and theological species and gravity* of these sins are the same as the evil deed itself in whose contemplation one rejoices.

As in morose delectation, so also sinful joy generally concerns the object in general, not its particular circumstances. Therefore, these latter generally need not be made a matter of confession.

b) It is *not sinful* to rejoice at the good effect of an evil deed or over the manner in which the evil deed was executed or at something which was formerly lawful or will later become licit.

Therefore, it is lawful to rejoice at the good child born of illicit relations, or over the freedom from temptations that follows voluntary or involuntary pollution. Neither is it sinful for a widow to reflect with a certain satisfaction upon past marital relations with her husband. Thus, too, the betrothed may think with joy upon the future fulfillment of the conjugal obligations. Yet such joy is often readily connected with sensual excitement and temptation and, therefore, with the danger of sinning.

108. — 3. *Evil desire* (desiderium) is the longing to do something forbidden.

An evil desire is efficacious if it develops into a firm intention or resolution. It is inefficacious if one would willingly carry out the deed, but is not really determined to do so, because, for example, he perceives its impossibility. — Desire can, furthermore, be conditional or absolute according as it is dependent upon a condition or not.

a) An *absolute desire* for what is sinful is always a sin of the same moral species and gravity as the evil action which one longs for, be the desire effective or not.

Since an evil desire usually concerns an action in the concrete, one wills the action with all its concomitant circumstances. These consequently have usually a determining influence on the immoral character of the action. Therefore, it is one thing to desire to strike a priest and quite another to desire to strike a layman. — But should the evil desire concern an action only in the abstract then such circumstances would not contribute any additional malice to the evil desire.

b) A *conditional desire* is not a sin if the condition added deprives the act of its malice. Otherwise, it is to be judged the same as unconditional desire.

The *removal* of the sinful character of an action by adding a condition to the desire is possible in all things that are forbidden by the positive law, and also in those things that are indeed forbidden by the natural law, but which may be lawful under given circumstances, e.g., if it were permitted I would eat meat on Friday; if it were necessary for my self-defense, or if God would allow it, I would kill another. — Such wishes, however, are often fraught with dangers.

The sinful character of those actions is irremovable if they are so intrinsically evil that even God cannot permit them, e.g., if on should say: I would blaspheme or give in to lewdness if it were not sinful. At times, however, such conditional desires merely mean that the natural inclination is so great that it would impel one to act if this were not forbidden. Such an avowal is no sin.

109. — II. The Capital Vices or **Sins** are evil in-clinations that are frequently the source of various kinds of sins.

These sins are called "Capital," not because of their gravity, but because of the greatness and the extent of their influence. — Whenever these inclinations produce their corresponding acts they become sins in the proper sense of the term. They are treated here in this latter sense.

1. **Pride,** or the inordinate desire for honor and dis-tinction, is a mortal sin *ex toto genere suo*, when it is of such a nature that one will not even be subordinate

to God. It is a venial sin *ex toto genere suo* if, with becoming subjection to authority, one longs inordinately for honor and distinction.

The latter kind of pride may accidentally be a mortal sin if it involves a grave injustice toward others or if it is the occasion of other mortal sins.

2. *Avarice,* or the inordinate desire for temporal goods, is a venial sin *ex toto genere suo.*

Avarice or covetousness becomes *mortally sinful* if, because of his cupidity, one violates the law of charity or any other commandment in a grave manner.

3. *Lust* is a grave sin *ex toto genere suo* if it is directly willed. For further details see 222.

4. *Envy,* or sadness because of the good fortune of our fellowman, which one looks upon as a diminishing of one's own possessions, is, like the sin against charity, a grave sin *ex genere suo.*

Envy is a *mortal sin* in him who begrudges his neighbor some valuable possession (natural or supernatural) and seriously wishes he did not have it so that the envious person himself might not suffer his imaginary disadvantage.

Merely to grieve that one does not have something that another has *is not envy;* neither is he envious who is depressed because another by reason of his possession, e.g., an office, is in a position to harm him; nor is it envy if there is sadness because a neighbor has something he does not deserve. Finally, it is not envy but *hatred* to begrudge our neighbor his possessions, not because these are looked upon as a diminution of our own good, but simply because we do not want him to prosper.

110. — 5. *Gluttony* is the inordinate longing for food or drink.

a) Immoderation in *eating* is in itself only a venial sin *ex genere suo.*

In itself this is true even if vomiting is induced. It may be a grave sin, however, for other reasons, e.g., injury to one's health, scandal, etc. (Cf. 208).

b) Intemperance in *drinking* which has as its immediate effect the loss of the use of reason is a graver sin than immoderation in eating.

a) Intoxication that results in a partial loss of reason is only a venial sin.

It may be a mortal sin because of scandal, injury to health, harm to one's family, etc.

β) Intoxication that ends in complete loss of reason is a mortal sin if brought on without a sufficient reason.

Complete loss of reason is presumed in him who can no longer distinguish good from bad, or if, after the drunkenness has passed, he cannot remember what he said or did while under the influence of drink, or if one does a thing which he never would have done when sober.

A sufficient reason to deprive oneself temporally of his use of reason would be to cure a disease or to counteract blood poisoning and the like. Merely to drive away the blues is not adequate reason.

To make *another person* completely drunk is also a grave sin, unless there is a sufficient excuse, e.g., to prevent him from committing a great crime. It is more readily permissible to be the *occasion* of another's intoxication, e.g., at a banquet.

c) Since *morphine, opium, chloroform* and similar drugs can also deprive one of the use of his reason temporarily, that which was said of intoxicating drinks holds also for narcotics (Cf. 165, 4).

a) To use narcotics in small quantities and only occasionally, is a venial sin if done without a sufficient reason. Any proportionately good reason justifies their use, e.g., to calm the nerves, dispel insomnia, etc.

Such use becomes gravely sinful if it creates an habitual craving for "dope" which is more difficult to overcome than dipsomania and more injurious to health.

β) To use drugs in greater quantities so as to lose

the use of one's reason is in itself a mortal sin; but for a good reason it is permissible.

Such a good reason is had in case of operations, i.e., that the patient be rendered insensible to intense pain, or that one might remain calm under the knife. In like manner one may administer opiates to one who is suffering greatly in order to alleviate his pain.

γ) In general it is forbidden to make a patient unconscious by the use of drugs in non-lethal doses in order that he may have a painless death (therapeutic euthanasia 211).

Such action is *lawful* if the sick person is well prepared for death and there is danger that he might otherwise fall into sin. Some authors allow such a procedure if the dying person is thus spared unusually great suffering and if one has reason to presume his consent. — According to the general opinion such a practice is not allowed merely to remove the ordinary anxieties that accompany the death agony. If the patient asks for such drugs in good faith and if there is no hope of teaching him otherwise, he should be left in good faith.

Such a practice is *never allowed* if the sick person is not prepared for death, and hope remains that he might eventually prepare for it. In such a case one must oppose as far as he can the doctors and relatives who desire to effect his dying while unconscious.

111. — 6. *Anger* is a disorderly outburst of emotion connected with the inordinate desire for revenge.

As an inordinate *outburst* of emotion, anger is only a venial sin, but might be a mortal sin if, for example, one would deliberately fly into such a rage that one could be thought to have lost one's reason.

As an inordinate desire for *revenge* anger is opposed to charity or justice, and is, therefore, a grave sin. It is a venial sin, however, if it concerns an insignificant evil.

Just anger is lawful, i.e., anger that is a righteous indignation over sin and which creates an orderly desire for punishment.

7. **Sloth** may be of a twofold nature.

a) It may consist in a *sluggishness* of the soul regarding the exertion necessary for the performance of a good work.

The good work may be a corporal task or a spiritual exercise of devotion.

Thus conceived sloth is not a sin specifically distinct from the transgression of a law because of indolence, e.g., the omission of the Sunday Mass because of laziness.

b) It may also consist in a *tedium* over the friendship of God because of the efforts necessary to maintain that friendship.

This kind of sloth is directly opposed to the love of God and is, therefore, gravely sinful *ex toto genere suo.*

112. Part V

THE VIRTUES

I. Concept. Virtue is a habit that perfects the powers of the soul and inclines one to do good.

II. Division. 1. According to their *source,* virtues are either natural or supernatural.

Natural virtues are acquired by human activity; supernatural virtues are infused by God.

2. According to their *object,* virtues are divided into theological (divine) and moral.

The *theological* virtues have God as their direct and immediate object. God is the object of faith because and in so far as He is infallible truth; of hope because and in so far as He is man's highest good; of love because and in so far as He is the good most worthy of all love. — The theological virtues are always supernatural virtues.

The *moral* virtues do not have God as their object, but something created, e.g., the assistance of a fellow-man, or the worship of God in so far as it is a moral good. — The moral virtues may be acquired by man or infused by God.

III. Cardinal virtues are those fundamental virtues

upon which all the other moral virtues in some way hinge (*cardo*: a hinge), and to which they may be reduced, namely, prudence, justice, temperance and fortitude.

Some authors consider the cardinal virtues as requisites and conditions that must accompany every virtue. Thus, whoever would perform an act of virtue must judge rightly about it (prudence), he must take regard to law and duty, and render to everyone his due (justice), he must endure difficulties and not give way to discouragement (fortitude), he must observe moderation and self-control (temperance).

113. — IV. Origin, Increase and Loss of Virtues.

1. The *natural virtues* are acquired and increased by practice, i.e., by repeated good acts. They are weakened and finally lost by frequent contrary acts.

Since the opposition of concupiscence is diminished by habit, a certain facility and joyousness are connected with the natural virtues. — A natural virtue is not lost by a single mortal sin against it.

2. The *supernatural virtues* are immediately infused into the soul by God. For their increase man must dispose himself by good moral conduct, the increase, however, being actually effected by God Himself. A supernatural virtue is lost by a grave sin against it.

The supernatural virtues give man's spiritual faculties a permanent capacity and an inner inclination for supernaturally good actions. Since they are not acquired by repeated exercise, there can be no habit through which the opposition of concupiscence is weakened, and thus they imply no external facility and pleasure in their practice.

The *loss* of faith is effected by a grave sin directly opposed to faith; hope is always lost together with faith, since it cannot exist without faith, as well as by every sin directly contrary to hope. Charity and the moral virtues are lost by every mortal sin.

114. — V. The Co-ordination of Virtues. 1. The *infused* and *acquired* virtues can exist independently of one another.

A baptized infant possesses the infused virtues, but not the acquired ones. Conversely, an adult may lose his infused virtues by a mortal sin and retain possession of his acquired virtues.

2. The *acquired* virtues are so **interconnected** that a person who possesses one of them to perfection, also possesses all the others. But as long as they are imperfect, one may be had without the others.

The reason is that prudence is the mother of all the moral virtues; he who possesses perfect prudence possesses all the other virtues. But as long as the virtues are imperfect, there is only a certain inclination, a predisposition to some definite moral activity, which does not necessarily imply an inclination to some other moral activity. Therefore, an unchaste person may be very generous.

3. The *infused* virtues of faith and hope can exist without the moral virtues; but love is inseparably connected with the moral virtues.

Faith and hope are given with the theological virtue of love, if they are not already had. Hope cannot exist without faith. Love cannot exist without faith and hope.

115. — VI. The Gradation of Virtues. The supernatural virtues rank higher than the natural. Among the supernatural virtues the theological virtues take precedence over the moral virtues, and among the three theological virtues hope stands higher than faith, and love higher than faith and hope.

That virtue is more perfect which brings us closer to our final end. The natural virtues regulate man with reference to a natural end; the supernatural, to his supernatural end. The moral virtues regulate the means necessary for the attainment of our eternal end, the theological unite us with our Eternal End Itself, Which is God. While faith makes God known to us, hope strives after Him and love unites us intimately with Him. Wherefore, the love of God is the most perfect and the Queen of all Virtues. It is the very essence of Christian perfection.

116. — VII. Christian perfection or the striving

after virtue is partly a duty and partly a matter of counsel.

In so far as it is a matter of counsel it is treated in Ascetics and Mystics. In so far as it is a duty it is dealt with in the teaching on the commandments. — The means of grace, especially the sacraments, are helps in earnestly and resolutely striving for virtue. They will be treated in the tract on the Sacraments.

Book II

117. THE COMMANDMENTS

We reach our eternal goal by observing the commandments which, for practical purposes, we shall divide into commandments that have their origin in the theological virtues, the ten commandments, and the commandments of the Church.

Part I

THE PRECEPTS
OF THE THEOLOGICAL VIRTUES

Chapter I

THE VIRTUE OF FAITH

Article I

Concept and Necessity of Faith

I. Concept. Faith is a supernatural virtue which, with the help of divine grace, enables us firmly to believe as true on the authority of God whatever God has revealed.

From the authority of God there arises the grave obligation to believe, at least implicitly, all that God has revealed, and also the duty to make an act of faith as soon as the revealed truth has been sufficiently presented for belief. — One must likewise make an act of faith repeatedly during life. It suffices that this be done by the practice of one's religion, e.g., by prayer, attendance at Mass, etc. — Besides this, one may be obliged to make an act of faith because of particular circumstances, e.g., if one has denied his faith, or if one cannot otherwise overcome a temptation.

118. — II. Necessary Knowledge of Faith. 1. By *necessity of means* (necessitate medii) every one who has attained the use of reason must know and believe that there is a God Who rewards the good and punishes the wicked. Probably one must also know and believe in the Blessed Trinity and the Incarnation.

Practically we must follow the safer opinion (Cf. 93). Therefore, one may not baptize or hear the confession of persons who have no knowledge of the Trinity or Incarnation, if these truths can still be sufficiently taught them. If a person doubts about the sufficiency of a penitent's knowledge it is generally recommended that the penitent be briefly instructed in the confessional. — Practically, however, confessions made in ignorance of the Trinity and Incarnation need not be repeated (Cf. 565).   — If a dying person cannot be further instructed he may be baptized or absolved although he only believes in God Who rewards the good and punishes the wicked. In such a situation Baptism is administered absolutely if the dying person undoubtedly has the intention of receiving Baptism; this condition, however, will seldom be realized in the case of such ignorance. Such a person should be absolved conditionally (si capax es). — *Idiots* who cannot even grasp the two fundamental truths are to be treated as infants.

2. By *necessity of precept* (necessitate praecepti) one is obliged to believe and have a knowledge of: the Apostles' Creed, the Our Father, the Ten Commandments, the Precepts of the Church and the necessary Sacraments (Baptism, Penance and Holy Eucharist) and also the other Sacraments if he desires to or must receive them.

The knowledge of nearly all these truths is required under pain of mortal sin. There is only a slight obligation in regard to several of the secondary truths, e.g., Christ's burial. There is no obligation to be able to repeat these truths by heart. A penitent ignorant of these truths may be absolved only if he seriously promises to be instructed, e.g., by diligently attending sermons, catechetical instructions, etc. A *more complete knowledge* of faith is necessary if the lack of such knowledge constitutes a danger of losing the faith. This is especially the case in our times. One may readily sin, therefore, by not knowing his catechism.

119.   *Article II*

Profession and Denial of the Faith

I. Profession of Faith may be demanded by divine and ecclesiastical law.

1. *Divine law* obliges one to profess his faith publicly if silence or evasion would imply a denial of faith, contempt of religion, an insult to God or scandal to one's neighbor (Cf. C. 1325).

When questioned by the proper authority one must confess his faith at the risk of his life. If such inquiry is illegal one may call attention to this fact and decline to answer. Questions by private persons may be answered by silence or evasion, if this would not be equivalent to a denial of faith, or does not give the impression that one is inconstant in his faith or ashamed of it.

Public defense of the faith is necessary if one can thereby avoid mocking and contempt of the faith. In itself flight is permissible in time of persecution. If the presence of priests is necessary for the welfare of the faithful these may not flee.

2. The *positive law* of the Church furthermore demands a public profession of faith at certain times.

α) C. 1406 requires that confessors and preachers make the profession of faith prescribed by the Holy See before they receive their faculties. According to a declaration of the Holy Office, March 22, 1918, this profession must be preceded by the oath against Modernism (confer AAS 10-136). — If one receives his preacher's patent and faculties for confessions at the same time, the profession need be made only once (Cf. 66). The profession need not be repeated with the renewal of jurisdiction, or when obtaining jurisdiction in another diocese.

β) The Church demands a "public" profession of faith from every adult about to be baptized, and also from every convert from heresy. The latter must make this profession before two witnesses and renounce his heresy. An exception is made if the danger of death leaves no time for this. The fact of conversion must be entered in the parish book. The conversion need not be made generally known. For some good reason one may keep his conversion secret for some time.

120. — II. Denial of Faith whether direct or indirect, is never allowed.

1. *Direct* denial of the faith is made by words, signs or actions which by their nature contain a denial of the true faith or a profession of a false faith.

He directly denies his faith who declares that he is no Catholic or that he is a Protestant; who sacrifices to idols, participates in a Protestant communion service or allows himself to be re-baptized. — It is not a denial of the faith, however, if a priest denies he is a priest.

2. An *indirect* denial of the faith is any action or omission which contains a denial of the faith, not in itself, but under the given circumstances.

He indirectly denies his faith who, when asked about his faith, remains silent while another replies that the person questioned is not a Catholic or that there is no Catholic among those present. — The same holds if one is instrumental in his being registered by authorities as a non-sectarian, failing thereby to reveal the truth. It is also an indirect denial of the faith if one frequents only non-Catholic services, to make others believe he has fallen away from his faith. — Some authors consider it a denial of faith to wear the masonic emblems or use the masonic handshake. Other authors do not admit this, but consider such actions lawful in certain instances.

3. *No denial* of faith is contained in the concealment thereof.

Therefore, a Catholic is allowed to eat meat on Fridays so as not to be recognized as a Catholic in order to avoid great vexation. The same holds for the omission of the sign of the cross at table prayers. Even the failure to kneel or genuflect in the presence of the Blessed Sacrament is in itself no denial of the faith, but it would likely be a sign of irreverence. It would be such a denial, however, if one, upon being challenged, would eat meat on a day of abstinence, etc., to show his contempt for the faith.

121.   *Article III*

Infidelity, Apostasy and Heresy

I. Infidelity is the lack of faith in one who is not
baptized. It is sinful in as far as one is responsible for it.

Inculpable infidelity is no sin. Whoever sinfully neglects to
acquire a knowledge of the true faith sins venially or mortally
according to the degree of his neglect. — One has no grave
obligation to make further investigation as long as he has no
reasonable doubt about his present religion. — Infidelity is always
a mortal sin for him who has had the true faith sufficiently
presented to him.

122. — II. Apostasy is complete defection from the
faith on the part of one who received the true faith in
Baptism (C. 1325).

One becomes an apostate by denying, for example, a personal
God or the Divinity of Christ. Affiliation with another form of
religion is not required.

123. — III. Heresy is an error of judgment in
consequence of which a baptized person obstinately denies
or doubts a truth revealed by God and proposed by the
Church for belief (C. 1325).

He *obstinately* denies a truth who does so deliberately despite
his knowing that the Church proposes it as divinely revealed.
He sins against faith, gravely or venially according to the degree
or negligence but is not a formal heretic who through sinful
ignorance does not know that the Church proposes a given truth
as divinely revealed. The same holds for the heretic who doubts
the truth of his religion, but fails to make further inquiry through
sinful carelessness or negligence. He becomes a formal heretic if he
neglects this inquiry because he is determined not to become a
Catholic, even though he would recognize the Catholic religion
as the true one.

He is guilty of the sin of heresy, but is not subject to canonical penalties, who denies a truth which he wrongly believes to
be revealed by God and proposed by the Church for belief; in
like manner, he who while having the faith denies such a truth,

but who is not baptized (e.g., a catechumen); also, he who interiorly denies the truth, but does not manifest his denial outwardly.

Since heresy is an *error of judgment,* he who only makes an external semblance of denying a truth of faith, but is, nevertheless, inwardly convinced of its truth, is no heretic, and does not incur the corresponding penalty, although he is considered a heretic in the external forum. Such a person, nevertheless, sins gravely by a denial of faith.

Although one is a heretic who deliberately *doubts* a truth of faith, he who merely suspends his judgment about a truth proposed as true, but does not postively doubt it, is no heretic; yet, he sins against his duty of making an act of faith. Whoever is tempted against faith and hesitates between assent and denial, and deliberately withholds his assent, sins venially by neglecting to resist the temptation.

Liberals, socialists and *communists* are heretics or not, depending upon the extent to which they profess the principles of these parties. Whoever, for example, professes the complete independence of the Christian State from the Church, or that the Church is subject to the State, is a heretic; similarly, he who maintains on principle that religion should have no influence on public life, or who would supplant matrimony with free love, or says private ownership of temporal things is an injustice. — Because of their ignorance such people are often in good faith. Whether the confessor may leave them in such faith depends upon the nature of their error and the amount of scandal they give. However, the episcopal regulations must be observed in this regard.

Since heresy presupposes *divine revelation,* he is no heretic who denies a truth that the Church in her capacity of infallible teacher proposes, but not as revealed by God; nevertheless, such a person sins gravely. — Whoever professes a truth which has indeed been condemned, but not by the infallible teaching of the Church, does not sin against faith, but against the obedience he owes the Church. as long as the contrary is not proved to certainty.

The Church's approbation of *private revelations* merely means they contain nothing against faith and morals. He never sins mortally who denies them because he is not convinced that they are from God.

N. B. *Schism* is usually associated with heresy.

If this is the case, what was said of heretics applies equally to schismatics. If not, schism is not a sin against faith, but against charity and obedience (Cf. 432).

124.   *Article IV*

Association with Non-Catholics

Association may be had with non-Catholics either in civil matters (communicatio civilis) or in religious functions (communicatio in sacris).

I. Association with non-Catholics in **civil affairs** is allowed as long as this does not constitute a danger to one's faith.

Because of the danger to faith it may be forbidden to work for those not of our faith, to join certain societies or attend non-Catholic schools. Since *debates* and *controversies* on religious subjects with those not of our faith are fraught with many dangers, especially if they are public, they are forbidden without permission of the Holy See, or in urgent cases, of the local Ordinary (C. 1325). According to a decision of the Holy Office on June 5, 1948, this prohibition holds particularly for the so-called "Ecumenical" Congresses. Disputes that arise from circumstances and only casually are not forbidden, e.g., with a travelling companion, etc. Neither are lectures or "Evidence Guild Talks" forbidden even though it is understood that any one present may heckle and make objections. It is forbidden to participate in assemblies, unions, lectures and societies that aim at a federation of all Christians. The promotion of all such projects is also forbidden (AAS 19-278).

125. — II. Participation in **religious worship** takes place when Catholics take part in non-Catholic services or permit non-Catholics to participate in Catholic services.

1. *Participation of Catholics* in non-Catholic services may mean that Catholics actually take part in the religious worship of non-Catholics or that they are only passively present at their sacred services.

a) Active participation in non-Catholic services is entirely forbidden (C. 1258).

The natural law forbids participation in services that are heretical. If the service is one that heretics have in common with us, even though no scandal comes from such participation, it is at least forbidden by Church law.

Therefore, it is forbidden to ask a heretic to baptize, to be a sponsor for a non-Catholic (even by proxy). In general it is unlawful to be best man or bridesmaid at a marriage performed by a non-Catholic minister, to receive Holy Communion from the hands of a schismatic. Some authors hold that in America it is considered only a sign of friendship to be selected as best man or bridesmaid at a non-Catholic wedding, not as officially witnessing the marriage contract. — In danger of death it is lawful to ask a non-Catholic to administer a Sacrament, provided there is no Catholic present who can do so, and if there is no scandal. — So, too, it is lawful with the required dispensation for a mixed marriage to allow a non-Catholic partner to administer the Sacrament of Matrimony to oneself and vice versa; but never before a non-Catholic minister.

It is forbidden to sing, play the organ or other instruments in the religious services of non-Catholics. — But it is not forbidden to pray or sing privately with heretics if the prayers or songs are not heretical and no scandal is given.

Whoever acts contrary to the prescriptions of C. 1258 and takes part in non-Catholic services is suspected of heresy (C. 2316).

126. *b) Passive attendance* at non-Catholic services is allowed for a good reason, e.g., due to one's position or for politeness, provided the danger of perversion and scandal is precluded (C. 1258).

Passive assistance implies that no part is taken in praying, singing, etc.

Under these restrictions it is permissible to attend a heretical Baptism, a marriage or funeral service conducted in a non-Catholic church. It is sometimes lawful to attend a non-Catholic service through mere curiosity, if the sect has long been established in the place. — A servant may also accompany his or her employers to a non-Catholic service if asked to do so. Soldiers and prisoners may attend such services if commanded to do so for the sake of order, but not if ordered *in odium fidei*. Attending the sermons of non-Catholic ministers may often be forbidden because of scandal or danger to faith; this latter holds also for

listening to such sermons on the radio, especially if done often.
—- A Catholic may not assist at the attempted marriage of a
Catholic before a non-Catholic clergyman since this would imply
a contempt for the Church's regulations and be a source of scandal.
One doing so, however, would not be "co-operating" in a manner
by which he would incur the excommunication mentioned in C.
2231.

127. — **2. *Participation of non-Catholics*** in Catholic worship can also be active or passive.

a) Active participation of non-Catholics in Catholic
services is forbidden in as far as it gives the impression
that there is no essential difference between Catholic and
non-Catholic faith or promotes indifferentism.

Protestants may not be sponsors at a Catholic Baptism. As far
as they belong to a sect they cannot perform this office validly
(C. 756). For a grave reason and if no scandal is given they
may, with the permission of the Ordinary, be witnesses at a Catholic
marriage. In as far as the Sacraments may be administered to
dying non-Catholics who are in good faith confer 558, 628. —
Neither may sacramentals be given them publicly. Hence, they should
not be given blessed candles on the Feast of Purification, ashes
on Ash Wednesday nor palms on Palm Sunday. It is not forbidden to give them holy water, blessed medals or to bless them
privately that they may receive the light of faith as well as health
of body (C. 1149). They may not carry candles at liturgical
functions, alternate at choir-prayers or participate in liturgical singing. For special reasons the Holy Office has allowed schismatic
girls to sing with Catholic girls at liturgical functions. — If no
Catholic organist is available, a non-Catholic may play the organ
for a time, scandal, however, being avoided. A priest may not
act as minister and accompany the corpse of a heretic to the
grave. For a good reason and apart from scandal he may accompany the corpse as a private person and lead some prayers at
the grave.

b) Passive attendance of non-Catholics at our services
is allowed. They may be invited to hear sermons.

128. Note.

1. ***Proximate and remote co-operation*** in sacred
services, confer 148.

2. The *reception of converts* into the Church is best done in the following order:

a) Thorough instruction in the Catholic faith.

b) Investigation into the validity of their non-Catholic baptism.

c) Notification of the Ordinary.

Reception into the Church is asked of the bishop in the name of the convert. If an adult is to be conditionally baptized the faculties to baptize without the ceremonies are usually requested at the same time, unless one has these faculties already by custom or general episcopal enactment. The ceremonies for the Baptism of adults are to be used if the convert has completed the seventh year (Cf. 483). In the U. S., however, the Rite for the baptism of infants is quite universally employed.

d) The actual reception differs according as the convert is to be baptized absolutely, conditionally or not at all.

In most cases the decision rests with the bishop whether and how Baptism is to be administered. Only when there is absolutely no doubt may the priest decide. If investigations are impossible conditional Baptism is allowed.

α) If Baptism is to be conferred absolutely nothing is required besides Baptism.

No adjuration of heresy nor absolution from sins or censures is necessary. The priest should see to it that the convert is sorry for personal sins.

β) If conditional Baptism is necessary the prayers indicated in the Roman ritual are first said, profession of faith is made, Baptism is administered conditionally, confession is heard and conditional absolution given.

The formula for the profession is found in the ritual. A record of the profession of faith is made and signed by the convert, two witnesses and the priest who took the profession. (Formulary Cf. 801.) Some diocesan regulations require conditional Baptism so

— 72 —

that the convert be more at ease and better disposed to contrition. But conditional absolution must follow the Baptism. This arrangement is possible if the convert confesses to the priest who is to baptize him, or if the priest arranges it with another confessor.

γ) If Baptism is not required profession of faith is made, absolution is given in the external forum from excommunication, and sacramental confession is made.

The absolution from the excommunication on account of heresy given in the external forum is valid also for the internal forum (C. 2251). If the formula is not contained in the diocesan ritual it is generally obtained from the chancery. No definite formula is necessary for validity. — Whoever has not completed his fourteenth year does not incur penalties l.s. and, therefore, need not be absolved from the censure.

e) *After the reception* the convert should immediately assist at Holy Mass and receive Holy Communion, unless grave and urgent reasons prevent this (C. 753).

"Immediately" is to be understood morally; any good reason would excuse from doing so right away. — Confirmation should be received in due time. — If a Catholic marriage follows, the *benedictio nuptialis* may be given and the *Missa pro sponsis* said.

N.B. In danger of death if time presses it is sufficient if the request to be received into the Church be recorded before two witnesses. Profession of faith follows. This can be made by merely answering questions. — Every priest is empowered to absolve from censures and sins in danger of death (Cf. 428, 579). To avoid embarassment at the funeral the non-Catholic minister should be informed of the conversion, preferably in the presence of relatives. — Episcopal authorities should subsequently be informed of the entire matter.

129. Chapter II

THE VIRTUE OF HOPE

I. Concept. Hope is a supernatural, infused virtue by which, with reliance on God's Omnipotence, Good

ness and Fidelity, we look forward to eternal salvation
and the necessary means to obtain it.

II. Necessity. Acts of hope are necessary for adults,
both by necessity of means and precept.

Acts of hope must be made on attaining the age of reason, i.e.,
when eternal happiness is sufficiently recognized as man's last end;
so, too, when one has sinned by despair; again if one cannot
otherwise overcome a temptation; if one must fulfill an obligation which presupposes an act of hope; finally, frequently during
life. One fulfills this duty by the exercise of hope implied in
leading a practical Christian life.

130. — III. Sins against Hope.

One sins against hope in the first place by not making the
acts of hope when required; furthermore, by having absolutely
no desire for the possession of God, and then by despair and
presumption.

1. He has **no desire** for the possession of God who
does not seek his final happiness in God.

He who would willingly renounce heaven in order to live
forever here on earth sins gravely if this attitude arises from a
preference for temporal things over the union with God. Such
statements, however, are often only an unfortunate expression of
an inordinate attachment to the things of this world and hence
they are not always mortally sinful. — One desiring to live forever
here on earth because he fears to be damned after death does
not always sin gravely (by despair) against hope.

131. — 2. *Despair* consists in giving up all hope
of salvation and the means necessary to be saved.

Despair must not be *confused* with the anxiety and fears that
may be entertained even by good people who are very conscientious in the performance of their duties. — Nervous and
hysterical persons often experience an apathy towards religious
exercises, which is an infirmity and not a sin against hope. Furthermore, the sensibly-perceptible feeling of despair is not a
voluntary defection from God, and if in such a state of soul
exaggerated expressions are sometimes used, they are not seriously
meant. — Habitual sinners who "despair" of their betterment,

are often only pusillanimous souls who despair rather of their own co-operation with grace than of divine assistance itself. If one "despairs" of receiving temporal things requested in prayer, this is likewise not a sin against hope, since God has not promised to grant them.

It is, moreover, not a sin against hope if one who is weary of life, wishes "out of despair" that he were dead. Sometimes there may be a sin, generally venial, against a different virtue. Such a wish is lawful if made with resignation to God's Will and if it proceeds from a desire for heaven or to be relieved from extraordinary suffering (Cf. 209).

132. — 3. *Presumption* is a sin committed by him who, in striving for eternal happiness, either trusts too much in his own strength or expects God to do something which, in keeping with His Attributes, He cannot grant, or which according to His divine plan He does not will to do.

He sins by *presumption* who hopes to reach heaven by his own efforts alone, or through the merits of Christ exclusive of all good works; likewise, who expects God to help him in committing sin, etc. or who sins because God is merciful.

It is *not presumption* to sin with the hope of being forgiven, since the real cause of such a sin is human weakness and not the hope of forgiveness. Even in the case in which a person would not so readily sin if the hope of forgiveness were not present to his mind, this circumstance would not be the cause, but only the occasion of sin. — It is likewise not presumption if one sins repeatedly because it is as easy to confess many sins as to confess only one, or if one postpones repentance in the hope of confessing later. This might readily be a sin against love of oneself.

133.   Chapter III

THE VIRTUE OF LOVE

Charity is a supernatural, infused virtue by which we love God as the highest good for His own sake and ourselves and our neighbor for God's sake.

Article I

The Love of God

I. The duty to make an act of love of God sometimes arises by necessity of means, more often by necessity of precept.

1. By *necessity of means* every adult is obliged to make an act of love of God if there is no other means of justification.

Other means to justification, besides martyrdom, are Baptism and the Sacrament of Penance with at least imperfect contrition.

2. By *necessity of precept* a person must make an act of love upon reaching the age of reason and when he must recover the state of grace and cannot do so by means of a Sacrament; likewise, when one cannot otherwise overcome a temptation. Furthermore, one must make frequent acts of love during life.

The state of grace is necessary, for example, in danger of death, when one must administer a Sacrament or receive a Sacrament of the living. — It is not known just how often such an act must be made during life. Moreover, one who leads a Christian life and avoids mortal sin, virtually at least, makes many acts of love.

II. Direct sins against the love of God are committed by omitting the above-mentioned acts of love and by hatred of God.

One sins by *hatred* of God if he has an aversion for God, e.g., because God forbids and punishes sin or permits suffering; furthermore, if one is hostile towards God, wishes Him evil, or wishes He would not exist, or were not omniscient or just; or if out of aversion for God one tried to destroy what gives God glory, e.g., by persecuting or suppressing the Church.

134.   *Article II*

Christian Self-Love

I. The necessity of supernatural self-love follows from

the command "Thou shalt love thy neighbor as thyself" (Matt. 22, 39).

Its necessity follows also from the fact that he who loves God will voluntarily love all that pertains to God and manifests the Divine Perfections.

II. Self-love is **practiced** by the very fact that one makes efforts to acquire supernatural, spiritual goods, and those things that are necessary for our corporal well-being, and external worldly possessions.

Since the natural virtue of self-love has its moral value we are not always obliged to act from a motive of supernatural self-love.

III. Sins against self-love are egotism and a hatred of oneself.

An *egoist* sins by preferring his own well-being to the glory of God or the common welfare. One sins by *self-hatred* if he does not reasonably provide for his body and soul. In fact every sin is a sin against a reasonable love of self. Since this is self-evident one need not specially accuse himself thereof in confession.

135.   *Article III*

The Love of Our Neighbor

§ **1. The Duty and Order of Fraternal Charity**

I. The duty of fraternal charity. 1. *In general* every one is bound out of love for God to love all creatures who are capable of receiving grace and enjoying eternal happiness.

This includes the Angels and Saints in heaven, the Suffering Souls in purgatory, sinners and the just here on earth; but not the damned in hell.

The moral virtue of fraternal charity also is ethically good; it consists in loving another because to do so is something naturally honorable.

2. *In particular* the duty of fraternal charity embraces also our enemies.

a) Forgiveness is, therefore, a duty even though one's enemy does not ask for it.

Enmity, hatred, desire for revenge and cursing are mortal sins if the matter is grievous. The following acts or dispositions are not to be confused with such sins: natural aversion for another, indignation at or dislike for the wicked or harmful conduct or quality of another. Cursing is not mortally sinful if, for example, on account of excitement, it is not fully deliberate, or if it is not seriously meant or if it concerns only a trifling evil. — We may wish our neighbor evil, even death itself, if we do so for his own good or some other equally great advantage, e.g., that a frivolous youth be not led astray and eternally lost, or that a father may not squander the family fortune.

An offender is bound to ask for forgiveness. If two persons have given mutual offence, he must first ask forgiveness who has offended first or who is the more guilty. It is best to advise both to do so. — The apology need not always be expressly made. In many cases it is implicitly contained in a special mark of attention or in a courteous greeting.

The offended must make an effort at reconciliation if the offender would otherwise remain in mortal sin or if scandal would ensue.

136. *b) External evidence* of forgiveness by the ordinary signs of friendship is necessary.

The ordinary signs of friendship differ according to persons, places and times, e.g., between brother and sister, relatives, authorities in the same community, residents of the same locality, fellow-students, confreres, etc. — In many places the common sign of love is the ordinary greeting. — Should the other not return the greeting, the one who gave it need not be the first to greet again.

a) Refusal to give the customary signs of friendship is a mortal sin if it proceeds from deep hatred or if the other is grievously hurt thereby or if great scandal results.

It is not sinful to avoid meeting our enemy in order not to become angry, if this does not scandalize or grieve our neighbor. It is not a grievous sin for two neighbors or confreres not to speak to or greet one another for a time because of some slight disagreement.

β) The ordinary signs of love may be omitted for some time for some good reason and apart from scandal.

Such reasons are the other's correction or just punishment, or to give evidence of the deep pain caused by the offence.

137. c) One need not renounce his right to *reparation* or *compensation* for damages.

Even though an offender has asked for forgiveness, judicial action may still be brought against him, but not out of hatred. — One would have to renounce his right to restitution if the damage inflicted were insignificant and the other's loss through restitution would be unduly great.

d) The obligation to love one's enemy does not require that *special signs of love* be shown him, even if such signs were previously mutually given. — In exceptional cases one might be obliged thereto for other reasons.

This would be the case, for example, if the refusal would be scandalous or if one had reason to believe that the giving of such signs would effect a change of heart in the other person. One need not undergo great sacrifice for this purpose.

138. — II. The order to be observed in loving our neighbor is determined by his need and our relation to him.

1. *The need* of my neighbor may be spiritual or temporal. Both may be extreme, grave or ordinary.

One is in extreme need if without the help of others he cannot at all, or only with extreme difficulty, avoid eternal or temporal death. Similarly, if one is in great danger of being placed in extreme need, or if he can scarcely escape a grave, enduring evil without the help of others, e.g., long imprisonment, loss of fortune or social standing, etc.

One is in grave necessity, if, without the help of others, he cannot without great difficulty avoid losing his soul, or if one suffers a great temporal evil or a not uncommonly great evil of long duration.

One is in common or ordinary need if threatened with a slight evil, or with a great one which can easily be avoided.

a) In *extreme spiritual necessity* we must assist **our** neighbor even at the risk of our life.

One need not *risk his life,* however, unless there is certain hope that our neighbor will be saved from his need by our assistance, or if there are others who can and will lend their aid, or if by our assistance the salvation of a number of others would be endangered. — Practically speaking, therefore, a mother cannot be obliged to undergo a caesarean operation, to make certain that her child be validly baptized; the reasons being that Baptism in the womb is probably valid, and that it is not certain the child will be extracted alive, nor that it will be saved if it dies as an adult. — It is never allowed to commit a sin, whether mortal or venial, to save others; since the will of God must be preferred to all else.

139. *b*) In *extreme temporal necessity* our neighbor must be helped even at our great personal inconvenience, but not at the risk of our life, unless our position or the common welfare demand the safety of the threatened party.

Such would be the duty of a physician appointed for a certain case. — It is lawful and laudable to endanger one's life to save a neighbor's life for a supernatural motive.

c) In *grave spiritual or temporal need* our neighbor must be helped in as far as this is possible without serious inconvenience to ourselves. Position, justice **or** piety may oblige one to make such a sacrifice.

Pastors must gravely inconvenience themselves for their parishioners if these cannot otherwise save their souls without great difficulty.

d) In *ordinary spiritual or temporal necessity* one is not obliged to help his neighbor in each and every case.

However, one must not be so disposed that he never comes to the assistance of another in such need. One must rather frequently help others if this does not imply a great disadvantage to himself. — One may forego a great spiritual good which is not necessary for salvation for the sake of our neighbor's spiritual or temporal welfare, e.g., postpone entry into a religious community, offer all **one's** good works for the Suffering Souls, expose oneself to remote danger of sin.

140. — 2. *Our relations* with our neighbor oblige us to help those who are nearest bound to us in case several are in similar need.

Since our connections with our fellowmen rest on different grounds, e.g., parentage, race, religion, we must prefer one to the other only in regard to those goods upon which the respective connection is based. Since blood relationship is the foundation of all our other connections, our relatives, at least those of the first degree, should be given the preference to others in a like case of need. The order, therefore, to be followed is: one's husband or wife, children, parents, brothers and sisters, other relatives, friends, etc. In extreme need our parents must be preferred to all others since we owe them our being.

141. § 2. Works of Charity

Among the various works of charity we here consider chiefly almsgiving and fraternal correction.

I. Almsgiving. 1. In a case of *extreme necessity* one is obliged under grave sin to help the poor even by sacrificing things necessary for our state of life.

One need not dispose of the things that are necessary for his own life or for those committed to his care.

a) The help *need not be more* than is required to alleviate the extreme need

If a loan suffices one need not make a donation.

b) One need *not do for others* what he is not obliged to do to save his own life.

One need not finance a change of climate for a poor man to save his life. A surgeon need not perform an extraordinary operation gratis. Neither is one obliged to renounce his social standing (Cf. 210).

2. In a case of *grave necessity* one must help the poor if it can be done without sacrificing things necessary for one's state in life. This obligation, generally speaking, is a grave one.

If a certain poor man can readily find help elsewhere, one would not have the grave duty to help him. But were only one particular physician or lawyer able to help him, he would have the grave duty to do so gratis. A man who possesses no superfluous goods, sins venially by not averting grave need from another if he can do so at slight inconvenience.

3. In their *ordinary need* one must help the poor in general from one's superfluous possessions; and according to the opinion of some authors, only under pain of venial sin.

One does not have to help all such paupers; it suffices that he aid several. Whoever annually contributes 2% of his superfluous income for this purpose does his duty by the poor. — They sin venially who, although they have only enough for themselves, never do anything for the poor. Note, however, that only the extreme limits of sin are indicated here. Whoever leads a truly Christian life will certainly do more than this for those in ordinary need.

N. B. Since great need is at the present day quite common, either at home or elsewhere, and since many modern charitable organizations make it easy to alleviate such need, one must expend considerably more than merely 2% of his superfluous possessions for charity. It is not necessary that one give all that he can spare to alleviate the need of a whole country stricken with extreme need (China, India). For, even should he give all he has, such a general evil would not be remedied. However, if all do their duty the individual will find it relatively easy to do his share.

142. — II. Fraternal Correction. 1. It is **a grave** *duty* to avert sin or the proximate danger of sin from another if the following conditions are simultaneously verified.

a) My neighbor must be in *actual spiritual distress.*

This is the case: if his sin or his determination to sin is certain; further, if my neighbor will not improve without fraternal correction; and, finally, if no one else, at least equally capable as myself, will undertake to correct him.

In as far as *no harm* will come of sins committed through *invincible ignorance* there is no duty in *charity* to correct anyone about to commit a material sin, e.g., by calling his attention to a day of fast or abstinence. But should such sins prove harmful either to the sinner himself (sins against the sixth commandment) or to others (failure to make restitution or scandal), there is a duty of charity to inform such as are in invincible ignorance. — Even should charity not oblige, the honor of God might impose a venial obligation to admonish another (to avert blasphemy). Besides, some are obliged in virtue of their office or out of piety to correct others.

b) The spiritual need must be *grave*.

This is always the case when mortal sin is involved. By way of exception a Superior may have the serious obligation to correct even minor failings of subjects if, for example, discipline is endangered by them.

c) There must be *well-founded hope* that the other will profit by the correction.

As a rule, therefore, there is no obligation to correct strangers. — A scrupulous person should not make fraternal corrections, since he is unfitted to do so. — If one foresees that greater good will come of fraternal correction at a later time, it may be postponed.

If there is *no hope* of improvement, fraternal correction is necessary only if omitting it would be scandalous.

d) The correction must be possible *without great personal detriment*.

It is generally not more than a venial sin to omit a fraternal correction because of very great timidity. — Bishops, pastors, etc., in virtue of their office, parents by reason of piety, are obliged to correct others even at the cost of great personal sacrifice. — Private persons, too, must do so if the omission would greatly harm the common welfare, e.g., if a perverted pupil were corrupting a whole institution, or if a priest were misleading the faithful.

143. — **2. The manner** of making fraternal correction. It can be done by words, glances, sometimes even by changing the subject of conversation or by withholding support from another.

3. *The order* to be observed in administering a fraternal correction is the following: first, one should correct privately, then, in the presence of one or two others; if this fails, one should report the matter to the proper authority. (Cf. Matt. 18, 15-17.)

Immediate denouncement is permitted: if the fault is public or will soon become public; if the common good or the good of another requires immediate manifestation of the fault, or if one would find personal correction very inconvenient, or if private correction would evidently be of no avail. Since one or the other of these conditions is usually verified in communities (institutions, seminaries, etc.) the matter can generally be referred forthwith to the Superiors.

144.   § 3. Sins Against Fraternal Charity

The principal external sins against the love of one's neighbor are seduction, scandal or co-operation.

I. Seduction. 1. The *direct and express* inducement of another to sin by words, signs or conduct, is a sin of the same theological species and gravity as the sin thus caused. It is, furthermore, a sin against charity.

In confessing sins which by their nature require an accomplice, e.g., fornication, one need not make special mention of seduction.

2. It is permissible to make a *request* which can be granted without sin, but which one foresees will be sinfully granted, provided one has a serious reason to make the request.

Thus one may ask a usurer for a loan; or a perjurer to take an oath. But if one can easily request the same from someone who will not sin in granting it one is obliged to do so.

We may never request anyone to do something which he cannot do without sin, e.g., to ask a tax-collector not to do his duty conscientiously.

3. *Advising a lesser sin* than the one a sinner is about to commit is ordinarily allowed, if the sinner

cannot otherwise be deterred from committing the greater sin.

This is certain if the lesser sin is contained in the greater, e.g., to advise a criminal to rob another rather than rob and murder him. Some authors also think it lawful to advise the lesser sin even if the sinner had no intention to commit that particular sin, e.g., persuade a murderer to rob, rather than kill another. — Concerning the unjust injury done to some definite person whom the sinner did not have in mind, confer 351.

145. — II. Scandal.

While seduction causes another to sin, scandal offers him the occasion to sin, sometimes, too, with the express purpose of causing him to sin.

1. *Unbecoming words or conduct* that are an occasion for another's spiritual ruin (scandal in the proper sense) are mortal or venial sins according as they give him occasion to sin seriously or not.

If the sin of another is intended, he who gives the scandal is guilty not only of a sin against charity, but also of a sin against the virtue he gives occasion to violate.

It is not necessary that the sin of the other actually follow; it suffices that the action can lead to sin. It is a mortal sin, therefore, to display obscene objects in a show window or public place. There is no question of scandal if those who witness a scandalous deed are either so depraved or so good that the thing has no influence upon them. — It is only a venial sin of scandal if the other sins gravely, but rather because of his own personal depravity than on account of some trivial occasion, which he uses as an opportunity to sin. Thus children are guilty of a venial sin of scandal, if, by slight disobedience, they occasion serious cursing on the part of their parents, or if girls by their trivial vanities, or their somewhat slightly unbecoming make-up or dress give young men an occasion to sin against holy purity.

146. — 2. *Actions good in themselves, which do not have the appearance of evil,* but which, nevertheless, give others occasion to sin, need not be omitted if the omission means great inconvenience.

It would be a *great hardship*, for example, for a girl to be compelled never to use a certain convenient street because someone living thereon sins gravely at the sight of her; but it would be only a slight inconvenience for her to choose another street once in a while. It would likewise be a great hardship to be compelled to give a large alms to a beggar in order to prevent his cursing, since others would soon imitate him.

A *slight inconvenience*, however, would not justify one to perform such an action, e.g., to inform another that one is eating meat on Friday because of a dispensation. So, too, one would be obliged to postpone the action or perform it secretly if this can easily be done.

3. *The observance of a positive law* may be omitted to avoid scandal. Ordinarily, however, one is not obliged to do this.

Thus a girl may miss Mass on Sunday to avoid being an occasion of sin to some certain young man. A pastor may say Mass on Sunday without fasting provided he cannot otherwise avoid scandal. Should a group of communists attempt to participate in an ecclesiastical funeral with their red flag, the pastor should try, in a becoming way to prevent it; if his efforts are in vain he may proceed with the funeral. If, however, against his will a red pall would be placed over the coffin, the priest should not conduct the funeral in the interest of the common good, even though the deceased were entitled to ecclesiastical burial according to C. 1239.

4. *Actions which are wrong in themselves* may never be done to avoid scandal.

It is not lawful to deny one's faith in order to avoid giving another an occasion to ridicule it; nor may one tell a lie to prevent an outburst of anger in another.

5. *Positing an occasion* of sin for another is lawful for a proportionately grave reason if the action itself is either good or indifferent.

Thus parents and employers may leave money lying about in order to test the honesty of their children or employees.

6. *The reparation of scandal* is an obligation in-

cumbent upon all who have scandalized others.

Ordinarily this is done sufficiently by receiving the Sacraments and giving a good example. Only in exceptional cases is a public statement necessary.

147. — III. Co-operation. 1. *Formal co-operation* in the sin of another, i.e., concurrence in which one takes part in the external sinful deed of another and at the same time consents to his evil intention, is always wrong.

2. *Immediate co-operation,* i.e., a concurrence in positing an action, which, according to its nature (ex fine operis) apart from the intention of one's accomplice (finis operantis) directly tends to produce the evil effect intended by the principal agent, is likewise wrong, even when done under grave moral duress. An exception is made when there is a question of damage to another's property, but only in certain cases.

Concerning co-operation in doing injury to another's external possessions, confer 354.

3. *Material co-operation,* i.e., concurrence in an action which is only a preparation to a sinful deed, is also wrong as a rule. It may be permitted if the preparatory action is good or at least indifferent, and a correspondingly good reason is had.

The *reason* must be greater, in proportion to the gravity of the other's sin, or the more certain it is that the sin will not be committed without one's co-operation or the greater one's obligation is to prevent the sin.

148. — 4. *Individual cases of co-operation.*

In these cases we take regard only to the sin of co-operation; besides this many things may be forbidden by reason of the scandal.

a) Co-operation in non-Catholic worship.

A servant may accompany his master to a Protestant church if doing so will not be interpreted as membership in the sect.

To sing or pray along in non-Catholic services is wrong because it is a participation in an illicit form of worship (Cf. 125). — Sisters in a hospital may not summon a non-Catholic minister for a dying person to assist him in death. For a very weighty reason (e.g., public welfare) they may inform the minister that a patient desires to see him. It seems lawful even for them to prepare a little table for his use in religious ministrations. — An architect may design churches for Protestants and synagogues for Jews for some very good reason; a lesser reason justifies the ordinary laborer to work on such buildings. In both cases, however, the supposition is that the heresy has long been practiced unmolested in that particular locality. It is lawful to sell pews, tables, carpets, lights, etc. to non-Catholics for their churches (if otherwise one would lose the profit). — A greater reason is required to sell works of art to non-Catholic churches since these serve to enhance their divine services and induce others to join the sect or remain in it. The Sacred Penitentiary declared it lawful to give money for the construction of Protestant churches if this will give Catholics the exclusive use of the church they at present share with non-Catholics. Congressmen may vote public funds for the erection of a Protestant church if it be in the interest of religious harmony. So, too, may private individuals for the sake of public peace among religious bodies attend bazaars, concerts, purchase chances, etc. in affairs conducted by Protestants for the building of a church, if the Protestants have extended the same courtesy to Catholics. Ringing the bells in non-Catholic churches, and giving notice of their services in the newspapers is looked upon by many authors as merely indicating the time of their services, and can be justified for any relatively grave reason.

149. *b) Donations for the building and maintenance of non-Catholic schools and orphanages.*

Since the principal purpose of such institutions is instruction and the exercise of charity one may contribute money towards such projects in mixed localities, provided no scandal results therefrom and the institutions will not be used for proselytizing.

c) Contributions to socialistic or liberalistic societies.

If the purpose of such societies is the care of the poor, sick, etc., one may contribute towards them for a reasonable cause. If their aim is opposition to the Church, or the election of a socialistic, liberalistic, or communistic candidate, it is wrong to support them.

150. *d) Co-operation in the publication of books, papers or magazines inimical to faith or morals.*

Printing, publishing or editing such literature is never allowed. Linotyping or proofreading the same is considered proximate co-operation, hence, permissible only for an extremely grave reason, e.g., if one cannot otherwise make a living. — Preparing and handling the paper, mixing the ink, servicing the presses, etc. is lawful for a time for a moderately grave reason. Selling ink, paper, machinery, etc. to such printing establishments is only remote co-operation and is lawful for the sake of profit. — To write a good article for an objectionable publication is to promote (although to a small extent) the interests of the magazine and is allowed only for a just and reasonable cause recognized as such by the bishop (C. 1386). In an urgent case the bishop's permission may be presumed. To contribute good articles regularly as an associate editor of an evil publication is to promote the same considerably and is lawful only for an extremely grave reason, e.g., if one cannot otherwise support himself or his family. Advertising in a disreputable newspaper is generally not a great aid to its publication and, therefore, lawful for any reasonable cause. Extensive advertising of an individual business man or a company may imply considerable assistance and is justifiable only for much more important reasons. One needs special faculties from the Holy See to sell irreligious literature; even then he may sell only to those who he has reason to think have faculties to read such literature (C. 1404. Cf. 400). In case of doubt one may presume the purchaser has the requisite permission (nemo malus nisi probetur). To others than these one may sell only to avoid an unusually great detriment, e.g., complete loss of trade. Professedly immoral literature may not be sold (C. 1404). Distribution of bad papers is considered proximate co-operation and is, therefore, justified only to avert great harm. Subscribing to such papers likewise requires a grave reason, e.g., great advantage to one's business. Merely to see what one's competitors have to say or sell is not a sufficient reason to receive such papers. To buy a copy now and then would be very remote co-operation and would be justified for an unimportant reason, provided no scandal would ensue. — In the reading of such literature the Church's laws on the prohibition of books must be observed (Cf. 397, 400 sqq.).

151. *e) Co-operation in immoral shows and dances.*

He sins mortally who takes part in, arranges, conducts, finances or invites others to mortally sinful shows and dances. If the same are only slightly indecent there would only be a venial sin in so doing. Musicians who play for immoral dances sin gravely unless excused by some weighty reason. — Policemen or watchmen who must be present on duty are excused. Those that keep the theater or hall in repair, etc. co-operate only remotely and are, therefore, excused for a less weighty reason. A very serious reason is necessary to rent one's place for such purposes, when his refusal to do so would prevent their taking place. Less reason suffices if other locations are easily available.

152. f) Co-operation of employees in the sins of their employers.

Domestics may by reason of their being employed prepare meat on a day of abstinence at the request of their employer, or serve drink in spite of the fact that they know he will become intoxicated. — Thus, too, may an employee purchase or procure immoral books or literature for his employer. For a proportionately good reason he may carry letters or gifts to a person with whom he knows his employer has illicit relations, or convey him thither or admit such a person into his employer's house. It is never lawful directly to induce another to sin; though for a serious reason a servant might invite such a person to visit his master, even though he knows sin will be committed; but not if such an invitation would be equivalent to seduction. — By order of the employer office help may make copies of accounts that will be injurious to others; for very good reasons they may even draft such statements themselves if ordered to do so. — Taxi drivers may give their services to those who ask to be conveyed to houses of ill-repute, because, on the one hand, they cannot hinder sin anyway, and, on the other, their refusal would mean considerable loss to themselves. — Clerks in a drug store may never advise customers in the purchase of contraceptives, but to keep their positions they may sell these things to those that ask for them.

153. g) Co-operation of laborers and tradesmen.

Seamstresses may for a reasonable cause and on request make unbecoming dresses, provided the wearing of them is not mortally sinful. Only a very weighty reason can justify the making of clothes that are gravely scandalous. Should one make such garments without being requested, merely to attract customers one would sin by scandal. — Merchants may sell things that can be misused, but the misuse of which is only foreseen in a general way, e.g., cards, dice, cosmetics, jewelry. A grave reason is necessary, not merely the loss of profits, if it is certain that the customer will abuse the articles. Tavern-keepers may not serve spirituous drinks to anyone who obviously will become intoxicated thereby, or who is already under the influence, unless they have a grave reason, e.g., to avoid great harm, cursing, fighting, etc. It is permitted, however, to serve intoxicating drinks to guests in general, even though one knows beforehand that some usually drink too much. Unless a dispensation is had, it is not lawful voluntarily to offer guests meat on days of abstinence. One may serve meat at their request. If a host is sure that a certain guest has no dispensation, he may serve the meat only to avert great harm. — Papers usually inimical to faith or morals may not be displayed even though they ask for them, and will otherwise fail to patronize the newsstand. One must also remember that such literature falls under the Church's prohibition (C. 1384, 1399). Should such literature only occasionally attack faith or morals it may be sold to individual buyers requesting it if the refusal would mean considerable loss of trade. Only if one knows from experience that nearly all customers ask for such literature and that they will not further patronize his place of business unless he openly displays it, may he do so. Good literature should then be displayed along with it.

154. h) Co-operation of the judge in executing an unjust law by passing sentence in accordance with the law.

A judge can never sentence one to do anything that is intrinsically wrong. Thus, for example, he cannot order one to live conjugally with a person to whom he is not married before God. — On the co-operation of a magistrate in contracting an invalid marriage confer 660, in obtaining a divorce, 766. — A judge may inflict a penalty on the transgressor of an unjust law if there is question of only a slight punishment and there is no prospect of the law's being repealed by concerted resistance on the part of the better citizens. In such a case the condemned cannot reasonably object to the sentence; this is especially applicable if the common good demands that a good judge remain in office. But a judge may never in such a case deprive a criminal of an inalienable right or possession, e.g., his life.

What has been said of the judge is generally applicable also to the impaneled and sworn members of a *jury*.

155. Part II

THE TEN COMMANDMENTS

The first three commandments of the Decalogue regulate our relations with God; the other seven, our relations with our neighbor.

In particular the first three commandments oblige us to show a becoming reverence to God with due submission to Him as the Creator and Supreme Lord of all things, i.e., to practice the virtue of religion. — The individual acts of divine worship are: sacrifice, adoration, prayer, vows, oaths, the sanctification of certain times, and the reception of the Sacraments.

Section I

The First Commandment

The first commandment requires that we worship God by sacrifice, adoration and prayer. It forbids us to dishonor Him by superstition and irreligion.

Chapter I

ACTS PRESCRIBED BY THE FIRST COMMANDMENT

I. Sacrifice.

In the new Law the worship of God demands the offering of the Holy Sacrifice of the Mass (Cf. 522 sqq.), at which the faithful are obliged to assist on occasions. (Cf. 159 sqq.)

156. — **II. Adoration.** 1. *Concept.* Adoration is the act of divine worship by which we acknowledge the Infinite Majesty and Dominion of God and our own dependence upon Him and submission to Him.

In a wide sense adoration may also mean the reverence shown to another person by reason of his pre-eminence.

2. Obligation. a) *Adoration in the proper sense*

(cultus latriæ) may and must be rendered to God alone.

It is rendered to Him *absolutely* when God Himself is worshipped (e.g., the Blessed Trinity, Jesus Christ, the Blessed Sacrament) because of His own excellence; it is offered to Him *relatively* when images of God, instruments of the Sacred Passion, etc., are venerated because of the excellence of God to Whom they have such a close relationship.

b) A special worship (cultus duliæ) is due to the angels and the saints, since as friends of God they participate in His excellence.

A greater worship (cultus hyperduliæ) than that offered to any other creature is due the Mother of God, because she also shares in a special manner in His excellence.

Saints may be venerated everywhere on earth with any act of the cult of dulia; the Blessed, only in those places where the Holy See permits their veneration and in the manner approved by it (C. 1277). The title "Venerable Servant of God" does not permit the practice of public veneration (C. 2115); private veneration of such a person is not forbidden.

The veneration of the Saints, etc., may also be *absolute* or *relative,* according as the Saints themselves are venerated, or only objects (pictures, relics) that have a close relation to them. — Only genuine relics may be exposed publicly in Church for veneration. Documents of authentication prove that relics are genuine (C. 1283). Ancient relics may be venerated according to custom unless it is altogether certain that they are not genuine (C. 1285). Exraordinary relics can neither be given away nor transferred to another church without permission of the Holy See. (C. 1281). Neither may they be kept in private homes or private oratories without the express permission of the local Ordinary (C. 1282).

157. — III. Prayer. 1. *Concept.* Prayer in a restricted sense is a request made to God for the granting of something that is necessary or useful for salvation.

In the *wide sense* prayer is any pious aspiration of the soul towards God or things divine. In this sense we distinguish prayers into prayers of praise, thanksgiving and petition. — God alone may be implored as the ultimate Author and Dispenser of all good. However, one may petition others for their intercession. Only the angels and those Saints and Blessed who have been acknowledged as such by the Church may be invoked publicly. Privately we may implore all the just in heaven and on earth, and in particular also baptized infants that die before attaining the use of reason, as also the Souls in Purgatory. — *Internal attention* is not necessary for the essence of prayer. One fulfills his duty in obligatory prayers (penance, Divine Office) even though he is voluntarily distracted when saying them, although such distraction is evidently a venial sin and a hindrance to the efficacy of prayer. A prayer said while performing external actions which are incompatible with internal attention ceases to be a prayer.

2. The *obligation* of praying is certain; how often one must pray is controverted.

Voluntary omission of daily prayers is seldom free from all fault, since it is the result of negligence and tepidity.

158. Appendix. The Divine Office.

1. *The obligation* of saying the Divine Office is a grave one for all clerics in Sacred Orders (C. 135), for those who have benefices (C. 1475), for religious who have solemn vows in communities that have the choir obligation, excepting the lay Brothers and lay Sisters (C. 610).

On the day of one's ordination to the subdiaconate the obligation to say the breviary begins, not with matins, but with that hour of the Divine Office which corresponds to the time when the order is received. If the ordinand had already said that part of the Office before his ordination to which he would only be obliged afterwards, he would have satisfied his obligation. — It is a grave sin to omit even one small hour or its equivalent. He who omits the entire Office of the day commits only one sin, provided he had previously made up his mind to omit it. Whoever omits his breviary on several successive days, commits as many mortal sins as days on which he neglects it. If one says his Office in English (e.g., the litany of Rogation Days) he does not fulfill his obligations (S. R. C. June 3, 1904). — It is disputed whether or not the litany on the Feast of St. Mark and the

Rogation Days obliges under grave sin. — In a well-founded doubt as to whether or not one has recited an hour of his Office he is not obliged to repeat it, much less must he do so if he doubts whether he recited the Office correctly. — If one has said the wrong Office by mistake, he has likewise done his duty (officium valet pro officio). If one discovers his mistake while praying he may continue the Office he has begun; but it were better to finish from the corresponding place in the correct Office. If one, for example, has said Sext twice and omitted None, he is still obliged to recite None. Other authors would excuse one from reciting None in this case, since the obligation of the breviary concerns the quantity rather than the quality, and the quantity of the two hours is more or less equal. If one has erroneously recited the wrong Office it were better that he does not say the one omitted on the day when the one already recited is due. — To intentionally interchange one Office for another of approximately the same length is not a grave sin, even though done frequently. — Merely to be able to pray with a companion or in choir where a different Office is being said is a sufficient reason to interchange Offices. — If one does not have the Proper Office at hand he must take the Office from the "Common." If there is no "Common" for the Office he must recite some other Office from his breviary. Concerning attention confer 157.

159. — 2. *The time* within which one must recite the Divine Office is the natural day, i.e., from midnight to midnight.

In reckoning the time for the private recitation of the Divine Office (not for choir prayer) one may follow any of the various ways of computing time (C. 33. Cf. 506 a). — Matins may be *anticipated* any time of the year after two o'clock P.M. The litany on the Feast of St. Mark and the Rogation Days may not be anticipated. — The priest should recite Matins and Lauds before his Mass. The present custom is to say the Little Hours in the forenoon, Vespers in the afternoon and Compline in the evening. In Lent and Passiontide Vespers are now said after noon both in choir and in common, and may fittingly be said at this same time when recited alone. — For any reasonable cause one may say the entire Office before noon or after noon. If one foresees a *hindrance* to the saying of his Office on the next day, it is very commendable for him to use his privilege of anticipating Matins, but there is no obligation to do so. But there is an obligation to say Vespers and Compline before noon if one cannot do so later in the day.

160. — 3. *The order* of the individual hours may

be interchanged without grave sin; an unwarranted interruption in the individual hours or between them is never gravely sinful; this is allowed for any good reason.

Matins may be anticipated in the afternoon or evening of the preceding day. Lauds are a morning prayer and are said in the early morning in choir or in common, and this rule may fittingly be observed by one reciting the Divine Office alone. Compline is appropriately said as the last prayer at the end of the day, even if one has anticipated Matins. In this case an examination of conscience (lasting a reasonable length of time) replaces the *Pater noster* before the *Confiteor.* — If one does not have the lessons at hand he may recite the parts of the Office available and supply the lessons later. So, too, one may recite the Little Hours before Matins, if he has only his "Horae Diurnae" with him at the time. — If one interrupts his Office, even in the middle of a psalm, he may resume praying exactly where he left off. The individual nocturns should not without reason be separated from one another over three hours.

161. — 4. *An excuse* from saying the Divine Office is constituted by either physical or moral impossibility, as also by dispensation.

Therefore, persons *seriously ill* or convalescing are excused; those also who can perhaps converse with others for an hour or two or are able to read for a length of time; since these latter occupations are relaxations and not exertions. Any serious indisposition (e.g., headache) excuses; scrupulosity, too, if it makes the Breviary obligation very troublesome. — Whoever is certain that he cannot say the entire Office and doubts whether he can say one or the other Hour is not obliged to say any part of the Office. — Whoever doubts if his illness is sufficient reason to excuse him from the recitation may follow the judgment of his superior, a reasonable physician or any other sensible person.

They also are excused from saying their Office who, either by reason of their office or for the sake of charity, undertake a task which is incompatible with their Breviary obligation. One need not sacrifice necessary recreation or necessary sleep to say his Office. Thus, a priest returning from an unforeseen sick call shortly before midnight need not give up his necessary sleep in order to say his Office. If he foresaw the situation and yet wilfully neglected to say his Office before the sick call, he sinned gravely. The same holds for those who are busy in the confessional until late at night.

A dispensation may be granted by the bishop according to

common law only when there is question of a dubium facti (C. 15), and in urgent cases which will not allow recourse to Rome (C. 81). This holds also for the superiors of exempt clerical religious communities. The bishop can, for a reasonable cause, dispense for a short period of time in virtue of a general custom.

162. — 5. *The penalty* for omitting Divine Office is determined for those whose obligation arises from a benefice, viz.: they lose their right to the income from their benefice in proportion to the length of time during which they omit their office (C. 1475).

Whoever, therefore, omits his Breviary one day loses his income for a day; whoever misses Matins and Lauds loses half a day's income. This holds only in case the beneficiary has no other obligation in virtue of his benefice than his breviary. If his income is a remuneration for other duties at the same time he does not lose all his income by reason of omitting the Office, e.g., a bishop or a pastor would scarcely lose more than a tenth part of it. — The income thus lost must be turned over to the church funds or to the diocesan seminary or given to the poor (C. 1475).

163.   Chapter II

SINS AGAINST THE FIRST COMMANDMENT

One sins against the first commandment in the first place by omission of the acts that it prescribes, and secondly by superstition and irreligion.

Article I
Superstition

Superstition is false worship of the true God or true worship paid to a false god. The former is called "cultus indebitus"; the latter, "cultus falsi numinis."

I. God is worshipped in a false manner if one mingles religious errors and deception with the worship of the true God (cultus falsus), or if God is worshipped by the practice of senseless, very unusual or ridiculous ceremonies (cultus vanus).

One sins by *false worship* if one worships God by the ceremonial rites of the Old Testament; if one fabricates miracles, visions, and revelations, exposes false relics for veneration, or tries to honor God by unbecoming actions. These are grave sins ex genere suo (Cf. 97); they may be venial by reason of ignorance, simplicity or smallness of matter.

One sins by *vain worship* of God if, contrary to the rubrics, he adds extra ceremonies to divine services, e.g., various signs of the cross, alleluias, etc., or if one seeks to introduce unusual and bizarre devotions. — Such actions are usually venial sins; though they may be grave by reason of scandal or violation of a grave precept of the Church.

164. — II. A creature is given divine worship both when it is worshipped directly as God (idolatry) or when powers are ascribed to it, which it does not possess according to the order of nature or grace (superstition in a restricted sense).

1. *Idolatry* is always a grave sin.

A grave sin is committed whether one intends actually to worship a creature as God (formal idolatry) or does it only externally through fear (material idolatry). Ignorance alone excuses from subjective sin, e.g., if one adores an unconsecrated host believing it to be consecrated.

2. *Superstition* in the restricted sense is committed by divination and sorcery.

Divination and sorcery are in themselves very grave sins, since they contain an explicit or implicit invocation of the devil. — One may sin by engaging in these practices oneself or by causing others to do so, e.g., to tell fortunes or have one's own fortune told, provided he himself or the other person is serious and not merely jesting.

Implicit invocation of the devil is also a grave sin. Even though one protests against the influence of the evil spirit, one still invokes him by using evidently inadequate means to produce some definite effect. If there is a possibility that the effect is the result of some unknown powers of nature, one may use such means if he protests against any diabolical influence. Such a protestation is unnecessary if one is certain the effect is produced by natural causes, even though the respective natural powers are little known, as happens, for example, in the use of the divining rod for the location of water or veins of metal. — At times there will be only venial sin, or no sin at all in the implicit invocation of the devil because of ignorance, simplicity or error, or because one does not really have faith in the questionable practice or because one engages in it more or less as a jest and provided no scandal is given. It will likewise be a venial sin or none at all if one does or omits something indifferent in itself because of certain information received, being prompted not by a belief in fortune telling, dreams, etc. but rather by some indefinite fear or by curiosity.

One may practice superstition also with the aid of *religious objects,* e.g., using the paten as a mirror and expecting thereby to recover from an illness; so, too, if one copies prayer leaflets and distributes them in order to obtain certain effects; furthermore, if one ascribes an infallible efficacy to a certain prayer or picture, etc., as frequently happens in the case of chain-prayers. Simplicity generally excuses one from sin in such cases.

165. — 3. *Rotating tables* may be connected with phenomena that may admit of a natural explanation or with such as cannot be so explained. Therefore, in some cases there may be superstition, in others, not.

It is conceivable that the tables are put into motion by purely natural powers. It is impossible, however, for such powers to manifest absolutely hidden things. Some authors believe they may reveal things that are known to at least one of the persons present. Such practices (e.g., the use of the ouija board) are, however, always to be discouraged, since they easily lead to superstition.

4. *Hypnotism* is not a sin against the worship due to God as long as it is not associated with superstitious intentions or a pantheistic philosophy of life.

Hypnotism is often forbidden by reason of its being dangerous to health and morals. Hence, for the lawfulness of hypnotic practices these conditions must be verified: a serious reason must be had (e.g., to cure certain ills); other unobjectionable means must not be available; furthermore, a thoroughly skilled and morally reliable hypnotist must conduct the hypnotizing; if possible it ought to be done in the presence of witnesses, and, finally, none of the participants may have superstitious intentions. The same principles apply to the modern practice of narcotherapy. Patients with the use of reason must first give consent to such treatment (Cf. 110).

5. *Spiritism* claims to be able to communicate with the spirit world and endeavors to establish such commerce with it. Although spiritism is for the most part fraud, still the intention alone to enter into communication with spirits is gravely sinful.

Therefore, it is mortally sinful to conduct a spiritistic seance or to act as a medium. even if one protests against all communication with evil spirits. It is also forbidden to attend a sitting as a mere spectator, even if one thoroughly discredits spiritism. Merely witnessing a seance may be gravely sinful because of scandal or because this would imply a promoting of spiritistic practices. — Apart from scandal, a scientist does not sin by attending seances for the purpose of studying the nature of spiritistic phenomena.

166.   *Article II*

Irreligion

Irreligion is a specific dishonoring of God, either in His own Person or in persons or things that are consecrated to Him. The sins of irreligion against the first commandment are: tempting God, sacrilege and simony.

I. Tempting God. 1. *The essence* of this sin consists in making an experiment of one of the perfections of God (His Wisdom, Power, etc.) without a good reason.

2. *The division.* This sin is divided into explicit and implicit tempting of God.

God is tempted explicitly if one does something or asks something of God for the purpose of ascertaining whether He possesses a certain power or here and now uses it. God is tempted implicitly if a person, without the express intention of experimenting with God, does a thing which according to its nature implies a tempting of God.

3. *The sin* of tempting God explicitly is always mortal. To tempt God implicitly may only be a venial sin by reason of the smallness of the matter.

taken apart. Chalices and patens *may be handled* ~~gy~~ and by those of the laity to whose care they ~~e.g.~~, sacristans. This also holds for used purificorporals before they have been washed. They ~~sed~~ out by a cleric in Sacred Orders before they ~~ymen.~~ The water used for rinsing is to be poured ~~m~~, or (if there be none) into the fire (C. 1306).

~~used~~ for divine service, but which are *not blessed* ~~,~~ may also be used for profane purposes, e.g., candelabra, cruets, the lavabo basin. The same ~~s~~ that are blessed, but not for divine services. may use blessed candles for studying, season his ~~ed~~ salt, etc. It is no sin to throw the bones of the shells of blessed eggs into the refuse container.

r use of the words of Holy Scripture.

sacrilegious to quote Scripture for sinful ends; to ~~r~~ jest is venially sinful.

ul appropriation of material things destined ~~·vices~~.

~~s~~ by usurpation or theft of ecclesiastical goods, or ~~ongings~~ of a private person which are about to be ~~:~~ services, e.g., a carpet or chair loaned for some ~~nity~~. — It is not a real sacrilege to steal an um~~eft~~ in church. Neither is it a sacrilege to seize the ~~y~~ of a cleric; nor to prevent certain things from ~~·e~~ ownership of the church, e.g., by not paying out

~~II~~. Simony. 1. *Simony of divine right* is ~~·e~~ will to buy or sell a spiritual thing, or a ~~ng~~ that is especially annexed to a spiritual temporal price (C. 727).

~~·g~~" and *"selling"* here mean any agreement ~~ne~~ wishes to oblige another to exchange a ~~ng~~ for a temporal thing or vice versa.

ecessary that the agreement be made explicitly. It be deducible from circumstances (C. 728). — The

— 104 —

Thus it would be a grave sin *expressly* to request Christ to show Himself in the consecrated Host if He be actually present. Should such an experiment proceed from a doubt against one's faith it would also be a grave sin against faith.

Even to tempt God *implicitly* can be a mortal sin, e.g., if a person, in impending danger of death, does not use the ordinary natural means of saving himself, but expects God to save him miraculously. The same holds for him who foolishly exposes himself to imminent danger of death and expects God to preserve his life.

He would not be tempting God who, out of levity or to show his courage, exposes himself to the danger of death (without expecting any special help from God), or who attempts an examination or a sermon without preparation. Such conduct may, however, be sinful for other reasons.

It is not sinful for one to look for extraordinary help from God, after natural means have failed, e.g., if a person voluntarily exposes himself to the danger of martyrdom in order to avert contempt of God. It is likewise not a sin for him who is slightly ill to expect to recover by the grace of God even without the use of medical remedies.

167. — II. A sacrilege is the unbecoming treatment of a sacred person, place or thing as far as these are consecrated to God.

In itself this *sin* is a grave sin, but it may sometimes be venial by reason of the insignificance of the object mistreated. — Specifically distinct sins are committed according as one maltreats a sacred person, place or thing.

1. *A personal sacrilege* is commited by unworthy treatment of a person consecrated to God. Under this head are included:

a) Every real injury inflicted upon a cleric or religious.

A cleric is one who has received tonsure (C. 108). Novices are considered religious. — The sin may be committed by killing, striking, pushing, trampling, throwing, spitting upon, etc., and, furthermore, by casting in prison or wresting something from sacred persons.

— 101 —

b) Every violation of the privilege of forum or immunity, by which a consecrated person, contrary to the prohibition of the Church, is summoned before court, or, e.g., forced into military service.

Concerning this privilege confer 409. — Sins committed by or against such persons, e.g., intoxication, calumny, etc., but which are not in any special manner contrary to their religious character, are not sacrileges.

c) Every sin of unchastity committed by or with persons consecrated to God by Holy Orders or Religious Profession.

Even sins of thought are sacrilegious. — A double sacrilege is committed if two such persons sin together. — The violation of a private vow of chastity constitutes a grave sin, but is not a sacrilege. — Only one sacrilege is committed if the person sinning is both a religious and a priest (Cf. 100).

168. — 2. A local sacrilege is committed by unworthy treatment of a sacred place.

Sacred places are localities destined for divine service or Christian burial by either consecration or benediction (C. 1154), thus: churches, public chapels and some cemeteries. — The sacristy is not a sacred place if it is built on to a church, neither are the church's storage rooms or attic, the church basement nor the church towers.

An unworthy treatment of such places occurs in:

a) Acts which, according to Canon Law, constitute a *pollution of the church.*

These acts are: murder, homicide (also suicide), grievously sinful shedding of blood, abuse of sacred places for godless and sordid purposes, burial of an unbeliever or an excommunicated person after a declaratory or condemnatory sentence has been passed. These acts must be certain, notorious and committed in the church itself. The pollution of a church does not pollute the cemetery beside it, nor vice versa (C. 1172).

b) Acts that are specially *repugnant to the sanctity of*

the place or which

These include: profan public banquets, fights, ing of candles, objects or church may be tolera the divine services. — P sity is not a serious sin. sacrileges. Therefore, th that such sins were comn the showing of stereopti 4—724). — The privi to the above-mentioned places permits taxes to b no sacrilege committed by confer C. 1179.

169. — 3. A rea honoring sacred thin

a) Unworthy recep of the Sacraments, es the Altar.

On unworthy administra confer 463. — *The Most B* neglecting to renew the Sa fully handling, or contemp if the chalices, corporals, see to it that the sanctuary If it were left unlighted committed.

b) Unbecoming trea sacred vessels, the holy

Therefore, he commits a or scornfully destroys the h objects, etc. It is no sin to b useless. — It is sacrilegious (which have been consecrated fane purposes, e.g., to use objects can, however, be use lost their original form, e.g.,

the vestments a only by the cle are committed, cators, palls an must first be r are washed by into the sacrari

Other objects for the purpo carpets, lamps, holds for thin Accordingly on food with bles blessed meat o

c) Improf

It is gravely do so in prop

d) Unlau for divine s

This happe even of the b used for divi religious solen brella that is private proper passing into t a legacy.

170. — the delibera temporal th thing, for

a) "Buy by which spiritual th

It is not suffices that

sin of simony is committed at the time when one makes such an intention; but the ecclesiastical penalties are only incurred when the contract is actually made, either expressly or tacitly (De internis non judicat Prætor). — Rendering some service merely in the hope that one may receive some spiritual good in return is not simony. But it would be simoniacal for one to do so for the primary purpose of giving another an occasion to return a spiritual good which he would otherwise not do.

171. *b) Spiritual things,* or *temporal things annexed to spiritual things* are called the "objects" of simony. They may be of various kinds.

a) Spiritual things are: graces, Gifts of the Holy Ghost, Sacraments, sacramentals, prayers, exercise of ecclesiastical jurisdiction, indulgences, blessings, consecrations, admission into a religious community, reception of an ecclesiastical office, etc.

He commits simony who sells relics, or who for a temporal price casts a vote for someone in an election to an ecclesiastical office. — It is not simony to accept something upon the occasion of a spiritual function, e.g., stolar fees, stipends (C. 730). — Whoever demands a higher stipend than is legitimately permitted commits an injustice and is obliged to restitute, but he does not sin by simony, since the prohibition against requiring a higher stipend is not made to prevent the appearance of simony, but to protect the people against excessive demands. — Neither does he commit simony who gives a priest money that the latter may not unfairly refuse someone a spiritual good, e.g., to administer a Sacrament. It is not simony to buy sacred objects to save them from profanation. Nor would it be simony if a cleric gave someone money as an inducement to recant a calumny, etc., which stands in his way of receiving some ecclesiastical office. But it would be simony to bribe a competitor against accepting an appointment to an office to which he is eligible according to Canon Law. — It is not simoniacal to give another a temporal good to persuade him to do something for his soul's salvation, e.g., to hear Mass, make his Easter. Finally, it is not simony to give a poor man an alms in order to induce him to pray for his benefactor in gratitude for the assistance given.

β) Temporal things may be annexed to spiritual things

either necessarily, so that the temporal things cannot exist independently of them: or accidentally, as partial objects of a contract (C. 727).

A necessary connection with a spiritual thing is had in a benefice which exists only because of the ecclesiastical office. A like relation is had between a spiritual function and the corporal work connected with it.

An accidental connection obtains between the consecration of a chalice and the gold of which it is made; the latter is valuable independently of the consecration. In selling such a chalice the consecration becomes a partial object of the contract if the price is raised because it is consecrated.

Therefore, he is guilty of simony who receives payment for the exertion connected with the celebration of Mass or a sick call. It would not be simony to require some compensation for saying a Mass at a late hour or in some distant place. Nor is it sinful to induce another by a monetary gift to sacrifice his attachment for a relic. — Neither is he guilty of simony who sells indulgenced rosaries or consecrated chalices if he does not increase the price thereof because of the consecration, etc. (C. 730, 1539). Objects lose their indulgences by being sold (C. 924); while blessed and consecrated things lose their blessing, etc. only when they are exposed for public sale (C. 1305).

172. *c*) *The temporal price given as an equivalent* for the spiritual thing may be money, other material goods (munus a manu), human intercession, praise, flattery or protection (munus a lingua), or personal service for temporal purposes (munus ab obsequio).

Therefore, it is simoniacal for a cleric to promise him who has the right of patronage to do secretarial work or give his children Latin lessons provided he receives the benefice from him. The same holds for a patron who will only confer a benefice at the request of a certain person because he sees therein some distinction for himself.

d) Simony of divine right is always *a mortal sin* ex toto genere suo (Cf. 97), because there is a grave irreverence in the comparison between temporal and spiritual things no matter how insignificant they may be.

173. — 2. *Simony of ecclesiastical right* consists in the exchange of things which the Church forbids because of the danger of irreverence to spiritual things connected with such exchange (C. 727).

This kind of simony is committed, e.g., by interchanging benefices against the prescription of C. 1487, or by demanding compensation for the expenses of celebrating Mass contrary to C. 1303 and without the bishop's permission.

Simony of ecclesiastical right is in itself *a mortal sin*, but may be venial by reason of the insignificance of the matter.

174. — 3. *Restitution* in case of simony. Since the contract of simony as also the simoniacal bestowal of office is void, it follows that whatever is given or received through such a contract, and all income received from an office conferred in such a manner, must be restored even prior to a judicial sentence (C. 729).

This obtains even in the case where the simony was committed by a third person without the knowledge of the person who received the benefice. An exception is to be made if the simony was committed fraudulently (e.g., to render the appointment invalid, etc.), or if restitution cannot be made. Therefore, since the application of a bination Mass cannot be cancelled one may keep the stipend accepted for such.

4. On *penalties* for simony confer C. 2392 and No. 437.

175.   *Section II*

Second Commandment

The second commandment forbids directly the dishonoring of God by profanation of His Holy Name. It also directs us thereby always to regard God's Name as sacred in the use of vows, oaths and adjurations and not to dishonor It by blasphemy or profanation.

Chapter I

VOWS

I. Concept. A vow is a promise made to God with

sufficient knowledge and freedom, which has as its object something that is possible, good, and better than its opposite (C. 1307).

1. A *genuine promise* alone is thus a vow, a mere resolution is not.

To know whether one made a real promise or a mere resolution is not so much determined from the words used as from the circumstance that one did or did not wish to oblige himself under sin. In a case of doubt one may presume that a resolution only was intended. — If one is firmly determined that any vow he might make without the advice of his confessor will be invalid, he is not held by a vow which he subsequently makes without such advice.

2. A vow is made to *God alone.*

Whoever vows something to the Saints, generally intends thereby to make a promise to God to do something in honor of the Saints.

176. — 3. *The knowledge required* must be at least as great as would be sufficient to commit a grievous sin.

Therefore, whoever does not have the full *use of his reason* cannot make a valid vow, e.g., infants, intoxicated persons or those half asleep. Likewise, a vow would not oblige one if it had been made altogether thoughtlessly. Neither is there any obligation in case of a well-founded doubt. — Ignorance and error also invalidate a vow if they concern the essence of the thing vowed, an essential circumstance or the principal motive for vowing. Thus, a vow to donate a certain chalice which one thinks is made of silver is invalid if it be actually made of gold. So, too, would a vow to make a pilgrimage on foot be invalid if the person believed it would take only three hours whereas it takes six. Again, no vow is really made if one vows something in thanksgiving for the recovery of his mother, and it turns out that she was not ill. — If the error concerns merely accidental circumstances public vows are valid, this being in the interest of the common good. Private vows would be invalid if with the knowledge of such a circumstance they would not have been made, unless there is question of something purely external. For this reason one would have to fast on a day he vowed to fast, even if he is invited out to dinner on that day and would not have made the vow had he foreseen the invitation.

177. — 4. *Lack of freedom* invalidates a vow that is made under the influence of fear that is grave and unjustly inflicted (C. 1307).

Therefore, a vow is valid if made under fear that is caused by some natural event, e.g., a thunderstorm, illness, etc.; likewise, if made out of inner spiritual anxiety.

5. *The possibility of the matter* vowed must be not only physical but also moral.

If the vow is partly possible and partly impossible of observance it must be kept as far as it can be, provided the matter vowed is divisible. Thus a married person who has made a vow of chastity may not ask for the marriage right. But if the vow is indivisible either in itself or according to the intention of the one vowing, it is invalid. Thus if one vows to make a pilgrimage to St. Ann's in Quebec, but cannot enter the Canadian Dominion he is not obliged to any part of the pilgrimage. — If a vow subsequently becomes impossible its obligation ceases.

6. A thing is *good or better* than its opposite either in itself or because of proximate circumstances.

Avoiding a house or a street is something indifferent in itself, and therefore, a vow to do so would be invalid in itself. But if such places are dangerous occasions of sin, the avoiding of them is something good, and a vow to do so would be valid. — Similarly, it is in itself better not to marry than to marry; therefore, a vow to marry is in itself invalid But if the marriage is necessary in order to make restitution for an injury or to avoid sin, then, to marry is better for the respective person than not to marry, and a vow to marry is valid. — One can also make a vow to do something which is already obligatory.

178. — II. The obligation. 1. Every vow obliges by reason of the virtue of religion either *gravely or venially* according to the intention of the person vowing or the matter vowed.

An insignificant thing can be vowed only under venial obligation, whereas an important matter may be vowed under venial or mortal obligation. — If one had no special intention to oblige himself lightly or seriously it is to be presumed that he assumed a grave obligation if the matter vowed is important. — Those things are considered important which the Church prescribes under mortal sin (hearing Mass, fasting, Holy Communion) or which redound considerably to God's glory or to the good of one's neighbor, or the person making the vow.

If the person making the vow had no intention to the contrary, various insignificant matters will generally *coalesce* to form a "materia gravis" if he made a real vow; but not if his vow concerns some personal service. Thus, whoever vows to give a small alms daily will sin mortally if he neglects to do so for many successive days. But whoever vows to say an Our Father daily will sin only venially even by neglecting his vow for a long time.

One who vows to do something already commanded, commits a double sin by violating his vow. He who doubts whether he had made a vow or not, or whether he has fulfilled it or not, is practically not obliged to do anything.

179. — 2. One can *bind* only *himself* by a vow, *not others* (C. 1310).

If parents, by a vow, dedicate their child to the religious life the child is not obliged to fulfill the vow; but the parents are obliged to give the child an equivalent education. — But if the vow concerns a matter regarding which the parents or guardians have a right to command, the child must obey, but not by virtue of the vow. If the forefathers or the heads of a community vow to hold a procession or observe a fast, future members of the community can be bound to observe it by ecclesiastical law, but not by virtue of the vow, unless they ratify the vow with the intention to bind themselves by it (Cf. *AAS* 29-343).

3. The obligation of a *real vow* descends to the heirs.

If a testator dies without having dispensed an alms he vowed to give, the heirs must give the alms; otherwise they sin against the reverence due to God, and sometimes also against justice, e.g., if the corresponding obligation is imposed upon them in the testament.

4. A *conditional vow* obliges after the condition has been fulfilled.

He sins against the vow who prevents the fulfillment of the condition by fraud; but he has no further obligation.

5. In a **disjunctive vow** one may always change the part chosen even after once making a choice, unless the part one desires to choose has meanwhile become impossible.

The vow *does not oblige* if before one makes his choice one of the parts becomes impossible through no fault of the person vowing, or even if after making a choice the fulfillment of the part chosen becomes impossible without his fault.

180. — III. The interpretation of a vow is made according to the intention of the person vowing. If this is not clear the vow is interpreted as broadly as possible.

Hence, he who vows in general to give an alms or donate a chalice, need not give a large alms nor an expensive chalice. — He who vows to fast a definite length of time need not fast on Sundays nor on days when his work, according to the laws of the Church, excuses him. — Whoever vows to say the rosary, may pray it alternately with a companion.

181. — IV. The fulfillment of a vow. 1. A vow is fulfilled by **doing what one has vowed.** The intention to fulfill it is not required.

Thus, whoever vows to say an Our Father every day, fulfills his vow if he says an Our Father without thinking of his vow. — This would not hold if while saying the prayer he deliberately did not intend to fulfill his vow (Cf. 63).

2. A **personal service** vowed must be fulfilled in person; whereas a *real vow* can also be fulfilled by another.

Wherefore, one person cannot fulfill another's vow to fast, but he can give the alms that the other person vowed. — But should the person who vowed the alms become incapable of giving it he has no obligation to ask another to do it for him. — Should another volunteer to perform the real service vowed the person who made the vow need only give his approval.

3. *The time* for the fulfillment of a vow. *a) If the time is determined* when the vow is made and the vow is not fulfilled within the time determined, then the vow need not be fulfilled later, provided the time fixed was "ad finiendam obligationem"; conversely, however, if the time was set "ad urgendam obligationem" (Cf. 67).

If the person vowing had not determined in what manner the time chosen was to be understood, we generally presume the time set was "ad finiendam obligationem" in all personal works vowed; and "ad urgendam obligationem" if real works were vowed. Therefore, if I do not fulfill a vow to give an alms next week, I must fulfill it the week after; but if I vow to fast next Saturday in honor of the Blessed Virgin Mary and do not observe the fast, I need not fast later.

b) If the time within which the vow is to be fulfilled *is not determined,* it must be fulfilled without delay.

Postponement is grievously sinful only when the value of the service or thing vowed is thereby considerably lessened or if delay constitutes a danger that the vow will later be rendered impossible or will be forgotten.

182. — V. The cessation of the obligation of vows through *external causes* occurs by annulment, dispensation or commutation.

For *internal reasons* a vow ceases to oblige if the final motive ceases (Cf. 176), by a substantial change of the matter vowed (Cf. 177) or by a lapse of the time which was attached to the vow for terminating the obligation (Cf. 181).

1. *The annulment of vows. a) The direct annulment* of a vow can be made by him who has power over the will of the person (domestic power) who made the vow. — Such an annulment is always valid, but a good reason is required to make it licit. — A vow directly annulled never subsequently revives (C. 1312).

A father has this power over the private vows of his children who are under age. — The mother can likewise do it, but with the proper subordination to the father, i.e., if the father does not object; the same holds for anyone who exercises paternal authority in default of the parents. — These vows can still be annulled after the children reach their majority and renew their vows, provided they do not intend thereby to assume an entirely new and independent obligation from that of their old vows. — So, too, superiors (which includes superioresses) may annul the private vows of their subjects made after simple profession. An exception to this rule is the vow to transfer to a stricter community. — This annulment may take place even though the superiors had previously approved of the vows and had given their permission thereto. — Whoever annuls a vow without a reason probably commits only a venial sin. — One may ask for an annulment on any reasonable grounds.

b) *An indirect annulment* of a vow is possible by one who has power over the matter of the vow. In this wise the obligation is not removed, but only suspended for such time as the matter vowed remains in the power of him who has declared the annulment (C. 1312).

Thus married partners may indirectly annul each other's vows which prejudice their mutual conjugal rights, even though the vows antedate marriage. In like manner a father can dissolve the vows of his adult children in as far as such vows hinder him in the free government of the family. — A similar power is enjoyed by a superior over the vows of his novices; the rector of an institution over the vows of his charges; the master over the vows of a servant. — With regard to the validity and lawfulness the same is true as was said of direct annulment. — All the vows that a person makes before entering a religious community are suspended by religious profession for the time he remains in the community (C. 1315).

183. — 2. *Dispensation* releases one from the obligation of a vow if it is granted by a competent superior for a just reason and in the name of God.

a) Those *competent* to dispense, besides the Holy Father, are the local Ordinary, the superior in an exempt religious community with reference to his own subjects, and those who have received delegated faculties from the Holy See (C. 1313).

Unless an explicit exception is made, *"Ordinary"* here includes, besides the Pope, the residential bishop for his diocese, an abbot and prelate *nullius* and their vicar-generals, the apostolic administrator, the vicar and prefect apostolic and those who hold these offices in cases of vacancy. In an exempt religious community the major superiors are the Ordinaries for their subjects. — By *"local Ordinary"* we understand all those above-named except the major superiors in religious institutes (C. 198). Concerning the faculties that regulars have for dispensing confer 416.

With the exception of the Holy Father, the persons named may annul only non-reserved vows, and only in case the annulment would not prejudice the acquired rights of others. *Reserved vows* are all public vows (thus all temporal and perpetual vows in a religious community, as also the implicit vow of chastity that is included in the subdiaconate), and besides these, the vow of perpetual and perfect chastity and the vow to enter a religious community that has solemn vows, provided these private vows are made absolutely and after the completion of the eighteenth year of age (C. 1309). For the formulary for dispensation, confer 799. — The following vows are not reserved: the vow to enter a convent, not to marry, to receive Holy Orders. Neither is a conditional vow reserved, nor a disjunctive vow if a part of the latter is not reserved. Nor is the vow that is made under the influence of even slight fear reserved; and, finally no vow is reserved to which one wished to oblige himself only under venial sin. — A vow made before the completion of the 18th year does not become reserved merely by the fact that it is simply renewed after completing the eighteenth year. If a reserved vow be legitimately commuted into a work that is not reserved, anyone who has faculties to dispense from the non-reserved vows can dispense from such a commuted work. — The *acquired rights* of others are prejudiced if the vow was made primarily for the benefit of others and was accepted by them. Furthermore, it is the practice of the Church in dispensing from vows to substitute some other work if they had been made with full deliberation.

b) The reason for granting the dispensation must be a moderately grave one.

Such reasons are: the welfare of the Church, great inconvenience in keeping the vow, grave danger of violating it, frequent scruples, rashness in making the vow. — In doubt whether the reason is sufficient the dispensation may be petitioned and granted; and the dispensation remains valid, even should one subsequently discover that the reason was insufficient. — But if one has absolutely no reason for asking, the dispensation is invalid.

184. — 3. *The commutation of vows* (i.e., the substitution of another work for the one vowed) that are not reserved may be made by the persons who made the vows if the work substituted is better or equivalent to the one vowed. Only one who has the power to dispense from a vow can commute it into a less good work (C. 1314).

It is always presupposed that no acquired rights of others will be violated. — In order to commute a vow into something of lesser worth there must be a reason, which need not, however, be as important as that required for a complete dispensation. — That work is better which under the prevailing circumstances is more pleasing to God, i.e., more conducive to the spiritual welfare of the person making the vow. — The worth of the work need not be physically equivalent, but only morally. Reversion to the original work vowed is always permitted. — Should the substituted work become impossible there is no obligation to resume the original work vowed if the commutation was made by ecclesiastical authority; but there would be such an obligation if the person himself commuted his own vow.

185.   Chapter II

THE OATH

Concept. An oath is an invocation of God as a witness to the truth of an assertion or to the honesty and fidelity of a promise.

The division is, therefore, into *assertory* and *promissory* oaths. Furthermore, as to the manner of taking an oath, God may be invoked immediately or mediately through some creature that bears some relation to God, as for example if one swears: "I call upon heaven and earth to witness..."

Article I

Conditions for the Validity and Lawfulness of an Oath

I. The validity of an oath requires:

1. *A formula.*

Unequivocal formulae are those such as: "I swear by God," "I call upon God to witness," "So help me God," "I swear by the Cross, by heaven, etc." — *Ambiguous formulae* are: "God knows," "God sees my conscience," "I speak in the sight of God." In the use of ambiguous expressions an oath is taken if the person using them intends to swear; in doubt as to whether one had such an intention or not it is presumed that no oath was taken. The following expressions are not oaths: "Upon my honor," "In honor and conscience," "As true as I live," "As sure as there is a God." The last expression is blasphemous if one wishes thereby to confirm a lie.

2. *The intention to swear.*

At least a *virtual* intention must be had (Cf. 8, 450). — *Without* such an intention no oath is taken even if one uses the formula of an oath. — Thus, such words as the following used at the reception into a religious institute, "I promise, vow and swear" is no oath, but merely a solemn declaration of intention. — If one uses an apt formula but without the intention to swear, which intention is not known to the bystanders, there is only a fictitious oath. It is only a venial sin to swear a fictitious oath provided a true assertion is thereby confirmed. But it is a grave sin of irreverence to God when such an oath is used to confirm a lie.

186. — II. Lawfulness requires:

1. That one be convinced of the **truth** of his assertion or that he have the firm purpose to keep his promise.

Perjury is always gravely sinful even though it be merely in confirmation of a jocose lie. — *A careless oath* is either venially or grievously sinful according as the negligence in inquiring into the truth is slight or grave. Whoever swears to something as true which he seriously doubts, sins gravely. — When *swearing in court* it is usually required that one have acquired the knowledge of his assertion by personal experience. To swear to a strict mental reservation is perjury (Cf. 369). To confirm a broad mental restriction with an oath is a mortal sin if it is done to the prejudice of those who have a right to know the truth; towards others one may do this with a grave reason, without which this would be venially sinful.

2. That the assertion be **morally lawful.**

To swear to a sinful statement (e.g., when detracting or boasting of sin) is a venial sin even though what is said be true. — To promise something evil under oath is mortally sinful, at least if the thing promised be gravely sinful.

3. That there be a *sufficient reason.*

To take an oath rashly is only a venial sin as long as there is no danger of swearing falsely.

187.   *Article II*

The Promissory Oath in Particular

I. The obligation. He who has sworn to do a thing is obliged by the virtue of religion to keep his promise (C. 1317).

A promissory oath, like a vow, obliges under mortal or venial sin according to the importance of the thing promised. — The obligation exists even if the oath is extorted by grave fear. In this case, however, an ecclesiastical superior can annul the obligation (C. 1317). No obligation arises from an oath to do something that is forbidden or useless (Cf. also 288).

II. The interpretation of a promissory oath depends chiefly on the intention of the person swearing. If the intention is uncertain the oath is to be interpreted broadly.

The oath to observe the statutes of an association merely means that one intends to be subject to them and ordinarily observe those regulations that actually oblige at the time, not that he will never transgress any statute. — For the rest, the meaning of the oath is interpreted according to the tenor of the promise, or contract, etc., which is being confirmed by oath (C. 1218). Should he to whom something is promised under oath relinquish his right to the thing promised the obligation of the oath ceases. An oath to keep a secret obliges only as far as does the secret itself.

188. *The oath of allegiance* or the *oath of office* as required of officials, etc., means that one intends to be subject to the law of the land, fulfill his office according to the prescriptions of the law, and not to undertake anything contrary to rightful authority; but it does not mean that one thereby binds himself under oath to observe every civil law.

If the civil laws contain provisions contrary to divine or ecclesiastical law an oath taken to observe them is made with the restriction: with due regard for the divine and ecclesiastical law. Since this condition is ordinarily implied, it need not be added expressly, unless this be necessary to avoid scandal.

III. The cessation of the obligation arising from an oath results from the same reasons and circumstances as that of a vow (Cf. 182 sqq.).

Whosoever has the faculties to annul, commute or dispense from a vow possesses the same power regarding the promissory oath (C. 1320). Note, however, that no privately made promissory oaths are reserved. The dispensation must not involve an injury to the acquired rights of others.

189.   Chapter III

ADJURATION

I. Adjuration in general. 1. _Concept._ Adjuration is the endeavor to persuade another to do or omit something by appealing to God, to a saintly person or sacred object.

God, the Blessed Virgin, the Saints and fellow men of equal standing are adjured in the form of a request. The devil can be adjured only imperatively. Irrational creatures may be adjured only indirectly, as far as God is requested to prevent any harm from coming through such things or to forbid the devil to misuse them to the injury of others.

2. _To adjure_ another **_lawfully_** one must be serious, have a sufficient reason and request only what is licit.

Should either of the first two conditions be lacking the adjuration would be venially sinful. Lack of the third condition is seriously sinful, at least if the thing desired is gravely forbidden.

II. Exorcism is an adjuration in which the devil is

either forced to abandon a possessed person or forbidden to injure someone.

It is forbidden to exorcise a possessed person without the special and express *permission* of the Ordinary (C. 115). — Not only a priest, but also a layman may privately conjure the devil from harming someone, e.g., by the use of sacramentals or by invoking the Name of Jesus.

190.   Chapter IV

DISHONORING THE NAME OF GOD

I. Blasphemy is any speech or gesture that contains contempt for or insult to God. It is always mortally sinful.

It suffices that a person be conscious of the meaning of the words or signs used; it is not necessary that he have the express intention to offer indignity to God. — Blasphemy may tend directly against God, or only indirectly, i.e., when the Saints or sacred things are reviled. — Furthermore, blasphemy may also include a heresy or a curse.

It is blasphemous to deny God's existence, call Him cruel or unjust, to shake one's fist toward heaven. One is guilty of blasphemy, too, by using sacred names and words with contempt or anger towards God.

It is not blasphemous, however, to utter sacred words in mere anger towards a creature (Cross, Sacrament); in themselves such utterances are only venially sinful. Much less is it blasphemous to use the word devil in anger. — Expressions like: the devil take you! may the lightning strike you! are not blasphemies but curses and quite often only venially sinful since they are not used seriously.

II. Profanity, or the disrespectful use of the Holy Name in anger or thoughtlessly, is in itself only a venial sin.

Profanity will be *seriously wrong* if the anger that causes it is directed against God or if it appears, objectively, at least, that one intends thereby to vent his anger against most sacred objects. It may also be seriously sinful because of scandal or an erroneous conscience.

N. B. The words *"cursing"* and *"swearing"* admit of various meanings. By accusing themselves of these sins penitents sometimes mean *a*) profanity, or the use of sacred names in anger against some creature (venial sin); *b*) blasphemy, the use of such names in anger against God or in contempt of Him (mortal sin); *c*) abusive language, which is not a sin against the second commandment but which may offend against charity or is a sin of anger.

191.   *Section III*

The Third Commandment

The third precept of the decalogue commands us to honor God on Sundays and Holydays by observing the Sunday rest and attending Holy Mass.

Chapter I

SUNDAYS AND HOLYDAYS
IN GENERAL

I. The duty to honor God at stated times is a precept of the natural law, the general prescriptions of which are outlined in detail by positive law.

In the Old Testament this proximate determination was found in the divinely instituted ceremonial law. In the New Testament God has entrusted the particular legislation to His Church. — So far as the obligation arises from ecclesiastical law it admits of dispensation.

II. The days which must be sanctified in a special manner in U. S. A. are, besides all Sundays, the Feasts of Christmas, Circumcision of the Lord, Ascension, Assumption of the Blessed Virgin Mary, All Saints and the Feast of the Immaculate Conception (Cf. C. 1247).

Canon Law, legislating for the universal Church, includes also the Feasts of Epiphany, Corpus Christi, Saint Joseph and SS. Peter and Paul.

III. The sanctification of Sundays and Holydays consists in observing the Sunday rest (i.e., abstaining from certain occupations) and attendance at the Holy Sacrifice of the Mass.

192.   Chapter II

THE SUNDAY REST

The Sunday rest requires abstinence from all servile work, judicial acts and commercial occupation. There are reasons that excuse.

I. Servile work (opera servilia) is occupation primarily performed by corporal powers and for material purposes.

Such works are: plowing, sowing, harvesting, etc.; sewing, cobbling, tailoring, printing, masonry work, etc.; all work in mines and factories, etc.

In some places *custom* justifies shaving, hair cutting, knitting, crocheting, etc.

It is also *permitted* to go walking, riding, driving, rowing, journeying, even though these be very fatiguing.

Liberal and *artistic works* (opera liberalia) are also lawful: studying, teaching, drawing, architectural designing, playing music, writing (also typing), painting, delicate sculpturing, embroidering, taking photographs. These works are lawful even if done for remuneration.

Servile works are forbidden even though done gratis, as a form of recreation or for some pious purpose. — About two and a half or three hours of such work, according to its arduousness, is *a grievous sin*. Thus, operating a modern washing machine, which consists in putting the clothes in the machine, pressing a button, removing and hanging clothes, would be only a venial sin if done for that length of time without an excusing cause or dispensation.

193. — II. Judicial acts are forbidden so far as they require juridical procedures or disturb the public rest.

Such acts are: summoning the defendant or witnesses, requiring the oath, publishing or carrying out the sentence. — The *gravity*

of the sin is determined not so much by the length of time
employed as by the importance of the action performed. — It is not
forbidden, however, to consult a lawyer, to grant a dispensation.
etc., on Sunday.

III. Commercial occupations are forbidden.

Forbidden in themselves are such activities as marketing, fairs,
buying and selling, public auctions, shopping in stores. Local
customs, however, justify some of these actions. It is not forbidden
for private persons to confer or agree on the purchase or sale of
cattle, lands, houses, etc.

**194. — IV. Causes excusing from the Sunday
rest** are: dispensation, religious services and one's own
or a neighbor's necessity.

1. *Dispensation* may be granted by the local Ordinary
or the pastor, but the latter only to individual parishioners or single families of the parish and then only in
particular cases (C. 1245).

Individual parishioners may also be dispensed when outside the
parish territory; but strangers only when they are within the
territory of the pastor granting the dispensation. — Superiors in
exempt religious communities have the same rights as a pastor over
the professed members, novices, candidates, pupils, the sick, convalescents, guests and those who reside in the monastery day
and night.

2. *Religious services* justify any work that is immediately connected with divine worship.

Thus, it is permissible to ring church bells, carry banners,
pictures, etc. in processions; but one may not sweep the church
or decorate the altars unless necessity requires this.

3. *Necessity* excuses from Sunday rest if a considerable harm or loss would otherwise be sustained by
oneself or one's neighbor.

Therefore, all indispensable housework is legitimate Sunday
occupation. Poor people may work on Sundays if they cannot
otherwise support themselves. If there is no time or occasion to

do so on week days one may mend clothes on Sunday. For the same reason working people may tend their little gardens on Sunday. Farmers may harvest their grain, hay, etc., or gather fruit on Sunday if a storm threatens. — Any necessary work is allowed in case of fire, flood, etc. — Mechanics may sharpen, repair, etc., tools that farmers and artisans need on Monday. Tailors may work on Sunday if they cannot otherwise finish mourning clothes for a funeral. Lighter manual labor is also probably lawful for charitable purposes or to avoid ennui.

195.   Chapter III

ATTENDANCE AT HOLY MASS

In order that *the grave obligation* of hearing Mass on Sundays and Holydays be fulfilled certain conditions are required on the part of the Mass and on the part of the attendants. — One may be excused from assisting at Mass for a proportionately good reason.

I. On the part of **the Mass of obligation** the following is required:

1. It must be *a complete Mass,* i.e., assistance at it must extend from the beginning of the Mass to the last blessing.

A venial sin is committed by voluntarily omitting an unimportant part of the Mass, e.g., from the beginning of the Mass to the Offertory exclusive, or the part that follows the Communion, or even the part which precedes the Epistle together with that which follows the Communion.

A mortal sin is committed by missing an important part voluntarily, e.g., that which precedes the Gospel together with what follows Holy Communion, the part extending from the beginning of the Mass to the Offertory inclusive, the part of the Canon that precedes the Consecration, or the part between the Consecration and the "Pater Noster," or the Consecration alone; but probably not the Communion alone. It is held that momentary and necessary withdrawal during the Consecration would be excusable. — Whoever misses an important part must supply this part in a later Mass on the same day.

The obligation to hear Mass *is not fulfilled* by him who is not present at the Consecration. But if one is present at the entire Mass except the Consecration, it may be presumed that the Church would not oblige him to attend another Mass. — If one, even though he be late for Mass arrives before the Consecration he must remain for the rest of the Mass in case he cannot assist at a later Mass, since he can still essentially fulfill his Sunday obligation; but if one were so late as to miss the Consecration he would not be obliged to remain for the rest of the Mass.

196. — 2. The Mass must be celebrated in a *church, public* or *semi-public oratory* or in the *open air.* One satisfies his obligation in a private oratory only if one has been granted this special privilege (C. 1249).

A *church* is a sacred edifice dedicated to divine worship and open to all the faithful for this purpose (C. 1161). — A *public oratory* is a chapel erected chiefly for the use of some college or for a group of individual persons, but which is open to the public at least during the time of divine services. — A *semi-public oratory* is one erected for the use of a community or for a certain group of the faithful, others having no right of admission (chapels in convents, monasteries, seminaries, schools, orphanages, hospitals, prisons, etc.). — *Private* or *domestic oratories* are erected in private homes for the exclusive use of a family or some individual (C. 1188).

Only he can satisfy his *Sunday obligation in a domestic oratory* who has received an indult to that effect; such an indult includes all relatives of blood or marriage to the fourth degree who live with him; furthermore, his guests and those servants that are necessary for himself or the priest during Mass. — Furthermore, all domestic servants are included, e.g., cooks, maids, baby-sitters, etc.; not, however, farm hands unless these would practically be members of the household. Canon Law allows anyone to fulfill his Sunday obligation at a Mass said in the private chapel of a cemetery (C. 1249) as also in the domestic oratory of a cardinal or a bishop (C. 1189). — He does not comply with his Sunday duty who attends a Mass said by a priest in a private home or a cabin on board a ship by virtue of a purely personal privilege. It would be otherwise, however, if the privilege is not purely personal, e.g., if the Holy See grants permission to say Mass in any becoming place in the missions or in non-Christian territory.

197. — II. On the part of **the attendant** the following is necessary:

1. *Corporal presence,* i.e., one's presence must be such that one may be reckoned among the attendants at divine service and that one be able to follow the Mass at least in its principal parts.

Wherefore, one *satisfies* his Sunday obligation by being present in church even if he cannot see the priest; so, too, if one is in the sacristy or close to the church, provided always that he is able to follow the main parts of the Mass. — Whoever is more than sixty feet distant from the church can no longer hear Mass even if he is still able to follow the priest at the altar, e.g., by means of a radio. An exception is allowed in the case where he is united to the church by a large crowd of people.

2. *Devout attendance,* i.e., he must have the necessary intention and attention.

The intention to hear Mass is sufficient. The intention to fulfill one's Sunday obligation is not necessary (Cf. 63). At least that degree of attention is required that one is aware of the progress of the Mass or of its principal parts. — Thus, one does not fulfill his obligation if he sleeps soundly during the Mass; whereas, he does who plays the organ, sings, or takes up the collection or who makes his confession during Mass; provided in each instance, however, that the person can in some way advert to the Mass; especially during the Consecration and Communion. Priests hearing confessions during Mass should pause for a while at the Elevation and Communion (Cf. also 67). — Where two or three Masses are being offered simultaneously one can assist at each, and even satisfy a multiple obligation, e.g., to hear Mass in virtue of a vow and as a sacramental penance.

198. — III. **Excuses** from assisting at Mass. Any moderately grave reason suffices to excuse one from assistance at Holy Mass, such as considerable hardship or corporal or spiritual harm either to oneself or another.

Therefore, the following are excused: the sick, convalescents, persons who cannot endure the air in church (e.g., certain neurotic persons and sometimes pregnant women in the first or last months of pregnancy); those that have a long way to church, people hindered by the duties of their state (e.g., shepherds, watchmen, policemen on duty, cooks, and those working in mills that may

not shut down over Sunday); women or children who would
incur the grave displeasure of their husbands or parents by attending Mass; servants whose masters do not permit them to attend
Mass (should this happen consistently the servants should seek
other employment); those that care for the sick, rescue workers
in time of fire or flood; and those who have reason to think that
by staying home they can hinder sin; or who would suffer injury
to their good name or possessions by going to Church. (Thus:
unmarried women who are pregnant, may remain at home if by
doing so they can avoid disgrace; similarly, those who lack clothing becoming to their social standing; those on a journey; those
who would suffer the loss of extraordinary gain by attending Mass).
One may miss Mass for the sake of a pleasure trip once or twice
if he has no other opportunity during the year, or if it is the
last opportunity he will ever have for a certain excursion. (Cf. 60.)
Finally, custom in certain localities excuses such as, for example,
lying-in women, widows in the first days of their bereavement,
engaged persons whose marriage banns are published in the only
Mass they can attend.

199.   *Section IV*

The Fourth Commandment

The fourth commandment determines explicitly the duties of
children towards their parents. Related to these duties are those
that children have towards anyone who participates in any way
in parental authority, as also the duties that parents and all superiors
have towards their subjects; hence, all duties obtaining in the
family and state.

Chapter I

DUTIES IN THE FAMILY

I. Duties of Children towards their Parents.
Piety requires that children show their parents:

1. *Reverence,* not only by internal sentiments but
also by external conduct.

Sins against filial reverence are committed by internal contempt,
offensive speech, disdainful deportment, striking blows. Even a trivial
but seriously meant abuse can be a grave sin. It is likewise a sin
against filial reverence to be ashamed of one's parents, to disown

or fail to recognize them because of their humble state, poor clothes, etc. — It is not against reverence to restrain one's parents even by physical force for some good reason and without interior contempt in case they have lost the use of their reason, e.g., because of insanity, old age or intoxication. Similarly, one may have good reason for not desiring to associate with his parents (because of some crime of theirs) provided, of course, that he looks out for their necessary support.

2. *Love,* in thought, word and deed.

Sins against the love due to parents are: indignation, hatred, cursing, speaking ill of them, injurious words or conduct, causing them anxiety, failure to pray for them or support them in spiritual or corporal necessity. — If children can assist their parents in grave need by remaining in the world they may not enter the religious life (Cf. also 255). — There is no obligation for children to pay their parents' debts after their death if the children have not inherited anything from them, even though the parents contracted these debts for the purpose of educating their children (Cf. also 321).

3. *Obedience* in all lawful matters which relate either to their training or to the domestic order.

Disobedience is a grievous sin if it concerns an important matter and the parents have given a real command. — In educational matters the obligation of obedience lasts until the children come of age. — *Minors* may not, therefore, undertake certain work or enlist in the army against the will of their parents. But in the choice of their vocation they are free. — Even *adult children,* as long as they stay at home, must obey in all things necessary for domestic order, e.g., to return home at a reasonable hour at night. — *Before marrying,* children should consult their parents. But even if they do not follow the sensible advice of their parents they generally commit only a venial sin.

200. — II. Duties of Parents towards their Children.

1. *Love.*

Love is the fundamental obligation of parents towards their children. All their other duties are rooted in it.

2. *Provision for life, health and well-being.*

Before birth they must ~~~~ anything that is injurious to the unborn child. After birth the mother should nurse her own child. Bottle feeding may be injurious to the child; if it is gravely injurious the mother would sin seriously by shirking her obligation unless there were a legitimate excuse. — Parents are also bound to provide their children with food, clothing and housing, and also to procure some degree of material security for them in the future by their industry and economy. — Both father and mother are equally obliged to support their *illegitimate children*. Most States place this responsibility on the father. If the court has sentenced him to do so, it becomes an obligation in conscience (for further details, confer 357). What is said of bottle feeding may be said likewise of engaging a wet nurse.

3. *Education.*

Parents have the natural and inviolable right and duty to give their children a good education. In virtue of this duty parents must educate their children according to their own social standing, accustom them to work and to help themselves at an early age, and provide especially for their physical, moral and spiritual welfare. This latter includes, therefore, the parental duty to set a good example and exercise correction and watchfulness. In the interest of a Catholic education attendance at *Catholic schools* is obligatory. According to canon 1374 Catholic children may not attend non-Catholic, non-denominational or mixed schools. Only the local Ordinary can decide under which circumstances and with which precautions attendance at such schools may be tolerated.

N.B. Since parents delegate a portion of their authority to teachers it follows that there are points of similarity in the duties between teachers and children and those of parents and children.

Children owe their teachers reverence, love and obedience in matters that pertain to their studies and good behavior. — Teachers have the correlative obligation of justice and charity to impart to their pupils proper knowledge and a good training.

201. — III. Mutual Obligations of Husband and Wife.

1. *Duties in common.* Husband and wife must love and help each other; they must grant the marriage right, observe marital fidelity and common life.

It is a grave sin for one of them to be absent for a long time against the will of the other, unless an important reason excuses. For more particulars confer 747. On the suspension of common life confer 764.

2. *The duties of the husband* are principally these: the government of the household and family, providing of food, clothing and shelter.

The husband sins by not making it possible for his wife to live according to her social standing, or by imposing work upon her that is not done by women of her state or condition.

3. *The duties of the wife* arise principally from her position as man's helpmate; she must manage the household affairs with proper subordination to her husband.

She sins by neglecting her domestic duties, by spending, against the will of her husband, larger sums from the common fund than is customary by women of her condition (Cf. also 253). — She may manage the house independently of her husband if he takes no interest in household affairs or if he is incapable of doing his duty in this regard.

202. — IV. Duties between Masters and Servants.

The servants belong to the family in a wide sense of the term. Apprentices, also, have the same standing in so far as they form part of the family circle. Their position in the family gives rise to corresponding obligations.

1. *The Duties of the Master. a)* *Justice* obliges a master to pay his hired help the wages agreed upon, not overburden them with work nor discharge them without a reason before their contract expires.

Violation of these duties carries with it the obligation of restitution. This obtains also in case the master is responsible for the servants leaving his employment prematurely, e.g., because of harsh treatment.

*b) **Charity*** obliges the master to look after the corporal, and especially the spiritual welfare of the hired help.

2. *The Duties of Servants. a*) *Justice* obliges servants to do their work conscientiously and not to leave their master's employment before the expiration of their contract unless there be a good reason for doing so.

If they do not prevent damage being done to the master's property they are obliged to restitution only in case they were hired to guard and protect his possessions.

b) *Piety* obliges them to show reverence, love and obedience to their masters similar to that of children towards their parents.

Their obedience extends to the domestic order, the duties of their position, and in particular to proper deportment and good morals.

203.   Chapter II

CIVIC DUTIES

I. Civil authorities have, as their first duty, to provide for the common welfare of their subjects.

Therefore, those in authority must, according to their ability, avert all harm from their country and promote its welfare; they must safeguard religion and morality, exercise justice in distributing rights and duties, legislate without respect to persons, appoint only worthy candidates to public office and remove therefrom the unqualified.

II. Congressmen and all **representative officials** must, like the supreme authority, endeavor to promote the common good in a positive manner, especially in those matters wherein they are expressly pledged to their constituents.

1. *Accepting an office* is forbidden to anyone incapable of filling it. If there is no valid excuse, he who possesses the ability, must accept a public office, if no

other capable person is available.

2. *Participation* in the deliberations and resolutions is obligatory.

This is especially true of those sessions where the successful passing of a good law or the prevention of an evil one is at stake.

3. *Co-operation* in evil legislation is sinful.

The only exception admitted is the case in which such representatives might avoid a greater evil by their co-operation (Cf. 144, 147); in such cases, however, they must make clear their position. — On their obligation of restitution confer 352, 355.

204. — III. Citizens' obligations embrace:

1. *Love of their country*, to which they owe protection and the opportunity to promote the common interests handed down to them by their forefathers.

This love for one's country should manifest itself particularly by the furthering of its welfare and by living in harmony with one's fellow-citizens. — One must especially beware of prejudicing the common good in favor of some particular class or clique.

2. *Respect for authority.*

Internal contempt for the governing body as such, i.e., for authoritative power (formal contempt) is a serious sin. Whereas internal contempt for the individual who is vested with authority is sinful according as similar contempt of any other person is sinful. The contumelious treatment of one in authority is gravely sinful especially when it occurs publicly or may easily become public; and, furthermore, when it occurs in his very presence.

205. — 3. *Election of good representatives.*

Voting is a civic duty which would seem to bind at least under venial sin whenever a good candidate has an unworthy opponent. It might even be a mortal sin if one's refusal to vote would result in the election of an unworthy candidate.

One may vote for an *unworthy candidate* only when this is necessary to prevent a still less worthy candidate from obtaining office; but in such a case one should explain the reason for his action if this is possible. In an exceptional case one may vote for some unworthy candidate; viz., if he can thereby avert some unusually great personal disadvantage.

4. *Loyalty* to lawfully constituted authority and *obedience* to law in general.

The secret escape of a prisoner is not positive opposition to civic authority and is, therefore, in itself not forbidden.

One may not obey laws that are immoral because they are contrary to the natural law and divine right; furthermore, one may exercise passive opposition towards their enforcement. — Open violence in such cases may be resisted by equal violence, provided that one has well-founded hope of success and that the common good does not suffer greater harm by such opposition than by the violence of the ruling powers. Some authors hold that in the case of extreme necessity the people may, after having exhausted all legitimate means of redress, lawfully depose the ruler and change the political constitution.

206. — 5. *Obedience to tax legislation* in particular. Where the tax laws are only penal laws they oblige in conscience only to accept the penalty inflicted for their transgression (Cf. 57). If they are not mere penal laws they oblige in conscience to the payment of the taxes even prior to a judicial sentence.

a) Indirect taxes are commonly held to be levied as penal laws.

Indirect taxes are the following: duties, customs and the excise taxes, e.g., revenues levied on alcoholic spirits, tobacco, etc.; and, according to some authors, inheritance taxes. Nevertheless, to default in the payment of one's taxes may be grievously sinful (by smuggling, etc.), especially if it be a question of a large sum because of the great dangers to which smugglers, etc., expose themselves and their families. Particularly in time of a depression a defaulter may offend against the common good.

b) Direct taxes are probably not levied by legislation which obliges in conscience prior to a judicial sentence.

Customary interpretation and the intention of the lawgiver would

seem to render an obligation in conscience highly questionable in
our country. Although citizens should be urged to pay their share
of the taxes, nevertheless, *post factum*, it is not necessary to urge
restitution.

Such taxes are personal taxes, real estate and property taxes,
industrial taxes and those that are levied for carrying on a trade
or business. — From this obligation there arises the duty to make
a corresponding declaration for assessment. A person need not be
scrupulous, however, in the appraisal of his possessions. One may
follow the general custom and declare his property in a manner
similar to that of the majority of taxpayers. The reason for this is
that the authorities make allowance for such a procedure in this
assessment. Should one deviate considerably from the customary
usage in appraising or declaring his goods he is guilty of disobedience to the law, but does not sin against commutative justice
and therefore has no obligation of restitution. This, however, would
apply only in the supposition that the law is not merely penal.
For details on restitution, confer 359.

IV. Soldiers who volunteer for military service are
obliged in commutative justice to keep their contract
and render their services.

The general laws of conscription in wartime oblige in conscience even where the legislator does not believe in a supernatural sanction and looks upon all laws as purely penal (Cf. 57).

207.   *Section V*

The Fifth Commandment

The fifth commandment forbids, in the first place, all unjust
killing either of oneself or of others. In the second place, it forbids all unjustified wounding or mutilation. Since death can result from the neglect of adequate care of one's health, the preservation of life and health is also a duty.

Chapter I

DUTIES TOWARDS ONE'S OWN LIFE

I. The direct taking of one's own life is a mortal
sin if done on one's own authority.

It is also forbidden to do something from which death will accidentally follow, if one has suicidal intentions in doing it, e.g., to smoke or drink immoderately in order to shorten one's life. — Suicides are deprived of ecclesiastical burial unless they manifest signs of repentance before death (C. 1240). — If ordered to do so by civil authority one would probably be allowed to carry out a legitimate death sentence upon himself.

II. Indirect suicide is in itself forbidden, but may be permitted for a proportionately grave reason.

One kills himself indirectly if, without the intention of committing suicide, he knowingly and willingly does something which not only has an intended good effect, but from which death also follows. It is presupposed that the good effect results from the action as immediately as does death.

Therefore, it is permissible to leap from a dangerous height to escape burning to death, especially if there is some hope of escaping death from the fall. A woman may also do so to avoid being seized and violated by a libertine. — Thus, too, it is lawful in wartime to blow up an enemy fortification or ship, although one forsees that his life will be lost in doing so.

208. — III. Endangering one's life is lawful only for an adequate reason.

The *reason* must be in proportion to the danger. To expose oneself to the remote danger of death without a sufficient reason would be only a venial sin. The care of the plague-stricken is permitted even at the risk of one's life. Steeplejacks, etc., may expose themselves to the dangers necessarily involved in their occupation. The imprisoned may attempt escape at the risk of their lives to avoid execution or a life-sentence. Dangerous tight-rope walking, etc., merely for motives of gain or vanity is forbidden. If practice or skill make the danger remote there would be no mortal sin in such action. — The same principles apply to all unreasonable wagering and daring one another, e.g., to eat or drink to excess, etc. — Prizefighting and wrestling are per se not immoral since the exposure to grave unjury or death is quite remote; but a reform in present boxing and wrestling regulations seems in place.

IV. Shortening one's life even for several years, or injuring one's health by leading a certain manner of life or doing certain kinds of work is lawful for an adequate reason.

Therefore, unhealthful *work* done in smelting plants or brass foundries, in the mines, glass factories and chemical plants is permitted. *Works of penance* are lawful as long as their practice is reasonable. *Immoderate indulgence* in food or drink is only a venial sin even though one forsees that he will thereby shorten his life to some extent. Immoderate use of drugs and narcotics, morphine, cocaine, etc. is mortally sinful if thereby one considerably shortens his life or ruins his health (Cf. also 110).

209. — V. Self mutilation is allowed only to save one's life.

Mutilation is usually a mortal sin. It is only venially sinful to remove a part of the body that has no important or vital function e.g., the earlobes. — *Castration* is a grave sin whether done to alleviate temptation or to preserve a soprano voice. — *Vasectomy, hysterectomy,* etc. (See No. 213) are mortally sinful if done to prevent offspring. — *Cancer, bloodpoisoning, infection,* etc. justify the amputation of a member of the body. — *Lobotomy* is permissible in cases of serious mental illness, but only as a last resort.

Organic transplantation (corneal, ovarian, renal, etc) according to the supreme law of charity, is probably lawful if it confers a proportionate benefit upon the recipient without depriving the donor completely of an important function. Nor does this seem to conflict with the teaching of Pius XII on the *Principle of Totality*. It is certainly lawful for a dying person to will his corneas to an eye bank.

An autopsy may be performed for an adequate reason. Thus medical science and a knowledge of anatomy is fostered by postmortem examinations. The dissected corpse must be treated reverently and properly buried.

VI. The desire to die is allowed for a reasonable cause and with resignation to God's Will.

Such a *reason* is the desire for the Beatific Vision or to be spared some extraordinarily great temporal misfortune or suffering, e.g., an unusually painful and prolonged illness. Seriously to desire death in order to escape the ordinary hardships of life is gravely sinful.

210. — VII. For the preservation of life and health one must employ at least the ordinary means.

Ordinary means are: proper food, clothing, housing and physical recreation; likewise medicinal remedies which are not beyond the means of the sick person; engaging a physician is also an ordinary means. It is understood that there be no question merely of some slight infirmity that will disappear of itself, and that there be a well-founded hope that medicinal remedies will be helpful.

Employing *extraordinary means* of preserving one's life is generally not obligatory. Therefore, even wealthy people are not obliged to go to a far-distant place or health resort; nor need they summon the best-known physicians even though they should otherwise die. Neither is anyone gravely obliged to undergo a very dangerous operation. — An exception to this rule is to be made if one is necessary for his family or his country and the success of the operation is morally certain. It would seem, therefore, that only in such cases has a father or superior the right to command those subject to him to undergo such an operation.

211.   Chapter II

DUTIES TOWARDS THE LIVES
OF OTHERS

Article I

Killing the Innocent

I. General Principles. 1. *The direct killing* of an innocent person is never allowed.

Euthanasia in a wide sense (therapeutic euthanasia) or the administration of non-lethal doses of narcotics to ease the pain that accompanies death is permissible under certain conditions (Cf. 110). *Euthanasia*, or "the termination of human life by painless means for the purpose of ending severe physical suffering" (definition formulated by the Euthanasia Society of America, Inc.) is not "merciful release" but murder. It is also wrong to hasten the death of a mother who is about to die in order to baptize her unborn child. — Physicians are forbidden, for the sake of experiment, to administer dangerous medicines to the sick in doses that may prove fatal. An exception to this rule may be made if the sick person cannot be saved by any other means and manifests his consent to the use of such a remedy. The same holds for surgical operations. — Puncturing the heart or bloodletting to prevent a person's being buried alive is forbidden under mortal sin. However, if it is certain the person is dead such action may be taken to allay the fears of the relatives.

2. *The indirect killing* of an innocent person, though in itself forbidden, is permissible for an adequate reason.

For the concept of indirect killing see 207. — Thus, if the brakes of an automobile fail and the machine begins dashing downhill the driver may, in order to prevent its going over an embankment, steer it aside even at the risk of running over someone. A city may be bombarded in time of war even though many innocent people will lose their lives. Likewise, during an insurrection one may return the fire of the rebels, even though they seek shelter behind a group of women and children, and many innocent lives are thereby lost, presupposing however, that there is no other way of silencing the fire of the insurrectionists.

212. — II. Foeticide. 1. *The direct killing* of the foetus is murder and therefore always gravely sinful.

Even though it be done to save the life of the mother, it is not permissible to destroy the living child, e.g., by craniotomy, embryotomy, etc. (Note, however, that it is possible today to perform certain cranial operations that reduce the size of the head and save the life of the child by allowing it to be born.) — So, too, it is always mortally sinful to procure an abortion, even though both mother and child will otherwise die. This holds also for ectopic gestation. There may be cases in which one may be left in good faith. Moreover, in most instances help may be rendered in a lawful manner by a caesarean section or similar operations. — All that is likewise mortally sinful which is done with the intention of effecting an abortion, even though this effect does not follow.

2. *Indirect killing* of the foetus is generally forbidden, but may be permitted for grave reasons.

Pregnant women sin gravely if, without a sufficient reason, they perform an action which they forsee will result in an abortion. A mother who is mortally ill may take medicine to restore her health, even though it causes an abortion, presupposing that there is no other remedy for the illness and that the restoration to health does not result from the abortion but from the medication. Similarly, it is lawful to remove a diseased uterus, even though a non-viable foetus be removed with it, provided the removal of the uterus is the only means that will save the mother's life. Under the same conditions it seems permissible to rupture the amniotic membrane and release the fluid in case of hydramnion while the foetus is still inviable, but only to replace into its proper position a retroflexed pregnant uterus incarcerated in the pelvic cavity. This seems lawful since the saving of the mother does not follow from the resulting abortion but from the replacement of the uterus. In other cases the puncture of the amnion is unlawful. (*Translator's note*: A number of moralists list the rupture of the amniotic membrane as unlawful in the foregoing instance since it is claimed that the malposition of the uterus may correct itself spontaneously and since obstetrical practice has other ways of rectifying the abnormality. Since hydramnion, infrequent as it is, usually is encountered only after the foetus is viable, the question is scarcely a practical one.) In like manner it seems that in case of an ectopic pregnancy which endangers the mother's life, the pathological formation may lawfully be removed, even though the foetus will be removed together with it, provided, however, one cannot otherwise save the mother and surgical intervention can no longer be postponed. Some authors go a step further and hold that whenever a tubal pregnancy exists, an operation to remove the tube is permissible, even though the danger to the woman is not imminent. The reason is that every such pregnancy constitutes a gravely dangerous pathological condition. It would seem that this can also be done in case one doubts whether the growth is a tumor or an extra-uterine pregnancy, and the matter will not suffer delay without endangering the life of the mother. It is never lawful, however, to attempt to kill the foetus, e.g., by the induction of an electric current. Medicines that only rarely result in an abortion may be taken even when the mother is in no imminent danger of death.

3. *Premature delivery* may be induced when there is a corresponding good reason since the child is viable.

One should delay such a delivery until it is morally certain that the child can live outside the mother's womb if this can be done without great danger to the life of the mother. If, however, the mother's life has reached a critical stage one may proceed to premature delivery as soon as it is probable that the child is viable. — Normally, a child is viable at the end of the twenty-eighth week of gestation. In a scientifically equipped hospital viability occurs slightly earlier, but the time of viability is a scientific, not an ethical problem, depending upon a number of variable factors.

Painless childbirth is a form of psycho-prophylactic therapy that "cannot be criticized from a moral point of view" (Pius XII). Nor does it contradict Genesis 3, 16 which can mean "Motherhood will give the mother much suffering to bear."

213. ETHICAL DIRECTIVES IN HOSPITAL PROCEDURE

LAWFUL PROCEDURES

I. In general, any procedure involving the reproductive tract is permissible if it is not undertaken for the sole purpose of sterilization.

1. **Orchidectomy** (removal of testes) for the treatment of carcinoma of the prostate when hormone therapy is not indicated.

2. **Oophorectomy** (removal of ovaries) for treatment of cancer of the breast.

3. **Vasectomy**, either by ligation or excision of the vasa deferentia when necessary, e.g., to prevent infection (of the epididymis) in prostatectomy.

4. **Salpingectomy** (removal of Fallopian tubes) for the cure or control of any serious disease.

5. **Hysterectomy** (removal of uterus) as a remedy for prolapse of the uterus, or to correct any other serious pathological condition.

6. **Indirect Sterilization** i.e., when sterility is an incidental consequence of an otherwise necessary procedure (e. g., in radiation therapy).

II. Any operation, treatment or medication during pregnancy directed to the cure or diminution of a serious pathological condition that threatens the life of the mother is permissible provided it does not constitute a direct attack upon the fetus.

1. **Hysterectomy** in the presence of pregnancy, provided the uterus is so seriously diseased as to endanger the life of the mother.

2. **Salpingectomy**, or the excision of a Fallopian tube containing a living, nonviable fetus, provided the action and intention is solely to correct the diseased pathological condition of the tube.

3. **Porro's Operation** under the conditions already mentioned.

4. **Caesarean section** for the removal of a viable fetus, and post-mortem in order to baptize a previable one.

5. **Premature delivery** after 28 weeks of gestation, or in a well equipped hospital, after 26 weeks.

6. **Paracenthesis**, or tapping, of fetal brain in case of Dystocia (difficult labor) resulting from Hydrocephalus.

III. Other operations or procedures injurious to the patient are moral if they can be justified according to the principle of Double Effect (Cf. No. 14) e. g., Appendectomy, Laparotomy, Narcotherapy (Cf. 165), etc.

UNLAWFUL PROCEDURES

1. **Direct Abortion** of a living fetus is always immoral, no matter what its "therapeutic" value. Therefore, neither eclampsia nor the toxemias of pregnancy (such as Morning Sickness) can justify direct abortion. Cf. 212.

2. **Curettage** of a pregnant uterus before the fetus is viable.

3. **Embryotomy** in any form, including Craniotomy, Decapitation and Evisceration, that is directly occisive of a living fetus.

4. **Direct Removal of a nonviable** fetus from a Fallopian tube in case of ectopic gestation.

5. **Premature Delivery** if labor is induced before fetus is viable.

6. **Direct Sterilization**, whether perpetual or temporary, either by removal or inactivation of any reproductive organ (vasectomy, orchidectomy, oophorectomy, hysterectomy, radiation, etc.) for the sole purpose of inducing sterility. Thus, e. g., hysterectomy is not permissible on the occasion of a caesarean operation, unless the womb is infected.

7. **Rupture of the Amniotic Membrane** in case of hydramnion while the fetus is still nonviable. Cf. 212.

8. **Dilation** of the mouth of the uterus (by the insertion of sounds, bougies or other instruments) before the fetus is viable.

9. **Artificial Insemination** (also advising, counselling or co-operating in the practice). Cf. 749.

10. **Unethical Procurement of Semen** for medical diagnosis or for the purpose of fecundation.

11. **Contraception.** Likewise advising or giving information on artificial contraceptive devices or practices. A physician may advise and explain periodic continence (Rhythm) to those entitled to such knowledge. Cf. 760.

12. **Radiation Therapy** of the ovaries, tubes, etc. during pregnancy unless this be necessary to save a mother's life by curing the pathological condition and not by attacking the fetus.

13. **Euthanasia** or "Mercy Killing" in all its forms. Cf. 211.

N. B. The Principle here involved is: The end does not justify the means.

214.   *Article II*

Killing the Criminal

I. A criminal may be executed if juridical proof has established the moral certainty that he has committed a grave crime for which the state, in the interest of the common welfare, inflicts capital punishment, and if someone has been authorized by the state to execute the sentence.

Lynching is, therefore, immoral where the "due process of law" can be observed. Only when ordered to do so may policemen, guards, etc., shoot a criminal condemned to death who attempts to escape. — Sentinels may shoot at one who refuses to obey when the challenge to halt is given, provided they have orders to shoot, and that they endeavor, as far as possible, merely to wound and not to kill. — Federal officers, border patrolmen, etc., may act in like manner toward smugglers who attempt to flee in spite of orders to halt. — A criminal must be given an opportunity to receive the Sacraments before his execution. If he refuses to receive them, the sentence may nevertheless be carried out.

215. — II. An unjust aggressor may be killed if the following conditions are verified:

1. *The goods* to be so defended must be of great value.

Such goods are: life, integrity of one's members, chastity, temporal goods of great value. — In defending temporal possessions of small value the aggressor may be killed only when he attacks the life of the owner. — One may defend the life and possessions of others even as he may defend his own.

2. *The aggression* must be actual and unjust.

If it is such the aforesaid defense is lawful even against one's parents, superiors or the clergy.

a) Actual aggression is an imminent or practically present assault which cannot be evaded.

Self-defense is, therefore, allowed not only when actually covered by the bandit's gun, but when the assailant reaches for his knife or revolver, sets his dog on one, summons his accomplice; not, however, if there is question merely of threatened or anticipated attack. After the aggression has taken place killing is no longer self-defense, but revenge. Consequently, a woman may not kill the man who ravished her. For the same reason it is wrong to vindicate one's honor by killing an offender at whose hands one has suffered real or verbal injury. — However, it is evidently a different matter when a thief is making off with a large sum of money.

b) Unjust aggression is had when the assault is at least materially unwarranted.

Therefore, one may also kill an insane or intoxicated person in self-defense.

3. **The defense** must be moderate, i.e., the assailant must not be injured more than is absolutely necessary to insure self-protection known as "moderamen inculpatae tutelae," or moderation of blameless defence.

Therefore, if one can save his life by flight he must flee, unless flight would be very disgraceful, e.g., in the case of an officer. Killing is unlawful if the assailant can be rendered harmless by wounding him. Because of his excitement the person attacked seldom sins gravely by exceeding the bounds of a blameless defense.

N. B. There is generally no obligation to defend one's self when this is possible only by killing the assailant.

One would be so obliged if one's life were necessary for the common good or if one were in the state of mortal sin, in which case, death would imply the loss of one's soul. — There may be a duty of charity to defend others (wife, children, parents, relatives) against an unjust aggressor. Officers of the law, etc. may be obliged to defend others against unjust aggression by reason of their office.

216. Chapter III

DUELING

I. Concept. A duel is a combat between two persons fought upon agreement with deadly weapons, i.e., such as are adapted to kill or seriously wound.

The concept of a *certamen singulare* is also verified in a contest between a few individuals. — The agreement concerns the time, place and weapons. — It is, therefore, not a duel if two persons, in sudden anger, withdraw to some appointed place and fight. Inflicting a mortal wound is mortally sinful. Fighting with sticks or clubs is not a duel. Dueling is illegal in American law. If death follows it is construed as either murder or manslaughter, with the seconds being liable as accessories.

II. Morality. 1. *Public authority* can justify a duel in the interest of the common welfare which would suffer great harm through war.

Public authority cannot, however, justify a duel for the vindication of an injury, to settle a private quarrel, etc.

2. Fighting a duel on *private authority* is mortally sinful.

This is true even if it is fought to escape the gravest evils, e.g., the loss of one's rank, position or means of livelihood.

217. — III. Penalties for dueling.

1. Excommunication reserved simply to the Holy See (Cf. 437).—2. Infamy of law ipso facto incurred by the principals and their seconds (C. 2351). Irregularity from defect is connected with this latter penalty (C. 984, No. 5).—3. Irregularity from crime, (in case death results) which both the murderer and his accomplices incur (C. 985), but which affects only the one who inflicts the wound in case only wounding occurs (C. 985).—4. Ecclesiastical burial is denied to those who die in a duel or from a wound received in a duel, unless they manifest signs of repentance before death (C. 1240).

218.   Chapter IV

WAR

I. Morality. Both offensive and defensive war are lawful for a just cause which must be serious enough to justify the great evils associated with war.

The *lawfulness* of war is evident from the fact that one is allowed to defend himself against an unjust aggressor or to prosecute his rights with force if there is no higher authority that will protect them. It is always presupposed that there is no other means to obtain justice, e.g., by arbitration, etc.

II. Participation in War. Anyone may volunteer for service in a war which is certainly just. — Both the soldiers already enlisted and the subjects conscripted by the state may fight in a war that is doubtfully just if the doubt cannot be solved. — No one may take part in an evidently unjust war.

In modern times it is almost always impossible for the private citizen to solve doubts concerning the justice of a war. — Whoever is forced to take part in an evidently unjust war may neither wound nor kill the enemy, unless his enemy attempts to kill him, notwithstanding his surrender.

219. — III. Methods of Warfare. In waging war anything necessary or useful for the attainment of the end is lawful provided it is not forbidden by either the divine or international law.

Therefore, ambushing or other strategy is permitted. International law forbids that non-combatants take any part in battle, that captured soldiers be killed merely because they are enemies, and that private property be looted. Valuables that the dead have about them belong to their heirs if these can be discovered. To levy a contribution or war tax to enrich oneself is unlawful. It is lawful to exact things necessary for war such as the rulers of a country themselves might demand in the interest of good government. With permission of the commander private soldiers may appropriate such things if necessary. If they have taken anything against the will of their officers they are bound to restitution, that is, if authorities have not consented in order to respect private property. There is no duty of restitution if the official's motive for withdrawing authorization was to prevent undermining discipline.

Atomic Warfare. The fourth condition required for positing an action that has an evil effect is that there be a sufficient reason, i.e., a proportionate resulting good, to permit the evil effect. The morality of using either the atomic or hydrogen bomb as a weapon of war is, therefore, not a question of principle, which remains unchangeable, but a question of fact, and the fact questioned is whether there can be a military objective so vital to an enemy, the destruction of which would be a sufficient reason to permit the death of a vast number of civilians who at most contribute only remotely and indirectly to the war effort. We think this proportion can exist 1) because today's concept of "total war" has greatly restricted the meaning of the term "non-combatant"; 2) because in modern warfare the conscription of industry, as well as manpower, greatly extends the war effort on the home front; and 3) because it is difficult to set limits to the defense action of a people whose physical and even spiritual existence is threatened by a godless tyranny. Therefore, while the use of atomic weapons must be greatly restricted to the destruction of military objectives, neverthelesss, it may be justified without doing violence to the principle of a twofold effect.

220.   Chapter V

CORPORAL PUNISHMENT AND CRUELTY TO ANIMALS

I. Corporal chastisement is lawful if done by, or with (at least tacit) consent of, competent superiors.

Public authorities have this power over malefactors, as also parents over their children. — By inflicting corporal punishment we may prevent one who has wronged us from injuring us again. There may also be circumstances in which a private individual may, in a reasonable manner, chastise another for the latter's betterment.

221. — II. Cruelty to animals. 1. Man has no *duties* towards animals since they have no independent personality. Being ordained for the service of man, animals may be used for any ethical purpose.

Such use is lawful even when it implies suffering and death for the animal. *Vivisection,* therefore, is lawful, provided it actually serves the advancement of science, and the animal is not made to suffer more than is absolutely necessary.

2. It is *sinful,* however, to cause an animal unnecessary pain.

The sinfulness does not lie in the violation of a right that an animal might possess, but only in the action's opposition to reason which forbids the needless causing of pain and death. In itself this would only be a venial sin. The action would be rendered seriously sinful by its brutalizing effect on the tormentor himself, and even more so by the gratification of sadistic impulses often connected with such conduct.

222.   Section VI

The Sixth and Ninth Commandments

The sixth commandment explicit forbids only adultery. Everything, however, that is contrary to the decent propagation of the human race is also prohibited, that is, every external sin against chastity. The ninth commandment prohibits unchaste thoughts and desires.

Chapter I

SINS OF IMPURITY IN GENERAL

I. Concept. By sins of impurity (luxuria) we understand the inordinate desire, for, or enjoyment of, sexual (carnal) lust.

Venereal delectation is the satisfaction which results from a commotion of the organs of generation.

The inordination consists in one's seeking sexual pleasure, be it conjugal or extra-marital, in a manner that frustrates the natural purpose of sex-life.

Immodesty in itself differs from impurity. Immodesty is the voluntary occupation with things that can readily stimulate the sexual appetite. Wherefore, immodest actions are often not distinguished from sins of impurity. For further particulars confer 234 sqq.

II. Division. Sins of impurity may be:

1. *Complete or incomplete.* The sin of impurity is complete if it leads to orgasm or the complete sedation of the sex impulse. It consists in the seminal emission in the male and the secretion of the vaginal fluid manifested by rhythmic contractions of the vagina in the female. Incomplete sins of impurity are those acts against chastity

that are not carried to their full termination.

2. *Natural or unnatural,* according as the natural purpose of sex can be attained thereby or not.

223. — III. Morality.

1. *All directly voluntary sexual pleasure* is mortally sinful outside of matrimony.

This is true even if the pleasure be ever so brief and insignificant. Here there is no lightness of matter. — Even the individuals in whom the sex urge is abnormally intense (sexual hyperesthesia) can and must control themselves. Mental aberration can diminish and even remove all imputability. Concerning the influence of passion confer 25.

2. *Indirectly voluntary sexual pleasure* is a mortal or venial sin or no sin at all according as the action causing it by its nature exercises a great or slight influence or none whatsoever upon the stimulation of the sexual appetite.

Carnal pleasure is indirectly voluntary if one undertakes an action which he foresees will result in sexual pleasure, but does not will this pleasure itself either now or later.

By their nature some actions stimulate the sexual faculty more or less intensely almost always, or rarely or never in a normal person.

In determining the sinfulness of such actions we abstract here from the danger of consent and from the presence or absence of an adequate reason for positing them. The reason for undertaking such an action must be in proportion to the influence that the action naturally has upon the arousing of sexual pleasure. Physicians, surgeons, nurses, etc. are excused from sin even should their occupation be the cause of pollution.

Actions which by their nature strongly tend to stimulate sexual activity are gravely sinful even though accidentally they do not have that effect. Only if one is certain from experience that he will not be much affected by such actions, is he excused from mortal sin if he posits such an action.

That which by its nature is no strong incitement to sexual

activity is not gravely sinful, even for such a person who knows that, due to his temperament, he is easily aroused, provided, however, there is no proximate danger of consent. But if such a person undertakes an action of that sort without a reason, he will usually do so with a bad intention and, therefore, it will be mortally sinful even though he may seek to deceive himself in the matter.

224. Chapter II

CONSUMMATED SINS OF IMPURITY

The complete sins against chastity may be natural or unnatural (intra vel contra naturam).

Article I

Natural Sins of Impurity

I. Fornication is voluntary sexual intercourse between unmarried persons, who are not bound by Holy Orders or vow and who are not related to one another by blood.

This mortal sin differs from other natural sins against chastity in this that aside from the sin of impurity it contains no other specific malice.

Sexual intercourse with a person engaged to someone else, according to many authors, is at least not a grave sin against the other engaged party and, hence, the fact of the engagement need not be mentioned in confession.

Concubinage and prostitution do not differ specifically from fornication, but since they imply a proximate occasion of sin and readiness to sin, they must be indicated, at least upon questioning by the confessor.

Thoughts, words, looks and touches that immediately precede or follow intercourse, need not be mentioned in confession since they constitute morally only one sin with the sin of fornication.

225. — II. Adultery is sexual intercourse with the husband or wife of a third person.

Adultery is *simple* or *double* according as only one or both parties are married. In some States of the U. S. adultery is by statute a crime for both parties, whether married or not; in others it is a crime for only the married person, and in still others, only when one of the wrongdoers is a married woman.

Besides the grave sin against chastity, adultery contains also another grave sin against justice. If both parties to the sin are married there is a twofold injustice. This specifically additional sin is present even if the innocent husband or wife consents to the sin. Should a child be born from adulterous relations there may be still another grave sin of injustice to the husband and legitimate children in as far as an innocent man will be obliged to rear another man's child and legitimate children be forced to share their inheritance with a stranger. Sinful desires, touches and kisses, but not mere glances, concerning a third person are adulterous; likewise, unnatural sins, even though a married person commit them with himself or his lawful spouse. The uneducated frequently are unaware of this specific malice. If there is no hope of their correcting such conduct the priest need not instruct them on the matter.

The *penalty* for public (notorious) adultery is exclusion from legitimate acts (C. 2357). Concerning legitimate acts confer C. 2256.

226. — III. Rape is illicit, consummated carnal knowledge of a woman against her consent.

Besides the mortal sin against chastity it is a grave sin against justice to ravish a woman. A double injury is committed in the ravishing of a virgin, namely, an unjust violation of her rights and the additional injustice of deflowering her of the precious possession of physical integrity. The contrary opinion is also probable.

Rape can be committed by the use of physical or moral force (grave fear, including reverential fear, fraud and deceit); likewise, by a sin committed with a woman who has not the use of reason (one who is insane or intoxicated).

To avoid sinning, a woman who is being ravished must offer internal and external resistance. She need not cry out when this cannot be done without danger to her life or reputation, unless she would otherwise consent to the sin. Rape is not so common.

IV. Abduction is the forceful taking of a person for the purpose of committing a sin against chastity with the same.

Besides the grave sin against chastity, abduction is, furthermore, a mortal sin against justice. Concerning abduction as a matrimonial impediment confer 703.

The force employed may be physical or moral and used either upon the person ravished or upon those under whose authority the person in constituted. The person abducted may be male or female, single or married, virginal or not.

227. — V. Incest is sexual intercourse between persons related by blood or by affinity within the degrees in which marriage is forbidden by the Church.

To the sin of impurity there is added another grave sin against piety. It is controverted whether or not the sins committed with persons related in the first degree of the direct or collateral line either by blood or by marriage constitute an additional and specifically different malice.

Even touches between such persons have the character of incest provided they proceed from sinful affection.

If a dispensation for contracting marriage has been granted such conduct is indeed a sin against chastity, but not incest.

VI. Sacrilege here is the violation of a person consecrated to God, or of a sacred thing or holy place, by a sin against chastity (Cf. 167 sqq.).

In addition to the sin of impurity there is an additional sin against reverence due to God.

228.   *Article II*

Unnatural Sins of Impurity

I. Pollution (self-abuse, masturbation; sometimes incorrectly called onanism).

1. *Concept*. Pollution is complete sexual satisfaction obtained by some form of self-stimulation.

By avoiding reference to "semination" our definition evades the various controversies concerning the specific difference of this sin in men, women, eunuchs and those who have not reached the age of puberty, since only men are capable of secreting semen in the proper sense of the word. Concerning the gravity of the sin, all authors agree that the following fundamental principles apply for men as well as for the others mentioned.

2. *The Malice of Pollution*. a) *Directly voluntary pollution* is always gravely sinful.

It matters not whether pollution is intentionally provoked or whether one takes voluntary pleasure in an involuntary emission. There is no obligation positively to suppress a pollution that occurs of its own accord. One may remain passive, provided there is no danger of consent. To promote a pollution intentionally is always gravely sinful even though it is done for other ends than sexual pleasure. — According to a decision of the Holy Office on Aug. 2, 1929, it is also forbidden directly to produce a pollution to obtain a semen specimen for the purpose of medical diagnosis (Cf. No. 242 and 749).

There is no new specific malice contracted by the various ways in which pollution is procured, but there can be such through various supervening circumstances (e.g., seduction, co-operation, desire to sin with others).

b) *Indirectly voluntary pollution* is a grave or venial sin or no sin at all, according to the principles laid down in 223.

Wherefore, it is lawful to wash, go bathing, riding, etc. even though one foresees that due to one's particular excitability in this regard, pollution will follow. Similarly, it is lawful to seek relief from itching in the sex organs, provided the irritation is not the result of superfluous semen or ardent passion. In case one doubts about the cause of the itching he may relieve it. It is likewise lawful in case of slight itching if only slight sexual stimulation is experienced therefrom. The supposition is always, however, that one does not consent to any venereal pleasure.

229. *c*) *Nocturnal pollution,* which is willed neither directly nor indirectly, is no sin.

This is true even when in a dream one takes pleasure therein. But if the pleasure is experienced while half-awake there would be a venial sin. The case of one's doing something before falling asleep with either the direct or indirect intention of procuring a nocturnal emission must be decided according to the principles governing the sinfulness of direct and indirect voluntary pollution.

N.B. Distillation is the emission of the subtle non-prolific, urethral fluid, the purpose of which is to facilitate the ejection of the semen. Distillation is possible also in impubescent and castrated persons.

It always precedes pollution and is conjoined with venereal gratification. Sometimes it takes place independently of pollution and with little or no sexual commotion or enjoyment. The emission is more prolific at the time of pollution; when distillation alone takes place very little fluid is lost. Habitual distillation which is due to organic debility is a pathological condition requiring the attention of a physician.

a) Distillation *without sexual gratification* is no sin.

There is no obligation to avoid its cause. The same must be said of passive pollution which consists in the emission of the semen upon very slight provocation (movement, touch, etc.). It is generally caused when awake and takes place without delectation.

b) Distillation which is *accompanied by venereal pleasure* is a sin of the same gravity and species as pollution.

What has been said about pollution applies here.

230. — II. Sodomy. 1. *Definition.* Sodomy is unnatural carnal copulation either with a person of the same sex (perfect sodomy) or of the opposite sex; the latter or heterosexual sodomy consists in rectal intercourse (imperfect sodomy).

Either kind of sodomy will be consummated or non-consummated according as semination takes place or not.

2. The *malice* of sodomy consists in the perverted affection towards the wrong sex or in the attraction towards the wrong method of sexual gratification.

If there is no such affection or attraction there is no question of sodomy, though two persons suffer emission from mutual touches, or from unnatural contact. Coition, unless rectal, between man and woman is not presumed to be sodomitical, but is fornication in affect and pollution in effect; whereas homosexual commerce is sodomy.

Perfect and imperfect sodomy are *specifically distinct* sins; so also are complete and incomplete sodomy (although authors do not agree on this latter in the case of women). — Probably there is no specific distinction between the sin of the active and passive agents, unless only one of the parties suffers pollution.

231. — III. Bestiality. 1. *Definition*. Bestiality is the coition of a human being with an animal.

It does not matter in what manner the act is performed.

2. The *malice* consists in the perverted affect towards an animal.

This is the *worst* of all the sins of impurity. — This sin is specifically the same whether committed with this or that kind of an animal and be it male or female. — If the immoral affect is lacking, the touching of an animal does not constitute bestiality, even though one thereby experiences sexual gratification or pollution.

232. Chapter III

NON-CONSUMMATED SINS OF IMPURITY

Incomplete sins of impurity may either be sins against chastity in themselves (sexual commotion) or they may be the cause of sins against chastity (immodesty). Cf. 222. Immodest acts may be external or internal.

Article I

Sexual Commotion

I. Definition. Sexual commotion is the pleasurable disturbance or excitement of the genital organs and the fluids that serve the purpose of generation. It is generally accompanied by an erection of the sexual organ of the male and the clitoral movement of the female.

To be distinguished from such commotion is the merely natural erection of the sex organ which arises from physical non-venereal causes without sense gratification. This is not sinful.

II. Morality. 1. Any *directly voluntary* sexual commotion is always gravely sinful be it ever so brief and insignificant.

2. *Indirectly voluntary* sexual commotion is a

mortal or venial sin or no sin at all according to the principles laid down in 223.

It must always be remembered that for adequate reasons some actions may be permitted which would otherwise be sinful, and that, because of the danger of consent something may be gravely sinful for one person which is only a venial sin or no sin at all for another.

233. — III. Resistance to involuntary sexual commotion is a duty only in so far as there is danger of consent. Whence it follows that:

1. It is best not to bother about *slight* and quickly passing carnal commotions.

To be concerned about them often arouses the imagination and aggravates the disturbance.

2. Some positive resistance is generally necessary in case of *vehement* carnal commotions.

An internal act of displeasure is often sufficient. Generally, too, one is obliged to renew one's determination not to sin or to make an act of love of God or to try to divert one's thoughts to something else or to endeavor to ward off the temptation by external occupation or conversation. If the temptation is of longer duration one is evidently not obliged to offer positive resistance without interruption, although a renewal of one's displeasure from time to time is advisable. — In exceptional cases one need not oppose a violent temptation by any positive resistance, if he knows from experience that the temptation will thereby only be aggravated.

3. If a *voluntary superfluous* action is the cause of the agitation one must offer resistance by desisting from the action.

Failure to resist in this manner is gravely sinful if the action concerned strongly tends by its nature to carnal lust. Only a venial sin is committed if the influence is slight. But if one voluntarily engages is such action for some length of time, a grievous sin will generally be committed, because of the great danger of giving consent.

234. *Article II*

External Sins against Modesty

Such sins are looks, touches, embraces, kisses, conversation, songs, and reading. In themselves these acts are morally indifferent. They become sinful through one's intention and especially because of their influence in exciting sexual pleasure.

I. Gravity of these Sins.

1. *The intention* to arouse sexual pleasure by such actions makes them gravely sinful every time.

2. *The influence* that these actions exert in stimulating carnal pleasure renders them gravely or venially or not sinful at all according to the extent of their influence (Cf. 223).

It is *presupposed* that these actions are performed without any good reason. If there be such a reason the actions are not sinful, provided one neither intends the sexual pleasure or pollution, nor consents to them if they arise spontaneously. — Furthermore, that must be observed which was already said in No. 223 of him who knows from experience that such things do not greatly affect him.

Because of the varying degrees of influence they may have in exciting sexual pleasure, the parts of the human body are sometimes divided into decent (face, hands, feet), less decent (breast, back, arms, legs) and indecent (sex organs and adjacent parts). That moralists are justified in dividing the parts of the body with reference to their influence in arousing sexual excitement, may be deduced from the fact that some civil authorities in the interest of public morality make a similar distinction. However, to avoid the implication that there is something morally objectionable about any portion of the human body, we will speak of parts that are public, semi-private and private.

In particular the following is to be observed regarding the sinful character of immodest actions:

235. *a) Touches.* α) For a reasonable cause one may touch even the private parts of his own person (e. g., in bathing, for healing purposes or to relieve irritation). Without a sufficient reason such touches are at most venial sins if one knows that he will not be sexually excited thereby. Should one without a reason continue these actions for a length of time he will usually experience sexual excitement; wherefore, such actions can readily become grave sins. For pedagogical reasons children should be taught to refrain from such touches entirely.

β) It is seriously sinful to touch the private parts of others (even over the clothing) without a reason, regardless of sex. Such touches are venially sinful only when done without an evil intention and in a hasty or casual manner and out of levity or in jest. Touching the semi-private parts of a person of the same sex is generally a venial sin at most, whereas it is usually a grave sin in case of the opposite sex. Even then there would be only a venial sin if it were done in a very perfunctory manner out of levity or jokingly.

γ) Touching animals indecently is generally not gravely sinful, unless it is done with an evil intention or for a long time or until the animal suffers pollution.

236. b) *Kissing and embracing.* α) Decent kissing and embracing as customarily done as a sign of politeness, friendship, relationship or of honorable love, are lawful even between persons of the opposite sex, but always on the condition that these actions are not done to excite sexual pleasure and that one does not consent to it or to pollution should these result. One should not readily consider young people guilty of grave sin when they kiss and embrace in their games and merrymaking.

β) Ardent, prolonged and repeated kissing is often a mortal sin. Not so, however, would be such kissing and embracing between parents and children.

γ) Kissing the private or semi-private parts of the human body is gravely sinful. So also is tongue-kissing (or soul-kissing) usually seriously sinful.

δ) Touching and kissing, innocent in themselves, but done with a bad intention, which one cannot hinder without embarrassment to oneself or another or without defaming another (e.g., when done publicly) may be permitted; in other cases one must prevent such actions.

237. c) *Looks.* α) It is lawful to look at the private parts of oneself for a reasonable cause. It is understood that one must not consent to any carnal pleasure that might result therefrom. Such glances out of curiosity or levity are venially sinful; they might easily become mortally sinful if prolonged without necessity.

β) It is venially sinful to glance at the private parts of another of the same sex or to look at them out of curiosity; to do so intentionally and for some length of time becomes seriously sinful, especially if this is connected with a certain affection for the other party. — For a good reason one may take light-, air- and sun baths, but as far as possible such bathers should keep the private parts of their bodies covered. — For the sake of modesty parents, swimming instructors, etc. should not permit little children to expose themselves to one another. To look at the semi-private parts of persons of the same sex is not wrong, unless it is done with sodomitical intentions.

γ) To look at the private parts of a person of the opposite sex is gravely sinful, unless done unexpectedly or superficially or momentarily or from a distance or if it is a question of little children. — In itself it is not very wrong to look at the semi-private parts of such persons, unless this is continued for some time. — In itself it is not lawful to use women and girls as models with only the genital organs covered. But if young artists in their training are compelled to attend art academies they do not sin by sketching such models. They must, however, not consent to any sexual commotion that may arise and must try to render the danger remote by prayer and renewal of their good intention. If women and girls have no other means to keep them from grave need they may serve as models, provided they employ the necessary precautionary measures.

δ) It is venially sinful out of curiosity to observe animals mating if no sexual pleasure is caused.

ε) To consider attentively and for a length of time nude pictures and works of art, giving special attention to the genitals, may easily become a serious sin, especially if they are modern works that are made to arouse sensuality.

238. *d) Conversation and songs.* α) Unchaste speech and songs are gravely or venially sinful according to the influence they exert in arousing carnal pleasure. Among adults of the same sex who have become somewhat cold in matters of the sixth commandment they are often only venially sinful. It is generally a grievous sin if young people engage in such conversation, or if adults do so with persons of the opposite sex, especially if they have an inordinate affection for each other. Besides, such conversation or songs may be gravely sinful on account of the evil intention or scandal or because of the sinful joy one derives from recalling past mortal sins. If scandal is given one need not, according to a probable opinion, indicate the number of listeners when confessing the sin (Cf. 104).

β) Voluntarily listening to evil talk and songs is gravely sinful if it greatly influences the arousing of sexual pleasure, or if doing so gives another occasion to indulge in such conversation or if one derives impure delight from listening to it. — It is only venially sinful if the matter has little influence in stimulating sexual pleasure and one listens out of curiosity or laughs with others out of human respect or perhaps even adds a word himself or laughs at the manner in which an off-color story or joke is told and not at the story or joke itself, provided, of course, no scandal ensues.

e) Literature. a) It is usually a mortal sin to read bad books, even though they are not entirely immoral, because this notably excites sexual passion. Such literature may be read, however, in order to acquire necessary knowledge. The greater the danger of consent is, the graver must be the reason.

β) In itself it is only a venial sin to read matter that is only slightly indecent. An evil intention may make it mortally sinful, or if one knows from experience that he will consent to the temptation that ensues from such reading. Young people should be dissuaded from reading love stories that are not of a noble type throughout.

239. — II. The Species of the Sin. Theoretically, unchaste touches, looks, conversation, etc. do not differ specifically, since they are sinful only in as far as they arouse carnal pleasure which contains the same specific malice no matter what be its cause. Practically, however, such carnal pleasure is usually accompanied by an unchaste affection towards another or connected with impure desires for the same; hence, these actions are done with an evil intention and, therefore, their proximate circumstances must generally be indicated (Cf. also 231 and 242).

III. The Number of Sins (Cf. 101 sqq.).

240. Scholion. 1. Company keeping with the intention of early marriage may be looked upon as a *necessary occasion of sin.*

No one can be expected to marry a complete stranger. Those

keeping company should take great care to make any proximate occasion a remote one. Consequently they should, as far as possible, avoid being alone, at least in such places where they might not readily be observed; neither should they meet too often. Furthermore, they should be zealous in prayer and in receiving the Sacraments. Should those who are engaged sin with each other they must be dealt with as those who are living in a necessary occasion of sin (Cf. 608).

2. As far as sexual liberties are concerned, engaged persons are *forbidden* to do anything which is not permitted to other single people.

They may touch, embrace or kiss each other in a becoming manner to manifest their mutual affection. Evidently, however, they may not consent to sexual pleasure that might be caused thereby.

241.   *Article III*

Internal Sins against Chastity

In general people refer to all internal sins against chastity as "impure thoughts." In matter of fact one may think of unchaste things speculatively (e.g., in study) or practically. In the latter instance one may imagine unchaste actions as present and take pleasure in the thought without the desire to actually do them (morose delectation) or with such a desire (unchaste desires).

I. Speculative thinking about what is unchaste.
1. It is gravely sinful to conceive such thoughts *with an impure intention.*

2. To provoke such thoughts *out of levity* or to entertain them out of negligence when they involuntarily come to our mind is a mortal or a venial sin, according as to whether such thoughts by their nature exert a greater or less influence in arousing the passions, or whether there is little or great danger of consenting to temptation.

If sexual passion is thereby aroused one must make an effort at resistance by diverting his thoughts to other matters.

3. For an *adequate reason* (for the sake of study)

it is not sinful to think of unchaste things speculatively, not even if this causes impure commotions or pollution.

But to consent to such effects is always seriously sinful.

242. — II. Morose delectation is the same kind of sin as the action one thinks about with pleasure and complacency.

III. Unchaste desires are always sins of the same gravity and moral species as the action which is sinfully desired.

Therefore, one commits a mortal sin or a venial sin according as the acts (looks, touches, etc.) one has in mind are venially or mortally sinful. — It is understood that consent to any carnal commotion is always seriously wrong. Concerning morose complacency confer 106. Sinful joy over an impure deed done in the past differs from morose delectation (Cf. 107).

This applies to both efficacious and inefficacious desires (Cf. 180).

One may not desire even a purely natural pollution which takes place involuntarily (either in a dream or when awake) for the sake of the carnal pleasure that accompanies it; but one may desire it for an ethical reason, e.g., to obtain relief from temptations. One is never allowed to do anything when awake with the intention of producing a pollution in sleep.

N. B. In *morose delectation* the mind usually abstracts from the proximate circumstances of the person, e.g., whether single or married. Hence, such circumstances need not be mentioned in confession. It would be otherwise if one took pleasure in the very fact that the person concerned is married or is a relative. — *Desire,* on the other hand, is concerned with these circumstances, and, therefore, to entertain unchaste desires for a single or for a married person is a specifically different sin.

Since ordinary people do not distinguish so precisely, it must be borne in mind that sins must be confessed as they are actually discerned. Abstracting from this, detailed questioning may often be interpreted in the wrong way and therefore, in such confessions there will be an excuse from the precept of material integrity (Cf. 567). — If people confess "impure thoughts" they should be asked if they took pleasure in them. If the answer is affirmative one may, according to the circumstances, inquire whether there were impure desires. If this, too, is answered in the affirmative, one might perhaps try to ascertain the specific malice by asking whether their desire referred to a single or a married person.

243. Chapter IV

SEXUAL PERVERSITY

I. Forms. 1. Sexual *paradoxia* consists in this that sexual commotions are experienced when, according to the general rule, the faculty to generate has either not begun to assert itself or has ceased to function, e.g., before the seventh year and in decrepit senility.

2. Sexual *anesthesia* is the inability to arouse the sexual appetite by any means.

People of this type are rarely found and because of impotency are unable to contract a valid marriage. Similar to them are those of a "frigid nature."

3. Sexual *hyperesthesia* consists of a morbidly intense sexual excitability.

This form of perversion is often conjoined with sexual paresthesia.

4. Sexual *paresthesia* is had when sex life is not affected by venereal matters, but by objects altogether foreign to sex life.

The following are forms of this perversion:

a) Sadism (named after the Marquis of Sade) is the venereal pleasure aroused by actions (real or imaginary) that are actively and vehemently cruel and inflict pain (striking, whipping, strangling, cutting, stabbing).

b) Masochism (named after the novelist Sacher Masoch who described this perversion in several of his works) is a type of sexual perversion in which sex pleasure is derived from the real or imaginary suffering of pain (e.g., in being struck, whipped, kicked, cut, etc.).

c) Fetishism is a perversity in which sexual passion is aroused by things which in themselves have no relation to sex and are not represented by the imagination as having any reference to any person, e.g., the imagination or the sight or touch of a hand, hair, a garment or shoe.

d) Homosexuality is the abnormal sexual attraction towards persons of the same sex. It must be distinguished from the sins committed with persons of the same sex which are sometimes committed by those who have no occasion to have relations with persons of the opposite sex. Homosexuality as contrary sexuality is found both in men and women.

244. — II. Imputability. Everyone, even the sexually abnormal and perverted, can and must control himself, since all actions are imputable to an individual as long as he has not lost all sense of responsibility and the actions are performed with knowledge and free will.

Mental diseases can, indeed, diminish and even destroy responsibility entirely (Cf. 36). — On the influence of passion confer 23, sqq.

Whosoever has a perverted attraction towards persons of the same sex should be dissuaded from accepting a position (e.g., teaching) in which he will scarcely be able to avoid the proximate occasion of sin.

N. B. It is to be noted that certain symptoms of perversity are sometimes found in those whose sex life is perfectly normal. The difference between these and sexual perverts is that the latter are affected only by abnormal objects.

245.   *Section VII*

Seventh and Tenth Commandments

The seventh and tenth commandments protect the right of ownership. Since it has already been shown in the general principles of morals (Cf. 105 sqq.) that sins of thought in their moral estimation must be considered equivalent to sins of action, there is no need of treating them here, and, therefore, a specific treatment of the tenth commandment is unnecessary. Wherefore, in the next four chapters we shall consider: Ownership in General, The Acquisition of Ownership, The Violation of Ownership, and Restitution.

On the concept of justice and its kinds confer 323.

Chapter I

OWNERSHIP IN GENERAL

Article I

Concept, Division, Origin and Object of Ownership

I. Concept. Ownership is the juridical faculty freely to dispose of something as one's own unless otherwise hindered.

An owner may sell, exchange, give away, destroy, etc., his property without thereby violating commutative justice. However, he may easily sin against other virtues by so doing, e.g., liberality, either by avarice or prodigality; furthermore, he may thereby sin against piety, charity, legal (social) justice, etc.

One may be *hindered* from freely disposing of his property by positive law (Cf. 246), or testamentary determination or by a contract. Because the strict rights of others may in some instances be violated one may thus sin against commutative justice and be obliged to restitution.

246. — II. Division. Ownership may be:

1. **Perfect,** i.e., the right to the possession and the complete use and disposal of a thing.

2. **Imperfect,** i.e., the right to the mere possession of a thing (*direct ownership*) or merely to its use (*indirect ownership*).

Possession differs from ownership. Possession is the actual corporeal holding of a thing with the intention of keeping it as one's own. A possessor is in good, bad or doubtful faith according as he is convinced that his possession is legitimate or illegitimate or as he has doubts about the same.

This right to the use of a thing may extend only to the simple use or usufruct. In either case the substance of the thing must remain untouched. Whoever has the use of a thing may enjoy its fruits for himself or his family; he who has the usufruct may also sell the fruits and thus enrich himself. Strictly speaking, use and usufruct seem to be mere subdivisions of what in modern legal terminology is known as servitude. Servitude consists in the necessity of one person's thing serving the utility of someone else (e.g., A must allow B the right of way on his property; specifically known as an easement).

3. The "right of eminent domain" is the competency of the State or some natural or legal person authorized by the State (e.g., a railroad company) to dispose of the property of a private individual in the interest of the common welfare for a sufficiently grave reason.

Strictly taken, this is not a right of ownership but one derived from the State's power of jurisdiction. — The damages inflicted upon the individual by the exercise of this right must be compensated in so far as possible. — The right is exercised by expropriation (e.g., when building a highway) or by transferring property in the interest of the common good (e.g., when finding a treasure-trove, confer 264) in prescription, 272 sqq., in certain auction sales, etc. confer 339, or when the State restricts the free exercise of property rights (e.g., in the case of minors, confer 254). — As on these occasions, the State may also restrict ownership rights in other cases of corresponding necessity. From this viewpoint we must judge the various reforms being attempted by Congressional land measures, housing legislation, etc.

247. — III. The Origin of Ownership.

1. **Natural law** is primarily the source of property rights, in so far as under present circumstances and the constitution of human nature many inconveniences would follow from the common ownership of this world's goods.

Accordingly, the teachings of the Manicheans, Waldensians, Albigensians, Socialists and Communists who deny the right of private ownership, are false. — Since the first purpose of the goods of this world is the maintenance of life, it follows that a person in extreme need may take from the possessions of another as much as is required to relieve his extreme need (Cf. 331).

2. *Positive Law* also is a source of property rights,

since the law of nature has not determined those rights in detail.

a) Positive laws that *establish a right* generally oblige in conscience even before the sentence of a judge.

For example, the law that supplies the lacking consent of competent authority in some contracts for the sake of the common welfare.

b) When positive laws merely *prescribe certain formalities* for legal actions, the legislator in most states does not thereby forbid the positing of informal action, neither does he deprive the action of its natural effects. But should someone dispute the illegal act and the judge declare it void, there would be an obligation in conscience to abide by the decision of the court.

This applies to civil testamentary legislation and legacies.

A legal transaction is null and void even before the court pronouncement if it is invalid already by the law of nature (e.g., a contract made with an insane person) — or if a valid action cannot later be voided (e.g., marriage between two infidels) — or if the purpose of the law is precisely to render an action void independently of any sentence — or if there is question of a gratuitous contract, since, in this instance the contractants only wish to oblige themselves in conscience in so far as the civil laws oblige them.

248. — IV. The Object of Ownership. 1. The *general object* of ownership is property, i.e., anything immediately and exclusively destined for a person.

The following axioms are deducible from the concept of ownership:

a) *Res clamat ad dominum,* i.e., the rightful owner is entitled to his property no matter into whose hands it has fallen. b) *Res fructificat domino,* i.e., the fruits of his property belong to the rightful owner. c) *Res perit domino,* i.e., a thing perishes at the loss of its owner. d) *Ex re aliena non licet ditescere,* i.e., no one has a right to enrich himself with the property of another.

2. *Special objects* of ownership are:

a) The goods of *body* and *soul* that constitute the nature of man himself. Man has not the direct, but only the indirect, ownership of these things.

Wherefore, no one may dispose of his own life. But one may place his corporal and mental powers at the service of others and accept pay for doing so.

b) *Honor, reputation* and the *goods of fortune.* Man has perfect ownership of these things.

Wherefore one may renounce his right to the reparation of his honor and good name, and he can remit another's obligation of making restitution for damage done.

249. *Article II*

The Subject of Ownership

An *owner* may be any person, either physical or moral (legal).

Accordingly, even the permanently insane, and unborn children may possess things; those not yet conceived cannot.

We shall consider only those owners who constitute a special problem for Moral Theology.

250. — I. Married People. 1. Property rights of married people are regulated according to the joint property rights of the respective State or according to the special agreement entered upon by the married couple. In practically all the States of the Union statutes have been enacted providing that all property, real or personal at the time of her marriage, or acquired by her thereafter, shall be and remain the separate property of the wife, free from the control of her husband.

The statutes of most States give married women the power to convey or dispose of their property; some States require that the husband join in the wife's conveyance of her land in order to make it valid. And in some States a husband has an inchoate interest in his wife's land, such as curtesy, statutory dower.

251. The wife's earnings in activities not connected with her household duties and damages which she may recover from torts committed against her are generally her separate property. She can usually use, manage and control her property as if she were unmarried, subject to certain restrictions on her power to mortgage her property. In practically all the States she can make a valid will disposing of her property. Corresponding to the husband's right of curtesy, the surviving wife has in most States rights to her husband's lands, known as dower, entitling her to one-third of all lands and tenements.

Dower and curtesy have been abolished and community property has been substituted therefor in the following States: Ariz., Cal., Ia., La., Nev., N. M., Tex., and Wash. The community property laws in these States provide that all real estate acquired by the husband or wife during marriage, except that acquired by gift, will, or descent shall be community property. They usually also provide that the husband shall have the sole right of management including the power of conveyance. Upon the death of either party, the property is used to pay the community debts and the remainder is divided equally between the survivor and the heirs or devisees of the deceased.

252. — 2. *Rights and Duties of the Husband.*

a) The wife's possessions, which the husband holds as property in trust, he is in justice bound to administer rightly.

Should he squander or dispose of such goods he is obliged to restitution.

b) Their common possessions he must likewise faithfully administer out of justice according to the stipulations of their agreement if the wife is in the strict sense a joint owner during the lifetime of the husband.

He is obliged to restitution if in the administration of such goods he transgresses legal regulations. No legal action can be brought against him for prodigal (or mal-) administration of such goods, but he might easily be obliged in conscience to make restitution because of squandering his wife's possessions. — Should the wife be entitled to half of their common possessions only after the death of her husband, he would not be obliged to restitution.

c) The husband must care for *his own possessions* with charity and piety.

By maladministration or squandering of the same he does not sin against justice and is, therefore, not subject to the obligation of restitution.

d) He is *obliged to supply his wife* with whatever is necessary for the proper care of the household.

For further particulars confer 253.

253. — 3. *Rights and Duties of the Wife.* *a*) The wife has a right to *support in keeping with her social standing,* even though when marrying she had no property of her own.

Proper support implies: Decent nourishment, clothing and recreation, the distribution of gifts and alms. It also includes the proper support of the children born of this marital union (confer 326). The wife's children of a former marriage, her parents and relatives who are in grave need, she must support out of her own possessions (if she has any) or from the common fund. If she and her husband have no common possessions, the amount she expends must not exceed considerably that which she — in keeping with the standing of her husband — is entitled to dispose of as alms; if more is needed she must have the consent of her husband. If this amount is unreasonably denied her, she may, nevertheless, support her children, parents, etc.; but she must compensate the heirs of her husband if possible from what she obtains after the death of her husband.

If her husband is squandering the family fortune, the wife may lay a considerable amount aside for the subsequent support of herself and the family.

If the wife foresees that, in default of children, the fortune will pass to others, she may lay something aside for herself and her becoming maintenance. But she must make provision so that whatever remains after her death will go to the heirs of the husband.

b) In the *absence* of, or in the *mental deficiency* of her husband, the wife must administer the household and make the necessary expenditures.

c) *Local customs* may give the wife still further rights, e.g., the care of the poultry and the benefits therefrom.

254. — II. Children. 1. *Minors.*

At *common law* persons under 21 years of age are infants or minors. In *some States* females attain their majority at 18 years of age, and in some States all minors attain their majority on marriage. One becomes of age at the first moment of the day preceding the twenty-first anniversary of his birth. Minors are the favorites of the law. To protect them the law grants them certain privileges and imposes some disabilities upon them. An infant or minor may not hold an office involving financial responsibility. Males at 14, and females at 12 years of age could make a valid will as to personalty only at common law; but in many of our States this is restricted by statute to those who are twenty-one.

The rights, duties and obligations arising from the artificial relation of *adoption* are by statute substantially the same as those arising from the natural relation of parent and child.

With regard to *illegitimate children* it may be said that to some extent the law recognizes bastards as children. Thus, a mother is entitled to the custody and the services of her illegitimate child as against the father or strangers (unless the welfare of the child requires the court to award its custody to another). The mother's domicile determines that of the child. The putative father is now by statute very generally compelled to support his illegitimate child. Although a bastard cannot inherit at common law, this rule has been greatly modified by statute.

a) Minors are *capable of acquiring ownership* from the first moment of their existence (confer 249).

b) The *administration* of the property of minors rests with the father or the one who takes the place of the father, except where provision to the contrary has been expressly made.

c) The *usufruct* of property obtained by gift or inheritance belongs to the minor.

255. *d*) The *earnings* of the child create a special problem. The wages of an infant or minor belong ordinarily to the father, or whoever takes his father's place; but he may be emancipated sufficiently so that he may be legally entitled to his own wages. A minor cannot claim wages for ordinary work done at home; he can do so, however, for extraordinary work. In the latter instance he cannot demand immediate payment.

That which a minor acquires independently of a mandate from his father and away from home (e.g., for running errands) or what he makes conducting some kind of business permitted him, is his own possession. Such a child is, however, obliged in justice to compensate his parents for bed, board and clothing. He is also obliged out of piety to help the other members of the family who are in straitened circumstances. If the work is done away from home and by order of the father, the fruits of the labor belong to the father. — If a son conducts a business with the goods of his father and without the latter's knowledge, the ownership of the profit depends upon the intention that the son had from the beginning. a) If he intended to act in the name of his father, the profit belongs to the father. b) If he acted in his own name, he sinned thereby, because he negotiated with his father's money without the latter's permission. The profit, however, belongs to the son. He must, however, have had the intention to be responsible for any risk and to stand good for any eventual damage. Since the son, as a rule, cannot do this, he sins also by exposing his father to the danger of suffering a loss. c) If the son presumed his father's consent to a kind of partnership towards which the father contributed money and the son the work, the gain must be divided between the two. d) If there is doubt as to whether he intended to act in his own or his father's name it is to be presumed that he acted in his father's name if the son ordinarily looks after the business of the father.

256. *e) Gifts. a)* A child acquires complete ownership over things that are given to him absolutely.

Such things are ordinarily given absolutely which are immediately consumed by use (primo usu consumptibiles), e.g., edibles, money for amusement, money for current expenses. Such money can also be used for becoming recreation. Expenses made against the will of the parents are sins of disobedience, but not of injustice.

β) A child does not acquire full ownership over things that are given to him for some definite purpose.

This includes money given a child for books, clothing, etc.

N. B. In general one should induce children to give their earnings to their parents, for in many instances they are obliged to do so at least out of piety. Similarly, parents should be warned against every appearance of exploiting their children. If the children have retained a part of what they have earned or have pilfered something from their parents, one should be slow, even in violations of justice, to oblige them to restitution, since parents ordinarily renounce their right to this.

257. — 2. *Adult* or *Emancipated Children. a*) *Acquisition of Ownership.*

a) What they acquire by independent occupation away from home belongs to them.

β) For ordinary work done at home in keeping with the standing of the parents even adult members of the family can claim no wages.

This is true even if there are others in the family, e.g., the sick, or students, who do no work; since the latter is purely accidental. However, it is advisable for the parents to compensate those who work in some manner.

γ) For extraordinary work done at home they acquire a right to compensation, except if they had agreed to do this work gratis.

But they cannot demand immediate payment, and they may ordinarily not resort to secret compensation. But if they have done so, they cannot easily be obliged to restitution. Generally, they are compensated by the parents by a larger share in the inheritance.

b) *Administration, use* and *usufruct* of their property belongs to them exclusively.

If an adult member still belonging to the parental household leaves the administration wholly or in part to his father the latter can use the fruits thereof at will.

258. — III. Clerics. 1. A cleric has full ownership over all *patrimonial* and *quasi-patrimonial property.*

To this classification belongs all that a cleric acquires as an heir, legatee, by gifts, contracts, secular office, etc. (bona patrimonialia). — Furthermore, Mass stipends, stole fees, teacher's salaries, pensions from the State or the Church, etc. (bona quasi-patrimonialia).

259. — 2. The *revenue of a benefice* (Cf. C. 1410) may be threefold:

a) Income necessary for a becoming maintenance. This belongs to the cleric without any restrictions (bona necessaria).

This is true even if the cleric has sufficient private possessions to support himself. A becoming maintenance implies not only the necessary food, clothing, housing, but also proper alms, recreation, hospitality, gifts, support of needy relatives, and provision for the future. Maintenance in keeping with one's standing is measured by the dignity of the person, the amount of the income and the living standards of the locality.

b) Savings that a cleric has accumulated from the revenue of his office by living in a more economic manner than he is obliged to do, belong likewise, without restriction, to him (bona parsimonialia).

c) A clergyman's *income that is not necessary* for his becoming maintenance must be given either to the poor or to some other pious purpose (bona superflua).

One's relatives may be numbered among the poor.

There is no obligation to apply these superfluous goods to pious purposes immediately at the end of the year. One may, therefore, allow them to accumulate for a pious endowment; but he must take absolute care that the goods be applied to such purpose immediately after his death.

To dispose of these goods in the manner indicated is *a grave obligation* imposed upon the cleric by strict law of the Church, not by justice. If therefore, he does not use the goods as he should, neither is he nor anyone else (e.g., an heir who receives them), obliged to restitution. Considerably more is required to constitute a mortal sin than is necessary for a grave sin of theft.

260. — IV. Authors.

By authors is here meant not only writers, but also artists, inventors, etc.

1. *Before publication* every author has by the natural law the right to the product of his talent.

Wherefore, one sins against justice and is obliged to restitution by publishing a manuscript or making public an invention against the will of the author or the inventor. — According to some moralists it is also an injustice to print for publication the notes of a professor or the sermon of a preacher against the will of these men. Other authors dispute this.

2. *After the publication* of a work or once a discovery or an invention becomes known, a new edition, translation or imitation is forbidden, at least by virtue of positive law, and, according to the opinion of many moralists, also in virtue of the natural law.

The *copyright laws* oblige in conscience at least in so far as they protect the author from loss. The same can be said of *patent laws,* as well as regulations prohibiting further editions during the lifetime and even after the death of the author. — However, it seems that those laws which restrict the use of a book rightly acquired in the exclusive interest of the author or publisher, e.g., by making the presentation of a musical selection dependent upon the permission of the composer, or by allowing a play to be staged only if as many copies of the play are bought as there are characters in the play (or by not permitting the books to be borrowed from another dramatic club), such regulations, in the opinion of conscientious Christians, beget an obligation of commutative justice only after a legal decision.

In the United States copyrights are granted for a term of 28 years from the date of first publication, with an extension of another 28 years if application for such renewal is made within one year prior to the expiration of the original term. Patents on designs are granted for 3½, 7 or 14 years; on devices, processes, compounds, plants, etc. for 14 years.

261. Chapter II

TITLES TO OWNERSHIP

As methods of acquiring ownership, the following are principally considered from the moral viewpoint: occupancy, accession, prescription and contract. Other titles can be reduced to these four.

Article I

Occupancy

Occupancy is the actual taking possession of a thing which belongs to no one with the intention of making it one's own.

The right to the ownership of real property was originally acquired by taking possession of it and keeping it. To a limited extent, this right may still exist in the western part of the United States, where unoccupied lands may be taken up by living on them for a certain length of time and filing a claim with the government. The things most liable to occupancy in our times are animals and chattels corporeal.

I. Occupancy of animals. 1. *Domestic animals* always belong to their original owners.

Both domestic animals and their offspring must always be restored to their primitive owner, even though they have strayed afar, and although their owner was previously unknown, and the animals would have died had not someone cared for them. He who does so may, however, demand compensation for his expenses and his labor. — Only in case the real owner remains unknown can such animals be claimed as other lost things by the title of occupancy.

262. — **2. *Tamed animals*** belong to their owner as long as they have not recovered their previous liberty.

Animals regain their liberty when they escape from their place of custody (e.g., birds from their cage, game from their preserve, fish from their pond), when they no longer return to their customary habitat (pigeons and bees), when it becomes morally impossible for the owner to exercise complete control over them or when he has given up their pursuit. More detailed determinations are generally contained in the individual State's legislation.

To give one's own animals better feed in order *to entice* a neighbor's animals is against justice. To feed one's own stock better without such an intention may (in rare cases) be a sin against charity, but not against justice.

It is lawful *to kill* another person's animals if this is done to prevent them from causing damage, provided the damage would be at least as great as the value of the animals killed and the damage cannot be averted by warning the owner of the animals or in some other way. The animals thus killed may be kept only in so far as doing so is equivalent restitution for the damage caused.

263. — 3. *Game* that enjoys its natural freedom belongs to no one.

Therefore, such game belongs to the first occupant. He has already occupied game who has either so cornered it or wounded it to the extent that it can no longer flee, or if it can no longer escape from a trap set by the occupant. This obtains even when the game is caught on another's property. The owner of the property can, however, forbid a hunter to trespass on his land, and in the event of poaching he may appropriate the captured animal himself.

At the present time all States have game laws requiring a license on the part of the hunter; and non-licensed hunting is forbidden.

Game laws are probably only penal laws. Many authors make an exception for the laws which forbid hunting out of season, maintaining that the common welfare requires that these oblige in conscience. The right of ownership is not violated by *poaching* on land that is not enclosed, since the owner of the land is not the owner of the game thereon. However, hunting may often cause damage to the property. Many authors require restitution in such instances, the amount of which is not determined by the value of the animals taken, but according to the degree of hope that the owner of the land himself had of catching the game. In capturing one or the other small game in a season when hunting is good the value of this hope would be so slight that there would scarcely be any question of restitution. Other authors, however, cannot see any violation of commutative justice in the damage done by hunting. Practically, therefore, one cannot be obliged to restitution. Professional poaching is a grave sin because of the dangers to which one exposes himself and his family. — What was said of hunting holds equally for *fishing*.

264. — II. Occupancy of Things or Chattels. 1. *Things never before possessed* by anyone (res nullius) belong to him who first seizes them.

To this class belong pearls on the seashore, gems, nuggets of gold, etc.

2. *A treasure,* or treasure-trove, by the right of nature belongs to him who finds it.

A treasure-trove is money, gold, etc., which, having been hidden in the earth or secret place so long that its owner is unknown, has been discovered by accident. The law in the United States seems to be, according to several adjudicated cases, that the finder of the treasure-trove has a title to it, and that the owner of the soil where it is found has no title thereto in virtue of his ownership of the land. The general rule, however, is that articles buried in the soil belong to the owner of the soil, unless the articles come under the definition of a treasure-trove, the definition of which is quite confusing. When the finder is a trespasser, the title of the treasure-trove vests in the owner of the soil. The subject is one of romance and adventure rather than of any practical value.

265. — 3. *Things freely abandoned* (res derelictæ) belong to him who first appropriates them after such abandonment.

Fruits are usually looked upon as abandoned if they are left in the field after harvest time, e.g., apples, nuts, grapes. The owner can also reserve the ownership of such to himself. — Since voluntary renunciation is necessary, things that are thrown overboard at sea in time of disaster, or goods lost after a shipwreck, or which in time of flood have been washed ashore (flotsam and jetsam) are not considered abandoned. If the owner can no longer be determined these things may be considered as lost articles.

If one dies intestate and without heirs his goods (bona vacantia) according to most laws revert to the State.

266. — 4. *Lost objects* (res amissæ) belong to their original owner as long as there is hope of discovering him.

If one finds an object he has no obligation of justice, but of *charity* to assume the custody of the thing. His duty of charity, however, does not oblige under grave inconvenience.

If the finder takes temporary possession of the thing, he thereby assumes as obligation of *justice* to try to find the owner, and to take good care of the thing meanwhile. He may claim compensation for his trouble and expense.

A finder who sinfully neglects to seek the owner of a lost article is and remains the unjust possessor and can never make a claim to its ownership, but must, in the event of the owner later becoming impossible of discovery, either give the thing to the poor or to some pious purpose.

267. According to *Positive Law* property is lost which has passed from the actual possession of the owner without his knowledge and contrary to his intention, and which has not passed at once into the possession of another. To acquire rights over such an object the finder must take such possession as the article permits.

Although obliged to ascertain the owner he need expend only ordinary time and money in doing so. All necessary and reasonable expenses incurred are recoverable from the owner. If he fails to ascertain the true owner when he has the means to do so, he may under the penal laws of some States be guilty of crime. If he takes possession of the object he thereby becomes the bailee for the owner, and, though his title to ownership is good against everyone except the true owner, he must on demand surrender the article to the true owner. *Finders* are not legally entitled to a reward unless one has been offered, in which instance the finder obtains a lien on the article, i.e., he can retain possession of the article until the reward is paid. We have no law stating a definite length of time after which the finder of lost articles becomes the owner, but the law of prescription would operate in this case. If the owner shows up before the time for prescription has elapsed and the finder has acted in good faith, the latter must return to the owner that whereby he has been enriched.

The opinion of authorities may be summarized as holding that the bailee status of the finder of a chattel is not affected by the character of the thing found, by the place or vehicle in which it is found, or by the relation of the finder to the owner of the place or vehicle. Lost things, therefore, lying where they fell in public places are not ordinarily deemed to be the possession of the owner of the locus; however, it may be as to private places.

Where the positive law determines the natural law in greater detail it obliges in conscience. When finding things of value it will usually suffice to notify the police or publish a notice in the newspaper.

268. Property which is simply *mislaid* is not considered lost property; consequently, the finder of such property does not acquire the qualified title as stated above, and does not become bailee for the owner.

For example, the finder of a mislaid article in a hotel should surrender the article to the proprietor, who is the proper custodian thereof. If it is morally certain from the very beginning that the owner of a found article cannot be determined, the thing may be considered as abandoned and appropriated immediately, e.g., a person finds a coin in a train after many passengers have alighted.

269.   *Article II*

Accession

Accession is a manner of acquiring the ownership of a thing which becomes united with that which a person already possesses.

The doctrine is founded on the rights of occupancy and is summarized in the axiom: *Accessorium sequitur principale,* i.e., the accessory follows its principal.

I. Natural Accession.

1. In *fruitage* produced without industry, and pregnancies of animals the increment belongs to the owner of the land or of the mother animal (Cf. also 339).

2. *Alluvion,* or land to land accretion, belongs immediately to the owner of the land adjacent to the waterway if the accretion has taken place slowly. But if a considerable portion of soil is washed away at one time the owner of the land where it settles becomes the owner

of the increment provided the original owner puts in no claim within the time specified by law.

270. — II. Industrial or Artificial Accession.

1. In accession by *specification,* or the working of a substance belonging to another, the new object belongs to the one who does the work, provided the work is more valuable than the material used. If the material is the more valuable, the finished product belongs to the owner of the material; but in either case the one must indemnify the other.

Wherefore, a statue which an artist carves from the wood belonging to another, belongs to the artist. Bread that a baker makes from flour belonging to another belongs to the owner of the flour.

If the material has been *stolen,* positive law frequently denies the workman the right to compensation for his labor.

2. In accession by *confusion* or commixture of various things belonging to different owners, each owner receives a portion commensurate with his original contribution provided the individual parts contributed cannot be separated from one another. If the one object is much more valuable than another with which it is mixed the owner of the more valuable object becomes the owner of the other also with the obligation of reimbursing the other owner.

The first supposition is verified, for example, when various kinds of flour, wine, oil, etc. are mixed together.

3. If a *building* is erected on one's own property with material belonging to another, or if it is erected on another's property with one's own material, the building belongs to the owner of the property who must indemnify the builder.

If the builder did not act in good faith, he loses, according to some positive laws, his right to indemnification.

271. — III. *Mixed Accession,* or accession by human activity in conjunction with the powers of nature.

If one sows or plants things on *land belonging to another* the growth belongs to the owner of the land who must compensate the sower or planter. That which is inserted into the movable property of another belongs to the owner of the more valuable object; however, there ensues the obligation of indemnifying the other, e.g., a gem is set into another's ring.

272.   *Article III*

Prescription

Prescription is a mode of acquiring title to ownership, immunity or obligation by reason of a lapse of time.

To avoid the necessity of proof of long duration the custom arose of allowing a presumption of a grant on proof of usage for a long term of years. In modern practice, the period of legal limitation for adverse possession of lands is generally adopted

I. Prescription in general is a title introduced by positive legislation, by which, under certain conditions, ownership is acquired (*acquisitive prescription* known in law as adverse possession) or another's legal right of action is barred (*liberative prescription* or limitation of actions).

Ownership may be perfect or imperfect, and it may extend to corporeal things or incorporeal hereditaments.

Positive laws may be civil or ecclesiastical Civil legislation does not in itself affect things that fall under ecclesiastical legislation. Nevertheless, according to C. 1508 the regulations of civil law are adopted by the Church, with the exceptions mentioned in Cc. 1509 —1512

273. — II. Acquisitive Prescription. In order that ownership be acquired by prescription or through adverse possession, five things are necessary:

1. *A thing* which, according to divine as well as human law, is subject to ownership.

Mass stipends, for example, cannot be acquired by prescription (C. 1509).

Things destined for divine worship either by consecration or blessing and which are not in the possession of private individuals cannot be acquired by private persons through prescription (C. 1510). Similarly, public squares, streets, public springs are not subject to the ownership of private persons by prescription, if the people have not ceased to use these things.

2. *Good faith,* that is, the conviction that the thing which a person possesses, is his own rightful possession.

A law which does not require good faith for prescribing has no effect in the realm of conscience. Prescription, therefore, does not take place if a person is convinced from the very beginning that the thing belongs to another. If this conviction is obtained during the course of time necessary for prescription, the latter is thereby interrupted. — In case of doubt one should endeavor to attain certainty. If certainty is impossible the possessor is considered as being in good faith. Slightly sinful negligence in investigating the truth has no influence on prescription.

274. — 3. *A title* is needed, i.e., a reason on account of which one is convinced that a thing belongs to him.

Prescription was originally based on the legal fiction that open, peaceful and uninterrupted possession for a long period of years raised the presumption of a grant. The doctrine is governed largely by statute in the United States. Evidence of adverse use must be clear and positive and usually it is a question of fact for the jury. Prescription is justified on the ground that public policy and convenience require that long possession should not be disturbed, and also because there is a social need of settling controversies and of affording relief to those who necessarily find it difficult to furnish proof of title on account of considerable lapse of time.

4. *Possession,* i.e., the taking or the appropriation of a thing or a right with the intention of retaining it as one's own.

Accordingly, a mere lease, tenure or usufruct furnishes no grounds for prescription. — Whoever possesses a thing in his own name, acquires it for himself by prescription; whoever possesses something in the name of another, acquires it for the latter, e.g., a guardian for his ward.

275. — 5. *A definite length of time* is required which varies according to the different laws.

Canon Law (C. 1511) requires one hundred years in case of immovable and precious movable objects and rights of the Holy See; thirty years when there is question of other moral persons in the Church. — For ordinary movable objects which constitute ecclesiastical goods, the time prescribed by the civil laws holds good in virtue of Canon 1508.

Three years are required for the prescriptions of a benefice unless there is question of simony (C. 1446), or if the title is lacking (C. 1509).

Formerly the period of possession necessary to give a title of prescription was from time immemorial, or "from the time whereof the memory of man runneth not to the contrary." Today the time is fixed in the United States by statutory regulation at twenty years for immovable goods in all the states except Me. (40), Ala., La. (30), Kan., Neb., Ohio, Pa. (21), Conn., Vt., Va. (15), Ind., Mich., Miss., Nev. (10), Fla., Ga., N. & S. Car., Tenn. (7), Cal. (5). For movable things the time required is less.

Interruptions and restrictions can intervene during the prescribed time.

If the period of time is interrupted the time which has elapsed before the interruption occurred is not reckoned, and a new period of time must begin; this takes place, for example, in a case of lost possession. In a case of restriction, or when the prescription is said to "sleep" the time both before and after the restriction can be added together. This would obtain, for instance, between the guardian and his ward during the time of the guardianship.

No interruption takes place when a thing, e.g., in virtue of a contract, passes from one possessor to another.

Therefore, the periods of time during which the previous possessors were in possession of the thing can be added up. But if a previous possessor was not in good faith, then he who is prescribing must have been in good faith for the entire length of time required by law for prescription.

276. — III. Liberative Prescription or Limitation of Action. Active and passive obligations are extinguished by a liberative prescription after a lapse of the length of time prescribed by the Statute of Limitation.

Limitation, as a measure of time, is a certain period prescribed by statute within which steps to enforce a right must be taken. Civil law contains various limitations, e.g., "Limitation of Actions" which is statutory restriction of the time within which action may be brought; "Limitation of Criminal Prosecutions" which determines the time within which indictment may be made for an offense.

Active obligation binds someone to do something, e.g., to pay his debts. By passive obligation one is bound to allow something to be done, e.g., that another have access to a spring.

The grounds for placing limitation on actions are the difficulty of preserving evidence for a long time, the death of witnesses, the probability that old claims are bad claims, the necessity of obviating uncertainties in titles and claims and the discouragement of long credits.

It is often doubtful whether the civil law intends to remove the obligation in conscience by a prescription, or whether it only intends to bar legal action thereby. Since most modern legislators do not concern themselves with obligations of conscience, in most cases it will remain doubtful as to just what the object of the law is. Practically, one may consider the obligation in conscience as being removed, provided all necessary conditions required by the moral law are present, e.g., good faith.

277. Liberative prescription requires:

1. *A demand* or a *claim* that is subject to liberative prescription.

Obligations arising from Mass stipends or Mass foundations are not subject to limitation action according to Canon Law (C. 1509).

2. *Good faith* is required which can be either positive or negative.

He is in *positive good faith* who is convinced, for instance, that he paid a debt. *Negative good faith* is present if one does not hinder another in the exercise of his right, e.g., if A does not hinder B from crossing A's property without B's calling A's attention to the fact that by a lapse of time A will eventually lose his right to object to such trespassing.

Negative good faith suffices for prescribing against passive obligations, and also against those active obligations which are based only upon a juridical (not moral) fault. — To prescribe against all other obligations, for example, the paying of one's debts, many authors require positive good faith. Some moralists, however, maintain, that the State can extinguish an obligation in conscience only in case of negative good faith, provided it is in the interest of the common welfare, e.g., in order that a creditor may not ruin his debtor by exacting full payment of debts for which he intentionally did not ask payment over a period of years in a deceitful manner. Practically, one may follow the milder opinion, except in cases wherein the creditor has reminded or for some reason purposely did not remind the debtor of his obligation; in such instances justice or equity forbid the debtor to appeal to liberative prescription.

278. — 3. *A certain length of time.*

According to C. 1511 the rights and claims, personal or real which belong to the Holy See are prescribed by a period of 100 years; in the case of other moral persons in the church thirty years suffice.

The legal limitations to the period within which actions may be brought usually vary in the United States from six years or less to twenty years. In actions on contracts not under seal, no action can be brought after six years; in actions on contracts under seal or actions affecting the title to real estate suit must be brought within twenty years. In actions of tort there is less uniformity, the statutes varying from two to six years.

A liberative prescription can be interrupted or restricted in the same manner as an acquisitive prescription.

279.   *Article IV*

Contracts

§ 1. Contracts in General

A contract is a binding agreement of the wills of two

or more persons manifested by some visible sign concerning one and the same contractual object.

Accordingly, in every contract the following elements can be distinguished: an object, capable persons, the contractual will and the effects of the contract.

I. The subject matter of the contract may be things or actions subject to the free and legitimate disposal of the contractants. The object of the contract must have the following qualities:

1. It must be *possible*.

No one can oblige himself to do the *physically* impossible; nor does anyone intend to oblige himself to what is *morally* impossible unless he explicitly states this. — If an action is *partially possible* and *partially impossible,* the former part should be observed if the character of the action remains substantially intact, or if the intention of the contractants so requires. — If an action becomes impossible after the contract is made the obligation to observe it ceases. Whoever renders a contract impossible through his own fault, becomes liable for any damage caused thereby.

280. — 2. It must *rightfully belong* to the disposing contractants.

No one can transfer the ownership of a thing which is non-existent nor can he sell what he does not own. It suffices, however, that one subsequently come into possession of the object of the contract. The transfer of an inheritance not yet possessed is void. The only exception to this principle is the doctrine of potential existence. This still exists in all those States that have not adopted the Uniform Sales Act. As the subject matter is non-existent (e.g., a farmer contracts to sell his future crop), all that is really contracted for is the expectancy. In exceptional cases the conveyance of another's property is valid.

3. It must be *morally lawful*.

We distinguish between illegal agreements, i.e., those that are forbidden by statute (e.g., gambling, Sunday agreements in Mass., Conn., N. J., Pa.) and agreements contrary to public policy which, though they do not contravene any law, are injurious to peace, morals, etc., so that the court will not enforce them (e.g., an agreement to break up a marriage, or one that tends to corrupt public officials).

Therefore, if a person obliges himself by contract to pay for something which is forbidden either by divine or human law, each contractant is obliged to withdraw from the contract *before its execution*. If one has previously received payment for such a thing he must return the money. If he cannot be legally forced to do so it would be a matter of pastoral prudence earnestly to exhort him to give a portion of the money to the poor or some other pious purpose. No one is obliged to return a voluntary gift which was made to him in the hope that he might be influenced to carry out some sinful action. *After an immoral contract has been executed* it is controverted whether the person fulfilling it can demand or retain the stipulated consideration. Most authors give him this right in virtue of the innominate contract "facio ut des." Since civil laws declare such agreements void (which holds probably only after a court sentence) they thus bar legal claim to the consideration. Wherefore, one cannot oblige a debtor in conscience to make payment, although the other contractant may retain what he has already received.

281. — 4. It must be ***estimable at a price*** or in monetary value if one of the contractants is expected to make payment.

Therefore, one may not ask payment for something which costs him no effort (e.g., for showing someone the way); a gift, however, may be accepted.

Monetary value may exist in an advantage of which one deprives himself, or in a new obligation which one assumes.

One may demand compensation for that to which he is already obliged out of *charity* (e.g., to care for the sick), since he thereby assumes a strict obligation of justice. Nevertheless, one might readily sin against charity by such a demand.

If one already has a *strict right* to some action of another, the latter cannot exact a price for the same (e.g., a judge cannot demand payment for passing a just sentence). If, however, a person is obliged out of justice to render some service to another he can make an agreement by which a third person will be obliged in justice to pay him for the same thing or action as long as the first contractant suffers no loss thereby. Thus, if one must run an errand for another, he can receive payment for the same trip from a third person, if he also accommodates the latter. The same reason (because an additional passenger is accommodated) obliges one in conscience to purchase a ticket for use on a railroad train, or to put good stamps on a letter. Those acting otherwise are bound to make restitution. On the contrary, one is not obliged to make restitution for disobeying individual postal regulations, or travelling rules, e.g., for giving someone else one's return ticket, riding in a better class coach than the ticket permits, including a written note when sending printed matter by third class mail.

282. — II. Persons competent to make contracts are all those who are capable of a perfect human act and who have the free disposal of the contractual object. Hence it follows that:

1. *No contract* can be made by persons who have not the actual use of reason.

This includes children before they attain the use of reason, those who are perfectly insane or completely intoxicated. Authors also include those who are only half awake or partially intoxicated.

2. *Limited capacity* to make contracts concerning goods that are not entirely subject to their free disposal is had by minors, married women and those legally restricted because of mental deficiency, prodigality or habitual drunkenness or who have been placed under provisional guardianship.

Minors have a qualified capacity to contract. With some exceptions minors may even annul a contract after it has been made and demand a return of the money. As a minor can disaffirm a contract (except in certain realty contracts) before he comes of age, so can he, when he becomes of age, confirm any contract made while a minor. Whereas a minor is thus protected against his own inexperience, he is not so protected against his own wrong-doing, hence, if he injures another's property he is liable for damages. After the recision of a contract a minor, even though he has in the meantime reached the age of majority, need not pay the debts he contracted during minority provided he has not thereby bettered his condition (e.g., if he carelessly squandered the money). He would have to do so, however, if he incurred expenses in keeping with his standing.

Married women have heretofore been restricted in their contractual capacity by common law, but these restrictions have largely been eliminated by statute. In most of our States a married woman may even make an enforceable contract with her husband, except with regard to her matrimonial status and the household services. It is safest to consult the law of the State in which one resides before entering into a contract with a married woman. All States allow her to act as agent for her husband.

One legally declared a *lunatic* cannot make a binding contract. No agreement made by him can be enforced. The same holds for those adjudged habitual *drunkards* and *spendthrifts*. A contract made by an *insane person* who is at large is voidable by the insane person himself during a lucid interval or by his guardian. The sane party to the contract does not enjoy the option of cancellation. In cases where a contract is rescinded the person with the qualified right to contract need only restore that which is still existent either really or equivalently. Such persons are justified in rescinding the contract even though they had expressly declared that they would not make use of this benefit of law. But if they were guilty of fraud in making the contract (e.g., by assuring the other contractant they enjoyed full contracting rights) they are liable for all damages.

283. — III. The contractual intention must have the following qualities:

1. It must be *actual* and *mutual.*

If one *has no intention* to make a contract, the same is void. In most cases of this sort the only manner of repairing the damage resulting from such a fictitious contract is by observing the contract. — If one's intention was actually to contract but *not to fulfill* the implied obligation, the contract is nevertheless valid.

That the contractual intention be *mutual* it is necessary that neither of the contractants revoke his intention before the other gives his consent. To avoid litigation, positive laws often determine a certain time within which one party must obtain knowledge of the other's consent. If he does not receive knowledge of the other's accepting his offer within that time his offer is considered revoked. — Positive law likewise determines at times that a contract is perfected by the very fact of accepting another's offer. A contract made by *proxy* is concluded the moment the procurator manifests the consent of his principal.

284. — 2. It must be adequately *manifested externally.*

An external manifestation of consent is required even by the natural law. It may be given in any manner preferred, even by silence itself in case of a gratuitous contract; also in case of an onerous contract if the other contractant easily can or should object in case he does not consent. Mere failure to return goods sent to one does not imply consent to the purchase thereof. — To avoid difficulties, however, positive laws often prescribe definite formulae. According to a well-founded opinion, however, such informal contracts oblige in conscience (with the exception of the matrimonial contract) until the invalidity has been declared by court. Wherefore, one who has received something through such an informal contract may retain it. But should the other desire legally to contest the contract the one who received something through it should freely renounce it in order to avoid unnecessary litigation.

285. — 3. It must be *fully deliberate* and *free.* Accordingly, error, force and fear can impair the validity of a contract.

a) Error. α) Every *substantial error* vitiates a contract.

An error is substantial α) if the nature of the contract is erroneously understood. Hence, a contract is void if one contractant considers it a donation and the other, a sale; or if one thinks that which is given to him is the payment of a legacy, whereas in reality it is a donation. — β) if the object of the contract is not really known. The object of a contract may also be that quality with which consent primarily concerns itself. Hence, a contract is void if one buys mere glass instead of a jewel; if one wishes to buy black goods for a soutane or suit, and the material in question is blue; or if one intends to buy wine for sacramental purposes and the wine he receives is slightly adulterated.

286. — β) An *accidental error* which is the cause of the contract (antecedent error), generally voids a gratuitous contract. According to some authors, however, such a contract is only rescindable.

Much depends upon the intention of the donor. Thus, if one would not have given a poor man alms if he had known that the beggar was a drunkard, he generally does not wish the gift to be invalid on that account. Similarly, if the donor is under the impression that the poor person is a relative of his.

γ) *Onerous contracts* are valid in spite of accidental errors. However, if the error is committed by the intentional deception of the other contractant or with his knowledge, the deceived party may rescind the contract, since the deceiver is obliged to make restitution for his injustice.

If the contract is not rescinded, at least that portion of the price must be restored which exceeds the limits of the highest price.

δ) If the accidental error did not give rise to the contract (*error concomitans*) the contract is not voidable at law.

The price must, however, be reduced to just limits.

N. B. Furthermore, the stipulations of positive law must be observed, even though they do not agree perfectly with the natural law, since the legislator can supply for the lack of consent by authoritative decision in the interest of the common welfare.

287. *b) Force* renders a contract void because of a lack of consent.

c) Fear. a) Any fear which destroys the use of reason (whether justly or unjustly inflicted) voids a contract.

Agreements made through intimidation or threat are void in conscience and also at law, if avoided within a reasonable time after duress has ceased. Hence, any payments made under duress are recoverable. The same can be said of other "undue influence."

β) Grave or slight fear which is unjustly inflicted by one of the contractants or with his consent gives the other contractant the right to rescind the contract.

If, therefore, money is extorted from one under threat of death the person thus threatened need not keep his contract.

γ) If the grave or slight fear is inflicted upon a contractant without the consent of the other contracting party, the party thus influenced can void the contract only if the fear was inflicted for the purpose of forcing him to make the contract.

If an individual, who is being attacked by a robber, promises a passer-by money for assistance he must keep his agreement.

δ) If the fear is not unjustly inflicted or if it is the effect of some necessary cause the contract is not voidable at law.

Accordingly, he who promises another money that the latter may not denounce him, or that the latter aid him in escaping a just sentence, must keep the contract.

288. — IV. Obligating Effects of a Contract.

1. A contract obliges in *justice,* either gravely or not, according to the nature of that which is contracted.

An exception to this rule is a gratuitous promise which, according to the intention of the promisor, may oblige only out of fidelity.

2. If a valid contract is *confirmed by oath,* the fulfillment of the contract is required not only by virtue of justice, but also of religion.

If the contract thus confirmed by oath is *invalid,* the oath itself does not bind, probably not even in case the contract is void only in virtue of positive law, because of the principle: *accessorium sequitur principale.*

If the contract confirmed by oath is merely *voidable* at law, one may not contest it. In contesting it, however, one would not sin against justice, but against religion. Since the other party obtains no strict right in spite of the oath, anyone who can dispense from oaths in general, can dispense from the oath referred to. — This obligation of not contesting the contract does not exist when there are reasons bespeaking the common welfare to the contrary, e.g., if minors have thus contracted (Cf. 282).

289. — 3. An added *condition* makes consent and consequently the validity of the contract dependent upon some extrinsic circumstance.

If the condition refers to something *past* or *present* the contract is immediately valid or void according as the circumstance, upon which the contract is made to depend, is verified or not.

A condition with reference to the *future* suspends the obligation arising from the contract, but obliges one to await the fulfillment of the condition. The contractant, who sinfully prevents the future condition from being fulfilled, thereby becomes liable to restitution for damages that ensue.

An *immoral condition* by which one obliges himself to sin, per se voids a contract. Positive Law in some instances regards such conditions as non-existent so far as the external forum is concerned, e.g., in last wills and in the marriage contract (Cf. 727). The same applies to impossible conditions (Cf. also 280).

4. A *burden* (contractus sub modo) makes some special action obligatory upon one of the contractants in a legal affair.

Such a burden is, for instance, the giving of a sum of money with the obligation of making a journey for the sake of study; a donation with the obligation of using it for the building of a church.

If there is a burden in the strict sense the non-fulfillment of the obligation renders the party liable to restitution. — If a gift is only for the advantage of the donee, there is no burden in the strict sense. Sometimes the donor merely intends to supply another with the means to attain some definite goal (e.g., the priesthood) but does not require its attainment. In such a case there is no question of restitution.

§ 2. Individual Contracts

Contracts are divided chiefly into gratuitous and onerous contracts according as one or both of the contractants benefit by the contract.

290. — I. A promise is a gratuitous contract in which one party (promisor) binds himself to give or do something or forbear from some act gratuitously for another (promisee).

1. A promise obliges either out of *justice* or by virtue of *fidelity* according to the intention of the promisor.

Until the contrary becomes certain, it is presumed that the

promisor intended to oblige himself only out of fidelity, and, therefore, only under venial sin. — Sometimes there is question only of a resolution or express intention, and not a real promise. — If by the sinful neglect to keep a promise one is the cause of loss to the promisee, he is obliged to repair such damage in so far as he foresaw this at least indistinctly. — Secret compensation may be resorted to in the case of non-fulfillment of a promise only in the event that the promise was made as a remuneration for rendering a special service.

2. The *obligation* of a promise lapses if the keeping of the promise becomes either impossible or immoral; when circumstances arise or become known in which the promisor would never have made the promise; and, in some instances, by death of either the promisor or promisee.

If the *promisor dies* a real promise, obliging in justice, passes on to his heirs, but this is not so if the promise was personal (Cf. 179). If the *promisee dies* the promise lapses provided it was made primarily as a favor to him; if it was made principally for the sake of his family the obligation does not cease.

291. — **II. A gift** is a gratuitous contract whereby the ownership (ius in re) of an object passes from one party (donor) to another (donee) without valuable consideration.

A gift may be made either *inter vivos* or *mortis causa,* according as the gift is to be delivered to the donee during the lifetime of the donor, or upon the latter's death.

A gift *inter vivos* is made without any prospect of immediate death. A gift *mortis causa* is made in prospect of death and on the implied condition that it shall be of no effect if the donor shall recover.

This latter form of gift is convenient when it is difficult or impossible for the donor to make a will, and it is claimed that it has been used to evade the inheritance laws. The gift is conditional and the recovery of the donor acts as a revocation without any formality. The donee to whom a gift has been made *mortis causa* may secretly appropriate the donated object after the death of the donor.

A gift that is made in consideration of death must be distinguished from a donation *mortis causa;* in the former instance ownership is transferred immediately.

A mere expression of an intention to make a gift *mortis causa* is not effectual, as when A gives his promissory note to B without consideration, payable in 90 days. The courts treat such actions as unenforceable. If the object has already been transferred in case of a gift *mortis causa* it is looked upon as a conditional donation, which is revoked if the donee dies before the donor.

1. Gifts of *insolvent persons* are valid but unjust.

If the donee is conscious of the actual condition of the donor, he is obliged to restitution in the event that he has been the cause of the donation; whether he is obliged to restitution in case he was not the cause of the donation is controverted. If he was not aware of the condition of the donor he is not obliged to restitution (Cf. also 363). Concerning gifts of persons who have become bankrupt, confer 367.

292. — 2. In virtue of the positive law the contract of a gift *can be voided* in certain instances.

Thus, for example, the law sometimes considers the gift contract voidable if the donor without grave personal fault falls into such need that he cannot decently provide for the support of himself, his wife and family. Again if the beneficiary proves grossly ungrateful to the donor, or if one of his close relatives is guilty of the same fault. The heirs of the donor have this same right when the donee deliberately and unlawfully causes the death of the donor or hinders the revocation of the gift. Gifts that are made to satisfy some moral obligation or for the sake of propriety, cannot be revoked, e.g., remunerative gifts and gratuities or "tips." When all the requisites are complied with the gift becomes irrevocable as between the parties, but under certain circumstances it may be attacked and set aside by creditors as in bankruptcy proceedings.

293. — III. A loan for use (Commodatum) is a form of bailment in which one contractant (lender) transfers an object to another (borrower) for a specified time and with the stipulation that the identical thing lent must be returned (Cf. 294).

1. The **borrower** must defray the ordinary expenses, and take the proper care of the commodity. Furthermore, he may use it in a manner in keeping with the terms of the contract, and must restore the thing itself to the owner at the end of the term specified.

Therefore, the borrower must pay for the feed of an animal loaned; but not the extraordinary expenses of a veterinarian. He is responsible for all damages arising to the object through his own fault, and even before the sentence of a judge if he be morally culpable; but only thereafter, in case of a juridical fault. He need not indemnify the owner for the ordinary deterioration the object suffers by wear and tear. Should the borrower put the thing to a use not stipulated in the terms of the contract and should the object suffer thereby, the borrower must compensate for the loss.

2. The **lender** must defray the extraordinary expenses and, at least out of charity, he is obliged to reveal the latent defects in the thing lent to the borrower. Neither may he abitrarily demand the return of the object before the term of the contract expires.

Although the lender should abide by his agreement, he may, nevertheless, avail himself of the benefit of the law should necessity arise, since loans are presumed to have been made in accordance with all legal dispositions.

294. — IV. A loan for consumption (Mutuum) is a contract that transfers objects (called "fungibles," as bread, wine, money) that are consumed in their use, with the understanding that their equivalent in kind be restored (Cf. 293).

1. The **borrower** becomes the owner of the thing loaned and has the duty to return in due time the equivalent of the loan in quantity and quality.

As owner he alone is liable for all damage and receives all profit made from the thing loaned.

2. The **lender** may not, as a rule, require a remuneration for the thing thus lent. For extrinsic reasons, how-

ever, which nowadays are always verified, in case money is lent, a just rate of interest may be charged.

In general one may be guided by the rate of interest established either by law or by custom. Only for special reasons may one demand more than this (e.g., if there exists unusually grave danger of losing one's money or a greater profit which one might otherwise easily realize). Anyone demanding a higher rate of interest without such reasons is a *usurer* sinning against justice and is obliged to make restitution to the borrower or his heirs, or, if these latter be unknown, to the poor.

295. — V. A **deposit** is a contract in which one of the contractants (depositor) places a movable object in the custody of another (depositary) who will later return it *in individuo*.

1. The *depositary* has the following obligations:

a) He must take *conscientious care* of the deposit and he must *return* it to the depositor upon demand.

The depositary is answerable for the effects of any grossly *sinful* neglect; not so in other cases unless he explicitly obliged himself thereto. Hotel keepers, etc., however, must answer for things entrusted to them even though their fault in the loss of such things is only slightly sinful. If the possessions of a depositary are *threatened together* with the things he has on deposit (e.g., in a fire), he may rescue his own possessions first, unless he had explicitly obligated himself to do otherwise or if he is being paid for the deposit or if the thing was placed on deposit for his own sake exclusively. The depositary is not obliged to return the goods to the depositor if they are ill-gotten, or if the depositor intends to use them to the harm of a third party, or if retaining them is the only manner in which he can obtain lawful compensation.

296. *b*) The depositary *may not use* the deposit without at least the presumed permission of the depositor.

If he has, nevertheless, used the deposit and has profited thereby, he may retain the increment as the fruit of his own industry. If the civil law determines that the depositary must pay interest on the money during the time that he uses it, he does not seem obliged thereto, if he uses the deposit without knowledge of the depositor and without paying interest, even though his use was not justified. But if it is a question of a company that makes it a business to use money left with it on deposit and retain only a portion thereof for security, the aforesaid procedure would be fraudulent.

2. The *depositor* must indemnify the depositary for all necessary expenses incurred and for whatever damage the latter may have suffered in keeping the deposit.

In case of legal fault the duty to compensate exists only after one is sentenced to do so; in case of moral fault even before this (e.g., if one conceals the sickness of an animal he places on deposit, although he foresees that the other's animals will become infected).

N. B. Our civil law distinguishes between simple deposit and sequestration. The latter obtains where there are two or more depositors, having each a different and adverse interest. Deposit money held for the winner of a wager can legally be recovered from the stakeholder, if before the payment, a party gives notice that he has cancelled the bet. Since many illegal wagers are not morally wrong, it follows that one who demands his money back after losing it to another is guilty of dishonorable action. The obligations of the stakeholder are ordinarily those of a depositary (confer also 308).

297. — VI. Agency is a contract in which one person (agent) is authorized to act for and in the name of another (principal).

1. An *agent* must exercise the proper care in the execution of his contract; hence, he must not act beyond the limits of his mandate and must turn all profits over to his principal.

Agents are frequently authorized to represent another person in business transactions. Since in our complex commercial life much of the world's business is transacted by proxy, this contract is of primary importance.

An agent must answer for losses that are the result of his gross neglect, even before the court obliges him thereto, if he is morally culpable. — In so far as he transgresses the terms of his contract he is liable for any ensuing damage but the gain made in doing so is his.

2. The ***principal*** must fulfill all obligations that the agent assumes in his name, and must defray all necessary and useful expenses incurred in the execution of the mandate, as well as pay for the damages that the agent suffers in the execution of the contract without personal fault.

If he revokes the contract he has these same obligations concerning all the agent has done before the revocation is made known to him. — He need not answer for damages accidentally befalling the agent (e.g., a railroad accident).

In conducting another's business *without a contract* of agency (negotiorum gestio), the same generally holds as was said of agency. The person conducting such an undertaking may require a just recompense for his labor. If that which is undertaken is for the purpose of averting a danger threatening him for whom it is undertaken the person undertaking the matter is liable to the other only for such damage as is purposely caused or which is the result of gross negligence.

298. — VII. Partnership is a contract relation subsisting between persons (principals) who have combined their property or labor in an enterprise for the purpose of joint profit or use.

Members of a *joint-stock company* are obliged at all general meetings to endeavor to carry on the business of the firm according to the precepts of morality and justice.

If the purpose of the firm is unethical but not in violation of justice (a firm publishing immoral literature), it is sinful to become a member of such a corporation, but the profit received by a stockholder of the firm may be retained. Members of a firm that conducts an unjust business (e.g., the manufacture of counterfeit articles; making unfair use of the patents of others) are liable for all damage that ensues, and generally their obligation of restitution is *in solidum* (Cf. 361). — If the purpose of the partnership is morally lawful but the methods employed are objectionable one must decide according to the rules of co-operation whether or not he may remain a member of the firm (Cf. 147). It is more readily permissible to remain a stockholder if one has only a small amount of stock in the firm and exercises little influence in its management and makes an effort to conduct the business honorably.

A number of States have adopted the Uniform Partnership Act approved by the Commission on Uniform Laws in 1914.

299. — VIII. Sale is a contract in which a seller freely agrees to transfer the ownership of a commodity to a buyer for a consideration called the price.

Among the uniform laws governing such transactions we have the Uniform Negotiable Instruments Law which has been adopted in all of the 48 States of the Union except Georgia, and the still more important Uniform Sales Act which has been adopted by a great majority of the States.

1. *The Commodity.* a) A *mistake* concerning the *nature* or a *substantial quality* of the commodity voids the contract of sale.

Such a mistake is made if buyer and seller, for example, believe an object to be an artificial jewel which in reality is a precious stone. — If neither buyer nor seller knows the real value of an object and both doubt whether the price paid represents the real value of the thing, the contract is valid, since in such an instance their agreement takes on the character of an aleatory contract. — If the value of the object is unknown to those generally familiar with the worth of such things and, therefore, would bring only a much lower price in ordinary commerce, but the buyer because of his shrewdness or by chance, happens to know its real value, the sale is valid and just even though the ordinary price be paid for it. The same is all the more true if the buyer discovers the real value of the thing only after buying it. Some authors are of the opinion that any price paid for things bought from a dealer in antiques is a just price. — If an object is found hidden in a thing that is bought and the owner thereof is unknown, the same rules are applied that were given for the discovery of a treasure or the occupancy of abandoned objects (res derelictae). — If the goods delivered are physically different from what the buyer desired to acquire, but are equally serviceable for his purpose, the contract remains valid: but if the price exceeds the limits of the highest just price for such a commodity it must be correspondingly reduced. — The same holds where there is a general custom of selling artificial instead of natural products (provided the buyer has not explicitly requested natural products) or if the goods are adulterated. Therefore, it is not unjust to adulterate unusually rich milk, if after the addition of water the milk is still as rich as that ordinarily sold by other dairymen.

300. *b*) A *mistake* about some *accidental quality* of a commodity does not void the contract of a sale, but in some cases renders it voidable at law (Cf. 286).

If the buyer *inquires* about the defects of the goods, not only the substantial, but also the accidental defects must be disclosed to him, be they occult or not. This would not be done, however, if the inquiry is a general one and the object will serve the purpose of the buyer equally well. — If the seller, in spite of the buyer's inquiry, does not reveal the accidental defects of the commodity, the contract is valid, but it can be rescinded if the buyer would not have bought the goods had he known of these defects; if he would have bought them in spite of such knowledge the price need only be brought within just limits. — If *no inquiry* is made concerning the accidental defects, there is no obligation to reveal them, provided the price is just and no fraud has been committed.

301. — 2. *The Price. a*) The price must be *just,* i.e., it must correspond to the value of the commodity.

An owner may sell a thing at this price even if, because of unusually advantageous circumstances, he bought it much cheaper. On the other hand, an individual may not sell a thing for more than the highest common price because of the extraordinary expenses he had in connection with it. — Even though a person sells a thing at a just price he will still sin against justice, if he fraudulently induces the buyer to buy (fraudulent advertising). The ordinary exaggerations of a merchant, however, are not deception.

b) A just price can be the *legally* fixed price, the common or *market price,* or the *conventional price.*

a) It is against justice to demand more than the *legal price* permits.

For instance, if a taxi driver demands more than the stipulated rate from an inexperienced client, he sins against justice. — There is an exception to this if the price, as the result of changed circumstances, is no longer just, or if the commodity is considerably better than the average, or if the price fixed is no longer observed by the majority of the people and those in authority silently tolerate the deviation from the legal price. — If the legal price has been fixed in the interest of the seller it is also a sin against justice for a merchant to sell for less if his fellow-merchants thereby suffer a loss.

302. β) If no legal price has been established the *market price* should be observed if there be one. The market price allows a considerable latitude (there is a highest, lowest and mean just price).

Where special reasons exist one may without sinning against justice, sell above the highest and buy below the lowest market price. Such reasons are, for example, to buy or sell at the present time *as a favor* to the other contractant, something that one might sell at a higher price or buy at a lower price at another time; likewise, if the seller has a *special attachment* to the thing. It is also probable that one may sell at a higher price because the buyer has a special attachment to the thing, or if the thing will be of special benefit to the buyer, provided he is not actually in need of the thing and the price asked is not exorbitant. — It is also permissible for a seller to deviate from the common price when, of his own accord, he offers something for sale, or if he must wait a long time for payment.

Whoever sells *below the market price* and thereby causes damage to other merchants, sins against justice towards his fellow-merchants only if he employs deception (sordid competition). Confer 334.

γ) If there is neither a legal nor a market price *any price* freely agreed upon is lawful.

This price is quite common in case of used articles, or of objects that are extremely rare or very precious (fancy price), although works of art, rare books, curios, etc. among those familiar with such articles have a species of market price which, however, allows of great latitude.

N. B. Whoever pays with *counterfeit money* which he himself received as payment, sins; but, according to a probable opinion, he is not obliged to restitution, if the one to whom he has given the money has already passed it on, and it is not known who actually suffers the loss by the transaction.

303. — 3. *Delivery of Goods.* Delivery usually indicates that ownership has been transferred; but the determining factor is the intention of the parties; for according to the natural law a contract is perfected by mutual consent.

The *tendency today* among business men engaged in selling is to pay closer attention to the standardized sales contracts. Rules have been formulated in the Uniform Sales Act to determine the intention of the parties as to the time when the title passes. In this connection the shipping terms are important. In domestic sales, selling terms are usually quoted as f.o.b., meaning, "free on board" i.e., delivered free of charge to the means of conveyance at mill, factory, etc. Where the Sales Act prevails the sellers may use the C.O.D. term which indicates that although he is transferring the title, he is reserving a lien on the goods and directing the common carrier not to make actual delivery until payment is made.

Purchase from one *not the owner* carries with it no better title than the seller possessed, for good faith does not create a title. However, in exceptional situations the innocent purchaser will be protected. One holding personal property under a voidable title can pass on a good title to an innocent purchaser for value, and the title cannot be avoided in the hands of the purchaser. Therefore, title acquired by fraud or from a minor may be reclaimed but not if the first purchaser has resold to an innocent purchaser for value.

Since a large volume of sales today is made on the *installment purchase plan,* in which the title passes only after the last installment is paid, it should be noted that some State laws (in order to obviate difficulties in cases of mortgage, etc.) require that these "Conditional Sales" be filed in an office of public records; in other States such sales are good against third parties without such acknowledgment.

With regard to the *destruction of the object* bought or sold the general principle *res perit domino* holds. Hence, if there has been an actual sale and the ownership of the goods has passed to the buyer, the loss is incurred by him if they are destroyed without the fault of the seller, even though they remain in the seller's possession. If the ownership still remains with the seller, the loss would be incurred by the seller, wherever the goods may be, even though on their way to the purchaser or in his hands. Where delivery is delayed due to the fault of one of the parties and the goods are partly or wholly destroyed, the loss must be borne by the party causing the delay, regardless of which party had title (Cf. Uniform Sales Act).

If a thing is sold to two buyers *consecutively* and delivered to the second buyer, the latter becomes the owner, since the first buyer only acquires the *ius ad rem;* however, the first buyer must be compensated. Where ownership is transferred by agreement alone, the second purchase is void.

304. — IX. Various Species of Sale.

1. *Monopoly* consists in the ownership or control of so large a part of the market-supply of a given commodity as to stifle competition, restrict the freedom of commerce, and give the monopolist control over prices.

a) State monopoly is a species of indirect taxation. Any price determined by State monopoly is just as long as it agrees with the rules of a just tax.

b) Private monopoly may result from one person's buying up all of a certain commodity. Similar to it is the agreement among manufacturers or merchants not to sell their wares under a certain price (trusts, rings). In all these instances the price determined will remain just, as long as it does not exceed the maximum price which would be just in case the monopoly did not exist, and provided other sellers are not hindered by fraud and deception from selling their wares at a lower price. — Monopolists may much more readily sin against charity, especially where the necessaries of life are monopolized.

In practice it is extremely difficult to determine the maximum just price. One may certainly designate a price as just which yields a moderate profit.

2. *Brokerage* is a form of sale in which one party (agent) is employed to make contracts in kind agreed upon in the name and on behalf of another (his principal), and for which he is paid a commission.

The concept of a broker, which implies some form of

sale through middlemen, is today vastly extended, and since the broker acts in the name of his company or principal he must follow the rules governing agency (297) and sale (299) and the practice of upright men.

Even as the agent, therefore, no broker or middleman may make a profit in connection with his agency, e.g., by dealing with tradesmen at discounts or selling at a higher price than he agreed upon with his company. He may do so, however, if the profit made is due to an altogether extraordinary effort on his part (e.g., by soliciting far-distant customers), or if his company permits him to retain such extra profits. He may likewise retain personal gifts from tradesmen or customers, e.g., those he receives as an inducement for him to do business with them.

3. *An auction* is a public sale of goods at which the highest bidder becomes the purchaser, provided there has been freedom in the competitive bidding.

Any price arrived at by auction will be a just price provided no unfair means have been used either to raise the bid or to keep it low since in our time the auction sale has more or less taken on the nature of an aleatory contract.

The *vendor,* according to the general custom today, may state a reserve price before the auction and thereupon take the article back if the desired, i.e., reserve price is not reached, and he may also in this case resort to fictitious bidding to raise the price. He may not, however, deliver something of lesser value than the commodity auctioned off.

The *buyers* may not employ force or fraud to prevent other prospective buyers from bidding. Present practice, however, justifies a person who makes an agreement with others that they either will not bid at all or that they will not bid beyond a certain price. In case of a forced auction (Sheriff Sale) such a pact would be a sin against charity.

The *auctioneer* sins against justice if he intentionally chooses a time for the sale when there can be only a few bidders present, or if he prematurely knocks down an article to a friend. In such instance he must make restitution to the amount of the difference between the bid accepted and the minimum just price.

305. — X. A lease is a contract whereby one person (lessor) conveys property to another (lessee or tenant) for a definite period of time, or at will, in consideration of a charge called rent.

The tenant is liable for all damage caused if he is morally responsible for it; for other damage only when he obliged himself to do so or is forced by court sentence. Statutory law determines the extent to which a renter must pay for repairs.

306. — XI. A work or building contract (locatio operis faciendi) is the letting out of work to be done to contractors, who frequently sublet portions to sub-contractors.

The contractor must complete the work he has undertaken at the price stipulated, and he must do so within the time specified and with the quality of material agreed upon in the terms of the contract.

If the contractor *cannot complete the work* at the price contracted it seems that he who let the contract is in justice obliged to pay him the minimum just price in case materials have gone up in price for reasons that could not have been foreseen so that no one could complete the work at the said price. This is true at least when the work is worth the additional amount to him who lets the contract.

The contractor is guilty of *injustice* if he uses cheaper material than that agreed upon, or if, to save himself from loss, he pays his employees less than a living wage. Furthermore, he is obliged to restitution if, due to his negligence, defective work is done.

It does *not* seem to be an *unfair practice* for contractors who compete for work, to agree among themselves that a job be done at a certain just price and that the one chosen by lot to do the work pay out a certain amount to his competitors as indemnity. The same may be said of the practice in which all competitors come to the agreement that they will raise their estimate by a certain amount, which amount is subsequently divided among those who do not get the work provided, again, that the overall estimate is just.

307. — XII. Employment (locatio operis); or the hiring of labor or services, is a contract in which one person (employee) obliges himself to do something for another (employer) for an agreed wage consideration.

1. The *employer* must as far as possible remove all physical and moral dangers from his employees; he must pay them a just wage and observe the terms of the contract in so far as they are just.

A *just wage* is one which under normal conditions is at least sufficient to support an honorable and frugal worker. A certain amount of provision for old age and for the days of unemployment must also be reckoned. A healthy, adult workman must also be able to earn sufficient to support decently an average-sized family. — Women are entitled to the same wages as men when their work is the same as that of men in quantity and quality.

A *lockout* is an injustice if it takes place illegitimately before the time stipulated in the contract has expired or if it is done to force the employees to accept less than a just wage. — In other instances it will be a sin against charity unless the employer is forced thereto by manifest necessity, e.g., if through a strike on the part of one class of workmen another group is unable to obtain material with which to work, or if those willing to work support those not willing, or if the employer can in no other manner reject the unreasonable demands of the workmen or protect himself from harm.

2. The *employees* are obliged to keep the labor contract which they have freely made in so far as it is just, and they must avoid whatever will cause harm to their employer.

A *strike* is unjust if a just contract is thereby broken or if its purpose is to obtain an unjust wage. In other cases it will be against charity, unless there are correspondingly grave reasons to justify the evils accompanying a strike. — In case the strike is just, there is no violation of justice if willing workers are kept from working provided this is done by persuasion or by threatening to exclude them from certain mutual benefits to which they have no claim. It is unjust to resort to force, lying, etc.

N. B. If the employment contract is unjust neither lockout nor strike is unethical before the termination of the contract. Likewise, the breaking of a contract on the part of the employer or employee may be warranted by a previous breaking of the contract on the part of the opposite party.

In practice *restitution* is seldom obligatory, since it is very difficult to determine whether justice has been violated by either lockout or strike, and because in the subsequent readjustment the obligation to restitution is usually implicitly condoned.

308. — XIII. A bet (or wager) is an aleatory contract in which something is staked or pledged on an event or contest, the outcome of which is determined by chance.

1. A bet is ***invalid*** if at the time it is made one party bets on a certainty.

If, however, A is sure of the outcome of the bet and informs B of his certainty and B, nevertheless, persists in betting, the contract is valid and equivalent to a free gift on the part of B.

2. A bet is ***unlawful*** if offered or taken on immoral matters.

Thus, a bet becomes immoral if one of the wagering parties thereby sins through prodigality or if the wager is laid upon the doing of something unlawful. Once the thing has been done the winner may accept the money wagered, although he cannot legally force the loser to pay (Cf. 280).

Where betting is proscribed by statute those betting cannot be forced to observe the wager; but when bets are won and the money has been transferred it cannot be recovered at law. Confessors may not, in such cases, threaten refusal of absolution to force losers to pay their wager.

309. — XIV. Gambling and Gaming when not indulged in as a mere pastime, are contracts of playing in which the contestants agree that to the victor belong the stakes.

In order that gambling be lawful as a contract all fraud or force must be excluded, the participants must have the free disposal of what they stake and they must all enjoy equal advantages.

In case of *fraud* or *coercion* the contract can be voided at the option of him against whom such means have been employed. Such a person may keep what he wins. If the cheater wins he is bound to restitution even if the other party does not rescind the agreement because of ignorance. He is guilty of cheating, e.g., who purposely takes such a position that he can see the cards in his opponent's hands. According to general practice it is not considered cheating to look at another's cards which he holds carelessly; neither does he cheat who simulates fear in order to allure his opponent to play or bid rashly.

The gambling contract is invalid for those who gamble with money or goods over which they do not have *the free disposal*. — He who cannot pay if he loses, may not retain the stake if he wins, since the lack of an object renders a contract void. — It is likewise invalid to play with one who is semi-intoxicated, since such a person cannot contract validly (Cf. 282). If the *inequality* of the players is so great that it is morally certain that one will win, the loser need not pay unless he knew beforehand of the superiority of his opponent. But one who is merely more experienced than the other may keep what he wins, even though his opponent was unaware of his superiority, unless the one who is more expert fraudulently induces the other to play.

Gambling is not countenanced by law, although betting on horse races is legalized in half a dozen States. Some forms of gambling are criminal offenses, but usually the only penalty for private gambling is the unenforceability of the transaction in the court. Most of our States have passed laws against gambling, some of them very severe. In almost all States of the Union *lotteries* are prohibited by law. There will always be difficulty in legally defining gambling and distinguishing between acts which violate the gambling laws and those which, while presenting questionable appearances, are yet not obviously to be placed in the same category.

310. — XV. Speculation, as distinguished from regular trade, is the act or practice of buying lands, goods, etc. in the expectation of a rise in price and of selling them at an advantage.

Speculation, in itself, as any other contract, is lawful, but fraught with many dangers of sinning against charity or justice. For these reasons it may often be sinful in practice.

He sins against *charity* who corners such vast quantities of goods that others thereby suffer need. — They sin against *justice* who raise the price of commodities by means of fraud, e.g., by spreading false reports. Others, however, even those who sell at the increased price do not seem to sin against justice, since speculation has much in common with games of chance.

Stock and produce exchanges have been used for gambling purposes. However, contracts for the buying and selling of "futures" and of stock "on margin" are, in all but a few of our States, considered as legitimate transactions on the theory that actual future delivery of the property is intended, but, in the case of the "bucket shop," where no delivery is ever intended, the transactions are unenforceable. Not only the fictitious nature of the dealings, but the duress which brokers employ against the producers, condemn gambling in "futures" as morally wrong.

311. — XVI. Insurance is a written contract (the policy) whereby one undertakes (the underwriter or company) to indemnify another (the insured) for an agreed consideration (the premium) against loss, damage, or liability arising from an unknown or contingent event.

The classification is very extensive, covering accident, burglary, casualty, commercial, employers, fidelity, fire, fraternal, industrial, life, livestock, marine, title, tornado insurance, etc., etc.

1. The *insurance company* is in justice bound to pay out the money stipulated in the terms of the insurance policy.

Consequently, such a company must be solvent.— The insurer may not employ duress in an effort to make the insured party satisfied with a lesser sum than is due him.

2. The *party to be insured* must make known to the insurer all circumstances about which inquiries are made and which are relevant and material to the contract, and he may claim only that sum of money which the company is obliged to pay.

Concealment of material facts, even innocent misrepresentations, will void the contract on the grounds of a substantial mistake if the knowledge thereof would prevent the insurance company from issuing the policy. But if the circumstance concealed is of such a nature that it would induce the company to demand a higher premium, the contract is valid, but the premium must be correspondingly increased. An insured person may claim *more insurance money* than he is entitled to if he does so in order to obtain at least that amount to which he has a right. That which the company freely pays him (e.g., as an advertisement) he may retain, even if it exceeds the extent of his losses. — The insured person may not accept compensation for things the destruction of which does not entail personal loss (e.g., in a fire) because they were already sold. An exception is had if the insurance company knows that such a merchant's stock is frequently valued at a greater or lesser amount than is covered by the policy.

An insured person has likewise no claim to insurance money if the loss sustained is due to his own *grave moral fault* or through the fault of close relatives mentioned in the policy. — If his fault was only slightly sinful he may claim and accept the money, unless a court sentence declares otherwise. — Neither may an insured person accept insurance money for losses which ensued without any fault of his, but which he *did not prevent* when he could easily have done so, e.g., by not extinguishing a fire. — In a case of *liability insurance* the company will stand good for losses caused even by the greatest carelessness, and the insured may accept the money in such instances. — Concerning *restitution* due to an insurance company, confer 362.

312. — 3. In a *life insurance* contract the insured party has in general the strict obligation in conscience to answer truthfully the questions proposed.

a) If one has *knowingly* made *false statements* the knowledge of which would have *prevented* the company from making the contract, such a contract is void. This obtains also when the physician consulted has deceived the company with the knowledge of the insured. In these cases the insured and his heirs have no right to the insurance money, but they have a right to the premiums paid together with the interest on them. In order to obtain this latter the insured party may accept the entire insurance money and hereupon restore the balance to the company, plus whatever expenses the company incurred, e.g., for medical examination, clerical work, etc. — If an important defect in health has escaped both the insured party and the physician the contract remains valid, since the company assumes such risks. The provision found in most life insurance policies (required in many States by statute) that declares a policy to be incontestable after a certain period, makes a policy that is invalid by reason of false statements valid after the lapse of a definite length of time. Hence, there is no obligation of restitution after such time has elapsed, not even if the insured party intentionally gave false information. — If the rules of the company declare a contract void because some facts were concealed which by the law of nature would not invalidate a contract, it seems that one may look upon the contract as void only after a court decision has declared it so; the premiums, however, would have to be increased in such a case as will be said under β). — Statutes that declare a policy void in consequence of any mistake whatsoever, no matter how insignificant, in the answering of the questions, are unjust. Hence, there is no obligation in conscience to consider such a contract void.

β) If the erroneous information is of such a nature that the company knowing the truth would nevertheless have made the contract but would have demanded a higher premium, the policy remains valid. The insured party, however, (or his heirs) must compensate the company for its loss, i.e., he must pay up the balance of the premium which the company would have required. — There is no obligation of restitution if the insured party lives as long as could be presumed, apart from the concealed defect; so, too, if he dies from some circumstance other than the one concealed.

γ) There is no obligation to reveal one's *occult sins;* hence, questions to this effect may be answered by mental reservations.

313. — 4. In case of *accident insurance* one sins against justice by accepting compensation for an accident which has not occurred at the work for which he is insured or which was caused intentionally.

Whoever has unjustly accepted such compensation must make restitution and discontinue receiving the money. If one cannot refuse to accept the money without great danger, e.g., of being penalized for deception, he may accept it but must give it to the poor. If he himself is poor he may retain it in whole or in part. An accident takes place "at work" also when one is injured on his way to work or during the lunch hour or during the rest period.

Unless the terms of the policy provide otherwise, one who receives a *sick benefit* need not spontaneously inform the insurance company when he again becomes capable of making a living. He is, therefore, not subject to restitution if he accepts a benefit beyond the stipulated time. He may not, after recovering his health and ability, employ fraud to prevent the withdrawal of his benefit; if he does so he would be liable to restitution.

314.   § 3. The Right of Succession

The right to succeed to the goods and rights (possessions) of one deceased is either by intestate law or by testamentary disposition. For the transfer of an inheritance acceptance is necessary from which arise special obligations.

I. Intestate succession takes place when an owner of property has left no will at his death, or has property which his will does not dispose of.

The will of the deceased is supplied by the will of the law known as statutes of descent when referring to real property, and statutes of distribution when referring to personal property.

1. *Statutes of Descent.* Upon the death of the intestate his *real estate* is deemed to vest at once in his heirs by operation of law, though it may be subject to contribute towards the payment of debts.

Intestate succession depends upon family relationship. The children of the deceased, if any, inherit his real estate in equal shares minus the dower, the descendants of any deceased child taking by right of representation the same share that he would have if living ("taking by stirpes"). Posthumous children of the intestate take as though they had been born in his lifetime. Illegitimate children may inherit from their mother; in a few States they may inherit from both parents. Half-brothers and half-sisters inherit alike as children of their common parent. Living children not provided for in the will usually inherit if their omission was unintentional. Children born after the making of the will, or those born after the testator's death, if not provided for in the will, usually take as heirs. The statutes ordinarily provide that an adopted child take the name of his adopting parent and shall become an heir at law. He may inherit from his natural parent by the general law. The natural parent may inherit from him, but not the adopting parent. The statutes differ concerning the inheritance by father or mother or both; brothers and sisters are sometimes given priority over parents as heirs. Husband and wife are made heirs of each other in most States. Where there is no living descendant or ancestor, the statutes provide for inheritance by the "next of kin," which means those most nearly related by blood. Where there is no one who under the law is entitled to take, the estate "escheats" to the State.

315. — 2. *Statutes of Distribution.* Upon the death of the intestate his *personal estate* does not at once descend to the heirs, but the title is deemed to vest in trust in the personal representative.

Debts are always the first charge upon the personal estate, whether the party died testate or intestate. *Legacies* are the next claim. If after this there is still something remaining it is disposed of according to the residuary clause of the will; but if there is no will or provision therein, it is disposed of by distribution. The statutes of distribution and descent are often similar, but not always. In some States there is a full and formal scheme of distribution marked out in the statutes.

316. — II. Testate Succession or the Right of Succession by Testamentary Disposition.

Testamentary disposition of property can be made by testamentary contract, a donation *mortis causa* and by last will and testament.

1. *A testamentary contract* or ante-mortem agreement with one's heirs, is a contract by which a testator cedes the right to the inheritance to the other contractants (or to a third party).

A testamentary contract can be revoked or changed with the consent of the other party or parties.

2. *Donation* mortis causa.

For the concept thereof, confer 291. It differs from a testament especially in this, that it must be accepted during the lifetime of the donor, and it agrees with a will and differs from a donation *inter vivos* in that it is revocable at will.

317. — 3. *Last Will and Testament.* a) *The ca-*

pacity to make a will is enjoyed by everyone who has the use of reason and the ability to bequeath according to statutory law.

The general rule is that every person of sound mind and memory and of the requisite age may make a will. The age at which one is competent to dispose of his property in this way is twenty-one years in the majority of the States. It is 18 years in Cal., Conn., Ia., Mont., Nev., Okla., N. D., S. D., Ut. In Col., Ill., Md., Mo., Wash., Wis., and D. C. it is 18 for females. In W. Va., Va., R. I., Ore., Mo., N. Y., Ark., Ala., persons of 18 (N. Y. females at 16) may dispose of personal property only. In Ga. 14, La. 16, Col. 17. The general trend and effect of the statutes is to put married women on an equal footing with men in making wills. Aliens may make wills, but they cannot devise land in many of the States.

318. *b) Formalities* are required by civil law for validity. The regulations of civil law apply also to testaments and bequests to pious causes. Canon Law requires all legal formalities to be observed in the making of such (C. 1513). Even if these formalities are omitted the heirs should ("moneantur" interpreted as preceptive. Cf. AAS 22-196) carry out the wishes of the testator. In a number of states bequests for Masses have been sustained as public trusts to advance religion, as a private trust imposed by the person named to have the Masses said, or as a direct gift to the priest. Legacies left for Catholic purposes are valid in conscience in spite of contrary statutes; they may be retained and cannot be set aside by co-heirs or other legatees without offending against justice.

Wills *irregular in form,* however, probably retain their binding force in conscience, until voided by court decree. Hence, one may retain what he has received in virtue of such a testament; an heir, nevertheless, has the legal right to prosecute his claim to the thing. Therefore, it is not permissible for an heir to correct subsequently a defect in the form of the testament (Cf. 334).

Formalities required for *oral* or *nuncupative wills*: testamentary capacity and intent are essential. Only personal property may be thus given except in Ga. and N. M. where devises of real property may be made. Two witnesses are required in most States. The time within which the will must be committed to writing varies from three to sixty days in the different States.

Formalities required for *written wills*: holographic wills are valid in Cal., Ia., La., Mont., N. D., Okla., S. D., and Ut. though not attested or subscribed by witnesses. Otherwise written wills must be attested by witnesses.

Wills so as to include the devising of *realty* must be in writing. The testator must sign his name to the will for validity. If unable to write he must make his mark. Most States permit another person to sign for the testator at the latter's express directions and in his presence. Two witnesses are required in all States except Conn., D. C., Ga., Me., Mass., N. H., S. C., and Va. which require three. La. has special rules. Persons over fourteen are presumed to be competent as witnesses.

319. c) *The obligation* to make a will is a conditional obligation.

Civil law sufficiently provides for the equitable distribution of the property in case of intestacy, except when peculiar circumstances render the making of a will morally obligatory.

Such *circumstances* are: when serious quarrels will ensue which can be obviated by a will, when the merits of the children differ so that an equal distribution by the law will work an injustice, when the poverty of one child or the unworthiness of another necessitates a will, etc. Likewise, when there are debts to be paid or restitution to be made which will not be taken care of unless there is a will.

320. d) *Duties of the Testator.*

a) The *natural law* obliges a testator who makes a will to leave a part of his possessions to his nearest kin, especially his wife and children who need assistance. There is, furthermore, a grave obligation from the law of nature to help a brother, sister or spouse (even in preference to pious causes) who is in grave need. It is a light obligation for him to help distant relatives in grave need, or a brother or sister who is in slight need.

When a will is necessary parents should make it in due time, taking care to provide for the repose of their own souls by appropriate directions. They must avoid favoritism among the children, and should not forget the poor and other charitable causes.

There is no obligation to leave everything to one's children or other near relatives, including the froward and the nonindigent. Where no reason for discrimination exists, charity and prudence counsel equal distribution among the children. — Certain reasons justify a parent in disinheriting a child, e.g., if a child lays violent hands on his parent, accuses or testifies against him in criminal court, if a son is guilty of incest with his mother, or if a daughter refuses an honorable marriage to live dissolutely, etc. The power to disinherit in some States has been restricted to the extent of limiting the proportion of the estate which can be willed to charitable purposes.

β) Our *positive laws* do not recognize necessary heirs, with the exception of the wife, to whom is due a third part of the immovable goods.

Hence, according to civil law a testator may select such of his children or other relatives as he pleases as his beneficiaries; or he may disregard them all and leave his whole fortune to strangers.

321. e) *Duties of the Heirs.* a) Upon acceptance of the inheritance heirs are obligated to payment of debts, legacies, etc., charged against the estate.

In order that heirs may not be bound to obligations beyond the amount of the inheritance, they may accept the inheritance under benefit of inventory, i.e., on the condition that legal inventory be made and that the obligations are all covered by the inheritance. It is probable, however, that an heir is not obliged in conscience to pay out claims beyond the value of the inheritance, even though he accepted the inheritance and has been declared liable to the obligations by court sentence. Hence, one cannot be obliged thereto. The creditors can, however, make legal claim for full payment.

β) In dividing the inheritance everything must be taken into consideration which the testator either explicitly or implicitly has designated to be reckoned as part thereof.

Thus, a father may indicate that the funds with which he set up his oldest son in business, or the money expended on his second son's professional training, be reckoned with their portions of inheritance.

γ) The heirs must pay out all legacies, bequests, etc., as soon as possible.

A legacy "for the poor" may be paid out to anyone who is actually poor. Thus, the relatives of the deceased, his fellow-citizens, etc. may be preferred. Even people of rank or high position may be considered as "poor" if they are unable to live according to their station. — If the object to be given is not definitely designated it suffices to give something of average value. If an object of art is specified, the least of its kind suffices.

322. *f) The revocation* of a testament is possible at any time.

In virtue of civil law, the promise not to revoke one's testament is void. Even though such a promise is confirmed with an oath, the testament may be revoked lawfully, since it is in the interest of the common welfare that such an oath be void (Cf. 288).

Revocation may take place *by an act of the testator.* This may be by a codicil by which further, different or inconsistent, provisions are added to the preceding will, extending, modifying or revoking it in part; it may be by a later will, by which the first is completely annulled, displaced, and superseded; or it may be by a revoking instrument which merely annuls the will. Furthermore, a testator may revoke his will or codicil by a destructive act, as burning, cancelling, tearing or obliterating it.

Revocation may also take place *by operation of the law,* but only when the testator's circumstances have radically changed, such as by marriage or birth of children.

For details concerning this, confer the Statute of Frauds and the statutory provisions of the individual States.

323. Chapter III

VIOLATION OF THE RIGHT OF OWNERSHIP

Article I

Injustice in General

I. Injustice is a violation of the strict right of another against his reasonable will.

Justice is a cardinal virtue (Cf. 112) which inclines us to give each one his due (suum cuique). It is divided into individual (or commutative) justice and social justice.

Commutative justice regulates the relations between man and man, whether as a physical or moral person. *Social justice* regulates the mutual relations between man and society (the State) and vice versa; as *legal justice* it requires the individual to render to the State what is its due; as *distributive justice* it obliges the State to render to the individual what is his due.

Injustice, in the proper sense of the word, is committed when a *strict right* (commutative justice) is violated. It may concern corporal or spiritual things, a person's honor or goods of fortune.

If the other party reasonably and voluntarily consents to the violation no injustice is committed. —It is unjust, however, if the other person cannot lawfully renounce his right.

Thus, A may not take B's life even with B's consent, nor may he allow B to have relations with his (A's) wife, nor may he appropriate to himself the possessions of an orphan child even with the latter's consent.

If *no strict right* is violated by an action no sin against commutative justice is committed, though one may sin against charity, e.g., if out of hatred one does not extinguish a fire that is destroying another's property.

324. — II. The gravity of the sin of injustice is measured according to the actual damage suffered either by an individual person or by the harm done to society.

In the first case (relative standard) there will be a grave sin if the sum involved is equivalent to the amount necessary to support the individual and his family for one day according to their condition of living or better still, if it is equivalent to one-seventh of his weekly wage or allowance. — In the second instance there will be a grave sin if the sum is about $100.00, even if the one suffering the loss be unusually wealthy. — In small things, that have no monetary value, there will be (absolute standard) a serious sin committed if the thing stolen, destroyed, etc. is highly venerable or very rare, e.g., a particle of the true Cross.

If neither an individual nor society suffers great harm, there will never be a mortal sin against justice, although charity may be seriously violated, e.g., if one is deeply grieved over the loss of some trifling remembrance to which he has a strong attachment.

325. — III. Specifically distinct sins will be committed if the rights violated differ specifically, e.g., life, body or external goods.

The right to external possessions is violated principally by theft and unjust damage.

Robbery and sacrilege contain a special malice besides the injustice contained in every violation of ownership. Robbery is also a personal injustice against the owner; sacrilege, a dishonoring of a sacred thing.

326.　　　　　　　*Article II*

Theft

I. Theft is the secret taking of a thing against the reasonable will of its owner.

1. The *taking* is done with the intention of keeping the ill-gotten object as one's own.

Therefore, cheating, the keeping of articles found, neglecting to pay one's debts, are considered equivalent to theft.

2. *"Against the reasonable will"* refers to the taking itself, not merely the manner of stealing.

Wherefore, it is not theft on the part of a trustworthy old servant, who is too timid to ask his master, to secretly give a poor man an alms, which his master himself would not have refused. The same holds if, under similar circumstances, food is given away which would otherwise go to waste.

3. An owner is ***not reasonably unwilling*** that a thing be taken if in justice or out of piety he is obliged to yield it.

Therefore, it is not stealing to take what is necessary in extreme need or as secret compensation; neither is it theft for a wife or for children to take what is necessary for their sustenance according to their social condition, nor if the wife takes money from her husband which he would otherwise squander to the neglect of his family.

An owner may be *reasonably unwilling* that a thing be taken from him secretly even though he has an obligation to yield it for some other reason, e.g., out of charity. Therefore, it is theft for a poor man to take things when only in grave need; likewise, for a person to take a book from the owner to prevent the latter's sinning. Unwillingness is even more "reasonable" on the part of an owner who, because of the danger of loss, does not desire an administrator or cashier to take money even with the intention of restoring it. In such cases the amount required to constitute a grave sin must be reckoned primarily according to the immediate circumstances, especially the certainty of the danger of loss and the extent of the administrator's obligations, e.g., if he conducts the administration as a favor or is hired to do so.

327. — II. The gravity of a sin of theft is in general reckoned as any other sin of injustice (confer 324). The following must be noted in particular:

1. *A greater amount* is required to constitute a grievous sin in the following circumstances:

a) If a *relationship* exists between the owner and the thief which renders the owner less unwilling to sustain a loss.

Therefore, a fourfold amount is often required for a wife to commit a mortal sin; a double amount in case of children. The more or less generous character of the father towards his wife and children must also be considered in the individual case, likewise, the assistance of these latter in the maintenance of the home, and finally, the purpose for which things are taken.

Half again as much for strangers is required in the case of religious who take things that belong to the community.

Servants seldom sin gravely by taking ordinary foodstuffs which they themselves consume. As to other things, especially such as are carefully guarded, servants sin no less gravely than strangers.

b) If *several persons* have joint ownership over the stolen goods and, therefore, the individual suffers a lesser damage.

It is immaterial whether the joint proprietors constitute a legal person (corporation) or not. If none of the individuals suffers a notable loss the absolute standard is applied, i.e., about one hundred dollars. (Cf. 324.)

328. *c*) If *the nature of the things taken* is such that the owner would not be very unwilling that they be taken.

For this reason *poor people* would seldom sin grievously by picking wild berries or gathering firewood on another's property. If it is a question of public property or a government reservation it would not readily be a grievous sin for the poorer members of the community even to cut down wood necessary for their home use, if this could be done without notable devastation.

d) If *the manner of taking* is such that the loss inflicted is not so great. This happens:

α) when petty thefts are *frequently repeated* without the intention of accumulating a larger amount.

If such thefts are committed at brief intervals, about double the amount is required to constitute a grave sin, no matter whether the loss is sustained by an individual or by society. Concerning the length of the intervals required to make petty thefts coalesce confer 330.

β) when several conspire to steal but the individual thieves do not obtain much and the person from whom the goods are taken suffers no great personal loss.

Under these conditions a grave sin will be committed only

if the whole amount taken and divided is double the ordinary amount necessary for a grave sin. The person robbed will not personally suffer a grave loss in all those cases in which an absolutely grave sum is required to constitute a mortal sin.

329. — 2. *Petty thefts coalesce* to form a grave sin in the following instances:

a) If one has the *intention* to accumulate a large sum by such pilferings.

In this case even the first petty theft is a grave sin. No greater amount is required to make a serious sin than in other thefts, not even if a long interval of time elapses between the pilferings. It should be noted, however, that more is necessary to constitute a grave matter in case the amount is taken from different owners in a way that none suffers a grave injury, but the common welfare does. — The individual thefts constitute only one sin (Cf. 103).

Thus, merchants, etc. may sin grievously by falsifying either quantity or quality in order to realize a larger profit thereby. Wine merchants or dairymen may usually be excused for adding water to wine or milk if such goods are thereupon sold at a lower price.

330. *b)* If frequently repeated thefts *automatically add up* to make a grave sum either because restitution is not being made or because the intervals between the thefts are short.

The greater the amount taken the greater must be the interval required to prevent coalescence. If the respective amount taken is almost a grave sum it would require about a two month interval to prevent its being reckoned with the next theft. If the sum is altogether trifling an interruption of a week would suffice to prevent coalescence. The constant nibbling of a servant scarcely ever becomes serious since such a practice causes neither grave damage to the employer nor much benefit to the servant. On the amount necessary to constitute a grave sin, confer 328, d.

In this manner tailors, millers, etc. may sin by retaining a portion of goods every time they make a sale thus acquiring a large amount. — Such a practice is permissible if sanctioned by local custom and if a smaller wage is accordingly paid them for their work.

c) If *several conspire to steal,* even if the individual

thief only obtains a small amount, but the aggregate sum taken is large.

If the person from whom something is stolen personally suffers grave damage no more will be required to constitute a grave sin than is necessary in any other kind of theft. Concerning the amount required for a mortal sin when the individual thief gets only a little and the person from whom it is taken personally suffers no great damage, confer 328 β.

If there is *no conspiracy* in the theft (e.g., children out walking come upon a cherry tree and strip it) none would commit a grave sin against justice, even though they should realize that the owner would suffer a grave loss from the small thefts. But should one of them induce the others to steal by his bad example he would sin seriously against charity.

331. — III. Reasons that permit one to take things belonging to another.

1. *Extreme need* justifies one in appropriating enough of another's goods to alleviate one's extreme need (Cf. also 247).

This holds also when one alleviates the need of a third party. Concerning *extreme need*, confer 138. — More may not be taken than is required to alleviate the said need; there must be no other way of acquiring what is necessary (e.g., by asking); the one from whom it is taken must not be in equal need; in many cases the things may only be taken after the manner of a loan. Consequently, if one has hopes of coming into better circumstances later, he must be determined to restore the value of the things he consumed in the time of need. If there was no such hope he need not restore anything, even though he unexpectedly becomes well-to-do.

Grave need does not justify such action. Nevertheless, a poor man may take things of small value if such things can alleviate his grave need and if he could get nothing by asking.

332. — 2. *Occult compensation* is permissible under the following conditions:

a) *A certain and strict right* to the thing concerned is required.

No such right is had, for example, if a servant has merely been promised a gift out of gratitude, or if one voluntarily undertakes to do some work to which he is not obliged by agreement, or if one freely does more work that he had contracted for.

Such a right does obtain if the stipulated wage is not paid, or if one has been forced by necessity or fear to contract for a wage that is certainly unjust. — It does not if one, without any need of help, employs another merely out of pity, or if the employee freely declares himself satisfied with such a wage, or if the low wage is compensated for by tips, better food, etc.

b) It *must be impossible* to obtain justice in any other way without great inconvenience.

Should one secretly compensate himself without this condition's being verified he would not thereby sin against commutative, but against legal justice and venially.

c) *No harm* thereby must be inflicted upon others.

Such injury would be casting the suspicion of thievery upon a third party. But since charity does not oblige under grave inconvenience such harm may sometimes be permitted. — Should the debtor later pay his debts the occult compensator must restore the value in some way.

N. B. In general a confessor should not readily permit a penitent to resort to occult compensation.

333.   *Article III*

Unjust Damage

Unjust damage consists in violating the property of another in some unjust manner without perceiving any advantage therefrom.

The harm may result either from destroying or injuring a thing that belongs to another or from hindering another's obtaining something, or from criminal negligence.

In hindering another from obtaining something an injustice is committed in two instances:

a) If the other is hindered in acquiring something to which he has a *strict right.*

This obtains if someone, for instance, induces parents to refuse to give a child an inheritance that belongs to it, or if one induces another (e.g., bribes an officer) to neglect his contractual or official duties, or finally, if, in a competitive contest, one, contrary to the clear rules of the contest, would not give the prize to the one who bests his competitors. The same holds for prizes in displays and exhibitions when these are of a competitive character; not, however, when they are primarily intended to demonstrate various accomplishments to persons interested therein.

If one has innocently undertaken an action which accrues to the detriment of another it would be *an injustice* not to hinder the evil effects thereof as soon as one becomes aware of the matter, provided he would not suffer a proportionately grave harm himself in hindering the effect. This is the case, for example, if one carelessly throws away a lighted match and a conflagration threatens as a consequence; if a druggist, by oversight gives a client poison instead of medicine; or a person in good faith gives harmful advice or erroneously attributes a crime to another.

334. *b) If one uses unjust means* to prevent another from obtaining possession of a thing which he may lawfully acquire.

Such means are force, fear, calumny, detraction, fraud, trickery, lies, persistent urging, bothersome flattery, etc. by which a person is hindered in the exercise of his freedom. It is immaterial whether such means be used against him who is to give or against him who is to receive.

Unjust damage is therefore committed if one, by detraction, calumny, etc., prevents another from receiving an alms or a position, or if, by intercepting another's mail, one causes him some disadvantage, or if one deceitfully validates an illegal testament. — Unjust damage is also caused in dishonest, but not in honorable competition. Unjust harm is committed by using force or cunning to prevent another from averting some loss to a third party. Should the other be obliged by contract to avert the harm, one causes unjust damage even though one merely induces him by petition to permit the harm (Cf. 333).

No unjust damage is done in preventing another's receiving an alms, legacy, etc., merely by petition. Neither is there such damage in keeping someone from acquiring a thing which is unlawful for him to have, even if unjust means are employed; thus, unjust harm is not done to another's external possessions by keeping him from receiving extravagant gifts through calumny, nor if one in this way keeps another from an office which he will certainly obtain by bribery, or to which he is unfitted. — It is evident, however, that calumny always unjustly harms another's reputation.

335.   Chapter IV

RESTITUTION

Article I

Restitution in General

I. Restitution is an act by which the goods which a man lost through a violation of commutative justice are restored to him.

Since commutative justice is not violated there is *no obligation* of restitution if, for instance, children, unmindful of their obligation of love, neglect to support their parents, or if a person defaults in the payment of his taxes.

Neither is there such a duty if that which belongs to another *cannot be restored* to him. Therefore, one is practically not obliged to compensate with money a violation of another's honor or the sin of adultery from which no child is born, etc. But should the court sentence one to pay an "equitable compensation" he would be obliged in conscience to do so.

If *no damage* results from the injustice, restitution need not be made. Thus, he who kills the father of a family who would shortly have died of an illness or who, by his habits of dissipation, was a burden to his dependents, need not make restitution to the family. — However, one would have to make reparation even if the damage would otherwise have been caused by a third party.

336. — II. The obligation of restitution is a grave one, but admits of lightness of matter.

Whoever cannot at all, or cannot immediately make restitution must at least have *the intention* to do so whenever this is possible. — If only a trifling amount is involved the duty to restore is a venial one even if in committing the damage one sinned gravely by reason of an erroneous conscience. On the other hand one is gravely obliged to give back a valuable object which he still possesses, even if he only sinned venially in stealing it, e.g., by thinking it was of little value.

III. The grounds, or so-called "roots" of restitution are: *wrongful possession* of another's goods and *unjust damage.*

Both may exist simultaneously as, for example, a robbed man besides losing the money stolen from him (which is in the unjust possession of the thief), likewise suffers the loss of the profit he could make with the money.

337.   *Article II*

Restitution on Grounds of Unjust Possession

The possession of another's goods may be materially, formally or doubtfully unjust. Accordingly, the duties of an unjust possessor who is *in good faith* differ from those of a possessor *in bad faith* and from the obligations of him *who doubts* about the lawfulness of his possession.

I. The possessor in good faith must immediately restore the goods of another together with the fruits thereof either actually or in their equivalent to the lawful owner, in as far as they have not become his own property by reason of the prescriptions of positive law. However, he may retain the fruits of his own labor. He may likewise deduct the necessary and useful expenses he incurred from the amount to be restored.

1. *The goods* themselves and their *fruits* are to be returned in the condition they are in at the time when he discovers their legitimate owner.

The possessor in good faith need not compensate the owner for any depreciation in the value of the goods even if they depreciate because of his sinful neglect. Neither may he retain a portion for himself if the goods increased in value while in his keeping.

338. — 2. *The equivalent* of such goods still exists if the possessor by the use or destruction thereof has become enriched either by profiting in some manner, **or** by sparing his own possessions thereby.

Some authors do not consider the money which a possessor **in** good faith has received by the sale of the thing as the equivalent of the thing itself. Practically, therefore, he may keep the purchase price even though the thing had been donated to him and the owner can no longer recover it either because it has since perished or the buyer cannot be found. It is advisable, however, that the entire gain be given back to the owner. But *should the buyer demand his money* either because he voluntarily or upon recommendation returned the object to the original owner, the possessor of the money must give it to him even though he would himself suffer the greater loss due to the impossibility of recovering the money he paid the thief. The only exception to this is when the buyer is the sinful cause of this impossibility, e.g., by premature restitution.

3. The object must always be given back *to the lawful owner* just as soon as he is discovered.

This holds without exception in case the owner reclaims his property. — If he does not claim it, for instance, because he does not know who has it, the possessor in good faith may return it to the thief from whom he bought it in order to recover his money if he could not otherwise get his money back. Should he be unable to find the thief he must give the object to its rightful owner though he would thereby suffer loss himself. — Whoever sinfully postpones restitution must compensate the owner for the loss he suffers in the meantime. If there is no hope of finding the owner the possessor in good faith may keep the goods.

339. — 4. *Positive law* ascribes the goods to the possessor in good faith by prescription and in several other instances.

For prescription confer 272 sqq. As soon as an object is prescribed its latest fruits are also prescribed.

A person buying a stolen object in good faith, and in market overt may keep it until the owner prosecutes the thief; if he sells it before such prosecution he is not liable to an action at the suit of the owner, although the owner can recover from the sub-purchaser. If the thing is not bought in market overt the buyer obtains no legal title and the rightful owner can recover.

5. *The fruits of labor* are the returns that things yield under the influence of human activity.

These include in the first place the fruits that result from human industry alone (fructus industriales), e.g., the profit realized from a business. Not included are those fruits which things produce of themselves (fructus spontanei) either by nature (fructus naturales), e.g., fruit, milk, wool, eggs, animal offspring, or as the result of a contract, etc. (fructus civiles), e.g., rent from a house. — Of the fruits that result partly from the activity of natural powers and partly from human industry (fructus mixti), e.g., grain, wine, butter, etc., the possessor in good faith may keep what corresponds to his labor.

The respective fruits must be restored to the owner even in the event that the owner would not have perceived them had the goods remained in his possession.

6. *Necessary and useful expenses* made for the maintenance or the improvement of the goods may be deducted when returning them to their rightful owner.

Wages for one's labor may also be reckoned as "expenses." Useless or extravagant expenses may not be deducted. If purely ornamental parts that have been added can be separated from the thing to be restored without injury to the latter this may be done.

340. — II. The possessor in bad faith must not only restore the ill-gotten goods together with all the fruits that they have naturally produced, but must repair all the ensuing damage which was at least indistinctly foreseen by him. The fruits of his labor he may retain. He may likewise deduct the necessary and really useful expenses he incurred.

1. *The object itself* must be returned; it is not enough to restore its value.

Should this betray the thief he may restore the thing's equivalent. — The chattel must be restored in the condition it is at present, even though it has meanwhile increased in value. Restitution is obligatory even if the thing would have perished for certain in the possession of the owner. Wherefore, everything which one has salvaged or stolen during a fire or flood must be restored Compensation for such salvaging may be deducted. Nothing need be restored if the goods were consumed or perished at a time when they were in danger of being lost and he who appropriated them foresaw that no one could have them. Whoever, under similar circumstances, would consume an army's provisions which would certainly have fallen into the hands of the enemy need make no restitution (Cf. also 342).

2. He, too, must restore the thing to its *lawful owner* who has received the thing from the thief.

If one who has knowingly acquired ill-gotten goods cannot otherwise recover the price he paid for the same, he may (like the possessor in good faith) return the goods to the thief (Cf. 338). Should the owner claim the goods from the present possessor in bad faith, the latter cannot demand the recovery of his money from the thief if he knew the goods were ill-gotten when he bought them, unless the contrary had been specifically stipulated in the sale.

341. — 3. *Losses* must be repaired to the extent that the owner receives as much as he would have had if the goods had not been stolen from him.

Losses may be sustained by the owner either by reason of his having had to buy other goods at a higher price or because of lost profit. The duty to restitute always implies the supposition that the losses were foreseen at least indistinctly. What is said of thieves is applicable to those *who do not pay their debts,* provided the creditors do not waive their right to compensation for damages.

If the thief no longer possesses the ill-gotten goods he must restore their value. If the goods fluctuated in value while the thief possessed them, (e.g., due to inflation, etc.) he must restore the equivalent of the value which the goods had at the time he consumed them or disposed of them. Some authors think it suffices to restore the value that the things had when stolen. Note in both cases that the thief must also compensate for the loss which the owner would have sustained if, for example, he had certainly sold the goods at a time when they commanded the highest price.

If the goods have perished nothing need be restored in case they would have perished while in possession of the owner for the same reason (e.g., due to some intrinsic defect or in a general flood). The same holds if the goods would indeed have perished at the same time, but for some other reason. — Some authors do not even require that the goods would have been lost at the same time if they had remained in the possession of the owner, and are satisfied, therefore, with the restoration of the fruits perceived by the thief in the meantime. But none of this holds if the goods would have been lost to the owner because of the fault of someone else, since the latter would then be obliged to compensate the owner. Neither does it apply if the goods would have perished in the hands of the owner, in case the loss was covered by insurance.

342. — 4. Concerning *the fruits* of labor and natural products, confer 339.

Whoever gambles with stolen money may keep what he wins; similarly, he who steals a lottery ticket from a seller. But if one steals such a ticket from anyone else he must restore what he wins, unless he had previously made up his mind to pay for the ticket even if he would not win anything. — Whoever steals young trees and plants them on his farm need not later return the grown trees but only the value of the small trees. Besides, he must compensate the owner for the cost of replanting. — So, too, he who steals eggs and has them hatched, need only restore the price of the eggs. In the opinion of certain authors interest may be considered an industrial fruit. Since every loss must be compensated, the possessor in bad faith may retain the interest only if the owner would not have put the capital out on interest. On the contrary, all emoluments must be restored which one has received, e.g., by renting a house, since rent is civil fruit.

N. B. A confessor should not be scrupulous in reckoning the value of things or the amount of losses incurred since a thief will often not even in a confused manner have foreseen the total result of his theft, and because in many cases nothing is accomplished by too strict demands. For the latter reason he may presume the owner's consent to a milder procedure.

343. — III. The Possessor in Doubtful Faith.

1. *A reasonable investigation* is required of him who seriously doubts the lawfulness of his possessing a thing, in order to obtain certainty.

This inquiry must be in proportion to the seriousness of the doubt, the value of the thing and the prospective success of the inquiry itself. If the doubt is slight there is no duty to investigate at all. — If the owner is found the same regulations are applicable as were given concerning the possessor in good faith (Cf. 337 sqq).

2. *If the doubt remains* after investigation the possessor may keep the object in question if he was in good faith from the beginning. According to some authors he may also keep it if he obtained it from someone whose good faith he doubted. But should he have taken it from someone against his will he must restore it to him if the latter was in good faith.

If he is certain that the present possessor is not the owner, but doubts as to which among several certain persons is the rightful owner, the goods would have to be divided ratably among them.

344. — 3. *Sinful negligence* in investigating is certainly a subjective offense against justice. Since from the outset it is not certain whether justice has been violated objectively the following distinction must be made:

a) *If the owner appears later* restitution must be made.

In this case it is certain that the sinfully negligent person also sinned objectively against justice. Wherefore, he must not only return the thing or its equivalent, but must also compensate for loss of profit which the owner sustained from the time that the doubt arose concerning the lawfulness of present possession; but he need not compensate for those suffered prior to that time. According to 348 he is only then obliged to make compensation under grave sin when the matter is important and if he sinned grievously in neglecting to investigate.

b) *If the doubt can no longer be solved* on account of sinful neglect to investigate he may follow the more lenient opinion and retain the goods in question, even if his doubt existed from the very beginning.

The reason is that in this case it remains uncertain whether justice has been objectively violated or not.

345.   *Article III*

Restitution Due because of Unjust Damage

In the case of unjust damage the obligation to make restitution obtains either by reason of the damage itself or because of unjust co-operation.

§1. Restitution Necessary because of the Damage Itself

I. The obligation of making reparation exists if the following conditions are verified:

1. The act of damage *must be unjust* in the strict sense (Cf. 333, 334).

Boycott is in itself not necessarily unjust; neither is it against charity if the end and means are good. It is sinful by reason of ill will, e.g., hatred, revenge, etc. — An injustice is committed if a person, by the use of unjust means, prevents another from obtaining something which he may lawfully acquire (Cf. 334).

346. — 2. The action must be *the real and effectual cause* of the damage.

Thus, no obligation of restitution arises from an action which is only the occasion of some damage, or a *conditio sine qua non* or the accidental cause thereof. — Accordingly, although seduction carries with it the duty of restitution, there is no such obligation when one has influenced another by bad example to injure a third person. Neither is one obligated to restitution if money one has loaned to another is used to cheat others. Furthermore, one need not repair damage caused by the wind accidentally carrying afar the sparks of his fire and starting a conflagration. Finally, no obligation of restitution exists on his part who has committed a crime for which an innocent party is being punished. However, if the criminal has deliberately thrown suspicion on the innocent person he is obliged to make restitution and must, if necessary, deliver himself up to save the innocent.

In case of doubt whether one's action has actually caused damage he is practically not obliged to make restitution (e.g., one doubts whether his detracting another has injured the latter's business). An exception to this rule is had in case one has knowingly and willingly caused the doubt, e.g., if two men have had adulterous carnal intercourse with a woman and were mutually aware of each other's action so that later on it is not known which of the two must father the child. — In a well-founded doubt as to whether a debt has been paid, the creditor may sue for payment; the possible debtor is, however, not obliged to pay before sentenced to do so by court.

347. — 3. The action must be *formally sinful*, i.e., deliberately and consciously unjust.

The sin may consist in the evil intention to cause damage or in sinful negligence. — Damage that is caused in the exercise of one's office, even though no formal sin be committed, must be repaired after a judiciary sentence.

If no sin is committed, but there is a *legal fault*, one is obliged to compensate only after being condemned to do so by court. Safety First laws (in building, etc.) that prescribe more than moral carefulness, do not oblige under sin; transgressing them constitutes the so-called *culpa juridica* or legal fault.

One is liable for the damage he voluntarily caused, even if he regrets this after positing the cause and cannot prevent the injurious effects.

If one involuntarily causes damage in the commission of a sinful act (wounding another while hunting on forbidden territory) he is not liable for this damage.

348. — II. The Gravity of the Obligation. One is obliged under *grave* sin to make reparation for grave damage, but only if he sinned mortally in causing the damage.

If, because of an erroneous conscience, one *sins mortally* in causing slight damage, he has only a light obligation to make restitution. — If, due to a wrong judgment, one sins only *venially* in inflicting a grave injury, restitution likewise obliges only under venial sin. If one's action was not a perfectly human act, even though venially sinful, he is practically not obliged to anything, since an obligation arises only from an act that is an *actus perfecte humanus*. But even in this case one must answer for a legal fault if one is sentenced to do so by the judge.

349. — III. The Amount of the Reparation. From

unjust damage caused to another there arises the obligation to repair *all the damage* which was *foreseen* at least indistinctly.

If one is obliged to repair *absolutely* all damage done, it should be borne in mind that the hope to obtain something is of lesser value than the thing itself. Therefore, whoever deprives another of his hope to obtain a thing, need not compensate him for the value of the thing itself, but only according to the measure of his hope. This latter is scarcely worth half as much as the thing itself. Only in case there had been absolute certainty of his acquiring the object must its entire value be restored.

If a person does not foresee even indistinctly the full injurious effect of his action (e.g., if he destroys a real work of art under the impression that it is a cheap product) such a one need only make restitution for the value of a cheap article. — It is disputed whether one would have to make restitution if, for example, intending to burn down his enemy's house, he actually destroys the house of his friend. Therefore, there is practically no obligation to make restitution, provided his ignorance was really invincible.

350.   § 2. Restitution in Cases of Unjust Co-operation

In order that one be obliged to make restitution because of co-operation it is required that, similar to cases of unjust damage, the action be unjust, that it be the actual cause of damage, and formally sinful.

I. Command. 1. Whoever induces another *by command* to do an injustice must make reparation for all the damage done *in his name*.

Accordingly, subsequent approval does not oblige one to make restitution. Whoever issues the command is responsible for all damage unavoidably inflicted in the execution of the command, but not for that which the person commanded caused by transgressing the limits of the mandate either out of malice or vincible ignorance, nor for the damage inflicted after the revocation of the command is intimated to the person so commanded. — Should anyone culpably hinder the revocation's being made known to the person commanded, this person would be obliged to restitution. The actual doer of the harm is bound in the second instance to repair the harm done.

2. Damage suffered *by the evil-doer* in the prosecution of the command must be borne by him who commands only if the command is unjust, i.e., imposed by force, fear, fraud or misuse of authority, and only in as far as the damage is at least indistinctly foreseen. Request, promise and threat entail the same obligation.

351. — II. Counsel. The counsellor must answer for the damage caused in as far as by his counsel he effectively persuaded another to do the unjust deed, or showed him how to do it.

1. One's counsel is *sinful* if he knowingly gives bad advice, or if he gives it officially (as confessor, physician) but with culpable ignorance.

Whoever gives evil counsel is in justice *bound to retract* it; if he gives it with excusable ignorance he must recall it only if this can easily be done. A counsellor is obliged in the second instance to repair the harm done.

2. There is *no effective influence* and, therefore, no duty to make restitution, if the person counselled was already determined to act unjustly and acted on his own initiative. — Neither is a counsellor responsible for damage caused in excess of that counselled. — Neither must A restitute for advising B to inflict a lesser damage than B originally intended, unless A advised that the damage be inflicted on some definite person whom B would otherwise not have injured at all. — Finally, no duty of restitution exists if the advice is effectively retracted in due time.

Retraction is very difficult when motives for doing the injury accompany the counsel, or when the manner and means are indicated, the knowledge of which brought about the inflicting of harm.

If the person counselled is determined to inflict the harm in spite of the revocation of the counsel, the counsellor is in justice bound to warn the one threatened, provided the person counselled is still acting under the influence of the counsel (e.g., by the use of means taught him); but should he proceed in virtue of his own malice, the duty to issue the warning is one merely of charity.

352. — III. Consent. He is an efficacious abettor of injustice and obliged to make restitution who, jointly with another, culpably causes harm in violation of commutative justice. He must make restitution in proportion to the efficacy of his consent.

Accordingly, they must make restitution who conspire to vote unjustly; likewise, all voters are so obliged where the voting is either by secret ballot or acclamation (e.g., by rising); furthermore, those who in voting successively cast their vote before the required majority is obtained, even though they foresee that the necessary number of votes will be cast without their own. — He is not obliged to restitution who consents to an unlawful action in order to avoid a greater evil which cannot otherwise be averted (Cf. 144).

353. — IV. Flattery. Whoever through praise or blame efficaciously causes another to commit an injustice or who deters another from making obligatory restitution, has the same obligation of restitution as the counsellor.

V. Concealing or Defending. Whoever shelters an evil-doer or receives and conceals ill-gotten goods is bound to restitution to the extent that he effectively co-operates in the injustice.

This occurs, for instance, if one promises a thief refuge before he steals; or conceals the stolen goods, and the thief does not restore because he has less fear of being detected. — This is not the case if one shields a thief because he is his friend, or because the one giving shelter can only in this way escape grave harm.

354. — VI. Participation. 1. Whoever possesses a portion of *the ill-gotten goods* is to be considered like the possessor in bad faith (Cf. 340 sqq).

2. Whoever takes an active part in *an injurious action* must repair the harm done if his efficacious co-

operation is formal, or if it is only material, but without sufficient reason.

Concerning co-operation confer 147. — *Immediate co-operation* in injuring another's possessions because of grave fear is justified provided one intends and is able to make reparation, or if the injustice will be committed also without his co-operation, or if the damage done is small. If none of these conditions is verified one may co-operate immediately only if he would otherwise suffer a very grave harm himself, e.g., loss of life. — *Mediate co-operation* in harming another is justified if a proportionately grave reason for the co-operation (proximate or remote) is had. Thus, remote necessary, or proximate free co-operation is justifiable to avert an equivalent harm; remote free co-operation is lawful even to avert some small harm.

355. — VII. Negative Co-operation. He is obliged to restitution who in virtue of his position, office or contract is in justice bound to prevent injustice, but instead of doing so is either silent or offers no resistance to the evil-doer, or does not denounce him although he could do so without great inconvenience.

Thus, parents *are liable* for the damages caused by their children who are under age, or by their animals due to a lack of necessary supervision. — Similarly, hired watchmen, game wardens, tax and toll collectors, are responsible for damage resulting from their negligence, unless it concerns an insignificant matter or the poor. They need not compensate for the fines that the State loses, and they may even keep the money they accepted as a bribe. The following are held to restitution: church trustees whose negligence is the cause of damage to the church, guardians who culpably fail to avert damage to the possessions of their wards, servants to whose special trust something is committed; finally, delegates who sinfully abstain from voting, and thus do not hinder a damage which they could have averted by their vote.

No restitution need be made if one's obligation to prevent harm to another is merely one of charity. This holds even in case one is paid to remain passive (e.g., by a thief). Therefore, a confessor is not bound to restitution if, because of reprehensible negligence, he fails to remind a penitent of his duty of restitution, unless his silence be equivalent to implicit counsel.

356. *Article IV*

Restitution in Individual Cases

I. Unjust Injury to Life and Health.

No compensation can be made for the loss of life and health, but it may well be made for the temporal damages connected with such loss.

Therefore, one need not *per se* pay smart-money (exemplary damages) until obliged by just legal sentence. But the expenses of the physician and pharmacist must be paid. Likewise, the monetary losses must be met which the injured man sustains during his convalescence. The injured may renounce his right to compensation, but forgiveness is not renunciation.

Likewise, indemnification must be made to the parents, children or wife of a murdered man for the harm actually done to them. No indemnification need be made to them if they have actually suffered no temporal harm, e.g., because the murdered man did not support them or because they are otherwise being cared for. Loss sustained by distant relatives, creditors, or the poor need not be compensated unless such loss was directly intended in the murder. Neither a life insurance company nor the State need be reimbursed for the loss suffered or pension to be paid to the widow, since no injustice was inflicted on them. — In like manner, no indemnification need generally be made for death or injury resulting from a duel; since the challenge or its acceptance removes the injustice toward the one killed. If the surviving duelist forced his opponent to duel, he is bound to make restitution; but in this case force usually is exerted by the so-called "court of honor."

357. — II. Fornication. 1. In case of **mutual consent** to sexual intercourse with a single person there is no obligation of restitution. The natural law, obliging a man to provide for his offspring, requires that he assist the mother in supporting the child.

If the man made no promise of marriage, no injustice is committed, but the woman may legally claim sustenance for the child. If he promised to marry her he is bound to do so, but only out of honor and fidelity. If his promise was fictitious, he seduced her and in justice must make compensation. Besides aiding equally in rearing and educating the child according to the social status of the mother, he must compensate her in some effectual way for the loss of her good name, if necessary even by marrying her.

2. In case of *rape* the man must make reparation for all damage done.

This includes all costs of the mother's confinement, the support, education, etc. of the child. Should the woman's chances of a successful marriage be lessened because of her having been de-flowered, such reparation would be required as would make it as easily possible for her to marry as it would have been before the offense. Reparation is best made by marriage if the woman agrees and the marriage probably will be a suitable and happy one.

358. — III. Adultery. 1. All harm sustained by the *lawful spouse* and the *legitimate children* in consequence of adultery must be repaired.

The husband must be indemnified for all expenses incurred in the support (food, clothing, etc.) of the illegitimate child. The legitimate children must likewise be compensated for the loss they suffer by being forced to share their inheritance with the illegitimate child in case their father dies intestate. — *If no child is born* of the adulterous relations, no monetary compensation need be made. — *In doubt* whether the child born is legitimate or not, no reparation need be made. — In doubt as to which of several adulterers is the father, confer 346.

The *adulterine child* may not (except to save its good name, etc.) accept what is bequeathed to it as to a legitimate child; but it need not believe any one individual witness testifying to its illegitimacy.

2. The *paramour alone* is held accountable for the damages if violence was used on the woman. If she freely consented, both are bound *in solidum* (Cf. 361) to make restitution. If the husband consented to his wife's infidelity, reparation need only be made in case the illegitimate child deprives the legitimate children of their rightful inheritance.

3. *An excuse* from restitution is had if reparation

cannot be made without disturbing domestic peace, education of children, etc.

If the wife obliged to restitution has no possessions of her own, about the only way she can make reparation is by curtailing her personal expenditures and by increased industriousness.

359. — IV. Tax Evasion. Because of the many theoretical controversies on the subject of taxes (Cf. 206) only those are obliged to make restitution who by means of bribery or violence (not by cunning) prevent tax-collectors from collecting a just tax, and the tax officials themselves who in some sinful manner do not collect just taxes.

Officials who do not report defaulters need not pay the fines that these would have to pay; they may likewise be indulgent towards the poor. — Should one bribe an official not to collect unjust taxes he is not obliged to restitution. — Neither would a notary have to make restitution if, for instance, in making out a deed for a sale he would not indicate the entire price paid and thus deprive the State of a part of its income. The reason is that the notary's duty is not to provide revenues for the State, but to confect legal documents.

V. — Soldiers, confer 206, IV.

360.   *Article V*

Making Restitution

I. The Order of Precedence. In the first place, he must make restitution who possesses another's goods (actually or in their equivalent). If this is not done or if it is a question of unjust damage, the next person obliged is he who commanded the unjust act; thereupon, he who executed it under orders; then all positive co-operators (by counsel, consent, etc.) and, finally, the negative co-operators.

He who, for his own advantage, *counsels* another to inflict damage, is as liable as one who commands. If the injury is equally advantageous to the counsellor and executor, both are jointly responsible for the entire damage, and in the event that one party does not make reparation, the other must make total reparation. If the counsel was only for the sake of the executor, he is liable for all damages, as the principal agent, the counsellor being secondary.

If he makes restitution who is *primarily* obliged to do so, those obliged in the second place are free; should those who are obliged secondarily make restitution the principal agent must compensate them. If the primary author of the damage is excused from making restitution, the secondary authors are likewise freed; but not vice versa.

If several individuals are obliged to restitution *in the same degree* and one restores in full, the others must compensate him. — Should the person to whom restitution is due excuse one of these from his *pro rata* obligation to make restitution, the others are not thereby freed from their obligation.

361. — II. The amount to be restored in case of several co-operators in causing unjust damage.

1. *The whole injustice* must be repaired (restitutio in solidum) by him who was the efficacious cause of the whole damage.

a) He has *an absolute obligation* to repair the entire injustice, i.e., he alone, and independently of others, must repair all the harm, who alone is the principal cause of the entire damage.

This duty rests on him who commands and on him who counsels for his own advantage. Should these default, the remaining co-operators are severally bound in the order indicated in 360, but they may demand compensation from him who was primarily obligated.

b) Co-operators have each a *conditional obligation* to repair the entire injustice, in the event that others who are co-equal causes (each one's part being sufficient to cause the whole harm) default in making restitution for their several parts. The one making restitution alone may demand compensation from the other agents.

One is considered to be equally with others the author of the entire damage done, if the damage is the effect of a strict conspiracy or if it could not have been caused without his co-operation. — This is not the case if his co-operation was neither necessary nor of itself sufficient to cause the damage. — If his co-operation was indeed sufficient, but not necessary, we must distinguish: if the co-operation was moral he is conditionally accountable with the others for the entire damage; if physical, he is probably only obliged ratably.

2. Only *a part of the injustice* (restitutio pro rata) must be repaired by him who was actually the author of only a part thereof.

Thus city folks on an outing may seriously damage a farmer's crop if each without conspiring with others enters a field of grain to gather a few flowers (Cf. also 330).

N. B. *In case of doubt* we may not impose upon anyone a graver obligation than can be proved with certainty. Wherefore, we may not oblige anyone to make total restitution if it is not certain that he was the sole cause of the entire damage, or if we have reason to believe that the others will stand good for their portion. — An unlettered person will not readily understand his obligation to repair the entire damage if others have co-operated and defaulted. Generally, such a person is to be left in good faith, and persuaded to repair at least a part of the harm done.

362. — III. Persons to Whom Restitution is Due.

1. *If it is known* to whom restitution is due, reparation must be made to him.

If this person is *dead*, restitution must be made to his heirs; in itself it is not sufficient to have a corresponding number of Masses said for him. — If the *State* is the injured party, restitution may be made to the poor; to some charitable institution, or (in the opinion of the translator) to the parochial school. The latter is generally permissible also when restitution is due an insurance company and it cannot be made without great danger of the offender's being discovered. This danger is greater if the insurance company is itself protected by insurance, which will generally be the case only when extremely valuable things are insured. In smaller mutual insurance companies, the members of which must pay premiums in proportion to the amount of losses sustained, there will generally be ways of making restitution without danger of being discovered. In large insurance companies the shareholders do not suffer any actual loss. Premiums are reckoned in keeping with the amount of the claims for damage, whether culpable or not. Therefore, those who suffer the injustice in this case are the policy holders who pay the premiums. Since one cannot make restitution to them, the money may be given to the poor or used for some charitable purpose.

2. **If it is not known** to whom restitution is due, or if the person is known but it is **impossible** to indemnify him, the possessor in good faith may keep the thing; but the possessor in bad faith as well as the author of unjust damage must make restitution to the poor or apply the amount to some pious purpose.

Restitution may also be made to the poor in cases where the person obliged to make restitution would otherwise suffer twice as much damage as the person to whom restitution is to be made suffers by the lack of restitution. — If it is not known to which one of several persons restitution must be made, yet if it is certain that one of them is entitled thereto, the amount must be divided proportionately among the probable owners if there are only a few of them. In case there are many probable owners restitution may be made to the poor. — In all cases where restitution should be made to the poor, he who is obliged to make it may keep the goods if he is himself poor. A person making restitution to the poor when he can do so to the injured party does not fulfill his obligation. Such a one may often be left in good faith.

363. — 3. If all creditors cannot be satisfied the prescriptions of the natural law and the positive law must be observed.

a) Natural law requires that:

α) *The lawful owner* be given the thing if it still exists *in re* and has not yet passed into the possession of the person to whom one is indebted.

This includes all objects loaned, rented, found or stolen.

β) Creditors who hold a *mortgage* are the next to be paid.

Payment is made in order of time, i.e., first mortgage, then the second, etc.

γ) The remaining creditors may be paid after these.

The remaining creditors may be paid off ratably as far as the credit reaches, or the debtor may pay off those in full whose claim is of longest standing. Later creditors may be paid prior to earlier ones if they are poor or if they sue for payment. For a just reason the debtor may also induce a later creditor to demand immediate payment.

He who cannot satisfy all his creditors commits *an injustice* by disposing of his goods in favor of his children or deeding all he has over to his wife, unless his wife herself is one of the creditors or if the amount transferred is necessary for her to live modestly according to her social status (Cf. also 291).

A *servant* knowing that his employer is insolvent may remain in his service and accept further wages if his service is necessary to preserve the respectability of his master; if such service is not necessary, and if the servant has until now been in good faith he may even accept back payment for wages and, for any reasonable cause, may continue in his service.

b) Positive law provides further regulations especially for cases of bankruptcy which oblige in conscience.

Our National Bankruptcy Act embodies several enactments supplementary to the natural law, e.g., in as far as it determines that privileged creditors be paid off even before mortgages. Thus, court costs, funeral expenses, doctor bills and servant fees must be paid first. Furthermore, it declares all payments made within three months prior to the declaration of bankruptcy invalid.

364. — IV. Manner of Making Restitution.
1. Restitution must be made in such wise that the equality of justice be *fully restored. The manner* of doing so is immaterial.

It may be done by additional or more diligent work, by a fictitious donation, provided the donor does not induce the reception of a favor return.—When restitution can be made to the poor, the person obliged to make it may reckon as payment all the alms he contributed after the time his obligation to make restitution began.

2. **The expenses and risks** involved in transmitting the amount to be restored are borne by him who is to receive it if the present possessor is in good faith; otherwise, this obligation rests on the one who has the obligation of making restitution.

If *an intermediary person* is chosen to transfer the payment with the consent of the creditor or the judge, the debtor is discharged from further liability. Likewise, if restitution is made through the confessor. For the rest, the penitent is rather to be left in good faith.

Should the confessor be unable to locate the creditor the amount must either be given to the poor or applied to some pious purpose. — Should the creditor refuse to accept the money, it belongs to the penitent. If the latter cannot be found the confessor may keep it.

365. — V. Time of Restitution. Restitution must be made as soon as possible and in full.

If total restitution cannot be made immediately, one is obliged at least to a partial restitution. — *Postponement* of restitution becomes a mortal sin only when the creditor suffers a new grave loss thereby. Whoever wishes to postpone restitution until his death generally sins seriously on account of the danger of its not being made at all. One should not readily disturb the good faith of such a person, but earnestly induce him to make a will wherein he fulfills his obligations of justice. — One may postpone restitution for a long time if the loss sustained by immediate payment is much greater than that which his creditor suffers by the postponement. In such a case the debtor need not compensate for the creditor's additional loss through postponement.

366.   *Article VI*

Causes Which Excuse from Restitution

I. Voluntary renunciation on the part of the creditor, and **condonation or remission** by the Holy

See free one from the obligation of making restitution.

Renunciation may be expressed or implicit, and sometimes even presumed, e.g., by the wife or children of the injured party or by servants, workmen or the poor who are guilty of petty thefts; likewise, if one is caught stealing and is reproved or punished and nothing is said about restitution.

Equivalent to renunciation is the *voluntary settlement* between creditor and debtor.

Remission on the part of the Holy See is obtained by one who has a good reason to be freed from the obligation of restoring church property. In those cases where restitution may be made to pious causes the Sacred Penitentiary has the faculty to remit at least a part of the obligation.

II. Physical or moral impossibility postpones the obligation of restitution and even remits it when such impossibility is perpetual.

Restitution is morally impossible if the debtor would thereby be constituted in really grave or very grave need (if by non-payment the creditor would suffer grave need). Likewise, if the debtor would thus lose the social status he has justly (not by cunning and cheating, etc.) acquired; and, finally, if he would thereby suffer some loss of a higher order, e.g., life, liberty, reputation, etc.

Confer 365 for reasons to postpone restitution; and 362 for reasons to make restitution to the poor instead of the lawful owner.

367. — III. Bankruptcy is declared when a debtor is not in a position to satisfy all his creditors and provides in this manner, while preventing a further dwindling of his possessions, for a just and equitable settlement of his debts.

1. *Before bankruptcy* is declared the debtor has definite obligations (Cf. 363).

Before bankruptcy is declared one may freely settle with his creditors (Cf. 366).

2. *When bankruptcy is declared* the debtor's entire possessions are subject to the regulations of positive law, which oblige in conscience as far as they do not conflict with the natural law.

The natural law allows an insolvent person to retain what is required to modestly support himself and his family according to their social status and to establish a small business. The same applies to the widow and children whose husband or father died subject to restitution, unless it be a question of insignificant things that have scarcely any value for anyone else, but which are highly treasured by oneself (e.g., keepsakes from one's parents). Futhermore, civil law provides for these interests.

An insolvent person can no longer make valid donations nor contract further debts.

3. *After bankruptcy* a debtor still has the obligation in conscience to pay his debts in full should he later come into possession of wealth. A discharge from subsequent payment is only by voluntary condonation of the creditors.

This latter may readily obtain in U. S. where the juridical opinion favors complete freedom in case of a bona fide bankrupt. According to this more lenient viewpoint, debts are contracted under the implied condition that they will cease in case of bona fide bankruptcy. Although the legal immunity guaranteed in phrases as "forever discharged from all debts and claims" does not apply to the internal forum, nonetheless, the law for all our States and territories "a discharge in bankruptcy shall release a bankrupt from all his provable debts..." is adduced as proof of the solidly probable opinion that a declaration of bankruptcy liquidates a bona fide bankrupt's debts also in conscience. — In voluntary or malicious bankruptcy restitution is obligatory already by reason of unjust damage.

Section VIII

368.   *The Eighth Commandment*

The eighth commandment forbids the giving of false testimony against our neighbor, and thereby safeguards the virtue of veracity. — This virtue is sinned against both by telling untruths and by unlawfully revealing what is true. Wherefore the following subjects are here treated: Lying, detraction and calumny, contumely, rash judgment and the violation of secrets.

Chapter I

LYING

I. Concept. A lie is a word, sign or action by which one expresses the contrary of what he thinks or wills (usually in order to deceive others).

It is also a lie to say what is true if one believes it to be false. But it is not a lie to say what is false if one thinks it to be true. A lie is called hypocrisy if it is expressed in actions.

II. Divisions. Lies are divided into malicious, officious and jocose lies.

A malicious lie is one that is injurious to another; officious lies or lies of necessity or excuse, are told for one's own or another's advantage; a jocose lie is told for the sake of amusement or diversion. — It is not a lie, however, if one jestingly tells such evident untruths that every reasonable person will readily discover the jest.

III. Morality. Lying is never allowed. It is in itself, however, only a venial sin.

Because a lie is *intrinsically* evil it may not be used as a means to avert even the gravest evil. Lying becomes *mortally sinful* if another virtue besides veracity (e.g., justice, charity) is thereby gravely violated.

369. — IV. Distinguished from the lie is:

1. *Mental restriction* (internal reservation).

a) Essentially it consists in this that a speaker puts a

meaning into words which is different from that which the words taken in themselves have in ordinary conversation.

Similar to mental restriction is *equivocation* or *amphibology*, i.e., the use of a phrase or idiom which in itself (not merely as the result of immediate circumstances) has a double meaning, e.g., to "beat" another may mean to strike him or to win from him in a contest.

b) Mental restriction is *divided* into the strict, and the broad, mental restriction.

A *strict mental reservation* is used when the actual meaning of the utterance can in no way be inferred from the external circumstances, e.g., one says: "I have not stolen"—and adds mentally—"with the left hand, but with the right."

The *broad mental reservation* is had if the real meaning of the expression can be inferred either from the circumstances of the question or the answer, or from customary usage, even if, as a matter of fact, such inference is not actually made; such as the conventional polite phrases, e.g., "the mistress is not at home," meaning "not at home to receive visitors."

370. *c*) *Morality.* α) The strict mental reservation is, like the lie itself, always forbidden.

β) The broad mental reservation is permissible, sometimes it is even obligatory, provided there is a sufficient reason for using it and the questioner has no right to know the truth. — For a grave reason this restriction may be confirmed with an oath.

A *sufficient reason* would be the safeguarding of anything necessary for body or soul or the evasion of annoying and unreasonable questions. — If officials are asked about matters of professional secrecy by persons without authority they may answer: "I do not know," i.e., "anything that I may communicate." This applies even more to matters of confession. So, too, if one is asked for a loan by another who cannot give surety he may answer "I have no money," i.e., "for a loan."

An *oath* may be taken to confirm the broad mental restriction because that which is affirmed is true, though misinterpreted. Consequently God is not being called upon to witness an untruth. A very good reason is necessary to justify such an oath, e.g., the safeguarding of some great good, or protection from some great harm (Cf. also 186).

If the other party has the *right* to know the truth, nothing may be concealed, because in this case one's right implies another's obligation. Therefore, the mental restriction is not allowed when one is justly questioned by a judge or by his superiors, or in making an onerous contract, etc.

An *accused criminal* need not confess his crime to the judge. Practically all authors allow a mental restriction here, and pleading "not guilty" is a conventional way of saying "I am not guilty before law until I am proved guilty." He may likewise say the accusation is a calumny, and may offer proofs for his pretended innocence. (Cf. also 374).

371. — 2. *Infidelity*, which consists in not keeping one's promises.

As truthfulness requires that our words correspond with our thoughts, so fidelity demands that our actions agree with our promises. — Whoever makes a fictitious promise sins by lying; if one does not keep his promise he sins by unfaithfulness. In itself infidelity is a venial sin; it is mortal if one has obliged himself under grave obligation, or if another suffers gravely thereby.

A *resolution* differs from a promise in this that by resolving, one merely makes an act of his will without thereby obliging himself.

372. Chapter II

DETRACTION AND CALUMNY

I. Concept. Detraction and calumny are unjust injuries to the good name of another with this distinction that detraction is committed by the revelation of true faults, whereas calumny is the imputation of false defects to another.

Talebearing is similar to the above and consists in reporting to a person something unfavorable said of him by another. This is often due to create enmity between the persons concerned.

1. *Good name* or reputation is the public estimation of a man's excellence.

Everyone has a *right* to his good name, even the deceased, and moral persons, e.g., a community — If his good name is genuine a man has an absolute right that no one injure it. One's right to a putative good name is relative and restricted, since the common good requires that secret faults generally be not revealed; however, there may be exceptional cases where the revelation of secret sins is not only useful but necessary.

373. — 2. There is no *injury* to reputation, and hence no detraction when the faults mentioned are already publicly known.

A crime is *publicly known* if its existence has been established by a legitimate sentence of the court, or if the fault was committed in the exercise of one's position as an official, a preacher, or professor, etc., or if it is commonly known or if it will soon be generally known.

A crime publicly known in a private or *exclusive community* (college, seminary, convent, etc.) may not be reported to outsiders.

A crime publicly known *in one place* and not yet known in another may be made known in the latter if it can be foreseen that it will soon become known there, or if the knowledge thereof will be beneficial to the persons to whom it is communicated.

A fault that was *formerly* a matter of public knowledge but is now forgotten, may not be brought to light again if he who was guilty of it has atoned for it.

374. — An *injury* to another's good name is committed by:

a) Every sin of *calumny.*

b) The *revelation of real crimes* in those cases where the revelation serves neither the common good nor private welfare.

Newspapers may publish crimes that are publicly known in some locality or which cannot long remain hidden. In the interest

of the general welfare they may also search out and publish the
secret faults of one who is seeking an official appointment of
which he is unworthy. They may likewise publish and criticize
the faults that public officials commit in the exercise of their office.
Historians may record the crimes of living persons for posterity,
and they may reveal the faults of the deceased, since history should
prove a tutor of life and a corrector of evil.

For the *benefit of an individual* such a revelation is allowed if
he who is guilty may profit thereby, or if harm can be averted
from a third person. It is lawful also for the sake of consolation
or advice to relate to a friend an injustice one has suffered. An
accused person who is actually guilty, but not yet convicted may,
in order to weaken the deposition of a witness for the prosecution,
reveal the true but secret faults of the witness if this be necessary
in self-defense, and the harm that will thereby accrue to the
witness be not proportionately too great (Cf. also 370).

375. — II. Sinfulness. 1. Injury to another's good name is a grave sin *ex genere suo* (Cf. 97) and it is against justice, whether it be detraction or calumny.

It is a *venial sin* if the other suffers only a slight injury to
his reputation. — The extent of the injury done depends upon the
nature of the matter revealed (impatience or adultery), upon the
person making the revelation (a newsmonger or a conscientious
man) and the person whose good name is injured (one who is
generally highly respected or a worthless fellow). Hence the criterion
quis, cui, coram quo detrahitur. The sin is greater or lesser in
proportion to the number of persons who hear the detraction or
calumny. To reveal a fault to one person who will certainly not
carry it further is practically only a venial sin, unless there is
some special reason why he who is guilty of it does not desire
that particular person to know of his fault. — Sometimes revealing
important matters is only a venial sin because of thoughtlessness.
— If a grave fault of a neighbor is already known it would not
be a grievous sin to relate another which customarily is associated
with it, e.g., to say of a public drunkard that he often gets into
fights.

Specifically, detraction and calumny differ only in this, that in
calumny there is superadded the malice of a lie. — Talebearing
is more grievous in so far as it instigates discord and enmity.

Numerically, there is only one sin committed if one should
defame another in the presence of many persons (Cf. 104).

376. — **2.** *Listening* to detraction and calumny is sinful:

a) If the other person is thereby *induced* to detract or calumniate.

In this case the listener becomes an accomplice in the sin of injustice; besides, he sins also by scandal. Generally the listener does not sin seriously if he merely desires to obtain this knowledge for himself and is firmly determined to see to it that the information will go no further.

b) If one *rejoices* in the fault — real or imputed.

c) If one *does not hinder* the defamation although he can do so.

Whoever acts thus sins against charity. However, since charity does not oblige under grave inconvenience and because the success of a correction is often very doubtful, the silence of private individuals under such circumstances is generally free from grievous sin at least. If one must listen to such talk against his will without being able to prevent it he commits no sin.

377. — **III. Restitution because of Damage Caused.**

1. The *obligation* to make restitution for damage unjustly caused by detraction or calumny is one of justice and includes the restoration of the injured person's reputation and the reparation of any material harm resulting therefrom if this was foreseen at least in a confused manner.

If the sin was venial because only slight harm was done, there is only a light obligation to make restitution. But if one has caused grave damage and sinned mortally in doing so he is obligated to restitution even at great personal inconvenience. If one foresaw that his defamatory manifestation would be carried further he would theoretically be obliged to restore the lost reputation in the mind of all those before whom the fault was revealed; moral impossibility, however, practically excuses from this obligation. — Whoever knowingly testifies falsely before court must revoke this testimony if the damage done cannot otherwise be repaired. (Cf. also the reasons that excuse from restoring another's reputation given below).

2. The *manner* of making restitution varies according as one has been guilty of detraction or calumny.

A *calumniator* must admit that he spoke falsely if the injured person's good name cannot otherwise be restored. — For the *detractor* to say so would be a lie; therefore, he must seek to restore the lost reputation in some other way, e.g., by excusing the faults of the detracted or by praising him for his good qualities.

If one has defamed another in a *newspaper,* he can generally make restitution only through the same medium.

3. The *reasons that excuse* one from making restitution for lost reputation are: if in some manner reparation has previously been made; if the matter has been forgotten; if it is foreseen that one will not believe the detraction; if restitution is morally impossible; if the defamed has been guilty of the same offense toward his defamer and refuses to restitute; if it can reasonably be presumed that the defamed renounces his right to the restoration of his good name.

Moral impossibility obtains if the defamer in retracting must suffer proportionately much greater harm than the one suffered whom he defamed. This holds also for him who has given false testimony before court. — Should one have acted in good faith he would more readily be excused. — Unless sentenced to do so by the judge, a defamer has no obligation to compensate, by payment of money, for the injury done to another's reputation when the restoration of his good name is impossible.

Renunciation of one's right to restitution is unlawful if such a renunciation is injurious to the common welfare or to one's relatives.

378.   Chapter III

CONTUMELY AND RASH JUDGMENT

Contumely is an injury to the honor due to another. Since even thoughts may be contumelious, authors usually treat *rash judgment* in connection with contumely.

I. Contumely. 1. *Concept*. Contumely consists in unjustly dishonoring another person in his presence and thus showing one's contempt for him.

A person may be physically or morally present according as he is actually present or only by proxy, picture, etc. — Dishonoring another may be done by words, deeds or omissions.

2. *Sinfulness*. Contumely is *ex genere suo* (Cf. 97) a grave sin against justice.

It is *venially sinful* to treat another with only slightly insulting words or gestures. — The gravity of the sin of contumely is determined by the words, actions or omissions employed and especially by the dignity of the person dishonored. Some expressions used among the less educated may be only banter, and, therefore, no sin; whereas among more cultured people they would imply a grave affront.

3. *Reparation* for an insult offered must be in keeping with the nature of the contumely itself, i.e., either public or private, and made in a manner that will indicate unequivocally that the injured person is really being honored thereby.

Toward superiors one should make reparation by asking pardon. Toward equals or inferiors it generally suffices to show special signs of esteem and good will. It might be necessary at times to ask explicitly for forgiveness for a grave insult even from an equal.

Other *damaging consequences* of a contumelious action likewise demand reparation if they have been foreseen at least indistinctly.

4. *Excuses* from the obligation of making reparation for contumely are: reasonable presumption that the dishonored person waives his claim to reparation; judicial punishment of the offender; if the offended has taken revenge; or if the contumelious action was mutual and equally grave on both sides.

379. — II. Rash Judgment. 1. *Concept.* Rash judgment is the firm mental assenting, without sufficient reason, to the existence of some moral defect in another.

Differing from a rash judgment is: α) *rash suspicion,* or the inadequately founded opinion that another has done something evil; β) *rash doubt* in which one withholds his judgment about the moral character of his neighbor without adequate reason; γ) the exercise of *caution* in practical life which is based on the fact that one may be deceived about the righteousness of his fellowman, and suffer from such deception.

2. *Sinfulness.* Rash judgment is *ex genere suo* a grievous sin against justice.

Conditions necessary for the sin to be grave: α) the matter in question must be important; β) there must be firm conviction; γ) the judgment must be fully deliberate and δ) without adequate reason.

Rash suspicions and *doubts* are generally only venial sins. Only then are they mortal sins when they concern some unusually serious crime and there are absolutely no grounds for assuming such an attitude of mind. — *Rash judgment,* too, is only a venial sin when one does not realize that the reasons for his assent are insufficient and does not advert to his duty of investigating the reasons, provided the judgment is not prompted by hatred.

To exercise *caution* in practical life is not sinful, since one does not think evil of one's neighbor, but merely reckons with the factual possibility of one's being deceived.

380.   Chapter IV

VIOLATION OF SECRECY

I. Concept. A secret is the knowledge of a thing which may not be divulged.

The thing, the knowledge of which may not be revealed, may be an invention, a transgression or some fact, e.g., financial embarrassment.

II. Division. Secrets are divided into:

1. *Natural secrets,* or those that must be kept by reason of the natural law.

Natural law requires that those things be kept secret, the revelation of which would injure or displease another.

2. *Promised secrets,* or those which one has promised to keep, after having received the knowledge thereof.

3. *Committed* or *rigorous secrets,* the knowledge of which one obtains only upon the condition that one will keep them secret.

The promise in a committed secret may be explicit or implicit. — To this class belong *professional secrets* to which one is obliged explicitly or implicitly in virtue of his accepting an office, as an editor, magistrate, pastor, physician, lawyer, midwife, etc.

381. — III. Violation of a Secret. 1. *In General.* It is never lawful to violate a secret by unjust means. It is permitted to acquire secret knowledge if one has a sufficient reason and uses fair means.

Therefore, one may not acquire the knowledge of an invention or some fact still unknown by unjust means, as burglary, eavesdropping, opening the letters of another, etc. Study, however, is a legitimate means. — Parents and other superiors may use lawful means to discover the failings of their children or subjects in order to correct them or to preserve others from harm.

Unjustifiable violation of a secret is in itself a *grave sin* against justice In trifling matters, however, it is only a venial fault.

382. — *Epistolary Secrets in Particular.*

a) *Violation* of epistolary secrets takes place by opening and reading others' letters or by reading those already opened, but kept in a secret place.

It is no sin to read letters that someone has discarded into some public receptacle; this is true even if the letter has been torn into small pieces and the finder reassembles them. But should one thus discover information that might prove injurious to another he would be obliged in charity to keep it secret. — Letters that have been lost may not be read.

b) Regarding the *sinfulness* the same holds here as was said about violating secrets in general.

c) It is *lawful* to open or read letters that have been opened:

α) with the permission of the sender or the addressee;

β) to avert grave damage to the common welfare, one's neighbor or oneself.

Wherefore, civil authorities may open letters, e.g., for the discovery of crime Parents, too, may read the letters of their children who are still under parental authority. Furthermore, it is the right of authorities in an educational institution to read the letters of their charges, but not if they contain family secrets or matters of conscience. The rights of a husband in this regard are determined by local usage. Anyone may read another's letters if he has a right to assume that they contain something unjustly and seriously harmful to himself.

γ) If the Rule or Constitutions of a religious institute grant this right to the superiors.

By his entrance into such a community the individual freely subjects himself to this regulation, thereby granting the authorities the right to read his letters. Canon 611 forbids superiors to read the letters that members send to the Holy See, the Apostolic Delegate, the Cardinal Protector, major superiors and their local superior if he is absent, to the local Ordinary and the Regular Superior to whom nuns may be subjected. Neither may the superiors read the letters that are received from these persons mentioned.

Whoever legitimately reads another's letters is obliged as by a natural secret not to communicate their contents to those unauthorized to know them.

Letters that contain matters of conscience or matter pertaining to the seal of confession may *never* be read. — If a superior doubts whether a letter contains a matter of conscience he may open it and read only enough to ascertain whether it actually does contain such material.

383. — IV. Revelation of a Secret. 1. To violate a

natural secret is a grave sin against justice or charity according as another is seriously injured or grievously offended by such revelation.

A venial sin is committed if the other person is only slightly harmed or slightly offended.

A sufficient reason for revealing a secret is the avoidance of a relatively great inconvenience to oneself or another, even though the other's harm suffered from the revelation of the secret be still greater. If one has unjustly obtained knowledge of a secret, he may reveal it only to save himself from an extremely great harm or as a defense against the other's unjust aggression.

An obligation to reveal a natural secret obtains when authorities legitimately request the information.

2. To reveal a *promised secret* is a venial or a mortal sin according as one pledges secrecy out of fidelity (under venial sin), or out of justice which in important matters obliges under grave sin.

In doubt as to how one intended to oblige himself a light obligation is presumed. In many cases, however, one will also be bound by a natural secret and that under pain of grievous sin.

A sufficient reason to reveal a promised secret is any great inconvenience in keeping it, unless one has explicitly obliged himself to keep it despite such inconvenience.

There is *an obligation* to reveal a promised secret if the competent superior rightfully requests the knowledge, as in case of a crime; this is true even if one took an oath to keep his promise of secrecy.

384. — 3. To reveal a *committed secret* is an especially grave sin. This is in still greater measure true of professional secrets.

A venial sin is committed if the matter is trifling.

Even *at the request of his superiors* one may not divulge this kind of secret, except for one of the following excusing reasons:

α) Serious harm to the common good. *β*) Serious and unjust injury to an innocent party threatening from him who communicated the secret. Therefore, if a man who is sexually diseased cannot be dissuaded from marrying by his physician, the latter may reveal the matter to his intended bride. One may not violate professional secrecy in order to testify against a criminal to save an innocent person from judicial condemnation if the criminal is not the cause of the condemnation (Cf. also 346). γ) To avert serious evil from him who has committed the secret; e.g., if he is knowingly bent on contracting an invalid marriage and cannot otherwise be dissuaded therefrom except by revelation of the secret. δ) A grave misfortune to oneself. No one can presume that a person would wish to oblige himself to such an extent, unless he has expressly promised to do so.

385. — V. Making Use of Secrets.

1. *It is unlawful* to make use of secrets the knowledge of which one has obtained unjustly.

To make use of a secret here means to employ the knowledge one has without thereby revealing the secret.

He who has unjustly opened business letters may not use the knowledge obtained to the disadvantage of his neighbor or competitor.

In an *exceptional case* one may do this; viz., if circumstances have so changed that it is now lawful to acquire the knowledge for a purpose which would be disadvantageous to another.

2. *It is lawful* to make use of secrets justly acquired (Cf. 381).

Wherefore, if one has accidentally come by business secrets from public conversation of business men, one may use the knowledge to one's own advantage even if another should thereby lose an opportunity of gain.

A *committed secret* may not be used to one's own or another's advantage if the one committing the secret reasonably objects to this.

386. ## Part III

THE PRECEPTS OF THE CHURCH

The universal disciplinary laws of the Church are contained in the Code of Canon Law (Codex Juris Canonici). Their treatment is principally the task of the canonist. We have heretofore made repeated references to some of these laws. Among those not yet mentioned we shall treat only those that find the most frequent application in daily life.

In the first place we are concerned with those laws that have come to be known as "The Precepts of the Church"; thereupon, we shall treat the ecclesiastical prohibition and censorship of books, the laws of the Church respecting the three principal states of life, and finally the penal legislation of the Church.

Section I

The Precepts of the Church

In the United States it is customary to single out the following chief precepts of the Church: 1. To assist at Mass and abstain from servile work on Sundays and Holydays of obligation. 2. To fast and abstain on the days appointed by the Church. 3. To confess our sins at least once a year. 4. To receive Holy Communion each year during the Easter Time. 5. To contribute to the support of the Church. 6. To observe the laws of the Church concerning Matrimony.

The sanctification of Sundays and Holydays has already been treated (Cf. 191 sqq.). We shall treat here only the laws pertaining to fast and abstinence, and the annual confession and Easter Communion, adding a note on the support of the Church and the marriage laws.

387. ## Chapter I

FASTING AND ABSTINENCE

I. The Days of Fasting and Abstinence.

In accordance with the provisions of Canon Law, as modified by the use of special faculties granted by the Holy See, the following regulations were adopted by the Bishops of United States.

1. ***Complete abstinence*** is to be observed on all Fridays of the year, Ash Wednesday, the Vigils of Immacu-

late Conception and Christmas.

In those dioceses where Holy Saturday (the entire day) is considered as another day of lent, meat may be taken at the principal meal.

2. *Partial abstinence* is to be observed on Ember Wednesdays and Saturdays and on the Vigil of Pentecost.

3. *Days of fast* are all the weekdays of Lent, Ember Days, and the Vigil of Pentecost.

Concerning the difference between complete and partial abstinence, confer 389.

It is to be noted that Ember Days and the Vigil of Pentecost are now days of partial abstinence. The special exclusion of the Vigils of Immaculate Conception and Christmas from this classification is noteworthy. These two Vigils are days of complete abstinence. — By distinguishing between complete and partial abstinence the benefits formerly granted to working people (Workingmen's Indult) are now extended to all who are obliged to abstain. — There is no longer any question about the interpretation of "workingmen" since the new formula makes no difference between manual workers, stenographers, white collar workers, students, seminarians, religious, etc. All may make use of the same privileges. — The purpose of these new regulations and important modifications is to enable those who are engaged in hard and exhaustive occupations, to keep the fast by enabling them to eat meat once on (partial) abstinence days. — Furthermore, Catholics serving in the Armed Forces, while they are in actual service, and their families, too, when eating with them, are dispensed from abstinence except on Ash Wednesdays, Good Friday, Holy Saturday (the entire day) and the Vigil of Christmas. — The Ordinaries of the United States may also dispense their subjects from the laws of fast and abstinence on civil holidays, but they are to exhort the faithful to make some offering, especially to the poor, by way of compensation. Bishops may dispense the entire diocese or any part of it (e.g., a town) for the special reason of a great concourse of people or for one of public health (C. 1245).

General custom allows one who is fasting to take a double portion of food at the collation on Christmas Eve (*jejunium gaudiosum*).

388. — II. Things prohibited by the laws of fasting and abstinence.

1. ***The law of fasting*** forbids more than one full meal a day. Meat may be taken at the principal meal on a day of fast except on Fridays, Ash Wednesday and the Vigils of Immaculate Conception and Christmas. Two other meatless meals, sufficient to maintain strength, may be taken according to each one's needs; but together they should not equal another full meal.

Eating between meals is also forbidden; but liquids, including milk and fruit juices, are allowed. The usual amount of cream in coffee or tea is permitted. Milk is understood as ordinary or homogenized, but does not include such combinations as malted milk or milk shakes. However combinations based on skimmed milk and a coloring or special flavoring such as "chocolate milk" are rather a drink than a food and, therefore, permissible. — The use of eggs and milk foods (*ova et lacticinia*) is permitted on all days on which there is both fast and abstinence. — Wine, beer, etc., are not considered nourishing drinks, though they may be contrary to the spirit of Lent. In order that a drink may not be injurious (*ne potus noceat*) a bite of food may be taken with it.

When health or the ability to work would be seriously affected, the law does not oblige. One who is not obliged to fast may eat meat as often as he wills on days when fasting alone is prescribed. In doubt concerning either fast or abstinence, one should consult his confessor or pastor.

The simultaneous use of fish and flesh at the same meal, and the interchange of the noon and evening meals (dinner and lunch) is permitted (C. 1251). For a just cause one may also interchange breakfast and lunch.

To interrupt the principal meal for more than half an hour without reason would be a venial sin; should the interruption last more than an hour it would be seriously sinful. For a proportionately good reason (e.g., to assist the dying) one may interrupt his dinner for several hours. In determining the amount that one may take for breakfast and lunch the following must be regarded: a person's physical constitution, the kind of work he does, the length of the fast and the severity of the climate. In general, a person may eat enough to enable him to do his work well and to continue the fast without considerable detriment to himself.

If one — either deliberately or by mistake — has eaten two full meals on a fast day, one can no longer observe the fast and, therefore, he may eat to satiety again.

389. — 2. *The law of abstinence* forbids the use of meat and soup or gravy made from meat.

On days of *partial* abstinence meat and soup or gravy made from meat may be taken only at the principal meal. These may not be taken at all on days of *complete* abstinence. The partial abstinence on a day of abstinence (e.g., an Ember Wednesday) is not to be confused with the partial abstinence prescribed on a fast day (e.g., the weekdays, other than Friday, in Lent).

The prohibition extends only to the flesh of mammals and birds, including the fat, blood, marrow, brains, heart, liver, etc. Lawful foods are fish, frogs, turtles, snails, mussels, clams, oysters, crabs, etc. — As seasoning one may use rendered lard not only to prepare food but also as a spread. Likewise lawful are margarine, and meat extracts that have lost the taste of meat or broth, e.g., gelatine; likewise gelatine products of animal origin, but not soup cubes that contain meat ingredients.

He who has once eaten meat on a day of abstinence may still observe the law and, therefore, he is not free to eat meat again the same day.

390. — **III. Subjects of the Laws. 1.** The law of **fasting** obliges all who have completed their twenty-first year and who have not yet begun their sixtieth year (C. 1254).

2. The law of **abstinence** obliges all who have completed their seventh year until the end of their life (C. 1254).

IV. The Gravity of the Obligation. The laws of fasting and abstinence in themselves oblige gravely. Slight violations of them are only venial sins.

One would certainly not sin mortally by eating about two ounces of food outside the meals allowed on a fast day; but it would be seriously sinful to take more than four ounces no matter whether taken at once or at different times of the day. Neither would it be mortally sinful to eat less than an ounce of meat on a day of abstinence; it would be gravely sinful to take two ounces. Slight violations of the law of abstinence do not coalesce to form a grave sin, unless one intends from the beginning to consume a large quantity.

391. — **V. Cessation of the Obligation. 1.** *Regula-*

tions of Canon Law. The laws of both fasting and abstinence cease on all Sundays and Holydays of obligation,
unless such a Holyday falls in Lent. Vigils are not anticipated. Lent ceases at midnight on Holy Saturday,
according to the regulations of the Restored Holy Week.

Therefore, should Christmas fall on Monday, the previous
Saturday is not a day of fasting and abstinence.

392. — 2. *Dispensations. a) General dispensations.*

b) Individual dispensations from the laws of fasting
and abstinence may be had from one's pastor, who may
dispense not only individuals but also individual families.
This same faculty is enjoyed by the superior in an exempt
Religious Community with regard to the professed members, the novices, servants, guests, etc., who reside in the
house day and night (C. 1245).

In some dioceses confessors have special faculties to dispense;
these faculties can often be used also outside the confessional.
Pastors and the above-mentioned superiors may also dispense themselves; confessors cannot do so if their faculties can only be
exercised in the confessional.

393. — 3. *Reasons Excusing from the Law.*
a) Physical or moral impossibility excuses from the *law
of fasting.*

Ill or convalescent persons in delicate health, and those that
are neurotic or who are subject to bad headaches or who cannot
sleep when fasting are excused therefrom; pregnant or nursing
women, and probably women during the period of menstruation;
the poor, who have not enough to eat at one time to satisfy their
hunger; hard-working people, e.g., farmers, millworkers, stone
masons, etc., provided they actually work a great part of the
day. They are also excused even if now and then they do not
have a hard day's work. Furthermore, professors, teachers, students,
preachers, confessors, physicians, judges, lawyers, etc. are excused
if fasting would hinder them in their work. Those, too, who
must make a strenuous journey by foot or wagon. Travelling by
train does not excuse. Distant journeys by car or bus usually
excuse, especially if it is impossible to get sufficient nourishment
at the proper time. — One may not undertake hard work merely

for the purpose of evading the law of fasting (Cf. 60).

394. — *b*) The following are excused from the *law of abstinence*:

The sick and convalescent, women who are pregnant and who require meat nourishment. Some authors allow such women a bite or two merely because of their craving for meat. Flesh meat may also be necessary for women who are nursing a child. Workmen doing unusually hard labor, especially work that gives one an appetite, as, at the furnaces, in the mines, etc.; poor people who have not sufficient Lenten food. Wives, children and servants are excused if the master of the house permits no other food. (Servants in such a case should seek employment elsewhere, unless another place would be even more disadvantageous spiritually.) An invitation to eat out where one would be expected to eat forbidden food may not be accepted. One could, nevertheless, accept such an invitation if the refusal would mean a great loss to himself or be gravely offensive to the one inviting, or if it would create enmity. The same can be said of him to whom unlawful food is unexpectedly served at a banquet. — If a meat meal has been prepared by mistake on a day of abstinence it may not be eaten if Lenten food is easily available and the meat can readily be kept for another day. If the meat prepared in such a case is of such a small quantity that it would not be forbidden, under mortal sin, the circumstance alone of having prepared it by mistake would excuse the eating of it from venial sin. — If the father (or another member of the family) is excused (or dispensed) from abstaining the others are nevertheless obliged to observe the law. Since it is often morally impossible to prepare separate meals, the whole family in this case is excused.

Note. The exhortation of the bishops "to attend daily Mass, to receive Holy Communion often, to take part more frequently in exercises of piety, to give generously to works of religion and charity, to perform acts of kindness towards the sick, the aged and the poor, and to practice voluntary self-denial especially regarding alcoholic drink and worldly amusements, and to pray more fervently, particularly for the intentions of the Holy Father" during periods of fast and abstinence should be understood as an integral part of the formula. — Public festivities during Lent and Advent are forbidden by the law of custom (Cf. 45). In determining the sinfulness of these one must consider the time (e.g., Good Friday), the kind of entertainment, the opinions of conscientious Christians and the possibility of scandal.

395.   Chapter II

ANNUAL CONFESSION AND COMMUNION

I. Confession. All the faithful who have reached the use of their reason must sincerely confess their sins at least once a year (C. 906).

This confession need not be made during the Easter time, but because of the prescribed Easter Communion it is practical to make it at this time Children who have the use of reason are also bound by this law even though they have not yet reached their seventh year. — Strictly speaking, however, only those are obliged by this precept who have committed a mortal sin. — One's obligation is not fulfilled by a sacrilegious confession. (C. 907). — If one has not confessed within the year one must do so as soon as possible. By so doing he would satisfy the precept for both years.

396. II. Easter Communion. All the faithful who have attained the use of their reason must receive Holy Communion at least once during the Easter season. It is earnestly recommended that they make their Easter Communion in their own parish church; if they do it elsewhere they should inform their pastor to this effect (C. 859).

1. The *obligation* extends also to children who have not yet reached their seventh year, provided they have the use of their reason.

The duty to see to it that children make their Easter Communion rests primarily upon the parents, guardians, confessors, teachers and the pastor (C. 860). Confer also 501.

The obligation is not satisfied by a sacrilegious Communion (C. 861). — If someone has not made his Easter duty for a long time, and this be publicly known, he is thereby a public sinner who loses his right to ecclesiastical burial (Cf. C. 1240).

2. The *Easter season* within which one must receive Holy Communion usually extends in the United States, from the First Sunday of Lent until Trinity Sunday.

Sometimes bishops have special faculties in this regard. —

Pastors and confessors may extend the Easter season for individual persons for any reasonable cause (C. 859), e.g., if the penitent comes to confession the Saturday before Trinity Sunday and is doubtfully disposed. There is a grave obligation to receive Holy Communion during this time. — Whoever has not communicated within the prescribed time must do so afterward.

3. The *place* to make one's Easter Communion, as mentioned above, is advisably one's parish church. If one makes it elsewhere he should endeavor to inform his pastor about this (C. 859).

Easter Communion may, therefore, be made in any church or chapel (even a domestic oratory) in one's own or in another parish district. — The duty to inform one's pastor when one communicates elsewhere is certainly not a grave obligation. Some authors consider it merely advisable.

N. B. I. The fifth precept of the Church obliges the faithful to support their Church. It is an obligation of justice to provide for the needs of God's ministers, and, hence, in itself a grave obligation. The faithful have thus the duty to contribute, according to their means, to the support of their pastors, their church and school. They have, likewise, the obligation in charity to support the home and foreign missions, Catholic Charities, orphanages, etc.

The fifth precept of the Church concerns both rich and poor (who can often render personal service), young and old. While their obligation is a grave one, we would not accuse anyone of grave sin who neglects to contribute his share, unless the clergy would thereby suffer want or other parishioners be greatly overburdened. Entrance into the church during divine worship must be absolutely free (Cf. C. 1181), and a parishioner has a right to the consolations of religion when dying regardless of his past neglect in supporting his church (Cf. Third Plenary Council of Baltimore, 292).

N. B. II. The sixth precept of the Church obliges the

faithful to observe the laws that the Church has made regarding marriage. These laws forbid the Nuptial Mass and marriage festivities during Lent and Advent, mixed marriages, marrying one's second cousin or nearer relation, attempting to marry otherwise except before a priest and two witnesses, etc. (Cf. 656 sqq.)

397.   *Section II*

Ecclesiastical Legislation on Books

The Church's laws concerning books are divided into those that treat of censorship, and those that deal with the prohibition of books.

What is said of "books" in the two following chapters applies also to newspapers, magazines and other publications, unless it is evident that "books" are to be understood in the strict sense (C. 1384). Pamphlets and leaflets, too, come under these regulations; but duplicated and mimeographed material is not included (unless it is published in this form), e.g., the duplicated lectures of a professor for the convenience of his students.

Chapter I

THE CENSORSHIP OF BOOKS

Censorship, in the strict sense, is the authoritative judgment of the Church on the contents of a book. The mere permission to have a book printed differs from censorship.

398. — 1. Books to be submitted to the Church's censorship, whether written by the clergy or the laity, are the following: i. the Books of Sacred Scripture as well as annotations and commentaries thereon; ii. books that treat of Holy Writ, Theology, Church History, Canon Law, natural theology, ethics and other cognate sciences; prayer books and books of devotion; books that contain religious, moral, ascetical, mystical or similar teaching, and other such books that are of special interest to religion and morality, even though their purpose is to foster piety; iii. sacred pictures, no matter by what process they are to be printed, and whether to be published with prayers or not (C. 1385).

Competency for granting permission to publish certain books is had only by the Holy See; generally, however, permission of the local Ordinary suffices. It may be the local Ordinary of the author, the printer or the publisher. Should one of these have refused the requested permission it may not be asked of the others, without mentioning the fact of the refusal (C. 1385). — Unless there is a good reason for the contrary the Ordinary refusing permission must state his reasons to the author if the latter should ask for them (C. 1394).

Permission for publication must be given in writing. The *Nihil Obstat* of the censor should precede the *Imprimatur* of the Bishop. Generally the name of the censor is also to be added (C. 1393). In the printed book itself the name of the censor need not be published; but the *Imprimatur* and the name of him who granted it must be indicated, as well as the time and place of the granting. This may be placed at the beginning or at the end of the book (C. 1394).

Translations and *new editions* (not mere reprints), require a new approbation. This is not required for the separate publication of articles that have appeared in periodicals (C. 1392).

399. — II. Permission without censorship is required for the publication of a work by:

1. *The laity* when writing for newspapers or magazines that are hostile to the Catholic religion or good morals (C. 1386).

This permission is granted by the local Ordinary. In as far as this entails *co-operation* in the sins of others, confer 150.

2. *The diocesan clergy* even when they write books on secular subjects or when they contribute to, or edit, periodical literature or daily papers (C. 1386).

The local Ordinary also gives this permission, which — unlike censorship — need not be obtained in every individual case; it may be given in general, either expressly or tacitly, and in some instances it may be presumed. Neither is it necessary to indicate this permission in the book itself. This permission seems to be required only in case one writes more or less constantly (or as an associate editor), not for one or the other article, if it is not a question of papers or magazines that attack faith or morals, or if the article is not of special significance to religion or morality.

3. *Religious* who must first obtain the permission of their major superiors and then that of the local Ordinary when they publish a book, or write for daily papers or periodical magazines or edit the same (C. 1385, 1386).

The "local Ordinary" is either the bishop of the diocese wherein the convent is situated or the bishop of the printer or the publisher.

III. The violation of these laws is usually a grave sin.

In less important matters there is only a venial sin, more so in case permission alone is required than when the work must also be submitted to ecclesiastical censorship.

400.   Chapter II

THE PROHIBITION OF BOOKS

I. The Extent of the Prohibition. A forbidden book is one which, without due permission, may not be published, read, retained, sold, translated, or in any manner whatsoever communicated to others (C. 1398).

A new edition of a forbidden book may be published if he who prohibited the book, or his superior or successor, has granted the required permission and the necessary corrections have been made (C. 1398). — *"Reading"* a book does not mean listening to its being read; wherefore, a professor may read significant passages from a forbidden book to his students before he refutes them. *"Retaining"* a book is not forbidden to the bookbinder while binding the book for someone who has permission to read it, or if he would otherwise suffer notable loss of trade. If several articles of a magazine are on the Index it would probably be allowed to keep the bound volumes thereof if the forbidden articles are inseparable from them. — *"Selling"* forbidden books is lawful to those who have permission to read them. An auctioneer who is disposing of a library may ask bids also on the forbidden books, but booksellers may keep such books in stock only if they have permission to do so from the Holy See (Cf. also 150). Forbidden books may not be loaned to others, not even to those of a different faith.

401. — II. Books forbidden by the common law of the Church are:

1. Editions of the original text of the Sacred Scriptures published by non-Catholics; likewise, translations of the same made or published by them.

2. Books that in any way defend heresy or schism or that tend to undermine the foundations of religion.

"Defend" does not merely mean to assert or command but to substantiate with alleged proofs. By *"foundations of religion"* is meant such fundamental truths as the existence of God, immortality of the soul, miracles, free will, etc.

3. Books which, of set purpose, attack religion or morals.

4. Books of non-Catholics which professedly treat of religion unless it is clear that they contain nothing contrary to Catholic faith.

5. Books published without due ecclesiastical approval which treat of Sacred Scripture, or contain annotations and commentaries thereon or translations thereof into the vernacular; books containing new apparitions, revelations, visions, prophecies or miracles or which seek to introduce new devotions.

6. Books which attack or ridicule any Catholic dogma, or defend errors proscribed by the Holy See; books which disparage divine worship, or seek to undermine ecclesiastical discipline, or avowedly defame the ecclesiastical hierarchy, the clerical or religious state.

Therefore, a book is forbidden which contains a collection of defamatory accounts concerning various popes or of the priestly or religious states, not, however, if the person of one individual pope or a certain religious Order is disparaged.

7. Books which teach or approve of superstition, fortune telling, divination, magic, spiritism and other such practices.

8. Books which declare duels, suicide and divorce to be lawful; furthermore, books that treat of freemasonry and similar secret societies, maintaining that they are useful or that they are harmless to the Church and civil society.

9. Books which, with avowed intention, treat of, describe or teach, lewd or obscene matters, such as the methods of birth control.

Medical or moral works on topics of sex, etc., written for a good purpose do not fall under this bann. — Those who cannot omit reading the obscene classics without great disadvantage to themselves are excused from this prohibition in as far as it is of ecclesiastical origin.

10. Liturgical books containing unauthorized changes so that they no longer agree with the authentic editions approved by the Holy See.

11. Books which contain apocryphal indulgences, or such as have been condemned or revoked by the Holy See.

12. Also forbidden are all images, however reproduced, of Christ, the Blessed Virgin, the Angels, Saints, or other Servants of God that are not in keeping with the sentiment and decrees of the Church.

N. B. Besides those named there are other books proscribed by the special decrees of competent authorities (Cf. C. 1395).

402. — III. Permission to read forbidden books may be had either according to the general rules of Canon Law or by special permission of a competent superior.

In virtue of the regulations of the Code of Canon Law all those who are in any manner engaged in *theological* or *biblical studies* may use the editions of the original text and all translations of Holy Scripture, provided the editions and translations are faithful and complete and they do not attack Catholic dogma in their introductions or annotations (C. 1400). This permission, therefore, extends to priests who continue their studies.

Cardinals, Bishops (including titular) and Ordinaries, e.g., the major superiors of a clerical exempt religious community, (Cf. C. 198) are exempt from the ecclesiastical prohibition of books. (C. 1401).

In *case of necessity* one may presume permission to read such books, if there is not sufficient time to have recourse to a competent superior for permission. — A forbidden book remains such even though it does not constitute dangerous reading in an individual case (Cf. 57).

403. — IV. The violation of the laws on the prohibition of books is in itself a grave sin; but in matters of lesser moment there is only a venial sin.

Reading forbidden literature is gravely sinful if the amount read would constitute a great danger for many people, even though it be harmless to the one reading. Therefore, according to the contents, one may read a greater or lesser portion of such literature without commiting a grievous sin. If the book is very obscene even half a page may be sufficient to constitute a mortal sin, whereas, if the book is not very dangerous, even the reading of thirty pages may not be gravely sinful. If a book is in itself harmless and is forbidden merely because it relates new revelations, etc., but is published without ecclesiastical permission, a person might commit only a venial sin by reading the entire volume. It is gravely sinful to read habitually forbidden newspapers and magazines, and even to read such literature a single time if one reads a considerable amount thereof (either in content or in quantity) directed against faith or morals.

To *retain* forbidden books is a mortal sin if one keeps them for more than a month. — It is not sinful to keep a book for a short time either because one intends to surrender it to the authorities or because he is awaiting permission to read it. For the *penalties* confer 433, 440.

404.   *Section III*

The Three Principal States of Life

The three principal states of life in the Church are: the clerical state, the religious state and the lay state. The distinction between the clergy and the laity is by divine ordinance. Religious may be clerics or laymen (Cf. C. 107).

Chapter I

THE CLERGY

"Clerics" are those who are assigned to the sacred ministry by the reception of first tonsure (C. 108). — In this chapter we shall treat of the obligations and privileges of clerics.

405.   *Article I*

The Obligations of Clerics

We are here concerned only with the general obligations of the clergy, not the special duties of a cleric who is a bishop, pastor, etc.

I. Holiness of Life. Clerics should lead a spiritual life more holy than the laity to whom they should be an example of virtue and upright life (C. 124.)

They are earnestly recommended to confess frequently, meditate, visit the Blessed Sacrament, recite the rosary and examine their conscience daily (C. 125).

It is obligatory for every priest to make a retreat at least once every three years, the Ordinary determining the place and duration thereof. A priest may be excused from this obligation only in a particular case for some important reason and with the explicit permission of his bishop (C. 126). Annual retreats are the order in most dioceses in U. S.

II. Clerical Studies. A cleric should continue his studies after his ordination especially his study of the sacred sciences (C. 129).

The Junior Clergy Examinations, as they are called, are obligatory for the secular clergy for at least three years after the completion of their theological studies (C. 130). — Priests engaged in pastoral work must, furthermore, attend the diocesan conferences that are held repeatedly during the year. If the conferences cannot be held, the solution of the questions proposed must be made in writing (C. 131).

III. Reverence and Obedience due to the Ordinary.

If an office has been assigned to a cleric by his bishop it must be accepted and faithfully discharged, unless a legitimate impediment excuses him (C. 128). — Without at least the presumed permission of his Ordinary no cleric may absent himself for a notable length of time from his diocese (C. 143).

406. — IV. Celibacy. Clerics in major orders are forbidden to marry; furthermore, they have the special obligation of living chastely. Even a merely internal sin against holy chastity is for them also a sacrilege (C. 132).

Clerics may not have women in their houses nor frequently visit those who might in any manner arouse suspicion. Therefore, clerics may not employ as maids or housekeepers young and especially strange or unrelated persons (Cf. C. 133).

V. The Divine Office. (Cf. 158 sqq.)

VI. Clerical Dress (C. 136). All clerics are obliged to wear a becoming clerical garb, in accordance with the legitimate customs of the country and the regulations of their bishops.

Custom in the U. S. is against the wearing of the tonsure. Care of the hair which savors of vanity is forbidden. Only those who have an apostolic indult to the effect may wear a ring (C. 136). The bishop's permission is required to wear a beard. The cassock must be worn when celebrating Holy Mass (C. 811). The Second Baltimore Council desired the wearing of the cassock in the rectory and about the Church, permitting a black secular garb when going out. The Third Plenary Council of Baltimore prescribed the wearing of the Roman collar both when at home and in public. Any good reason excuses one from wearing the clerical garb. It would be venially sinful not to wear it once or twice without any reason. To do so habitually is grievously sinful and under certain circumstances punishable by severe ecclesiastical penalties (Confer Cc. 136, 188 No. 7, 2379).

VII. Clerical Decorum. Clerics should refrain from all amusements and occupations unbecoming to their sacred calling (C. 138).

Engaging in unbecoming arts or occupations is forbidden, as also are games of chance and gambling. — Clerics may carry arms only in case of necessity. — Ordinary hunting is not forbidden unless it is overdone or if scandal ensues; but the chase is expressly prohibited. In case of necessity or for any other reason approved by the local Ordinary they may enter taverns, night clubs, etc. (C. 138). They may not attend theatrical performances, dances and shows which are unbecoming to their state or if their attendance thereat would be a source of scandal to others. (C. 140.)

407. — VIII. Occupations Specifically Forbidden. 1. *Medicine and surgery* may be practiced by the clergy only with an apostolic indult (C. 139).

He practices medicine who, after the manner of physicians, makes diagnoses and prescribes remedies. — It is not forbidden to recommend some remedy known to be good for a certain ailment without having made the diagnosis referred to. It is lawful also to care for the sick under the direction of a physician, as is done, for example, by the religious in some communities. — By "practicing" the Code seems to imply frequent exercise so that it would not be sinful for one to use his knowledge of medicine on rare occasions. — Neither does it seem to be forbidden for some member of a religious community to make use of his medical knowledge in the case of his fellow religious after the manner of a parent and his children.

2. *Public offices* that imply the exercise of lay jurisdiction or administration may not be held by clerics (C. 139).

The office of notary public may be exercised by a cleric only in ecclesiastical court. A cleric may not compete for, nor accept the office of senator or representative without the permission of his bishop (C. 139). The Third Plenary Council of Baltimore forbids priests to meddle in political affairs, unless the defense of morality and sound principles is at stake. — If military service is compulsory they may volunteer for military service only with their bishop's permission in order to be sooner freed from their military obligations. — They may take no part whatever in a civil war or popular uprising (C. 141).

3. *Legal avocations* are forbidden to clerics; wherefore they may not appear as counsel or attorney. They should not act as witnesses in important criminal trials except in case of necessity (C. 139).

Only if their own affairs or those of the Church are concerned may they exercise the office of solicitor or advocate.

4. *Private administration* of the goods and property of lay people and secular offices that impose the obligation of rendering an account are forbidden to clerics without the permission of the bishop (C. 139).

This prohibition includes the assuming of a guardianship or the office of executor of a testament for the laity, as also a position on the board of directors or any office of warrant or under bond in a savings bank or credit association.

408. — 5. *Business enterprises* are forbidden to clerics whether conducted personally or through others, either for their own benefit or for the sake of others (C. 142).

By *"business"* is here meant any trading or commercial transaction in which goods are bought and sold for profit, whether the goods are sold unaltered or are changed by hired labor (as in a factory). — Thus, it is not forbidden for a clergyman to sell the products of his own fields, garden, etc. even if he must hire help to alter them (e.g., he may sell the wine he makes from the grapes of his own vineyard). So, too, he may sell things that he previously bought and made over, etc. by his own labor, e.g., he may sell a picture that he painted. It is likewise lawful for him to buy stocks and bonds and, according to an opinion that is practically certain, not only when there is a question of companies that concern natural resources, but also of commercial or industrial corporations. It is necessary, however: a) that the cleric remain only a shareholder and is thus not held responsible for the value of his stocks; b) that the stock company be engaged in some legitimate business; c) that the cleric take no part in the administration of the company. At a meeting of the stockholders he may at most allow another to represent him and look to the unobjectionable administration of his business; d) that he does not make a business of trading in stocks and especially that he avoids gambling on the Stock Exchange. It is not forbidden, however, for a cleric either to sell or exchange his stocks in as far as this is necessary for the reasonable administration of his possessions, e.g., if he sees his stocks devaluating.

N. B. Concerning literary occupation confer 399; sponsorship, confer 381; the celebration of Mass, confer 453; the duty of giving one's superfluous income to charitable purposes, confer 259.

409.   *Article II*

The Privileges of Clerics

I. The "Privilegium canonis" protects clerics against personal injury. Whoever inflicts a personal injury on a cleric becomes guilty of a sacrilege (C. 119).

Concerning this sacrilege, confer 167; its penalties, confer 431, 434, 438.

II. The "Privilegium fori" exempts clerics from appearing before civil court without the permission of the competent ecclesiastical superior in all civil suits and criminal prosecutions (C. 120).

If, without the bishop's permission, a cleric is summoned to the secular court he may appear in order to avoid greater evil, having first informed his respective superior and obtained his permission (C. 120). Concerning the penalties, confer 434, 435, 442.

III. The "Privilegium immunitatis" exempts the clergy from all civil duties and offices alien to their state (C. 121).

This pertains especially to military service.

IV. The "Privilegium competentiae" permits an insolvent cleric to retain what is necessary to live in accordance with the clerical state (C. 122).

The duty to pay one's creditors as soon as possible evidently remains. — A similar benefit of the law is accorded to civil officials by state law.

N. B. No individual may renounce these privileges of the clerical state. They are lost by the cleric's being reduced to the lay state (C. 213) and also by his being perpetually deprived of the right to wear the clerical garb (C. 2304); and by degradation (C. 2305).

410. Chapter II

RELIGIOUS

Religious are those who have taken vows in a religious community (C. 488). In the following articles we shall treat only of the duties and the privileges of religious.

Article I

The Duties of Religious

Only the principal obligations of religious are here considered.

I. The general obligations of the clergy also bind the religious unless the contrary is evident either from the context of the law or the nature of the matter (C. 592).

For further particulars, confer 405 sqq. — These obligations are in some instances more severe for religious. Can. 595 accentuates their obligations to strive for perfection by prescribing that the superiors take care that the religious make an annual retreat, attend daily Mass, make their daily meditation, etc., unless they are legitimately hindered; that they confess at least once a week and receive Holy Communion frequently. The obligation rests immediately on the superior and, therefore, unless the superior has given a command to do so, the individual religious will not sin against this law by omitting these prescribed exercises. The superior is not obliged, however, to give a specific command concerning these matters; it suffices that he give his subjects appropriate exhortations, admonitions, etc. He would sin if, by his negligence, he were the cause of the general non-observance of these regulations.

In the interest of the sacred sciences religious who are priests must make an annual examination for at least the first five years after completing their theological studies (C. 590). In every formal house the theological conferences must be held at least once a month (C. 591). Confer also C. 131.

411. — II. Striving for perfection is an obligation incumbent upon all religious.

It is a mortal sin to neglect this obligation by habitually violating the vows or other precepts obliging under grave sin; by contemning perfection to the extent that one positively resolves not to strive for it, or if, by one's example, he seriously offends against religious discipline and observance.

III. Observance of the Vows. 1. The *vow of poverty* covers all things that have monetary value. The *simple vow* of poverty forbids the use of such things independently of one's superior; the *solemn vow* of poverty deprives the religious of all right of ownership and invalidates all acts contrary to the vow.

Objects of the vow of poverty are not such things that cannot be bought for money, e.g., a good reputation, relics, etc. — *Manuscripts* that one has prepared while under vows may not be given away or disposed of under any title whatsoever, if they have been prepared with care and can reasonably be presumed to be fit for publication. It is not certain whether the destruction of such manuscripts is a sin against the vow of poverty or against justice, e.g., it would be against justice if the religious were assigned to literary activity, or if the community went to any expense in their preparation.

The vow of poverty is *violated* by every independent act of ownership; by accepting, keeping, using or disposing of things without the knowledge of the superior; donating, alienating, loaning things, or by using them for a longer period or time than authorized by the superior; by using things for purposes other than those the superior designated; by negligence in caring for or using things destined for the members of the community. — The superior's permission need not always be obtained explicitly; sometimes it may be presumed.

A *mortal* sin is committed if the value of the thing concerned be equivalent to a grave sin in a case of theft (Cf. 327). But when there is a case of the forbidden use of a thing the value is estimated not according to the value of the thing itself, but the value of its use. — A far greater amount (perhaps even four or five times as much) is required to constitute a mortal sin for one with simple vows, in disposing of things regarding which he still retains ownership.

Restitution can be made by a religious to his community by cutting down on expenses that he might otherwise legitimately make. He need not, however, deny himself anything necessary for his reasonable maintenance. One may frequently presume the superior's condonation of the obligation to make restitution.

412. — **2.** *The vow of chastity* obliges the professed religious, because of the virtue of religion, to abstain from every sin, even a purely internal sin, against holy chastity and to renounce all that which would be lawful in valid marriage.

Solemn vows not only render marriage unlawful, but invalid. (Cf. 702.) Solemn profession dissolves a marriage that has not been consummated (Cf. 761).

3. *The vow of obedience* obliges the religious to obey his respective superior in all things which, in keeping with the Rule and Constitutions, are commanded him in virtue of obedience.

The vow of obedience obliges only when one is explicitly commanded "in virtue of obedience" or by the use of other like-meaning words. But even where there is no question of an obligation in virtue of the vow, a religious may sin in various ways by the violation of some regulation, e.g., by scandal, formal contempt, etc.

413. — **IV. The law of enclosure** prohibits certain persons from entering a religious house and forbids the religious from leaving the same except under certain conditions.

The law of enclosure embraces the entire house in which the religious family dwells, including the garden, orchards, etc. which are reserved exclusively for the religious. — The church is not included in the enclosure, nor is the sacristy if it immediately adjoins the church; the guest quarters and parlors are likewise exempt (C. 597). The choir — if it adjoins the church — is a part thereof, and therefore (in communities of men) is not enclosed.

1. *Papal enclosure* is observed in houses of religious men and women with solemn vows.

Differing from the members of a religious Order are the members of a Congregation, i.e., those who take only simple vows, be they temporary or perpetual.

a) No woman of whatever age, rank or condition may enter the enclosure of orders of men under any pretext whatsoever (C. 598).

The only exception in our country is the wife of the president or the governor (of the state) and her female retinue (C. 598). — For penalties confer 436.

b) No one may enter a *convent of nuns* (i.e., Sisters with solemn vows) regardless of age, sex, standing or condition without permission of the Holy See (C. 600).

Exceptions to this law are: a) The confessor or his representative when the Sacraments are to be administered to the sick or dying. In the absence of the confessor, any priest who is celebrating Mass in the convent may give Holy Communion to the sick. b) The president or the governor of the state together with his wife and attendants. c) Physicians, mechanics, etc. may enter with the permission of the local superioress and the approbation of the local Ordinary (C. 600). For penalties confer 436.

Nuns in convents subject to papal enclosure are also forbidden to leave the enclosure under any pretext whatsoever even for a brief period of time (C. 601).

Exceptions to this rule are justified by the danger of death or other very grave emergencies.

2. The law of *enclosure* for the houses of *religious congregations* forbids the admittance of persons of the opposite sex into the enclosure (C. 604).

The exceptions to this law are the same as those mentioned for papal enclosure; furthermore, the superior may for a just and reasonable cause admit others (C. 604).

414. — *Recitation of the Divine Office* in common is obligatory in all houses of religious communities of men and women who have the obligation of choir, if at least four of the members so obliged, who are not legitimately hindered at the time, are available. If fewer than four of the religious are available the obligation exists only if the Constitutions so prescribe (C. 610).

This regulation of the Code obliges both male and female religious, but not those whose "choir obligation" consists in praying the Little Office of the Blessed Virgin.

Two religious are probably sufficient to satisfy the choir obligation; likewise, it can also be done by the novices alone. Lay brothers cannot, however, fulfill the choir obligation. Concerning the obligation of praying the Divine Office when one is unable to attend choir, confer 158.

415.   Article II

The Privileges of Religious

I. The privileges of the clergy (i.e., the privilegium canonis, fori, immunitatis, competentiae) are enjoyed also by religious (C. 614).

Brothers, Sisters and novices likewise share these privileges.

II. The privilege of exemption is enjoyed by all religious with solemn vows and it includes their houses and churches with the exception of the cases expressed in law (C. 615).

This privilege, too, is enjoyed by the novices, but not by those nuns who are not subject to a regular superior. — Members of Congregations do not enjoy this privilege, unless it has been granted to them explicitly (C. 618), e.g., the Redemptorists and Passionists.

III. The privilege of questing is accorded to all those Orders that were founded as mendicants and actually are such (C. 621).

As soon as mendicants found a house in a diocese they may collect alms throughout the diocese with the sole permission of their superior. If they wish to quest in another diocese they need the permission of the local bishop (C. 621).

Congregations of pontifical right require a special papal indult in order to quest for alms. Even with such a privilege they must obtain the written permission of the local Ordinary, unless their papal indult provides otherwise (C. 622). Diocesan Congregations must have the written permission of the bishop of the place where their house is situated and also of the bishop in whose territory they wish to collect (C. 622).

By *"questing"* Canon Law does not understand appeals made by mail or the collection of contributions and gifts at some private gathering. Neither does it include collections made in churches, nor the visiting of one or the other charitable person or family in the hope of getting some help or even asking them for assistance. They do "beg," however, who, although they do not go from house to house, yet inquire what people are generous in supporting good works, perhaps acquiring a list of such people, subsequently visiting them for the purpose of asking alms.

416. — IV. Some Special Privileges of Regulars.

"Regulars" are religious who belong to an Order, i.e., who have taken solemn vows.

1. *Holy Mass* may be celebrated by Regulars two hours before dawn and two hours after midday.

Furthermore, in their own churches they may, for a just reason, celebrate Mass and permit visiting priests to do so two hours after midnight and three hours after midday. — On reckoning the time of dawn confer 544.

2. *Confessors* that are Regulars have the following faculties:

a) They can *dispense* lay people (sæculares) from *non-reserved vows,* provided the acquired rights of a third person are not thereby violated.

This obtains even though the vow is confirmed by an oath. — The dispensation can be given in the internal forum, whether in or outside of confession.

b) They can *dispense* for the internal forum from *irregularities* arising from an occult crime, but not from the irregularity of one who commits voluntary homicide, or who effectively procures an abortion, or who is an accomplice to these crimes.

This dispensation covers both the reception and the exercise of Holy Orders, but holds only for the diocesan clergy. — An occult crime is one that is not publicly known and presumably will not readily become publicly known (Cf. C. 2197).

c) They can *absolve* in the internal forum from censures reserved by common law to the Ordinary.

If a reconciliation is necessary in the external forum (e.g., in case of marriage before a non-Catholic minister) the confessor should not give absolution. (Cf. 427.) — The most practical application of this privilege is absolving from excommunication incurred by procuring an abortion. — Regulars, however, cannot absolve from censures that the Ordinary has reserved to himself.

417.   Chapter III

THE LAITY

I. The duties of the laity arise chiefly from the natural law, the positive divine law and the precepts of the Church.

Although these duties are also enjoined and determined in greater detail by the Code of Canon Law, they will not be specifically treated here since they have been considered when treating the respective precepts. For further particulars, especially on the duties of the different stations in life, etc., see the alphabetical index under words: "subject," "defendant," "laborer," "physician," etc.

II. The rights of the laity are largely reducible to the fundamental right to receive from the clergy the spiritual goods necessary for salvation, according to the rules of ecclesiastical discipline (C. 682).

For particulars, the various treatises in Sacramental Theology and Canon Law may be consulted. — Besides, the laity may possess special rights, e.g., the right of patronage.

These rights may be greatly restricted, e.g., by a person's joining some non-Catholic sect or by incurring an ecclesiastical censure, especially excommunication (C. 87). But a baptized person can never be deprived of any of the rights he has in virtue of the indelible character of Baptism nor can he lose his inalienable claim to the Church's special solicitude, and, in danger of death, if he is rightfully disposed, to the Sacraments necessary for salvation.

418. — III. Associations of the Faithful. 1. *The founding* of an ecclesiastical society may be made by private persons or by the Church (Cf. C. 684 sqq.).

A society founded by private persons is "ecclesiastical" only if it has a spiritual purpose and is founded with the consent of the Church, or is at least approved by the Church. Consequently, lay associations may be highly commended by Church authorities and even enriched with indulgences without their being "ecclesiastical," e. ., the Saint Vincent De Paul Society, the Seraphic Work of Charity and the Confraternity of Christian Mothers. They are subject to the bishop only in keeping with canon 336.

By the formal *Decree of Erection* issued by the legitimate ecclesiastical superior a society becomes a legal (moral) person, in the Church (C. 687). Such associations are obliged to submit an annual financial statement to the bishop (C. 691). — A society of this kind is called a "sodality" if it constitutes an organic body with hierarchial organization (C. 707), and with an elected director (prefect, president) and assistants.

2. *Reception* into a society is made according to the statutes of the association. Entry in the society's register is sufficient proof of reception. If the organization is a legal person, registration is required for the validity of membership (C. 694).

Clerics may also belong to such associations. Though registration suffices as proof of membership, to enjoy the rights, privileges, indulgences and other spiritual favors, one must also perform the pious works which are legitimately prescribed, according to the Code Commission, Jan. 4, 1946 (AAS 38-162).

419. — 3. *The division of ecclesiastical associations* is made, according to their purpose; hence these are Third Orders Secular, Confraternities, and Pious Unions (C. 700).

a) Third Orders aim at directing tertiaries living in the world along the way of perfection according to the spirit of some Order and in a manner compatible with their life in the world (C. 702).

Third Orders remain under the guidance of a Religious Order and have a Rule approved by the Holy See.

The *General Absolution* that tertiaries receive on certain feasts is a plenary indulgence gained under the ordinary conditions. Any confessor can impart the general absolution privately (in confession). It may be imparted also on the vigil of a feast as well as throughout the octave following. The following formula suffices in the confessional: *Auctoritate a Summis Pontificibus mihi concessa plenariam omnium peccatorum tuorum indulgentiam tibi impertior in nomine Patris et Filii et Spiritus Sancti. Amen.*

b) Confraternities have as their purpose the promotion of public worship. Other aims may also be united to this one (C. 707).

Confraternities are always founded as sodalities (C. 707). — An Archconfraternity is a sodality that has the right to affiliate to itself other associations of the same kind (C. 720). By this aggregation the affiliated society participates in all the indulgences, privileges and spiritual favors that the Holy See has directly conferred upon the Archconfraternity. The Archconfraternity does not in any manner acquire power or governing authority over the affiliated body (C. 722). Sometimes the name "Archconfraternity" is conferred upon an association as a mere honorary title (C. 725).

c) Pious Unions are erected for the purpose of practicing some work of piety or charity (C. 707).

Primary unions have the right of aggregating other similar associations (C. 720). The effects are similar to the aggregation of a confraternity to an archconfraternity (C. 722). The title of Primary union is likewise sometimes given by the Holy See as a mark of honor.

420.   *Section IV*

Penal Legislation

In the following chapters we shall treat ecclesiastical penalties only in as far as the knowledge thereof is absolutely necessary for the confessor. We shall first consider penalties in general, and then the individual censures incurred by anticipatory sentence (latæ sententiæ or l.s.).

Chapter I

ECCLESIASTICAL PENALTIES IN GENERAL

I. Concept. An ecclesiastical penalty is the deprivation of some good inflicted by legitimate ecclesiastical authority for the betterment of the delinquent or in punishment of an offense (C. 2215).

An offense (delictum) is an external and morally imputable violation of a law to which there is at least an indeterminate sanction attached (C. 2195).

421. — II. *Division.* 1. Penalties are *medicinal* or corrective (censures) and *vindictive* or punitive according as they are primarily ordained for the betterment of the offender or as a punishment for his offense.

a) The *individual censures* are: excommunication, interdict and suspension (C. 2255).

An excommunication is always a censure, whereas an interdict and a suspension can be inflicted as censures or, as vindictive penalties (C. 2255).

Censures may be reserved or non-reserved. A censure inflicted *ab homine* (Cf. 423) is reserved to him who inflicted it, as well as to his superior and successor. Censures imposed *a jure* may be reserved either to the Ordinary or to the Apostolic See. According to the facility with which censures inflicted by law may be removed they are distinguished into censures reserved *simpliciter*, *speciali modo* or *specialissimo modo* (C. 2245).

a) An excommunication excludes a person from the communion of the faithful and carries with it certain other consequences (C. 2257).

An excommunicated person may not administer the Sacraments or sacramentals (C. 2261). Neither may he receive any Sacrament nor (after a judicial sentence) a sacramental. He is likewise excluded from ecclesiastical burial if he dies without having manifested signs of repentance (if a declaratory or condemnatory sentence has been passed) (C. 2260). Furthermore, he does not share in any indulgences, suffrages or general prayers of the Church. But the faithful may pray for him, and a priest may celebrate Mass for him privately (Cf. 526 and C. 2262). An excommunicated person may not exercise any act of ecclesiastical jurisdiction, etc. (C. 2264). Confer also 417 and 454.

422. — β) An interdict deprives the faithful of certain

spiritual goods without their being denied communion with the Church (C. 2268).

An interdict is personal or local according as it affects a person immediately or only indirectly through a place (C. 2268). A local interdict does not forbid the administration of the Sacraments to the dying if the respective regulations are observed; but, with several exceptions, it prohibits the celebration of divine services in the interdicted territory (C. 2270). Those who are personally interdicted may not take part in any divine service, nor even attend such, except the hearing of sermons. Similar to the excommunicated, they may neither administer nor receive the Sacraments or sacramentals, nor be given ecclesiastical burial nor exercise any act of jurisdiction, etc. (C. 2275). — The interdict *ab ingressu ecclesiae* prohibits the celebration of any divine service reserved to the clergy, the assistance at such, as well as the reception of ecclesiastical burial (C. 2277).

γ) Suspension is a censure depriving a cleric of the right to exercise the duties of his office and his power of orders, or to perceive the fruits of his benefice, or both (C. 2278).

There are various degrees of suspension.

b) *Vindictive penalties* may be inflicted upon all members of the Church (clerical and lay), or they may be applicable only to the clergy whenever they restrict the rights proper to the clerical state.

The first class includes some interdicts, infamy of law, deprival of Christian burial, denial of the sacramentals, exclusion from legal ecclesiastical acts (e.g., administration of ecclesiastical goods, the office of sponsor in Baptism, etc., confer C. 2256 No. 2), withdrawal of the right of precedence, pecuniary fines, etc. (C. 2291). — If one is denied Christian burial, other ecclesiastical solemnities are thereby also excluded, e.g., funeral or anniversary Mass (C. 1241). However, a priest may say Mass privately for him (Cf. 526). — Cases that imply the loss of ecclesiastical burial are mentioned in Nos. 207, 396, 421, 432, 435, 437. Furthermore, this right is forfeited by one who orders his body to be cremated (C. 1240).

Vindictive punishments applicable only to clerics are: suspension, penal transfer from an office, determination of residence, deprivation of the clerical garb, deposition and degradation (C. 2298).

423. — 2. Penalties are either *latae sententiae* (l.s.) or *ferendae sententiae* (f.s.), according as they are incurred *ipso facto* by the commission of an offense, or must be inflicted by the judge (C. 2217).

A censure l.s. may be said to be imposed by *anticipatory sentence;* a censure f.s., by *condemnatory sentence.*

3. Penalties may be either *a jure* or *ab homine* depending upon whether the punishment (l.s. or f.s.) is designated in the law itself or is expressly imposed by special precept or by a condemnatory judicial sentence (C. 2217).

Before the condemnatory sentence is issued a penalty f.s. that is determined by law is *a jure* only; after the sentence, it is *a jure* and *ab homine,* but is treated as a penalty *ab homine* (C. 2217).

424. III. Incurring a Penalty. 1. For a *delin-quent* to incur an established penalty it is required: *a*) that there be an external act (Cf. C. 2195), *b*) that the offense be complete, according to all the characteristics of such a transgression, *c*) that a mortal sin be committed (C. 2218), *d*) that the delinquent (in case of a censure) be obstinate (C. 2241).

In *doubt* whether one of the four conditions obtains it is presumed that the penitent has not incurred the censure. Concerning absolution confer 429, d.

Merely attempted offenses may be punished with appropriate penalties (C. 2235).

2. *Accomplices* incur the same penalty as the principal agent even though they are not expressly mentioned in the law, provided they really conspire and physically concur in the execution of the offense, or provided the offense is of such a nature that it requires an accomplice, or if without their co-operation the offense would not have been committed (C. 2231).

Therefore, if one induces another to attempt marriage before a non-Catholic minister (C. 2319) or to undertake an abortion (C. 2350), he incurs an excommunication reserved to the Ordinary, if without such inducement these sins would not have been committed.

If the law expressly declares that accomplices are included in the penalty, as in the case of a duel (C. 2351), it is evidently not necessary that any of the aforementioned conditions for co-operation be verified in order to incur the penalty.

425. — IV. Excuses from Penalties. 1. *Affected ignorance* does not excuse from any penalty l.s. whether the ignorance concerns the law itself or only its penalty (C. 2229).

Ignorance is affected or pretended if one purposely desires (or intends) to remain ignorant that he may more readily sin without remorse of conscience or may have an excuse for his action.

2. Words as: *"whoever presumes,* dares, knowingly, deliberately, rashly, advisedly,"* etc. used in the text of a law indicate that any diminution of imputability, either on the part of the intellect or the will, exempts one from incurring penalties l.s.

Accordingly, therefore, one evades the penalty when acting under the influence of fear, if intoxicated, if he does not employ the care prescribed according to circumstances, if he is mentally deficient, or carried away by passion. This still holds even if the deed remains subjectively a grave sin. The same is generally true if a minor (C. 88) is guilty of an offense the imputability of which is, according to C. 2204, diminished by the age of minority, in case it is not certain that the minor is in full possession of his mental faculties.

3. *Ignorance* of the penalty or of the law does not excuse from a penalty l.s. if expressions like those mentioned above are not used in the text of the law and the ignorance is crass or supine; but if the ignorance is not crass or supine it excuses from censures l.s.; not, however, from vindictive penalties (C. 2229).

Ignorance is said to be crass or supine if it results from gross carelessness in contradistinction to other ignorance which, although grievously sinful, is not the effect of great negligence.

426. — 4. *Grave fear* does not excuse from penalties l.s. if the law contains no expressions such as "whoever

431. Chapter II

CENSURES LATAE SENTENTIAE

Article I

Individual Excommunications

I. An excommunication *specialissimo modo* reserved to the Holy See is incurred by him:

1. *Who profanes the Sacred Species* by discarding Them or who carries Them off or retains Them for an evil purpose (C. 2320).

Thus: he incurs this censure who, in plundering a church, would throw the Consecrated Hosts on the floor out of contempt; but not the thief who places Them on the altar out of wholesome fear or, one who, out of gravely sinful negligence, drops a Consecrated Host.

2. *Who violently attacks the person of the Holy Father* (C. 2343).

3. *Who absolves or feigns to absolve his accomplice* in a sin of impurity (C. 2367). Cf. 587.

4. *The confessor who presumes to violate directly the seal of Confession* (C. 2369).

The confessor alone incurs this censure and only by directly violating the seal (Cf. 619). Concerning "presumes" confer 425.

5. *A bishop who consecrates to the episcopacy one who has neither been appointed by the Holy See nor expressly confirmed by it, and the person who receives such consecration,* even though coerced by grave fear (Holy Office, April 9, 1951).

432. — **II.** An excommunication *speciali modo* reserved to the Holy See is incurred by:

1. *Every apostate, heretic or schismatic* (C. 2314).

Concerning apostasy and heresy confer 122 sqq. — A schismatic is one who refuses to be subject to the Supreme Pontiff or who declines to have communication with the members of the Church subject to the Holy Father (C. 1325). Affiliation with some independent religious body or the founding of such is not necessary. — He is a schismatic, for example, who leaves the Church to avoid paying his church dues, but not every one is a schismatic who simply refuses to obey the Holy Father even for a long time.

Absolution can be imparted by the local Ordinary for the external forum (C. 2314). Absolution from the sin can then be given by any confessor (Cf. 2251). Furthermore, all notorious apostates and adherents of heretical or schismatical sects are denied Christian burial (C. 1240).

433. — 2. Those who *publish, defend,* or who *knowingly read* or *retain* without the requisite permission books of apostates, heretics or schismatics, or books *nominally proscribed* by Apostolic Letters, provided such books have actually been published (C. 2318).

By "books" in this connection we understand publications of (approximately) 160 pages in octavo. Small pamphlets and tracts are indeed forbidden (Cf. 401) but not under excommunication. — The concept of apostasy, etc., implies that one is a Christian; pagans and Jews are, therefore, not included. — A book is not written in defense of error if it merely contains some erroneous statements; more than that is required, namely, there must be an attempt to convince the reader by some manner of proof. It is sufficient, however, if one individual proposition is defended, even though the subject matter of the book is otherwise not of a religious character. — An Apostolic Letter is some writing of the Holy Father himself; thus books forbidden only by some decree of a Congregation are not thereby proscribed under excommunication. — The publisher incurs the penalty only after the book is rendered accessible to the public. — The printer is not excommunicated, neither is the linotypist. — A book is "defended" by him who praises its contents and undertakes to uphold it, declares it to be opportune or who preserves the book from destruction; but not one who merely praises the style of the author. — He is excommunicated by "reading" who reads a sufficient amount to constitute a mortal sin (Cf. 403). The same obtains for "retaining" a book. A book is said to appear when it becomes accessible to the public. Proof readers are not excommunicated. — Since the reading and retaining must be done "knowingly," minors are exempt from the excommunication in case it is not certain whether they are in full possession of their mental faculties (Cf. 425).

434. — 3. Whosoever, not being a priest, simulates saying Mass or hearing Confession (C. 2322).

4. Whoever appeals from the laws, decrees or mandates of the reigning Pontiff to a General Council (C. 2332).

5. Whoever has recourse to the secular power to impede letters or other communications of the Holy See or its legate, or whoever prevents the promulgation or execution of such letters, etc., or because of them injures or intimidates others (C. 2333).

6. Whoever issues laws or decrees against the liberty and rights of the Church, or **impedes the exercise** of ecclesiastical jurisdiction by appealing to the secular authority (C. 2334).

The civil authorities that accept such a recourse and take measures against the exercise of the Church's jurisdiction, or the executive body do not incur this excommunication; but the members of the legislature who vote for such legislation do.

7. Whoever dares to cite a cardinal, legate of the Holy See, or major officials of the Roman Curia or his own Ordinary before the secular court against the prescriptions of canon 120 (C. 2431).

8. Whoever lays violent hands on the person of a cardinal, legate, patriarch, archbishop or bishop (C. 2343).

9. Whoever usurps or retains for himself property or rights of the Roman Church (C. 2345).

10. Whoever fabricates or falsifies writings of the Apostolic See, or knowingly uses such (C. 2360).

11. Whoever falsely denounces a confessor to his superior as guilty of solicitation (C. 2363). For further particulars confer 599.

12. Whoever usurps an ecclesiastical office, benefice or dignity, or permits himself to be unlawfully placed in, or who retains any of the foregoing.

13. Whoever conspires against legitimate ecclesiastical authority or in any way strives to undermine it.

The censure is incurred also by those who in any way, directly or indirectly, participate in the delicts mentioned in 12 and 13 (*Sacred Congregation of the Council,* June 29, 1950).

14. Whoever (clerics or religious) either personally or through others **engages in trading or business** of any kind, even by currency transactions, in violation of C. 142 (*S. Cong. of Council,* March 22, 1950). Religious here includes members of recent secular institutes. Clerics seriously involved may be degraded. That an individual act of trade or business is not censured is implied in the word "engage." See 408.

435. — III. An excommunication *simpliciter* reserved to the Holy See is incurred by him:

1. Who makes profit from indulgences (C. 2327).

He "profits" from indulgences who makes a temporal gain by granting or publishing an indulgence, or who sells indulgenced objects at a higher price because of the indulgence attached, even though the gain be for a good cause.

2. Who joins the Masonic or other similar associations which plot against the Church or the legitimate civil authority (C. 2335).

In such societies it is required that their members or leaders be bound to secrecy regarding the organization, purpose and program of the society; but it is not necessary that they bind themselves thereto by oath. — Thus, the nihilists and anarchists are included, not socialists. — Adherents of such societies lose their right to Christian burial (C. 1240).

To be *reconciled* to the Church such a person must sever all connections with the society and promise he will never again pay the required dues and, as far as possible, to repair the harm done by scandal. He must be resolved to notify the society of his resignation from membership as soon as he can do so without grave inconvenience to himself. Books, papers, and insignia of the society must be handed over to the confessor who will forward them to his Ordinary or, if this cannot be done conveniently, they must be burned.

3. Who presumes to absolve without the necessary faculties from an excommunication that is *specialissimo modo* or *speciali modo* reserved to the Holy See (C. 2338).

4. Who lends any aid or extends favor to an excommunicated person in the offense for which the latter has been declared a *vitandus;* as also the cleric who knowingly and deliberately holds communion with such an excommunicated person in sacred functions or allows him to take part in divine services (C. 2338).

5. Who dares to cite a bishop (not already mentioned under

II, 7), or abbot or prelate *nullius* or a major superior of a religious institute of papal right before the secular court against the prescription of C. 120 (C. 2341).

436. — 6. *Who violates a major pontifical enclosure of nuns,* no matter what the person's rank, condition or sex may be; and who introduces or admits such persons into the enclosure (C. 2342).

The same holds for violating a minor pontifical enclosure in as far as it pertains to those parts of the enclosure reserved for the nuns.

Papal enclosure obtains in convents of religious women who have solemn vows. — The entrance to such convents is also forbidden to women. Concerning the exceptions confer 413.

7. *A nun who unlawfully leaves a major pontifical enclosure* (C. 2342).

This likewise holds for a nun who unlawfully leaves the "septa monasterii" in the case of a minor pontifical enclosure. For further particulars, see 413.

8. *Women who violate the papal enclosure* of religious men in solemn vows as also the superiors and all others who introduce or admit women of any age whatsoever into the enclosure (C. 2342).

Although girls under the age of puberty do not incur the censure (Cf. 426) yet they do so who introduce or admit even infant girls into the enclosure. They are said to "admit" persons who, in virtue of their office, should prevent such entrance; while others may "introduce" someone into the enclosure, i.e., to send within, invite or permit a person to enter. — He does not incur excommunication who sees a woman within the enclosure and does not expel her.

9. *Whoever presumes* to convert to his own use or usurp ***Church goods*** or whoever prevents those to whom such goods belong from enjoying them (C. 2346).

"Church goods" here means any temporal goods belonging either to the church as such or to any legal person in the Church (C. 1497). — He does not incur the penalty who does not pay his Church dues, since, as long as they are not paid, they are not Church goods, and the non-payment is not a positive action which is required by the word "prevent." He would, however, incur the penalty who would appropriate to himself the contents of the collection basket.

437. — 10. *Whoever engages in a duel* or who either challenges another to a duel or accepts such a challenge, or whoever, in any manner, aids or seconds a duel, or is intentionally present as a spectator, or permits or does not prevent it if he can do so (C. 2351).

Whoever challenges another to a duel is excommunicated even if the challenge is not accepted, as also is he who accepts the duel even though it does not take place. One who only feigns to challenge or accept, but who is firmly resolved not to fight, is not subject to the censure. — Because of their assistance and support, promoters, seconds, physicians, the priest who agrees to remain nearby for immediate assistance, the judges and whoever places money, arms, place, etc. at the disposal of the principals or who stand watch, and, furthermore, those onlookers whose presence is an encouragement for the duellists or an approval of duelling. — The penalty does not embrace the priest or doctor who is called for help after the duel, nor cab drivers who are at the service of all who request their services.

Those who die in a duel or from a wound received in a duel, without manifesting any sign of repentance must be denied ecclesiastical burial (C. 1240). Concerning the consequences of this denial confer 422. — Duellists and their seconds are, furthermore, automatically branded with infamy (C. 2351) and are irregular (C. 984).

11. *Clerics* in major orders and solemnly professed religious *who presume to contract marriage*, even by a mere civil ceremony, and also those who marry such persons (C. 2388).

12. *Whoever commits simony* in the conferring, assuming or resignation of any ecclesiastical office or benefice or dignity of any kind (C. 2392).

13. *Whoever withdraws*, destroys, conceals or substantially alters any *official document* of the episcopal curia (C. 2405).

438. — IV. Excommunications reserved to the Ordinary are incurred by:

1. *Catholics* who *contract marriage* before a *non-Catholic minister* (C. 2319).

According to a *Motu Proprio* of Pius XII (1954) *any* marriage contracted by a Catholic before a non-Catholic minister acting in his religious capacity involves this excommunication.

It matters not whether the marriage takes place in a church or private home. — Neither does it make any difference whether the marriage be valid or invalid.

2. *Catholics marrying* with the explicit or implicit

agreement to educate some or all of their offspring outside the Catholic Church (C. 2319).

3. Catholics who knowingly dare to *offer their children* to a non-Catholic minister for Baptism (C. 2319).

4. Catholic parents, or those who take their place, who
knowingly have their children or wards educated or
brought up in a non-Catholic religion (C. 2319).

It matters not whether the education take place in a school or
privately, in connection with profane instruction or apart from it.

5. *Whoever manufactures,* knowingly sells, distributes or
exposes *false relics* for public veneration (C. 2326).

6. *Whoever lays violent hands on the person of
any cleric* or religious (man or woman) not already
mentioned in 431 and 434 (C. 2343).

The penalties are more severe if such injury is inflicted on higher
ecclesiastical dignitaries, (Cf. 431, 434). Laying violent hands includes: striking, shoving, snatching things from, tearing the clothes,
imprisoning or otherwise detaining, vio'ently preventing from pur-
suing a journey, etc. Verbal injuries are not punished by censure.
— The Ordinary to whom this excommunication is reserved is the
Ordinary of the offender.

439. — 7. *Whoever procures an abortion,* if the
effect is produced (C. 2350).

There is question here of aborting an inviable fetus. — Should
the effect not follow, the censure is not incurred. — If one is
absolved from his sin before the effect takes place the censure is
likewise not incurred. — It is immaterial what method is used
or by whom (the pregnant woman herself or anybody else) the
abortion is procured. Abortion due to carelessness would not
entail the censure. — If the mother is induced to the crime out
of grave fear she does not incur the censure (Cf. 426). Anyone
may incur the penalty as an accomplice (Cf. 424).

8. *Apostates from a religious institute* (C. 2385).

In exempt clerical religious communities the censure is reserved

to the major superior, in other communities to the local Ordinary.
— An *apostate* is one who, with perpetual vows, illegally leaves
the monastery with the intention of not returning, as well as one
who leaves lawfully, but does not return in order to withdraw
himself perpetually from monastic obedience (C. 644). This intention must be manifested externally. It may be rightly presumed
if the individual concerned does not return within a month or
manifest an intention of returning (C. 644).

9. Religious with simple perpetual vows *who contract
marriage and those whom they marry* (C. 2388).

This includes female religious also (Cf. 490). The penalty embraces those also who are dismissed but whose vows still bind.

440. V. Non-reserved excommunications are in-
curred by:

1. The *authors and publishers* of the books of Sacred Scripture,
or of Annotations and Commentaries thereon, who have not obtained the requisite permission from the Ordinary before publication
(C. 2318).

2. Those who, contrary to the prescription of C. 1240, command
or compel the *ecclesiastical burial* of an unbaptized person,
apostate, heretic, schismatic or others, either excommunicated or
under an interdict (C. 2339).

3. All who in any manner knowingly are responsible for the
alienation of Church property without the necessary apostolic
permission (C. 2347).

4. Whoever *compels anyone to embrace the clerical
state* or to enter the religious life or make religious
profession (C. 2352).

This penalty is especially applicable to parents, relatives, guardians, etc.

5. One who knowingly *neglects to denounce* within
a month the priest who solicited the said person (C. 2368).

On the meaning of "knowingly" confer 599.

441.   *Article II*

Individual Interdicts and Suspensions

I. Individual Interdicts.

1. *Legal bodies* (e.g., universities, colleges, etc.) appealing from the laws, decrees, etc. of the reigning Pontiff to a General Council incur an interdict *speciali modo* reserved to the Apostolic See (C. 2332).

2. An interdict *ab ingressu ecclesiae* **reserved to the Ordinary** is incurred by him who voluntarily grants Christian burial, contrary to the prescriptions of canon 1240, to infidels, apostates, heretics, schismatics and other persons excommunicated or interdicted (C. 2339).

3. A *non-reserved* interdict is incurred by him a) who knowingly holds or permits divine services to be held in interdicted territory, or who admits clerics who are excommunicated, suspended or interdicted by a declaratory or condemnatory sentence to the celebration of divine services that are forbidden under censure. The interdict is, furthermore, *ab ingressu ecclesiae* (C. 2338).

b) Whoever causes a place, community or college to be put under an interdict is himself personally interdicted (C. 2338).

442. II. Individual Suspensions.

1. A suspension *reserved to the Holy See* is incurred by

a) The cleric who promotes or is promoted to Orders simoniacally or who through simony administers or receives any other Sacrament (C. 2371).

b) One who presumes to receive Orders from anyone who is excommunicated, suspended or interdicted by a declaratory or condemnatory sentence, or from a notorious apostate, heretic or schismatic (C. 2372).

2. A suspension *reserved to the Ordinary* is incurred by

a) A cleric who dares to cite before the civil court anyone enjoying the *privilegium fori* contrary to canon 120, in as far as he has not incurred one of the more severe penalties already mentioned in Nos. 434, 435.

b) A cleric in major orders who is a fugitive from a religious institution (C. 2386).

3. A suspension **not reserved** is incurred by:

a) A priest daring to hear confessions without the requisite jurisdiction (suspended *a divinis*) or to absolve from reserved sins (suspended from hearing confessions) (C. 2366).

b) One who is maliciously ordained without dimissorials or with falsified ones or before the canonical age or without observing the legitimate sequence of orders (*per saltum*) (C. 2374).

c) A cleric daring to resign an ecclesiastical office, benefice or dignity into the hands of a layman (C. 2400).

d) An abbot or prelate *nullius* who does not obtain the abbatial blessing, contrary to C. 322, is suspended from the exercise of his jurisdiction (C. 2402).

e) A vicar-capitular who issues dimissorial letters for ordination contrary to the regulation of C. 958 (C. 2409).

f) A religious superior presuming to send his subjects to the bishop of another place not in accordance with law (C. 2410).

Book III

443.   # THE SACRAMENTS

Part I

THE SACRAMENTS IN GENERAL

A *Sacrament* is an external sign instituted by Christ to signify and effect the sanctification of man.

Accordingly we treat in this first part: the external sign, the effects, the minister and recipient of the Sacraments.

444.   Chapter I

THE EXTERNAL SIGN

I. Concept. The outward sign in the administration of the Sacraments consists in the matter (i.e., some sense-perceptible thing or perceivable action) and in the form (i.e., words or signs) by which the matter receives its proximate sacramental determination.

The remote matter is the thing used, e.g., water for Baptism, oil for Extreme Unction, etc. The proximate matter is the use or application of the remote matter, e.g., the ablution in baptizing, the anointing with oil, etc.

II. Requirements. 1. A *union of matter and form* is required and it must be such that it actually constitutes one individual sacramental sign.

In the Holy Eucharist this union must be physical. In the other Sacraments a moral unity suffices, and this may vary according to the nature of the Sacrament.

Wherefore, in the Holy Eucharist the matter must be present when the priest commences to pronounce the form. — In Baptism, Confirmation and Extreme Unction, there must be at least a partial union of matter and form. Should the form be spoken immediately following the application of the matter, one may theoretically consider the Sacrament as valid, but in practice the Sacrament should be repeated conditionally. The Sacrament is invalid if matter and form are separated for the space of an "Our Father." — In the Sacrament of Penance the union which a judicial act requires is sufficient; for Matrimony a union required for contracts is enough.

445. — 2. *One and the same person* must employ the matter and apply the form.

Wherefore, Baptism is invalid if one person pours the water and another pronounces the words. (Cf. AAS 8-478 sq.)

3. Matter and form must be *certainly valid.*

Hence, one may not follow a probable opinion and use either doubtful matter or form. Acting otherwise one commits a sacrilege.

An *exception* exists only in case of necessity when there is no certainly valid matter at hand, because of the principle *sacramenta propter homines*. In a case of extreme necessity one is obliged to use such doubtful matter, e.g., to baptize with tea. If the reception of a Sacrament is very beneficial one may also use doubtful matter. Hence, a sick person, having confessed, may be anointed with the oil of catechumens; likewise, one may absolve an idiot who has confessed only doubtful sins (Cf. also 551). The exception referred to, however, does not apply to the Holy Eucharist because of the danger of idolatry. — When Sacraments are administered in doubtful cases the administration is conditional.

446. — 4. Matter and form must be used *unchanged.*

a) Substantial change invalidates the administration and is gravely sinful if voluntary. An *accidental change* does not invalidate but is venially or mortally sinful according to the magnitude of the voluntary alteration.

A substantial change in the matter for Baptism would be the use of wine instead of water; an accidental change would be the mixture of a small amount of perfume with the water. — A substantial change in the form of absolution would be this: "Ego te abluo..." But to use those words in baptizing would only imply an accidental change.

It would also imply a substantial change if one were to write the words when the Sacrament requires spoken words. — Moreever, that the Sacrament may not be exposed to the danger of invalid administration the words must be spoken in such manner that the minister may hear himself.

b) Separation of individual *words* and *syllables* constitutes a substantial change if the interval is long enough to alter the meaning of the sentence.

Thus, the form remains valid if one says "Ego te baptizo," coughs and then completes the form. Similarly, if one interrupts the form by some incidental remark, as "Turn the page," "Keep quiet," "This water is too cold." The formula of absolution is likewise valid if the confessor, after saying: "Ego te absolvo," notices the penitent leaving the confessional and says: "Come back! Never leave before the priest finishes! — a peccatis tuis."

The form is invalid if interrupted for several minutes, e.g., after saying: "Hoc est enim corpus," one has a coughing spell, after which he should add "meum."

If *individual syllables* are separated a shorter interruption makes the form at least doubtfully valid; thus, if after saying "Hoc est enim cor-" one should sneeze several times and then conclude "pus meum." In such cases the word begun should be repeated.

c) In *judging* whether a form has been altered substantially or only accidentally one must consider whether the minister acted inadvertently, i.e., mispronounced the form by mistake or whether he intended to give the form a different meaning.

Thus Baptism is valid if one out of ignorance says: "Baptizo te in nomine Patris et Filia et Spiritu Sancta." — Consecration is valid if one says: "Hoc est colpus or copus meum"; or if one says "calis" instead of "calix"; or uses the masculine instead of the neuter form, as "corpus meus." If, however, he should use the term "hic" in the sense of "here," the consecration would be invalid.

447.   Chapter II

THE EFFICACY OF THE SACRAMENTS

I. All the Sacraments either produce or increase sanctifying grace *ex opere operato,* i.e., by reason of the

Rite itself. At the same time they also confer the habit of the supernatural virtues and the gifts of the Holy Ghost.

The Sacraments instituted to produce sanctifying grace (Baptism and Penance) are called Sacraments of the dead. Whoever receives these Sacraments in the state of grace receives an increase of sanctifying grace.

All the other Sacraments were instituted to increase sanctifying grace and are called Sacraments of the living. He who is not in the state of grace but having imperfect contrition receives a Sacrament of the living in good faith is thereby restored to the state of grace. This is certain in the case of Extreme Unction and probable in the case of the other Sacraments of the living.

II. Each Sacrament confers, furthermore, a special, sacramental grace, peculiar to itself.

According to the general opinion this is none other than sanctifying grace adapted to the purpose for which the respective Sacrament was instituted.

III. Baptism, Confirmation and Holy Orders imprint an indelible character on the soul.

Consequently, these three Sacraments, unlike the others, cannot validly be repeated.

448. — IV. An obstacle may prevent a Sacrament from being either fruitful or valid.

1. A Sacrament is *unfruitful* (i.e., does not convey sanctifying grace) if it is received without the necessary moral dispositions.

A Sacrament may be validly received and yet be unfruitful (sacramentum validum sed informe). In spite of this, Baptism, Confirmation and Holy Orders nevertheless would imprint their character and could not be repeated. — Whoever knowingly receives a Sacrament unworthily commits a sacrilege.

Should one recover the proper dispositions after receiving a Sacrament fruitlessly, sometimes the Sacrament *revives,* i.e., its corresponding graces are subsequently conferred.

Reviviscence is certain in case of Baptism. As to Confirmation, Holy Orders, Extreme Unction and Matrimony it is highly probable. In the case of the Holy Eucharist it is probable as long as the Sacred Species remain present; while it is questionable regarding Penance.

For the reviviscence of a Sacrament, that *disposition* is in general necessary which is required for its valid and licit reception.

Thus, should a Sacrament of the living revive, it is required that either perfect contrition be had or imperfect contrition with sacramental absolution. In Extreme Unction alone imperfect contrition suffices. — For the reviviscence of a Sacrament of the dead, imperfect contrition suffices. If a sacrilege was committed in the reception or a mortal sin subsequently, perfect contrition or imperfect contrition and confession are necessary, because the efficacy of the Sacrament unfruitfully received does not extend to these sins.

449. — 2. The reception of a Sacrament is *invalid* if administered to one who is incapable of receiving it or who does not will to receive it.

Examples: if an unbaptized person is confirmed, a person in good health is anointed, or a woman is ordained. A Sacrament invalidly administered never revives. Such a Sacrament can be administered absolutely when the obstacle has been removed. — To administer or receive a Sacrament invalidly is a much greater sin than to administer or receive it unfruitfully.

450.   Chapter III

THE MINISTER OF THE SACRAMENTS

Article I

Requirements for Valid and Lawful Administration

I. Valid administration requires:

1. *Divine authorization,* since only God can unite inner grace with the sacramental action.

The faculty to baptize is given to all men, even to the heathen. Power to administer the Sacrament of Matrimony is granted to all the faithful who are not prevented by a diriment impediment. Faculties to administer the other Sacraments are received through the Priesthood.

2. *The right intention*, since the administration of a Sacrament must be a human act (actus humanus).

a) The intention must exist *when* the Sacrament is administered, since man, as the instrumental cause, administers the Sacrament under its influence.

It is best to be conscious of one's intention (intentio actualis) at the moment of administration; this is not necessary, however, as long as it is administered under its influence (intentio virtualis). A virtual intention is had, e.g., if one, for the purpose of saying Mass, goes to the sacristy, vests, etc., but is completely distracted, even voluntarily, at the subsequent consecration.

If *external attention* is lacking, the intention to administer a Sacrament is implicitly revoked, making the administration invalid. External attention is lacking if one undertakes an external action that is incompatible with internal attention.

The administration of a Sacrament is invalid if one previously, indeed, had the requisite intention, which here and now no longer exists and thus exercises no influence on his action, even though he did not revoke it (intentio habitualis). Thus there is no consecration if a priest in the delirium of a fever pronounces the words of consecration over bread and wine on the table at his bedside; the same holds for any one attempting to confect a Sacrament while intoxicated, insane or asleep.

It is still less sufficient for validity if one neither has nor ever had the required intention even though one would have made it if he had thought about it (intentio interpretativa).

451. *b*) The intention must be *to perform the respective sacramental action.*

The intention may be included in another intention. Accordingly, Baptism is valid if administered by a Jewish physician who acts with the intention of doing what the Church does, or as Christians do. But no Sacrament is confected if one merely performs the sacramental action for practice (e.g., a seminarian baptizing or saying Mass) or as a mockery.

Baptism, as conferred in the sects of the Disciples of Christ, the Presbyterians, the Congregationalists, the Baptists and the Methodists, as far as the intention of the minister is concerned, is to be presumed valid when rendering matrimonial decisions, according to the Holy Office (AAS 41-650). Some other sects, too, may confer Baptism validly, but the Holy See was only asked concerning these five.

c) The intention must affect a *definite person* or some *definite matter*.

The person is sufficiently specified if the minister merely intends to baptize or absolve the person present, even though the child is not, as the priest thinks, a girl, but a boy; or the penitent is not Mr. Smith, but Mr. Jones. — So, too, the matter is specific enough if the priest intends to consecrate the bread he has in his hands, even though instead of one host he holds two by mistake; similarly, if he intends to consecrate the hosts in the ciborium and there are six hundred, instead of four hundred as he believes. The matter is undetermined if one intends to consecrate only four hundred of the six hundred hosts he knows are in the ciborium.

452. *d*) The intention may be *absolute* or *conditional*.

If the condition refers to the past or present the Sacrament is valid or invalid according as the condition is objectively verified or not. If only God knows whether the condition is realized or not the validity of the Sacrament is highly doubtful, e.g., "I now baptize this child, if it will otherwise die before a priest arrives to baptize it." — If the condition refers to the future the sacrament is invalid (except in case of Matrimony).

α) A reasonable cause is required for the conditional administration of a Sacrament.

Whoever administers a Sacrament conditionally without such a reason sins gravely; but if he is convinced that the condition is fulfilled, only a venial sin is committed. — Whenever a Sacrament is administered under circumstances that render its validity doubtful, conditional readministration is obligatory (Cf. 445).

β) The condition, like the intention, need not be expressed in words, except in administering Baptism and

Extreme Unction where verbal expression is prescribed by the rubrics.

Some authors think that condition also suffices which is contained in the intention to administer the Sacrament as it should be administered according to the mind of the Church.

3. Faith and the state of grace are *not required.*

All other requirements being given a Jewish doctor, therefore, validly baptizes, although he neither believes in Baptism nor in Christ. Concerning the state of grace see 453.

453. — II. Lawful administration of the Sacraments requires:

1. *The state of grace.*

A *layman* administering a Sacrament in the state of mortal sin commits only a venial sin.

An *ordained minister* in conscious mortal sin confecting a Sacrament without necessity commits a mortal sin. In the case of the Holy Eucharist this holds only for "confecting" the Sacrament. Thus a priest sins mortally by saying Mass, solemnly baptizing, hearing confessions or anointing the sick while in the state of mortal sin; likewise a bishop who would thus confirm or ordain. — But whoever on one occasion hears several confessions, or confirms a number of people successively thereby commits only one grave sin (Cf. 103). — But an ordained minister who is not in the state of grace sins only venially by administering a Sacrament privately, i.e., without the prescribed ceremonies (e.g., Baptism), or in a case of urgent necessity when he cannot first recover the state of grace (e.g., absolving or anointing in an accident), or if he merely distributes Holy Communion without confecting the Sacrament. Much less would it be mortally sinful for a priest in sin to assist at marriage or give Benediction of the Blessed Sacrament.

The state of grace may be recovered by eliciting an act of perfect contrition. Confession is prescribed only before celebrating Mass (Cf. 504).

454. — 2. *Internal attention.*

Voluntary distraction does not invalidate a Sacrament, but is venially sinful. It is gravely sinful if it exposes the minister to the danger of omitting something which is prescribed under grave obligation. — If *external attention* is lacking the administration is invalid. Cf. 450.

3. *Avoidance of unnecessary repetition.*

For particulars see 458.

4. *Freedom from censures and irregularities,* observance of the *rubrics* and possession of the required *permission.*

An *excommunicatus vitandus* or an *excommunicatus per sententiam declaratoriam vel condemnatoriam* may not confer a Sacrament on anyone who is not in danger of death. In danger of death one under such censure may only give absolution (C. 822); however, he may administer the other Sacraments at the request of the faithful if no other minister is present (C. 2261). The same holds for one who is suspended from administering the Sacraments *per sententiam declaratoriam vel condemnatoriam* (C. 2284). — Other excommunicated or suspended persons may administer any Sacrament at the request of the faithful (C. 2261), provided they have recovered the state of grace. — The permission sometimes required is treated in the sections dealing with individual Sacraments.

455.   *Article II*

Obligations and Faculties of the Minister

I. Administering the Sacraments. 1. Whoever has the care of souls must, *by reason of his office,* administer the Sacraments not only in charity, but also in strict justice, at the reasonable request of his charges.

Thus bishops, pastors, chaplains, vicars and superiors of clerical religious communities have this obligation. A *reasonable* request is not only one made in danger of death, but one made before some special Feastday, or if made to recover the state of grace, or to obtain the grace necessary to overcome temptation, or to gain some large indulgence, etc. — An unreasonable request is sometimes made by scrupulous or "pious" souls at altogether unreasonable hours.

The *gravity of the sin* of refusing a Sacrament is measured by the spiritual loss sustained by the petitioner through the denial of the

Sacrament. Thus he who would once or twice refuse to hear a confession or give Holy Communion to one who is not in spiritual need would sin only venially. — It would be gravely sinful to frequently confer the Sacraments grudgingly, or to refuse as a matter of principle on ordinary weekdays, or to administer the Sacraments only reluctantly to the grievously ill. — Pastors, etc. must administer the Sacraments even at the risk of their lives to those under their care who, without the Sacraments, could only with great difficulty avoid losing their souls. This might be practical in the case of one weak in faith and in danger of death and for whom an act of perfect contrition is very difficult.

456. — 2. He who is not obliged to do so by virtue of his office must administer the Sacraments *out of charity*.

Sins against charity can evidently be mortal sins. — Since charity generally does not oblige under great inconvenience, an ordinary priest must risk his life to administer the Sacraments only in case it is certain that the petitioner can otherwise scarcely save his soul and that the hope of saving him by conferring the Sacraments at least counterbalances the danger to which the priest must expose himself in administering them.

457. — II. Refusal of the Sacraments. Whoever administers the Sacraments to an unworthy recipient co-operates in the sin of another. But co-operation in the sin of another is lawful in certain instances (Cf. 147). From this the following conclusions may be deduced:

1. An *occult sinner* must be refused the Sacraments if he secretly requests them. If he asks for them in the presence of others he may not be refused, lest his good name be lost and the other faithful be deterred from receiving the Sacraments.

If a priest knows only from confession that one is unworthy to receive the Sacraments, he must administer them even though the sinner requests them secretly.

2. A *public sinner* must always be refused the Sacraments, whether he wishes to receive them publicly or secretly.

Exception is always made for the Sacrament of Penance if the sinner is rightly disposed. For a very serious reason a pastor may assist at the marriage of a public sinner (Cf. C. 1066).

Should a public sinner ask to receive the Sacraments at a place where his crime is unknown, they must, nevertheless, be refused him, if his sin will soon become known in that place; but if it can be foreseen that his sin will remain unknown there, the Sacraments must be given him.

That one be no longer considered a public sinner, it is generally sufficient that he be known to have gone to confession. If he is living in a proximate, voluntary occasion of sin (e.g., in concubinage) he must, as a rule, first give it up. In the example given he must likewise first repair public scandal (e.g., by disapproving of a wayward life).

458. — III. Repetition of the Sacraments. 1. It is *forbidden* under grave sin to repeat a Sacrament, even conditionally, if it has certainly been administered validly.

Neither the entire Sacrament nor the form nor a part of the form may be repeated. Wherefore, it is not permissible to repeat the form merely because one does not recall having uttered it. Because of their perplexed conscience scrupulous persons often do not sin by such repetition; but they are obliged to avoid scrupulosity to the best of their ability.

2. It is *lawful* to repeat any Sacrament conditionally if there is a doubt about its validity.

3. It is *obligatory* to readminister a Sacrament conditionally if its validity is doubtful and either the virtue of religion, justice or charity requires that it be validly administered.

Hence, conditional repetition is obligatory; in case of consecration because of the danger of idolatry; in case of Holy Orders so that all subsequent Sacraments conferred by the ordinand be valid; so also in baptizing and in absolving a dying person, or in anointing an unconscious person who is dying and in the state of grave sin in order that these persons be not eternally lost.

IV. Simulation and Dissimulation of the Sacraments.

459. — 1. *Simulation* of a Sacrament is never allowed, not even to save one's life. — It consists in performing the sacramental action without the intention of conferring a Sacrament, although others think a Sacrament is being administered.

It is unlawful, therefore, to fictitiously go through the action of baptizing without the intention of baptizing, or to use non-sacramental wine at the consecration. — It is not really simulating a Sacrament to give a communicant an unconsecrated host; but it is unlawful since this gives others an occasion of idolatry and since the communicant (if he knows the host is unconsecrated) will at least externally feign to adore the unconsecrated bread.

2. *Dissimulation* of a Sacrament is permissible for a grave reason. — It is pretending to administer a Sacrament or the performing of a non-sacramental action under such circumstances that bystanders think a Sacrament is being administered.

Hence, it is permissible in confession to make the sign of the cross with the words *Misereatur tui* ... without the formula of absolution over a penitent who is incapable of being absolved, so that others may not know absolution is being refused him or lest the seal of confession be broken. For an extremely grave reason a priest may by prearrangement with a person who will approach the Communion rail pretending to receive, make the sign of the cross with the consecrated Host say the words *Corpus Domini nostri* ... and then put the Host back into the ciborium.

460. Chapter IV

THE RECIPIENT OF THE SACRAMENTS

I. Requirements for Valid Reception. 1. The recipient of a Sacrament must be in *the wayfaring state* and (except in case of Baptism) validly baptized.

Baptism here means the Baptism of water only.

2. The required *intention* must be present.

In order that those who have not yet attained the *use of reason* (be they infants or adults) may validly receive those Sacraments of which they are capable the intention of the Church is sufficient. But he who has attained the use of reason (even though later on he may have lost it) must personally have the corresponding intention.

He who receives a Sacrament merely as a jest does not receive it validly; whereas he does who receives it under the influence of grave fear (with the exception of Martimony), provided he has the intention of receiving the Sacrament.

461. *a) The implicit habitual intention* is in itself sufficient for the valid reception of a Sacrament. If in some instances more than this is required, it is not by reason of receiving a Sacrament, but because of the nature of the respective Sacrament.

Concerning the habitual intention see 450. — An implicit intention is one that is contained in another intention, e.g., in the will to live like a Christian.

An habitual implicit intention certainly suffices for Confirmation, Viaticum and Extreme Unction. — If a priest may presume that a person has not revoked his will to die a Christian, the last Sacraments may be given him though he be unconscious or even oppose the administration in delirium or insanity. The habitual intention even takes precedence over the actual if it is stron er than the latter. Thus, a person who absolutely wants to receive Extreme Unction before death, but here and now does not want to be anointed, thinking he is not yet in danger of death, can be validly anointed.

b) The explicit habitual intention is required in order that ordination be certainly valid, since the intention to assume a new state and new burdens is not readily included in another act of volition. Similarly, some authors require the same intention for the Baptism of adults while others think the implicit habitual intention suffices.

c) A virtual intention is necessary for Matrimony, since here the recipient is also the minister.

Probably such an intention is also necessary for confession since many authors believe the acts of the penitent are the matter for this Sacrament. One may, however, conditionally absolve a dying unconscious person even though he has merely an implicit habitual intention.

462. — 3. Valid reception does *not require* faith, the state of grace nor attention, not even external attention.

The Sacrament of Penance is an exception.

Therefore, an unbeliever who so desires may be validly baptized even though he have no faith.

Whoever receives a Sacrament with voluntary distraction, e.g., absolution, sins venially.

463. — II. Requirements for the Lawful Reception. 1. The *Sacraments of the dead* require at least imperfect contrition.

2. For the *Sacraments of the living* the state of grace is a grave obligation.

It is best to recover the state of grace by confession. This is obligatory for receiving Holy Communion. For the other Sacraments it suffices to elicit an act of perfect contrition.

3. If it be known that the *minister will sin* gravely by administering a Sacrament, one may neither request nor still less receive a Sacrament at his hands.

When the minister is able to confer a Sacrament without sinning if he so wills (e.g.. by first recovering the state of grace) the faithful may ask him to administer the Sacraments, for any reason that justifies co-operation in the sins of others (Cf. 147). Such reasons are: reception of the Sacraments by the sick, fulfilling a command of the Church, Baptism of a child, confession in order not to remain longer in grave sin, etc. — In as far as *excommunicated* or *suspended* clerics may not administer the Sacraments, and, consequently, in how far the faithful may not request them to do so, confer 454. — Because of the danger of scandal or perversion, only one in extreme spiritual need may ask a *heretic* or *schismatic* to administer Baptism or give absolution provided no other minister is available.

Part II

464. THE INDIVIDUAL SACRAMENTS

Section I

Baptism

Baptism is a sacrament by which one is spiritually reborn through washing with water and the use of the appropriate form. — Besides the Baptism of water there is also the Baptism of desire and of blood (Cf. 470).

Chapter I

THE OUTWARD SIGN OF BAPTISM

I. The Matter. 1. The *remote valid matter* for Baptism is natural water (C. 737).

In judging what is "water" we do not have recourse to chemical analysis, but rather to the estimation of ordinary people.

a) Certainly valid matter: rain and sea water; spring, well and drain water; water from melted ice, snow or hail; mineral and sulphur water; dew and water from sweating walls and recondensed steam; distilled water if by distillation only foreign matter is removed; muddy water or water mixed with any other substance as long as the water certainly predominates by far.

b) Certainly invalid matter: milk, blood, amniotic liquid, tears, saliva, foam, fruit juices, wine, beer, oil, thick broth, ink.

c) Doubtful matter is thin soup, weak beer, coffee, tea, water from dissolved salt, sap from vines and other plants, rose water and similar liquids extracted from vegetative matter.

465. — 2. The *remote lawful matter.*

a) In danger of death, if one cannot have certainly valid matter, any kind of water is lawful which is not certainly invalid.

One may only baptize conditionally with doubtful matter. — If one must baptize and two kinds of doubtfully valid matter are available he is obliged to use the more probably valid. After using doubtful matter Baptism must be repeated conditionally. Even in a case of necessity pure water must be preferred to water containing other ingredients in small quantity. If a child is to be baptized in the womb a small quantity of bichloride of mercury (quicksilver) or similar sublimate may be used as a prophylactic.

b) In private Baptism ordinary water may always be used. Some authors recommend, however, that baptismal or at least holy water be used.

Private Baptism is Baptism administered without the prescribed ceremonies.

c) In solemn Baptism there is a grave obligation to employ baptismal water.

Solemn Baptism is that which is administered with the prescribed ceremonies, even though it take place in a private home.

If the supply of baptismal water runs low plain water may be added, but only in lesser quantity. This may be repeated. However, the interval between additions must not be so short as to constitute a moral unity. — At the request of the parents a little water from the Jordan may be added. — Cold water may be warmed.

If baptismal water becomes putrid it is still valid, but should one be unable to renew it in an emergency, then out of reverence to the Sacrament, pure, natural water is preferable. Holy water or ordinary unblessed water may be used for solemn Baptism if one is in a hurry and has no baptismal water. But if time permits one should bless baptismal water according to the formula given in the Roman Ritual.

466. — N. B. *The Blessing of Baptismal Water.*

In all churches with a baptismal font water must be blessed on Holy Saturday, even if plenty old water remains. The water blessed previously is to be poured in the sacrarium. — In blessing baptismal water those holy oils are used which were blessed by the bishop in the current year. If the new oils have not yet arrived on Holy Saturday the water is blessed without them, the oils and corresponding prayers being privately added later. If Baptism is to be administered before the new oils arrive, the old are mixed with the blessed water. If the priest foresees the necessity of baptizing before the arrival of the new oils, the old oils may be used at the blessing of the baptismal water. — If for any reason whatever a blessed

Easter Candle is not available for the blessing of the baptismal water on Holy Saturday, an ordinary candle is blessed (benedictione candelarum extra diem Purificationis) and used instead.

In case of necessity baptismal water may be blessed at other times also. The Ritual, however, prescribes a special formula for such occasions. — In churches (e.g., mission stations) where solemn Baptism is administered, but where there is no font, the solemn blessing of baptismal water according to the ceremonies of the Missal is not permitted on Holy Saturday.

467. — 3. The *proximate valid matter* of Baptism consists in the actual washing of the person to be baptized by the one baptizing.

The washing may be done by immersion, aspersion or infusion.

A definite *quantity* of water is not required; it suffices that the water flow over the one being baptized. Several authors hold the flowing of one or two drops insufficient. — Baptism is doubtful and must be repeated conditionally if administered by rubbing wet fingers across the forehead or by merely making the sign of the cross thereon with a wet finger. The same holds for the use of a damp cloth, sponge or wet hand when the water does not actually flow. Likewise, if administered by aspersion as when sprinkling with holy water if the drops do not flow over the skin but remain where they fall.

The water *must touch* the one to be baptized. Baptism is invalid if the water merely comes in contact with the clothes, or the uterus or fetal membrane in case of uterine Baptism. It is likewise invalid if only a head scab or a mucuous excretion on the head is contacted. — If the hair alone and not the skin is touched the baptism is doubtful.

Baptism is certainly valid if administered on the *head* (if the hair is very thick it would be better to baptize on the forehead). Baptism is valid even if the head is entirely covered with sores. It is probably valid if one were to baptize on the breast, neck or shoulder; probably invalid if administered on the hand, arm or the foot.

Validity also requires that *one and the same person* apply the water and pronounce the words. The washing may be done by infusion or by holding the one to be baptized in standing or flowing water (e.g., in a spring or in the rain).

4. The *proximate lawful matter* in the Western Church consists in the triple infusion, i.e., the one baptizing pours water three times on the head of the one being baptized while pronouncing the form.

This practice obliges under mortal sin.

468. — II. The form of Baptism prescribed for the Latin Church reads: *"Ego te baptizo in nomine Patris et Filii et Spiritus Sancti* (I baptize thee in the name of the Father and of the Son and of the Holy Ghost)."

"Amen" is not added, though validity is not affected by adding it. — The following form would also be valid: "I baptize thee in the Name of the Father, Son and Holy Ghost," or " I baptize Your Highness in the Name ..."

Such forms as these are *invalid*: "I baptize thee in the Names of the Father and of the Son ...." or "I baptize thee in the Name of the Most Blessed Trinity"; or "In the Name of the Triune God"; or "In the Name of Christ"; or "I administer the Sacrament of Baptism to you in the Name of the Father and of the Son ...."

These forms are *doubtfully valid*: "I christen thee in the name ..." or, "I baptize thee in the power of the Father ...." or "I baptize thee in the Name of the Father and of the Son (and) Holy Ghost," or "I baptize thee by the Name of the Father ..."

Ambiguous forms often allow a heretical as well as orthodox interpretation. These are valid or not according to the intention of the minister. Thus the form "I baptize thee in the Name of the Father and in the Name of the Son and in the Name of the Holy Ghost" is valid unless one would wish to indicate thereby a difference of Nature between the Persons of the Trinity (Cf. also 446).

469.   Chapter II

THE EFFECTS AND NECESSITY OF BAPTISM

I. The effects of Baptism are the remission of both original and personal sins and the punishment due to sin, the imprinting of the baptismal character, the infusion of sanctifying grace, the supernatural virtues and the gifts of the Holy Ghost, and especially the conferring of a right to the graces necessary to lead a Christian life.

Personal sins and the punishments due to them are remitted only in connection with at least imperfect contrition. Wherefore, if an adult is to be baptized he must be exhorted to elicit an act of contrition.

470. — II. Baptism of water is **necessary** for the attainment of salvation as an indispensable means for reaching that end. Only in exceptional cases can the Baptism of desire or of blood take its place.

Baptism of blood consists in suffering death for Christ. It operates *quasi ex opere operato*, i.e., no subjective act is required, and hence, even infants can be justified in this wise. The *Baptism of desire* consists in an act of perfect contrition or perfect love, which acts somehow include a desire for Baptism. — Neither the Baptism of desire nor of blood imprint an indelible character. The obligation to be baptized by water still remains (Cf. also 460).

Conditional Baptism is always necessary whenever there is a doubt, even a slight doubt, about the validity of the Baptism received, because this Sacrament is indispensably necessary for salvation.

If there is no doubt about the validity of the Baptism received, one may not be baptized, even conditionally, though Baptism was administered by a lay person or heretic. — Before one rebaptizes conditionally because of a doubt he must try to remove the doubt by investigation. Only moral impossibility excuses from such investigation. If nothing can be learned about the Baptism of one converting to the Faith conditional Baptism is necessary. — In the case of foundlings a thorough investigation must be made to determine whether they are baptized or not; if it cannot be ascertained that an abandoned child is certainly baptized, conditional Baptism is necessary (C. 749). An accompanying note asserting that the child has been baptized is not a conclusive proof.

471. Chapter III

THE MINISTER OF BAPTISM

I. Minister of Solemn Baptism. 1. The *ordinary minister* is any priest. Baptizing is a pastoral right. The local Ordinary or pastor can permit others to baptize. Permission may be presumed in case of necessity (C. 738).

Apart from the case of necessity it is mortally sinful to baptize without at least the presumed permission of the pastor.

In his own parish the pastor may baptize only his own parishioners and the homeless (vagi). He may baptize others only if they cannot easily or soon be baptized by their own pastor (C. 738). — However, a pastor may not solemnly baptize his own parishioners in another parish without the required permission (Cf. C. 739).

The Baptism of adults should, when feasible, be referred to the local Ordinary, so that he may personally administer the Sacrament if he so wishes or delegate another (C. 744).

In territories where parishes or quasi-parishes are not yet legitimately established, the right to baptize in the whole territory or any part thereof by anyone beside the Ordinary is determined by particular legislation or by custom (C. 740).

2. The *extraordinary minister* is the deacon. He may use his power only with the permission of the local Ordinary or the pastor. This permission may be granted for any reasonable cause (C. 741).

Reasonable causes are, for example, when the pastor is absent or when he is busy in the confessional or preaching, etc. — In emergencies this permission may also be presumed (C. 741).

A deacon baptizing must use salt and baptismal water previously blessed by a priest. If no blessed salt is at hand the deacon may bless it.

A deacon baptizing without the required permission sins gravely. A cleric inferior to a deacon furthermore becomes irregular (C. 985).

472. — II. *The minister of private valid Baptism* is any person. Therefore Baptism administered by unbelievers and heretics is valid (Cf also 750). Concerning the intention confer 451.

Lawfully however the laity may baptize only in danger of death and then only when there is no priest present (C. 742).

To do otherwise is mortally sinful. — An *exception* is permitted and even necessary when a child is to be baptized in the mother's womb. — A contrary custom prevailing in mission districts, where catechists or other trustworthy lay persons baptize outside the case of necessity as often as no priest is present, may be continued.

If possible, two or at least one *witness* should be present in private Baptism, so that the administration of Baptism can be attested to (C. 742). Witnesses should observe everything closely that they may testify to the validity of the Sacrament conferred. — *Parents* may baptize their own child only when the latter is in danger of death and no other minister is at hand (C. 742). This prescription obliges only under venial sin, and does not oblige at all if the others present are less skillful and instructed than the parent. — The *ceremonies* omitted in private Baptism must be supplied in church as soon as possible (C. 759). — The local Ordinary may permit the omission of the ceremonies but only in conditional baptism of adult heretics (C. 759).

473.   Chapter IV

THE RECIPIENT OF BAPTISM

Any human being in the wayfaring state not yet baptized is *capable* of being baptized (C. 745).

I. Adult Baptism. The *valid* Baptism of anyone with the use of reason requires the intention to be baptized.

In *doubt* about the required intention of one in danger of death, Baptism is administered conditionally (si capax es).

An *explicit habitual intention* certainly suffices, e.g., if one has expressly asked for Baptism before becoming unconscious. Some authors say an *implicit habitual intention* is insufficient (Cf. 461). Because this opinion is not certain, one may baptize in danger of death when there is only an implicit habitual intention present. If it is later possible to evoke an explicit intention the person is to be rebaptized conditionally. — It is controverted as to just what acts of the will include the intention to be baptized. Nearly all authors agree that the desire to embrace the Christian religion includes the desire for Baptism. Many deny that this desire is included in an act of perfect contrition. According to a decision of the Holy See a missionary may not baptize a dying Jew or pagan who, he may suppose, has only imperfect contrition; but it is necessary that the

missionary may reasonably infer from positive indications that the
dying person desires Baptism or has the intention to be received
into the Church. (S. Off. 18. sept. 1850; 30 mart. 1898.)

**474. — 2. *Licit* Baptism requires furthermore that
the person to be baptized be properly instructed and be
sorry for his personal sins.**

Except in danger of death thorough instruction in the truths of
the Catholic Faith is necessary (Cf. C. 752). If, in danger of
death, one cannot be completely instructed it suffices that he somehow shows that he believes those truths, a knowledge of which is
necessary (necessitate medii) for salvation (Cf. 118), and that he
sincerely proposes to lead a good Christian life. (C. 752). — Concerning the reception of non-Catholics into the Church see 128. —
Should there be a doubt about the necessary *knowledge* or *contrition*
of a person to be baptized in danger of death, Baptism is administered absolutely, because of the reviviscence of the Sacrament
(Cf. 448).

475. — *N.B. Baptism of the Insane.*

The insane may be baptized if they never attained the use of
reason. The formula for infants is used (C. 754). — If they have
lucid intervals they may be baptized during one of these if they so
desire (C. 754). — If they have become insane after attaining the
use of reason they are to be baptized in danger of death provided
they desired Baptism while they still had the use of reason (C. 754).

**476. — II. Infant Baptism. 1. *Children of Catholic
parents* should be baptized as soon as possible (C. 770).**

Postponing Baptism without a reason is sinful. Many authors
hold that the delay of one month without any reason or more
than two months with a reason, is mortally sinful.

**2. *Children of non-Catholic parents* may or may
not be baptized according as it is foreseen that they will
or will not die before reaching the age of reason, and
furthermore, whether they have already attained the use
of reason or not.**

"Non-Catholic" here means unbelievers, heretics and schismatics.

What is here said about non-Catholics generally holds also for children of apostate Catholic parents (C. 750, 751).

a) One may baptize such a child against the will of its parents if it is foreseen that the child will *die* before attaining the *use of reason* (C. 750).

If death is certain the child must be baptized unless a greater detriment would follow to religion. If death is only probable one may baptize (S. Offic. 18 jul. 1894). When a contagious disease breaks out a healthy child is not to be considered in danger of death merely because it is in danger of infection (S. C. de prop. fide. 17 aug. 1777).

b) *Apart from the danger of death* such children may be baptized if their Catholic education is assured and the consent of the father or mother, grandfather or grandmother or guardian is had, or if there is no one who has parental authority over the child or who can exercise such authority (C. 750).

If the Catholic *education* of the child is not assured Baptism is forbidden even should the parents request it. If the Catholic training is assured the child may be baptized at the request of one party even though it is foreseen that the other party will have the child baptized again by a Protestant minister.

If *one of the parties* in authority *is Catholic* and a promise is made to rear the child a Catholic, Baptism should be administered provided there is hope that the child will actually be reared a Catholic (S. Offic. 6-8 jul. 1898 ad 4).

c) If such children have *attained the use of reason* and ask to be baptized and are sufficiently instructed in the Catholic Faith, they can and must be baptized even against the will of non-Catholic parents provided there is sufficient guarantee that they will live as Catholics.

Should grave detriment to religion follow such a Baptism its administration may be postponed.

477. — 3. Prematurely born children, if certainly alive, are to be baptized absolutely no matter what their stage of development. In case of doubt as to whether an aborted human fetus is still alive Baptism is administered conditionally (C. 747).

Even though miscarriage take place before the fortieth day Baptism is administered absolutely if life is certainly present.

4. *Monstrosities,* or monstrous forms, however misshapen, that are alive must be baptized. If one doubts whether there be one or more individuals, one is to be baptized absolutely, the other conditionally (C. 748).

The condition reads: *Si non es baptizatus.*

478. — 5. *Children in the womb* may not be baptized as long as there is hope that they will be born in the normal manner and that Baptism will be possible (C. 746).

If the head alone is delivered and there is danger of death, Baptism is administered thereon, no conditional repetition being subsequently necessary (C. 746). If death threatens after some other member is presented, Baptism is administered conditionally upon it (si capax es). Should the child survive birth, Baptism must be repeated conditionally (si non es baptizatus) — If no part of the child is delivered it can be reached with a syringe and baptized (the child itse'f being reached and not merely the amniotic membrane confer 467). Baptism is administered conditionally (si valet), since many doubt the validity of such a Baptism. If the child is thereafter born alive, Baptism is to be repeated conditionally.

Should the mother die before the child is born there remains the grave obligation of charity to baptize if there is any hope that the child is still alive. Such a hope is generally not had if the mother dies within the first four months of gestation. Should the pregnant woman die and the child still probably be alive, it should first be baptized conditionally in the womb as best it may and then extracted and conditionally rebaptized. — The priest should not fail to remind the deceased mother's relatives of this obligation. — To avoid legal implications and scandal the priest should neither order a Cæsarean operation nor undertake to perform it himself.

479.   Chapter V

THE SPONSORS

I. Necessity of Sponsors. 1. For *solemn Baptism*
there is a grave obligation to have a sponsor (C. 762).

If only one sponsor is had it may be a man or woman. If two
are had, one must be a man and the other a woman (C. 764). If
two men or two women stand for a child it would be a venial sin
if both sponsors are of the same sex as the child. It is not certain
whether in other cases there would be a grave sin since the new
Code. — Not more than two sponsors are permissible (C. 764). If
the parents have designated more than two the superfluous ones
may be admitted as honorary sponsors or baptismal witnesses.

2. *In private Baptism* there should also be a sponsor
if one can easily be had; if one is not employed a sponsor
should at least be present when the ceremonies are supplied (C. 762).

3. If in *conditional repetition* of Baptism the same
sponsor can be had who was present for the first Baptism,
he must be engaged. In other cases where Baptism is
conditionally repeated no sponsor is necessary (C. 763).

If the sponsor for the first Baptism is unavailable a different one
may be procured. A sponsor must be secured when the ceremonies
are to be supplied if there was no sponsor for the first Baptism
(Cf. C. 762).

**480. — II. Conditions for Valid and Lawful
Sponsorship.** 1. *Validity* requires the following conditions for the godparent (C. 765).

a) He must be *baptized,* have the *use of reason* and
the *intention* of acting as sponsor.

b) He must not be a member of any heretical or
schismatical *sect;* nor be *excommunicated* by condemnatory or declaratory sentence, nor *infamous* by law, and

not be barred from legitimate ecclesiastical acts. Likewise no *deposed* or *degraded* cleric may be sponsor.

c) The godparent must not be the *father, mother* or *spouse* of the one to be baptized.

d) He must be *designated* as the sponsor either by the person to be baptized or by his parents or guardians; in default of these, by the minister of Baptism.

If the parents choose as sponsor one who has not the qualifications required for valid and lawful sponsorship the minister may reject him and designate another. Should the person rejected nevertheless touch the child during Baptism he would not thereby become the godparent. — If no one has been chosen as sponsor, but someone nevertheless touches the child with the intention of acting as sponsor his action does not make him sponsor.

e) He must physically *hold* or *touch* the one being baptized or *receive* the baptized person from the sacred font or from the hands of the minister.

It is not required that the sponsor answer the questions. — One can be sponsor also by proxy.

481. — 2. *Lawfulness* requires the following conditions in a sponsor (C. 766):

a) He must be *fourteen* years of age.

For a reasonable cause the minister may require someone more advanced in age or admit someone under fourteen.

b) The sponsor must not be *excommunicated* for some notorious crime nor be *barred* from legitimate ecclesiastical acts nor be *infamous* by law.

If a judicial sentence has been inflicted sponsorship would be invalid.

He must not be under *interdict* nor known as a *public criminal* nor be *infamous* in fact.

c) A godparent must know the *fundamental truths* of Faith.

d) He must not be a *novice* or a *professed religious*.

An exception is made in case of necessity if the local Superior gives express permission.

e) If in *major Orders* he requires the express permission of his Ordinary.

N. B. If the pastor doubts whether one may validly or lawfully act as sponsor, he should consult the Ordinary if time permits (C. 769).

482. — III. The Effects of Sponsorship. 1. Sponsors must be solicitous for the *spiritual welfare* of their godchild during his entire life if the parents neglect their duty and the child is in need of this attention (C. 769).

2. Sponsors contract a *spiritual relationship* with their godchildren.

This relationship arises whether the Baptism is solemn or private, provided it is valid; not, however, if one acts as sponsor only when the ceremonies are supplied (C. 769). — If Baptism is readministered conditionally neither the sponsor at the first nor the sponsor at the second Baptism contracts this relationship; unless the same person is sponsor at both Baptisms (C. 763).

483.   Chapter VI

THE ADMINISTRATION OF BAPTISM

I. The Obligation of the Baptismal Rite. 1. *Solemn Baptism* is obligatory both for children and for adults. Exception is made only in danger of death.

The omission of an important ceremony is *mortally sinful*, e.g., the anointings with the oil of catechumens or chrism, breathing upon the subject, the use of salt, the Creed. The use of old oils is also mortally sinful unless one cannot obtain new oils. According to a decision of the Sacred Congregation of Rites, the use of saliva may be omitted for a reasonable cause of hygiene, or when this ceremony would constitute a danger of contracting or spreading disease (Jan. 14, 1944).

If the hair is very thick it should be parted so that in *anointing with chrism* at least a little of the oil touches the scalp; one may also anoint very high on the forehead.

The *formula for infants* is used for all who have not attained the use of reason (children before completing their seventh year, the insane). For all others the formula for adults is used (Cf. The Ritual and C. 745). For a grave and reasonable cause the local Ordinary may permit the use of the formula for infants in baptizing adults (C. 755). — He may allow Baptism *without the ceremonies* only in the case of conditional Baptism of adult heretics (C. 759).

The *questions* and answers must be recited first in Latin; they may then be repeated in the vernacular for the sponsor. (Some dioceses have the privileges of asking the questions in the vernacular only.)

When a priest or deacon baptizing *in danger of death* omits the ceremonies he should, if time permits, add the ceremonies that follow Baptism (C. 759).

484. — 2. *A Christian name* should be given a person in Baptism.

If pastors cannot persuade parents to do this they should add the name of a Saint to the one chosen by the parents and enter both names in the baptismal register (C. 761). — In Confirmation another name may be added to the baptismal names.

3. For the Baptism of adults it is becoming that both minister and subject be *fasting*. Unless there are important reasons to excuse them, adults should *assist at Mass* and *receive Holy Communion* immediately after Baptism. (C. 753).

The fact that salt has been taken in Baptism is no hindrance to the reception of Holy Communion.

4. The *prompt supplying* of the ceremonies omitted is a grave obligation (C. 759).

One is excused from this if a ceremony was omitted by mistake and cannot be supplied without causing scandal or gossip.

It is not customary to supply the ceremonies in the case of a convert whose former Baptism was certainly valid.

If the Baptism is repeated conditionally the ceremonies must be supplied only when they were omitted in the first Baptism; in other cases repetition of the ceremonies is permitted (C. 760).

485. — II. The Place of Baptism. 1. The proper place for *solemn Baptism* is the baptistry of a church or public oratory (C. 773).

In an exceptional case and for a reasonable cause the local Ordinary may permit Baptism in a private home (C. 776). — He can more readily allow Baptism in the sacristy. — If a child cannot be taken to church without great detriment to the parents (e.g., defamation) or to itself, and if it is impossible to have recourse to the Ordinary, this permission may be presumed.

The Second Plenary Council of Baltimore (237) committed it to the prudence and conscience of missionaries in towns and villages where there is no church to *baptize babies in the home* if they cannot be taken to the nearest church or mission station because of bad weather, difficult journey (at least 3 miles in some dioceses), poverty of parents or other grave cause. Such Baptisms must be administered in a becoming place (C. 776) and with all the ceremonies (AAS 17-452).

2. *Private Baptism* may be administered in any place (C. 771).

Concerning private Baptism see 465.

486. — III. Recording the Baptism. After Baptism the *pastor* must enter the necessary data in the *baptismal register* without delay (C. 777).

Even when another priest baptizes, the entry into the register must be made by the pastor or by his representative, e.g., the *vicarius oeconomus* or *substitutus*. It is sufficient, however, if the pastor countersigns the entry made by another.

The following data must be entered: The *name* of the baptized, his parents, sponsors and the minister; the *place* and *date* of Baptism (C. 777).

In case of an *illegitimate child* the name of the mother is entered if her motherhood is publicly known or if of her own accord she requests in writing or before two witnesses that her name be entered. The name of the father is entered if he, like the mother, freely requests this or is known to be the father by some public authentic document. In other cases the baptized is entered as the child of an unknown father, or of unknown parents (C. 777).

487. *Section II*

Confirmation

Confirmation is the Sacrament in which, through the imposition of hands and anointing with chrism together with the use of certain sacred words, a baptized person receives the Holy Ghost in order to steadfastly confess his faith by word and deed.

Chapter I

THE EXTERNAL SIGN AND EFFECTS OF CONFIRMATION

I. Matter. 1. The *remote valid matter* is chrism, a mixture of olive oil and balm blessed by the bishop.

It is controverted whether the addition of balm, and whether the blessing by a bishop is necessary. Practically, the faculty to bless the chrism is never given to those priests who obtain faculties to confirm (C. 781). — It is likewise doubtful whether Confirmation would be valid if administered with the oil of catechumens or the oil for anointing the sick.

Lawfulness requires that the chrism be blessed on the previous Maundy Thursday.

For an urgent reason older chrism may be used.

2. The *proximate matter* is the anointing with chrism in the form of a cross and the simultaneous imposition of the hand.

Validity requires only that imposition of the hand which accompanies the anointing; not the extension of hands at the beginning nor the one at the end of the Confirmation ceremony. Anointing may not be done by means of an instrument (C. 781).

II. The form used in the Latin rite is *Signo te signo*

crucis et confirmo te chrismate salutis in nomine Patris et Filii et Spiritus Sancti.

The words "signo te" and "confirmo te" are certainly necessary for validity; the others are at least required for lawfulness.

III. The effects of Confirmation are: an increase of sanctifying grace and of the Gifts of the Holy Ghost, a strengthening of faith to combat the enemies of salvation, and the impression of an indelible character which marks the recipient as a soldier of Christ.

488. Chapter II

MINISTER AND RECIPIENT OF CONFIRMATION

I. The ordinary minister of Confirmation is the Bishop (C. 782).

A bishop *validly* confirms the faithful at any time and place. *Lawfully* a bishop confirms only within his own diocese, not only his own subjects, but also strangers, unless the Ordinaries of the latter have expressly forbidden this. — Outside his own territory he must have at least the reasonably presumed permission of the respective Ordinary. Without the said permission he may confirm his own subjects outside his own diocese provided he confirms privately, i.e., without the staff and mitre (C. 783).

II. The extraordinary minister of Confirmation is a priest to whom the faculty to confirm has been given either by common law or by a general or special indult of the Holy See (C. 782).

1. In virtue of the regulations of *common law* the following can confirm:

Cardinals, abbots and prelates *nullius,* vicars and prefects apostolic who have not been consecrated bishops (C. 782).

The said local Ordinaries cannot validly confirm after the expiration of their term of office, nor outside their respective territories, even should the local Ordinary of such another territory give them permission (C. 782). Within the territory of their jurisdiction they may also confirm strangers, except in cases where the Ordinary of such strangers has explicitly forbidden it (C. 784).

2. By *general indult* of the Holy See, the faculty to confirm as extraordinary ministers, only in the cases and under the conditions mentioned below, is given to the following priests by a Decree of the Sacred Congregation of the Sacraments, September 14, 1946:

Pastors having their own parochial territory, *Vicars* mentioned in C. 471, *Administrators* (vicarii oeconomi) and *Priests* to whom the full care of souls with all the rights and duties of pastors has been entrusted in an exclusive and permanent matter in a certain territory with its own definite church. These priests can validly and lawfully confirm all the faithful in their territory who by reason of grave illness are in danger of death.

Pastors here does not include *personal* or *family pastors* who have not been assigned their own proper territorial limits. Even pastors of language or *national parishes* do not have the faculty in virtue of this Decree, *unless* they have their own territory. In our country a priest who is pastor of all the Germans, Italians, Poles, the Colored, etc. of a city, or district, does have a territory, even though it is cumulative with that of another parish or number of parishes, and, therefore, such pastors have the faculty to confirm. *Vicars*, i.e., priests who are assigned to exercise the actual care of souls in parishes united *pleno jure* to a religious house, cathedral chapter, or to some other moral person, and who have all the rights and duties of pastors. *Administrators*, i.e., priests who are appointed by the local Ordinary to administer vacant parishes until proper pastors can be appointed to them.

These priests cannot delegate their faculty to confirm (C. 210).

The following do not have the faculty to confirm: The *assistant priest* or curate (vicar co-operator, C. 476); the *vicar substitute*, who with the approval of the Ordinary takes the place of the pastor during the latter's absence (C. 474); the *vicar adjutor* who is assigned to assist an aged or infirm pastor (C. 475) even though he has all the rights and duties of a pastor, and though he may be canonically (C. 451) designated as "pastor." Neither does the

Vicar General of a diocese, nor the *Vicar Capitular* who governs the diocese during its vacancy, have the faculty to confirm unless he is at the same time pastor as described above.

Neither is this faculty enjoyed by *rectors* to whom the care of souls is assigned in a certain part of a parish. (The so-called "rectors of churches" are priests who have charge of some church that is neither parochial, nor capitular, nor annexed to a house of a religious community. They cannot confirm because they do not have the exclusive care of souls, since the pastor, for example, can also validly assist at marriages in their district; generally, rectors do not have all the rights and duties of pastors, e.g., the obligation to apply the *Missa pro populo*.)

The "faithful in danger of death" may be either adults or children who have not yet attained the use of reason. — To validly confirm the faithful of an Oriental rite a special indult is required according to C. 782. Such an indult was granted in a Decree of May 1, 1948 concerning those Orientals who are entrusted to the care of the Latin clergy. (AAS 40-422.) In the Apostolic Constitution of November 30, 1894 it was specified that "every Oriental outside the territory of a Patriarch is under the charge of the Latin clergy."

At the request of the U. S. Hierarchy the faculty to confirm in danger of death children and infants (not the mothers) under their care was extended to the head chaplain in hospitals with maternity wards and foundling homes, but on the condition that not only the bishop, but even the local pastor is not available or is lawfully impeded from conferring the Confirmation. (Oct. 25, 1948.)

Similar to Extreme Unction, Confirmation can be administered to one in danger of death from a mortal wound, or, an injury received in a serious accident, or in consequence of being poisoned either by himself or by others.

If the extraordinary minister, for good and solid reasons, judged a person to be in danger of death and administered Confirmation, the sacrament is both validly and lawfully conferred, even if as a matter of fact no such danger of death was present.

These priests can confirm only within their own territory. Within their territory they confirm any Catholic, even strangers and pilgrims.

They may confirm the sick even if these are brought into their district temporarily for the sole purpose of being confirmed, being brought in, for example, from a neighboring parish whose pastor refuses to administer the sacrament. In their own territories these priests may confirm persons who are staying in places which have been withdrawn from parochial jurisdiction, e.g., seminaries, hospitals, sanitaria, guest-houses, and similar institutions, including religious Institutes howsoever exempt.

By overstepping the limits of this mandate priests act invalidly and incur the penalties mentioned in C. 2365.

Since this privilege is not granted to these priests for their personal advantage they have a duty to administer the sacrament.

Only then may the priests mentioned use this faculty to confirm if no bishop, even a titular bishop, is available; or if the bishop is impeded from conferring Confirmation in person. Under these conditions priests may confirm in the episcopal city itself.

Should a priest falsely, but in good faith, assume that no bishop was available or that the bishop present was prevented from confirming, the Confirmation is valid. — If he does not act in good faith, he incurs the penalties mentioned in C. 2365, and loses the faculty to confirm. However, since he incurs the penalties only by "daring" to confirm, any circumstance that lessens his liability excuses him from the penalties according to C. 2229. Confirmation thus administered would be valid, even though the priest was not in good faith.

The Rite for this extraordinary administration of Confirmation is found in the Appendix to the Roman Ritual.

According to C. 798 this administration of Confirmation shall be recorded in the parish confirmation register.

The notation in the register shall be followed by the remark: *Confirmation conferred by Apostolic indult, the person being in danger of death from grave illness.* Ordinaries are frequently satisfied with the simple remark: *Confirmation of necessity.* Besides, the minister must also enter his own name with the name of the one confirmed. If the one confirmed is not a parishioner, this, too, must be mentioned stating to which parish or diocese he does belong. Likewise, the names of the parents and sponsors, the day and the place of Confirmation are also recorded.

The Confirmation is likewise to be entered in the baptismal register. Should the confirmed belong to another parish, the pastor thereof shall be notified of the confirmation with an authentic document containing the data mentioned.

In addition to this the extraordinary minister shall immediately notify his proper diocesan Ordinary of the Confirmation in each individual case by means of an authentic document, mentioning all circumstances that affect the case.

3. In virtue of a *special indult* priests of the Latin rite other than those mentioned above under 2, are sometimes also empowered to administer Confirmation to members of another rite.

Unless such an indult explicitly provides otherwise, priests of the Latin rite can validly confirm only the faithful of their own rite (C. 782).

III. The Recipient. 1. *Valid* reception of Confirmation requires that the subject be baptized. Of those who have attained the use of reason it is furthermore required that they have at some time made at least the implicit intention to be confirmed and have not revoked this intention.

2. *Lawful* reception requires the state of grace. Whoever has reached the age of discretion must furthermore be adequately instructed (C. 786).

Grace in this instance need not be recovered by confession. — Confirmation should generally be received not long after attaining the use of reason. For grave reasons Confirmation may be given at an earlier age (C. 788). Such a reason would be a well-founded fear that the child would otherwise have to wait very long before being confirmed. — Adults who are baptized on their deathbed, should not be confirmed if they can no longer be given instruction sufficient to awaken a desire for this sacrament (S. Offic. 10. april. 1861, C. 786). — Neither fasting nor Holy Communion is prescribed for the reception of Confirmation.

3. A *grave obligation* to be confirmed cannot be proved with certainty.

He sins gravely, however, who refuses to be confirmed out of contempt. Great stress should be laid upon the reception of this holy Sacrament by reason of the increased paganizing influences of our times.

489. Chapter III

SPONSORS AND RITE OF CONFIRMATION

I. The Sponsors. 1. It is a *serious obligation* to have a sponsor for Confirmation if this be possible (C. 793).

Each confirmand should have only one sponsor. One should not be sponsor to more than one or two persons to be confirmed. For a reasonable cause the minister may make an exception to this rule (C. 794).

2. *Valid* sponsorship for Confirmation demands the same requisites as sponsorship for Baptism (Cf. 480); moreover, the sponsor must be confirmed (C. 795).

3. *Lawful* sponsorship likewise requires the same conditions as for Baptism (Cf. 481). But the sponsor for Confirmation may not be the confirmand's godparent, unless Confirmation is administered immediately after Baptism. The Confirmation sponsor must furthermore be of the same sex as the one to be confirmed. The minister may dispense from these latter two regulations for some reasonable cause (C. 796).

4. *The effect* of sponsorship is a spiritual relationship between sponsor and confirmed, which, however, is not a matrimonial impediment (Cf. C. 1079). It likewise creates an obligation to look after the spiritual welfare of the person confirmed (C. 797).

490. — II. The Rite. 1. *Solemn* Confirmation is administered by the bishop with miter and staff.

An ordinary priest should wear at least the alb and stole. If he has an Apostolic indult to confirm he must first read this to the faithful in the vernacular. But he who has faculties from the Code need not refer to this. The Second Plenary Council of Baltimore (252) prescribes the use of cards from which the pastor reads the confirmation names to the bishop confirming.

2. In the *private* administration of Confirmation the stole alone suffices for any good reason (S. Offic. 12. feb. 1851).

N. B. Confirmation may be administered on any day and at any hour; the most appropriate time, however, is the Pentecostal season (C. 790). — The church is the most proper place in which to confirm. For a good reason any other becoming place may be chosen (C. 791). The reception of Confirmation, like that of Baptism (Cf. 486), should be recorded in a special Confirmation book by the pastor. The respective names should be entered, and notification thereof should also be made in the baptismal register. — Should the one confirmed belong to another parish, the name of this parish and the diocese must also be entered. Furthermore, his pastor must be notified with an authentic certificate containing all the required data.

491. *Section III*

The Holy Eucharist

Since the Sacrament of the Holy Eucharist in its confection is inseparably bound up with the offering of an oblation, we here treat of the Holy Eucharist as a Sacrament and as a Sacrifice.

First Division

THE HOLY EUCHARIST AS A SACRAMENT

The *Most Blessed Sacrament* of the Altar is the Sacrament in which the Body and Blood of Christ are present under the forms of bread and wine for the spiritual nourishment of our souls.

Chapter I

THE OUTWARD SIGN OF THE HOLY EUCHARIST

I. Matter of the Holy Eucharist. 1. The *remote valid matter* is wheat bread and grape wine.

a) The *bread* must be made of wheat flour mixed with natural water and baked by the application of heat.

Bread made of any *other grain,* e.g., barley, oats, millet, buck-wheat, corn, etc. is invalid matter. Rye bread is doubtful. Bread made from any *variety of wheat* is valid, e.g., smooth, bearded, summer or winter wheat. In some localities spelt is used without scruple.

Invalid matter is bread made with *milk, wine, oil, butter,* etc. — If only a small portion of such ingredients were added, so that one might still say the bread is made with water, the matter thus prepared would be valid but unlawful.

Unbaked dough is invalid matter, as also is dough *fried* in butter or *cooked* in water.

b) The *wine,* to be valid, must be made of ripe grapes.

Invalid matter is verjuice (wine made from unripe grapes), wine from which the alcohol has been extracted, brandy, cider, etc.

492. — 2. The ***proximate valid*** matter of the Holy Eucharist is bread and wine *physically present* and *properly designated* by the intention of the priest.

The matter is *physically present,* and consecration valid, even though the priest does not perceive the host, e.g., because of blindness or because he forgot to uncover the ciborium. To leave the ciborium covered intentionally is a venial sin. — Consecration is doubtful if the hosts are locked in the tabernacle, or if they accidentally get between the pages of the missal, under the corporal or chalice. — The matter is no longer physically present if it is too far removed (more than 50 or 60 feet) from the altar. Neither is matter physically present for consecration if it is behind the altar.

The matter is not *properly designated* and therefore not consecrated if it is present on the altar but unknown to the priest. — If the priest intends to consecrate half of the hosts in the ciborium w thout determining which ones, none are consecrated. If the priest m stakes the number of hosts, all of them will, nevertheless, be consecrated provided his principal intention is to consecrate all the hosts in the ciborium or on the corporal, or if he has the intention to consecrate what he holds in his hands. If he discovers at the time of Communion that there are two large hosts stuck together, he may rest assured that both are consecrated (Cf. 451).

If the priest has only a *general intention* to consecrate, the individual drops of wine clinging to the inside of the chalice are probably not consecrated. The same holds for the minute fragments that detach themselves from the hosts before the consecration, but which to all appearances are still attached to the hosts. Drops of wine adhering to the exterior of the chalice, and fragments that before the consecration do not cling to the host are not consecrated. If it is uncertain whether they were completely separated from the host before consecration they must be handled with proper reverence.

If, by mistake, consecrated hosts become *mingled* with unconsecrated ones, the priest should consecrate them all at a subsequent Mass, his intention being to consecrate all those that are not already consecrated.

493. — 3. Remote Lawful Matter

a) *Bread* is lawful matter under these conditions:

α) If it is made without the admixture of any other substance besides wheat flour and water.

If only a relatively small quantity of another substance is added consecration will still be valid; the admixture of a larger quantity will render the consecration invalid.

β) If it is fresh or recently baked.

If the bread has just begun to mold it is still valid matter. Hosts that are completely moldy are no longer valid matter, because the mold fungus is imperceptible to the naked eye, and that which we usually designate as "mold" is, so to say, only its blossom. The decomposition of bread takes place more or less rapidly according to the humidity of the climate. Generally speaking, hosts for consecration should not be more than a fortnight or a month old. On the renewal of the Sacred Species, confer 520.

γ) In the Latin Church hosts must be unleavened and circular in form. Hosts for the Sacrifice of the Mass should be larger than those used for the Communion of the faithful. All hosts must be clean.

Leavened bread may be used in the Latin rite only to complete the Sacrifice already begun; not to confect the Sacrament for Viaticum.

It is venially sinful to consecrate a *disfigured* or *soiled* host; should one observe these defects only after the offertory, he may consecrate such a host. — If no large host is available the priest may celebrate Mass with a small host even though it be a Mass of private devotion; provided, of course, that no scandal will ensue. No grave reason is required.

494. b) *Wine* is lawful matter if it is unadulterated, fermented, unspoiled and clear.

Additions and *adulterations* render the wine invalid or unlawful according to the greater or lesser amount thereof. It is not lawful to add potash or tartar in order to make the wine more palatable. — On the contrary, one may add *alcohol* in order the better to preserve the wine. It is required, however, that the alcohol be derived from grapes and that the admixture take place while the wine is still very young (when violent fermentation has begun to subside). Only so much may be added that the sum total of the alcoholic content will not exceed 12%; should the alcoholic content naturally exceed that amount one may fortify it up to 18%. — It seems lawful to clear cloudy wine if this be done with isinglass or albumen, because these substances together with the impurities contained in the wine settle to the bottom of the container and can be removed with the sediment when the wine is drawn off. The use of tannic acid for this purpose is illicit since it is impossible subsequently to completely separate it from the wine.

Raisin wine may be lawfully used for sacramental purposes. The raisins are left to swell in water and are then pressed. Wine so made must have the color, taste and odor of wine. Wine made by a *second pressing* is invalid matter if water has been added.

A little water must be added to the wine during the Holy Sacrifice. Should a priest forget to do so at the offertory, this must be done sometime before consecration; it may never be done after the consecration of the chalice. A single drop of water is enough to comply with the rubic. If the water added should exceed a third part of the wine the latter would become doubtful matter; light wine would thereby become invalid.

Unfermented wine (must, grapejuice) is unlawful matter. Wine is sometimes cloudy because it is still working; such wine may be used for Mass without hesitation. Disturbances arising from the presence of acetic or lactic acid or from mold render the wine invalid matter.

Wine just *beginning to sour* is valid but unlawful matter. Only in the very first stages of its turning sour is such wine permissible if no other is available. Americans should not mistake dry wine for sour wine.

495. — 4. *Proximate Lawful Matter.* Under penalty of a mortal sin the bread and also the wine to be consecrated must be present on the altar (i.e., on the altar stone) and on the corporal.

Matter to be consecrated need not be in immediate contact with the corporal. It suffices that at the moment of consecration it be either in the hand of the priest or in an open consecrated vessel. If no ciborium is available one may not place hosts to be consecrated upon another corporal besides the one used for the Mass, even though it be placed upon the latter. — If the altar stone is quite small, it suffices that a part of the base of the ciborium rest on the stone. — If the priest has the intention to consecrate the hosts in the ciborium they will be consecrated even though at the time of consecration the ciborium is not on the corporal.

Hosts to be consecrated for the faithful had best be placed on the altar *at the very beginning* of the Mass; they should be present at least at the offertory. — If they are brought only after the offertory they are to be offered mentally. For some reasonable cause hosts may be brought out shortly after the offertory; a grave reason is necessary if the Preface has already begun; after the Canon has commenced only a very grave cause would be a justifying reason, e.g., if otherwise a large number of the congregation could not communicate. If only one or the other person would thus be deprived of Communion a small particle of the large host may be given him.

496. — II. Form of the Holy Eucharist. The **essential** words for the consecration of bread are: *Hoc est corpus meum;* and for consecrating the wine: *Hic est calix sanguinis mei.*

All the other words are prescribed under grave sin except the word *enim,* the omission of which is only a venial sin.

The priest should heed the exhortation of the Missal and not be disquieted if he cannot recall having correctly said everything which is required for consecration. — If it is certain or doubtful whether some essential part was omitted, the form should be repeated absolutely or conditionally. If the priest notices this at the time of consecration the form alone is repeated, but if he adverts to it only later in the Mass he should repeat beginning with the words *Qui pridie.* If the consecration of the wine alone is concerned, then he starts with the words *Simili modo.* — Only when the doubt is well-founded is there a duty to repeat. In itself it is a grievous sin to repeat the form without a just reason; but a perplexed conscience may excuse one from all sin.

497.   Chapter II

EFFECTS OF THE HOLY EUCHARIST

I. The particular effects of the Holy Eucharist consist primarily in this, that It nourishes and strengthens the spiritual life of our souls, unites us most intimately with Christ and His Mystical Body, the Church, increases sanctifying grace in us, weakens our evil inclinations and confers upon us a pledge of eternal life.

These graces are essentially the same whether one receives a large or small host; or whether one receives under one or both species. Evidently one obtains a greater measure of graces by a better preparation.

II. The time when these effects are produced is not the moment the Sacrament is confected, but when It is received; hence, when the Sacred Species are consumed.

The confection and reception of the Sacrament of the Holy Eucharist are not simultaneous. — If the Sacred Species are retained in the mouth until They are dissolved one does not receive the Sacrament. — If one vomits the Sacred Species, one has, nevertheless, received the Sacrament. — It is not certain whether the sacramental graces are imparted when the Sacrament is received by methods of artificial nutrition. However, in 1886 and 1919 the Holy Office in particular responses said this should not be done. Moreover, it is certain that there is no obligation to administer the Sacrament in this manner. — It is disputed whether the measure of grace *ex opere operantis* is increased if, after receiving Holy Communion, the disposition of the recipient becomes more fervent while Christ is still present in the Sacred Species. About eight or ten minutes are required for the Species to decompose in a healthy stomach. Although more time is required in case of the sick, nevertheless, they may take a stomach lotion three hours after receiving Holy Communion without any fear of irreverence to the Sacred Species.

498.   Chapter III

CONSECRATOR AND MINISTER OF THE HOLY EUCHARIST

I. The consecrator of the Blessed Sacrament is every priest, and only a priest.

Even heretical and schismatical priests can validly consecrate. — Several priests may co-consecrate one and the same matter but only at an ordination Mass and at the consecration of a bishop. Should one of the co-celebrants accidentally finish the form sooner than the others, these still consecrate, because such consecrations are

considered morally simultaneous, since each intends to consecrate
together with the others.

II. The minister of the Holy Eucharist must be
possessed of the power of jurisdiction besides that of
Holy Orders.

1. With reference to the *power of orders* we distinguish the ordinary and the extraordinary minister.

a) The *ordinary* minister of Holy Communion is every
priest (C. 845).

For the sake of devotion a priest may give himself Holy Communion outside of Mass, but only in case he cannot celebrate and
no other priest is available to administer the Sacrament to him.

b) The *extraordinary* minister of Holy Communion is
the deacon; but he needs the permission of the local
Ordinary or the pastor. This permission should be given
only for a grave reason. In case of necessity it may be
presumed.

The rector of a church is, in this respect, equivalent to a pastor.

A reason justifying *this permission* would be, for example, if the
priest were occupied hearing confessions, etc. — In distributing Holy
Communion the deacon wears the stole after the manner of a
deacon; otherwise he observes the same *rubrics* as the priest. Thus
he gives the blessing with the Blessed Sacrament after communicating the sick. At the *Indulgentiam* and after distributing outside
of Mass, according to the new ritual, he gives the blessing with
his hand.

Should anyone distribute Holy Communion who has not yet
received the diaconate he thereby becomes irregular (C. 985). —
In extreme necessity, however, even a layman may administer
Communion to others or to himself, if this can be done without
scandal. If in certain sicknesses the administration of Viaticum
requires special skill the priest may allow the Sister infirmarian
to administer It, using a spoon.

499. — 2. The *power of jurisdiction* may be had in
virtue of one's office or by reason of special regulations of
Canon Law.

a) In virtue of their office the following are empowered to distribute Holy Communion; the local Ordinary in his diocese, the pastor in his parish, and the superior in a clerical religious community.

The *pastor* has the special right to take Holy Communion publicly to the sick in his parish. Other priests may do so only in case of necessity or with at least presumed permission of the pastor (C. 848). Likewise, only the pastor may administer Holy Viaticum to the sick within his parish either publicly or privately (C. 850). It makes no difference whether the sick are his parishioners or not (C. 848, 850). — This pastoral right extends only to that first administration of Viaticum prescribed by Divine Law. Should a sick person thereafter desire to receive the Sacrament repeatedly in the same illness, other priests may administer It, but only according to the norm indicated in the following number.

Religious are an exception to this rule. In clerical religious communities the superior has the right and obligation to administer Viaticum to all his professed subjects, to the novices, and to all who remain in the cloister day and night, as servants, students, guests, sick or convalescents. — In convents of nuns this right is reserved to the ordinary confessor or his representative. — In communities of Sisters and Brothers it is again a pastoral right, unless the bishop has entrusted these lay religious to the care of a chaplain (C. 514).

500. *b)* In virtue of *common law* any priest may distribute Holy Communion during his Mass and, in celebrating privately, also immediately before or after Mass (C. 846).

The local Ordinary may prohibit the distribution of Holy Communion during a Mass said in a private chapel (C. 869). In order to distribute Holy Communion *outside of Mass* one must have at least the presumed permission of the rector of the church (C. 846). One appointed as assistant priest has this requisite permission. — Any priest may take Holy Communion to the *sick* privately (not the prescribed Viaticum) with the presumed permission of the priest to whose care the Blessed Sacrament is entrusted (C. 849). Holy Communion may be taken to the sick privately for a just reason (Cf. C. 847).

501.   Chapter IV

THE RECIPIENT OF HOLY COMMUNION

I. Person of the Receiver. 1. Every baptized person is *capable* of receiving the Holy Sacrament of the Altar.

An unbaptized person consuming the Sacred Species receives the Body and Blood of Christ, but not a Sacrament.

2. Holy Communion is *lawfully* received only under the following conditions:

a) The recipient must have attained to the *use of reason* and be possessed of the *requisite knowledge.*

Children who are so young that they have neither knowledge nor understanding of this Sacrament may not receive Holy Communion (C. 854). — Children in danger of death must be given Holy Communion if they are able to discriminate between the Blessed Sacrament and ordinary bread and if there is no danger of irreverence. — Outside the danger of death more complete knowledge of the Christian teaching and better preparation are required. Children must have a knowledge in accordance with their mental capacity of those truths of faith which are necessary for salvation by necessity of means (Cf. 118) and they must be able to approach the altar with a devotion in keeping with their years. — The judgment in this matter belongs in the first place to the child's confessor, then to his parents or guardians. Pastors, however, have the duty to see to it that children do not receive Holy Communion before they reach the age of discretion or before they are properly prepared. If necessary, they may make sure of this by an examination. The admission of children to their First Holy Comunion is not a pastoral right. In some places, however, it is a pastor's right to decide which children may take part in the solemn celebration of First Holy Communion.

Insane persons who have never had the use of reason may not be given Holy Communion. If they have lucid intervals they may receive at such times. Imbeciles and persons who have become feeble-minded by old age may be given Holy Communion several times a year if they are able to distinguish Holy Communion from ordinary food. During the Easter season and in danger of death It must be given them. — Those who, after attaining the use of their reason, become completely insane may be given Communion only in danger of death if one has reason to think they previously desired this and are in the state of grace. However, there is no duty to administer the Sacrament to them. — The same holds for the unconscious. — Furthermore, the following requisite is often lacking in such cases.

502. b) There must be *no danger of irreverence*.

In case of *mortal illness* there must be probability, at least, and in case of ordinary sickness one must be almost certain, that the Sacred Species when received will not be dishonored.

He who is subject to violent *coughing* may communicate between coughing spells if these permit him to swallow the host, since that which is expectorated when coughing does not come from the stomach or gullet, but from the lungs or windpipe. — However, if one is subject to consistent *vomiting* he may not communicate as long as there is danger of the Sacred Species being emitted. If the vomiting has gradually begun to subside (e.g., in dysenteric and cholera cases), a two- to four-hour, or at least a six-hour cessation would seem to indicate a change in the patient's condition and that the slight irritation to the stomach caused by the presence of the Sacred Species would not readily result in another vomiting spell. Should the vomiting occur at irregular intervals (e.g., in injuries and illnesses of the brain, nervous disorders, abdominal inflammation, strangulated hernia or in cases of incessant vomiting of the pregnant) an intermission of approximately twelve hours is required for giving Holy Communion without danger of inducing further vomiting. — It is best (in danger of death) first to give the sick person a small portion of solid or liquid food to see whether his stomach can retain it. If possible a physician should be consulted. Since ice diminishes the irritation that causes vomiting it is advisable to give the patient either ice water or a small piece of ice (about one-half square inch in size). — Often a doubt arises as to whether vomiting will not set in when an anaesthetic is taken before an operation. In such cases Holy Communion may not be administered shortly before the narcotic is given. — Pregnant women, especially in the first months of pregnancy, sometimes experience a nausea that causes them to vomit in the morning; they must not receive Holy Communion until a few days' cessation of the ailment indicates improvement of their condition. — Alcoholics, too, occasionally experience the same disorder brought on by a sickness of the stomach. The only thing for them to do is to rise earlier on Communion days and defer going to church until they have this ordeal over with.

503. — 3. There is an *obligation* to receive Holy Communion during the Easter time (Cf. 396) and in danger of death (C. 864).

It matters not whether death threatens from illness or from an external cause, e.g., before a battle, dangerous operation or execution, etc. — The formula *Accipe Viaticum corporis Domini...* is used only when giving Holy Communion to those who are dangerously ill and then only once, and furthermore, in the case of one condemned to death. In order to spare a sick person's feelings one may always give Holy Communion with the ordinary formula *Corpus Domini...* If one has already communicated on the day when danger of death sets in he is not obliged to receive again that same day; but he is to be earnestly advised to do so (C. 864).

Should the danger of death continue for a length of time it is lawful and fitting that the sick person receive Viaticum also on subsequent days (C. 864). In administering the Sacrament, the priest uses the formula prescribed for Viaticum, unless a reasonable cause excuses him. — Sacrilegious reception of Viaticum does not satisfy the obligation. To avoid infamy Holy Communion may be given secretly to one who has previously received Viaticum sacrilegiously.

504. — II. Spiritual Disposition. 1. The *state of grace*, the *right intention* and a *becoming devotion* are required and sufficient for receiving Holy Communion.

Whoever communicates in conscious mortal sin commits a sacrilege. — He commits a venial sin and is deprived of many graces who receives from some slightly sinful motive (vanity, human respect) or is voluntarily distracted while receiving.

2. If one is conscious of being in a state of mortal sin he must recover the *state of grace* by sacramental confession. — Perfect contrition suffices only in case there is no confessor present and there is an obligation to communicate or celebrate Mass. — A priest thus celebrating must go to confession as soon as possible (C. 807, 856).

a) If one doubts whether or not he has sinned seriously

he need not go to confession; neither must he do so if he has forgotten to confess some grave sin in confession.

If there is a reasonable doubt about one's being in the state of grace one must make an act of perfect contrition. Moral certainty concerning the genuineness of one's sorrow suffices.

b) A confessor is *not considered available* if one cannot obtain any confessor at all without great inconvenience.

Lack of choice between several confessors is *no excuse;* neither is he excused who cannot confess to his regular confessor.

A grave difficulty that is extrinsically connected with confession, *excuses* from confession. Thus if one cannot approach a confessor because of urgent work, infirmity or great distance (about an hour's travel in good weather, presupposing good roads and good health), or because of the danger of scandal or defamation or (according to some authors) if for some extraordinary reason confession to the only available confessor would be invincibly repugnant, e.g., if a priest would have to confess to his nephew. Another excuse from confessing would be if the only grave sin to be confessed is of such a nature that the knowledge thereof would constitute a grave spiritual harm to the confessor. — Great difficulty that is intrinsically connected with confession does not excuse, e.g., the shame one feels in confessing to an acquaintance or one much younger than oneself or to one's subject (a pastor to an assistant).

505. *c*) *A necessity* to celebrate or communicate obtains if Mass or Communion cannot be omitted without scandal, defamation of character or injury to another.

Thus one may have to say Mass so that the faithful may be able to fulfill their Sunday obligation or that one may confect the Eucharist for Viaticum; likewise, if one remembers that he is in the state of sin only when at the altar or Communion rail, or if one is scheduled for a nuptial or funeral Mass.

d) The precept to *confess as soon as possible* (quam-primum) means a priest must confess within three days.

It is supposed that the priest has the oportunity to confess within this time; one need not undertake a long journey for this purpose. — One is obliged to confess on the first day if he foresees that he will not have the opportunity to do so on the two following days, or if he will have to say Mass again on the following day and now has the opportunity to confess. There is *no obligation* for a priest to confess within three days if he has sacrilegiously celebrated, e.g., either because he said Mass without necessity or because he did not avail himself of the opportunity to confess or because he did not make an act of contrition. — If such a priest does not intend to say Mass for a while, he does not sin by not confessing in the meantime.

3. *Daily Communion* requires nothing more than a good intention and the state of grace; however, one should ask the advice of his confessor.

The confessor should pay special attention to the motives of the penitent and see to it that the latter will not neglect his or her duties in consequence of going to Communion every morning. The confessor should above all instruct the communicant regarding the fruitful reception of the Sacrament.

506. — III. Corporal Disposition. 1. The celebrant and communicant must be *fasting.*

a) The essence and duration of the fast. Priests and faithful, before Mass or Holy Communion respectively, must abstain for three hours from solid foods and alcoholic beverages, and for one hour from non-alcoholic beverages. Water does not break the fast. (Pope Pius XII, MOTU PROPRIO, *Sacram Communionem,* March 19, 1957).

The meaning of this rule would be obscured by detailed comment. Therefore, we merely observe that no special circumstances nor excusing causes are required; neither is the consultation of a confessor necessary.

The length of the fast must be measured from the moment of Communion for the laity and from the start of the Mass for the priest saying Mass.

Since both priests and people are earnestly exhorted (*At enixe hortamur*) to observe the former legislation on fasting, we have retained the table for reckoning the time of midnight. The table is practical also for the recitation of Divine Office and the observance of abstinence.

506a. TABLE FOR RECKONING THE TIME OF MIDNIGHT

The following table shows how many minutes our clocks are ahead of (+) or behind (−) true local time, which may be followed in the private celebration of Mass, for the private recitation of Divine Office and in observing the laws of fast and abstinence. The "plus" minutes may be added to our clock time at midnight in the following cities that indicate an addition.

EASTERN TIME

Albany, N. Y. .... −5	Grand Rapids, Mich. .. +42	Raleigh, N. C. .... +14
Altoona, Pa. .... +13	Harrisburg, Pa. .... +7	Richmond, Va. .... +9
Baltimore, Md. .... +6	Hartford, Conn. .... −9	Rochester, N. Y.... ... +10
Boston, Mass. .... −16	Lansing, Mich. .... +38	Saginaw, Mich. .... +36
Brooklyn, N. Y. .... −4	Markette, Mich. .... +49	Savannah, Ga. .... +24
Buffalo, N. Y. .... +15	Miami, Fla. .... +20	Scranton, Pa. .... +2
Burlington, Vt. .... −7	Montreal, Canada ..... −6	St. Augustine, Fla. .. +22
Camden, N. J. 0	Newark, N. J. .... −3	Springfield, Mass. .... −9
Charleston, S. C. ...... +19	New York, N. Y. ...... −4	Syracuse, N. Y. .... +4
Cincinnati, Ohio ...... +38	Ogdensburg, N. Y. .... +2	Tampa, Fla. .... +30
Columbus, Ohio .... +32	Paterson, N. J. .... −3	Toledo, Ohio .... +34
Cleveland, Ohio .... +26	Philadelphia, Pa. 0	Toronto, Can. .... +13
Detroit, Mich. .... +32	Pittsburgh, Pa. .... +20	Washington, D. C. ..... +8
Erie, Pa. .... +20	Portland, Me. .... −19	Wheeling, W. Va. ..... +23
Fall River, Mich. .... −15	Providence, R. I. ...... −14	Wilmington, Del. ...... +2

CENTRAL TIME

Alexandria, La. ...... +10	Galveston, Tex. ...... +19	Oklahoma City .... +30
Amarillo, Tex. ...... +47	Green Bay, Wis. ...... −8	Omaha, Neb. .... +23
Atlanta, Ga. .... −22	Indianapolis, Ind. .... −15	Owensboro, Ky. .... −11
Belleville, Ill. 0	Kansas City, Mo. .... +18	Peoria, Ill. .... −2
Bismark, N. D. .... +43	La Crosse, Wis. .... +3	St. Cloud, Minn. ..... +16
Chicago, Ill. .... −9	Lafayette, La. .... +8	St. Joseph, Mo. ...... +19
Corpus Christi, Tex .. +30	Leavenworth, Kan. .. +19	St. Louis, Mo. .... +1
Covington, Ky. .... −22	Lincoln, Neb. .... +27	St. Paul, Minn. .... +12
Dallas, Tex. .... +27	Little Rock, Ark. ...... +9	San Antonio, Tex. ... +31
Des Moines, Ia. ...... +14	Louisville, Ky. .... −17	Sioux City, Ia. .... +25
Dubuque, Ia. .... +2	Milwaukee, Minn. .... −8	Superior, Wis. .... +8
Duluth, Minn. .... +8	Nashville, Tenn. ...... −13	Tulsa, Okla. .... +24
El Paso, Tex. .... +66	Natchez, Miss. .... +5	Wichita, Kan. .... +29
Fort Wayne, Ind ...... −19	New Orleans, La. 0	Winnipeg, Can. .... +26

MOUNTAIN TIME

Boise, Ida. .... +45	Great Falls, Mont. .... +25	Salt Lake City, ... +27
Cheyenne, Wyo. .... −1	Helena, Mont. .... +28	Santa Fe, N. M. ...... +4
Denver, Col. 0	Phoenix, Ariz. .... +28	Tucson, Ariz. .... +24

PACIFIC TIME

Baker City, Ore. ...... −8	Portland, Ore. .... +10	San Francisco, Cal. .. +10
Fresno, Cal. 0	Reno, Nev. 0	Spokane, Wash. .... −10
Los Angeles, Cal. .... −7	Sacramento, Cal. ...... +6	Seattle, Wash. .... +9

APPROXIMATE ESTIMATION FOR SMALLER TOWNS

N. B. For every fifteen miles east of any city indicated on above table sun time is approximately 1 minute less than the time here shown (and for every 15 miles west, one minute more). Thus a Pittsburgher attending a Thursday night banquet may continue to eat meat until 20 minutes past midnight (clock time); whereas a person in Boltz, Indiana Co., Pa. (60 miles or 1 degree east of Pgh.) may do so only until 16 minutes past midnight, while one in Paris, Washington Co. (30 miles west of Pgh.) may eat meat until 12:22 a. m. Friday morning according to the clock.

ADDITIONAL MINUTES PERMITTED BY SOLAR TIME

The following table shows the minutes that true local time is ahead of solar time on various days of the year. Dates omitted are minus. Thus, one may add these minutes (indicated by bold type) to those above. From Feb. 6 to 18 a Pittsburgher may eat meat until 12:34 a. m. Friday.

DEC. 27 add **1** min., 29:**2**, 31:**3**, JAN. 2:**4**, 5:**5**, 7:**6**, 9:**7**, 12:**8**, 14:**9**, 17:**10**, 20:**11**, 24:**12**, FEB. 1:**13**, 6:**14**, 18:**13**, 26:**12**, MAR. 3:**11**, 7:**10**, 11:**9**, 15:**8**, 19:**7**, 22:**6**; 25:**5**, 28:**4**, APR. 1:**3**, 4:**2**, 7:**1**, JUNE 20:**1**, 24:**2**; 29:**3**, JULY 4:**4**, 11:**5**, 21:**6**, AUG. 1:**5**, 11:**4**, 17:**3**, 21:**2**, 25:**1**.

Water does not break the fast, i. e., any drink which in popular language is called water. This includes mineral water, sulphur water, water that is chemically purified or made drinkable, such as fluorinated water. One may himself add the necessary powder. Carbonated water is also permitted, i. e., water to which gas has been added to make it effervescent. One may slake his thirst immediately before going to Holy Communion.

The fast is broken by taking solid food or alcoholic beverages within three hours and non-alcoholic beverages within one hour before receiving Holy Communion or beginning the celebration of of Mass, even if it be done unintentionally. — In doubt whether one has done so he may receive or celebrate with a quiet conscience. Communion is forbidden under grave sin to one who has broken his fast by taking even a small amount of food or forbidden drink.

507. *b) The precept of fasting* forbids the taking of *solid food* and *beverages* (other than water).

a) The concept of eating.

The following conditions are implied in the concept of eating: **α)** The matter consumed must be taken from without. Therefore, swallowing blood from bleeding gums, etc. does not break the fast. However, if one swallowed the blood sucked from a bleeding finger the fast would be broken. According to the Roman Missal the fast is not broken by voluntarily or involuntarily swallowing the particles of food that remain located in or between the teeth. One who wishes to receive at ten o'clock breaks his fast by placing candy in the mouth before seven and letting it dissolve and be swallowed during the three-hour fasting period. But should one take a coughdrop *long* before seven and accidentally fail to dissolve it completely before seven, he might communicate even though he swallowed some of it (like the remains of food above) after seven. Neither is the fast broken by taking things in the mouth and spitting them out again, e. g., mouth wash, or food and drink for the sake of determining whether they are properly seasoned or cooked. Chewing tobacco is unbecoming and unless done with a good reason is forbidden under venial sin: the fast, however, would not be broken thereby unless one intentionally swallowed some of the tobacco or juice. — **β)** That which is taken must according to the common opinion be digestible. Hence, the fast is not broken by smoking, swallowing a hair, a few grains of sand, a piece of chalk, iron, wood, and probably not by swallowing pieces of fingernails, wax or straw. — **γ)** There must be actual eating. Therefore, the fast is *not* broken by intravenous feeding nor by a nutritive enema, nor by a stomach lotion even though a portion of the liquid or some lubricating grease from the instrument remains in the stomach.

β) *Three hours without solid food or alcoholic drink.*

To communicate or say Mass, morning or night, afternoon or evening, all (including the sick) must abstain from solid food and alcoholic beverages for three hours immediately preceding Communion or the start of Mass. Prior to these three hours the faithful and priests are free to take any kind of food and even alcoholic beverages at meals or between meals even though they have no difficulty in observing the traditional fast, provided they respect the rules of temperance and the obligations of days of fast and abstinence.

Alcoholic beverages are excluded, whether taken in greater or lesser amounts for three hours before communicating or starting Mass. These beverages include hard liquors, straight or mixed, wine, beer, cider, etc. They are forbidden even when mixed with another drink, e. g., coffee.

γ) *One hour without non-alcoholic beverages.*

The celebrant and communicant may continue to take liquids provided they are without alcohol, even after having eaten, up until one hour before Mass and Communion. Such liquids are (according to the Holy Office, September 7, 1898) all beverages and *liquid nourishment* which can be drunk from a glass without mastication. Thus a porridge or puree is not permitted for three hours before receiving or starting Mass. But one is said to drink a broth, coffee, milk, fruit and vegetable juices, and other liquids, even though sweetened or mixed with another substance such as bread crumbs, or into which an egg is broken, as long as that which one drinks has not lost its liquid character. One can drink a raw egg or one that has been slightly boiled. So, too, liquids that contain solid substances in suspension, as chocolates. Care must be taken, however, not to drink meat broths on days of abstinence. — This rule applies to all Masses and Holy Communions, including the Paschal Vigil, the midnight Mass on Christmas and all evening Masses.

508. — *c*) *The Infirm,* even if not bedridden, may take non-alcoholic beverages and that which is really and properly medicine, either in liquid or solid form, before Mass or Holy Communion without any time limit. *Motu Proprio* as before.

The sickness must be real, not merely a slight indisposition or fatigue. It is not necessary, however, that a doctor diagnose the illness. It matters not whether it be grave or slight, acute or chronic, dangerous or not, painful or not painful, whether it be physical, psychic or both. Hence, a violent headache or toothache suffices; likewise the weakness of old age. The patient need not be bedfast. The word "sick" is to be understood in a wide sense and does not suppose grave illness. Hence, if one needs medication without delay because of an indigestion, a bad cold or a hacking cough, he may take it. Likewise, he may take any non-alcoholic liquid for sustenance; and he may do so up to the very moment of Mass or Holy Communion.

Canon 852, 2 is now abrogated by a ruling of the Holy Office (Oct. 21, 1961) on the authority of Pope John XXIII which allows sick persons unable to leave their homes for a week, to receive Holy Communion in the afternoon or evening, even if they are not bed-ridden or in danger of death. They must observe the Eucharistic fast as above. The local priest judges the reasonableness of the request.

True medicine. That which is "really and properly medicine, either in liquid or solid form" may be taken by the sick at any time. Here, too, popular estimation determines what is medicine. Even medicine with an alcoholic base is permitted. So also are pills, tablets, pastilles and any pharmaceutical prescription of a doctor; but not that which is occasionally taken as a medicine, as cognac or a diet of prescribed food.

509. *d*) The fast is *not broken* by that which is taken together with the Sacred Species.

Thus if a priest swallows a piece of cork from the wine bottle or a fly at his first Mass on All Souls' Day he may say the other two Masses. Likewise to one who cannot otherwise swallow the host a little wine may be given even though the wine actually be swallowed first. According to many authors the purification of the ciborium and the consumption of the small fragments contained therein is still allowed for a good reason even after one has consumed the *ablutio digitorum* made with wine and water.

N. B. *Eating* immediately after receiving Holy Communion (within eight or ten minutes) without an urgent reason is an irreverence toward the Blessed Sacrament, and, therefore, a venial sin.

The concluding words of this epoch-maknig *Motu Proprio* should not be overlooked: "All those who will make use of these concessions must compensate for the good received by becoming shining examples of a Christian life and principally with works of penance and charity." Although these words add on specific obligation, they are as worthy of attention as the privileges granted.

510. — 2. *Reasons excusing* from Eucharistic fast:

a) *The danger of death* (C. 858).

One who is in probable danger of death from illness may receive Communion even daily without fasting, even though he did not communicate so frequently when in health. Should it be easy for such a one to fast it would be laudable if he did so. He who is not sick, but is in danger of death may receive without fasting only if it is inconvenient for him to postpone the reception of Holy Communion until the following day. — A priest may say *Mass without fasting* in order to confect the Holy Eucharist for Viaticum.

511. b) *Completion of the Sacrifice of the Mass.*

This may happen if the priest only recalls after the Consecration that he has broken his fast, or if after the Consecration he is unable to finish the Mass and the only other priest available is one who has broken his fast; or if at the Communion one becomes aware that he has consecrated with invalid matter and has already consumed it either entirely or in part. So, too, a priest may consume the small particles he discovers on the paten, etc. after his Mass and before he divests. If he has already taken off his vestments or if it is a question of an entire host, or if the particles are those remaining from a different Mass, he may consume them only when there is no becoming place to reserve them.

c) *Necessity of avoiding irreverence to the Blessed Sacrament.*

This may happen when the Sacred Species must be saved from desecration by unbelievers, bombardment in wartime or from a fire. In such emergencies either the priest or laymen may consume the Sacred Species.

512. d) *Avoidance of defamation or scandal.*

Thus a priest who has broken his fast may ordinarily offer the Holy Sacrifice in order that the Sunday Mass be not omitted. — A newly ordained priest may also use epikeia in the case of his

First Mass celebration. Some authors also allow this on the occasion of First Holy Communion. However, scandal must always be avoided. — So, too, one may receive Communion if, after reaching the Communion rail, he recalls having broken his fast, and cannot leave the rail without defaming himself.

e) Dispensation.

Further dispensations from the Eucharistic fast can be granted by the Holy Office in order to say Mass (C. 247), and by the Congregation of the Sacraments for the reception of Holy Communion (C. 249). The provisions of the *Constitution* in 510. supersede all existing contrary regulations, reprobate all contrary customs and abolish all former faculties and privileges, both personal and territorial, granted by the Holy See. Moreover, the provisions of the said document are to be interpreted strictly.

513. — 3. *External cleanliness* is also required for the reception of Holy Communion.

Thus, one may not appear at the Holy Table in soiled, torn or unbecoming clothes. — The face, hands, and whole body must likewise be clean. If one has some visible and repulsive sore that will heal in a short time it is becoming to postpone Communion; not, however, if it will be long in healing. — Women may communicate during their menstrual period or after giving birth to a child; marital relations and involuntary pollution are likewise no hindrance.

514. Chapter V

DISTRIBUTION OF HOLY COMMUNION

I. Place. 1. *Ordinarily* Holy Communion may be received in any place where Mass may be said (C. 869).

The permission to say Mass aboard ship includes the permission to distribute Holy Communion. — The local Ordinary may prohibit the distribution of Holy Communion in individual instances (C. 869). — The priest may not distribute Communion to the faithful during Mass if this necessitates his going out of sight of the altar. (C. 868).

2. Concerning **Easter Communion** see 396.

515. — II. Time. 1. With certain restrictions Holy Communion may be received on *any day of the year.*

On *Maundy Thursday* Holy Communion may be distributed both during the Mass or Masses and immediately afterward. Exception is made for the sick and for Holy Viaticum. On *Good Friday* and the *Paschal Vigil* Communion may be distributed only during the liturgical functions and to those in danger of death.

2. The *time of the day* when Holy Communion may be distributed should correspond to the time when Mass may be said (Cf. 544)

An exception is made for a reasonable cause (C. 867). Those who communicate in the morning, afternoon or evening are now held only to a fast of three hours from solids and one hour from liquids (other than water), even when they receive apart from the Mass. If a priest cannot visit the sick in the morning he may do so in the afternoon and bring them Holy Communion.

The celebrant, or another priest, may distribute Holy Communion during an afternoon or evening Mass, or immediately before or after. To communicate at such a Mass one need not actually attend the Mass or be a member of the group for whose advantage the Mass is said. One may not receive Communion in a Mass after midday who has received in the morning. See 544. One may receive at an afternoon Mass even if he could easily have received at a morning Mass. People may receive during the Christmas *Midnight Mass,* unless the local Ordinary has forbidden it, according to Canon 869. Only in necessity may Communion be carried on the street at night.

516. — III. Rite. 1. *General Prescriptions.*

To distribute Holy Communion without wearing any *sacred vestment* is a grave sin when done without necessity; it is a venial sin to do so without a stole or surplice. During Holy Mass, as well as immediately before or after, Holy Communion is distributed while wearing the sacred vestments required for Mass. If the priest is vested in black he does not give the blessing after distributing Communion, and he omits the *Alleluia* during the Easter season. — If Communion is distributed outside of Mass the priest should wear a stole of the color corresponding to the office of the day (not the Mass) or white. — Omission of the *prayers* before or after the distribution is a venial sin. — Two *candles* must be lighted on the altar. Violation of this requirement is a venial sin. — In distributing Holy Communion the priest must use his *thumb* and *index finger,* or, for a serious reason, one of the other fingers. — Every priest must distribute Communion under the form of *leavened or unleavened* bread according to his rite. A priest may distribute hosts of another rite if no priest of that rite is present;

but he must observe the ceremonies of his own rite (C. 851). Every Catholic has the right to receive Holy Communion even for devotion's sake in the *rite* of any church in union with the Church of Rome. It is advisable that each receive his Easter Communion in his own rite. The Viaticum, however, must be received in one's own rite, but urgent necessity excuses from this precept (C. 866). If the *number of hosts* is insufficient they may be divided; but not into more than two or three parts each, lest the particles be too small. The priest may break a part from his own host to communicate one or two people. It is forbidden to give any person *more than one* host to promote his devotion. This may be done for other reasons, e.g., because the priest is unable to consume all the remaining particles. Only in case of necessity may the host that is consecrated for Benediction of the Blessed Sacrament be given to the faithful. — If no *server* is present the priest says all the prayers himself. — The *purification of the ciborium* is best done by pouring wine into it and turning it carefully in a slow circular motion without using the finger either before or after to brush the particles into the chalice.

517. — 2. *Communion for the Sick.*

The prescriptions of common law requiring *external pomp* when Holy Communion is taken to the sick do not oblige in the United States. Even in places that are exclusively Catholic present custom excuses the priest from observing the public ceremonies of the Roman Ritual.

The danger of irreverence, great dislike of the patient or his family for publicity, lessening of respect for the Blessed Sacrament due to the fact that It would be daily carried on the street, etc. justify taking Communion to the sick *privately*. (Cf. Concl. Plen. Balt. II, N. 264). In carrying Communion to the sick privately the priest should wear the stole under his coat (not in his pocket), carry the Bl. Sacrament on his breast in a pyx placed in a burse suspended from his neck by a cord. In this country it is not customary that someone accompany the priest. For the formula to be used in giving Viaticum see 503.

518. — 3. **Defects.**

If a Host *falls on the floor* the priest should indicate the place with a purificator or pall and subsequently wash the place and pour the water into the sacrarium. To avoid creating a sensation he may wait until the people have left the church. Washing is omitted if the Host falls on the chin, hands, clothes, etc. of the communicant. Should It fall into a woman's clothing she should extract It, hand It to the priest who in turn will administer It to her. The same procedure should be observed if the Sacred Host should fall behind the grille in an enclosed convent, though in this case the priest may also enter the enclosure (Cf. C. 600 No. 4).

Should a patient *vomit* after receiving and the Sacred Species be still easily discernible, they should be put in a clean vessel with either water or wine and placed in a becoming place in the church until they have decomposed, and then poured into the sacrarium. If the Species are no longer recognizable the emission should be gathered up with clean gauze or cotton and burned and the ashes put into the sacrarium.

If a patient *dies* with the Holy Communion still lying on his tongue It should be removed and treated like a host that has been vomited.

519.   Chapter VI

RESERVATION AND EXPOSITION OF THE BLESSED SACRAMENT

I. Reservation of the Holy Eucharist. 1. *Necessary conditions.*

a) Wherever the Blessed Sacrament is kept there must be someone to whose *special care* It is entrusted (C. 1265).

This person may be a layman. The tabernacle key need not necessarily be kept by a priest, but the priest in charge of the church or chapel is responsible for its safe keeping (C. 1269).

b) *Mass* must regularly be said at least *once a week* where the Blessed Sacrament is reserved (C. 1265).

An occasional exception is allowed in extraordinary cases.

2. *Place* of Reservation (C. 1265). *a*) The Blessed Sacrament *must* be reserved in the cathedral church, in the principal church of an abbey or Prelature *nullius,* vicariate, the prefecture apostolic, in every parish or quasi-parish church and in a church attached to exempt religious Institutes of men or women.

b) The Eucharist may be reserved in collegiate churches or in the principal oratory (public or semi-public) of a pious or religious house or ecclesiastical college *with permission* of the local Ordinary.

c) For keeping the Blessed Sacrament in other churches or chapels an *Apostolic indult* is necessary. The local ordinary may permit such churches and public chapels to reserve the Holy Eucharist for some good reason but only *per modum actus,* i.e., as long as the reason exists (C. 1265).

While a parish or similar church or chapel is being restored the local Ordinary may allow the Blessed Sacrament to be kept temporarily in another church or chapel, since the latter takes the place of the former.

520. *d*) *It is forbidden* to reserve the Blessed Sacrament anywhere in a religious or pious house except in the church or principal oratory (C. 1267).

Should the inmates of the house hold their religious exercises in another chapel, this becomes the principal oratory and the Holy Eucharist may be reserved there. If the church has another title to reserve the Blessed Sacrament, it retains this right also. — The Blessed Sacrament may never be reserved in several oratories in the same house, unless there are several communities living separately in the house (AAS 10-347). Such a condition may obtain in a seminary where, in addition to the seminarians, there are resident Sisters in care of the house.

e) For a good reason, recognized by the bishop, the Holy Eucharist may be taken from the church, etc. and kept in some safe place *over night.* In this case it is necessary that It be placed on a corporal and that the sanctuary lamp burn before It (C. 1269).

The *sanctuary lamp* must be fed with olive oil or beeswax. Where no olive oil is available the local Ordinary may permit the use of other oils. As far as possible vegetable oil should then be used (C. 1271).

3. *Renewal of the Sacred Species.* Hosts must always be fresh, and, therefore, frequently renewed, to avoid danger of decomposition (C. 1272).

The humidity of the climate and the condition of the church determine the frequency of renewal. Hosts should never be consecrated if more than five or six weeks have elapsed from the time they were baked. The greater number of authors teach that, as an ordinary rule, the consecrated hosts should be renewed within a period of one month after being baked.

521. — II. Exposition of the Blessed Sacrament (C. 1274). 1. *Private exposition* of the Blessed Sacrament is lawful without the bishop's permission for some reasonable cause in all churches and chapels where the Holy Eucharist may be reserved.

Private exposition is done by opening the tabernacle and drawing the ciborium forward for the adoration of the faithful, but without taking it out of the tabernacle. Incensation is not prescribed. Appropriate and approved prayers are then recited before the Blessed Sacrament. The priest wears a surplice and white stole. At the conclusion the *Tantum ergo,* the *Panem de coelo,* and the oration *Deus qui nobis* are sung or recited. Whereupon the tabernacle is closed. It is also permissible to incense the Blessed Sacrament and give Benediction. While giving Benediction the celebrant wears the humeral veil, and covers the ciborium with it. — Private exposition is permitted for a private reason, e.g., the special request of a family, or when one of the parishioners is dying. For the sake of his own private devotion a priest is not allowed to open the tabernacle, say his prayers and then close it.

2. *Public exposition* of the Blessed Sacrament is permitted during Mass or Vespers only on the feast of Corpus Christi and within its octave. — At other times Benediction is allowed only with permission of the local Ordinary for a good and weighty reason.

Exempt religious must also obtain this permission. — The permission of the bishop may be tacit, e.g., for Benediction services that are customary in the respective diocese. — The *exposition of the ciborium* in the repository is prohibited in the Roman rite. Where it is tolerated it must be considered a public exposition.

522.   Second Division

THE HOLY EUCHARIST AS SACRIFICE

The *Holy Sacrifice of the Mass* is the real and true Sacrifice of
the New Testament in which Christ is offered under the appearances of bread and wine, thus continuing the Sacrifice of the
Cross in an unbloody manner.

Chapter I

ESSENCE AND VALUE OF THE MASS

I. Essence of the Sacrifice of the Mass. 1. Sacrifice
of the Mass consists *essentially* in the Consecration; Holy
Communion, however, is an integral part of the Sacrifice.

Because the Church commands attendance at the entire Mass,
he does not fulfill his Sunday obligation who is present only at
the Consecration (Cf. 195). — At his Communion the priest must
consume the host he himself has consecrated during the Mass he
is saying; thus he may not exchange this host for one previously
consecrated for exposition and consume only the latter. — The
small hosts consecrated at Mass should not be distributed to the
faithful before the priest has consumed the large one, unless there
is a necessity of distributing earlier and no other hosts are available.

523. — 2. Whether the *Consecration of both species*
is essential to the Sacrifice is controverted. But it is never
permitted to consecrate only one species.

Should the priest observe *before Consecration* that either the
bread or wine is missing or invalid (Cf. 491 sq.) he must discontinue the Mass if no valid matter is available. If he discovers
the invalidity after the Consecration he should wait until valid
matter is procured, if it is obtainable within a short time. If no
other matter can be had, he continues with the Mass leaving out
the words and signs that refer to the missing matter. If he perceives
the invalidity only after leaving the altar there is nothing to be
done ordinarily, lest there be scandal or irreverence to the Blessed
Sacrament. Some authors say nothing can be done about it since
the Mass is ended.

If there is a very serious doubt about the validity of the matter *after Consecration*, other matter should be supplied. (Not every doubt that would require a priest to replace the doubtful matter before Consecration suffices to oblige him to replace it thereafter.) The supplied matter must be consecrated conditionally; it is to be consecrated absolutely only when one is morally certain that the matter previously used was invalid.

The duty regarding the *application* of the Mass is not fulfilled if only one species is consecrated. In such cases, therefore, Mass must be offered a second time or (if this is not feasible because of the great number of them) recourse must be had to Rome (Cf. 542).

524. — II. Value of the Mass. 1. *In itself* the Mass has an *infinite value*, since Christ is both Priest and Victim.

God is likewise given infinite praise, thanks and propitiation by the Mass.

This is not quite the case in respect to the effects which the Holy Sacrifice has *ex opere operato* in relation to man, namely, as regards the impetratory (the obtaining of spiritual and temporal goods), propitiatory (divine reconciliation), and satisfactory (remission of temporal punishment due to sin) effects.

2. The *effects* of the Mass are *not diminished* for the individual by the fact that several take part in or assist at the Holy Sacrifice.

The fruits of the Mass that benefit those who take part in the Sacrifice and attend the Mass are called *fructus speciales*. Extensively they are without limit. — The same is to be said of the effects that every Holy Mass has on the entire Church (fructus generales).

525. — 3. The *effects* of the Mass that are received by an individual in consequence of the *special application* of the priest (fructus ministeriales) are, according to a rather widespread opinion, both *extensively and intensively finite* in virtue of the positive will of Christ.

Wherefore, the greater the number of persons for whom the Mass is being said, the less fruits will the individuals receive. And the more Masses that are applied for a person the greater will he benefit thereby.

The fruits of the Mass *ex opere operato* may be increased *ex opere operantis,* i.e., by the worthiness and devotion of the celebrant and the faithful who are joint offerers. — A still greater increase of the fruits may result from the special prayers of the Church (e.g., in a Requiem Mass) or because of greater external solemnity (a Solemn or High Mass).

A priest must offer a Mass for each stipend received, and he may not satisfy another obligation by a Mass for which he has accepted a stipend (C. 825), not even if he wishes to apply the spiritual benefits accruing to himself (*fructus specialissimi*) to others. — The priest may accept additional compensation for a Mass besides the stipend for the application, but only if it is certain that the added remuneration is given exclusively for the celebration and not for the application of the Mass (C. 825).

Since it is not absolutely certain that the effects of the Mass as explained in No. 3 are limited, a priest may conditionally (i.e., if the one giving the stipend suffers no loss thereby) offer the Mass for several other intentions provided he does not intend to fulfill an obligation of justice by these conditional applications.

526.   Chapter II

APPLICATION OF THE MASS

Article I

General Remarks

I. Persons for whom Mass may be Offered.

1. With some restrictions the Holy Sacrifice may be offered for *all the living* and for the **Souls in Purgatory** (C. 809).

The application of the Mass for the *damned* is absolutely invalid. — We may implore an increase of the external, accidental veneration of the *saints* in Heaven through the Mass; besides, thanks may be offered to God for the grace and glory He has bestowed upon them. Finally, we may entreat God at Mass for spiritual and temporal blessings through the intercession and merits of the saints. — It is an article of faith that the Holy Sacrifice helps the *Suffering Souls.* It is not certain, however, that the fruits will be given to just that soul for whom the Mass is applied. Neither do we know to what extent the Mass is beneficial to the faithful departed.

2. Mass may be offered privately for the *excommunicated*, provided no scandal is given. In the case of an *excommunicatus vitandus* the Mass may be said only for his conversion (C. 2262).

Mass is offered privately if it is not announced or if only the priest or at most one or two others know for whom it is being applied. —What is said of the excommunicated can be applied also to heretics and schismatics. Care must always be taken that the application be not public. This also applies in the case of a deceased Protestant Ruler. — In itself it would not be wrong to offer a Mass, even publicly, for a living, unbaptized person; but it would often be forbidden because of scandal.

3. Mass may not be applied publicly for those to whom the Church denies *ecclesiastical burial* (C. 1241).

Private application in this case is not forbidden.

527. — II. Manner of Application. 1. The application must be made by the *celebrant* of the Mass and at least *before the consecration* of the wine.

Application made contrary to the command of a superior is valid but unlawful. — The application need not be made expressly before every Mass; on the contrary, it suffices that the celebrant has not revoked an intention previously made (*intentio habitualis*). Wherefore, it is lawful to make such an intention for a whole week, or month or several months.

2. The application must be *exactly* determined, at least *implicitly*.

Invalid, therefore, is the application with the intention: according to one of the ten intentions I have noted in the Mass book. The following would be valid: according to all the ten intentions I have noted. If one says Mass ten times with this intention he has done his duty.

The celebrant himself need not know the respective person or purpose for which his Mass is being applied. It suffices that the application be *implicitly* determined, e.g., according to the intention of my superior, the first intention noted in the book, according to the intention of him who offered the stipend first, etc. —

It is *unlawful,* and perhaps even invalid, to apply the Mass: according to the intention of him who will first give me a stipend (C. 825); in this case one may not retain the stipend when later received. — If a priest, hearing that a person has died, knows for certain that someone will shortly request a Mass for the deceased, such an application would certainly be valid. But after receiving the stipend he is freed from the obligation of applying another Mass only if the person offering the stipend knows what has been done and agrees to it.

If a celebrant makes two *contrary intentions* for the application of a Mass, the predominant intention prevails. That intention is the stronger which the priest would have preferred had he adverted to this contradiction. Since certainty can scarcely be had in the matter, it is advisable to make the second application according to the intention which has not been satisfied.

If one erroneously applies a Mass *pro defuncto* instead of *pro defuncta* the application is valid, since the celebrant has primarily the intention of fulfilling his duty.

528. *N.B.* In itself it is very advisable that the priest know at every Mass for whom or for what intention the Mass is being applied. Since it is sometimes impossible to note all the individual intentions (e.g., at places of pilgrimage), especially when the intentions are passed on to other priests, it is sufficient to apply the Mass: *according to the intention of him who has the first right to it.* Thus the Masses will ordinarily be said in the order in which the stipends were received. If various stipends are received simultaneously a corresponding number of Masses are said conjointly according to the intentions of all those who gave the stipends. If the stipends are *passed on* to other priests, he who applies the Masses will do best by saying them according to the intention of him from whom he received them, and, in case the latter has made no intention, according to the intention of him who has prior right thereto. — According to a decision of the Sacred Penitentiary (Dec. 7, 1892) a priest fulfills his obligation if he says the Masses *according to the intention of him who gave the stipend,* without expressly thinking of any definite sequence. Herein, namely, is the implicit intention of applying the Masses in the order corresponding to the rights of the donors of the stipends.

529. *Article II*

Obligation of Applying the Mass

One may have an obligation to apply a Mass because of an office, a chaplaincy or a stipend.

I. The pastoral office requires that Mass be offered on certain days for the faithful committed to their care by residential bishops, vicars capitular, abbots, prelates *nullius*, vicars and prefects apostolic, pastors and certain parish vicars (C. 451) and quasi-parish priests.

Parish vicars chiefly include the following: the parish administrator (vicarius oeconomus), and sometimes also the parochial vicar who substitutes for the pastor (C. 474). Quasi-pastors (C. 451) are those in charge of quasi-parishes, i.e., part of a vicariate or prefecture apostolic, at the head of which there is a priest in care of souls (C. 216). There are no quasi-parish priests in the U. S.

Titular bishops are *not obliged* to apply the *Missa pro populo* (C. 348), nor are Superiors in a clerical exempt religious institute, although it is becoming, esecially in the case of the latter, that these should say Mass occasionally for their subjects. Neither are the following so obliged: chaplains, curates, vicarii adjutores (C. 475), rectors of seminaries, and priests merely sent to assist a pastor.

The *Missa pro populo* is said only for the *living members* of the congregation, not for the deceased. — *The Holy Mass* that is thus applied need not necessarily be the High Mass; a low Mass suffices. It is only the application of the Mass that obliges under grave sin. The day designated, the parish church where it is to be said, or the person appointed to say it are prescribed under venial sin only. It would be mortally sinful, however, to deviate from these regulations habitually.

530. — 1. The *days* on which the *Missa pro populo* must be said. Bishops (C. 339), vicars capitular (C. 440), abbots and prelates *nullius* (C. 323), pastors (C. 466), as well as some parish vicars (C. 451), are obliged to apply a Mass on all Sundays and Holydays, including the suppressed Feast Days (C. 339). Vicars and prefects apostolic (C. 306), as also quasi-parish priests (C. 466), must apply a Mass at least on Christmas, Epiphany, Easter, Ascension Day, Pentecost, Corpus Christi, the Feast of the Immaculate Conception, the Assumption of the B. V. M. and on the feasts of SS. Joseph, Peter and Paul and All Saints (C. 306).

Only one *Mass* need be applied for the people *on Christmas,* likewise, when a Holy Day falls on Sunday (C. 339). In like manner, only one Mass need be applied in case another diocese or parish is *aeque principaliter* connected with one's own, or if one has charge of a second parish (C. 339, 466).

If a *feast is transferred* to a day on which the hearing of Mass and abstaining from servile work are commanded, the Mass must be applied on that day. If the office and Mass alone are transferred then the *Missa pro populo* is to be said on the original date of the feast (C. 339).

531. — 2. *Those obliged* to say the *Missa pro populo* must do so *in person* if possible. If lawfully hindered they must have another priest say the Mass in their stead. If this, too, is impossible, they must say the Mass either personally or by proxy later on and as soon as possible (C. 339, 466).

Illness *excuses* from the personal application of the *Missa pro populo* but not a contrary custom, nor the circumstances that the faithful readily attend a certain Mass, thinking it to be said for them, nor the fact that a Requiem, a nuptial or a funded Mass is scheduled for that day, provided the Requiem, etc. can without great inconvenience be said by another priest or be postponed to another day.

3. The *place* for applying the *Missa pro populo* for a parish is the parish church. For special reasons an exception may be made (C. 466).

If the pastor is lawfully absent he may use his own judgment in deciding whether he will say the Mass where he happens to be or have someone else say the Mass in his parish church (C. 466).

532. — II. A priest in charge of a **chaplaincy** with which the application of Masses is connected, must likewise apply the Masses or have someone say them for him.

This is a *personal* obligation only when it is expressly so determined in the documents of the chaplaincy. — If he must personally apply all the Masses and every day at that, he need not make up for those he omits because of illness if the illness is of short duration (not more than a month or two). The same rule obtains if he misses some Masses on account of a short trip or because of his annual retreat. Furthermore, he is allowed five or six Masses annually for himself and his relatives; but he may not take a stipend for any of these free Masses.

If the rules of the chaplaincy do not require the personal application on the part of the chaplain, he must see to it that another priest applies the Masses even when he is ill. In this case the chaplain has no free Masses. If he has another priest say the Masses for him he need only give the regular diocesan stipend, unless the regulations of the chaplaincy state otherwise. If there is question not of funded Masses, but of Masses requested by private persons, he must give the entire stipend received to him who says the Masses.

533. — **III. A stipend** is a contribution toward the support of the priest upon whose acceptance the priest assumes a grave obligation in justice to offer the Holy Sacrifice of the Mass for the intention of the contributor.

1. *Amount of the Stipend.* The local Ordinary may determine the amount of manual stipends. Where such a determination does not exist the custom prevailing in the diocese must be observed. Exempt religious are bound by the diocesan regulations in this matter (C. 831).

Manual stipends as distinguished from funded stipends are given to the priest, as it were, from hand to hand. — The bishop can forbid the acceptance of a *smaller stipend* (C. 832); in individual cases, however, a priest can make an exception to such a prohibition in favor of the poor. — The local Ordinary cannot prohibit the acceptance of a *larger stipend*. But it is forbidden to demand a larger stipend and whosoever does so is bound to restitution. A larger stipend may be asked only because of special inconvenience in saying Mass, e.g., a *Missa cantata* or saying Mass at a distant place or at a very late hour; but not because of special graces connected with a Mass, e.g., saying Mass at a privileged altar or at some shrine of pilgrimage. One may, however, give preference to the higher stipend and even tell the people that such stipends will be given first attention.

If someone gives a sum of money for Masses *without designating their number* it must be presumed that the number corresponding to the diocesaon stipend is desired. An exception to this rule is justified only in case the priest may lawfully presume the donor had a different intention (C. 833).

534. — 2. *The obligation of justice* remains even though the stipend be lost without any fault of the priest who is obliged to say the Mass. This obligation extends also to the special circumstances specified by the donor regarding the celebration of the Mass (C. 833).

The *non-observance* of such circumstances is a serious matter only when the omission is of importance, e.g., saying Mass at a privileged altar or singing a High Mass. If the matter can be adjusted only by the application of another Mass, the priest is obliged to do this. The non-observance of other stipulations (Mass on a certain feastday, a votive Mass, etc.) is only a venial sin, not entailing any obligation of restitution. If one has a good reason it is no sin to disregard such stipulations, — If in some churches (e.g., at popular shrines) because of the special devotion to the place people request more Mases than can be said there, a notice should be posted informing the faithful that as many Masses as possible will be said there and that the remaining stipends will be turned over to other priests (C. 836).

If one has not expressly requested any such *accidental circumstances*, it is presumed he merely wants the application of a Mass (C. 833). Accordingly, it is not forbidden to make the application for a living person while saying a Requiem Mass, or to apply the ferial or feastday Mass for someone deceased. The former is, nevertheless, unbecoming if done without a reasonable cause. Similarly, it is not necessary to say a votive Mass if the one giving the offering requests a Mass in honor of some mystery or saint.

535. *Gregorian Masses* must be said uninterruptedly on thirty successive days. Only one Gregorian Mass of a series may be said on Christmas Day. The last three days of Holy Week do not constitute an interruption on the part of the priest who is saying the Gregorian Masses if he is not celebrating any of the liturgical Masses on these days. If the Gregorian Masses are interrupted without any fault of the priest he must begin the series anew if he has received more than the ordinary stipend for them; if the latter is not the case one cannot insist on such an obligation, especially if one or the other of the Masses is said at a privileged altar. —It is not required that one and the same priest say all thirty of the Masses, nor is it necessary to say Requiem Masses even on those days when the rubrics permit them (Cf. also 786).

A plenary indulgence is granted to the suffering Soul for whom a Mass is said at a *privileged altar*. The Mass must be applied for that Soul; it can also be applied for other Holy Souls at the same time. The indulgence is never gained if the Mass is offered at the same time for the living. If one has accepted the obligation of offering such a Mass, he need not say it at a privileged altar, if he enjoys the privilege of a personal privileged altar. — Other priests do not fulfill their obligation by saying such a Mass at a non-privileged altar, not even if they gain a plenary indulgence for that soul. Only when a priest has made a bona fide mistake and said the Masses at some non-privileged altar may he compensate for each Mass thus said by applying a plenary indulgence to the souls concerned (Cf. also 785).

536. — 3. *The time for satisfying obligations* concerning stipends. *a)* If the donor has explicitly or implicitly *designated the time,* the Masses must be said within the time limit assigned (C. 834).

If, for example, the Mass is requested for a successful operation, a happy death, successful lawsuit or examination, etc., there is an obligation of restitution if the Mass is said only after these events have taken place.

b) If no definite time is mentioned the Masses should be said within a short time relative to their greater or smaller number (C. 834).

If the offering is from *one and the same person* an entire month is allowed within which to say the Mass in case of only one stipend; at least two months are granted for 20 Masses; 40 Masses should be said within about three months, 60 within four months, 80 Masses within five months, 100 Masses within half a year and 200 within one year. — But should 20 *different people* each request one Mass they must all be said within one month. Should one receive stipends from heirs, executors of wills, and other persons who are obliged to have a certain number of Masses celebrated, the date from which to reckon the time for saying Masses is the day on which the priest who is to say them receives the stipend, unless some other arrangement is demanded by special circumstances. — If the Masses are said considerably later (e.g., one or two months) than the time prescribed one sins gravely, but is not obliged to restitution.

c) If the donor expressly leaves it to the priest to say the Mass when he wishes, he will satisfy his obligation if he says the Mass within a year (C. 834).

A priest may not accept more stipends than he can satisfy within a year (C. 835). Should one person give a priest 400 stipends requesting that he say the Masses personally, the priest may accept them, since it is evident that more than a year's time will be required to comply with the request.

537. — 4. *Satisfying the Stipend Obligation.*
*a) Only *one stipend* can be satisfied by the application of only *one Mass* (C. 825).

For particulars, confer 525. — If a priest receives money from someone who asks to be *remembered* at Mass, the priest need not apply a Mass for him, and may therefore accept a stipend for the Mass in which he makes the memento.

b) It is forbidden to accept an *offering for the celebration* of a Mass and *another for the application* thereof, unless it is certain that the one contribution is given only for the celebration and not also for the application (C. 825).

If *no offering* whatever is given for a nuptial Mass, the Mass need not be applied for the couple, and the celebrant may satisfy any other stipend obligation thereby (S. Off. Sept. 1, 1841.) The same holds for a funeral Mass (S.C.C. April 27, 1895), although it is very becoming that such Masses be applied for the poor gratis (Cf. C. 1235).

c) A priest saying *two Masses* a day may satisfy an obligation of justice by only one of them (C. 824).

It matters not for which of the two Masses he accepts the stipend. — If one of the bination Masses is said *pro populo* no stipend may be accepted for the other. — One may accept a stipend for one of the Masses if the other, in fulfillment of an obligation of charity (e.g., which one has as a member of some confraternity) is said for the deceased. — For some *extrinsic reason* (late hour, great distance, etc.) one may accept an additional compensation, for this is not a stipend. This holds also for the second and third Masses on All Souls' Day. — Since the law contained in c) aims at averting every *danger of simony,* he who transgresses it sins gravely by *simony;* but is not guilty of an *injustice* and may, therefore, retain the stipend, since the Mass has been said. A priest may accept three stipends for his three *Christmas Masses* (C. 824); on *All Souls' Day* he may accept only one stipend, which may be for any one of the three Masses (Cf. 546).

538. — 5. *Transmission of Stipends. a*) Persons having the free disposal of Mass stipends may *lawfully* forward them to priests whom they personally know to be in good standing or who are recommended by their own Ordinary (C. 838).

Thus Mass stipends may not be passed on to the laity (e.g., booksellers) for further disposal. — Without special faculties from the Holy See no bishop can prohibit the sending of stipends to priests outside his diocese. — However, it is forbidden to send stipends directly to Oriental priests or superiors of Oriental Religious Institutes. This must be done either through the Congregation for the Oriental Rite or through the Apostolic Delegate or through prelates having ordinary jurisdiction in the Oriental Church.

b) There is an *obligation to forward* to the respective Ordinary all stipends that cannot be satisfied within a year (C. 841).

It is not said hereby that one may lawfully wait a year before transmitting them. Moreover, a priest who has Masses that are to be applied by others must pass them on as soon as possible (C. 837). — This twofold obligation of forwarding stipends and doing so without delay, affects not only priests, but also the laity, especially those who by accepting an inheritance must see to it that a number of Masses are said annually. — In the case of funded

Masses which must be forwarded (*ad instar manualium*), the obligation to transmit them to the Ordinary *begins* at the end of the year in which they should have been said; as to manual stipends this duty begins one year from the day they were received, unless the donor has designated otherwise (C. 841).

539. *c*) Regarding the *amount* of the stipend to be forwarded, we distinguish between manual and funded Mass stipends.

a) *Manual Mass stipends* must be transmitted in their entirety. Some part of them may be retained only when the donor explicitly permits this or if it is certain that the amount exceeding the regular diocesan stipend is given as a personal gift (C. 840).

No deduction may be made even for a pious purpose.

In transmitting Mass stipends every appearance of *trading and barter* must be avoided (C. 827).

Therefore, Mass stipends may not be exchanged for other things (books, merchandise, subscriptions, etc.), but must be handed on *in propria specie*.

Stipends are given as a *personal gift* (intuitu personae) when they are given out of gratitude, friendship or because of needy circumstances, etc. — It is not forbidden that he to whom the stipends are forwarded should make a *donation* in favor of the one forwarding them by renouncing a part of his right to the stipend, but this must be done with absolute freedom. For the same reason two priests may voluntarily interchange intentions, each retaining his original stipend. — Whoever unlawfully retains part of a stipend is obligated to make *restitution* according to the more common opinion of moralists.

If an extraordinary stipend (on the occasion of a wedding or funeral, etc.) constitutes the *pastoral allowance* or if it forms part of the *stolar fee*, the pastor may, if he has the Mass said by another priest, give the latter only the regular stipend for a Mass at such an hour and retain the rest (S C. C. July 25, 1874).

540. *β*) *Funded Mass stipends* which cannot be satisfied according to the terms of the foundation, are to be transmitted to others (*stipends ad instar manualium*).—

In transmitting these stipends only that amount need be sent which corresponds to the regular stipend in the diocese where the Masses are said, provided that that which is in excess constitutes a part of the endowment of the benefice or pious foundation. But even in this case the entire stipend must be forwarded if the founder has so ordained (C. 840). Funded Mass stipends that are not *ad instar* are not to be transferred.

By the diocese "where the Masses are said" is not understood the one in which the benefice or pious foundation is erected, but the diocese where the Masses will be said.

d) Stipends are transmitted to others at the *sender's risk* and this responsibility lasts until he receives notice from the addressee that the latter has received the stipends and assumed the obligation of saying the Masses (C. 839).

Oral information suffices; but not merely the postal money order receipt. The signed and cancelled check would probably be sufficient.

541. — 6. Regulations insuring the certain application of Mass intentions. *a) All priests* must keep an *exact account* of all the Mass intentions they receive and which they have already satisfied (C. 844).

Likewise, *bishops* and *religious superiors* who distribute intentions to others must accurately note in their books all Mass intentions together with the offerings made (C. 844). Similarly, *rectors of churches* and those in charge of pious places who receive Mass stipends (C. 843).

b) The *right* and *obligation* to see that Mass stipends are satisfied belong to local Ordinaries and religious superiors according as churches are entrusted to them.

Ordinaries also have the obligation to *inspect* annually the records that church rectors, etc. must keep according to C. 843.

542. — 7. Reduction and Condonation. *a)* A *reduction* of the number of Masses is made when a foundation, without any fault of its administrator, becomes so devaluated that the endowment no longer suffices to supply the stipends for the Masses designated in the foundation. It may be granted only by the Holy See (C. 1517).

If the principal has been completely lost the obligation to say the Masses ceases automatically. If manual stipends are lost the obligation remains (C. 829).

b) A *condonation* takes place when Masses which should have been said in the past have not been said and can no longer be easily said. The fruits of the Masses thus unapplied are supplied from the spiritual treasury of the Church. Condonation is granted only by the Holy See.

Condonation may be granted for Masses that were obligatory by reason of a foundation or of manual stipends. — Whoever petitions this favor must indicate "ex stylo curiae" whether he has previously received a condonation. — If one has omitted saying the Masses in the hope of receiving a condonation he must likewise mention this fact, so that the customary clause "dummodo malitiose non omiserint animo habendi compositionem" may be omitted in the rescript. The maliciously negligent will scarcely obtain a condonation.

543.   Chapter III

PARTICULAR REGULATIONS ON THE MASS

I. Eucharistic Fast.

The same fasting regulations given for the reception of Holy Communion (506ff) apply also for the celebration of Holy Mass.

Priests *binating and trinating* may consume the ablutions made with water. On *Christmas* and *All Souls Day* they must observe the rubrics prescribed for ablutions. Should a priest consume an ablution mistakenly made with wine, he may still say another Mass.

For further reasons excusing a celebrant from fasting, see 510ff.

II. Obligation to Say Mass. 1. Every priest is *gravely obliged* to say Mass several times a year (C. 805).

A priest must, therefore, celebrate Mass at least three or four times each year, and in such a manner that there be not too great an intermission (half a year) between the Masses. — Who says Mass more rarely can sin gravely by scandal or spiritual sloth.

2. *Bishops* and *religious superiors* must see that their priests celebrate at least on Sundays and Holydays (Ibid).

A command is not needed; admonition and encouragement suffice.

III. Time for Saying Mass. 1. A priest may say Mass *any day* of the year. See the regulations of November 16, 1955 for the ceremonies of the **Restored Holy Week.**

544. — 2. The *time of day* for celebrating Mass. One may not begin Mass earlier than one hour before dawn and not later than one hour after noon (C. 821).

Dawn is about two hours before sunrise. Where the days dawn very late one may follow the custom of commencing Mass earlier.

Only a *gross deviation* from this rule (about two hours) is gravely sinful if done without a sufficient reason, especially if done habitually. Confer 416 for the privilege of regulars.

On *Christmas Day* the conventual or the parish Mass may commence at midnight. In chapels of convents and pious institutions wherein the Blessed Sacrament may be permanently reserved a priest may say all three Christmas Masses at midnight (C. 821).

3. *Afternoon and Evening Masses.* Ordinaries of places, excluding vicars general who are not in possession of a special mandate, may permit Holy Mass to be celebrated *every day after midday,* should this be necessary for the spiritual welfare of a considerable number of the faithful. —Pius XII, MOTU PROPRIO, *Sacram Communionem,* March 19, 1957.

The Ordinary of the place is the residential bishop, an abbot or prelate nullius, Vicar and Prefect Apostolic. The Ordinary can delegate the deans to give this permission in their deaneries, either for a long period or "ad actum," or for a group of churches or a certain area.

The spiritual welfare must involve the common good, not just a private family. A considerable number of the faithful would be twenty or thirty people.

The number of Masses permissible depends on how many are necessary to satisfy the devotion of those seeking to assist at Mass and receive Holy Communion. Thus on special occasions the bishop may permit a Mass for mothers early in the afternoon, another for children after class is dismissed and a third in the evening for those who work during the day.

The hour of the Mass may be any time after noon, though the most practical hours will be between four and ten p. m. Since the "Christus Dominus" has not been abrogated, some think that permission from the Holy Office or the Congregation of the Sacraments should be obtained if Mass is to be celebrated *habitually* before four o'clock in the afternoon.

545. — IV. Place for Saying Mass. 1. Mass may be said in any *church* and public or semipublic *oratory*.

Churches and public oratories (C. 1191) must be previously consecrated or at least solemnly blessed (C. 1165). — Blessing is not required in order to say Mass in a semi-public oratory. Nevertheless, it may be blessed with the ordinary house blessing. It is not forbidden, however, to consecrate or bless it like a church.

2. In *private oratories* Mass may be said habitually only with the permission of the Holy See (C. 1195).

Private oratories need not be given the regular *church blessing,* but may be given the ordinary *benedictio loci* or house blessing (C. 1196). — In the indult of the *Holy See* permission is generally granted for a low Mass each day exclusively of the greater feasts. On such feasts, however, the bishop may grant permission for a Mass, but only for reasons other than those for which Rome granted the indult, and only by way of exception (per modum actus, C. 1195).

The *local Ordinary* may grant permission to say only one Mass in a domestic oratory and that only on some extraordinary occasion and for a reasonable cause, provided he has either personally or by proxy first inspected the oratory and found it properly adapted for Mass. Only for the cemetery chapel may the bishop grant permission to say Mass regularly (C. 1194).

3. Bishops and Ordinaries may permit Mass to be said in a *room* which is neither a church nor chapel, and in the *open,* but only for one or the other time and for a reasonable and extraordinary cause (C. 822).

However, they may never permit Mass to be said in a bedroom (C. 822). — Mass may be said aboard ship only with permission of the Holy See obtainable through the Apostolic Delegate. —

If, however, there is a chapel on board ship, erected by permission of the competent Ordinary, any priest may celebrate Mass therein, even without an Apostolic Indult, provided he observes the regulations for celebrating Mass at sea, e.g., only when the sea is calm. — Field Masses on the occasion of political celebrations are not permitted (AAS 16-370).

546. — V. Bination. 1. A priest may say Mass only *once a day*, except on *Christmas* and *All Souls Day*.

Three Masses are *permitted* but not prescribed on these two days. — He who says only *one Mass* on Christmas Day must take the Mass corresponding to the time of day. On All Souls' Day the first Mass formulary of the day for all the faithful departed is to be taken. This regulation holds also for sung Masses; but in this case, the priest may say the other two Masses first.

A stipend may be taken for each Mass on Christmas Day, but only one on All Souls' Day.

2. A *second Mass* may be said on Sundays and Holydays (with the bishop's permission) if a considerable number of people could otherwise not hear Mass (C. 806).

This permission may be granted if approximately thirty people could not otherwise fulfill their Sunday obligation. — If another priest is available who is prepared to say the second Mass, bination is not permitted. — The faculty to binate is not given to any particular priest, but only with reference to the faithful; hence, any priest supplying for one who has faculties to binate, may also say a second Mass. — Should the need of a second Mass arise unexpectedly the bishop's permission may be presumed. The matter must subsequently be brought to his attention, unless some general regulation anent this matter obtains in the diocese. — On feasts that are not of obligation a priest may not binate, not even if the people attend Mass in large numbers. — A pastor of two parishes can, with the bishop's permission, hold the functions of Holy Week in each (*Cong. of Rites,* March 15, 1956). Particular indults to binate may include First Fridays, occasions of weddings and funerals and to renew the Sacred Species in oratories, if no other priest is available.

A further concession to binate is granted to one celebrating the Easter Vigil and bishops celebrating the Holy Thursday *Chrism Mass.*

547. — VI. Mass Servers. 1. A priest *must* have a server to assist him at Mass and answer the prayers.

This is a grave obligation. *Necessity excuses,* e.g., Mass of obligation for either priest or people, Mass to confect Viaticum, or if the server leaves after the beginning of the Mass and does not return. — One is more readily allowed to say Mass with a server who does not know the prayers. — If the server answers the prayers badly, the priest should answer himself if he can do so without becoming confused. — Indults permitting a priest to say Mass without a server now include a clause requiring the presence of someone to assist at the Mass.

2. No **woman or girl** may serve Mass. An exception is made when no man or boy is available and a just reason is had. In no case may the woman serve at the altar; she may only answer the prayers at a distance.

A Sister may do this even though the Mass is said *devotionis causa* in a convent chapel; although this would be venially sinful if a man or boy were easily available. — It would be a grave sin, however, for any woman to serve at the altar.

548. — VII. Sacred Furnishings. 1. *Episcopal consecration* is required for the altar, chalice and paten.

2. A **special blessing** must be given the three altar cloths, amice, alb, maniple, stole, chasuble, corporal and very probably also the cincture and pall.

Among others the pastor has faculties to bless these things for the churches and oratories within his parish limits; rectors of churches for their churches; superiors in a religious institute and the priests of their organization, whom they delegate; but only for the furnishings of their own churches and oratories and for those of nuns subject to the regular superior (C. 1304).

3. No **blessing** is required for the purificator, chalice veil, burse, missal, cross, the two wax candles or finger towels.

The *cross* must be provided with an image of the Crucified. In Masses during which the Blessed Sacrament is exposed the crucifix may be removed from the altar or may be left upon the altar; but it must be removed during exposition outside of Mass. —The two wax *candles* should be made for the most part of beeswax. Extra candles may be used only because of some solemnity (parish or conventual Mass, a priest's First Mass, etc.), but not in deference to the celebrant, unless he be at least a bishop. — To say Mass with only one candle is a venial sin;

without any it is a grave matter. A recent decree of the Sacr. Congr. of Rites (Aug. 18, 1949) states the *minimum* number of beeswax candles required as two for a private Mass, four for a chanted Mass, a solemn Mass and for the exposition of the Blessed Sacrament, the deficiency to be supplied by other forms of light. — It is forbidden to use *gas* or *electric lights* together with the prescribed candles or in place of them.

549. — VIII. The rubrics prescribed for the rite of the Mass itself oblige (preceptive) under sin; those indicated (directive) for recitation *before* and *after* do not.

The prayers given as a *preparation* for or as *thanksgiving* after Mass do not oblige under sin.

Vestments of the color prescribed oblige under venial sin. — It is also venially sinful to take a *different Mass* from the one permitted by the rubrics.

Omission of those parts of the Mass that recur in every Mass is more readily a grave sin than the omission of the other parts. It is gravely sinful to omit the prayers at the foot of the altar, the epistle with the tract, gradual, etc., or one oration in the canon, etc. — It is venially sinful to omit the Gloria, Credo, Commemorations, etc. — *If the priest forgets* something that obliges only under venial sin he should not supply it; the same holds in case one reads the wrong epistle or gospel. If one has entirely omitted (not merely interchanged) something that obliges under mortal sin, he should supply it if this can be done without attracting attention and if the mistake is noticed shortly after the omission.

To insert a short prayer or ceremony for the sake of private devotion is venially sinful. — After the priest's Communion a brief exhortation to the communicants is permitted. In distributing Holy Communion during the Mass the celebrant may not go out of sight of the altar according to canon 868.

The Prayers after Mass (according to a Decree of the Sacred Congregation of Rites, March 9, 1960) may be omitted: 1) after a Wedding Mass or on the occasion of first Communion or a general Communion, of Confirmation, or ordination, or of religious profession; 2) when Mass is followed immediately and with due propriety by some other sacred function or "pious exercise;" 3) when a homily is given during Mass; 4) after a dialogue Mass, but on Sundays and feast days only. (AAS 52-360) — A sacred function follows immediately after the Mass if the same priest who has the Mass also conducts these services, especially if he does not retire to the sacristy to change his vestments. Such services are, for example, Benediction of the Blessed Sacrament, a conference, some Confraternity devotion, the *Libera* after Mass, etc. — The "feast days" mentioned in connection with the dialogue Mass refers to first and second class feasts, according to a private response given to the Bishop of Fargo, December 7, 1960 (See *The Jurist,* April, 1961, page 276.) No restriction was made concerning Masses at which a homily is preached; therefore, the prayers may be omitted at such a Mass on any day. — On All Souls' Day and Christmas Day the prayers may be omitted after the first and second Masses if the priest stays at the altar and says the Masses uninterruptedly.

A priest obliged to omit or alter some things *because of illness* need have no permission for this if it concerns something insignificant, e.g., the use of a cane, necessity of supporting oneself on the altar with both arms, inability to elevate the Sacred Host at elevation. If it concerns a grave matter he needs the permission of his respective superior to say Mass, e.g., if he must sit during Mass or be supported by another.

550.   *Section IV*

The Sacrament of Penance

Penance is the sacrament in which the sins of a repentant sinner committed after Baptism are forgiven by the absolution of a priest.

Chapter I

THE OUTWARD SIGN OF THE SACRAMENT

I. Matter of the Sacrament of Penance. 1. The *remote matter* is all sins committed after Baptism.

It is called *materia circa quam.* The acts of the penitent and sacramental absolution are concerned with it.

a) Necessary matter is all mortal sins committed after Baptism that have not been directly remitted by the Power of the Keys.

Should one confess other mortal sins *immediately after* receiving absolution (e.g., forgotten sins, circumstances that change the nature of a sin, a considerably larger number of sins) absolution must be given again.

Sins committed *during the reception* of Baptism (e.g., sacrilegious reception) would ordinarily remain in the perverted will and would, therefore, have to be confessed. Should, however, a sin be committed at the very moment of its reception this sin would be removed by the subsequent reviviscence of Baptism. Practically speaking, such a sin need not be confessed.

When *converts* are baptized conditionally the sins committed after their first Baptism are doubtful matter for confession. These sins must, nevertheless, be confessed in the United States in virtue of the decrees of the Baltimore Councils. Absolution is given only conditionally.

551. *b) Free and sufficient matter* is all venial sins committed after Baptism (whether already confessed or not), and also all mortal sins already rightfully confessed and directly remitted.

A *general accusation* suffices when free matter alone is had. But for the sake of a beneficial confession (direction of the penitent, contrition, purpose of amendment) it is very advisable that some definite sin or species of sin be mentioned. — If one confesses other venial sins *immediately after being absolved* one may (but need not) be absolved anew.

c) Insufficient matter is all sins committed before Baptism, imperfections and doubtful sins.

If one confesses only sins committed before Baptism or mentions only imperfections, one cannot be absolved at all. — If only doubtful sins are confessed, (e.g., by children, idiots) absolution may be given conditionally. Conditional absolution is obligatory if one doubts whether or not a mortal sin has been committed. But if one should doubt whether there is question only of venial sin or imperfections, absolution should be given only rarely (at most once a month). — The difficulty can often be remedied by having the penitent include one or the other certain sin previously confessed.

552. — 2. The *proximate matter* consists of the acts of the penitent, namely, contrition, confession and the intention to accept the penance. By these acts the sins are subjected to the Power of the Keys for the purpose of remission by absolution.

Thomists regard these acts as proper matter of the sacrament; *Scotists* consider them as the *conditio sine qua non* which (according to some) need not even be perceivable. Practically, one may follow the second opinion in as far as one may conditionally absolve a dying person who has not previously given any signs of contrition and is now incapable of doing so, or who is even unconscious (so that contrition can only be habitual). For particulars on the acts of the penitent, confer 559 sqq.

553. — II. Form of the Sacrament of Penance. 1. *Form of Absolution.*

a) The form comprises the words: *Ego te absolvo a peccatis tuis in nomine Patris et Filii et Spiritus Sancti. Amen.*

Certainly valid would be the form: *Te absolvo a peccatis tuis.* — If several persons are to be absolved simultaneously, e.g., on the occasion of a catastrophe, the formula to be used is: *Ego vos absolvo a peccatis vestris in nomine . . .*

b) The prayers *Misereatur . . . Indulgentiam . . .* and *Passio . . .* should not be omitted without a just cause (C. 885).

Such a reason would be, for example, lack of time or a great number of penitents.

These prayers are not prescribed under sin.

Since the prayer "Passio..." possibly gives the works of the penitent a special satisfactory value, it should not be omitted. It may be said while the penitent is withdrawing from the confessional.

Moreover, it is a pious custom to bless the penitent before confession with the words: *Dominus sit in corde tuo . . .*

c) The raising of the hand from the *Indulgentiam* until the *Passio* and also the sign of the cross are not prescribed under sin, but are very becoming.

d) The absolution from censures is required under sin

if the penitent certainly (or probably) has incurred a censure.

The word *suspensionis* is *omitted* in absolving the laity and (usually) those in minor orders. If he is certain that no censure has been incurred the priest may omit the absolution from censures ("Dominus noster ...").

554. — 2. *Manner* of giving Absolution. Absolution must be given:

a) Orally:

Absolution in writing or by means of other signs is invalid.

b) To one personally present:

α) Absolution is certainly valid if the penitent is still near enough to enable the confessor to speak with him (even though he should have to raise his voice).

St. Alphonse thought a distance of less than twenty paces sufficient. — It is not necessary for the confessor to be able to see the penitent, or that the latter actually hear the former giving absolution. — Absolution is doubtfully valid if the priest and penitent are in different rooms between which there is no communication.

β) As long as the penitent can in some manner be perceived by the confessor, even though he may not actually be perceived because of some momentary obstacle absolution is probably valid.

Under such circumstances absolution must be given conditionally if there is a case of necessity. — In extreme need a penitent may even be absolved by telephone, since there is a slight probability that such absolution is valid.

N. B. Should the penitent *leave* the confessional before receiving absolution he may still be absolved as long as he is near the confessional. Otherwise, he should be recalled. If this is impossible, absolution may be given either absolutely or conditionally as long as there is moral certainty that absolution can still be given. If the penitent has completely disappeared the matter should be left to God. Should the same person come back to confession later the confessor should exhort him to be sorry for all his past sins and then absolve him.

555.   Chapter II

EFFECTS AND NECESSITY OF THE SACRAMENT OF PENANCE

I. Effects.

1. *Forgiveness of sins* through the infusion of sanctifying grace.

All mortal sins are either directly, or indirectly forgiven by a worthy confession. As to venial sins, only those are forgiven for which one is truly sorry.

2. *Remission of the punishment* due to sin. All the eternal, and at least part of the temporal punishment, is remitted.

3. *Infusion of sacramental graces.*

These graces enable us to do worthy works of penance and prevent us from relapsing into sin.

4. *The reviviscence* of the merits (due to good works) lost by mortal sin.

556. — II. Necessity.

1. *As a necessary means* (necessitate medii) of salvation this Sacrament must be received by all who have fallen into mortal sin after Baptism. If it cannot actually be received the desire for its reception suffices.

That *desire* is sufficient which is included in supernatural perfect contrition. The desire to confess as soon as possible is not required. It suffices to have the resolution to confess one's sins when the divine law requires it (e.g., in danger of death) or when the Church commands it.

Venial sins may be forgiven outside of confession and without the desire to confess. For their remission it is highly probable that the nobler motives of imperfect contrition are required (e.g., because venial sins are contrary to the obedience due to God; or because they defer the Beatific Vision). The less noble motives of imperfect contrition remit venial sins only in conjunction with some other Sacrament, e.g., Extreme Unction, Holy Communion.

2. *By virtue of ecclesiastical law* annual confession is of obligation (Cf. 395).

Religious superiors are obliged in conscience to see to it that their subjects confess weekly (C. 595). Superiors need not actually command their subjects to do so; it suffices that they call attention to and encourage this in their exhortations. As long as no real command is given, religious do not sin by omitting weekly confession.

Bishops are likewise obliged in conscience to see to it that their seminarians confess weekly (C. 1367). This obligation is similar to that of religious superiors. Furthermore, bishops shall see to it that *all clerics* confess frequently (C. 125).

557. Chapter III

THE RECIPIENT OF THE SACRAMENT OF PENANCE

Every person who has committed a mortal or venial sin after Baptism can receive the Sacrament of Penance. — Contrition, confession and satisfaction are required for the valid and fruitful reception thereof.

Article 1

The Recipient

Practical difficulties arise especially in the case of the unconscious dying recipient, and concerning heretics.

I. Those Dying While Unconscious.

1. If the dying person gave *signs of repentance* before becoming unconscious or asked for a priest, he must be absolved.

2. If he is *no longer capable* of giving any sign of contrition he must be absolved conditionally if he led a Christian life.

He may also be absolved conditionally although he led an evil life, even if death overtakes him in the very act of sinning.

Absolution may not be given to one who refuses the ministrations of the priest to the very last moment of consciousness. Once such an unrepentant sinner becomes unconscious, according to a few authors, he may be absolved conditionally, since there is still a possibility that he may have changed his attitude and acquired the dispositions proper for the reception of the Sacrament. There is, however, no obligation to absolve such a person. Furthermore, one must always guard against irreverence and scandal.

3. An *apparently dead* person may be conditionally absolved under the foregoing conditions.

Since, according to the findings of science, death does not follow immediately after the last breath has been drawn, the priest can and must absolve a person within half an hour after he has stopped breathing, if death ensues after a long illness. In case of sudden death absolution may still be given within two (or more) hours after breathing has ceased.

4. *In doubt* whether the dying person is a *Catholic* or not, absolution may be given conditionally.

N. B. Since one cannot know for certain whether a person is really or only apparently unconscious the priest should speak to such a person, informing him which Sacraments he is about to administer. Furthermore, the priest should recite with him the acts of faith, hope, charity and contrition.

558. — II. Heretics and Schismatics. 1. *Outside the danger of death* no Sacraments may be administered to heretics or schismatics even though they request them in good faith (C. 731).

2. *In danger of death* a heretic or schismatic may be absolved conditionally if he is in good faith and cannot be convinced of his error. As far as possible scandal must always be avoided.

One should previously try to awaken in the non-Catholic acts of faith, hope, charity and contrition, give him an opportunity to acknowledge that he is a sinner and induce him to desire that the priest help him as far as possible, or at least that the Will of

Christ be carried out in his behalf (Cf. 561). — Absolution is given without his observing it. One may deal similarly with an unconscious non-Catholic. — For security's sake one should try to induce a dying non-Catholic to make an act of perfect contrition (Cf. also 628).

559. *Article II*

The Acts of the Penitent

§ 1. Contrition and the Firm Purpose of Amendment

I. Contrition. 1. *Concept.* Contrition is sorrow of the soul and aversion for past sins with the resolution not to sin again.

This resolution not to sin again is at least implicitly contained in the sorrow of the soul and the hatred of sin. Because of its importance it is treated separately.

2. *Division.* *a*) Perfect contrition is had when the motive of our sorrow is the love of God as the highest Good and for His Own sake.

Thus we are sorry for mortal sins because by them we have offended the greatest and most lovable Good. — Such contrition justifies the sinner before the actual reception of the Sacrament of Penance when it includes at least implicitly the will to confess.

b) *Imperfect contrition* or attrition is that sorrow which does not proceed from the love of God, but from some other supernatural motive that refers to God (e.g., heinousness of sin, fear of eternal or temporal punishment that God inflicts upon sinners).

Together with confession it suffices to remit mortal sin. — For the forgiveness of venial sins outside of confession confer 556.

560. — **3. *Characteristics*** of contrition. For the valid reception of the sacrament of Penance contrition must be:

a) *True or interior.*

The penitent must genuinely regret his past sins. Mere recital of the act of contrition is not enough. — A sensible feeling of sorrow is not required; contrition is primarily a matter of the will. In most cases they who are disturbed because they cannot feel sorry are certainly contrite; if such penitents have the firm intention to avoid mortal sin they should be absolved without hesitation.

b) *Formal or explicit* and in some manner *made manifest.*

Although an act of perfect love of God justifies a sinner outside the Sacrament, and although contrition is included in such an act of love, one may not rest satisfied therewith when going to confession; but must make an explicit act of contrition, since contrition probably constitutes the (partial) matter of the Sacrament (Cf. 552). For the same reason contrition must be manifested externally (e.g., by a repentant confession, request for absolution, etc.).

c) *Supernatural.*

Contrition must proceed with the aid of grace from some supernatural motive.

d) *General.*

Sorrow must extend at least to all mortal sins not yet forgiven. No sins are forgiven without contrition; nor can any one mortal sin be forgiven apart from the other mortal sins. — Contrition need not concern itself expressly with each mortal sin; it suffices that one be sorry for some general motive (e.g., fear of hell, love for God). — Contrition need not embrace the venial sins, since mortal sin may be remitted without the remission of venial sin. — However, if one confesses only venial sins one must be sorry for at least one of them to safeguard the validity of the Sacrament.

561. e) *Supreme or sovereign* (appretiative summa).

Thus the contrite must consider and hate sins as the greatest of evils. — One need not have the highest degree of sorrow (intensive summa). Such sorrow is not within our power.

f) *Sacramental.*

Contrition must at least implicitly refer to the Sacrament of Penance and be virtually present during absolution.

Contrition refers *implicitly* to confession if conceived during the preparation for the Sacrament or if, as a consequence of sorrow, one resolves to confess or if one in some manner expresses one's sorrow in confession. — According to some authors, the will to do what Christ requires for the forgiveness of sin suffices, e.g., as is had by a dying heretic. — If sorrow were conceived only after the accusation of sins this would be sufficient.

Contrition endures *virtually,* e.g., in the intention to confess, in greater watchfulness. If contrition endures in this fashion it may have been conceived hours, and even days, before absolution is given. — In like manner one need not make a new act of contrition if, after being absolved, one confesses a forgotten mortal sin and is absolved again. — According to some authors it suffices merely that the contrition be not revoked (habitual continuation); wherefore, in extreme necessity absolution could be granted conditionally in such circumstances. — Contrition is certainly revoked by every mortal sin. It is uncertain whether contrition based on some general motive is revoked by a venial sin when one has only venial sins to confess; it would certainly not be recalled if the new venial sin is not as great as the venial sins for which one is contrite.

562. — II. Purpose of Amendment. 1. *Concept.* The firm purpose of amendment is the earnest will not to sin again.

In itself that good resolution *suffices* which is contained implicitly in a contrition conceived from some general motive; it would be better, however, to make a resolution explicitly.

2. *Characteristics* of the purpose of amendment are that it be:

a) Firm, i.e., the penitent must have the sincere will to amend.

Should one immediately after confession fall into the same mortal sins one confessed there would be good reason to fear that one's purpose of amendment was not firm. — But if one fears or is even convinced that one will sin again one may, nevertheless, have a firm purpose of amendment.

b) Efficacious, i.e., the penitent must be resolved to use the means necessary to avoid sin and its proximate occasions, and to repair according to his ability the evil one has caused.

c) Universal, i.e., the resolution must extend at least to all mortal sins in general.

One need not think of all sins individually. It is enough that the contrition or resolution be based on some general motive (love of God, punishment for sin). — Regarding *venial sins* the purpose of amendment need not be universal. But if one confesses only venial sins one must at least be resolved either to avoid some definite venial sin or that he will not commit the sin as often or as deliberately as heretofore. — Those who are accustomed to confess only venial sins should, for the sake of greater spiritual progress, also make some very definite resolution.

563. § **2. Confession**

I. Concept. Sacramental confession consists in the telling of our sins to a duly authorized priest with the intention of being absolved by him.

That confession also is *sacramental* which remains incomplete or which is sacrilegious.

No sacramental confession is made when one knowingly tells his sins to a priest who, he knows, has no jurisdiction. Likewise, if one confesses to a priest who has jurisdiction, but does so merely for mockery or to seek counsel or consolation. Should one later change his mind and really desire absolution he would at least have to make a general accusation of the sins previously confessed.

564. II. Qualities. Confession must be:

1. Secret, i.e., one is never obliged to confess his sins when others can overhear them.

Should one, in danger of death, be able to confess only in a way that others will hear, the priest may absolve him even though he merely indicates by some sign his desire for confession. — If one wishes to confess publicly one may do so.

2. Oral, i.e., by means of the spoken word.

Before the appearance of the Code of Canon Law the necessity for this quality was derived from custom. The Code says nothing about it. — It sufficed even before the Code that the penitent submit to the priest a written list of his sins saying verbally that he wished to accuse himself of the sins there written. — Any good and reasonable cause excuses one from an oral accusation.

3. *Sincere,* i.e., the penitent may not lie in confession.

It is a *grave sin* to lie about some circumstances necessary for the accusation or in an important matter concerning which the confessor lawfully questions the penitent. The same is true if one is silent about such matters or conceals them in any manner. In all these cases confession is invalid. — In itself the same holds for exaggerations in such things. But in this regard ignorance usually excuses.

It is *venially sinful* to be untruthful about optional matter for confession or in things that do not belong at all to confession. Confession remains valid except if the lie is such that it would be a grave sin outside of confession.

It is *not forbidden,* especially when making a general confession, to include sins committed since the last confession with others already forgiven so that they cannot be distinguished from each other. Upon questioning by the confessor, however, the truth must be told, e.g., if the priest asks the penitent in order to discover if he is an habitual sinner or a recidivist.

565. — 4. *Entire,* i.e., one must confess all grave sins committed after Baptism which have not been directly remitted by the Power of the Keys (material integrity), at least in as far as under given circumstances one is not excused from confessing them (formal integrity).

Doubtful sins (i.e., if one doubts whether he has committed a sin, or whether he has sinned gravely, or whether a sin committed has been confessed) practically speaking need not be confessed. Persons with a lax conscience should be made to confess them (Cf. 90), the scrupulous should never do so, and others are to be advised to confess them.

Whoever purposely confesses to a certain priest in the hope that *not* all his mortal sins will *be understood,* sins mortally against the law requiring an entire confession.

Forgotten or lawfully *omitted sins* (Cf. 567) must be mentioned in the subsequent confession. One need not on this account confess sooner, and one may communicate in the meantime if no other obstacle presents itself.

Repetition of previous confessions is a duty when there is moral certainty about their invalidity. In doubt, repetition is advisable; only in the case of scrupulous persons is it harmful and to be omitted. — Should one make a general confession to his regular confessor who remembers at least indistinctly the sins already confessed, a generic accusation is sufficient. — If, after making invalid or sacrilegious confessions, a penitent, without repeating these, makes other confessions in good faith (e.g., through ignorance or inadvertence) these latter confesssions are valid. The previous invalid confessions however, must be repeated, since the sins thus confessed were not directly remitted.

566. a) *All mortal sins* are properly confessed only when their number and lowest species, together with the circumstances which change the species of the sins, are exactly indicated.

α) If the number cannot be given exactly it must be given as nearly as possible.

If in indicating the number of sins one erroneously minimizes, the mistake must be corrected in the following confesssions.

β) The species of sin must be indicated to the extent in which the penitent recognized the specific malice in the sinful action.

If in confession one is conscious of another grave sin to be confessed, but cannot remember what kind of sin it is, he must at least mention the fact that there is another grave sin to be confessed. Should he recall the sin after confession, he must tell it in his next confession.

γ) The external act of sinning (not only the internal sinful intention) must be confessed.

The effect of a sinful act so far as it no longer depends on the free will need not be mentioned unless such accusation be necessary by reason of special circumstances, e.g., to determine the extent of the harm done, the obligation of restitution, or when a censure is incurred *effectu secuto*.

567. *b*) Impossibility *excuses* from confessing all mortal sins provided confession to this particular confessor must be made immediately.

In such cases the sins are indirectly remitted (by the infusion of sanctifying grace), but they must be told in the subsequent confession in which this excuse does not exist.

a) Impossibility may be physical or moral.

It is *physically impossible* for the following to make an integral confession: a dying person who has lost the use of speech; people who can no longer remember their sins. Physical impossibility also prevails before a battle, during a conflagration or shipwreck; in time of a contagious and serious epidemic, if individual confession is impossible; the mute and those who must confess with the aid of an interpreter are likewise excused from confessing all their sins (Cf. 570).

Moral impossibility obtains if the accusation is connected with a very unusual difficulty which is not intrinsically connected with the nature of confession.

Shame, embarrassment or repugnance in confessing sins to a confessor whom one knows are intrinsic to the nature of confession; so also is fear of a reprimand. Such difficulties do not justify making an incomplete confession.

568. The following are the principal extrinsic difficulties excusing from integrity of confession: *a*) Danger of violating the seal of confession, e.g., if others can recognize from the conduct of the priest in confession that some certain sin is being confessed. *β*) Danger of defamation, e.g., if others (in the infirmary) can overhear the sins, or if the confession lasts so long that others necessarily conclude the penitent has many grave sins to confess. *γ*) Danger of scandal or sin to priest or penitent, e.g., in the accusation of sins against the sixth commandment. Special care must be taken not to teach children sins when questioning them. *δ*) Danger of serious spiritual or temporal detriment (to oneself or others), e.g., a scrupulous person becomes more confused by repeating confessions or by a prolonged examination of conscience; if a lengthy confession is injurious to the health of the penitent; if there is real danger of infection during a contagious epidemic; or if there is danger that the penitent will die before completing his accusation.

569. β) Confession must be made here and now and to this particular confessor if no other confessor is available to whom one can confess without the aforesaid difficulties, and if otherwise the penitent would either die or be obliged to remain in mortal sin for a long time, or if by omitting confession he would give scandal or suffer a loss of reputation.

Wherefore, people are *not excused* from making complete confessions if so many penitents gather for confession before some feastday that it is impossible to hear them all. According to an Instruction of the Sacred Penitentiary on March 25, 1944 (AAS 36-155) priests may give sacramental absolution to many at the same time, or to individuals who make only a partial confession if some grave and urgent necessity arises, which is proportionate to the gravity of the divine precept, for example, if the penitents otherwise without any fault of their own would be deprived for a long time of sacramental grace and of Holy Communion. The case is practical in places where there is no priest, and a visiting priest arrives, but cannot remain long enough to hear the confessions of all the penitents. — A general absolution may likewise be given to soldiers when a battle is imminent or in progress, or if this is impossible, then as soon as it is judged necessary. The same holds for civilians and soldiers in danger of death during hostile invasion. (AAS 32-571).

570. *c*) From the fact that confession must be complete it follows that one must use all the corresponding *ordinary* (not the extraordinary) *means* to insure its integrity.

α) The principal ordinary means is examination of conscience.

As much *care* must be given to this examination as is customarily given to matters of importance. It will vary according to the time over which the examen extends, conditions in which the penitent lives, and his intelligence. Confession is invalid if mortal sins are omitted because of gravely sinful negligence in this matter.

If one fails to confess mortal sins by reason of venially *sinful negligence* the confession remains valid. — He who is morally certain that he has no necessary matter for confession is not at all obliged to make an examination of conscience, although this is advisable to insure genuine contrition and especially an earnest purpose of amendment.

The *writing* of one's sins is never obligatory, not even if one knows beforehand that he will otherwise forget some of them.

β) Since the use of extraordinary means is not obligatory no one is required to confess by means of an interpreter; nor do the dumb need to write out their confession.

However, this is usually advisable for peace of soul. Besides one must remember that a materially incomplete confession is lawful only in case of necessity (Cf. 569).

It should be noted that the hard of hearing are generally obliged to confess in the place designated for them if the integrity of confession requires it. If they have an unusually great aversion toward confessing in such a place, they should not be compelled to do so. — Should the confessor notice at the very beginning of the confession that the penitent is hard of hearing, he should invite the penitent to follow him to the place for hearing such confessions. This should not be done once the confession is partially made lest the bystanders suspect the penitent of having to confess some extraordinary sin. In such cases the penitent is simply absolved, since there is an excuse from the integrity of confession (Cf. 568).

571.   **§ 3. Satisfaction**

I. Concept. Sacramental satisfaction is some penitential work imposed by a confessor in confession, through which atonement for sin is made to God and the penitent is granted a remission of the temporal punishment due to sin.

It is an integral part of the Sacrament of Penance and must, therefore, be imposed by the confessor and accepted by the penitent. Its efficacy is not only *ex opere operantis*, but also *ex opere operato*.

II. Duties of the Confessor. 1. In itself the duty to *impose a penance* is a grave one.

This obligation admits of a *smallness of matter* (parvitas materiae), so that the confessor sins only venially if he does not impose any penance for venial sins confessed. — If the penitent is altogether *unable* to perform a penance, none need be given. If the penitent is not unconscious, at least a small penance should be imposed, e.g., kissing the crucifix or repeating the ejaculation: "My Jesus, Mercy!" — If the penitent confesses an *additional mortal sin* immediately after receiving absolution, a new penance need not be imposed, as long as the first penance given may still be said to correspond to the kind and number of the sins confessed.

572. — 2. The penance must be in keeping with the *number* and *nature* of the sins confessed, with due consideration for the *ability* of the penitent.

Wherefore, in itself a grave penance must be imposed for grievous sins. A "grave" penance is the performance of a work which the Church can prescribe under mortal sin, e.g., hearing Mass, receiving Holy Communion, fasting, recitation of the rosary; but not a mere five Our Fathers. — Intense sorrow of the penitent, zeal for gaining indulgences, and especially the danger that the penitent will not perform a large penance or will be estranged from the reception of the Sacraments, are some of the reasons sufficient to excuse the priest from imposing a grave penance. — Furthermore, works that are obligatory may be given as a penance, e.g., hearing Mass on Sunday.

3. It is best to impose the penance *before imparting absolution;* this is not prescribed, however.

573. — III. Duties of the Penitent. 1. In itself it is a grave obligation for the penitent to *accept and perform* any reasonable penance imposed upon him in a valid confession.

It is *a mortal sin* not to perform a grave penance which has been imposed *sub gravi* for mortal sins. If the penitent before receiving absolution does not intend to perform such a penance, his confession would be invalid. — It is a venial sin to omit a light penance which has been imposed for either mortal or venial sins. If it is not entirely or not exactly performed as imposed, the penitent would only then commit a grave sin if he omitted a very important part of it. Accordingly, if one is told to recite the

rosary on his knees, he would sin venially by reciting it standing
or by voluntarily omitting a few Hail Marys. — One does not
sin by not performing a penance which is not in keeping with
present church practice or which is unreasonably grave. In such
cases it is best to have the confessor commute the penance in
the subsequent confession.

If one, with or without sin, *forgets the penance* imposed, he
is strictly speaking not obliged to perform any penance. It is very
advisable however, to return and ask the confessor what the penance was; if he thinks the priest no longer remembers the penance
he can receive a new penance in the following confession after
giving the confessor a general idea of his previous confession, or
he can say as penance the prayers usually imposed upon him for
such sins as he confessed.

**574. — 2. It *suffices* that the penance imposed be per-
formed in the manner in which the confessor imposed it.**

The *intention* to perform the penance is not necessary (Cf. also
63). — One may perform his penance *while fulfilling another
obligation*. Thus, a rosary imposed as penance may be said while
hearing Sunday Mass. — If a work *already prescribed* is imposed
as penance, e.g., hearing Mass, the penance cannot be fulfilled
by hearing a Mass of obligation, unless the confessor has expressly
declared this to be sufficient. — If prayers are imposed that are
frequently said *alternately* (the rosary) one does his duty by thus
saying them. — *Voluntary distractions* while saying a penance do
not hinder the fulfillment of the obligation; but as irreverence
during prayer they are venially sinful. — A penance can still be
performed after the penitent falls into *mortal sin*. — By performing a work given as penance one can also gain indulgences connected therewith (C. 932).

**574. — 3. In itself there is no definite *time* pre-
scribed for the performance of a penance.**

Therefore, a penance might be *postponed* until after the following confession. If the confessor has designatd a certain time for
its performance the penance should be performed within that time.
— In both the foregoing cases it would be a *grave sin* to postpone
a penance if the delay would constitute a danger of one's entirely
forgetting a grave penance that is imposed under serious obligation, or if it would make its performance impossible, or if the

value of the penitential work were considerably diminished by the postponement.

IV. Commutation of a penance is lawful for a reasonable cause and may be made by any confessor who has at least an imperfect knowledge of the penitent's state of soul.

A reasonable *cause* is any spiritual benefit to the penitent himself. — *Commutation* into an equivalent or less valuable work may be made at, or even without, the request of the penitent.— The confessor who imposed the penance may also commute the penance outside of confession; any other confessor can do so only in confession. The penitent himself cannot exchange the penance given him for one considerably better. — Knowledge of the previous penance may be sufficient information about the *state* of the penitent's soul.

576. Chapter IV

THE MINISTER OF THE SACRAMENT OF PENANCE

The priest alone is the minister of the Sacrament of Penance (C. 871). We shall consider his faculties and obligations.

Article I

Powers of the Minister

A confessor must be possessed of the powers of Orders and Jurisdiction (C. 872). The power of Orders is treated primarily in dogmatic theology. Moral theology is concerned chiefly with the power of jurisdiction.

§ 1. Jurisdiction in General

Jurisdiction may be ordinary, delegated (ab homine **or a iure**) or supplied.

A. Ordinary Jurisdiction.

I. The subject of ordinary jurisdiction is one with whose office jurisdiction is connected by law, e.g., residential bishops, pastors and superiors of exempt clerical religious institutions in keeping with their constitutions.

Religious superiors should hear the confessions of those subjects only who freely request this. Only for a grave reason should they do so habitually (C. 518).

II. The extent of ordinary jurisdiction covers the entire district committed to one's care, and in case of superiors it extends over their subjects.

Whoever has ordinary jurisdiction can absolve any of the faithful *within his territory,* but outside his district only his own subjects (C. 881). Custom also gives the pastor delegated jurisdiction anywhere within the diocese outside his own parish. In the U. S. Ordinaries usually give *diocesan* faculties.

The following are subjects in an exempt clerical *religious community* with regard to confessional jurisdiction: all professed members, novices, servants, pupils, guests, the sick and the convalescent, provided they reside within the enclosure day and night (C. 514; 875).

III. The cessation of ordinary jurisdiction takes place by the loss of office; also by excommunication, interdict or suspension from office after a declaratory or condemnatory sentence (C. 873).

577. B. *Jurisdiction Delegated ab Homine.*

I. Power to grant delegation is vested in the local Ordinary (C. 874) and the superiors of clerical exempt religious institutes designated by their constitutions (C. 875).

Penitentiaries (C. 401) and pastors (AAS 11-477) cannot delegate.

Exempt male religious confessing for peace of conscience, may be absolved by any confessor approved by the local Ordinary from sins and censures, even those reserved in the community (C. 519), without the obligation of having recourse afterwards.

II. Delegation must be explicit, either in words or writing (C. 879). Hence, it may not be presumed.

It should not be given to anyone known to be intellectually unqualified. Certainty in this matter is usually obtained by an examination (C. 877).

578. — **III. The extent** of delegated jurisdiction is restricted to the boundaries of the respective territory.

Hence, unlike the pastor, one delegated for a certain territory cannot absolve outside of that territory. — It is to be noted, however, that due to an arrangement among bishops, a priest delegated for his own diocese is often delegated for the *bordering diocese*. In case of a religious this delegation usually lasts only as long as one is stationed in a house situated in the respective diocese.

IV. Cessation of delegated jurisdiction occurs by expiration of the time or exhaustion of the number of cases for which delegation was given; by the fulfillment of some commission, by the delegating superior's revocation directly conveyed to the delegate; by renunciation of the delegate made directly to the delegating party and accepted by him; and by cessation of the chief cause (for which delegation was granted), but generally not by the delegating party's retirement from office (C. 207).

Should the one delegating *die* or *retire from office,* delegation would cease only if the jurisdiction had been given for some definite person and the confession had not yet been commenced when the delegating party died; or in case this had been expressly mentioned when jurisdiction was granted by such clauses as "donec ego vixero" or "ad beneplacitum nostrum." Such a restriction is not contained in the clause "usque ad revocationem." He absolves validly who *does not advert* to the fact that the time of his delegation has expired or the number of cases for which he received jurisdiction has been exhausted (C. 207).

579. *C. Jurisdiction Delegated a Iure.*

I. In danger of death any priest may validly and lawfully absolve any penitent from any sin or censure including those that are reserved or notorious although he is otherwise not possessed of any jurisdiction; and even in the presence of an approved confessor (C. 882).

The *danger of death* may arise from illness or from some external cause, e.g., fire, battle, shipwreck, etc.

Every priest has this power, even the irregular, censured, apostate, schismatic or heretical priest, provided he has been validly ordained. To avoid scandal one may be forbidden to call such a priest if an approved priest is available. Absolution may also be given by one of the above-mentioned in the presence of a priest who has special faculties for the respective reservations.

Confer 428 regarding the obligation of *having recourse* when censures are absolved in danger of death. Concerning the confession or absolution of non-Catholics confer 558.

The only exception concerns absolving an accomplice.

The absolution of an accomplice is always valid when the accomplice is in danger of death, but it is lawful only under certain conditions (Cf. 589).

580. — II. On a sea voyage priests may absolve all fellow passengers if they have lawfully received confessional jurisdiction either from their own bishop or from the bishop of the harbor whence they embarked or from the bishop of any intermediate port where the ship puts in. This obtains also if the ship passes or stops at various places subject to the jurisdiction of different Ordinaries. — As often as the ship puts in at port priests may hear the confessions of the faithful who for any reason whatever come aboard, or whom they may meet on land if they go ashore. These same faithful may also be absolved from cases reserved to their local Ordinary (C. 883).

These faculties are in force at the beginning of the voyage and expire as soon as those to whom they are granted definitely leave the ship, even though they journey farther inland. The faculties may also be exercised on land if the priest tarries one or two days ashore, even though he transfers to another ship. However, this would not be the case if the priest stays ashore longer than three days and can easily approach the local Ordinary (AAS 16-114).

III. Priests **travelling by air** have the same faculties for confessions as those who take an ocean journey, appropriate adjustment of the clauses to fit the case being made. (Pius XII *Motu Proprio*, Dec. 16, 1947.)

581. — IV. Delegation *a iure* takes place in two instances concerning **Sisters' Confessions.**

A particular delegation by law is required since special jurisdiction is necessary for hearing the confessions of religious women (C. 876).

1. *For peace of conscience* any Sister may validly and lawfully confess to any priest approved by the local Ordinary for hearing confessions of women in any church, public or semi-public oratory, as also in any place legitimately appointed for hearing confessions of women (C. 522; AAS 12-575).

Every sincere confession is made for *peace of conscience.* — This confession may also be made in the Sister's own church or convent chapel. The Sister may also summon such a priest to come and hear her confession. If the confession is not made at one of the places mentioned it is invalid (AAS 20-61).

2. *In grave illness* a Sister may confess to any priest approved for confessions of women as often as she pleases (C. 523).

Danger of death is not necessary.

582. *D. Supplied Jurisdiction.*

Supplied jurisdiction is a form of delegation imparted in the very act of confession, so that a confession once begun becomes valid.

I. In common error the Church supplies jurisdiction (C. 209).

One may follow the opinion which holds that *a common error* is had when some public act is posited which in itself is capable of leading, not one or the other, but all people indiscriminately into error, even though perhaps one or the other because of his special information may be aware of the lack of jurisdiction. — Absolution is valid even though the penitent realizes the priest's lack of jurisdiction.

Although absolution thus given is valid, it remains *gravely forbidden,* since the Church supplies jurisdiction only for the sake of the common welfare. — Absolution is lawful only for a very serious reason (e.g., for a reason that would permit one to say Mass without fasting).

II. Doubt of law or fact (*dubium iuris vel facti*) is another case in which jurisdiction is supplied (C. 209).

A dubium iuris is had if the law itself is doubtful (if, for example, there is a controversy regarding the meaning of *error communis*). *A dubium facti* obtains if the doubt concerns a fact (e.g., whether he who committed a crime, punishable by a censure l.s., possessed the requisite imputability). — Absolution may be given without a special reason, since in this instance the Church supplies jurisdiction for the sake of the confessor and the penitent and only *ad cautelam.*

III. If jurisdiction has expired and the priest, without adverting to the fact, continues to hear confessions, jurisdiction is likewise supplied (C. 207).

583.   § 2. Restriction of Jurisdiction by
Reservation

I. Reservation of sins is the limitation by a competent superior of an inferior's power of absolution so that the latter cannot absolve certain sins for want of jurisdiction.

Superiors (C. 895; 896) may reserve at most, three or four of the more grievous, atrocious, and external sins which must be specifically determined. The reservation should not remain in force longer than is necessary to eradicate some inveterate vice or to restore decadent Christian discipline (C. 897). — Confer also C. 898 and C. 2247.

Reservation directly affects the confessor, so that a stranger can be absolved in another diocese from a case reserved in his home diocese, even though he goes to the other diocese solely to be absolved (C. 900), but he cannot be absolved from cases reserved in the other diocese.

The reservation lasts only as long as the sin is necessary matter for confession (Cf. 550). — It probably ceases as soon as a confessor, having faculties for the reserved case, passes judgment on the sin though the confession be invalid or sacrilegious, or even if the sin be inculpably omitted.

584. — II. To incur a reservation it is required that: the sin be complete in its species; that it be formal and external; it must be mortal both as to the external act and the internal act of the will; and finally, there must be certainty, not only that all these conditions are verified, but that the reservation affects this particular sin.

Any confessor reasonably *doubting* whether one of the foregoing requisites is lacking may absolve from the reserved sin since the Church supplies jurisdiction in case of a doubt (Cf. 582).

Ignorance of the reservation very probably does not excuse one from incurring it, although the contrary opinion extrinsically may be more probable. Nevertheless, in some dioceses knowledge of the reservation is expressly given as a condition for incurring it.

III. Reservations cease in confessions of the sick who cannot leave the house, and when couples confess in preparation for marriage; as often as the superior does not grant faculties for a particular case when asked; when, according to the judgment of the confessor, the superior cannot even be approached without great harm to the penitent or violation of the seal; if the penitent goes to confession outside the diocese where the case is reserved (C. 900); finally, in danger of death (C. 882).

Great harm may be done to the penitent by simply constraining him to remain in sin for a longer time.

In the cases mentioned the reservation ceases no matter whether the sin is reserved to the Pope or to the Ordinary; but it must be borne in mind that we are here concerned only with reserved sins, not reserved censures (for the latter, see 427 sq.).

585. — IV. Absolution from reserved sins can be given in virtue of ordinary power by him who makes the reservation, by his successor or superior; in virtue of delegated power, by him who has received special faculties from a competent superior.

The law grants faculties to absolve from diocesan reserved cases to the Canon Penitentiary in a cathedral or collegiate church (C. 899), to pastors during the entire paschal season (even though the penitent has already made his "Easter confession") and to missionaries during the time of a mission (C. 899). What is said of missions may be applied also to public retreats. Local Ordinaries are obliged to grant at least to deans the habitual faculties to absolve from reserved sins and the power to subdelegate in some specific and more urgent case (C. 899). If sins are reserved in an exempt religious community, several confessors in every monastery must be given faculties to absolve (C. 518).

586.   § 3. Abuse of Jurisdiction

A. Inquiring about the Name of an Accomplice

The Prohibition. The confessor must guard against asking the name of the penitent's accomplice (C. 888).

He commits a *grave sin* who, with the intention of learning the name of a penitent's accomplice (*inquisitio formalis*), asks for his name or about circumstances from which he will recognize him.

But it is *lawful* and even a *duty* to ask about proximate circumstances which are necessary for the integrity of the confession or for the correct direction of the penitent, even though one recognizes thereby the sinner's accomplice.

For the sake of the common welfare the confessor may demand, under penalty of refusing absolution, that the accomplice be denounced to the proper superior outside of confession.

587.   B. Absolution of an Accomplice

The Prohibition. A priest's absolution of his accomplice in a sin of impurity is invalid. The only exception is in danger of death; even then it is illicit except in case of necessity, according to the rules of the Apostolic Constitutions, especially the Constitution of Benedict XIV. *Sacramentum Poenitentiae* of June 1, 1741 (C. 884).

I. The accomplice may be a person of either sex, whether an adult or a child under the age of puberty.

The law includes the case in which both were children when the sin was committed and the confessor at that time never thought of becoming a priest. The following conditions must obtain.

588. — II. The sin must be one against the sixth commandment, and must be internally and externally grave for both parties.

1. *Against the sixth commandment* means that sins against any other law or virtue are not included in the prohibition.

A completed sin against chastity is not required. Unchaste touches, looks or speech suffice (S. Offic. March 18, 1873).

2. *Externally* means the sin must be apparent.

Merely internal sins (e.g., sins that might accompany a conventional kiss of greeting) do not fall under this prohibition.

3. It must be *a grave sin* externally as well as internally.

A sin is *externally grave* if the party externally manifests consent, e.g., by making no earnest resistance to gravely sinful touches.

The case is *not* verified if the external action is only very unbecoming, but not gravely sinful. — Neither does the law include an action that is externally a mortal sin, but is not so internally, e.g., due to insufficient advertence or consent. Finally, it does not include the case where one internally consents but outwardly offers earnest resistance.

4. The action must be *mutually* a grave sin.

Thus, sins committed with a sleeping person, with one fully intoxicated or insane, or with one who is entirely too ignorant to know that such conduct is gravely sinful, are *not* included. Confer, however, the recent restriction of the Holy Office (AAS 26-634) in 590. — Furthermore, it is not enough that one only mediately takes part in the sin, e.g., by making the sin possible; he must be an immediate accomplice in the sin.

5. *Certainty* is required concerning the presence of the above-named conditions.

In doubt whether an act was objectively a grave sin, or whether one party sinned gravely this law would not apply.

589. — III. Restriction of Jurisdiction. 1. *Apart from the danger of death* all jurisdiction over the sin in question is withdrawn from the priest accomplice as long as the sin has not been directly remitted.

The sin is *indirectly* absolved if the penitent inculpably omits confessing it or confesses other sins together with it to the priest accomplice. Even though such indirect absolution is valid if the penitent is rightly disposed it is, nevertheless, forbidden under grave sin for the priest to impart it. — If the penitent has already been directly absolved by another confessor the priest accomplice recovers jurisdiction over this sin, although it is not advisable that he again hear the confession of his accomplice. Superiors may sometimes forbid the priest ever again to hear the confession of his accomplice.

2. *In danger of death* a priest accomplice always has jurisdiction over the sin in question. But absolution is lawful only in a few instances.

Such instances are: if there is no other priest present or available, not even one without jurisdiction; if another priest refuses to hear the sick person's confession or if the penitent refuses to confess to any other priest; if another priest cannot be called without scandal or defamation. — The priest accomplice should try to avoid scandal or defamation if possible, e.g., by going on a journey.

590. — IV. The penalty for absolving (or feigning to absolve) an accomplice is excommunication reserved *specialissimo modo* to the Holy See. This applies also in case the accomplice is validly, but unlawfully absolved in danger of death (C. 2367).

Hence, *the penalty* is incurred if the penitent confesses the sin and the confessor absolves or pretends to absolve him directly or indirectly. It is likewise incurred if, upon direct or indirect inducement of the confessor, the penitent fails to confess this particular sin which has not yet been directly remitted, and the priest absolves or feigns to absolve him (C. 2367). According to a decision of the Holy Office, for the priest to tell a person before committing the sin that a certain unchaste act is not a sin or at least not a serious sin, constitutes an indirect inducement for the penitent to be silent about it in confession (AAS 26-634).

The priest commits a grave sin but is not excommunicated if he absolves his accomplice who culpably or inculpably omits to tell the sin without the confessor's in any way inducing the omission.

Ht neither sins nor is penalized if, when his accomplice confesses in the presence of others, he is mindful of his lack of jurisdiction and merely dismisses the penitent with a blessing to avoid defaming him.

A confessor is excused from sin and penalty if he absolves his accomplice to avoid self-defamation. This may happen when the penitent is not aware of the identity of his accomplice; not, however, if the penitent knows who the accomplice is, but does not know that he is about to make his confession to him. — The confessor is likewise excused from both sin and censure if he doubts whether a certain person is his accomplice, and cannot attain certainty without defaming himself.

Another excuse from sin and excommunication is had if the priest's accomplice (e.g., in some out-of-the-way place) never has an opportunity to confess to another priest, or if the penitent must confess but cannot go to another priest without great danger of defamation or scandal. The confessor must then tell the penitent that this sin will be remitted only indirectly and that it must be confessed later to another priest.

When *recourse to Rome* is had, the information, whether or not the respective priest was ever absolved from this censure before must be given. If there have been three transgressions since the last absolution from censure, Rome demands that the priest cease hearing confessions (S. Poenit. March 5, 1925). — If the penitent cannot abstain from his office of confessor, the first petition to the Sacred Penitentiary may contain a request that this requirement be omitted, giving the reasons for the request (Formulary for petition confer 797).

If the priest, after incurring the excommunication, unlawfully exercises his Sacred Orders, he becomes irregular (Cf. 648). On dispensation from irregularity confer 643, 644.

591.   *C. Solicitation.*

The law. According to the laws of the Apostolic Constitutions, especially that of Benedict XIV. *Sacramentum Poenitentiae* of June 1, 1741 a penitent must denounce a confessor who is guilty of solicitation in confession. The denunciation must be made within one month either to the local Ordinary or to the Congregation of the Holy Office. The confessor has a grave duty to inform the penitent of this obligation (C. 904).

I. The sin of solicitation consists in this, that a priest in connection with confession attempts to seduce a penitent to some grave sin against chastity, or holds unlawful or unchaste conversation with the same or makes arrangements to commit such a sin.

The sin is also committed if the penitent commences the solicitation and thus induces the confessor to sin so that the solicitation eventually becomes mutual.

592. — 1. *A sin against the sixth commandment* is the first requisite.

Neither the sex nor the age of the penitent matters, nor whether the penitent is personally solicited or is used as an intermediary for the solicitation of a third person; nor whether the penitent is induced to sin with the priest or with another person or with himself or herself; nor whether the sin is to be committed forthwith or later. Even unlawful or indecent words or appointments suffice.

Solicitation can be made by words, signs, gestures or touches; or by writing that is to be read immediately or later. Unchaste talk or appointments constitute solicitation in so far as the confessor thereby wishes to gratify his evil inclinations. Solicitation occurs not only when the priest expressly induces the penitent to sin against the sixth commandment, but also if his bearing or manner of speech, by their very nature either induce the penitent to commit such sins or confirm him in the practice of committing them, e.g., if he says: in difficult family conditions conjugal onanism is not a grave sin; pollution is lawful for considerations of health.

593. — 2. The second requirement is that the sin be *a mortal sin.*

It is *not necessary* that whatever takes place in connection with confession be objectively a grave sin. In itself it may even be good or indifferent, but, as the eventuality indicates, done with a gravely sinful intention. Hence, it may be difficult to have certainty as to whether or not the gravely sinful intention existed already in the confessional, e.g., if the confessor merely asks about the penitent's place of residence or makes an appointment with her in his room. If no other plausible reason for such action could be given, the confessor must be denounced; however, if some honorable motivation might be construed, e.g., because the confessor actually had some very important matters to discuss with the person, the evil intention can usually not be proved and, therefore, in virtue of canon law no denunciation need be made. — The obligation of denunciation exists whether the *penitent consented* to the solicitation or not; even if the penitent at the time (because of innocence) in no way realized the solicitation; likewise if the solicitation was *on the part of the penitent* and the confessor consented and sufficiently manifested his reaction externally.

If the confessor induced the penitent to do something slightly improper, there is no obligation to denounce him. — Neither does such a duty exist if the confessor says or does something unbecoming, not maliciously, but in *innocent simplicity.*

594. — 3. There must be *a connection between confession and solicitation.*

Solicitation when administering the other Sacraments does not come under this law.

Such a relation obtains if:

a) Solicitation takes place *during the confession* itself.

This includes the time before absolution, beginning with the preliminary blessing. It is not necessary that absolution be actually given. That which takes place during the confession may be objectively indifferent; it is sufficient if later on it becomes evident that the action was prompted by a gravely sinful intention (Cf. 593).

b) Solicitation is committed *immediately before* **or** *after* confession.

This is the case if no action intervenes between solicitation and the actual confession, or only such action as has reference to solicitation.

c) Solicitation takes place *on the occasion of confession.*

This is so, if the penitent begins with the serious intention to confess, but confession does not actually follow because the penitent, having been solicited, either indignantly leaves or consents to the solicitation, thus discontinuing his confession. — One has *no duty to denounce* a priest who solicits him outside of confession when he asks the confessor to hear his confession the following day (not immediately); nor if the confessor uses confessional knowledge to solicit a penitent later, but in no wise reveals his evil intention in the confessional.

595. *d*) Solicitation is done *under the pretext of confession.*

Denunciation is in place, for example, if the confessor visits a sick person on the plea of hearing her confession, and then solicits her. *No obligation to denounce* obtains if the sick person calls the priest on the pretext of going to confession, but in reality only wishes to seduce him. Neither need the confessor be denounced if the person is bent on sinning and uses confession as a mask to shield the confessor in the eyes of others, e.g., by alleging confession as the reason for the priest's visit.

e) Solicitation takes place *in the confessional,* or in a place permanently *designated* for hearing confessions, or where confessions are heard *temporarily,* provided that in all three instances both participants act as though confession were being made.

A place where the hard of hearing go to confession is permanently designated for confessions. Confession is heard temporarily, e.g., in the sacristy, chapel, any room in case of a crowd, a sick room or sick bed. — In a confessional or place permanently set aside for confessions, there is a pretense of confession by the very fact that one is present there, unless it is evident that he does not intend to go to confession. In a place where confessions are heard only temporarily a pretense of confession requires some positive act, e.g., a blessing is given as at the beginning of confession or the priest inclines his head as though he were hearing the penitent's accusation.

4. Finally, *if there is certainty* that the conditions just mentioned are verified.

596. — II. The Denunciation. 1. Any priest guilty of solicitation *must be denounced.*

Even a priest devoid of jurisdiction; or when the penitent first solicits and the confessor consents, provided the latter gives external evidence of his consent; even if the sin is postponed till later; or if the matter is long past and has remained secret; or if the priest has long since repented and made amends; or if the penitent at the time did not realize the solicitation; or if the priest shortly after beginning the solicitation discontinued and was sorry for his sin. — The obligation ceases after the death of the priest.

2. The *duty to denounce* rests on the person solicited. Others are not obliged by the Code, but they may be summoned as witnesses.

The denunciation must be made even though the penitent only in later life realizes the evil intention of a confessor; no matter if the solicitation can be proved or not; or if others have already denounced him; or if the penitent consented to the solicitation or commenced it (the denouncing person need not metion his own sin). — The priest need not denounce himself; he will be treated with much greater leniency, however, if he does.

Even if the requirements of canon law are not given, the natural law may still oblige one to denounce. Thus, one is gravely obliged in charity to denounce a priest if by doing so a grave sin or great harm can be averted. Grave personal inconvenience excuses from this duty of charity. Should the conduct of the priest be to the serious detriment of the community, the natural law would oblige one to denounce him even at the cost of great personal inconvenience.

597. — 3. Denunciation obliges under *grave sin* and must be made *within one month* reckoned from the time one becomes conscious of the obligation.

A priest hearing a solicited person's confession is obliged to instruct the penitent concerning this duty; the soliciting confessor alone is excused from this obligation. Before a confessor obliges a penitent to this denunciation he must make sure that the penitent is trustworthy. — He must impose the obligation even if the penitent is now in good faith, and even if it can be foreseen that the obligation will not be fulfilled. However, he need not do so if the penitent is in danger of death or if the confessor who solicited, no longer hears confessions.

4. The denunciation is made to the *Holy Office* or to the *local Ordinary*.

According to an Instruction of the Holy Office, June 9, 1922, he is the local Ordinary in whose territory the soliciting priest has his residence. — The denunciation would quite naturally be made to the Ordinary of the place where the penitent resides, but he in turn must transmit the sworn accusation to the Ordinary of the soliciting priest. — Religious superiors, even exempt, are strictly forbidden to accept such a denunciation.

5. The denunciation is made in the juridically prescribed *form*.

It is best first of all briefly to inform the respective superior of the fact, either orally or in writing. He should be told of the time of the solicitation and the immediate circumstances (e.g., whether during confession or on the occasion of confessing, etc.) In order that the denunciation be valid it is absolutely necessary that the penitent sign his name and give his address. If the confessor helps the penitent in this matter he must take great care not to discover the name of the priest denounced. The penitent should insert the soliciting priest's name in the letter drafted by the confessor. — The juridical denunciation itself takes place only when the person denouncing, at the request of the local Ordinary or his delegate, confirms the accusation with an oath and his signature.

598. — III. Excuses from the obligation of denouncing are impossibility or unusually great harm.

Natural shame and embarrassment are no excuse; neither is gratitude nor fear of the ill will of the person denounced; but great danger to one's life, health or livelihood excuses; as also does the circumstance that the priest is a close relation or a very good friend. — But should the common welfare demand denunciation no consideration of livelihood, relationship or friendship would excuse. — If denunciation cannot be made within a month, it must be done as soon as possible.

599. — IV. Penalties. 1. *Solicitation* is punished by very grave penalties *ferendae sententiae* (C. 2368).

2. *Failure to denounce* is automatically penalized by excommunication not reserved to anyone, provided the penitent knowingly neglects to denounce within a month reckoned from the time he becomes conscious of his obligation (C. 2368).

The penitent may be absolved from the censure by any confessor in the sacramental forum (Cf. 428), but only after making the denunciation or solemnly promising to do so (C. 2368). Should the promise not be kept, the excommunication does not revive, but the grave obligation to denounce remains.

3. *False denunciation* is penalized by excommunication specially reserved to the Holy See (C. 2363).

They also incur this censure who are instrumental in causing someone else to make a false denunciation (Cf. 424). — This penalty is incurred by juridical denunciation, even in case no action is taken against the priest. — The penalty is not incurred by merely sending a letter, signed or anonymous, to the bishop; neither is it incurred if the denunciation is made to a religious superior.

Absolution from this censure can be given only after the false denunciation has been formally retracted and reparation made as far as possible. Moreover, a severe and prolonged penance must be imposed (C. 2363). One may absolve from this censure in an urgent case after the penitent has signed a retraction or has disavowed his accusation in the presence of two witnesses.

The *natural law* requires that calumny be retracted and restitution be made for the harm inflicted even in those cases where excommunication has not been incurred.

Absolution from the sin of false denunciation is reserved to the Holy See and it is the *only* sin that is reserved *ratione sui*.

Again it is only the juridical denunciation that is reserved. The reservation is incurred even when the excommunication is not, e.g., due to ignorance (Cf. 425). — Concerning the cessation of this reservation confer 584.

600.   *Article II*

Duties of the Minister

As teacher, physician and judge the confessor must be possessed of sufficient knowledge to administer profitably the Sacrament of Penance. He must teach the penitent, properly judge the state of his soul, absolve him, correct mistakes and safeguard the seal of confession. Special difficulties are involved in fulfilling these duties toward some penitents.

§ 1. Acquisition and Preservation of Necessary Knowledge

The confessor must have at least that knowledge which is required to judge immediately and properly the cases that ordinarily occur in his locality; in rare and difficult cases he should know enough to doubt and to be conscious of his obligation not to judge without either consulting his books or seeking counsel from others.

More knowledge is required in cities than in country districts.

A priest commits a *grave sin* if he hears confessions when he knows that he does not possess the requisite knowledge. If he doubts his ability he may follow the judgment of the one who grants faculties. — A superior sins gravely if he approves a priest as confessor who is intellectually unqualified for the office. Should a superior reasonably doubt the ability of a priest to whom he has granted jurisdiction, he must examine him anew, even though he be a pastor (C. 877). — The penitent, too, sins seriously by intentionally seeking an ignorant confessor, although simplicity may often excuse him.

601.   § 2. The Confessor as Teacher

I. There is an **obligation** to instruct the penitent:

1. If the penitent's ignorance concerns matters, the knowledge of which is a *necessary means* for salvation, or the knowledge of which is necessary for the *fruitful reception* of the Sacrament.

It matters not whether the knowledge of these respective truths is certainly or only probably necessary for salvation. Instead of teaching the penitent in the confessional the Sacrament may be postponed till the penitent has studied his religion for himself; such procedure, however, is usually not advisable.

2. If the penitent's ignorance is *invincible* and the priest forsees that instruction will be profitable either now or later.

An exception is had where the harm will be greater than the benefit.

3. If the penitent through *vincible* and *gravely sinful* ignorance thinks that what is a mortal sin is no sin at all or only venial.

The same holds for actions, etc. of whose gravely sinful character the penitent cannot much longer remain in ignorance.

4. If the penitent *doubts* whether something is mortally sinful or not.

The penitent is usually in doubt when he *asks questions,* and therefore he is no longer in good faith and must be taught. He may be in good faith if he asks a question merely to manifest a scruple or because he considers something venially sinful. — Sometimes one should not answer more than is asked; e.g., if one who has taken a vow of chastity, asks whether it is lawful to render the marriage debt, one may simply answer "yes," withou. adding the fact that in this case the debt may not be requested.

5. If the ignorance or error of the penitent is the cause of *great harm.*

This happens if the penitent erroneously thinks something is sinful, which is not, or thinks a thing mortally sinful which is only a venial sin; if the penitent is in danger of contracting some sinful habit or is living in the proximate occasion of sin.

6. If the *public welfare* would suffer by the silence of the confessor.

Thus, if the invalidity of a marriage is commonly known the penitent must be told even though he has till now been in good faith, and even if it is foreseen that he will not pay any attention to the information.

602. — II. Instruction may be omitted if the ignorance of the penitent is invincible and no benefit can be expected from such instruction, and if the lack of instruction is not harmful to the penitent nor to the community.

It may also be omitted though the omission be to the detriment of a private individual, e.g., if it can be foreseen that the penitent will not make any restitution in spite of being told of his obligation. — It may also be omitted if the penitent would obey, but if the harm of doing so would outweigh the benefit, e.g., if the children would suffer greatly through a confessor's telling a penitent of the altogether unsuspected invalidity of his marriage. — In a doubt whether the instruction would be more harmful than beneficial it is ordinarily not given.

603. § 3. The Confessor as Judge

As judge the confessor must pass judgment on the penitent before absolving him. For this reason it is sometimes necessary to ask questions.

I. In passing judgment the priest must consider both the sins and the disposition of the penitent.

1. *Sins* are judged according to their quantity and quality.

An implicit judgment suffices, such as a confessor forms who hears confession with the requisite knowledge and attention.

2. A penitent may be absolved if the confessor reasonably judges that he is probably *disposed*.

It may often be considered a sufficient indication of a good disposition if a person confesses of his own accord. He is very doubtfully disposed who, without making any resistance, always falls into his old sins, does not avoid the proximate occasion of sin, or uses no means for improvement. This doubt may be outweighed, however, by the fact that the penitent now confesses with much greater contrition than formerly; or if he has been aroused from his state of indifference by a mission, a death, etc; or if at present he confesses some sin which he formerly concealed; or by his fulfilling some grave obligation, e.g., making restitution.

604. — II. Questioning the Penitent. 1. *The obligation.* Questions are necessary primarily to insure the integrity of confession, less frequently to discover the disposition of the penitent.

a) To insure integrity the priest must ask questions as often as he reasonably doubts whether a confession is complete, no matter whether the penitent fails to confess sins either culpably or inculpably.

An act need only be confessed in as far as it was known to be sinful. Hence, the confessor must in the first place ascertain to what extent the penitent sinned subjectively. If this is impossible he may leave the entire judgment to God. — The confessor should pay special heed to C. 888: "he should avoid putting inquisitive or useless questions, especially concerning the sixth commandment; and take special care not to question young people imprudently about things of which they are ignorant." Confer 606 on what the confessor must do when he doubts the sincerity of the penitent.

b) The penitent's answers to questions regarding his *disposition,* may be accepted if he is evidently in earnest and sincere.

The proposition which held that a priest may absolve any penitent who merely says he is disposed, even though there are serious reasons to believe otherwise, has been condemned by Innocent XI.

2. *Gravity of the Obligation.* In itself this obligation is grave. A confessor sins grievously by failing to ask questions if he neglects this duty to such an extent that he does not learn to know the penitent's spiritual state of soul, or is unable to direct him properly, or if the Sacrament is thereby exposed to the danger of invalidity.

The duty of the confessor to ask questions is not as grave as the penitent's obligation to examine his conscience and accuse himself properly. As the effort of penitents in examining their conscience varies with their respective abilities (Cf. 570), so the confessor's duty to put questions differs with various penitents (e.g., the ignorant, the gravely ill, etc.). He need not apply additional care even though he could hope thereby to discover still other sins.

605.·   § 4. The Duty to Absolve

I. A properly disposed penitent must be absolved without delay (C. 886).

Concerning the required disposition confer 603. — Absolution may be *postponed* only if the penitent can offer no reasonable objection, e.g., if the priest has good reason to believe that the penitent subsequently will not fulfill some grave obligation (e.g., of restitution).

If, regarding his obligations, a penitent wishes to *follow an opinion* which the confessor thinks false, the latter must nevertheless give absolution if reputable moralists consider such an opinion probable. If however, the penitent alone considers such an opinion probable (e.g., the lawfulness of conjugal onanism) the confessor may not absolve him.

II. A certainly indisposed penitent must be refused absolution.

The confessor can frequently dispose such a one in the confessional and thereupon absolve him.

III. A doubtfully disposed penitent *per se* must be refused absolution; in exceptional cases and only for a grave reason may or must he be absolved conditionally.

Such serious reasons are: the danger of defamation or estrangement from the Sacraments, necessity to receive a Sacrament (Matrimony, Confirmation), or danger of death.

If the confessor cannot *decide* whether a penitent is doubtfully or certainly disposed, he should do what, as far as he can foresee, will be most beneficial to the spiritual welfare of the penitent (Cf. also 609).

606. — IV. In doubt about the sincerity of penitents who do not confess grave sins when the confessor has reason to expect that they should do so, a distinction must be made:

1. *Conditional absolution* must be given if it can be assumed that the penitent has *forgotten* the sins, or has *already confessed* them, or has a sufficient **reason to omit** confessing them (Cf. 567).

2. *In other cases* we must again distinguish:

a) If the confessor knows of the penitent's sins from the *statement of others* he may refuse absolution provided he is morally certain of the truth of their assertion, in spite of the contrary protestation of the penitent.

b) If the *confessor himself witnessed* the sin and if all error is out of the question he may not absolve, though the penitent stubbornly denies it.

c) If he has the knowledge from the *confession of an accomplice,* he must above all beware of breaking the seal by imprudent questions. Because of the different opinions of moralists he may absolve either absolutely, or conditionally, or not at all without the penitent's becoming aware of the fact.

607.   § 5. Duties Towards Occasionists Consuetudinarians and Recidivists

I. Occasionists. 1. *Concept.* An occasion of sin is some external circumstance that leads one to sin. Hence he is an occasionist who sins in consequence of such a circumstance.

We do not consider the remote, but *the proximate occasion* of sin, e.g., that person, place or thing with which great danger of sin is connected, whether for people in general (absolute occasion) or for some particular person because of his individual disposition (relative occasion). — We do not consider the remote occasion here, since for a reasonable cause one may expose himself to such an occasion.

The proximate occasion may be *free* or *necessary*. The former can be easily avoided. A necessary occasion is one which is physically or morally impossible to avoid without great danger to life, health or reputation. One necessary proximate occasion of sin is company keeping with the prospect of an early marriage.

2. *Absolution* of those in the proximate occasion of grievous sin.

a) Whoever does not want to give up a *proximate free occasion* of sin cannot be absolved.

This is true even if the penitent is willing to try to make the occasion remote by means of prayer, etc.

Whoever *sincerely promises* to give up such an occasion immediately may be absolved without delay. — If the penitent has repeatedly broken his promise he is doubtfully disposed. Generally speaking a penitent cannot be absolved before he has actually given up a continuous occasion of grievous sin (Cf. 605). If avoiding the occasion requires great moral effort (e.g., dismissal of a person, giving up a position) the confessor may postpone absolution the very first time until the occasion is made remote.

608. *b)* If one does not abandon the *proximate necessary occasion* of sin, but is willing to use adequate means to make it remote, he may be absolved.

Such means may either strengthen the penitent spiritually (prayer, Sacraments, consideration of the eternal truths) or lessen the influence of the ocasion (guarding the eyes, avoiding intimate familiarity or the opportunity of being alone with another).

If one continually relapses into sin in spite of taking such precautions, he cannot be forced to give up the occasion at all costs; however, he must be vigorously encouraged to be more zealous in the use of such means that will make the occasion remote. — Should the occasion constitute a proximate danger to his eternal salvation he must abandon it even at the price of his life. One who is *not willing* to use the means that will render such an occasion remote, cannot be absolved.

N. B. There are various intermediary stages between the remote and proximate occasion. The greater the danger of sinning, the more serious must be the reasons to justify one in not avoiding the occasion of sin.

609. — II. The consuetudinarian or **habitual sinner** is one who frequently commits the same sins over a longer period of time without there being a long interval between the individual sins.

If, without a sufficient reason, one does not avoid an occasion which, though no longer remote, is not yet proximate, he commits at least a venial sin.

The consuetudinarian *differs* from the recidivist principally in that he has not yet relapsed into the same sin after repeated confessions.

An habitual sinner, actually well disposed must be absolved without delay and without his having made any previous improvement.

III. A recidivist or backslider is one who, in spite of repeated confessions, always relapses into the same sins without making any earnest effort towards improvement.

Ordinarily the *general rules* for absolving are here applied (Cf. 605). The difficulty consists in determining the sincerity of the backslider.

As a rule one is *well disposed* who sins through weakness, who in general has an aversion towards sin, resists temptation, and detests his sin shortly after committing it (this happens frequently in case of self-abuse). Sometimes one may easily determine whether a penitent is well disposed by asking, not only how often he has given way to temptation, but how often he has overcome it. Those recidivists are usually ill disposed in whom there is some stubborn sinful attachment (e.g., illicit friendship, attachment to ill-gotten goods, habitual birth prevention). But even such a person may be adjudged well disposed if he is actually more earnestly contrite than he was in previous confessions.

A *doubtfully disposed* recidivist should usually be absolved if he relapses because of weakness since he needs the grace of the Sacrament. But those should generally be refused absolution who relapse into sin because they will not comply with a serious duty (e.g., make restitution, discontinue an unlawful intimacy).

610. § 6. The Duty to Correct Mistakes

The mistakes of a confessor may concern the validity of absolution, the integrity of the confession and the duties of the penitent.

I. The valid imparting of absolution is an obligation of justice on the part of the confessor.

In a doubt whether or not one has absolved, or has done so validly, conditional absolution must be given.

1. The *culpable omission* of this obligation obliges the confessor to correct his mistake at great inconvenience if the penitent will otherwise suffer serious harm.

2. The *inculpable omission* of this duty obliges the confessor only to correct his mistake at great inconvenience when there is danger of the penitent's dying in the state of mortal sin.

3. The *correction* is made by giving valid absolution without the penitent's repeating his confession, provided his previous contrition continues (C. 561).

If *contrition has not continued* and the penitent of his own accord returns to confession after some time, it suffices to have him make a general accusation of his previously confessed sins and be sorry for them. — If the penitent must be informed of the invalidity of absolution outside of confession there is no question of the seal of confession being involved, if the confessor alone is the fault of the invalidity (e.g., because he had no jurisdiction).

611. — II. The integrity of confession may suffer either because of some positive action of the confessor or in consequence of some omission for which the confessor is personally at fault or not. — In no case need he correct his mistake at his grave disadvantage.

If he is the *positive cause* of the mistake he must correct it even outside of the confessional; but, because of the seal, he must first obtain the penitent's permission. He will generally be excused from doing so because such procedure is usually very disagreeable either to himself or the penitent.

III. Mistakes Affecting the Duties of the Penitent. 1. If the confessor by some *positive action* which was *gravely sinful* has led the penitent into an error regarding an obligation of justice he is obliged even at his own grave inconvenience to repair the harm caused thereby to the penitent or to a third party.

The same holds if a confessor has innocently made a false decision, but in a gravely culpable manner has neglected to correct his mistake when he could have easily done so.

The harm may be spiritual (e.g., if the confessor tells a penitent he need not avoid a proximate occasion of sin), but more frequently it will be temporal (e.g., the priest erroneously obligates the penitent to restitution).

The harm must also be repaired outside of confession. But should the seal of confession be involved it is always necessary first to obtain the penitent's permission to discuss the matter.

If the confessor *has not sinned gravely,* there is no grave obligation of justice to repair the harm (Cf. 348).

2. If the confessor causes harm to a penitent by some **omission** (e.g., failure to instruct), his obligation of reparation is only one of charity, even though he should have sinned gravely by his negligence.

He is, therefore, generally not obliged to make good his omission under proportionately grave inconvenience (Cf. 139).

The only *exception* is when his silence is equivalent to positive approbation. Hence, in this case we apply what was said of the confessor who causes harm by some positive action.

612. § 7. The Seal of Confession

By the *seal of Confession* we understand the strict obligation to maintain silence concerning that which is disclosed in sacramental confession, the revelation of which would render confession odious.

We shall consider the obligation, the subject, the object and the violation of the seal of confession.

A. The Obligation of the Seal of Confession.

I. Origin of the Obligation. 1. This obligation is **based** on the natural law, the positive divine law and canon law.

The purpose of the seal is to exclude, as far as possible, from the institution of confession everything which might make confession burdensome for the penitent.

2. The *obligation applies* only to what is disclosed in sacramental confession (Cf. 563).

Hence, it arises from a confession that is only commenced, a sacrilegious confession and one in which absolution is refused or deferred.

No obligation arises from a confession knowingly made to one who is not a priest, neither from a mock confession, nor from a conversation one holds with a priest without the intention of confessing, for instance, to seek advice, etc., even though in doing so the person intends to confide certain matters to the priest "under the seal of confession." In such cases there will generally be a natural or a committed secret. Scandal must always be avoided.

613. — II. Extent of the Obligation. 1. The confessor must safeguard the seal of confession towards *all persons*, including the *penitent;* as to the latter, however, only outside of confession.

Thus, two confessors to whom a penitent has confessed the same sins may not speak thereof to each other. — The confessor may not even speak to the penitent himself of his sins outside of confession without the latter's permission. In a subsequent confession, however, the priest may speak to a penitent of what he previously confessed without his permission; likewise, if the penitent, after leaving, immediately returns to the confessional. Confessional secrecy must be observed even after the death of the penitent.

The seal does *not forbid* the priest to reflect upon matters confessed, or to try to discover who is making his confession to him, or to ask a third party for the name of a penitent. However, the latter is a violation of the seal if others thereby get the impression that the confession dealt with something extraordinary.

2. *With permission of the penitent* one may speak of sacramental matters with the penitent himself and with others, even outside of confession.

Such permission can be given, e.g., that the confessor may

consult someone more experienced concerning a difficult case.

Presumed permission is insufficient. — Should the penitent of his own accord begin speaking of such matters with the confessor outside confession, he thereby implicitly gives the priest permission. — Only rarely and for serious reasons should such permission be requested. The penitent must give it altogether freely. — In confession the penitent may be compelled even under threat of the penalty of being refused absolution, either to divulge some matter pertaining to confession or to give the confessor the requisite permission to do so. If the penitent refuses to comply, the priest nevertheless must respect the seal.

614. — III. Gravity of the Obligation. The seal of confession always obliges under mortal sin.

1. There can be no slight *direct violation* of the seal.

Concerning direct and indirect violation confer 619.

2. *No exception* is ever made, not even to save one's life or for the common welfare.

When questioned the confesser should reply with an evasive answer, e.g., "What is that to you?", "I did my duty," or employ a broad mental reservation, e.g., "I don't know" (i.e., with communicable knowledge). He may even confirm such an answer in court with an oath, if by refusing to testify suspicion might arise. — If a confessor cannot confess a sin of his own without breaking the seal he must omit it in confession.

If a confessor is asked by the sacristan or by the Sister in charge of patients at a hospital, etc., whether someone who had just confessed wants to communicate the priest should direct such an inquirer — to safeguard the seal — either to the penitent himself, or answer only with permission of the penitent.

Great prudence is especially necessary when a patient who is not disposed should receive Viaticum. If he is a public sinner it is best to ascertain before hearing his confession whether or not he is properly disposed (e.g., prepared to repair public scandal). If the lack of the necessary disposition is discovered only in confession, the priest should induce the patient (also in confession) to abstain from Holy Communion. If the latter consents, the priest may somehow conceal the Sacred Particle in his clothes and inform the bystanders or relatives that everything necessary has been taken care of by the confessor. Should the patient, never-theless, insist on receiving Holy Communion, It must be given him. — But if the patient explains that he asked for the priest only for the sake of respectability there is no question of a sacramental confession, and consequently no obligation of the seal. Natural law, however, obliges one to observe all possible secrecy in these matters.

3. In a *case of doubt* the priest must always do the safer thing (i.e., favor the seal), since he must absolutely see to it that no one be deterred from confession.

Hence, if it is controverted whether a matter falls under the seal of confession or not, one may not follow the more lenient opinion. The same holds if the priest doubts whether a penitent has given him permission to use sacramental knowledge, or whether a confession was sacramental, or whether he has also acquired the knowledge outside of confession.

615. *B. Subject of the Seal of Confession.*

I. The confessor is bound in the first place by the seal of confession (C. 889).

This holds true even in the case where a layman was er-roneously taken for a confessor.

II. All who in any way **obtain knowledge from confession** are likewise obliged by the seal (C. 889).

Therefore, the following are so obliged; interpreters; the superior who is requested for faculties to absolve from a reserved case or to whom a penitent has recourse after being absolved from a censure; anyone who reads a letter concerning such a case or censure; he who, with the penitent's permission, is asked for counsel unless the penitent has freely exempted this latter from the obligation of the seal; he with whom the penitent has dis-cussed a matter of conscience in order to confess to him later (but not if the penitent intended to confess to someone else); those who acidentally or intentionally overhear something being said in confession (not, however, if the penitent knows he is speaking so loudly that others might hear him — such a one voluntarily renounces his right); all those to whom a person who is bound by the seal, either unintentionally or sacrilegiously, communicates sacramental knowledge (moreover, these may not even discuss the matter among themselves); whoever reads the written list of sins a penitent gave the confessor or which is found in the confessional, or which the confessor has lost, not, however, one who reads the list before it has been given to the confessor, or which the penitent keeps or loses after confession.

616. — III. The penitent is not obliged by the seal of confession; not even with reference to what the confessor has told him.

He who discloses matters to the detriment of the confessor sins by violating a natural or a committed secret, unless the private welfare or common good requires such manifestation.

617. C. Object of the Seal of Confession.

With reference to the extent of the obligation one may distinguish a threefold object of the seal of confession: sins; things said in explanation of sins confessed; matters whose revelation would be disagreeable to the penitent.

I. All sins confessed fall under the seal, even public sins, unless the confessor knows them from sources other than confession.

They may be mortal or particular venial sins. — In itself, it is *not wrong* to say that someone has confessed sins (since this is the case in every confession), or that so-and-so hardly ever committed a sin.

The confessor may not speak of any sins as long as he knows of them only from confession, even though he is convinced that they are commonly known. — The priest may speak of the sins he knows from sources *apart from confession,* but he must beware of representing something as certain which previous to hearing confession he considered only probable, and he must refrain from correcting inaccuracies in virtue of his confessional knowledge.

II. All that is said for the better explanation of sins likewise falls under the seal, unless the confessor knows these things also outside of confession, or if it is a question of matters commonly known.

It matters not whether that which is said to clarify sins is *necessary, useful or superfluous.* Thus, if a penitent says he sinned against the sixth commandment and thereby committed a sacrilege because of his vow; she had a fight with her husband because he was drunk; he was ashamed of his parents because of their poverty; or he missed Mass on account of some sports event: these circumstances come under the seal.

If these circumstances are *commonly known* (e.g., the game, the vow, etc.) the confessor may speak of them although he himself gets the information only through confession, provided others do not get the impression that the penitent has accused himself of these things in any way.

618. — III. Anything else which is known only from confession is protected by the seal, provided it is not commonly known and the revelation thereof **will prove disagreeable** to the penitent.

It is theoretically *controverted* whether this really falls under the seal of confession; practically, one must follow the stricter opinion (C. 614).

The obligation of the seal, therefore, extends, for example, to scrupulosity or those natural defects of a penitent, which are not commonly known; faults the penitent committed in the act of confessing (e.g., impatience; not, however, an act of theft which the penitent committed while going to confession).

The virtues and graces of the penitent *are not matters for the seal,* provided they are not manifested in order more clearly to declare the sins themselves, e.g., the gravity of ingratitude towards God. — In itself, even the fact of one's confessing does not fall under the seal unless others may conclude from this fact that the penitent must have committed some specific sins. — In itself, one may also say he gave so-and-so absolution.

619. *D. Violation of the Seal.*

I. The Sin of Violation. Direct violation of the seal of confession is always a mortal sin; indirect violation may be only a venial sin.

Violation of the seal is always a sin against the reverence due to the Sacrament of Penance; hence, it is a sacrilege. It is furthermore always a violation of an implicit contract, and often also an injury to reputation.

II. Manner of Violating the Seal. 1. The seal is *directly* violated if some object of the seal together with the identity of the penitent is revealed without the latter's permission.

This might readily happen if a confessor were to say what kind of grave sin was confessed to him today.

It matters not whether the penitent be known to those to whom the revelation is made or not, or if he will forever remain unknown to them. — He also violates the seal who, for instance, while standing close to the confessional *purposely* tries to overhear what the penitent is saying.

2. The seal is *indirectly* violated if from a story that one relates or an expression he uses there arises the danger that someone will acquire a knowledge of that which is protected by the seal of confession.

620. — 3. *Any use* of knowledge derived from confession which is burdensome to the penitent, is considered by some moralists as an indirect violation of the seal. Others deny this. All, however, are agreed that such an act is forbidden under grave sin (Cf. 890).

Not even for the sake of averting the gravest harm from the common welfare, may knowledge be used in such wise, (e.g., in elections, distribution of offices, ordinations, administration of Sacraments) even if no one, including the penitent himself, should discover the divulging of such knowledge. — The confessor may not refuse to hear anyone's confession if he knows only from confession that the person is very hard to dispose for absolution or that he can become very troublesome in confession. — Still less may a priest dismiss an employee because of what he has learned about him in confession, or hide a key in order that the penitent who confessed a theft may not have further access to a certain room, etc.

It is not forbidden, however, to use confessional knowledge in a manner which is not burdensome to the penitent. Thus, a priest may use knowledge thus obtained to be more friendly towards the penitent, to correct his own faults, to pray for the penitent, to consult books, to use the knowledge to his own spiritual advantage, etc. Missionaries may preach of matters which they would otherwise not have spoken about without violating the seal (observe, however, 621). As to what a priest must do who knows from some other confession that the present penitent has committed a certain sin which he now denies, confer 606.

621. — III. Differing from the violation of the seal is the suspicion or the appearance of such a violation which must likewise be avoided.

The Holy Office has condemned the practice of some confessors of speaking without necessity either in private conversation or in sermons for the supposed edification of the hearers about things they have learned only from confessions, even though they avoid everything that might actually endanger the seal. Superiors are gravely obliged to see to it that their subjects observe this regulation (S. Offic. 9 June, 1915).

IV. A penalty l. s. is incurred only by the direct violation of the seal (Cf. 431).

N. B. 1. One and the same manifestation may or may not constitute a violation of the seal *according to circumstances*. It is wrong to say that a certain sin is committed in a certain community if the fact is not commonly known, or if the community is small (a certain amount of defamation is thus inflicted on each individual); not so, however, if the community is large. — It is not sinful for a pastor in consequence of his knowledge from confession to tell missionaries of certain sins about which they should make special mention, provided the congregation is a large one or if there is question of sins commonly committed in that locality. If only one or the other individual of the place is guilty of such a sin, such action on the part of the pastor is always unlawful, since these few may be hurt when they realize that the pastor has spoken to the missionaries about sins which he knows only from confession.

2. In some places it is customary to give the penitent *a card* after confession testifying that he has received the Sacrament. If the penitent requests this it must be given him even though he did not receive absolution. If the certificate expressly says the penitent has been absolved, these words may not be struck out. — A priest may always give this card to the penitent if it is requested in confession, and he must do so if his refusal would become known to the by-standers who would in consequence suspect that the penitent had been refused absolution.

622.　　　　　　　*Section V*

Extreme Unction

Extreme Unction is the Sacrament through which the health of the soul and often that of the body is restored to one dangerously ill, and which is administered by anointing with consecrated olive oil together with the prayer of the priest.

Chapter I

THE OUTWARD SIGN AND RITE

I. Matter of Extreme Unction. 1. *Remote Matter.*

a) *Valid matter* is olive oil blessed either by the bishop or by a priest having special papal faculties (Cf. C. 945).

It is probable that the oil must be blessed for this very purpose (*oleum infirmorum*). In case of necessity one may anoint conditionally with chrism or the oil of catechumens; but if Oil of the Sick can subsequently be had the Sacrament must be repeated conditionally. If the oil supply runs low one may add unconsecrated olive oil, but in lesser quantity. This may be done repeatedly, even if ultimately the sum total of the oil added exceeds that which was originally blessed by the bishop (Cf. C. 734); but the additions may not succeed each other so closely as to constitute a moral unity.

b) *Lawful matter* is Oil of the Sick that the bishop of the respective diocese has blessed during the current year.

Except in case of necessity the use of old oil is forbidden under grave sin; likewise (according to some authors) the use of oil that has been blessed by some bishop other than one's own Ordinary.

623. — 2. *Proximate matter* is the anointing with oil.

a) *Validity* requires only one anointing, provided the form employed refers to all the senses.

In case of necessity it is sufficient to anoint only one of the senses, or preferably the forehead, with the prescribed short form. If time permits the individual anointings are supplied (C. 947), and not conditionally but absolutely. This is not done if the sick person has meanwhile died, or probably not if the person in danger still lives, but an hour has passed since the last anointing.

b) *Lawfulness* requires that the anointing be made with the thumb of the right hand or at least with one of the fingers — in the form of a cross — in the following sequence: eyes, ears, nose, mouth, hands, feet — beginning with the right member in case of double organs.

All this, with the exception of the individual anointings, seems to be prescribed under venial sin. — Any good reason excuses from anointing the feet (C. 947). — In grave necessity one may also anoint by means of an instrument (rubber glove, ball of cotton, etc.) (C. 947). — The eyes and (or) ears must be anointed even if the sick person has been blind and (or) deaf from birth. If an organ (hand, ear, etc.) has been lost the anointing is made nearby using the regular form; a patient in a paroxysm or fury is anointed near the mouth.

c) *Manner of Anointing.*

The eyes are anointed on the lids, the ears on the lobes, the nose either on the ridge towards the point or at the side on either nostril. If the mouth cannot be closed, it suffices to anoint the upper or the lower lip. The hands of a priest are anointed on the back, those of the other faithful on the palms. The feet may be anointed on the soles or still better on the instep.

624. — II. Form of Extreme Unction. 1. *In ordinary cases:* *Per istam sanctam unctionem et suam piissimam misericordiam, indulgeat tibi Dominus quidquid per visum (auditum, odoratum, gustum et locutionem, tactum, gressum) deliquisti. Amen.*

Naming the respective sense is not necessary for validity. — In anointing double organs the form is said only once, but it should not be completed before both members are anointed. (Nevertheless, the anointing would also be valid if the form were repeated individually for each of the organs.)

2. *In cases of necessity:* *Per istam sanctam unctionem indulgeat tibi Dominus quidquid deliquisti. Amen.*

Confer 623 on supplying the individual anointings. If time permits the prayers should also be supplied, beginning with the prayers before the anointing.

III. Rite of Extreme Unction.

It is gravely sinful (except in case of necessity) to administer this Sacrament without any liturgical vestment, i.e., without stole and surplice. — The server and candle do not seem to be prescribed under sin. If no man is available, it would seem that a woman may answer the prayers. — It is seriously sinful to omit a considerable part of the prayers without necessity. — If several persons are to be anointed at the same time, the prayers before and after the anointings are said in the plural; but the prayers that accompany the anointing are said in the singular number. — If the patient is also to receive Holy Communion the present day practice requires that the anointing follow the Viaticum. This practice obliges only under venial sin.

625. Chapter II

THE EFFECTS OF EXTREME UNCTION

I. The health of the soul is effected by strengthening of the soul through grace and by the remission of sin and the punishments due to sin.

Strength is restored to the soul by the infusion or increase of sanctifying grace and the right to those actual graces which are necessary for final perseverance.

The sins remitted may be venial or mortal. Imperfect contrition at least is always required. — The forgiveness of mortal sins is, however, only a secondary effect; wherefore, the person to be anointed should if possible be in the state of grace before receiving this Sacrament (Cf. 447 and 631). Hence, if the sick person appears to be unconscious he should be absolved before being anointed. If a person who has been anointed does not die, he must, of course, confess his mortal sins.

The punishment due to sin, at least in part, is immediately remitted *ex opere operato.* Besides this, actual graces are given which enable one to obtain the remission of the temporal punishment due to sin.

II. The health of the body is effected by assisting

natural causes, not after the extraordinary manner of a miracle.

If, therefore, Extreme Unction is delayed until life can be saved only by a miracle, this effect cannot be expected. Furthermore, physical health is restored only when this will be conducive to eternal salvation.

626. Chapter III
THE MINISTER OF EXTREME UNCTION

I. The Minister. 1. Every priest, and only a priest, can *validly* administer Extreme Unction (C. 938).

Concerning conditional administration confer 631.

2. The *lawful* minister may be either ordinary or extraordinary.

a) The ordinary minister is the pastor of the parish where the sick person happens to be.

As a rule, other priests may not administer this Sacrament. In a clerical religious community it is the right and duty of the superior, either personally or through his representative, to administer the Last Rites to his professed subjects, the novices, candidates and lay persons who remain permanently in the convent either as servants, as students, as guests, as patients or as convalescents (C. 514). Confer C. 397 on the administering of this Sacrament to the bishop.

b) The extraordinary minister is any priest who anoints in case of necessity or with the reasonably presumed permission of the pastor or bishop.

627. — II. Duty of the Minister. 1. The *ordinary* minister is gravely bound in justice to administer Extreme Unction either personally or through others to the sick people in his territory who request it, unless he is excused for some just reason. If there is danger that the sick person will be eternally lost without this Sacrament he must administer it even at the risk of his life.

This latter may happen if the dying person has not confessed for a long time and is unconscious.

Whoever has the spiritual care of others by reason of his position, has also the grave obligation to tell them when they are seriously ill so that they may receive this Sacrament in due time.

2. The *extraordinary* minister is obliged only in charity.

Charity generally does not oblige under grave inconvenience. Should a dying person be in danger of losing his soul without this Sacrament, the extraordinary minister would likewise be obliged to give the Last Rites at the risk of his life.

628.   Chapter IV

THE RECIPIENT OF EXTREME UNCTION

I. The valid reception of Extreme Unction requires that the recipient be alive and baptized, that he have attained the use of reason and be in danger of death through sickness or old age, and that he have the requisite intention.

1. The *apparently dead* may be anointed.

According to medical science an apparent death precedes actual death. A person dying after a long illness may be anointed within about half an hour after he has drawn his last breath; anointing may be done as long as two or three hours after sudden death. Concerning the absolution of the dying, confer 557.

2. *In doubt* whether the dying person has been *baptized* he may be anointed conditionally; but there is no obligation to do so, e.g., an unknown person in an accident.

Conditional administration is also permitted if the person is *unknown*, even though the non-Catholic minister had been or will be in attendance.

An adult dangerously ill may and should be anointed *imme-*

diately after Baptism since this Sacrament is also beneficial to a newly-baptized person by supporting him in his illness and strengthening him for the hour of death. — In mission countries Extreme Unction should not be given to those who are baptized on their deathbed, if they have not yet learned that there is a special Sacrament for the dying.

629. — 3. The subject must have attained *the use of reason* because Extreme Unction removes the consequences of sin, and one who has never had the use of reason has likewise never sinned.

Thus children before the age of reason may not be anointed, neither may the insane who have never had lucid intervals; children, however, who have not yet made their first confession or Communion may be anointed.

630. — 4. *The illness* must be so serious that death may reasonably be feared.

If one is in danger of death but is not ill, he may, indeed, receive Viaticum; but may not be anointed, e.g., before an execution or a battle; before an operation, unless death already threatens in consequence of illness. — The mortally wounded, the poisoned, women before a dangerous parturition, and also those who suffer from the weakness of old age, may be anointed. — In doubt whether there is illness of some kind connected with the danger of death Extreme Unction may be given conditionally (C. 941). — Death need not be imminent; hence, the Last Rites (e.g., in mission districts) may be given though it be foreseen that the invalid will live a month, or even a year. This Sacrament can only be received once during the same danger of death (C. 940). This is true also where a new danger of death supervenes (e.g., if pleurisy is contracted by one sick with pneumonia). — If this Sacrament is received validly but without fruit, it will very probably revive. That it may do so it is necessary that he who received it sacrilegiously go to confession or make an act of perfect contrition. If it was not received sacrilegiously, imperfect contrition suffices (Cf. 448).

Extreme Unction may and should be *repeated* during the same illness if after the anointing, the patient rallies to the point where the danger of death no longer exists, and his condition thereafter again becomes critical. But in such a case, there is no obligation to repeat the Sacrament if the relapse follows within a short time (less than a month) after the previous crisis. In doubt whether one may repeat it or not one may generally decide in favor of repetition.

5. *The intention* necessary for Extreme Unction must be at least the habitual implicit intention (C. 943).

On habitual intention confer 450. The intention to be anointed is *implicitly* contained, e.g., in the will to live and die a Catholic. — Thus one may anoint him who has lived a Christian life; and, one, too, who has not lived much like a Christian or even whom death overtakes in the act of sinning. *In doubt* whether an unconscious person remains impenitent and consequently whether he has the intention to be anointed. Extreme Unction is administered conditionally, e.g., "si capax es" or "if you have the intention" (C. 942 Cf. also 557).

631. — II. The lawful reception of Extreme Unction requires the state of grace. If it is impossible to recover the state of grace by confession or perfect contrition, Extreme Unction with imperfect contrition will remit mortal sin.

Although the state of grace can be recovered by perfect contrition, a person in sin who is in danger of death is obliged to confess by divine command. — If only after being anointed one who is in sin elicits the necessary contrition (Cf. 630) Extreme Unction very probably revives. Therefore, it should never be administered with the condition "si dispositus es," but with the condition "si capax es."

III. The duty to receive Extreme Unction does not in itself oblige under serious sin.

One might sin gravely by contempt of the Sacrament or by the scandal he gives in neglecting it.

Whoever, either by reason of his office or of piety, has the spiritual care of one who is ill, has the grave obligation to tell him when he is seriously ill and thus make it possible for him to be anointed. — Others have a serious obligation only if a patient would otherwise lose his soul.

632.   *Section VI*

Holy Orders

The clerical state is acquired by *tonsure* (C. 108). The giving of tonsure is not an ordination but a sacred ceremony.

The *four minor orders* are: the order of porter, lector, exorcist, and acolyte (C. 949). According to the general opinion they are not sacramental in character.

The *three Major Orders* are: the subdiaconate, diaconate, and priesthood (C. 940). The subdiaconate is probably not a sacrament. The diaconate and priesthood are certainly Sacraments; and not only the simple priesthood, but also the episcopate. Holy Orders is not physically, but only morally one Sacrament.

Holy Orders may be *defined* as the Sacrament by which spiritual power is conferred together with the grace to exercise properly the respective office.

This *spiritual power* in case of minor orders, subdiaconate and diaconate refers to functions that have a more or less intimate relation to the Sacrifice of the Mass and also to the imparting of certain blessings and the performing of exorcisms. — Priesthood confers the power to consecrate the Body and Blood of Christ, to forgive sins and administer Extreme Unction. — The episcopate gives power to ordain and confirm.

633.   Chapter I

THE OUTWARD SIGN OF HOLY ORDERS

I. In minor orders the matter is the handing to the cleric the symbols of the office required for the exercise of the respective order. The form consists in the words which accompany this action.

II. For subdiaconate the matter is the handing over of the empty chalice with a superimposed paten without a host. The form is contained in the accompanying words of the bishop.

According to many authors the handing of the Epistle book (missal) with the corresponding words is essential. Practically this opinion must be followed.

III. For the diaconate, priesthood and episcopacy it was formerly disputed as to what precisely constituted the matter and form. This controversy was settled by an epoch-making decree in the Apostolic Constitution *Sacramentum ordinis* of His Holiness, Pope Pius XII, November 30, 1947 AAS 40-5). It is now certain that the matter, and the only matter, of the Sacred Orders of the diaconate, the priesthood, and the episcopacy is the imposition of hands; and that the form, and the only form, is the words which determine the application of this matter, which univocally signify the sacramental effects— namely the power of Order and the grace of the Holy Spirit—and which are accepted and used by the Church in that sense.

In conferring each Order the *imposition of hands* must be done by physically touching the head of the ordinand, although a moral contact is sufficient for validity.

The *traditio instrumentorum* remains prescribed for the future, but is not required for validity.

The provisions of this Constitution have *no retroactive force.* If, because of former controversies, a doubt arises over the validity of Orders already conferred the matter must be submitted to the Holy See.

634. — IV. The following principles concerning the matter and form of the diaconate, priesthood and episcopacy apply:

1. **For the diaconate** *the matter* is the one imposition of the hand of the bishop which occurs in the Rite of that Ordination.

The form consists of the words of the *Preface*, of which the following are essential—and therefore required for validity: *Emitte in eum, quaesumus Domine, Spiritum Sanctum, quo in opus ministerii tui fideliter exsequendi septiformis gratiae tuae munere roboretur.*

2. **For the priesthood** *the matter* is the first imposition of hands of the bishop which is done in silence.

The continuation of the same imposition through the extension of the right hand and the last imposition which is accompanied by the words "Accipe Spiritum: quorum remiseris peccata, etc." do not belong to the matter.

The form consists of the words of the *Preface*, of which the following are essential—and therefore required for validity: *Da quaesumus, omnipotens Pater, in hunc famulum tuum Presbyterii dignitatem; innova in visceribus eius spiritum sanctitatis, ut acceptum a Te, Deus, secundi meriti munus obtineat censuramque morum exemplo suae conversationis insinuet.*

3. **For the episcopacy** *the matter* is the imposition of hands which is done by the consecrating bishop.

The form consists of the words of the *Preface*, of which the following are essential—and therefore required for validity: *Comple in sacerdote tuo ministerii tui summam, et ornamentis totius glorificationis instructum coelestis unguenti rore sanctifica.*

Although for the validity of episcopal consecration only one bishop is required and sufficient, nevertheless the prescriptions of the *Roman Pontifical* must be observed. Therefore, all the co-consecrating bishops must employ both matter and form, i.e., each must impose hands, touching the head of the bishop-elect with both hands, while saying the form, and having formed the intention of conferring episcopal consecration together with the bishop who is consecrator (Apostolic Letter, November 30, 1944, AAS 37-131).

635.   Chapter II

THE MINISTER OF HOLY ORDERS

I. Holy Orders can be **validly** conferred by either **an** ordinary or an extraordinary minister.

1. *The ordinary minister* is a consecrated bishop (C. 951).

2. *The extraordinary minister* is a person who lacks the episcopal character but has faculties to confer orders either by common law or by an indult of the Holy See (C. 951).

Canon law gives the faculties to confer tonsure and the minor orders to: a) Cardinals, provided the candidate has dimissorials from his Ordinary (C. 239). b) Vicars and prefects apostolic, abbots and prelates *nullius,* during their term of office, if the candidate is their subject or has dimissorials from his Ordinary (C. 957). c) Regular abbots entrusted with the government of an abbey, if they are priests and have legitimately received the abbatial blessing, and the candidates are subject to them at least in virtue of simple profession (C. 964).

636. — II. The lawful administration of the episcopate requires that the consecrator be a bishop who has received a special mandate from Rome (C. 953). As to the other Orders a distinction must be made between candidates of the diocesan clergy and religious.

1. *Diocesan clerics* must be ordained by their own bishop (C. 955). If he is lawfully hindered they may be ordained by another bishop if they are provided with dimissorial letters from their proper Ordinary (C. 955).

That bishop is the *proper minister* for ordination who is the Ordinary of the territory where the ordinand has his domicile and place of origin, or domicile only. In the latter case he must confirm with an oath his intention to remain permanently in that diocese. This oath may be omitted in case the cleric has already been incardinated into the diocese by tonsure or is destined for service in another diocese (C. 956).

Dimissorial letters are statements giving a subject permission to be ordained by a bishop other than his own Ordinary. They may be granted by one's own bishop to any other bishop of the same Rite in communion with the Holy See (C. 961).

637. — 2. *Religious* are to be ordained by the bishop of the diocese where the religious house to which they belong is situated.

a) *Exempt religious* cannot be ordained by any bishop

without the dimissorial letters from their own major superior (C. 964).

The dimissorials may be sent only to the bishop of the territory where the religious house to which the ordinand belongs is situated (C. 965). The superior may send the dimissorials to another bishop if the local Ordinary gives permission, belongs to a different Rite, is absent, or is not holding ordinations at the next regular time according to C. 1006, or if the diocese is vacant and the administrator has no episcopal consecration. The ordaining bishop must be certain that one of the preceding conditions really obtains; an authentic document from the episcopal curia of the ordinand will establish this certainty (C. 966). Those who have only temporary vows may be given dimissorial letters only for tonsure and the minor orders (C. 964).

b) *Non-exempt religious* are governed by the same laws as diocesan clerics with regard to ordination (C. 964).

However, they do not take the oath to remain in the diocese. — Sometimes the superiors of these communities have the *privilege* of granting dimissorials for their subjects, but if the latter take only temporary vows such letters may not be given for Major Orders (C. 964).

638. Chapter III

THE RECIPIENT OF HOLY ORDERS

In order that one may be ordained, certain requirements are demanded and one must be free from irregularities and impediments.

Article I

Requirements of the Ordinand

I. Validity requires that the candidate for an ordination be a baptized male who, if an adult, must have at least the habitual explicit intention to receive the Sacrament of Holy Orders.

Hence, the ordination of children before the use of reason is valid, so also the ordination of those who are forced into receiving

Orders by grave fear. — Those, however, who have been forced into receiving Major Orders by grave fear, and who are able to prove the existence of such fear, can be reduced at their request to the lay state and freed from the obligation of celibacy and from the duty of saying the Divine Office, provided they have not (i.e., after the fear has ceased) tacitly ratified the obligation by the exercise of their Orders (C. 214). — They cannot be said to be "forced" who receive ordination in order to escape a life of poverty at home.

639. — II. Lawfulness of ordination requires:

1. The *intention to receive all Orders* including the priesthood in their proper sequence (C. 973).

Thus, if one intends to receive only tonsure and minor orders they may not be given him. — Whoever, after receiving minor orders, changes his mind and does not desire to receive the Major Orders cannot be compelled to do so by the bishop (C. 973).

2. The *state of grace.*

He alone commits a mortal sin (a sacrilege) who, in the state of mortal sin, receives an Order which is certainly a Sacrament.

3. The reception of *Confirmation.*

It is not certain that this is a grave obligation.

4. A *moral life* in keeping with the Order to be received.

Thus, one is specially unfitted for the priesthood who habitually sins against holy chastity. Whoever foresees that he will continue to lead such a life after ordination, sins gravely by receiving a Major Order. A confessor will generally do well to advise such a one to discontinue at the very beginning of his seminary career, since later on this will become more difficult, and because the candidate, fearing dismissal, may live continently for some months before ordination, but after ordination he will revert to his old habit. This advice should be given particularly in the case of a candidate who leads a lukewarm life or of one in whom there are manifest signs of pronounced neurasthenia or other psychopathic disorders. If the evil habit has not been overcome after the second or third year in the major seminary the confessor should request the candidate to leave.

640. — 5. The *canonical age.*

For the subdiaconate one must have completed his twenty-first year; for the diaconate the twenty-second; and for the priesthood he must have completed his twenty-fourth year (C. 975). For an important reason a dispensation will be granted to ordain one to the priesthood a year or eighteen months earlier. A certain age is indirectly prescribed for minor orders, in as far as it is required for the course of studies, as seen in the next paragraph.

6. The *requisite knowledge.*

One may not receive tonsure before beginning his theological studies; subdiaconate may be conferred only toward the end of the third course of theology; diaconate may not be given before beginning the fourth year and priesthood not before the end of the first semester of the fourth year of theology. Theological studies may not be made privately (C. 976). — A corresponding examination must be undergone before receiving Orders (C. 996).

7. The *reception of previous orders* (C. 977).

641. — 8. The *observance of the intervals* (C. 976).

a) The length of time between *tonsure* and the *first minor order* and the time between the individual minor orders is left to the prudent judgment of the bishop.

Tonsure may not be given together with a minor order, nor may all minor orders be conferred on one day (C. 978). The contrary custom, however, is not condemned.

b) Between the order of *acolyte* and the *subdiaconate* there must intervene at least one year. Between the *subdiaconate* and the *diaconate,* as also between the *diaconate* and the *priesthood* there must be an intermission of at least three months unless necessity or utility of the Church according to the bishop's judgment demand otherwise.

Minor orders may never be conferred together with the subdiaconate, nor may two Majors Orders be given on the same day. Every contrary custom is condemned (C. 978).

9. A *canonical title,* in case of Major Orders.

The title for ordination is to guarantee a permanent and proper maintenance for the ordained.

a) The secular clergy have the title of a benefice or, if this is lacking, that of patrimony or pension (C. 979). If neither of these is had the title of "service of the diocese" may supply the deficiency and in countries subject to the Propaganda, the "title of the mission" (C. 981).

b) Religious have the following titles: Regulars have the title of solemn profession, or, as it is called, the title of poverty; religious of simple perpetual vows have the title of common life (*Titulus mensae communis*) or the title of the Congregation or a similar one according to the Constitutions; all other religious are governed by laws for the secular clergy in this matter (C. 982).

642.   *Article II*

Irregularities and Simple Impediments

§ 1. General Observations

I. Concepts. 1. An *irregularity* is a canonical impediment of a permanent nature which directly renders it unlawful to receive ordination and indirectly forbids the exercise of orders received.

"Orders" here include tonsure. — An irregularity is not a penalty, but a means to safeguard the dignity of the clerical state and office by excluding those who are unqualified for the service of the altar. If observing a prohibition to exercise orders irregularly received would defame him, one may exercise such orders, but must seek a dispensation without delay. Compare with C. 2232.

2. A *simple impediment* differs from an irregularity in this that it is not of a permanent nature.

An irregularity can only be removed by dispensation, whereas a simple impediment eventually ceases of its own accord.

II. Division. *Irregularities* arise either from defect

(*ex defectu*) or from crime (*ex delicto*).

An irregularity from defect is the lack of qualification required for ordination for which the candidate is not responsible; while an irregularity from crime is an impediment based on a grave sin of the candidate.

643. — III. Origin. Irregularities *from defect* and simple impediments arise *ipso facto* and are incurred also by those who are ignorant of them.

Irregularities *from crime* arise only as a consequence of mortal, external (public or occult) sins committed after Baptism (C. 986). Hence, if one by his evil deed has nevertheless not sinned gravely bcause of his good faith or because there is question of some small matter, he does not become irregular.

Irregularities and impediments are *multiplied* if they arise from different causes, not, however, from a repetition of one and the same cause. The only exception is voluntary homicide(C. 989).

In a doubt about an irregularity we distinguish between a *dubium juris* and a *dubium facti*. If the doubt is of law there is no irregularity; if there is a doubt of fact it is advisable to apply for a dispensation, since one would otherwise be forbidden to exercise the order received, as soon as the existence of the irregularity should be established.

IV. Dispensation.

1. The *competent authority.* *a*) *The Holy See* can dispense from all irregularities and impediments to ordination.

The Holy See dispenses very rarely from some irregularities and impediments. — The Congregation of the Sacraments dispenses in public cases (C. 249), the Sacred Penitentiary in occult instances (C. 258).

b) *Ordinaries* can dispense their subjects *α*) from irregularities that are doubtful *dubio facti* in case the Pope is wont to dispense from such irregularities (C. 15).

β) from irregularities arising from an occult crime,

except voluntary homicide and abortion and those offenses
that have been taken to court (C. 990).

By "Ordinary" is here meant the diocesan bishop and the major
superior in a clerical exempt religious community. Ordinaries may
also empower others to grant the dispensation.

644. — *c*) *Confessors* may dispense in the cases mentioned under β), but only if the matter is occult and
urgent and there is no time to apply to the bishop; also
if there is danger of grave harm or loss of reputation,
and only in order that their clerical penitent may lawfully exercise orders already received (C. 990).

Subsequent recourse to the bishop or to the Holy See is not
required. — Neither is any definite formula prescribed for the
dispensation; any clear manifestation of one's will suffices. The
danger of infamy might excuse from the observance of the irregularity arising from homicide or abortion. But one is obliged to
apply to the respective superior for dispensation as soon as possible.

Concerning the faculties of regulars confer 416.

2. The *petition for dispensation* must indicate all
irregularities and impediments incurred. If this is not
done a general dispensation would, nevertheless, be valid
for those omitted in good faith, except voluntary homicide, abortion and co-operation in these crimes, and those
crimes that have already been presented to a court. The
dispensation, however, would not cover those concealed
in bad faith (C. 991).

3. The *effect of the dispensation* extends also to the
reception of major orders if it is a general dispensation
"for the reception of Orders."

The dispensed cleric may obtain a benefice to which the care
of souls is attached, e.g., a parish; but no consistorial benefice may
be given him. He cannot be made a cardinal, bishop, abbot or
prelate *nullius*, nor can he be made a major superior in a clerical
exempt religious institute (C. 991).

645.   **§ 2. Individual Irregularities and**
Impediments

I. Persons Irregular from Defect (C. 984).
1. *Illegitimates* — whether the defect is public or
occult — may not be ordained unless they have been
legitimated or have made solemn profession.

On legitimation by subsequent matrimony see 748.

2. *Bodily defectives* who on account of debility
cannot safely, or on account of deformity cannot becomingly, minister at the altar. If one is already ordained a greater defect is required to impede him from
exercising his Orders; those actions are not forbidden
him which can be properly performed in spite of the
defect.

Accordingly, those are irregular who have no thumb or index
finger; who tremble in such wise that there is danger of their
spilling the Precious Blood; whoever has an artificial leg, in as
far as this defect cannot be concealed; the blind or mute, the
deaf who cannot hear the answers of the server; those who
stammer so as to excite laughter or derogatory remarks; those who
are seriously deformed by mutilation, or otherwise, e.g., if the
last three fingers are missing; those so hunchbacked that they
excite laughter, or who cannot stand upright. — The absence of
the left eye does not constitute an irregularity if the deformity
can be rendered unnoticeable by an artificial eye.

If corporal deformity *arises only after ordination,* the celebration of Mass is not forbidden, e.g., because of deafness. The
purblind may obtain a papal indult to say daily either the Votive
Mass of the Blessed Virgin or *missa quotidiana defunctorum.*
Should such a one lose his sight completely he may say Mass
only with the assistance of another priest and with a new indult
if in the first indult these words are found: "dummodo orator
non sit omnino caecus." — Private celebration is permitted to
one who cannot stand at the altar without a cane or support, or
who has Hansen's disease (leprosy) or a similar illness.

In a doubt as to whether or not a defect constitutes an irregularity the decision rests with the bishop.

646. — 3. *Epileptics,* the *insane,* the *diabolically possessed* even after they have been cured.

If such an affliction overtakes one only after ordination and if he is certainly perfectly cured, his Ordinary may permit him to exercise the orders he has received. — Should the one so afflicted suffer attacks only every fortnight or even more rarely he may apply to the Holy See for dispensation.

4. *Bigamists,* i.e., those who have successively married at least twice.

Simultaneous bigamy constitutes an irregularity from crime.

5. The *infamous* who have incurred infamy of law.

Cases of *infamia juris* are mentioned in canons: 2310, 2314, 2328, 2343, 2351, 2357 and 2359.

6. *Judges* who have pronounced a *death sentence.*

Jurymen do not become irregular since they only affirm the imputability and do not pass sentence. It is here presumed that the sentence is actually carried out.

7. *Executioners* and all voluntary and immediate assistants in the inflicting of the death penalty.

Soldiers who have been commanded to join a firing squad and excute a court-martialled criminal are not irregular; neither are their officers, since such action does not make them official executioners; neither are they irregular who prepare the instruments for execution since these do not take an immediate part in carrying out the sentence.

647. — II. **Persons Irregular from Crime** (C. 985). 1. *Apostates, heretics* and *schismatics.*

He is not criminally irregular who has been a member of a non-Catholic religious sect in good faith. But because of the presumption of formal sectarianism, etc. in the external forum he must obtain a dispensation *ad cautelam.*

2. *Whoever has allowed himself to be baptized*

by a non-Catholic, except in case of extreme necessity, becomes irregular.

3. *Those who attempt marriage* or go through the civil ceremony, while bound by a valid marriage bond, Sacred Orders, or simple or solemn religious profession; or any man who attempts marriage with a woman who is bound by such a religious profession or marriage.

One in simple vows may marry validly, but he thereby becomes irregular.

4. *Voluntary murderers* and those who have effectively procured abortion and also all accomplices.

5. *Those who have mutilated themselves or others,* or have *attempted suicide.*

Mutilation here means the removal of a member or organ of the body which has its own proper function, e.g., eye, ear, hand, foot; but not a finger, earlobe or tooth. The irregularity is not incurred if the organ is not amputated, but merely disabled; neither is it incurred if the amputation is necessary, since this is not sinful.

648. — 6. *Clerics who practice medicine or surgery without an apostolic indult,* if the death of a patient has followed such practice.

The irregularity follows if death has ensued, even though the cleric be possessed of the necessary knowledge and has used every requisite precaution.

7. *Those who abuse Sacred Orders* by performing acts of Orders reserved to the clergy in Major Orders when they have not received the respective Orders, or if they have received them but are forbidden to exercise them by reason of a canonical penalty.

Thus, he is irregular who "says Mass" or "absolves," in spite of the fact that he is no priest. Furthermore, an excommunicated priest who hears confessions or says Mass against the prescription of C. 2261 becomes irregular. — A priest does **not** become irregular by absolving without the necessary jurisdiction, since he does not thereby abuse the power of Orders, but that of jurisdiction. Neither is a deacon irregular who distributes Holy Communion or baptizes solemnly without permission.

Clerics with only tonsure or minor orders may for a reasonable cause take the place of a subdeacon at a Solemn Mass. But they may not wear the maniple, put water into the wine at the offertory, uncover the chalice after consecration nor purify it after Communion. — Such a cleric would become irregular if he would carry out the rubrics exactly as a subdeacon, and if, in doing so he were guilty of a grave sin; he would not, however, if he would wear the maniple but would not perform the functions mentioned, nor if he would perform the functions without wearing the maniple.

649. — III. Simple Impediments to Ordination (C. 987).

1. *Children of non-Catholics,* as long as their parents remain in their error.

According to an interpretation of the Code Commission, July 14, 1922, the term "children" signifies only the descendants in the paternal line, and these only in the first degree.

The same Commission on July 30, 1934, decided that the term "non-Catholic" embraces not only persons who belong to a non-Catholic sect, but also persons who belong to an atheistic sect.

The impediment also affects the children of mixed marriages, even though the marriages are contracted with the required nuptial promises and a dispensation. In keeping with the aforesaid reply of the Code Commission it is presupposed that it is the father who is the non-Catholic.

The impediment ceases as soon as both parents are Catholics; probably also after they have died in their error.

2. *Married men,* as long as their wives are living.

3. *Those who occupy an office or administrative position forbidden to clerics* and of which they are obliged to render an account, may not be ordained until they have given up the office or position and have discharged all their obligations.

4. *Slaves,* properly so-called, until they have been emancipated.

5. *Men liable to ordinary military service* until they have finished their term of service.

They are not prevented from ordination who have served their term and have been discharged from active service, but who will later be recalled from time to time to serve a short term; neither are they hindered from ordination who are liable to conscription in case of war.

6. *Neophytes* may not be ordained until, according to the judgment of the bishop, they have sufficiently proved themselves.

Converts to Catholicism from a non-Catholic sect are not included here, not even if they have been baptized conditionally. However, confer also 647.

7. *The disreputable* or those who suffer from infamy of fact until they have, in the judgment of the Ordinary, recovered their good reputation.

One may lose his good name in consequence of a crime or bad morals; it may even happen that an innocent person may incur infamy of fact. Reputation is recovered either by amendment or by proof of innocence.

650.   Chapter IV

PREPARATION FOR ORDINATION, THE RITE, TIME, PLACE AND REGISTRATION OF ORDINATION

I. Preparation for Holy Orders includes: a seminary education, presentation of various testimonials, examination, publication of names, and retreat.

1. *The seminary education* (C. 972). Care must be taken that candidates for the priesthood be trained from

an early age in a seminary. They must at least make their theological studies in a seminary.

Dispensation from living in a seminary may be given by the Ordinary only in particular cases and for a serious reason. Those who are dispensed must be entrusted to the watchfulness and spiritual direction of an able and pious priest.

651. — 2. *The testimonials* to be presented vary according as the candidates are diocesan clerics or religious who are likened to them in this matter, or members of an exempt community.

a) Secular clerics and religious, who in this regard are governed by the laws for seculars, according to C. 993 must present: *α*) a testimonial of their previous ordination; for the reception of tonsure their baptismal and confirmation certificates; *β*) a testimonial of studies concerning matter prescribed by C. 976; *γ*) a testimonial of good moral conduct either from the rector of the seminary or from the priest to whose care the candidate was entrusted outside the seminary; *δ*) testimonial letters from all the bishops in whose dioceses the candidate lived long enough to contract a canonical impediment; *ε*) a testimonial from his major superior if the candidate is a religious.

The time within which a candidate after reaching the age of puberty can contract a canonical impediment is, as a rule, three months for men doing military service and six months for others (C. 994). The time of residence must be morally uninterrupted. — If a candidate cannot obtain a testimonial letter because he is not known to the bishop or because he changed his place of residence too often, he can be made to declare under oath that he has not contracted any irregularity or impediment to Holy Orders (C. 994). A religious candidate whose superior has the privilege of writing out dimissorials, need not present all these testimonials, since in this respect he is likened to exempt religious.

b) Exempt religious must present dimissorials from their major superior (C. 964).

In these dimissorials the religious superior must testify that the candidate has made profession and belongs to the religious house subject to the said superior, that he has completed the prescribed course of studies and is possessed of all other qualifications required by law (C. 995).

652. — 3. *The examination* before ordination covers the order to be received, and, in case of candidates for Major Orders, several tracts in theology (C. 996).

The bishop determines the matter and method of the examination and appoints the examiners (C. 996). — If the dimissorials state that all examinations have been passed the ordaining bishop may rest satisfied with this, but he is not obliged to do so (C. 997).

4. *The publication* of the names of those to be ordained is done in the home parish church of each candidate and before each of the Major Orders.

In some places it is customary law that the public announcement be made only once or not at all. — The Ordinary may dispense wholly or in part from this obligation or substitute for it an announcement posted at the door of the church. It is omitted for religious with perpetual (simple or solemn) vows. — The faithful who know of an impediment to ordination must notify the bishop or pastor (C. 999).

5. *The retreat* before tonsure and the minor orders must last three full days, before Major Orders at least six full days (C. 1001).

If several Sacred Orders are received within half a year the bishop (or major superior in an exempt religious community) may reduce the retreat for the diaconate to three days (C. 1001). The bishop cannot do this for the other Major Orders even if they are received within a month, unless they follow so closely upon one another that it is impossible to have the retreats (AAS 20-359 sq.).

N. B. The Profession of Faith, including the oath against Modernism, must furthermore be made before receiving the subdiaconate (C. 1406; Cf. 119).

653. — II. The Rites of ordination prescribed by

the respective liturgical books must be accurately observed (C. 1002).

Those ordained to Sacred Orders must receive Holy Communion at the Ordination Mass (C. 1005).

At the end of the ordination ceremony *certain prayers* are imposed on those ordained. Candidates who have received tonsure or minor orders must recite the seven penitential psalms, together with the litany, versicles and oration. The newly ordained subdeacon and deacon must recite a nocturn of the Divine Office. Whoever is ordained to the priesthood must, after the First Mass, say the following Masses: first, the Mass of the Holy Ghost, then that of the Blessed Virgin and finally one for the Suffering Souls. The newly ordained shall also pray for the bishop.

The psalms with the litany, etc., are found at the end of the Breviary. — The nocturn imposed may be either the respective ferial nocturn or the first nocturn of the feast or Sunday office, if the ordination takes place on these days. The bishop may determine a different nocturn or one from another day. A nocturn here means the psalms and antiphons, not the lessons, invitatory or hymn. — The Masses enjoined are Votive Masses, unless there occurs a feast of the Blessed Mother or if a Mass of the Holy Ghost is otherwise prescribed. A stipend may be accepted for these Masses; but it is laudable to offer them for the Church and the Holy Souls.

These prayers do not oblige under sin.

654. — III. Time. Episcopal consecration is conferred on Sundays or on Feasts of the Apostles and during Holy Mass. — Major Orders may be given only during Mass on Ember Saturdays or on the Saturday before Passion Sunday or on Holy Saturday. For a grave reason the bishop may confer them on a Sunday or Holyday of obligation. — Minor orders may be given on any Sunday or feast of double Rite but only in the forenoon. — Tonsure may be given any day and at any hour (C. 1006).

According to a declaration of the Code Commission, May 15, 1936, the Holydays of obligation on which under certain conditions Sacred Orders may be conferred are not those formerly obligatory feasts which the Code has suppressed for the universal Church (AAS 28-210).

IV. Place (C. 1009). 1. *Major Orders.*

a) *General ordinations* should be held at the cathedral church. If ordinations are held in another city, as far as feasible the most prominent church should be chosen and the local clergy should be present.

b) *Particular ordinations* may take place in other churches, even in the chapel of the bishop's residence or in a seminary chapel or monastery choir.

2. *Minor orders* and *tonsure* may be conferred in a private oratory.

655. — V. Registration. 1. There must be a special record in the *curial archives* of the diocese where the ordinations are held in which the names of the newly ordained, the minister and date of ordination are entered (C. 1010).

2. The *newly ordained* are given a certificate of ordination. If they are ordained by a strange bishop with dimissorials from their own Ordinary they must show the certificate to the latter that he may enter the ordination in his own register (C. 1010).

3. Ordination to the subdiaconate must also be entered in the *baptismal register.*

For this reason the pastor of the place of Baptism must be notified of the ordination by the local Ordinary or by the major superior in the case of religious who are ordained with dimissorials from the superior (C. 1011).

656.   *Section VII*

The Holy Sacrament of Matrimony

Chapter I

THE NATURE OF MARRIAGE

I. Concept. 1. The *marriage contract* is a contract by which two competent persons of opposite sex give to each other the exclusive and irrevocable right over their bodies (*ius in corpus*) for the procreation and education of children.

Besides this primary purpose marriage has as *secondary ends* the mutual material and spiritual assistance to the married parties and protection against the abuse of sex life (C. 1013). The primary purpose of marriage is essential for its *validity* to the extent that the right to marital commerce may never be excluded. Nevertheless, it is lawful to renounce the exercise of that right by mutual consent (the so-called *Josephsehe* or virginal marriage). The marriage contract is valid even when it is certain that there is no possibility of having children. — If the primary purpose mentioned is not excluded the contract is *lawful and valid* even though the contractants personally have another lawful purpose in view, e.g., the settling of quarrels.

657. — 2. The *sacrament of matrimony* is the marriage contract between baptized persons which Christ elevated to the dignity of a Sacrament (C. 1012).

Accordingly, if baptized persons have been validly married they have also received the Sacrament of Matrimony (C. 1012). The explicit intention to receive a Sacrament is not necessary for its reception; it suffices to intend contracting a valid marriage. This intention makes the contract valid and a Sacrament, even though one is convinced that the marriage is no Sacrament. A legitimate marriage between two non-baptized persons becomes a Sacrament when they are baptized without their renewing matrimonial consent.

The *matter* of the Sacrament is the outward manifestation of the mutual conferring of the marriage rights; the *form* is the external expression of the acceptance of the same. — Accordingly, the essence of Matrimony consists in the marital consent (Cf. also 718).

The *ministers* of Matrimony are the matrimonial partners only, and not the priest. The latter's presence is necessary for validity, in the same manner as the presence of a notary is sometimes required for a valid contract.

On the *effects* of this Sacrament confer 746 sqq.

658. — II. Division. 1. Marriage between *Christians* or between *non-baptized persons.*

Marriage between Christians is called *"matrimonium ratum"* until it has been consummated; thereafter, it is designated as a *"matrimonium ratum et consummatum"* (C. 1015). Marriage between non-baptized persons is called *"matrimonium legitimum"* (C. 1015) and is not subdivided, since consummation does not give it any greater indissolubility.

2. *Valid* and *Invalid* Marriage.

If the marital contract has certainly been made, or if two persons are commonly considered husband and wife, and if a doubt arises as to the validity of the marriage, the marriage must be upheld until the contrary has been proved (Cf. C. 1014). This also holds for the marriage of heretics and non-baptized persons. Exception is made only in favor of the *privilegium fidei* (C. 1127). Concerning this confer 762.

An invalid marriage may be *putative* or *attempted* according as the invalidity of a person's marriage is known to him or not. One and the same marriage may be putative for one partner (the one who contracted the marriage in good faith) and attempted for the other. The Code Commission (Jan. 26, 1949) settled an old controversy by stating that a marriage can be putative only if celebrated in the Church (coram Ecclesia).

3. *Public* and *Clandestine* Marriage.

Marriages are thus divided according as they are contracted with the canonical formalities required for validity or not.

A marriage of conscience differs from a *clandestine marriage* in this that it is contracted without previous publication of the banns, but before the pastor and two witnesses who are obliged to secrecy in the matter. For particulars confer 745.

659. — 4. *Ecclesiastical* or *civil* marriage, according as the marriage is contracted before the Church or civil authorities.

Since Catholics cannot validly marry before a civil magistrate, any civil ceremony is for them a mere formality observed at most only to share in the merely civil effects of marriage. Wherefore, Catholics may not conduct themselves as married people before they are married in the Church, and still less may they rest satisfied with a civil ceremony alone. Although some States in the U. S. have laws regarding the manner of contracting marriage, nowhere is there a law requiring any definite ceremony to be observed by all. The only thing generally required is that matrimonial consent be mutually expressed before some authorized agent. Some States explicitly ordain that the priest or parson observe the ceremony required by his religion. A few States permit the civil official to follow any ceremony he wishes. No priest will be prosecuted in the U. S. for not observing a certain civil marriage formality. States rightly require certain formalities, e.g., registration, as a condition for granting legal value to a canonically valid marriage and punish the omission of those requirements. A COMMON LAW marriage is one entered into without ceremony of any sort, but where man and woman live together as man and wife and give themselves out as such to the world. Twenty-two states and D. C. recognize such marriages as valid. See p. 496.

660. — III. Matrimonial Jurisdiction. 1. As to marriage *baptized persons* are subject to the exclusive jurisdiction of the Church, since their marriage is always a Sacrament (Cf. 657).

Therefore, unless otherwise stated, the marriages of baptized non-Catholics are also subject to ecclesiastical legislation. Such exceptions principally concern the impediment of mixed religion (Cf. 701) and the form (Cf. 736). The State has authority over the marriage of Christians only with regard to the merely civil effects of marriages (e.g., property rights, testamentary rights). The State cannot establish impediments, etc., for them.

As a *civil official* a Catholic may without further ado co-operate in a civil marriage if the parties are willing to be married in the Church immediately after the civil ceremony. A grave reason is required for such co-operation if he is certain that they will not be married subsequently in the Church. Some authors even think he may co-operate for an *extremely grave* reason when there is an impediment present which will not admit of a dispensation, for example, the bond of a previous marriage. See 696.

2. The marriage of *unbaptized persons* is subject to the State.

Therefore, the State may determine impediments for the unbaptized provided they are not contrary to the natural or positive divine law. The bond of such a marriage cannot be dissolved by the State, since this is forbidden in the New Testament by positive divine law to which the unbaptized are also subject (Cf. 50). — The Church has no jurisdiction over such marriages. Hence, Jews and neo-pagans are not bound by the matrimonial legislation of the Church.

661. Chapter II

ENGAGEMENT

I. Concept. Betrothal or engagement is a promise made with mature deliberation by which one person obliges himself to enter into marriage with another person of the opposite sex.

A promise of marriage is *unilateral* of one person only thus obliges himself towards another who accepts the promise; it is *bilateral* or *betrothal* if both parties mutually thus oblige themselves (C. 1017).

II. Necessity. There is no necessity to make a valid betrothal before marriage.

To increase the sense of responsibility, however, one should induce those who are seriously keeping company to make a promise of marriage in a form that would be valid before the Church.

662. — III. The form of the marriage promise. Validity requires that it be made in writing and signed by both contracting parties, and by either the pastor (or local Ordinary) or at least by two witnesses (C. 1017).

The pastor (local Ordinary) validly *assists* at all canonical engagements within his territory, even though both contracting parties are strangers; but outside his territory he cannot validly assist at the betrothal of even his own parishioners. It is not forbidden that he act as one of the two witnesses, since witnesses alone suffice without the parish priest.

Neither the pastor nor Ordinary has power to *delegate*. But he who has full pastoral faculties (Cf. 729) can assist validly without delegation.

As a *witness* anyone may be employed who has sufficient mental maturity and can countersign the document. Both witnesses may be men or women, and they need not be Catholics.

The *formulary* may be written, printed, or reproduced in any mechanical manner. — The signatures must be made by hand and in the presence of all participants. — According to the common opinion the date and probably also the place are required for validity and, therefore, should never be omitted.

If one or both of the contractants cannot write, this fact must be noted in the document itself, and a third witness must sign it (C. 1017).

If the betrothal is validly made without the assistance of the parish priest the latter should be informed of the fact so that he can enter it in the marriage register.

663. — IV. The principal effect of a valid canonical engagement is the obligation to marry in due time.

Legal action to force marriage cannot be brought before the ecclesiastical court on the grounds of a valid promise of marriage; but a breach-of-promise suit can be brought for possible damages (C. 1017). — There are no grounds for indemnification if the betrothal is invalid, unless the damages have been unjustly caused, e.g., by fraud or deceit.

It is controverted whether the sexual relations of one of the engaged parties with a third person constitutes a sin against justice as well as a sin against chastity. Hence, in confessing the matter the circumstance of being engaged need not be mentioned.

Probably one does not sin gravely by unjustifiably breaking off a canonical engagement, since according to some authors, it obliges only out of fidelity. Others think it obliges gravely out of justice, either to marry the person or settle for damages. Hence, absolution cannot be denied a penitent guilty of broken faith if, in spite of the confessor's admonition, he intends marrying a different person.

664. — V. Dissolution of the Promise of Marriage. An engagement may be broken by mutual agreement; and also because of some important change of circumstances which takes place after the promise has been made or only then becomes known.

Examples of such a significant change are: a supervening prohibitive or diriment impediment, choice of a more perfect state of life, unjustified delay of marriage, a grave sin with a third person, syphilis, tuberculosis, insanity, irreligion, theft, murder, loss of reputation, social standing or considerable possessions. For a just reason an engagement may be broken on one's own authority, unless this be forbidden by some particular law; scandal must always be avoided. The party affected by the change of circumstances, in many cases remains bound by the promise if the betrothed partner does not renounce the engagement. — *Per se* the party culpably responsible for such a change must compensate the other party who on that account withdraws from the engagement.

Anything which would cause great damage to the other party must be *manifested* before the engagement is made, e.g., a contagious disease. The same is to be said of a fiancee who is pregnant by another man, since her future husband cannot be expected to rear a strange child. Instead of revealing her disgrace the girl may simply break off the engagement. — Those things which will not inflict a serious injury on one's future consort, but which make marriage less desirable, (poverty, ineptitude, etc.) need not, *per se*, be revealed unless it can be foreseen that the subsequent marriage will thereby become an unhappy one, in which case one is obliged in charity either to break off the engagement or reveal the unfavorable circumstances.

665.   Chapter III

PRECAUTIONS AGAINST INVALID AND

UNLAWFUL MARRIAGE

Before marriage is contracted it must be ascertained that there is no obstacle to its valid and lawful celebration (C. 1019). To attain this end there are required: Pre-nuptial investigation, baptismal certificate, banns and instruction of the parties to be married.

In *danger of death* the sworn statement of the contractants that they are baptized and free from all impediments suffices, provided one cannot have other proof and there are no indications that the contrary is true (C. 1019). — The oath need not be taken before witnesses nor need there be any record made of it.

I. Pre-Nuptial Investigation.
The parish priest whose right it is to assist at the marriage must, before publishing the banns, prudently and separately question the bride and groom, inquiring whether there be some impediment and whether they — especially the bride — are entering upon marriage freely (Cf. C. 1020).

The *pastor of the bride* generally undertakes this investigation (Cf. 735). If the groom cannot go to see the pastor of the bride, the pastor of the groom should be asked to conduct the examination.

Occult impediments need not be revealed to the pastor. A dispensation therefrom is absolutely necessary; but this may be obtained through the confessor. The pastor must also examine any papers, records or testimonials presented by the couple, e.g., certificates of Baptism, Confirmation, death of previous consort.

666. Besides, the pastor must make sure that the prospective husband and wife are *adequately instructed* in the Christian faith. He need not catechize them if they are known to be well-instructed Catholics (C. 1020). In case of gross ignorance the pastor must instruct them. If they refuse to take instruction he may not on that account refuse to marry them, but should treat them as public sinners (Cf. 672).

If they are not yet *confirmed* the pastor should induce them to receive this Sacrament before marrying if this can be done without inconvenience (C. 1021).

Those *under age* should be admonished not to marry without the knowledge, or against the reasonable objection of their parents. If they do not heed his advice the pastor should not assist at their marriage without first consulting the Ordinary (C. 1034).

All States of the Union have laws that require parental approval for the marriage of minors. Though they only render marriage unlawful, some of the laws are sanctioned by fines as high as $1,000 plus 3 years imprisonment. Of the 53 States and Territories 46 require this approval when the prospective husband is under 21 (if under 20 in N. H., 18 in Ia., N. C., S. C., Tenn., Mich., in

Ga. 17), and the girl under 18 (if under 21 in Conn., Fla., Ky., La., Mo., and perhaps in O., Pa., R. I., Va., W. Va., Wyo., and Puerto Rico). A few States make an exception when the girl lives away from home. Generally these laws affect the civil official granting the marriage license; but some States expressly mention the minister before whom the marriage is contracted. Hence, great caution is necessary. See Schema page 496.

667. — II. A baptismal certificate must under grave obligation be exacted by the pastor if Baptism was not administered in his parish (C. 1021).

The certificate must be of recent date (six months) in order to attain its purpose. It must contain information from the baptismal register concerning Confirmation, previous marriage, subdiaconate or solemn profession (Cf. C. 470). — Frequently this certificate cannot be obtained from baptized non-Catholics; if requiring it involves great difficulties it need not be procured (Cf. 56, 89).

III. The banns of matrimony are published in order that by public proclamation others may have their attention called to the impending marriage and be given an opportunity to reveal possible impediments known to them.

1. *Necessity.* In itself publication of the marriage banns is prescribed under grave sin.

This is true even if in an individual case there is certainly no impediment, since the law is made *ad praecavendum periculum commune.* Nevertheless, the omission of one publication, and perhaps even two, is only a venial sin. — *Dispensation* may be granted by the local Ordinary for a legitimate reason, also from the publication which should take place in another diocese. If one has several local Ordinaries, that one is competent to dispense in whose diocese the marriage is to be contracted. If the marriage is to take place outside the proper dioceses of the parties, any proper Ordinary can grant the dispensation (C. 1028). — As to what is to be done in *danger of death* confer 665. — Marriage with *a non-Catholic* must not be announced without the bishop's permission (C. 1026).

668. — 2. *Place.* a) The marriage must be announced

in *all places* where the parties have a pastor (Cf. C. 1023).

Hence, the proclamation must be made where the betrothed have a domicile or quasi-domicile (Cf. C. 92-25) or where they are staying for the time being, if they have no domicile or only a diocesan domicile (C. 94).

b) If the person about to be married has lived six months in another place after reaching *the age of puberty* (Cf. C. 88) the pastor must turn the case over to the Ordinary who will prudently judge whether the banns shall be published in that place or whether other proofs shall be gathered regarding the party's freedom from impediments (C. 1023).

The pastor shall likewise consult the Ordinary if suspicion arises about an impediment even in cases of residence lasting less than six months (C. 1023). — The oath of the parties is admissible as evidence. — As a rule, one must have recourse to the Ordinary in every such case.

Responsibility for the publication of banns rests on the pastor who is to assist at the marriage, since he cannot assist until he is certain there is no impediment (Cf. 1019; 1030). — The results of the proclamations made elsewhere must be communicated immediately to this same pastor (C. 1029). If he gets no report he must consult the bishop. If time does not permit and he has moral certainty that no impediment exists he may apply epikeia and celebrate the mariage.

669. — 3. *Time*. The banns must be published on three successive Sundays or feastdays of obligation; publication must be made in church during Mass or other divine services which are frequented by the faithful (C. 1024).

A *short interruption* without a reason would not be a grave sin; it would even be advisable if Holydays immediately succeed one another. — Banns may be published on feastdays that are local and, with special permission of the bishop also on the suppressed Holydays if a relatively great number of people attend services. — Banns may be published during Advent and Lent. The church need not necessarily be the parish church. Publication may also be made outside of church, e.g., at a field Mass or sermon in the open.

Between the last publication and the wedding there should be *an interval* of at least three days (C. 1030), e.g., the wedding may not take place before the Thursday following the last Sunday of publication (Cf. C. 34). A good reason justifies an exception (C. 1030). — The pastor is judge in the matter. — If marriage does not take place within six months after the last proclamation publication of the banns must be made anew, unless the bishop decides otherwise (C. 1030).

670. — 4. *Form.* Banns are usually published orally (C. 1024). The Ordinary of the place may permit the posting of the names of the parties at the church door as a substitute for oral publication (C. 1025).

The baptismal and family name and place of residence are to be mentioned; likewise the number of the publication, and whether a dispensation from an impediment has been granted. Nothing should be said that would defame the couple.

The notification at the church door must remain at least eight days (e.g., from Saturday evening until the second subsequent Monday morning). The notice must remain there over at least two Sundays or obligatory feastdays.

5. *Duty of the Faithful.* The faithful have the serious obligation to inform the local pastor or bishop in good time of an impediment known to them (C. 1027).

This holds if a dispensation from the banns is obtained, even if no one else has knowledge of the impediment so that it cannot be proved before court. One is excused only if the manifestation of an impediment means great harm to oneself, one's family or the state. — There is no obligation if a dispensation from an impediment has been granted, or if one only suspects an impediment, or if it cannot be revealed without violating the seal of confession or professional secrecy.

671. — 6. *Procedure of the Pastor.*

If *in doubt* about the existence of an impediment the pastor may begin and proceed with the publication of the banns. He must try to settle the doubt by further inquiry. If this is impossible the pastor must refer the matter to the bishop (C. 1031), who may dispense if there is a *dubium facti*, provided the impediment is one from which Rome usually dispenses (C. 15). If it is a *dubium juris* the bishop may authoritatively judge that such a doubt of law actually exists and that, (if there be question of an ecclesiastical impediment) marriage may be contracted. Such a doubt always exists in case of transients (*vagi*); hence, (except in case of necessity) the pastor may never assist at their marriage before obtaining permission of the local Ordinary (C. 1032). The same obtains for the marriage of emigrants who are either *vagi* in the new country or are little known there (AAS 13-348).

If there is *certainty* concerning the existence of an impediment, we distinguish: a) if the impediment is occult the pastor commences (or proceeds with) the publication of banns, meanwhile placing the matter before the bishop or Sacred Penitentiary without revealing any names; b) if public, he must not commence the publication before obtaining a dispensation in the external forum, even though he knows a dispensation has already been granted in the internal forum. If publication of the banns has already begun, he proceeds, meanwhile reporting to the bishop (C. 1031).

If *no impediment*, either certain or doubtful, is discovered the pastor must permit the marriage to take place (C. 1031). Concerning the marriage of public sinners confer 672.

The *necessary documents* must be obtained before the wedding takes place (C. 1030), viz., baptismal certificate (667), authentic document on the publication of the banns and its results if the marriage was announced in a different parish (668), marriage license, death certificate of former spouse, etc. If these documents are not received in time and the wedding cannot be postponed without harm, a priest should consult the Ordinary or use epikeia, provided he is morally certain that there is no impediment.

Concerning the interval between the last publication and the wedding, confer 669.

672. — IV. Instruction of the Spouses. The pastor should not fail to instruct the couple on the sanctity of the Sacrament of Matromony, their mutual marital obligations and the duties of parents towards their children. Besides, he should urge them to go to confession and Holy Communion before their marriage.

This instruction may best be given shortly before the wedding, but should never be given in the confessional. Regard should be had for the varying conditions of bridal couples. — If a *public sinner* refuses to confess, or one notoriously under censure refuses to be reconciled to the Church, the pastor may not assist at his marriage except for a serious reason and after consulting, if possible, the Ordinary (C. 1066) Cf. also 693. — If a general Confession is made it should precede the wedding by several weeks on acount of dispensation from possible occult impediments. — Holy Comunion may be received during the nuptial Mass, hence, after the mariage is actually contracted.

673. Chapter IV

MARRIAGE IMPEDIMENTS IN GENERAL

Article I

Concept, Division and Author

I. Concept. A marriage impediment is an external circumstance that prohibits marriage, rendering it invalid or at least unlawful.

Therefore, some impediments are incapacitating laws, others merely make marriage unlawful. — Before the Code most authors employed the term "impediment" more comprehensively, so that the words "matrimonial impediment" included the lack of marital intention (in one who could otherwise validly and lawfully marry) and failure to observe the form required by law for validity.

Inculpable *ignorance* of a diriment impediment does not make marriage valid (Cf. C. 16).

II. Division. Matrimonial impediments are:

1. *Prohibitive* or *diriment* according as they render marriage only unlawful or unlawful and invalid.

2. *Absolute* or *relative* according as they prohibit marriage absolutely or only between certain persons.

3. *Public* or *occult* according as they can be proved in the external judicial forum or not.

4. *Temporary* or *perpetual* according as they cease automatically or not in the course of time.

5. Of *major* or *minor degree* according as a dispensation therefrom will be invalid or not when false reasons are alleged as grounds for dispensation or certain circumstances are concealed (Cf. 680).

6. Of *divine* or *human right*.

674. — III. Author. 1. *God* has established certain impediments by the natural and the positive divine laws.

These impediments affect all men, even the unbaptized; the latter are also bound by the authentic determinations of the divine law made by the supreme ecclesiastical teaching authority (C. 1038).

2. *The Roman Pontiff* (or General Council in union with the Pope) may establish impediments in the form of general or particular laws.

These impediments oblige only the baptized (C. 1038), also non-Catholics, unless they are explicitly excluded.

3. *Local Ordinaries* cannot establish real impediments. But in a particular case, for a just reason and for as long as the reason obtains, they can forbid marriages to any person in their territory and to their own subjects even elsewhere (C. 1039).

A marriage contrary to this prohibition is valid but unlawful. The Holy See can add an invalidating clause to such a prohibition (C. 1039).

4. *The State* can establish marriage impediments only for the unbaptized (Cf. 660).

The civil concept of an impediment is similar to that which was common among authors before the Code (Cf. 673). Special attention must be paid to the difference between our "void" and voidable" laws on this matter; we shall note the civil law under the several impediments.

N. B. The Use of Epikeia can only be made in exceptional circumstances when there is question of a difficulty in obtaining a dispensation from an ecclesiastical impediment from which the Church is wont to dispense, e. g., in time of persecution. If the impediment is disparity of worship, a marriage without a dispensation would be valid only if the demands of the natural law are satisfied: there must be moral certitude that the children will be reared Catholic, and there must be no danger to the faith of the Catholic party.

675.   *Article II*

Dispensation from Matrimonial Impediments

§ 1. The Author of the Dispensation

I. The Roman Pontiff can dispense from all ecclesiastical impediments (C. 1040); but not from those of divine law.

Others have only that power to dispense which the Holy Father grants them either by common law or by personal indult.

The Pontiff generally acts through the Roman Congregations when dispensing; e.g., the Holy Office for the impediment of mixed religion and disparity of cult and also in questions touching the Pauline Privilege (C. 247); the Congregation of the Sacraments for all other public impediments of those subject to the Latin rite (C. 249); the Congregation for the Oriental Church if there is question of a marriage between two Orientals or between a member of the Oriental, and one of the Latin Church, excepting those matters that pertain to the Holy Office (C. 257); The Sacred Penitentiary for occult impediments (C. 258). — Concerning the continuation of faculties to dispense during a vacancy of the Apostolic See, confer C. 61.

676. — II. Local Ordinaries. 1. *In urgent danger of death* local Ordinaries may for peace of conscience or for the legitimation of offspring, dispense from the form and from all impediments of ecclesiastical law, whether public or occult, simple or multiple. The only exceptions are the impediments of priesthood and affinity in the direct line if the marriage is consummated (C. 1043).

The danger of death may be due to an extrinsic cause or to illness. Dispensation can probably be granted even if recourse to Rome is still possible. It matters not whether the impediment affects the sick person or the one who is well (e.g., the subdeacon or his "wife") — Scandal must be avoided. — The usual guarantees (*cautiones* No. 694) must be obtained in dispensing from mixed religion or disparity of cult. — Faculties to dispense are applicable to all persons in the respective territory including strangers, and to subjects when absent therefrom.

2. *In urgent necessity* (*casus perplexus*) local Ordinaries may dispense from the same impediments as in danger of death and under the same conditions, provided the impediment is discovered only after everything has been prepared for the wedding and the marriage cannot, without probable danger of grave detriment, be postponed until a dispensation be obtained from Rome (C. 1045).

It is doubtful whether a dispensation from the form can be granted. — An impediment is "discovered" if it was previously unknown to either the pastor, the local Ordinary or the couple, even though others knew of it, or if the couple has concealed it maliciously. — In the United States it is estimated that about two months are required for a dispensation from Rome. Recourse by telephone or telegram does not come under consideration. If recourse is made and no reply is obtained in time for the wedding, the bishop can dispense in virtue of C. 81 if there is question of an impediment from which Rome dispenses and there is danger in delay. On account of C. 204, however, the case must be reported to Rome.

677.— 3. *As to convalidation* of an invalid marriage, Ordinaries have the same faculties as in urgent cases if recourse to Rome is impossible and a similar danger obtains (C. 1045).

On renewal of consent for convalidation confer 767 sqq.

4. *In dubio facti* Ordinaries may dispense from impediments from which the Apostolic See usually dispenses (C. 15).

A *dubium facti* is had if the facts that give rise to an impediment are doubtful.

5. In virtue of their *Quinquennial Faculties,* local Ordinaries have special delegated powers.

678. — III. Pastors, Priests Assisting according to C. 1098 No. 2, and Confessors.

Confer 730 regarding priests assisting according to C. 1098 No. 2.

1. *In danger of death* the aforenamed possess the same faculties as local Ordinaries (676), provided the same conditions exist and the Ordinary cannot be reached in time. Confessors have the faculties only for the internal forum in the act of administering the Sacrament of Penance.

For *recourse* to the local Ordinary telephone and telegraph are not considered. One need not employ any extraordinary means, e.g., auto, train, airplane. One should usually figure on a week for recourse to the bishop unless his residence is not far distant.

If the *confessor* dispenses, he does so validly even if absolution is invalid or refused. — Whether he can dispense from public impediments is disputed. *Per se* one can ascribe this power to him in virtue of C. 209. Since dispensation in the sacramental forum cannot be proved, thus making the validity of the marriage contestable, such a dispensation is usually designated as unlawful. If the pastor or his delegate cannot be reached the confessor may act as assistant priest and dispense in the external forum. If either of them can be reached he must be called to assist at the marriage unless the confessor also dispenses from the form. There will usually be no difficulty in manifesting a public impediment to him for the purpose of obtaining a dispensation.

One who is *delegated* to assist at a marriage (e.g., a chaplain delegated *ad universitatem causarum*) does not enjoy the faculties of the assistant priest referred to in C. 1098, since of the latter it is said *si haberi ... nequeat ... sacerdos delegatus*. In virtue of C. 200, however, we presume that a pastor delegating another to assist at a marriage also delegates his respective powers to dispense.

Notification of the local Ordinary must be made (C. 1046) by the pastor or assistant priest immediately (i.e., within 2 or 3 days) if either of them has dispensed in the external forum. The dispensation must be entered in the marriage register. If granted in the internal non-sacramental forum it must be noted in the secret archives of the episcopal curia (C. 1047).

679. — 2. *In urgent cases* when the impediment is discovered after everything is prepared for the wedding which cannot be delayed without probable danger of great inconvenience and one can no longer have recourse to the local Ordinary, or only at the risk of violating a secret, the aforesaid persons have the same faculties as the local Ordinary (Cf. 676), but only for occult cases (C. 1045).

Concerning recourse to the Ordinary confer 678.

The *secret* whose violation is risked can be either the confessional or professional secret or any other secret.

"Occult cases" also include impediments that are by nature public, but actually occult (AAS 20-61), e.g., consanguinity registered in public records, but actually unknown.

Granting of the dispensation by the pastor or the assisting priest mentioned may also take place outside of confession. This is even necessary if the impediment is probably known in the external forum so that the marriage is liable to be contested. — In this case the dispensation must be entered in the marriage register (C. 1046). If granted in the internal non-sacramental forum the dispensation must be recorded in the secret archives of the episcopal curia (C. 1047).

3. *For convalidation* of marriages the same faculties obtain as in urgent cases, provided the same danger exists and there is no time to refer to the local Ordinary (C. 1045).

For *registering* the marriage the same applies as for urgent cases.

680.   **§ 2. Grounds for Dispensation**

I. Necessity. The validity of a dispensation always requires a sufficient reason (C. 40, 80). Only in case of minor impediments does a dispensation remain valid when none of the reasons alleged are true or when false reasons are advanced (C. 1054).

The reason must exist at the moment when the dispensation is actually granted. Thus, if an executor is appointed, the reason must exist when he dispenses, not necessarily when the executor is appointed. Concerning the necessity of a reason confer 73.

Impediments of minor degree are: consanguinity in the third degree of the collateral line (second cousins), affinity in the second degree of the collateral line, public decency in the second degree, spiritual relationship, adultery with either the promise of, or the attempt at marriage (C. 1042). If the consanguinity or affinity mentioned touches the first degree the impediment, according to many authors, is of major degree.

681. — II. Individual Reasons for Dispensation:

The woman's limited prospects of marriage (angustia loci), hence if the locality of the bride has fewer than 1500 Catholic inhabitants, and she therefore can find no other man equally acceptable; her super-marriageable age (aetas superadulta), i.e., if the bride has not been married before and has completed her twenty-fourth year; her lack or insufficiency of dowry; the poverty of a widow (burdened with numerous small children); the advantage of peace; danger to faith; the danger of a mixed marriage or of the celebration of the marriage before a non-Catholic minister; the danger of a civil marriage; the danger of incestuous concubinage; the danger of some spiritual harm; the cessation of notorious concubinage; the removal of grave scandal; the perpetuation of a noble family; excellence of merits; legitimation of offspring; excessive, suspected and dangerous familiarity; cohabitation that cannot easily be broken up; the evil repute of the woman, even though it be based on a false suspicion; the convalidation of an invalid marriage; the fact that the woman petitioning the dispensation is bereft of one or both parents; the fact of illegitimate birth; the presence of an infirmity or deformity in a party; the fact that the girl has been deflowered by another man; if a widower is seeking a good mother for his children; if a certain man and woman need each other's aid to run a businesss, etc; the fact that everything is prepared for the wedding; the fact that it is widely rumored that a certain couple will be married; the exemplary lives of both parties; the fact that a marriage proves suitable to the parties; some special advantage in the marriage; the welfare of the parents, e.g., if the father or mother of one or both parties is in need; mutual help and companionship in advanced age.

It is recommended that all existing reasons for a dispensation be mentioned in the petition, since: *quae non prosunt singula, multa iuvant.*

682.   § 3. The Petition for Dispensation

I. The petition may be made by the bridal parties
themselves. However, it is generally done by the priest
who is authorized to assist at their marriage in case of a
public impediment and by the confessor if the impediment is occult. The petition is usually addressed to the
Ordinary who will either himself dispense or forward
the petition to Rome.

Should a petition sent to the Ordinary endanger the Seal of
Confession, the penitent's attention should be called to this and
the necessary permission be obtained.

A petition to Rome is addressed to the Holy Father himself
(Beatissime Pater) if the dispensation is to be granted either by
the Holy Office or by the Congregation of the Sacraments; it should
be addressed to the Major Penitentiary (Eminentissime Princeps) if
the petition goes to the Sacred Penitentiary.

683. — II. Composition of the Petition. The following must be indicated: the number and lowest species
of impediments, reasons for the dispensation and the
exact address of the person to whom the rescript is to
be sent. It must furthermore be indicated whether or
not the marriage has already been contracted, and, if
so, whether the prescribed form was observed; whether
it was entered into in good faith, or with the conviction
(or in the hope) that a dispensation would more readily
be granted after the publication of the banns.

Furthermore, the names of the contractants, their
parish and diocese are to be mentioned when the petition
is made for the external forum. Besides, the customary
statement must be added respecting the financial condition of the petitioner. Cf. 689.

To avoid error, the request for a dispensation from the impediment of consanguinity or affinity, should be accompanied by a
diagram of the family tree (AAS 33-302).

If the *lowest species* of impediment is not mentioned, e.g., affinity instead of consanguinity, the dispensation is invalid, even

though it is a question of only minor impediments. An error regarding the *degree of impediment* does not invalidate the dispensation, if the existing degree is inferior to the one indicated (e.g., if the second is mentioned instead of the third degree); it does invalidate it if a more remote degree is mentioned (C. 1052), unless one has included the family tree and indicated thereon the exact relationship. — If the *number of impediments* is not mentioned in case of consanguinity or affinity the dispensation is invalid, unless the impediment not indicated is of the same or a more remote degree than the one mentioned (C. 1052). The Code Commission (July 8, 1948) declared that such impediments not indicated are also removed by the dispensation. Since *occult impediments* may not be indicated when applying for a dispensation in the external forum the public impediments must also be mentioned in the petition to the Sacred Penitentiary, and it must be indicated that a dispensation from the public impediment is also being sought in the external forum.

In a petition for the *internal non-sacramental forum* addressed to the Sacred Penitentiary no names are mentioned, but the dispensation is subsequently sent to the episcopal curia, the names being mentioned, so that a record thereof may be filed in the secret archives according to C. 1047. If the Seal of Confession is involved permission of the penitent is necessary. In petitions sent to the bishop it is beter to mention the names immediately. — In a petition *pro foro sacramentali* names are never given.

A formulary is given in No. 800.

684. § 4. Granting of the Dispensation

I. Mention of Apostolic See. Whoever dispenses in virtue of faculties delegated to him by the Holy See must mention the papal indult in granting the dispensation (C. 1057).

II. Dispensation in Virtue of General Delegation.

1. If one has general faculties to dispense from some *particular* impediment he can dispense even if the impediment is multiple unless the contrary is expressly mentioned in the indult (C. 1049).

2. Whoever has a general indult to dispense from *various impediments* may dispense also from all of them when several impediments occur in one and the same case (C. 1049).

3. Faculties may not be used when *application has already*

been made to the Holy See (C. 1048). An exception is permitted for a grave and urgent reason, but Rome must subsequently be informed of the matter (C. 204).

4. If an impediment from which one *cannot dispense* exists with one or more public impediments from which one can dispense by an indult, one must apply to Rome for all of them. Should one discover the impediment from which he can dispense only after applying to Rome for the other he may use his faculties (C. 1050).

5. The pastor or assistant priest dispensing in danger of death or urgent cases shall see to it that the dispensation *pro foro externo* is entered in the *marriage register* of the parish archives; if the dispensation is granted *pro foro interno non-sacramentali*, the entry must be made in the secret archives of the diocese (C. 1046, 1047).

685. — III. Dispensation on the Grounds of a Petition made to the Holy See.

Since dispensations here dealt with are granted almost exclusively *in forma commissoria*, no consideration is given to those granted *in forma gratiosa*.

1. An *error* in the rescript concerning the names of the petitioners, their diocese or parish or the subject matter of the petition does not invalidate the rescript if, according to the judgment of the Ordinary, there is no doubt about who or what is meant (C. 47).

If an error is made about the lowest species of the impediment or about the degree or number in case of consanguinity or affinity the same holds as was said in 683 about the petition (Cf. C. 1052).

2. The executor cannot grant the dispensation until he has *actually received* the rescript authorizing him to dispense unless he has been officially notified of his appointment as executor by the Congregation granting the indult (C. 53).

Dispensation granted before the rescript is received is invalid. In this case a second petition is not required, but the rescript must be executed anew. If the rescript is lost before the executor receives it a new petition must be filed. Confer 687 concerning the case wherein the penitent presents himself only after the destruction of the rescript.

3. Before executing a rescript for dispensation the executor **must make certain** that the reasons for the same actually obtain.

If this is not done the dispensation is valid provided the reasons actually exist. — In the external forum one may accept the results of another's investigation. In the sacramental forum the confessor must believe the penitent unless he knows from another source that the reasons alleged are fictitious.

4. If the executor makes a **mistake** that invalidates the dispensation he can again execute the rescript (C. 59).

686. — IV. Dispensation in the External Forum.

1. Execution should be made **in writing** (C. 56).

This is not required for validity but for lawfulness.

2. The document by which the bishop grants the dispensation should be sent to the pastor who will preserve it in the **parish archives.** — The dispensation itself must be recorded in the **marriage register.**

The rescript of the Apostolic See together with a record of its execution is kept in the diocesan archives.

V. Dispensation in the internal non-sacramental forum must be recorded in the bishop's secret archives, unless the rescript of the Sacred Penitentiary determines otherwise (C. 1047).

Hence the names of the petitioners are to be made known to the Ordinary (Cf. 683). — If the impediment later becomes public no further dispensation is necessary (C. 1047).

VI. Dispensation in the Sacramental Forum.

1. The confessor chosen by the penitent must **carefully read** the rescript and observe exactly all that is required for validity.

It is best to do this before confession (C. 796).

2. Thereupon the petitioner makes his *confession.*

Sacramental confession is necessary for the validity of the dispensation. The dispensation remains valid even if the confession is invalid or sacrilegious or if absolution is not imparted. If the impediment affects only one of the contracting parties (e.g., by reason of a vow of chastity) or if only one of the contracting parties is guilty (e.g., through public concubinage with the mother of the bride), then only this party is obliged to go to confession. If, however, the impediment affects both parties and if both are guilty (e.g., in case of adultery with the promise of marriage) it is necessary for the lawfulness of the dispensation that both parties confess and accept a penance.

3. *Information* concerning the veracity of the reasons alleged for the dispensation follows (Cf. 685).

687. — 4. Thereupon a *penance* is imposed for the transgression which was the cause of the impediment.

This penance differs from the sacramental penance. Neither imposition nor the acceptance thereof is required for validity.

5. *Dispensation is granted* orally, preferably in Latin (e.g., *Auctoritate Apostolica dispenso te super impedimento hoc criminis*); it may also be given in any other language.

Dispensation is probably also valid if granted implicitly, e.g., if the executor says: the petitioners may marry.

6. Destruction of the rescript by *burning* or *tearing* it up must take place *sub gravi* within three days after dispensation has been granted.

Failure to do so is penalized with excommunication l.s. For the sake of information, however, one may make a copy of it; but the place, date and names must be omitted. — If the impediment subsequently becomes known, the marriage of course remains valid; but a new dispensation is necessary for the external forum. — Should the penitent fail to appear at the appointed time, the rescript may be kept as long as there is hope that he will appear. If he should present himself only after the rescript has been destroyed, it may still be executed. — If only one of the contracting parties is affected by the impediment (e.g., vow of chastity) this party alone need appear before the confessor. If both are affected by it (e.g., adultery with the promise of marriage) both must present themselves; although the dispensation would be valid if only one did so. If it is known beforehand that one of the parties will not present himself, this should be noted in the petition.

688. — VII. Effects of the Dispensation. Besides removing the impediment a dispensation has the following effects:

1. *Legitimation* of offspring (except adulterous or sacrilegious) already born or conceived when a dispensation from a diriment impediment is granted in virtue of ordinary power or of a general indult (C. 1051).

Legitimation does not follow when the faculty to dispense is delegated for a particular case; in such instances it must be petitioned separately.

2. *Dispensation* without further requirement from the impediment of *adultery* with the promise of, or attempt at marriage, but only when the Holy See either dispenses from a *matrimonium ratum et non consummatum* or gives the surviving party permission to contract a new marriage because of the presumed death of the former spouse.

Should the bishop permit a new marriage because of such a presumed death the permission does not automatically contain a dispensation from a possible impediment of adultery. — In *dubio facti*, however, the local Ordinary can dispense (Cf. 677).

689. N.B. *The Fees.* A definite offering must, as a rule, be made for Apostolic rescripts containing a dispensation for the external forum, but not for those pertaining to the internal forum, except when one applies to the Sacred Penitentiary through the Ordinary or the

Roman agency, in which case the postal expenses alone need be paid.

Offerings are divided into *alms* (fixed by way of a fine called *componenda*) and *taxes*. The *componenda* is a sum of money sent by the petitioner to the Holy See for works of piety and as reparation for the non-observance of the law. The taxes are contributions towards the support of officials and for defraying the expenses of the Roman Curia. The offering must be in proportion to the possessions of the petitioner and the gravity of the impediment. The *destitute* need only pay the postage; the *poor* (i.e., those who live by manual labor, e.g., workmen, artisans, etc.) pay no *componenda*, but only a moderate tax; the *quasi-poor* (people of moderate means) pay the tax for the poor and a small *componenda*, while the *rich* pay in proportion to their wealth. If one's wealth is not truthfully indicated in the petition made to Rome, there is an obligation of restitution, but the dispensation is valid. C. 1056 forbids Ordinaries to charge for dispensations. A small contribution for chancery expenses is permitted, from which the very poor are dispensed. According to present-day practice, Ordinaries send a definite sum of money to the Holy See at the end of the year to defray the expenses of the Congregation issuing matrimonial indults.

690. Chapter V

INDIVIDUAL IMPEDIMENTS

Article I

Prohibitive Impediments

Prohibitive impediments render marriage unlawful but not invalid.

I. The simple vow of virginity, the vow of perfect chastity, the vow not to marry, to receive Sacred Orders or to embrace the religious state render marriage unlawful (C. 1058).

The simple vow of *perfect chastity* also includes the public vow as made in simple profession.

The vow *to enter the religious state* is the vow to enter an Order or Congregation, whether these be of papal or episcopal right (Cf. C. 488), having either temporal or perpetual vows.

For the *penalties* incurred by religious who marry after having made perpetual vows confer 439.

After marriage the vow must still be observed as far as this is compatible with the marital obligations, and the nature of the matter permits. — Accordingly, the vow not to marry ceases entirely. If one has made a vow of virginity he must render the marriage debt, but may not request it as long as virginity is not irreparably lost (either by consummation of the marriage or voluntary pollution). — He who has vowed to receive Sacred Orders or enter the religious state must render the marriage debt. Since a non-consummated marriage is dissolved by solemn profession (Cf. 761), it is gravely sinful to petition the debt before the consummation of the marriage in case one has either vowed to enter a religious community with solemn vows or if there is reason to hope that the other party will take this step, i.e., enter such a community. — If later on one is freed from his matrimonial obligation one must keep his vow. — Whoever has vowed perfect chastity may render, but may not request the debt (Cf. 751). In most cases it is advisable to seek a dispensation from the vow as soon as possible.

This impediment *ceases* when the vow ceases (Cf. 182 sqq.). Whoever has vowed to receive Sacred Orders or to enter the religious state, but is refused admittance through no fault of his own, has no further obligation (the matter vowed must be possible. Cf. 177). If he is rejected through his own fault he must make another attempt to fulfill his vow.

691. — II. Legal relationship (adoption) is an impediment in church law in so far as it is an impediment in civil law (C. 1059).

Thus, *adoption* is in the eyes of the Church a diriment or prohibitive impediment, or none at all acording to State law. No State in the U. S. recognizes any impediment of marriage arising from legal adoption. In Puerto Rico it is a diriment impediment. Foreigners residing in the U. S. temporarily without giving up their former domicile, remain subject to the laws of their country. Legal adoption is a diriment impediment, therefore, for such who come from Italy, Spain or Poland; prohibitive for those from France, Germany, Hungary, Switzerland and Belgium.

Before the Code adoption was a diriment ecclesiastical impediment where civil law corresponded substantially to the Roman law; its extent was considerable.

692. — III. Mixed Religion. 1. Concept. This impediment exists between two baptized persons of whom one is Catholic and the other a member of an heretical or schismatic sect. If such a union constitutes a danger to the faith of the Catholic party or to the offspring the marriage is also prohibited by divine law (C. 1060).

a) *The Baptism* of both parties must be certain or presumably certain. If the non-Catholic party is not baptized there exists then the diriment impediment of disparity of worship (Cf. 701).

If either the fact or the validity of the non-Catholic's Baptism be really doubtful dispensation from the impediment of disparity of worship must be obtained *ad cautelam*. After the marriage has been contracted its validity must be upheld until it is proved that one party was baptized and the other not (C. 1070).

693. *b*) *Apostasy* from the Catholic faith or *joining forbidden societies* but without formal enrollment (*adscriptio*) in a non-Catholic religious sect does not constitute this impediment.

Th faithful should, however, be *deterred* from marrying such persons. — The pastor may not assist at notorious cases without first consulting his Ordinary, who may permit such a marriage for weighty reasons and when he can reasonably assume that there will be no danger to the Catholic education of the children (C. 1065). The same holds for non-sectarians. Condemnation for heresy or schism alone does not constitute this impediment.

The *impediment* exists between a Catholic and a fallen-away Catholic who has officially been enrolled (adscriptus) in an heretical or schismatic sect. According to an interpretation of the Code Commission (AAS 26-494) that which is said of a non-Catholic sect applies also to the adherents of an atheistic sect. Thus the impediment exists between a Catholic desiring to marry an apostate Catholic or a non-Catholic Christian who has joined an atheistic sect. The same would have to be said of a Catholic who intends to marry a Christian who has joined a theistic religious society, e.g., Judaism or Mohammedanism. — It would seem that the impediment does not exist between a Protestant who has become non-sectarian and a Catholic; but, as in the case of public sinners, the pastor may not assist at such a marriage without having previously consulted with the Ordinary.

Catholics who embrace or propagate the materialistic doctrines of communism are apostates, and, therefore, the marriage of one such with a Catholic is to be looked upon as a mixed marriage, requiring the ante-nuptial agreements, dispensation and the absence of sacred Rites. (AAS 41-42.)

694. — 2. *Dispensation from the Impediment.*

In so far as this impediment rests upon divine law the Church does not and cannot dispense from it.

If there is no danger of perversion for the Catholic party or the offspring, the Church will dispense from the law of the Church under the following conditions (C. 1061):

a) If *just and grave reasons* urge the dispensation.

b) If the following *guarantees* (*cautiones*) are had:

α) The non-Catholic party must promise to avert all danger of perversion from the Catholic party.

Thus, absolute liberty to practice the Catholic faith must be permitted.

β) Both parties must promise that all children will be baptized and reared as Catholics.

These promises do not affect the children of the Protestant partner by a former marriage, neither do they affect children already born before the celebration of the marriage. Nevertheless, the parties to the marriage are to be warned of their grave obligation under the divine law to see to the Catholic education also of children who are already born (Holy Office, Jan. 16, 1942. AAS 34-22).

The Catholic must be reminded of the obligation of charity prudently to bring about the conversion of the non-Catholic party (C. 1062); but there need be no special promise made to this effect.

c) If there is *moral certitude* that the promises will be kept.

The promises must ordinarily be made in writing (C. 1061). — The petition for dispensation may be made only after the promises have been given.

695. *Civil law* does not acknowledge the impediment of mixed religion. Hence ante-nuptial pacts or promises concerning religion have no more civil effect than any other agreements.

696. — 3. *A marriage ceremony before a non-Catholic minister* either before or after the Catholic wedding is forbidden.

A pastor who is aware that the parties are contemplating such a ceremony or that they have already done so may not assist at their marriage. An exception is admissible for very serious reasons if no scandal will arise and the Ordinary is consulted. Nowhere in the U. S. is a civil ceremony required by law (C. 1063).

4. *Invalidly contracted mixed marriages* cannot be rectified unless the promises are made.

According to a decree of Jan. 14, 1932 (AAS 24-25) this applies also for dispensations granted in danger of death — In extremely difficult cases the bishop may, in virtue of his quinquennial faculties, grant a *sanatio in radice* without the promises being made.

5. *Penalties.*

Catholics presuming to contract a mixed marriage without a dispensation (even though the marriage be valid) are automatically excluded from positing lawful acts (actus legitimi) and from the reception of the Sacraments, until they have been dispensed by the bishop (C. 2375). Concerning *actus legitimi* confer C. 2256. — On censures l.s. that may be incurred confer 438.

N.B. Concerning marriage with public sinners and those under notorious censure confer 672; with fallen-away Catholics who have not affiliated with any non-Catholic religious sect, confer 693.

697. *Article II*

Diriment Impediments

I. Nonage. A boy who has not completed his sixteenth year and a girl who has not completed her fourteenth year cannot validly contract marriage (C. 1067).

Age is reckoned according to Can. 34. Thus a girl born at five o'clock A.M., May 5, 1926 cannot contract a valid marriage before May 6, 1940. She cannot marry till the day after her fourteenth birthday.

Puberty has nothing to do with the validity of the marriage. An earlier marriage is invalid though both parties are fully developed physically. It is valid if contracted after the age limit even though they have not attained to puberty. — *Unbaptized persons* are not affected by this impediment. — Where *mentality* is lacking (confer 717) marriage is invalid, whether the person be baptized or not, even though the party has long since passed the canonical age and has reached puberty. — An invalidly contracted marriage does not automatically become valid upon the parties reaching the required age; marital consent must be renewed in the manner prescribed (Cf. 767 sqq.).

Young people should be restrained from marrying before they reach the age customary in their *respective country,* even though they have reached the age required by Church law (C. 1067).

Great discrepancy obtains among the *statutes of our States* on the marriage impediment of "nonage." In the states where there is no provision in the statutes for either a minimum age of consent, or provision for parental consent, then the common law rule of a minimum age of 14 for males and 12 for females would be applied. It should also be noted that in no state will parental consent, if obtained, *validate* a marriage where the male is under 14 or the female is under 12.

Marriage below the minimum marriageable age is void in some States; in others it is voidable. Particular statutes and exceptions abound (e.g., if the girl is pregnant). In 31 States and D. C. marriage under 21—18 requires parental consent (Cf. Schema p. 496).

State	With parents' consent		Without parents' consent		Recognize Common Law Marriages	Miscegenation Prohibited	Blood Test Days valid	Waiting Days	License Valid Days
	(M)	(F)	(M)	(F)					
Alabama	17	14	21		A	B	C30		30
Arizona	18	16	21	18		B			Indef
Arkansas	18	16	21	18			C30	3	60
California	18	16	21	18		B	C30		Indef
Colorado			21	18	A	B	C30		30
Connecticut	16	16	21	21			C40	5	60
Delaware	18	16	21	18	A		C30		Indef
D. C.	18	16	21	18	A			5	Indef
Florida	18	16	21	18	A	B	C30		30
Georgia	17	14	21	21		B	C30		
Idaho	15	15	18	18	A	B	C30		
Illinois	18	16	21	18			C15	1	30
Indiana	18	16	21	18	A	B	C30		60
Iowa	16	14	21	18	A		C20		20
Kansas			21	18			C30	3	Indef
Kentucky			21	21		B	C15	3	30
Louisiana			18	16		B	C7	3	
Maine			21	18			C30	5	365
Maryland	16	14	21	18		B		2	180
Massachussetts			21	18			C30	5	60
Michigan	18	16	18	18	A	B	C30	5	30
Minnessota	16	15	21	18	A		C30	5	180
Mississippi			21	18		B		5	Indef
Missouri	15	15	21	18	A	B	C15	3	10
Montana	18	16	21	18	A	B	C20		Indef
Nebraska	18	16	21	21	A	B	C30		Indef
Nevada	18	16	21	18	A	B			Indef
N. Hampshire	14	13	20	18			C30	5	90
N. Jersey	18	16	21	18	A	B	C30	3	30
N. Mexico	18	16	21	18			C30		Indef
N. York	16	14	21	18	A		C30		60
N. Carolina	16	16	18	18		B	C30		60
N. Dakota	18	15	21	18	A	B	C30		60
Ohio	18	16	21	21	A	B	C30	5	60
Oklahoma	18	16	21	18	A	B	C30		10
Oregon	18	15	21	18		B	C30		
Pennsylvania	16	16	21	21			C30	3	60
Rhode Island			21	21	A		C40		90
S. Carolina	16	16	18	18	A	B		2	Indef
S. Dakota	18	15	21	18		B	C20		20
Tennessee	18	18	18	21		B	C30		Indef
Texas	16	14	21	18	A	B	C15		Indef
Utah	16	14	21	18		B	C30		
Vermont	18	16	21	18		B	C30	5	60
Virginia	18	16	21	21		B	C30		Indef
Washington	14	15	21	18		B		3	Indef
W. Virginia	18	16	21	18		B	C30		Indef
Wisconsin	18	15	21	18			C15	5	30
Wyoming	18	16	21	21		B	C30		

B - States that prohibit marriage between whites and negroes; B - States include Orientals or Mongolians. Five States (La., Nev., N. Car., S. Car., Va.) also forbid marriages between whites and (American) Indians.

699. — II. Impotency. Antecedent and perpetual impotency renders marriage invalid by virtue of the natural law, whether it be on the part of the man or the woman, whether it be known to the other party or not, and whether it be absolute or relative (C. 1068).

a) Impotency is the inability to exercise complete normal sex-relations. — It is absolute if sexual intercourse with anyone is impossible; relative, if it is impossible only with a certain person; perpetual, if it does not cease of itself or cannot be removed by natural or morally lawful means, or at least not without probable danger to one's life.

Because of the progress of medical science impotency may at one time or place be perpetual, at other times or places only temporary. — Impotency arising after marriage is contracted does not invalidate the marriage. — Lack of testicles constitutes impotency. According to many authors he also is impotent on whom complete or double vasectomy has been performed, provided the mutilation cannot be rectified by a new operation which is not dangerous to life or seriously injurious to health. This opinion is shared in a decision of the Roman Rota, Oct. 25, 1945, which declared such a marriage invalid. If, however, the condition is remediable, at least at the time of marriage, the marriage would be valid. As to the dissolution of a marriage not consummated by reason of impotency, see 761. — The impediment of impotency remains even though conception is possible by artificial insemination (Allocution of Pius XII, Sept. 29, 1949. Cf. 749).

b) In doubt (whether of law or fact) about impotency, marriage may not be prohibited (C. 1068).

A legal doubt exists, e.g., concerning a woman devoid of womb or ovaries. — A factual doubt must be solved, e.g., by consulting a conscientious physician. Cases of hermaphroditism must be referred to the bishop, who will render a decision only after consulting competent authorities on the matter. — After contracting marriage the parties may attempt to perform the marriage act as long as impotency remains doubtful, even though the seed be lost.

c) When married people become certain of the existence of antecedent perpetual impotency they must discontinue further use of marriage rights, since their marriage is invalid.

Marriage can in such cases be juridically pronounced invalid. Since antecedent permanent impotency is very difficult to prove it is often better to seek a dispensation from a *matrimonium ratum non consummatum*. — When both parties are in good faith it may be advisable *not* to disturb them. If good faith is wanting they might, in very exceptional cases, be permitted to live together as brother and sister.

d) Sterility neither invalidates marriage nor makes it unlawful (C. 1068).

Wherefore even very aged people may marry as long as they can somehow consummate the marriage.

N. B. Civil law. In all States of the union except Conn., La., and S. C. a marriage which is invalid because of incurable impotence can be civilly dissolved either by a declaration of nullity or by divorce, provided action is brought within the time limit specified by law. Though sterility does not legally incapacitate one for marriage, yet a woman made barren by surgical operation is under legal and moral obligation to disclose the fact to an intended husband.

700. — III. Existing Marriage Bond. A person once validly married cannot marry again as long as the prior marriage has not been dissolved, even though it has not been consummated (C. 1069).

Death alone can *dissolve* a consummated marriage between Christians (C. 118). Protestants, too, married according to civil law, cannot contract a valid marriage before God as long as a former marriage partner still lives. Marriage of the unbaptized, whether consummated or not, can be dissolved by the Pauline Privilege; in other cases the second marriage of the unbaptized is invalid if the first party still lives, even though a civil divorce be obtained. — *The second marriage* is also invalid when contracted with the firm conviction that the first spouse is dead, even if the second marriage is contracted according to canon law, and the Church has authorized it because of the presumed death of the absent spouse.

A new marriage is unlawful until the nullity or dissolution of the prior marriage has been legally and certainly established (C. 1069). — A civil declaration of death (e.g., prolonged absence by reason of war) is not sufficient to authorize one's entering upon a new marriage. — If the former partner died in another parish the pastor thereof must supply a death certificate; if this cannot be had the case must be referred to the bishop.

701. — IV. Disparity of Cult. 1. *The Impediment.* Marriage is null and void if contracted between an unbaptized person and one baptized in, or converted to, the Catholic Church (C. 1070).

Baptized in the Catholic Church are the following: *a)* adults who freely convert to Catholicism and receive Baptism — *β)* children whose parents or guardians (be they Catholic or not) have them baptized, either privately or solemnly, with the intention of making them members of the Catholic Church. — Those children also are bound by the impediment who are born of non-Catholics, but who, in keeping with C. 750, receive Catholic baptism in danger of death, even despite parental objection, but who from infancy have grown up in heresy, schism or without any religion. Most authors think children are not included if, born of non-Catholics, they are baptized by a Catholic contrary to the rulings of C. 750 and 751 and brought up as non-Catholics.

Those, too, are considered to be *converts* to the Catholic Church who, though not baptized in the Church, have been reared as Catholics from childhood, and who have for some time at least lived as Catholics, and thus have not objected to membership in the Catholic Church.

An apostate Catholic (even though he join another religion) remains bound by this impediment even as one who remains a Catholic from youth or is a convert to the Church.

Heretics and schismatics who never belonged to the Catholic Church are not bound by the impediment; still less are catechumens.

In doubt about the validity of the Baptism of a Protestant, etc. whom a Catholic desires to marry, a dispensation from disparity of cult is required *ad cautelam* (Cf. 692).

Before the Code (May 19, 1918) the impediment existed between all unbaptized and validly baptized persons even though the latter never belonged to the Catholic Church.

2. *Dispensation* is granted under the same conditions as those required for a dispensation from mixed religion (Cf. 694 sq.). The reasons, however, must be more weighty.

702. — V. Major Orders. Clerics in Major Orders cannot marry validly (C. 1072).

Major Orders are subdiaconate, diaconate and priesthood (C. 949). — Clerics in Minor Orders can validly marry, but in doing so they *ipso iure* lose clerical status (C. 132).

The impediment presupposes that Orders were received validly, with full knowledge of all concomitant obligations and without duress. The impediment also binds one who, induced to take Sacred Orders by grave fear, has (after the fear has ceased) ratified his ordination at least implicitly by the exercise of his Orders. If he has not so ratified his ordination he may be reduced to the lay state by a sentence of the judge and be freed from all obligations of celibacy and the divine office (C. 214). — Concerning *censures* l.s. confer 437.

VI. Solemn Vows. Whoever has taken solemn vows in a religious institute cannot validly marry. The same holds for those who have taken simple vows which, by special disposition of the Holy See, invalidate marriage (C. 1073).

If the profession was null and was not subsequently validated the marriage is valid. Lawfulness, however, requires that the profession be authoritatively declared invalid. — *Secularization* removes the impediment (Cf. C. 604). A secularized religious may, therefore, marry provided he has not received Major Orders. Regarding *censures* l.s. confer 437.

703. — VII. Abduction. A man who abducts a woman in order to marry her cannot validly do so as long as she is within his power. The same holds if either in her own home or at a place whither she has freely gone, he forcibly detains her with the purpose of marrying her (C. 1074).

Violence may be physical or moral, e.,.g fraud, deception, threats.

— The abductor may act personally or by proxy. — The impediment exists even if the girl is engaged to him. — No impediment obtains when the girl, induced by gifts or flattery, elopes with her abductor to marry him.

No impediment exists if a woman abducts a man or if a man abducts a woman merely to satisfy lust. — Such a marriage, however, may be invalid by reason of grave fear (Cf. 723 sqq.).

The impediment ceases if the abducted woman is liberated from the power of her abductor and restored to a place of safety where she can act freely. Prior to this the marriage would be null even though the abducted would gladly consent to it. — Concerning rape as a sin against chastity confer 226.

Civil law. In nearly all of our States grave penalties are inflicted upon an abductor as a precautionary measure against marriages which are void because of violence or duress.

704. — VIII. Crime. The impediment of crime invalidates marriage with the accomplice of crime in the following cases.

1. *Adultery with the Promise of Marriage.* Persons who, during one and the same legitimate marriage, have committed adultery and mutually promised to marry one another cannot contract a valid marriage (C. 1075).

a) Adultery must be:

α) Real.

The impediment does not arise from a putative marriage. A *matrimonium ratum* alone suffices; likewise in the case of separation from bed and board, and if the parties are civilly divorced.

β) Complete.

Sexual intercourse must be the normal act by which generation is possible; onanistical or sodomitical copulation is insufficient. If there has been sexual intercourse it is presumed to have been complete until the contrary is proved.

γ) Formal.

Both parties must be conscious of the fact that at least one of them is married. — The impediment does not seem to arise if one party is a divorced non-Catholic who does not consider the action adulterous.

705. *b*) The *promise* must be:

α) Real.

A mere desire or purpose does not suffice. — It is not necessary, however, that the canonical form be observed in making the promise.

β) Absolute, or (according to most authors) one that has become absolute through the fulfillment of a condition before the death of the lawful spouse.

γ) Serious.

No impediment arises if a promise is made in jest or fictitiously. If the promise has been made it is presumed to have been seriously made, unless there are reasons to the contrary.

δ) Free.

It must not have been made out of grave fear or in consequence of a substantial error.

ε) Mutual.

Each must promise and accept the other's promise in some externally perceivable manner.

ζ) To marry after the death of the lawful spouse.

The promise to marry while the lawful spouse is still alive, e.g., after a civil divorce is obtained, does not give rise to the impediment.

706. *c*) *One and the same marriage* must be violated consciously and unjustly by adultery and promise of marriage.

It matters not whether the adultery or the promise be first in order of time. — No impediment exists if A promises to marry B, a single person, and then after B marries C, A commits adultery with B; or if A commits adultery with H while H's first spouse is living and then promises to marry H during H's second marriage; or if A commits adultery with K and makes the promise to L. Neither does the impediment arise if a man promises to marry a married woman whom he thinks single, and then after he learns of her marriage commits adultery with her; should he subsequently confirm his promise the impediment arises. — No impediment arises if before the sin of adultery the promise is seriously made and then revoked in such a manner that the other party receives knowledge thereof; but the impediment remains if the promise is revoked only after adultery has been committed.

If each is married unknown to the other no impediment arises. Culpable ignorance regarding the marriage of the other party excuses from the impediment unless the ignorance is affected (Cf. 16).

707. — 2. *Adultery with Attempted Marriage.* Whoever during one and the same lawful marriage commits adultery with, and actually attempts to marry another person, cannot validly marry that person (C. 1075).

a) Marriage is attempted when both persons in any form whatsoever give their marriage consent, be it before a competent pastor, a non-Catholic minister, a civil official or only privately.

Concubinage without connubial intentions does not constitute this impediment. — In the first case of impediment of crime the promise is made to marry after the death of the lawful spouse, whereas here the attempt is made while that spouse lives. — The impediment arises even though the marriage were otherwise invalid, e.g., due to consanguinity; not, however, if the marriage were null because of grave fear.

b) Adultery is understood as in 704.

c) One and the same marriage must be consciously violated by adultery and attempt at marriage.

Number 706 also applies here. — If one learns that the rightful spouse of his accomplice is still alive only after attempting marriage, he incurs the impediment, provided after acquiring a knowledge of this fact, he does not revoke the marital consent and commits a formal sin of adultery.

708. — 3. *Adultery with Conjugicide*. The marriage of two persons is null if during the same legitimate marriage they mutually have committed adultery and one of them commits conjugicide (C. 1075).

Conjugicide must actually follow from an action of one of the adulterers; mere attempt to murder is insufficient. — It matters not whether an adulterer murders his own spouse or the spouse of his accomplice. The marriage must be valid, not merely putative. If one hires another to do the killing the impediment arises, but not if the murder is only subsequently approved. — The murder must be committed with the intention of marriage with the surviving widow or widower. Probably this intention to marry the survivor must somehow also be manifested externally, and according to some authors made manifest to or at least be known by the accomplice in adultery. Because of the uncertainty of the law, the impediment in this instance practically does not arise by reason of C. 15. The requisite intention is juridically presumed until the contrary is proved. — The impediment does not arise when the murder is committed out of revenge or to satisfy base lust more freely.

Concerning the *adultery* the same holds as in 704. Adultery must precede conjugicide; otherwise, there is no adultery.

709. — 4. *Conjugicide by mutual, physical or moral co-operation* prevents two people from validly marrying (C. 1075).

Conjugicide presupposes valid marriage. — Conspiracy may be by command, counsel, persuasion, etc.; there is no conspiracy if one party learns of the murder only later and approves of it. — The intention to marry the accomplice in crime must be in the mind of at least one of them and in some manner manifested externally. Such an intention is presumed before law until the contrary is proved.

Multiplication of the Impediment.

Multiplication of the impediment is effected when to adultery with the promise of marriage there is added the attempt at marriage and if, furthermore, there is conjugicide either with conspiracy or by only one of the adulterers. — The impediment is multiplied, too, in the case of adultery with the promise of, or attempt at, marriage when both parties were married and each knew of the other's marriage or if there has been double conjugicide. — There is no multiplication if during one and the same marriage, adultery is repeatedly committed or the promise of marriage is made repeatedly. — All impediments must be indicated in the petition for a dispensation.

Concerning a dispensation granted implicity confer 688.

Before the Code (May 19, 1918) it was not quite certain whether the impediment arose when the guilty persons had no idea that such conduct constituted an impediment to future marriage. Since the Code has gone into effect it is certain that ignorance does not excuse one from incurring the impediment (Cf. C. 16).

Unbaptized persons do not contract the impediment, not even if they marry only after their Baptism; nor in case one part of the crime takes place after Baptism (e.g., the promise required for the first form of the impediment). — If one party is baptized and the other not, the impediment arises, except in the third form (adultery with conjugicide) if the unbaptized person commits the murder.

710. — IX. Consanguinity. 1. *In the direct line* marriage is invalid between all ascendants and descendants, whether legitimate or natural (C. 1076).

The direct line embraces all blood relatives originating from each other by procreation: son (daughter), father (mother), grandfather, etc.

2. *In the collateral line* marriage is invalid between blood relatives to the third degree inclusive (C. 1076).

In the collateral line persons descend, not from each other, but from a common ancestor, e.g., brothers and sisters, cousins, etc. Blood relatives may have the same father and the same mother (full brothers, cousins, etc.), or only the same father or the same mother (half brothers, half sisters). The degree is the measure of distance between blood relatives. In the collateral line there are as many degrees as there are generations in one of two equal branch lines (or as many degrees as there are persons subtracting the common ancestor). Thus brother and sister are related in the first degree, cousins german in the second. To determine whether or not the parties to be married are related in the third degree one need only observe whether or not their grandparents were brothers and sisters. If the branch lines are unequal there are as many degrees as there are generations in the longer line. Thus uncle and niece are related in the second degree (touching the first). (Cf. C. 96.) Relationship in the fourth degree touching the third, etc. is no impediment. In requesting a dispensation from the second or third degree one should indicate the fact if these degrees touch the next nearest degree. When the second degree touches the first the practice of the Roman Curia requires that this be mentioned in the petition for a valid dispensation (Cf. AAS 23-413).

711. — 3. _Multiple consanguinity_ is had with every additional common ancestor.

The impediment is multiplied: a) if the parents and (or) grandparents are blood relatives (Diagram I). Francis and Mary (uncle

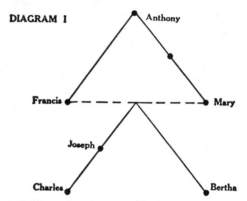

and niece) marry. They have two children, Joseph and Bertha. Charles the son of Joseph desires to marry his aunt Bertha. They are doubly related: through Francis and Mary they are related in the second degree touching the first; furthermore, they are related in the third degree through Anthony.

The lineage of Charles can also be traced back to Anthony through Mary, and Bertha's through Francis. Thus they are related in the fourth degree touching the second. The longer line to the common stock is not considered in determining the marriage impediment.

b) if blood relatives have children from blood relatives (Diagram II). Christian and Jude are brothers. Mary and Jane are sisters.

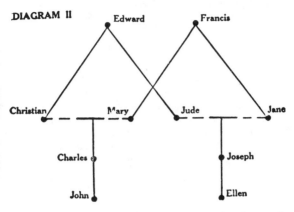

DIAGRAM II

Christian marries Mary and Jude marries Jane. John, the grandson of the one marriage desires to marry Ellen the granddaughter of the other marriage. Both have two common ancestors (two grandfathers Edward and Francis) and are thus twice related in the third degree collateral line.

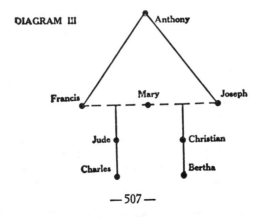

DIAGRAM III

c) if one has children from several blood relatives whom he marries successively (Diagram III). Mary first marries Francis and after his death she marries his brother Joseph. Charles is a grandson of the first marriage who desires to marry Bertha, the granddaughter of the second. Charles and Bertha have the same grandmother, Mary, and are thus related in the second degree. Furthermore, they have the same great-grandfather, Anthony, and are related in the third degree through him.

712. — 4. *Dispensation* from this impediment is never granted, in as far as it is certainly (first degree direct line) or probably (all other degrees of the direct line and the first degree collateral line) of divine law (C. 1076). Neither is it ever granted if there is a good reason to doubt whether two persons are actually related in this manner.

Dispensation is seldom granted when a more remote degree touches the first (Cf. 710). On error and dispensation confer 683.

Before the Code (May 19, 1918) the impediment extended to the fourth degree inclusive in the collateral line. Multiplicity existed not only when there was a plurality of common ancestors, but also when two persons descended in different ways from one common ancestor. Thus in our first diagram Charles and Bertha were thrice related: once in the second degree touching the first, again (through Francis and Mary to Anthony) in the third and finally in the fourth degree touching the second. Though these impediments no longer exist, yet a marriage thus invalidly contracted before 1918 is not automatically validated by the Code, but must be convalidated (Cf. 767 sqq.).

Unbaptized persons are affected by the impediment in so far as it is of divine law. Where the divine law is uncertain and public scandal is avoided they may be left in good faith after their Baptism for the sake of avoiding greater evil. Canon Law obliges when one party is baptized and the other is not. The unbaptized are obliged by the civil law. In all our States marriage of relatives within the prohibited degrees is a diriment impediment of the first class, ("void") except Ala., Fla., Ohio, S. C., Tenn., Tex., Va., Wash., W. Va., where it is a second class impediment ("voidable"). While the State laws concerning marriage differ, nevertheless, marriages in all States are forbidden between relatives in the direct line; likewise marriages in the collateral line to the second degree touching the first according to the Church's method of computation (e.g., uncle and niece). The following States permit first cousins to marry: Ala., Cal., Conn., Fla., Ga., Ky., Me., Md., Mass., N. J., N. Mex., N. Y., R. I., S. C., Tenn., Tex., Vt., Va., D. C. Grave penalties are inflicted on those guilty of the crime of incest and on the assisting minister. Dispensation from ecclesiastical authorities is not sufficient.

713. — X. Affinity. 1. Affinity invalidates marriage in all degrees of the *direct line* and in the *collateral line* to the second degree inclusive (C. 1077).

Affinity is a relationship arising from a valid marriage of Christians and exists between the husband and the blood relatives of the wife and between the wife and the blood relatives of the husband (C. 97). Wherefore affinity is possible only when at least one of the parties is or has been married. — The consanguinity underlying affinity may be full or half blooded; the blood relatives may be born before or after the marriage. — The marriage must be valid, whether consummated or not.

Since there is no affinity between them, two brothers of one family may marry two sisters of another, or a brother and sister may marry a brother and sister. A stepson may marry his stepmother's mother or sister as well as her daughter by a former marriage. The surviving widow and widower of a brother and sister, respectively, may marry each other, but a widow may not marry her deceased husband's brother, i.e., her brother-in-law.

Affinity is computed in the same manner as consanguinity. Therefore, in the same line and degree in which a man is related to others by blood, is his wife related to them by affinity, e.g., a man is related in the first degree of affinity to his wife's sister, in the second degree to her cousin; in the direct line he is related by affinity in the first degree to his stepmother and stepdaughter.

714. — 2. *Multiple affinity* arises by multiplication of the impediment of consanguinity and by successive marriages with blood relatives of the deceased spouse (C. 1077).

Regarding error and its effects on a dispensation from this impediment confer 683.

Before the Code (May 19, 1918) affinity was based on sexual intercourse, whether marital or not. — The impediment of public honesty arose from a non-consummated marriage. — The impediment of affinity from marital intercourse extended to all degrees of the direct line and to the fourth degree inclusive of the collateral line; from extramarital intercourse to the second degree inclusive both in the direct and collateral lines. Concerning the convalidation of such a marriage confer 767 sqq.

Unbaptized persons are only indirectly bound by this impediment, e.g., an unbaptized woman desiring to marry her deceased sister's widower if theirs had been a Christian marriage. This impediment does not exist between two unbaptized persons or between an unbaptized and a baptized person; but it does if their marriage is Sacramentalized by the Baptism of both parties (or of the unbaptized party if the other has already been baptized).

In twenty-five of our States affinity is no marriage impediment. In Ga., Ky., Me., Md., Mich., N. H., Okla., Pa., R. I., S. Dak., Tenn., Vt. affinity within varying degrees voids marriage; whereas marriage in Ala., Del., Mass., Tex., Va., W. Va. is voidable on the grounds of affinity. In some instances jurisprudence renders the written law doubtful. Penalties are usually less severe than for incest.

715. — XI. Public decency is an impediment arising from an *invalid marriage* and from *public or notorious concubinage;* it annuls marriage between one party and the blood relatives of the other in the first and second degrees of the direct line (C. 1078).

Therefore, the impediment extends to the parents, grandparents, children and grandchildren of the other party.

The *marriage* may be consummated or not, putative or attempted (confer 658). — It is doubtful whether the impediment arises from a marriage that is invalid from lack of consent.

If persons bound to the canonical form contract a *civil marriage* or marry before a non-Catholic minister, their union is not even considered an "invalid" marriage and the impediment arises only from their subsequent cohabitation (public concubinage).

In doubt about the existence of *public concubinage* the matter must be submitted to the Ordinary according to C. 1031 (Cf. 671).

The impediment *remains* after the concubinage or invalid marriage ceases. — It is controverted whether it remains after the invalid marriage or concubinage has been converted into a valid marriage or whether it merges with the impediment of affinity. In such cases one may rest satisfied with a dispensation from the impediment of affinity.

Before the Code (May 19, 1918) the impediment arose: a) from a valid engagement and remained even after the engagement was broken off by death or in any other way. It invalidated marriage in the first degree of the direct and collateral lines. b) from a non-consummated marriage, whether valid or not, except when the marriage was invalid from lack of consent. Marriage was invalid to the fourth degree of the direct and collateral lines.

The unbaptized are not bound by this impediment if they marry invalidly among themselves or live in public concubinage. But if a Christian man lives in public concubinage with an unbaptized woman he cannot marry her mother or daughter.

716. — XII. Spiritual relationship invalidates marriage between the person baptizing and the baptized and between the baptized person and the sponsors (C. 1079).

This applies also to private Baptism. The Baptism must be valid. Conditional rebaptism gives rise to the impediment between the baptized and the sponsors provided the latter sponsored both Baptisms (Cf. 482). — The same holds for the minister. — To incur the impediment one must be a valid, though not necessarily, a lawful sponsor (Cf. 480).

Before the Code (May 19, 1918) the impediment existed between the minister and the person baptized or confirmed and his parents; furthermore, between the sponsors and the one baptized or confirmed and his parents. Spiritual relationships existing before the Code remain since the Code went into effect, but the impediment ceases in as far as it is no longer covered by the Code's legislation. However, marriage invalidly contracted before the Code remains invalid. For convalidation confer 767 sqq.

An unbaptized person who baptizes another is not affected by the impediment if he himself later receives Baptism. Unbaptized sponsors are not considered since they cannot validly act as sponsors (Cf. 480).

XIII. Legal Relationship (Cf. 691).

717. Chapter VI

MATRIMONIAL CONSENT

Article I

**Nature, Necessity and Manifestation
of Matrimonial Consent**

I. Nature. Matrimonial consent consists essentially in giving and accepting the perpetual and exclusive right to the body, i.e., the right to acts suitable for the propagation of the human race (C. 1081).

Because this right must be given for always, a marriage would be invalid if the parties were to give it only for those times when conception will not follow intercourse. However, if, by mutual agreement, they merely intend to use their rights (given for always) at those times, their marriage would be valid.

In contracting marriage it suffices that each party be asked if he will "take" the other, since this can only be done if each is willing to "give" himself.

One does not marry validly if one *refuses to give* the matrimonial right or accepts its corresponding obligations (C. 1086). The marriage is valid if one accepts the corresponding obligations with *no intention to fulfill* them, e.g., if one intends to abuse marriage onanistically or to separate from the other party in case of adultery. While a marriage is invalid if the parties intend to contract it (matrimonium ratum et consummatum) in such wise that it can be dissolved by divorce ("trial marriage"), on the other hand, a marriage is valid (although illicit) if the parties contract it with the intention of abusing it onanistically. — The marriage is valid also if the wife before marrying undergoes a contraceptive operation.

The *knowledge* that marriage is a permanent union of man and woman for the procreation of children is a prerequisite for true matrimonial consent. This knowledge is presumed in every one who has reached the age of puberty (C. 1082). Whoever alleges ignorance thereof must prove its existence. — If one is aware of the nature of marriage but is ignorant of the manner in which it is consummated, his marriage is considered valid. If the marriage has not been consummated it may be dissolved by papal dispensation in case of insuperable repugnance to intercourse. See 761.

718. — II. Necessity. Because marriage is a contract

(Cf. 656, 657) and the essence of every contract is the contractual will, it follows that matrimonial consent is the essence of marriage.

No human power can supply matrimonial consent (C. 1081); consequently, there is no sanation of "marriage" possible if one party refuses consent.

He who has not the use of reason (children, the insane) cannot validly marry because of the lack of matrimonial consent. He does not marry validly who, upon making the contract, does not intend to marry even though externally he simulates matrimonial consent.

It is always presumed that one's intention corresponds with his words until the contrary is proved (C. 1086). — The intention need not be actual at the time marriage is contracted. It suffices that the internal matrimonial will virtually perseveres (Cf. 8) while the matrimonial intention is being manifested, and that it has not been revoked, thus making it at least habitual (Cf. 8) until the other party manifests matrimonial consent. — He who marries without giving consent can, as a rule, only repair the harm done to the other party by subsequently giving the consent necessary to make the marriage valid (Cf. 769).

719. — III. External manifestation of matrimonial consent is required for validity, because marriage is a contract and because it is a Sacrament.

Whoever is *not bound by the laws of the Church* need not manifest consent by words, but may do so by equivalent signs (gesture) or by letter.

Church law demands that consent be expressed by the spoken word. Observance of this regulation, however, is not required for validity. Whoever cannot speak may manifest his consent in other ways (C. 1088). One may employ an interpreter (C. 1090). — Since May 19, 1918 Canon Law requires that both parties be present either personally or by proxy for contracting a valid marriage (C. 1088, 1089). The Holy Office (Sept. 6, 1949) authoritatively declared that this provision of the Code binds also in the case of marriages of baptized non-Catholics. — Only for a grave reason may a pastor assist at a marriage which is contracted by proxy or through an interpreter, and only if he has no doubt about the authenticity of the proxy's commission and the trustworthiness of the interpreter. If time permits he should consult the Ordinary (C. 1091).

720. *Article II*

Ignorance and Error Concerning
Matrimonial Consent

What is here said of ignorance also applies to error and vice versa. Erroneous notions may concern the nature of marriage, its properties, the possibility of marrying or the other party.

I. Nature of Marriage.

For the effects of ignorance concerning the nature of marriage confer 717.

II. Properties of Marriage. 1. *Simple error* regarding the unity or indissolubility or the sacramental character of marriage does not vitiate the matrimonial consent even though such an error is the cause of the contract (C. 1084).

A simple or theoretical error is had when the mistake is only in the mind and is not expressed by any positive act of the will. — Wherefore, Protestants, Jews and the non-baptized who think marriage is a soluble contract marry validly, even though they would not marry if they knew the truth. Error is presumed to be merely theoretical until the contrary is proved.

2. A positive act of the will in which a simple error finds its expression invalidates marriage (C. 1086).

Hence, marriage is invalid in the case of one who expressly states that he intends to contract a dissoluble union or that he would rather renounce marriage than receive a Sacrament. — Such a positive will can sometimes be inferred from the form used in contracting marriage, or from other of the attendant circumstances, e.g., if a formula which excludes indissolubility is read aloud before consent is given.

721. — III. Possibility of Contracting Marriage. Certain knowledge or opinion about the nullity of the marriage about to be contracted does not necessarily exclude matrimonial consent (C. 1085).

Wherefore, if two persons think there is a diriment impediment to marriage but nevertheless desire to be man and wife if possible, they actually marry validly if in reality no impediment exists. — The same holds when contracting a civil marriage if, for certain reasons, one is not bound to the form. But if such persons merely intend to perform a civil ceremony or live in concubinage there is no marriage.

IV. The Other Party (C. 1083). 1. Error regarding the *identity of the person* voids marriage even by natural law.

Thus the marriage of Jacob was invalid because the veiled Lia was given him instead of Rachel.

2. Error regarding the *quality of a person* invalidates marriage if the mistake amounts to an error about the person or if the other party is a slave.

a) A mistake *amounts* to an error concerning the person if one is deceived about a definite qualification which serves to identify the person substantially.

It is therefore required that this quality be proper to only one person in the world, that one does not have a personal knowledge of the person and that one wishes to marry him for this one and only reason. Such a marriage is null and void by natural law.

722. *b)* *Slavery* invalidates marriage if it is contracted by a person who is free with a person who is in a condition of proper servitude whom one believes to be free.

On the other hand, marriage is valid if two slaves intermarry, or if the free party knows that the other is not free. — Slavery here means the servile state properly so called. Those held in bondage or who are serving a life sentence are not included.

In this form the impediment is purely ecclesiastical; therefore, it does not exist between two unbelievers. It does exist when a baptized free person wishes to marry an unbaptized person who is not free. It is disputed whether or not there is an impediment when the unbaptized party is free and the baptized person is a slave.

c) *All other errors* concerning the qualities of the other person do not invalidate marriage not even if the error is the cause of the marriage.

Therefore, a marriage is valid which one contracts with a person of whom he wrongly thinks that she belongs to the nobility, is rich, in good health, honorable, etc. even if the most cunning deception is practiced.

723.   *Article III*

Matrimonial Consent Vitiated by Violence and Fear

I. Violence invalidates marriage (C. 1087).

Thus, if one is physically forced, e.g., to nod the head as a sign of consent while not consenting interiorly the marriage is null, even between unbaptized persons (Cf. 718).

II. Fear voids a marriage that is contracted under the influence of a fear that is grave and unjustly caused by an external agent and from which one can free himself only by choosing marriage (C. 1087).

In such instances marriage is invalid although there is interior consent, provided that at the time the marriage is contracted one is still under the influence of fear and does not, because he is now better acquainted with the other party, very glady marry the other person. — If only one of the four conditions mentioned is lacking the marriage is valid even though contracted under the influence of fear.

1. Fear is *grave* if caused by a grave evil which is proximately imminent.

Moral certitude suffices. Fear may be absolutely or relatively grave (Cf. 21). Marriage is invalidated also by relatively grave fear if one would have to say that a like degree of fear (not the same evil) would greatly influence a prudent person. Reverential fear can be grave if conjoined with certain attendant circumstances, as threats, blows, importunate entreaties, indignation, permanent displeasure of parents, etc. It matters not whether the evil threatens one of the contractants or his relatives or whether the other contractant or a third person resorts to threats. In doubt whether fear is grave or light we presume the latter.

724. — 2. Fear is caused *externally* if it does not arise from illness, qualms of conscience, fixed ideas, hallucinations, etc.

That fear is not induced externally which a girl harbors because of the anger of her father, if the father has done nothing to engender the fear.

3. Fear is *unjustly induced* when not only charity but justice is violated by the threat.

Wherefore, since an uncle has no obligation of justice towards his nephew, the latter's marriage will be valid if entered into because his uncle threatens to ignore him in his will if he does not marry. — But since no one has a right to kill him who disgraces a girl, a threat to do so (unless he marry her) would be unjust. It would not be unjust to threaten to sue him for support. — Although engagement gives the right to contract marriage a man has no right to force a girl who is guilty of a breach of promise to marry him. Should he do so, fear would be unjustly inflicted and the subsequent marriage invalid. — Since injustice presupposes a free agent, fear arising from acts of God (e.g., a thunderstorm) or hard times (e.g., impoverishment, unemployment) is to be disregarded.

725. — 4. One is said to be *forced to marry* in order to be free from fear when he has no alternative save marriage to rid himself of the fear.

From the history of C. 1087 it is evident that the present wording of the law settles an old controversy, namely, that marriage is invalid not only when he who inflicts fear does so with the intention of forcing another to marry; but also when circumstances are such that the one marrying is under the impression that he is contracting marriage to escape unjust threats. Marriage is likewise invalid when one desires to extort money from another and the latter marries the extortioner's daughter as the only alternative to escape the extortion.

Validation of a marriage is possible after the fear has been removed. Confer 769 for particulars.

Unbaptized persons also, according to the more probable opinion, are bound by this impediment, since it is probably based on the natural law. Since there is a real *dubium iuris* here the general presumption in favor of validity should prevail. Marriage between a baptized and an unbaptized person is certainly always invalid no matter which party is influenced by the fear.

726. *Article IV*

Conditional Matrimonial Consent

I. Concept. By a condition is meant a circumstance upon which one makes his consent depend in such wise that consent stands or falls with the circumstance.

It is not sufficient that one would have given conditional consent if he had thought of doing so.

The condition need not be expressed externally. It suffices that it exist only virtually when the contract is made (Cf. 8). — Conditions may concern a present, past or future event or circumstance.

II. Lawfulness. Only an extremely important reason justifies conditional matrimonial consent; if possible the bishop's approval must be had.

The condition must be expressed before the pastor or two witnesses either in the act of contracting marriage or beforehand, and in such wise that it can be juridically proved. It is sinful not to do so; but the legal consequences follow, nevertheless. It is extremely difficult to prove the addition of a non-expressed condition. Whoever adds a condition without the knowledge of the other party commits a grave sin of injustice.

727. — III. Effects. 1. A condition concerning the future. *a)* If something lawful is the object of the condition, the validity of the marriage is suspended until the condition is fulfilled (C. 1093).

Thus a girl who marries a man on the condition " if you pass the Bar examination," is not his wife before that event. As soon as he passes the examination she is his wife without any further declaration of any kind, provided neither has revoked the consent given. — The obligations arising from a conditional contract are: not to hinder the fulfillment of the condition and reasonably to await its fulfillment. Should one meanwhile marry another person this latter marriage would be valid but unlawful.

b) If something *necessary, impossible* or *unlawful,*

but not contrary to the substance of marriage, is the object of the condition, it is presumed that the condition was not seriously added and is, therefore, non-existent (Cf. C. 1092).

Such a marriage is considered valid in the forum of law, even though the condition is not fulfilled. However, if one proves that such a condition was seriously added, the validity of the marriage contract is suspended in the juridical forum until the condition is verified. In the forum of conscience everything depends upon whether the condition was actually made or not.

c) If something *contrary to the substance of marriage* is the object of the condition the marriage is invalid (C. 1092).

That is against the substance of marriage which militates against the unity or indissolubility of marriage or which excludes the right to the use of matrimony or the right to preserve the children from death. Whoever adds such a condition absolutely has not the required matrimonial intention (Cf. 717) and cannot validly marry even according to natural law. — Often the so-called "matrimonial bargain" or "understandings" (e.g., that they will not have more than two children) do not imply a real condition, but are merely a purpose. Such marriages are valid, since the right to the use of matrimony is not excluded, but only the intention of not fulfilling the marital obligations properly is expressed.

728. — 2. A *past or present condition* does not suspend the validity of marriage. The marriage is forthwith valid or invalid according as the condition is actually fulfilled or not (Cf. C. 1092).

This applies also to an impossible condition provided it was seriously made. — If the object of the condition is something unlawful the marriage is immediately valid or void according as the condition is fulfilled or not (e.g., "I will marry you if you are willing to use contraceptives"). But if the immoral condition makes the validity of the marriage dependent upon the *obligation* to an immoral action, the marriage is invalid since no one can oblige himself to sin. — In any case where marriage is contracted under a past or present condition the contractants may not live as married people until they are certain that the condition has been verified.

729.   Chapter VII

THE MATRIMONIAL CONTRACT

Article 1

The Ordinary Form

I. Requisites for Validity. Only those marriages are valid which are contracted before the parish priest or the local Ordinary or a priest delegated by either of them and before two witnesses (C. 1094).

The Church supplies pastoral jurisdiction when by *common error* someone is considered a pastor (Cf. C. 209); consequently such a one validly assists at a marriage.

Parish priests are not only those who are actual pastors, but also quasi-pastors in missionary countries and all vicars who have full parochial powers. The Holy See has issued special regulations for army chaplains (C. 451).

Parish vicars are: α) the actual vicar, i.e., who rules over a moral person (chapter, monastery) to which a parish is attached (C. 471); β) the administrator of a vacant parish (vicarius oeconomus) (C. 472); γ) the substitute (vicarius substitutus) who is put in charge when the pastor is absent from his parish over a week (C. 465). He has all the rights of a pastor in spiritual matters unless restricted in some way by the Ordinary or the pastor (C. 474). He assists validly at marriages only after the Ordinary has approved him as substitute and has not made any reservations regarding his powers. If the pastor for some grave, unforeseen reason must leave the parish for over a week the substitute can assist at marriages without special approval of the Ordinary (AAS 14-257). He must inform the Ordinary of the arrangement as soon as possible; δ) the assistant priest (vicarius adjutor) who is assigned to a pastor who cannot take care of a parish due to age, illness, etc., provided the vicar takes the pastor's place in all things (C. 475). ε) Included also are those parish vicars (as for example, curates, rectors) to whom is entrusted the care of a certain district which in public juridical matters is completely separated from the mother church.

When the bishop sets apart a definite part of a parish, granting the right to assist at marriages, among other pastoral rights, without raising the district to the status of a legal parish, the priest put in charge of such a place (rector, parish vicar) is also empowered to assist at marriages. If, however, such a district is separated from a parish as a "filial congregation" or "chapel congregation," but not erected as an independent curacy or filial congregation, whilst being committed to a special priest with full pastoral powers, the priest in charge can validly assist at marriages only when delegated by the Ordinary or the competent pastor.

730. — 1. *Assistance at Marriages by the Pastor or Local Ordinary* (C. 1095). To assist at marriages validly:

a) They must have *taken canonical possession* of their benefice or *have entered upon their office.*

They must not be excommunicated, interdicted or suspended from office by a court sentence (sententia condemnatoria) nor declared such by an ecclesiastical tribunal (sententia declaratoria).

b) They must assist *within their own territory.*

They cannot validly assist at the marriage of their subjects outside their own territory; within their territory they can assist validly at the marriages, not only of their own subjects but also at those of others. — The exempt churches of regulars are here considered as part of their territory.

c) They must be *free from force and fear* in asking for and receiving the declaration of consent.

The required questions must also be asked in the case of mixed marriages; otherwise, they would be invalid. — But a marriage is valid if a competent priest is induced to assist by fraud or deceit.

731. — 2. *Assistance at Marriages by a Delegated Priest. a*) The pastor (or Ordinary) *can delegate* only when he himself is able to assist validly at marriages, and he can delegate only for his own territory (C. 1095).

The quasi-pastor and parish vicar can also delegate if they have full parochial powers.

Subdelegation may be given by missionaries who have general delegation from the Vicar or Prefect Apostolic where no quasi-parish has yet been erected. — The assistant priest may also sub-delegate if he has a general delegation from the pastor or Ordinary according to C. 1096; and they also who are delegated for a special case if the faculty to subdelegate has been expressly granted them (AAS 20-61).

b) Delegation can be given only to a priest. It must be given to a definite priest for a definite marriage. Assistant priests alone may obtain a general delegation but only for the parish to which they are attached; otherwise, delegation is invalid (C. 1096).

A priest need not have confessional jurisdiction.

The Church *supplies jurisdiction* in the case of a priest assisting at a marriage without delegation, according to the prescriptions of Canon 209, i. e., if there is question of a common error or positive doubt about the delegation. (*Code Commission,* March 26, 1952)

A priest is definitely designated either by mentioning his name or his office if no mistaking the person is possible, e.g., the first assistant at St. Augustine's Church in Pittsburgh. — Delegation by the pastor would be invalid if made thus: "the priest whom the religious Superior will send to supply in my absence" (AAS 16-115). Several priests may be delegated for the same marriage.

Since the marriage must also be exactly designated, delegation would be invalid if given for "the weddings that will take place next week" or for "the next five weddings." Delegation may be given for several weddings, but they must be distinctly designated as must be the assisting priest.

Assisting priests should not be given a general delegation; they can, however, be given such. — The Vicar and Prefect Apostolic may give missionaries a general delegation in those localities where a quasi-parish has not yet been erected. — This general delegation does not cease with the death or transfer of the delegating pastor or missionary superior. However, a new pastor or new superior of the missions can revoke the delegation at any time.

732. *c) Delegation must be given expressly* (C. 1096).

This is required for validity. — Tacit or presumed delegation or mere tolerance is insufficient. On the contrary, delegation need not be made in writing. Unless particular law requires a written document for lawfulness, it may be given by words or unambiguous signs. Delegation may be made by telephone or telegraph. Sometimes this is forbidden by particular law.

It seems that acceptance of a delegation "ab homine" is necessary for validity. The person delegated implicitly accepts delegation by the fact that it is requested with his knowledge and consent. In such a case marriage is valid but unlawful if the delegation is granted but the witnessing priest does not yet know of it. If the delegation was requested without his knowledge and he has not been told of its concession the marriage is invalid.

733. — 3. *The witnesses* must be able to observe and testify to the contracting of the marriage, and, together with the assisting priest, they must be present when matrimonial consent is expressed.

Therefore, they must have the use of reason, but they need not be adults. Nothing is prescribed about the sex or religion of the witnesses, nor is it required that they be free from censure; scandal, however, must always be avoided. — Marriage is valid even if they do not hear the parties taking each other as husband and wife as long as they recognize by some equivalent sign that marriage is being celebrated. — Witnesses need not have the explicit intention of acting as witnesses to a marriage. It is sufficient if they do so accidentally, even though the contractants are not aware of this; although not necessary for validity, they should be requested beforehand to act as witnesses. — Marriage is also valid if the witnesses are forced to assist by violence, fear or deception. The contracting parties have the right to choose the witnesses.

734. — II. Requirements for Lawful Assistance at Marriages (C. 1097). Before the local Ordinary or pastor may assist at a marriage they must be certain:

1. *That there is nothing against the valid or lawful celebration of marriage.* This certainty must be attained in the manner prescribed by law.

Private conviction is insufficient; certainty must be acquired by the means prescribed by law (examination of the parties, publication of the banns). — In case of delegation the one delegating must acquire this certainty (C. 1096).

735. — 2. That at least one of the parties has *a domicile or quasi-domicile* in the respective parish or that he has resided there for at least *one month.*

Concerning domicile and quasi-domicile confer Cc. 92-95. — The month's residence must be morally continuous. Residence is not interrupted by a day or two of absence, neither must the days absent be supplied. — It suffices also that one actually resides in a parish for a month, even though he had no intention of doing so.

Should a pastor wish to assist at a marriage in which neither of the parties has observed the required residence in his parish he must get permission from the pastor who is competent to marry them. This permission, which differs entirely from delegation, may also be general. Whoever assists at a marriage without this permission may not retain the stole fee, but must send it to the competent pastor. Permission is not required in case of grave necessity or if it is a question of the homeless who, for the time being, have no residence. — Even though a pastor is empowered to assist at the marriage of transients he must, nevertheless, according to C. 1032, apply to the bishop (except in case of necessity) since he can never have certainty that there is no impediment (Cf. 671).

Ordinarily the wedding is held before the pastor of the bride; a reasonable cause excuses, however. If the bride is Protestant, the wedding is held before the pastor of the groom. — If Catholics of different Rites marry the wedding is performed, unless particular law determines otherwise, according to the Rite of the man and before his pastor.

736. — III. Persons Affected by the Form (C. 1099).

1. This form *is obligatory* for all who have been baptized in the Catholic Church and converts to Catholicism from heresy or schism (even though they later fall away from the Church), no matter whether the Catholics marry among themselves or with Orientals or non-Catholics, be the latter baptized or not. It obliges also those who receive a dispensation from mixed religion or disparity of worship.

Confer 701 for particulars about those "baptized in the Catholic Church" or "converted" thereto, but note the following exceptions.

2. This form is *not obligatory* for *non-Catholics* marrying among themselves, whether baptized or not.

According to Canon 1099 persons born of non-Catholic parents and baptized in the Catholic Church, but who from infancy had grown up in heresy or schism or infidelity or without any religion, were not bound to observe the canonical form of marriage when marrying non-Catholics. Pope Pius XII in a *Motu Proprio,* August 1, 1948, abrogated this exception and decreed that these persons be obliged to observe the form after January 1, 1949.

However, these children who have been baptized in the Catholic Church were and are, nevertheless, bound by the impediment of disparity of cult (Cf. 701). — Childhood here means the time before attaining the use of reason. Children of mixed marriages who were baptized as Catholics but reared from infancy in heresy, etc. were likewise not bound by the form (AAS 21-573); the same held for children of apostates (AAS 22-195).

737. The Law before the Present Code.

a) The law *Tametsi* (obliging from the Council of Trent until 1908) which had full force in the U. S. only in the Province of Santa Fe prescribed that *all baptized* persons observe the form. The law was local in as far as it obliged all persons in the territory where it was promulgated; it was also personal, in that it obliged anyone who had a domicile or quasi-domicile in that same territory, even though at the time he happened to be in an exempt territory. Any party not bound by the law communicated his immunity to the other party. Furthermore, in the Province of New Orleans, San Francisco, the diocese of Vincennes (Ind.) and the city of St. Louis, where the *Tametsi* was modified by the Benedictine Declaration, only *Catholics* were obliged to the form, and then only when marrying other Catholics. The pastor competent to marry those bound by the form was the parish priest of their place of residence, not the place of the wedding. The form did not oblige anyone else in the U. S.

b) The Decree *Ne Temere,* in force since April 19, 1908, prescribed that all Catholics are bound by the form no matter whom they marry; and that non-Catholics are not bound by the form except when marrying a Catholic.

738. PERSONS IN THE U. S. BOUND BY THE MATRIMONIAL FORM AND IMPEDIMENTS.

		FORM	IMPEDIMENTS
The "TAMETSI" Affecting persons married before April 19, 1908.	1. All baptized persons in the Province of Santa Fe. See N. B. 1 below.	Bound by the matrimonial form.	All Catholics and all baptized Protestants bound by all other marriage laws and impediments.
	2. Catholics in the Provinces of New Orleans and of San Francisco. N. B. 2.	Bound by the form only when marrying another Catholic (Not when marrying a Protestant).	
	3. Everyone else in the United States.	No form needed.	
The "NE TEMERE" For those married after 1908 and before 1918.	1. All Catholics.	Bound by the form when marrying anyone.	
	2. All non-Catholics.	Bound by the form only when marrying a Catholic.	
The "CODE" Obliging persons marrying since May 19, 1918.	1. All Catholics.	Same as under the "Ne Temere"	All Catholics and all baptized Protestants, with the exception that only those who are baptized in the Catholic Church are bound by the impediment of Disparity of Cult.
	2. All non-Catholics.	Same as under the "Ne Temere"	

N. B. 1. Now comprising the diocese of Santa Fe, Gallup, & Tucson.

N. B. 2. The Tametsi modified by the Benedictine Privilege applies in the diocese of Alexandria, Amarillo, Corpus Christi, Dallas, Galveston, Indianapolis, Lafayette, Little Rock, Los Angeles, Mobile, Monterey-Fresno, Natchez, New Orleans, Oklahoma City-Tulsa, Reno, Sacramento, San Antonio, San Diego, San Francisco, partly in Belleville, Denver, El Paso and Salt Lake City and the city of St. Louis. It also holds for Ireland.

Furthermore, it should be remembered that the words "non-Catholics" as used in the Code in this matter until January 1, 1949 included all those born of non-Catholic parents, who, although they were baptized in the Catholic Church, had grown up in heresy, schism or infidelity or without any religion.

According to the Code Commission the words "non-Catholic" also include: a) the children of mixed and disparate marriages; and b) the children of apostate parents. (AAS 21-573 and 22-195).

739.   *Article II*

The Extraordinary Form (C. 1098)

I. In danger of death two people may validly and
lawfully marry without the assistance of the competent
pastor, but before at least two witnesses, provided they
cannot without great inconvenience either send for
(*haberi*) or go to (*adiri*) the pastor, local Ordinary or
delegated priest.

If *another priest* can be had he should be called so
that he may assist at the marriage together with the two
witnesses. Marriage would, nevertheless, be valid even
if he were not summoned.

The danger of death may arise from illness or any external cause,
e.g., a battle, flood, etc. — It suffices that only one of the parties
be in danger of death. — If one has made a mistake in regard
to the danger of death, marriage remains valid, provided he did not
act with absolute rashness. — In such cases marriages may be
contracted even though not necessary for the peace of conscience,
legitimation of children, etc.

The *great inconvenience* may affect the parties about to be
married, the pastor, a third person, or the common good. It may
concern life, health, liberty, reputation, or material possessions.
It does not seem that one would be obliged to use an automobile,
telephone or telegraph to obtain delegation for a priest who is
available. — Concerning the absence of the pastor confer 740. It
should be noted that in danger of death one can also dispense
with the form (Cf. 676, 678).

The *witnesses* need not ask the parties for their matrimonial
consent, it suffices that they hear them declare it.

740. — II. Apart from the danger of death marriage may also be validly and lawfully contracted before
two witnesses alone if a competent pastor or delegated
priest can neither be summoned nor approached without
great inconvenience, and one may reasonably presume
that this state of affairs will last for a month. Lawful-

ness, however, requires as in the preceding instance that a priest, even though not empowered to assist at the marriage, be present if possible.

Regarding the *great inconvenience* confer 739. — In order that marriage be validly and lawfully contracted in such cases there must be moral certainty that no competent priest can be approached or summoned without great inconvenience. The fact may be notorious or certainty may be acquired by investigation (AAS 17-583). — It suffices that the bride and groom be unable to approach or summon the competent priest; it is not required that this be generally impossible. — The marriage is valid even if shortly after being contracted a competent priest (e.g., a missionary) unexpectedly appears. — Marriage may not be contracted in this manner if the two parties can easily go to the pastor of another place. — This arrangement holds only for the physical absence of the pastor or local Ordinary (AAS 20-120). The pastor and local Ordinary are considered physically absent if, though materially present in their districts, they cannot assist at the marriage without great inconvenience (AAS 22-388). In such cases one should call the bridal party's attention to this extraordinary form of marrying only after obtaining the Ordinary's judgment on the presence of the necessary conditions so that there will be no doubt about the validity later.

Before the Code the time was reckoned from the past: a month must have elapsed since a competent pastor was available.

741. Article III

Individual Regulations Concerning Marriage

I. Time (1108). 1. *Marriage* may be contracted at any time of the year.

Three days should intervene between the last publication of the banns and the wedding (Cf. 669). Marriage is contracted in the morning because of the nuptial Mass; it may also take place in the afternoon or evening. Some bishops have forbidden afternoon and evening weddings.

2. *The nuptial blessing* is forbidden from the first Sunday in Advent until Christmas Day inclusive, and from Ash Wednesday till Easter inclusive. For a reasonable cause the local Ordinary may permit it during

these seasons but the liturgical regulations must be observed. The couple should be reminded to abstain from all worldly display.

If the bishop allows the nuptial blessing during the forbidden time the votive Mass "pro sponso et sponsa" may be said, but not on those days when a votive Mass is ordinarily forbidden (Cf. 743).

On All Souls' Day and Good Friday the nuptial blessing may not be given.

742. — II. Place (C. 1109). 1. *Catholics* should be married in the parish church; with the permission of the bishop or pastor they may also be married in another church as well as in a public or semi-public chapel.

Only in an extraordinary case may the bishop allow a wedding to take place in a private home for some lawful and reasonable cause. In churches and chapels of seminaries and convents of women, Ordinaries may allow a wedding only in urgent cases, proper precautions being taken.

2. *Mixed marriages* should not be held in Church.

The local Ordinary may dispense from this regulation to avoid greater evil. Such a dispensation does not include a dispensation from the prohibition of sacred Rites at a mixed marriage (C. 1102). To avoid greater evil the bishop may permit some of the usual sacred ceremonies, but never the celebration of Holy Mass. A great difference in practice obtains in our country. Frequently the marriage ceremony takes place at a side altar or at the Communion rail outside the sanctuary gate.

III. Rite. 1. *In general.* Except in case of necessity marriage should be celebrated according to the Rite found in the Roman Ritual or introduced by lawful custom (C. 1100).

In the U. S. the Roman Ritual is to be followed. — The priest wears a surplice and white stole. If the wedding precedes or immediately follows the nuptial Mass he may wear the vestments including the chasuble.

743. — 2. Nuptial Blessing. *a)* The *minister* is the pastor (C. 462). He may also commission another priest to give it.

b) The pastor *shall take care* that the parties receive the nuptial blessing (C. 1101).

It may also be given long after the parties have been married. — It is not prescribed under grave sin. If they have been married a long time there does not seem to be any obligation to receive it. — The nuptial blessing may not be given when the bride is a widow who received it at her first wedding. It may be given, however, (where it is customary) if the groom is a widower even if it was given on the occasion of his first marriage.

c) It *may be given only* after the couple is wedded and during Holy Mass.

The nuptial blessing may be given only when both parties are present. If the *Missa pro sponsis* is prohibited, the nuptial blessing may be given in another Mass. In this case the *oratio pro sponsis* is added *sub unica conclusione*. The *Missa pro sponsis* is forbidden on Sundays, Holydays of obligation, feasts of the first and second class, privileged octaves of the first order (Easter and Pentecost) and of the second order (Epiphany and Corpus Christi), privileged ferials (Ash Wednesday and Monday, Tuesday and Wednesday of Holy Week) and the vigils of Christmas, Epiphany and Pentecost. The nuptial blessing may not be given in a Requiem Mass. — The Mass itself need not be applied for the couple. — The nuptial blessing may be given to several couples at once. — The parties are not required to receive Holy Communion during their Nuptial Mass. — In some places the nuptial blessing may be given apart from the Mass in virtue of a special indult. A special formula is then used which is not the form given in the Mass. — As to the prohibition of the nuptial blessing during forbidden times confer 741. Although the nuptial blessing may not be given at the wedding of a widow (C. 1143), nevertheless, the *Missa pro sponso et sponsa* may be celebrated.

3. In *mixed marriages* the questions eliciting consent must be asked; all sacred ceremonies are forbidden. To avoid greater evil the Ordinary may allow one or the other ecclesiastical ceremony, but never the celebration of Holy Mass (C. 1102).

Per se the use of a surplice and stole is also forbidden; likewise the simple blessing after the betrothal and the use of candles. — In most places, however, local Ordinaries allow exceptions. They may never permit Mass to be said as a conclusion to the ceremonies (AAS 17-583). When Mass is forbidden, the nuptial blessing is likewise forbidden.

744. — IV. Registration (C. 1103). 1. The Marriage must be entered in the *matrimonial register* as soon as possible by the pastor or the priest who takes his place.

Entry must be made of the names of the bridal couple, and assisting priest, the place and time of the wedding. — Diocesan regulations often require the dates of birth of the couple and the names of their parents. — The priest who assisted at the marriage by delegation does not register the marriage. Should he do so the pastor must countersign the entry. — (Cf. also 684).

2. Entry must also be made in the *baptismal register* by the pastor of the place of Baptism.

The pastor who assists at the marriage of one who was not baptized in the parish where the wedding takes place must, either personally or through the episcopal curia, inform the pastor of the place where that party was baptized, of the marriage. — In a mixed marriage this naturally holds only for the Catholic party. — Entry must also be made in the matrimonial and baptismal registers in cases of convalidation, *sanatio in radice* and declaration of nullity.

3. In those *exceptional cases* where marriage is contracted without a priest empowered to assist, the entry must be made in the books as soon as possible by any priest who happened to be present; if no priest was present or if he neglects his duty the witnesses and the married parties have the obligation to see to this.

For the cases when an exceptional form is permitted confer 739 sqq.

745. — V. Marriage of conscience may be permitted only by the local Ordinary for very serious and urgent reasons (C. 1104).

A *marriage of conscience* is one contracted before the competent pastor and two witnesses, but without any previous proclamation of banns and secretly so that the assisting priest, the witnesses and the local Ordinary have the strict obligation to keep the marriage secret. Each of the married parties has the same obligation as long as the other is opposed to the disclosure (C. 1105). — Under special circumstances the local Ordinary may publish the marriage (C. 1106). — This marriage may not be entered in the usual marriage and baptismal register, but must be noted in a special book in the secret archives of the diocese (C. 1107).

746. Chapter VIII
EFFECTS OF MARRIAGE

The effects of marriage are partly of a general character and party concern marital intercourse.

Article I
General Effects

The marriage contract has the following general effects:

1. It produces a *bond* which is by nature *indissoluble* and *exclusive of every other marriage bond* (C. 1110).

Indissolubility here means that the bond cannot be dissolved while both parties are living; it is automatically dissolved by death (C. 1118). — This absolute indissolubility holds only for consummated marriages between baptized persons. Marriages of the unbaptized, even though consummated, may be dissolved by the Pauline Privilege, but not by the State. — Under certain conditions the Church can dissolve non-consummated marriages of baptized persons.

The *exclusion of every other marriage bond* means that no one can have a second husband or wife while the first one still lives. Polyandry is absolutely and directly contrary to natural law;

polygamy is indirectly opposed to natural law and in the New
Testament it is also forbidden by the positive divine law.

2. **Sanctifying grace** is increased in the married
couple and they receive special *sacramental graces* in
keeping with their state, in as far as there is no obstacle
to the reception of these graces (C. 1110).

For particulars confer 447 sqq.

747. — 3. *Cohabitation* and *care of the children*
are obligations imposed upon married people.

A long absence of the husband even against the will of his
wife is lawful for a very important reason, e.g., the welfare of
the community or the care of important family affairs. The husband must take his wife with him if she requests this and if it
can easily be done. He may, however, absent himself from her
against her will for a short period of time without a serious reason.
— Since the husband is the head of the family the wife cannot
leave him against his will unless great harm would otherwise
threaten her. — By mutual consent married people may renounce
the use of the marriage right (Communio tori) if there is no
danger of incontinence for either party. — *The choice of residence*
belongs to the husband. An exception would be justified if, when
marrying, they had agreed upon a certain domicile and there were
no good reason to change the agreement; or if the husband should
desire to change the place of residence for an evil purpose; or if
the wife could not follow him without serious physical or moral
harm; finally she need not follow him if he has the wanderlust
unless she knew of this before she married him. — The wife may
request a change of domicile if their present residence is seriously
harmful to her either physically or morally. *Care of the children*
refers to their education, both religious and moral, as well as
physical and civil, and to the provision for their temporal welfare
(Cf. 200).

748. — 4. The *husband* receives *domestic and
paternal authority.*

5. The *wife shares in the status of the husband*
as far as canonical effects are concerned (C. 1112). She
has the **obligation to obey** him and the **right to his**

protection and support in keeping with her social state.

By special stipulation the wife may be excluded from sharing the social standing of her husband. — For particulars on support confer 201, 252.

6. The ***legitimation of their ante-nuptial children*** follows marriage as far as canonical effects are concerned, unless, in special instances other arrangements have been expressly made. It is required that during the time of conception, pregnancy or birth the parents were able to contract a valid marriage (C. 1116, 1117).

Children legitimized by subsequent marriage are not considered equal to those born in lawful wedlock when there is question of receiving the cardinalate (C. 232), the episcopate (C. 331), or the dignity of a prelate or abbot *nullius* (C. 320).

749.   *Article II*

The Use of Marriage

§ 1. Lawfulness

I. Marital intercourse is lawful for the procreation of children or for other honorable reasons.

Such reasons are: promotion of mutual love and harmony, restoration of peace, avoidance of incontinence in oneself or consort, etc. — Marital intercourse remains lawful even if it is certain that no offspring is possible (e.g., in case of aged or sterile people); if the wife has had her ovaries or uterus removed, or if a stillbirth or premature delivery will result; or if because of indisposition either fecundation is impossible or the semen would go to waste. Some authors believe marital intercourse is also lawful if the parties become impotent after contracting marriage provided coition is still possible, e.g., if the husband has undergone the operation of complete castration or double vasectomy.

Artificial Insemination. 1) *Outside of marriage* artificial insemination is absolutely immoral. Both the law of nature and the positive divine law decree that the procreation of new life may only be the fruit of marriage. 2) *In marriage* artificial insemination is immoral a) if the semen is derived from a third person (donor), since the procreative rights of married partners are exclusive, nontransferable and inalienable. Thus practiced, artificial insemination is a revolting procedure involving the sins of pollution and adultery, b) if the active principle is derived from the husband by acts contrary to nature. Obviously, a marriage invalid by reason of the impediment of impotency, is not rendered valid in this manner. 3) *In marriage* artificial insemination (in a wide sense) is not forbidden if by it we mean the use of artificial means either to facilitate the natural act or enable the natural act, performed in a normal manner, to effect conception (Cf. 228).

II. Marital intercourse is unlawful:

1. If it *impedes procreation.*

Hence no attitude or position which does not prevent conception is gravely sinful. If generation is thereby only made more difficult, assuming such a position would be a venial sin if there were no sufficient reason to justify it.

750. — 2. If it is *injurious to health.*

Marital intercourse is seriously sinful if it constitutes a proximate danger of death. — A grave reason is required to make it lawful when it results in great harm or remote danger of death, e.g., such a reason would be the preservation of marital fidelity of the one party during the prolonged illness of the other, or the preservation of domestic peace. In such circumstances there is no obligation to render the debt even though the other party requests it (Cf. 756). For a serious reason one who is sexually diseased may request the marriage debt from a healthy consort after the latter has been informed of the disease. If the person in health is willing to make the sacrifice he or she may do so, but there is no obligation. In general the sexually diseased should be advised not to have intercourse. — Tubercular patients may lawfully use their marriage rights with moderation. Intercourse is generally forbidden under grave sin within two weeks after childbirth, and under venial sin for the following four weeks; but it is lawful while the mother is nursing, and during pregnancy unless there is danger of an abortion. — It is lawful but not advisable during menstruation. It may be gravely injurious during protracted cases of certain ailments on the part of the woman. A physician should be consulted. — The prospect of weak or ailing children or the probability that they will die before birth does not render marital intercourse sinful.

751. — 3. If it is *spiritually harmful.*

Marital intercourse is gravely sinful in the presence of others. It should be interrupted if someone unexpectedly appears, even though pollution should certainly follow; but one may not consent to the latter. Whoever has taken a vow of chastity may not request the marriage debt, unless the other party is in danger of incontinence and too embarrassed to request it; at the request (even implicit) of the other party the one who has made the vow must render the debt, even though the other party has taken a similar vow. — Intercourse is gravely sinful when the marriage is invalid, even though only one of the parties is aware of its invalidity. — When one seriously doubts about the validity of the marriage he is obliged to investigate the matter. While investigating one may not request the marriage debt, but must render it at the request of the other party who entertains no doubt about the validity of the marriage. If the doubt cannot be solved the marriage may be considered valid.

N.B. *Sacred Times.*

Marital relations are lawful at any time, although during seasons of penance temperance is advisable. — It is also lawful the night before going to Holy Communion although they who communicate rarely will do well to abstain at this time: when requested by the other party, however, it is a duty to render the marriage debt. Wives should beware of fulfilling their obligation grudgingly.

752. — III. Imperfect acts that are sexually stimulating (kissing, embracing, etc.) are lawful or forbidden according to the following rules:

1. They are always lawful *in connection with the marriage act,* whether as preparatory thereto or as a completion thereof.

This pertains to looks, kisses and touches. — Wives who do not obtain complete satisfaction may procure it by touches immediately before or after coition since the husband may withdraw immediately after ejaculation. Some authors believe she may do so also when the husband withdraws in an onanistic manner. The same cannot be said of the husband should the wife withdraw since the seed would thus be wasted.

753. — 2. Apart from the marriage act which the couple either cannot or do not desire to perform:

a) Mutual acts that are sexually stimulating are lawful when done with a just cause (e.g., as a sign of affection) if there is no danger of pollution (even though this should sometimes accidentally follow) or even if there is such danger but there is also a reason justifying the action (e.g., to avert suspicion, to restrain one's consort from adultery, in obedience to a request).

What is said of the danger of pollution holds if the acts naturally tend to have such an effect; not, however, if such an effect is only accidental, e.g., on account of the peculiar disposition of a person (Cf. 223). Actions apt to result in pollution are grave sins if performed without a just cause; actions unlikely to have this effect would not be more than venially sinful, unless performed with the intention of pollution. — Consent to the delectation of even an involuntary pollution is gravely sinful; many do not realize this nor is it expedient to inform them.

b) Solitary acts which are sexually exciting are mortal sins if by their nature they greatly influence pollution or if done with the intention of procuring pollution; if there is no such danger or intention they cannot be prohibited under penalty of grave sin.

c) Morose delectation (excluding the danger of pollution) is either no sin or a venial or mortal sin for married people according as that in which they take pleasure is lawful or prohibited for them under venial or mortal sin.

The same holds for desires. — The pleasure that accompanies the merely speculative thinking about sex matters is not gravely sinful for married people as long as it does not constitute a proximate danger of pollution or is not a serious danger of their consenting to morose delectation or desires that are seriously sinful.

754. § **2. The Obligation of the Marriage Act**

I. Rendering the requested marriage debt is a grave obligation, especially when the petitioner is in danger of incontinence or would have to make a great sacrifice to overcome temptation.

The husband usually petitions the debt expressly while the wife does so implicitly, e.g., by showing signs of affection. — It is only a venial sin to refuse the debt (provided the other party is not placed in danger of sinning gravely), if the petitioner will readily renounce his right, or if rendering it is only briefly postponed, or if the use of the marriage right is frequent and its refusal is only rare, e.g., once a month. Elderly women and mothers of many children should generally be left in good faith if they think they sin gravely only when they almost always refuse to render the marriage debt or only if by such repulse, the huband is put in danger of grave sin. — In general one should rather call women's attention to the gravity of their obligation and remind husbands to be moderate.

755. — **II. Excuses** from rendering the debt are:

1. *Adultery* on the part of one's consort.

The adultery must be certain and committed with knowledge and consent. Thus no excuse arises if one's partner has been raped; or if the crime has been pardoned, e.g., by voluntary rendering the debt in spite of the knowledge of the adultery.

2. *Non-support* of wife and children.

If the husband squanders his income and compels his wife to provide for their livelihood, she need not render the marriage debt. But if the family must live in poverty through no fault of the husband, there is no reason for refusing the debt; neither does the circumstance that more children would necessitate greater restrictions on the family constitute such a reason.

3. *Lack of the use of reason* on the part of the petitioner.

Hence, the marriage debt may, but need not, be rendered to the insane nor to the completely intoxicated.

756. — 4. *Unreasonable demand.*

This is principally the case when one party desires such frequent intercourse that the constitution of the other suffers greatly. Judgment should be passed by a conscientious physician.

5. *Great danger to health or life.*

Such a danger would be given in the case of gravely infectious diseases, of a very weak heart, etc. — The ordinary hardships of pregnancy, childbirth, nursing, and care of children, such as intense but brief pains, prolonged but mild headaches, etc., are not a sufficient excuse. Neither is the fear of a miscarriage or stillbirth, which the wife knows from experience will follow conception. For particulars confer 750.

6. *Spiritual welfare.*

For particulars confer 751. On rendering the debt to a husband who practices onanism confer 758.

757.   § 3. The Sins of Married People

The principal grave sins that married people commit are: sins against prenatal life (Cf. 212), adultery (Cf. 225), conjugal intercourse under circumstances that make it unlawful (Cf. 749, 750, 751), acts posited without sufficient reason and which gravely endanger pollution, and acts undertaken with the intention of effecting pollution (Cf. 752, 753), refusal of the marriage debt (Cf. 754 sqq.), acts that frustrate the principal purpose of matrimony. — It remains for us to consider only the latter sins. They are sodomy, onanism and the use of contraceptives.

I. Imperfect sodomy, i.e., rectal intercourse, is a grave sin when the seminal fluid is wasted.

Excluding the sodomitical intention it is neither sodomy nor a grave sin if intercourse is begun in a rectal manner with the intention of consummating it naturally or if some sodomitical action is posited without danger of pollution. — *Positive co-operation* on the part of the wife in sodomitical commerce is never lawful, hence, she must at least offer internal resistance. However, she may remain externally passive, provided she has endeavored to prevent the sin. She thus applies the principle of double effect and permits the sin to avert the danger of a very grave evil which cannot otherwise be averted; it remains unlawful for her to give her consent to any concomitant pleasure.

758. — II. Onanism is practiced in various ways:

1. *Naturally,* i.e., if after intercourse is begun the husband withdraws and thus wastes the seed.

Husband and wife commit a *grave sin* by onanism. Since nothing sinful takes place before the withdrawal, the wife may co-operate materially (Cf. 147) for a moderately grave reason. Such a reason would be: domestic peace, or fear that the husband will commit adultery. If abstinence is gravely inconvenient for her the wife may lawfully request the debt from a husband who will render it onanistically (Cf. 144 for the reason). She may consent to the concomitant pleasure, but not to the sin of her husband. She has an obligation of charity to admonish him at times against committing the sin; however, she is excused from making this fraternal correction if it would constitute a grave danger of discord or indignation, etc. — There is no obligation to render the debt to a husband given to the practice of onanism, except in the case where charity would oblige her to do so, e.g., to prevent discord or keep her husband from committing adultery. — A grave sin is committed by interrupting intercourse even though the woman alone experiences the orgasm, except it be a case of necessity, e.g., if the husband in this instance is incapable of semination.

It is *not sinful* to interrupt intercourse: a) on account of some unforeseen necessity, e.g., the arrival of a third person; b) if done by mutual consent and for some reasonable cause and if there is no danger of either party suffering a pollution; for this would merely constitute an act of touch. (Cf. 752.) But it is gravely sinful if done against the will of either party, even though there is no danger of pollution. *"Reserved" coitus* can be sinful because of the danger of pollution or a sinful intention to avoid conception. Hence, the *Holy Office* warned priests never, either spontaneously or upon being questioned, to presume to speak of the "amplexus reservatus" as though it were morally unobjectionable. (June 30, 1952).

759. — 2. *Artificially,* i.e., by the use of contraceptives.

a) The method may be by the use of a device on the part of the man or woman to *prevent insemination.* When a male protector or sheath is used in intercourse it is unlawful from the beginning; hence, the wife may not even co-operate materially but must conduct herself in the same manner as if the husband intended to commit sodomy. — The same must be said of the use of a vaginal sheath.

b) Onanism is practiced also by the use of instruments or chemical substances which *prevent conception*.

This is done especially by: a) the vaginal douche, used to expel the spermatozoa; b) by the introduction of an antiseptic, a medicated suppository, etc., that kills the spermatozoa; c) by applying pressure on the vagina to expel the semen; d) by rising, walking, dancing, hard work, especially lifting, etc., with the same intention; e) by the introduction of a spermicidal jelly or diaphragm (or both) to occlude the mouth of the uterus and thus prevent the entrance of the spermatozoa; f) by the use of hesperidin, a drug taken in pill form which directly sterilizes by rendering the ovum impenetrable. The conjugal act performed while the drug is operative is onanistic in nature.

α) A woman sins gravely by expelling the seminal fluid or preventing its entry into the uterus. It is not sinful to do so if she has been the victim of rape or deception provided she does so before conception, since in this instance the semen is equivalent to an unjust aggressor.

Urination after coition does not prevent conception and hence is not sinful; however, one may sin gravely by resorting to it with an evil intention. — It seems lawful to use a vaginal lotion after an hour or two provided it is done without an evil intention, since generation is not impeded thereby; it is unlawful, however, to do so immediately after intercourse, even though it be done to alleviate great pain.

β) The husband must use all his marital authority to prevent such practices on the part of his wife.

If he cannot hinder her from doing so, he must conduct himself in a manner similar to that of a woman in regard to a husband given to the practice of onanism. A few authors consider this lawful also in the case where his wife uses a diaphragm, etc.

760. N.B. *Treatment of Onanism in the Confessional.*

a) *Questioning* the penitent is of obligation as often as there is a well-founded suspicion in this regard. In such instances the question may be: "Does your conscience reproach you in regard to the sacred character of matrimony?" "Have you done anything contrary to the purpose of marriage?"

b) Instructing the penitent on the gravity of such sins is necessary, even though the penitent has heretofore been in good faith. Good faith will scarcely be found in this matter nowadays, except in extremely difficult circumstances, e.g., if a reliable physician tells a woman that another pregnancy will endanger her life. In such instances the confessor may omit the instruction if he foresees that sins which are now only material will become formal sins.

c) Whoever is not firmly resolved to avoid the sin is not disposed and cannot be absolved. Being intrinsically evil, conjugal onanism is gravely sinful even when—to avoid it—married people would have to practice lifelong continence. From early times Christians were called upon to make heroic sacrifices. When God demands a sacrifice He gives the grace necessary to make it.

d) Recidivists who assure the priest that they had the best intentions are to be handled as recidivists living in the proximate occasion of sin; those who, furthermore, cannot have more children (e.g., because of the illness of the wife or extreme proverty) should be treated as those who are living in the proximately necessary occasion of sin (Cf. 608); whereas those who do not desire more children because they are unwilling to make sacrifices, should be handled as those living in a proximate free occasion of sin (Cf. 607).

e) Conception, according to the opinion of physicians, follows only when marital relations take place at certain times, i.e., during the period of fertility on the part of the woman. Abstaining from intercourse during this period has come to be known as the **Rhythm Method of Birth Control.** For a proportionate reason and with the mutual consent of husband and wife it is lawful intentionally to practice periodic continence, i.e., restrict intercourse to those times when conception is impossible. Physicians are not agreed as to the exact extent of the so-called "safe period." In recent times the opinion is gaining more adherents which holds that a woman is sterile in the last eleven days before menstruation, and that conception only follows if intercourse is had between the nineteenth and tenth days before menstruation. Since some women have irregular cycles and since illness may in some cases cause a disturbance of the regularity, the confessor should refer women who have a sufficient reason to avoid pregnancy to a conscientious physician who may give them biological details regarding the sterile period.

Periodic abstinence, misnamed "Catholic Birth Control," is, therefore, lawful only under certain conditions: 1) Both parties must freely agree to the restrictions that it involves. 2) The practice must not constitute an occasion of sin, especially the sin of incontinence. 3) There must be a proportionately grave reason for not having children, at least for the time being.

761.   Chapter IX

DISSOLVING THE MARRIAGE BOND AND
ABANDONMENT OF COHABITATION

I. Solution of the marriage bond between baptized
persons is possible only if the marriage has not been
consummated; the Pauline Privilege can dissolve the
marriage of unbaptized persons even though it has
been consummated.

1. A non-consummated marriage between *baptized
persons* is dissolved by solemn religious profession or
by dispensation of the Holy See (C. 1119).

The *non-consummation* of the marriage must be conclusively
proved. — A non-consummated marriage is *ipso iure* dissolved by
solemn profession. — The *dispensation* must be petitioned by the
married parties themselves (C. 1973). It can also be granted when
only one party requests it, even against the will of the other
partner (C. 1119). — Grounds for dispensation are: doubt concerning impotence, impotence subsequent to the contracting of
marriage, crime committed by one of the parties, invincible aversion
of the married parties toward each other or against marital relations. If the woman has been forced even though only once by the
husband to the complete conjugal act, their marriage is thereby
consummated and cannot be dissolved (Cf. 746).

762. — 2. Legitimate marriage between *unbaptized
persons,* even if consummated, can be dissolved by the
Pauline Privilege (C. 121).

The *Pauline Privilege* is based on I Cor. 7, 12—15. In virtue
of this privilege such a marriage can be dissolved if one party
receives Baptism and the other party either departs from the converted partner or refuses to live with him (or her) without serious
danger of grave sin against Faith or morals (sine contumelia
Creatoris). The baptized party can still use this privilege even after
having continued marital relations with the infidel party after
Baptism (C. 1124). But the privilege is not applicable to a marriage contracted between a baptized and an unbaptized person with

a dispensation from the impediment of disparity of worship (C. 1120). — (However, it seems that the marriage bond may be dissolved by papal dispensation when a baptized non-Catholic marries an unbaptized person.) — The Pauline Privilege cannot be applied as long as the believing party is still a catechumen, but not yet baptized.

Before the baptized person may marry again he must *interpellate* the unbaptized person and ask whether she will convert and be baptized or at least live with him *sine contumelia Creatoris* (C. 1121). The interpellations should generally be made by authority of the local Ordinary. In exceptional cases, however, they may be made privately, but in such wise that the fact can be proved in the external forum (C. 1122). The interpellations are required for the validity of the second marriage, unless the Apostolic See makes an exception (C. 1121).

The first valid marriage is *dissolved* only when the baptized party remarries (C. 1126).

763. Special Faculties have been granted by the Constitution *Altitudo* of Paul III, the Constitution *Romani Pontificis* of St. Pius V, and by the Constitution *Populis* of Gregory XIII. C. 1125 extends these to the whole world.

Paul III allowed converts in the West Indies who, as pagans, had several wives, to keep the one they preferred if they could no longer remember which one they married first. — Dispensation from the interpellations is granted *ipso iure;* and the marriage is to be contracted in the customary form.

Pius V allowed some converts of India to retain the wife who would consent to be baptized, provided the residence of the first wife was unknown and it was extremely difficult to find her. The facts had to be proved summarily in extrajudicial form. Dispensation from the interpellations is granted *ipso iure* in such cases.

Gregory XIII made still further concessions regarding the marriages of those pagan couples, one or both parties of which were carried off by enemies into distant lands so that when one converted it was impossible to make the interpellations. For such cases the Pope gave certain priests (since the Code this applies especially to local Ordinaries, pastors, and quasi-pastors) the faculties to dispense from the interpellations, after it was summarily and extrajudicially proved that the unbaptized party either could not be interpellated or did not answer the interpellation within the time determined. — Under such circumstances the new marriages must be contracted in the prescribed form, and may be entered into with any member of the Faith. (One need not, as in the two preceding cases, have previously lived as husband or wife with the respective person.) These marriages are valid even if it later becomes known that the other party was unable to answer the interpellation or was even baptized.

764. — II. Separation from bed and board, the bond remaining, (divorce in a limited sense) is possible by mutual agreement, and in some cases also against the will of one of the parties.

1. *Mutual consent* suffices for separation if there is a just cause (Cf. C. 1128).

Such a reason is invincible mutual aversion. — Two people may also separate for some higher motive, be the separation complete or in part, perpetual or temporary. In doing so they must pay due regard to the welfare of their children and the danger of incontinence.

2. *Without mutual consent* separation may take place because of adultery or on other serious grounds.

a) Adultery is cause for perpetual separation (C. 1129).

The adultery must be formal, complete and morally certain. Sodomy and bestiality are equivalent to adultery. It is always presupposed that the innocent party did not consent to the adultery nor induce its commission (e.g., by frequent refusal of the marriage debt, abandonment of common life; quarrelling or serious lack of love is not sufficient), nor is guilty of the same crime, nor has explicitly or implicitly condoned it. Tacit forgiveness is had if the innocent party with full knowledge of the adultery nevertheless freely consents to conjugal relations; forgiveness is legally presumed if within six months the guilty party has not been dismissed nor deserted nor duly denounced (C. 1129). Separation may be made on private authority if the adultery can be proved to a certainty or is publicly known; but it is advisable to take judicial action at least subsequently (C. 1130). — The innocent party retains the right to admit or recall the guilty partner to married life, unless with the consent of the innocent party the latter has chosen a state incompatible with matrimony (C. 1130).

765. b) *Other reasons* justify only a temporary separation.

Such reasons are: if one's partner joins a non-Catholic sect or educates the children as non-Catholics, if he leads a criminal and disgraceful life, or is the cause of physical or spiritual danger to his consort, or if his cruelty renders common life too difficult, etc. (C. 1131). — Separation on private authority is lawful only when the grounds are certain and there is danger in delay; otherwise one must have the approval of the local Ordinary (C. 1131). Sometimes a person who fails to have recourse to the bishop may be left in good faith. — Restoration of married life is a duty when the reasons for separation cease. If the local Ordinary has declared a separation for a definite or an indefinite length of time the innocent party is not obliged to resume common life until the period has elapsed or until ordered to do so by the bishop (C. 1131). After the separation the education of the children belongs to the innocent party; but if one of the. parties is a non-Catholic the right to the education of the children belongs to the Catholic party. In both instances, however, the local Ordinary can decide otherwise if this is to the best interest of the children and their Catholic education is safeguarded. (C. 1132).

766. N.B. *Catholics and the Civil Law.*

Most States not only recognize the right of separation, but also complete dissolution of the marriage bond, even though it be a consummated marriage between Christians. Such a "divorce" has no effect before God.

A suit for the *complete divorce* of validly married persons is not allowed even though the plaintiff has no intention of remarrying. Such a suit would give the divorced person an opportunity to remarry invalidly. Such procedure is lawful only when one cannot otherwise obtain certain civil effects to which he has a right (e.g., separation from bed and board), provided he had no intention of remarrying. Before one sues for divorce he should obtain permission of the ecclesiastical authorities and promise in writing that he intends only to procure its civil effects.

A *Catholic judge* who by reason of his office must accept a divorce case may, according to a probable opinion, co-operate in granting the divorce, since he may consider the divorce a mere civil formality like civil marriage itself. The judge must avoid scandal as far as possible and remind the Catholic parties of the law of the Church. The Holy See at times has passed strict regulations for special cases of scandal.

A *Catholic attorney* may not accept an unlawful divorce suit. If appointed to give gratuitous legal service to the poor, that which was said of the judge also applies to him. — Likewise, Catholic lawyers may take part in a divorce suit when the interest of religion is at stake. This obtains if there is hope that the parties will have recourse to Catholic attorneys and these in many instances can bring about a reconciliation. Scandal must be avoided as far as possible.

767. Chapter X
VALIDATION OF INVALID MARRIAGES

Validation of a marriage consists in this, that a marriage already contracted, but null and void, in subsequently made valid. The two ways of doing this are simple validation and *sanatio in radice*.

I. Simple validation consists in removing the cause which made the marriage invalid and renewing matrimonial consent. From the moment consent is renewed the marriage is valid.

The *renewal of consent* must be a new act of the will ratifying a marriage known to have been invalid from the beginning (C. 1134).

Validation differs according as the marriage is null by reason of a diriment impediment, lack of consent or defect of form.

1. In case of a *diriment impediment* validation requires:

a) *That the impediment be removed.*

The impediment may cease either automatically (nonage, marriage bond), by a dispensation (consanguinity, affinity) or by a change in legislation. Thus if marriage was invalidly contracted by reason of affinity, which was invalidating only before the present Code went into effect, this impediment requires no dispensation since May 19, 1918. The marriage does not become valid, however, before consent has been renewed in the manner prescribed.

If the impediment *cannot be dispensed* from and both parties are in good faith, they should be left so if one has reason to fear they will not separate, or if separation would cause great harm to the children. — If one party is no longer in good faith one should try to have the ecclesiastical court declare the marriage null. If no proof is available the couple should be induced to separate from bed and board. In very exceptional cases they might be permitted to live together as brother and sister, if this can be done without danger of incontinence or public scandal.

768. b) *That the matrimonial consent be renewed* (C. 1133).

Renewal of consent is necessary even if at the time they attempted to contract marriage, both parties gave their consent and never revoked it (C. 1133).

Confer 767 as to what is meant by renewal of consent.

The *manner* of renewing consent varies:

a) If the impediment is *public* both parties must renew their consent in the prescribed manner (C. 1135).

A public impediment is one that can be proved in the juridical forum. — In this case a compeltely new marriage takes place, but without the proclamation of banns, the nuptial blessing or blessing of the ring. — If the impediment is public, but unknown in the respective place, it may often be advisable to avoid scandal by remarrying before a pastor and two witnesses who will be obliged to observe secrecy. However, the validation must be entered in the church books.

β) If the impediment is *occult* and *known to both parties,* it suffices that they renew their consent privately and secretly (C. 1135).

γ) If the impediment is *occult* and *known to only one party* it is enough if this party renews consent privately and secretly, provided the consent of the other party continues (C. 1135).

In a case of doubt the continuation of consent is presumed (C. 1093). — Consent is not necessarily revoked by the reception of a civil divorce nor by abandonment of cohabitation.

δ) If the impediment is *secret* and *unknown to both parties* it suffices to acquaint one of them with the fact who will then renew the matrimonial consent.

If neither can be informed without great danger of their separation to the grave detriment of the children, one should apply for a *sanatio in radice*, mentioning the fact that the impediment is unknown to the parties and that they cannot be informed thereof.

769. — 2. *Lack of consent* renders the following necessary for validation:

a) The *party that did not give valid matrimonial consent* must do so.

On renewal of consent, confer 767.

The renewal may, and at times, must be:

α) *Purely internal* if the defect of consent was purely internal, e.g., in the case of dissimulation.

β) *External,* if the want of consent was also externally recognizable. It is then renewed in the form prescribed for contracting marriage. Renewal must also be external if the lack of consent was public; it is done privately and in secret if the defect was occult (C. 1136).

One or the other of these alternatives will obtain according to circumstances in cases of fear or conditional consent. — Lack of consent is public if it can be proved in the juridical forum.

b) The *party that gave consent must not have revoked it* in the meantime (C. 1136).

Renewal of consent is, therefore, not required of this party.

3. *Defect of form* makes it necessary that the parties contract marriage anew in the manner prescribed (C. 1137).

If a party refuses to reappear before the pastor he should be induced to act by proxy (Cf. 719). If he cannot be persuaded to do this a dispensation from the form should be applied for, (in danger of death the pastor can dispense under certain provisions, Cf. 678), or an application for a *sanatio in radice* made.

770. — II. Sanatio in radice is an act by which, after an impediment has ceased or been dispensed from, marriage is validated and the law of renewing consent is dispensed with and by a fiction of law, marriage is considered as having been valid from the beginning (C. 1138).

The act is called *sanatio in radice,* or "radical sanation" because it now "heals," i.e., makes valid, the matrimonial consent (the "root" of matrimony) which was previously invalid, so that it can produce its natural effects and thus becomes a valid marriage. — Accordingly, the Sacrament of Matrimony is received at the moment the sanation is granted. — The sanation has retroactive power in regard to the canonical effects, just as though the marriage had been valid from the beginning, unless the contrary is expressly stated in the rescript (C. 1138). — If the impediment has not already ceased of itself, the sanation likewise dispenses from it.

1. *The power* to grant a *sanatio in radice* is reserved to the Holy See (C. 1141).

With certain reservations the Apostolic See delegates this power to local Ordinaries in their quinquennial faculties. — The Holy See grants a sanation both in the juridical forum and in the forum of conscience; whereas, local Ordinaries can usually do so only in the juridical forum.

771. — 2. The conditions required for obtaining a *sanatio in radice* are the following:

a) A grave reason.

Such a reason is, for example, if neither of the parties can be told of the invalidity of their marriage without very great harm; if one party really consents to marriage but cannot be induced to express it in a manner valid in the eyes of the Church. — The petition for the sanation must contain the reason.

b) Invalidity of the marriage because of a *diriment impediment of ecclesiastical law* or *lack of form* (C. 1139).

No sanation is granted if the invalidity is due to an impediment of divine law (e.g., the marriage bond). Marriage is not validated *in radice* if such an impediment is removed (e.g., by the death of the previous consort), not even from the moment when the impediment has ceased (C. 1139).

c) *Continuation of matrimonial consent,* i.e., of such consent as would be required by natural law for a valid marriage (C. 1139).

If neither or only one of the parties consents to the marriage, a sanation cannot be granted, whether the consent was lacking from the beginning or was only revoked later (C. 1140). — Consent may still exist though both know they cannot contract a valid marriage, and it may still continue though both are resolved to separate should it be possible. — Concerning the continuation of matrimonial consent confer 768. — If consent was wanting in the beginning but given later, validation can be granted from the moment the consent was given (C. 1140). — A sanation may be granted with the knowledge of both parties or only of one, or of neither.

APPENDIX

772. Chapter I

SACRAMENTALS

I. Concept. Sacramentals are objects or actions which the Church uses, in imitation of the Sacraments, to obtain favors, especially spiritual ones, through her intercession (C. 1144).

Sacramentals, therefore, have their power primarily through the intercession of the Church; but much depends upon the disposition of the minister and the recipient. — Sacramentals never directly confer an increase of sanctifying grace or remission of sins, but they give us the help of grace necessary to make it easy to obtain an increase in sanctifying grace or the forgiveness of sin.

773. — **II. Division.** 1. Sacramentals may be sacred *objects or actions.*

Objects (holy water, scapulars, blessed ashes, etc.) enable us to obtain certain divine favors by using them.

By actions the blessing of God is immediately invoked upon man.

2. Actions may be *blessings or exorcisms* according as they are employed to effect some supernatural positive effect or to overcome the power of the devil.

a) Blessings are *constitutive* or *invocative* according as through them persons or things are permanently set aside for the service of God, or the blessing of God is merely called down upon them.

b) Constitutive blessings are either *consecrations* or *simple blessings* according as they are given with the holy oils or not.

c) Concerning exorcism confer C. 189.

774. — **III. Minister.** The legitimate minister of the sacramentals is a cleric to whom the Church has given the corresponding faculties and to whom the exercise of these faculties is not forbidden (C. 1146).

The power to *consecrate* is given only to bishops and to those who have received a special apostolic indult (C. 1147).

All *other blessings* which are not reserved may be given by any priest (C. 1147). Special faculties are necessary to attach an indulgence to a blessing. — Whoever, without special faculties, gives a reserved blessing (not an indulgence), does so illicitly but validly, unless the contrary is especially mentioned in the reservation (C. 1147). Consecrations are always excepted (C. 1147). — An ordinary priest can, therefore, bless fields, fruit, etc. privately. But without the pastor's permission he may not give the nuptial blessing, nor bless baptismal water; neither can he solemnly bless fields, fruits, etc., since these blessings are reserved to the pastor.

A deacon can bless the Easter candle. The Ordinary or pastor for a good reason can also allow him to conduct a burial service; but in doing so he must wear the stole after the manner of deacons. He may not wear the cope, but does everything else the same as a priest. — Concerning Baptism and the distribution of Holy Communion by a deacon confer C. 471 and 498.

Lectors may bless bread and fruits.

775. — IV. Recipients. 1. Sacramentals are to be administered primarily to *Catholics* and *catechumens* (C. 1149).

Excommunicated or interdicted persons may not receive them if they have incurred these censures by a declaratory or condemnatory sentence (C. 2260, 2275).

2. Non-Catholics may also receive sacramentals unless they are excluded in individual cases (C. 1149).

Thus one may give them blessed candles, palms or ashes. One must always beware of superstition. It is forbidden to give non-Catholics the nuptial blessing.

V. Rite.

The Rites prescribed by the Church must be observed for the valid administration of sacramentals (C. 1148).

776.   Chapter II

INDULGENCES

Article I

Indulgences in General

I. Concept. An indulgence is a remission of the temporal punishment due to sin granted by the Church after the guilt of sin has been remitted (C. 911).

The guilt of sin and the eternal punishment are remitted by sacramental absolution or by perfect contrition. The temporal punishment which remains to be expiated either here on earth or in purgatory may be remitted by the Sacrament of Penance, by other voluntary works of satisfaction, and especially by indulgences. — By granting indulgences the Church remits the satisfaction for sin which is due to God by drawing on the merits of Christ and the Saints.

II. Division. 1. Indulgences are *plenary or partial* according as they remit all or only a definite amount of the temporal punishment due to sin.

If one does not fully gain a plenary indulgence he gains a partial indulgence in keeping with his dispositions (C. 926).

By a partial indulgence of a certain number of specified days or years one receives a remission of as much temporal punishment due to sin as he would have expiated by performing the canonical penance in the early Church for the corresponding length of time. Since the penitential discipline of the forty-days fast was much stricter than on other days more punishment was thereby expiated. Wherefore, an indulgence of seven quarantines was formerly added to an indulgence of seven years to indicate the remission of temporal punishment commenurate with the canonical penances which were performed during the fasting season. Just as the canonical penances formerly remitted punishment in proportion to the earnestness of the penitent's disposition, so also in gaining an indulgence, more punishment is remitted if the disposition of the penitent is more sincere.

777. — 2. Indulgences are *for the living or the*

dead according as they can be gained for the living or also for those deceased.

All indulgences granted by the Apotolic See may be gained for the Holy Souls, unless otherwise specified. No one can gain an indulgence for another living person (C. 930).

The Church grants indulgences to the living by way of absolution, and to the deceased by way of suffrage. — The effect of an indulgence for the living is, therefore, infallible, provided all required conditions obtain. Indulgences for the dead are infallible only in so far as all prayer is infallible. Therefore, it cannot be determined whether, or in how far, a certain soul benefits by an indulgence.

3. Indulgences are *personal, real or local* according as they are immediately applied to a person (e.g., a confraternity) or are immediately attached to an object (e.g., rosary, crucifix) or to a certain place (e.g., church, altar).

The object to which an indulgence is to be attached must be solid and not easily breakable. Rosary beads may be made of solid glass. (AAS 18-24).

The indulgences attached to a rosary or other object are *lost* if the object is entirely destroyed or sold (C. 924). Thus if one has already gained indulgences with a blessed rosary he can give it to another (lend it or give it away) who may also gain the indulgences attached to it. But as soon as such a rosary is sold it loses its indulgences. A buyer can have a bought rosary blessed with indulgences, even though he has not paid for it. — A rosary can be rechained without losing its indulgences; and in doing so the beads need not be strung in any particular succession. Neither are the indulgences lost if a few beads (4—5) are lost and replaced by unblessed beads; in this manner all the beads may by and by be replaced. — Indulgences attached to a church do not cease by the complete destruction of the church provided it is rebuilt within fifty years on the same or nearly the same spot and under the same title. (C. 924.)

778. — III. Gaining an indulgence requires a person competent to gain it, the intention to gain it, and the performance of the prescribed work.

1. *He is competent* to gain an indulgence who is baptized, free from excommunication, in the state of grace at least when he performs the last of the prescribed works, and who is a subject of him who granted the indulgence (C. 925).

It is controverted whether one must be in the state of grace to gain an indulgence for the dead.

2. *The intention* required to gain an indulgence must at least be a general one (C. 925).

According to a practically certain opinion an implicit habitual intention suffices (Cf. 450). However, it is advisable to renew the intention at least every morning.

779. — 3. *The prescribed works* are principally confession, Communion, visiting the church, and prayers.

When it is specified that an indulgence is to be gained on *the usual conditions* the following are necessary: Confession, Holy Communion, Visit to a church or public chapel (according to Canon 929 a semi-public chapel is also meant), and prayers for the Holy Father's intentions.

If the contrary is not expressly mentioned one cannot gain an indulgence by doing a good work which he is *already bound to perform by law or precept*. However, by doing a good work enjoined as a penance in confession one can likewise gain any indulgences that may be attached thereto (C. 932). — *By repetition* of one and the same work to which a plenary indulgence is attached one cannot gain more than one plenary indulgence each day, unless the contrary is explicitly permitted (C. 928), e.g., the Portiuncula Indulgence. But by the performance of a different work to which a plenary indulgence is attached one can gain another plenary indulgence the same day. — A partial indulgence may be gained repeatedly the same day by repetition of the same work, unless the contrary is explicitly stated (C. 928).

One cannot gain more than one indulgence by one and the same work which has been enriched with several indulgences on various titles. Confession and Communion are exceptions to this rule, as well as other special concessions to this effect (C. 933).

a) Confession is also required of those who have no mortal sins to confess.

It may be made within eight days preceding the day for gaining
the indulgence or within the octave following; it may be made
any time within the octave following a triduum, a novena, retreat,
mission, etc. — Those who confess at least twice a month or communicate almost daily (5 times a week), unless they are legitimately
hindered, need not make a special Confession to gain an indulgence
(C. 930).

780. *b) Holy Communion* may be received the day
before (e.g., Aug. 1, for Portiuncula) one intends to
gain the indulgence as also during the octave following
the feast, triduum, novena, etc. (C. 931).

According to Canon 933 it seems that this *one* Communion
(similar to what was said about confession) suffices for all the
indulgences that one wishes to gain during the novena, octave, etc.

The prescribed confession and Holy Communion need not be
made in the church where one intends to gain the indulgence. —
The obligatory Easter Communion also suffices, except for gaining
a Jubilee indulgence. — Confession and Holy Communion are not
prescribed for gaining the Indulgences attached to saying the Stations of the Cross; perfect contrition suffices.

c) The visiting of a church which is sometimes required may take place any time between noon of the
preceding day and midnight of the day set for gaining
the indulgence (C. 923).

This "visit to a church" may be combined with one's assistance
at a *Mass of obligation,* since during a Mass at which one is
obliged to attend (e.g., on Sundays) he may pray for any intention
he pleases, and since one may attend a Mass of obligation also
outside the church.

If one *cannot enter* the church either because of the crowd of
people making visits or because the doors happen to be locked
at the time, he may say the prayers outside. When the visit to a
church or public chapel in general is required persons who, living in
a convent, orphanage, hospital, sanatorium or educational institution, either leading a community life or residing there to serve
the inmates, may gain the indulgence by visiting the chapel of the
institution where they can fulfill their Sunday obligation, provided

they perform the other works prescribed and provided their institution has been erected with the consent of the Ordinary (C. 929). This concession does not hold when the visitation of a particular church or chapel is prescribed, as, for example, for gaining the Portiuncula Indulgence. Neither does it hold for those institutions which are erected by secular authorities without the co-operation or consent of the Ordinary, even though the latter has permitted a chapel to be erected therein. Finally, the concession does not apply to those who are detained in prison.

781. *d) The prayers* to be said according to the intentions of the Holy Father are left to the choice of the person gaining the indulgence, unless certain prayers are prescribed. The prayers must be said orally, at least in part; meditation alone is insufficient (C. 934).

If an indulgence is gained on condition that one "prays for the intention of the Holy Father" it suffices, according to a declaration of the Sacred Penitentiary, Sept. 20, 1933, to say an *Our Father, Hail Mary* and *Glory be to the Father,* or another prayer of similar length (AAS 25-446; 26-108). — To gain the *Portiuncula Indulgence* and all *toties quoties* indulgences which require that a church be visited one may not substitute any other prayers for the six *Our Fathers, Hail Marys* and *Glorys.*

If a *special prayer* is prescribed it may be said in any language. It must be certain, however, either by a declaration of the Sacred Penitentiary or local Ordinary that the translation is exact. If anything is added, omitted or interpolated one does not gain the indulgence (C. 934). However, indulgences are not lost, according to a declaration of the Sacred Penitentiary, Nov. 26, 1934, by every addition, subtraction or interpolation, but only by those that alter the substance of the prayer (AAS 26-643).

One may *alternate* with another in saying the prayers or mentally follow while another recites them (C. 934). *Mutes* can gain an indulgence attached to public prayers if together with the other faithful they devoutly raise their hearts to God. They may recite private prayers either mentally or by the sign language or merely read by sight (C. 936).

Indulgences attached to *ejaculations* can be gained by all the faithful even if they are not recited orally, but only mentally (AAS 26-35).

782. *e*) A confessor can *commute* the prescribed work for one legitimately hindered from performing it (C. 935).

The prescribed work in this case must be commuted into a work that is morally its equivalent, with due regard for the abilities of the person, for whose sake the commutation is made.

This commutation may be made by any priest approved for hearing confessions, even apart from confession. Thus a confessor may change a prescribed Holy Communion into some other good work for children who have not yet made their First Holy Communion or for such as are hindered from communicating, e.g., by illness. — The conditions alone may be commuted, not the object nor the reason for the indulgence.

Only the things prescribed as conditions for gaining the indulgence may be commuted; not, however, the object nor the objective of the indulgence. Thus if making the Stations is to be substituted by another work the use of a specially blessed cross is positively necessary. In like manner frequent Communion cannot be interchanged for some other good work if the indulgence is granted precisely on account of frequent Communion. The same holds for gaining indulgences granted for visiting shrines of pilgrimage. — On the other hand, the visiting of a designated church, which is prescribed for gaining a *toties quoties* indulgence or the Portiuncula Indulgence, can be commuted into some other work (AAS 32-62).

783.   *Article II*

Some Special Indulgences

I. The Death Indulgence is gained at the moment when the soul is separated from the body. It can be gained in various ways.

1. *The Apostolic Blessing at the moment of death.*

Any priest assisting the dying (even though not approved) is *authorized* to give this blessing according to the formula of the ritual (C. 468). — *Any one* in danger of death may receive it (the sick, soldiers before battle, those to be executed). It must be refused to excommunicated persons, to the impenitent and those dying in public mortal sin. — The *essential conditions* for gaining this plenary indulgence are: α) that the sick person call upon the Name of Jesus, orally if possible, but at least in his heart (e.g., "My Jesus, Mercy"). It is here a question of an indispensable condition; β) that he accept sickness and death with resignation to God's Will. (Both conditions will be fulfilled if the dying person recites the prayer: "Jesus, for Thee I live; O Jesus, for Thee I die, etc."); γ) if possible the person should also receive Holy Communion. — If the conditions were not fulfilled, e.g., in one unconscious, they may be supplied later. — The Apostolic Blessing can be given *only once* in any grave illness with danger of death, even though the illness may be prolonged and Extreme Unction may be repeated because a new danger of death has set in. (Cf. 630). Neither is it to be repeated if the sick person was in the state of mortal sin when it was given or sins gravely thereafter; since it suffices that one be in the state of grace at the moment of death. — The Apostolic Blessing may be repeated only in case the sick person recovers and is then placed in a new danger of death; however, repetition is not necessary to gain the death indulgence.

784. — 2. *The Possession of an object of devotion to which Apostolic Indulgences are attached.*

Among these Apostolic Indulgences is the plenary indulgence at the hour of death. — The sick person should if possible confess and communicate and accept death with resignation to God's Will, and with a contrite heart call upon the Name of Jesus, orally, if possible; furthermore, the dying person must have the object of devotion with him. He need not necessarily touch it; it suffices that the article be on the bed or at the bedside, even though the sick person does not advert to the presence of the object.

3. *The Crucifix to which there has been attached the death indulgence toties quoties.*

This differs from other objects of devotion to which the Apostolic Indulgences are attached in this, that the dying person must kiss the crucifix or touch it in some way. The cross need not, however, belong to the dying person; on the contrary, it may be presented to many dying persons all of whom can gain the indulgence.

Furthermore, the following conditions are also required: Confession, Communion, invocation of the name of Jesus and accepting death with resignation to God's Will as above.

4. Finally, a plenary indulgence may be gained by the dying who say *certain prayers* or belong to *certain confraternities.*

785. — II. The Papal Blessing with a plenary indulgence may be given twice a year by the Ordinary of the diocese (C. 914).

Conditions for gaining this indulgence are: the reception of the Sacraments and prayers for the intention of the Holy Father.

Regulars who have the privilege of giving the Papal Blessing may do so only in their own churches and in the churches of nuns and tertiaries legitimately affiliated to their Order; but not on the same day and place (village or city) on which the bishop grants it (C. 915). This regulation does not apply to the Papal Blessing which is given, e.g., at the end of a mission.

The formula which regulars must use is found in the Roman Ritual, Title VIII. c. 32. According to a decision of the Sacred Congregation of Rites, March 12, 1940, this same formula must be used by *all priests,* whether secular or regular, who have a special indult from the Holy See for imparting the Papal Benediction with the plenary indulgence. If the indult requires that the blessing be given at the end of the sermon, then one makes the sign of the cross with the crucifix, saying: *Benedictio Dei omnipotentis, etc.* (Rom. Rit. Appendix. Bened. faciendae a sacerdotibus Ap. Indultum habentibus.)

III. The Privileged Altar is an altar at which a priest can gain a plenary indulgence for a soul in Purgatory for whom he says Mass at the altar.

No other condition is required save offering the Holy Sacrifice. — This indulgence differs from other indulgences principally because it is more certain of being gained. For particulars, confer 535.

It is becoming, though not necessary, that a Requiem Mass be said when the rubrics permit.

On All Souls' Day, November 2 (and during the octave of the commemoration of All Souls), all Masses that are celebrated are as those said at a privileged altar. All altars in a church are privileged during the time of Forty Hours Adoration (C. 917). — Some priests enjoy the personal right of a privileged altar.

786. — IV. The Gregorian Masses are thirty Masses said on thirty consecutive days for a deceased person.

From very early times the faithful have piously believed that God will free the respective soul from Purgatory at the intercession of Saint Gregory. However, there is no plenary indulgence connected with these Masses. For details confer 535. — In some places six Masses said consecutively are designated as Gregorian Masses. This custom is laudable, but not expressly sanctioned by the Church, nor is it so well-founded as the thirty Masses regarding the effects hoped for.

787. — V. The Station Indulgences are those gained by visiting the stations of the Way of the Cross in Jerusalem.

According to a recent decision one can gain a plenary indulgence as often as (toties quoties) one makes the Stations with a contrite heart and according to the prescriptions of the Holy See; besides, one can gain another plenary indulgence if one receives Holy Communion on the day he makes the Stations. — If for any good reason one is unable to finish the Stations once he has begun, an indulgence of ten years is gained for each Station visited. — This holds as well for those who gain the station indulgence by the use of the Station Crucifix (Cf. 790). If for any reasonable cause one is unable to finish reciting all the *Our Fathers,* he gains an indulgence of ten years each time he says the *Our Father, Hail Mary* and *Glory be to the Father.*

1. *Conditions for gaining these indulgences: a) meditation* even though it be brief, on the Passion of Christ. This meditation can be on the Passion in general, though it is better to make it on the theme of the respective Station.

b) Corporal movement from station to station. This is always required for the private praying of the Stations. — Whenever it might cause confusion (for the whole crowd to attempt to pass from station to station) each one may remain in his own place while the priest with two servers or choristers goes from station to station, pausing at each to recite the usual prayers, the faithful staying at their places and responding alternately. In the oratories of religious, where on account of lack of space all the religious cannot move together from station to station without causing a disturbance, they can gain the station indulgences if one religious, man or woman, walks around and recites the usual prayers at each station, while the others remain in their places and there rise and genuflect for each station. The faithful living in common as mentioned in C. 929 can gain the indulgences of the Way of the Cross under the same circumstances as those described for religious if one man or woman passes from station to station and recites the usual prayers (Sacred Penitentiary, March 20, 1946, AAS 38-160). Those indults which contain further concessions in this regard and which were given to some dioceses are not revoked by this decision. Accordingly, if it is hard to understand the priest who goes about from station to station, a second priest may lead the prayers from the pulpit or from some other advantageous position, while the people stand and kneel at each station, or stand and at least genuflect. According to an indult granted to some dioceses it suffices that only one priest be present who leads the prayers from the pulpit while the faithful, remaining at their places, stand and kneel as the individual stations are prayed.

c) *No temporal interruption* is permitted while visiting the stations. A brief interruption (of about ten minutes) would not affect the gaining of the indulgences.

788. — 2. *Erection of the Stations.* a) According to a decree of March 12, 1938 (AAS 30-111) the written documents formerly required for validity *before erecting the stations* are no longer required. Validity requires only that the priest have the necessary faculties to erect the stations and be requested to erect them. In the interest of ecclesiastical discipline, however, it is altogether proper that (unless the place enjoys exemption) the permission of the Ordinary of the respective district be obtained whenever the stations are erected. If time does not permit one to apply to the local Ordinary one must be able reasonably to presume his permission. — Delegation to bless the stations is granted by the Sacred Penitentiary, to which one must apply with a recommendation from his own Ordinary (AAS 25-170). Members of the Franciscan Order can also obtain permission from their competent Superiors.

b) *The Blessing and Erection of the Stations.* The Rite prescribed in the ritual for this purpose is required for validity. It is not prescribed that the making of the stations follow the blessing. — Validity demands that the crosses be made of wood; wooden crosses encased in crosses made of iron would be invalid. Pictorial representations of the Passion of Christ are not necessary. — In blessing the Stations the priest must be morally present in the place where they are to be erected. The blessing may be done from the altar. In the convents of women with papal enclosure the blessing may be done at the grill. — The crosses may be blessed either before or after they are fixed in their proper place. — The crosses may be put in place either by the priest or by the others, even privately and without any ceremony.

c) After erecting the Stations the priest who erected them must make a memorandum, in which he indicates that he erected the Stations and by whose power he did so. He must sign the document, which is thereafter kept in the parish archives. If he received delegation from the Ordinary the latter must receive a certificate. — Exhibition of the memorandum and conservation of documents are not necessary for validity.

789. — 3. *A sanation* for all validly erected Stations was granted by the Sacred Penitentiary on March 12, 1938. Such a general sanation seems only to refer, as former general sanations, to the blessing, legal formalities and documents; not to those cases where, for instance, crosses made of iron were erected.

4. *Cessation of the Indulgences.* The indulgences are lost: a) if at least seven of the crosses are destroyed or removed either at one time or one after the other; b) if the stations are transferred to a morally different place.

One or the other cross may be replaced without a new blessing's being necessary.

Changing the sequence of the crosses or rearrangement of the stations in the same church or place is allowed. — The stations may be removed entirely for a short length of time. If the stations are renovated (e.g., new crosses are inserted) at the same place where they were erected they may be blessed by a lawfully delegated priest; the consent of the Ordinary, etc. need not be obtained.

790. — 5. *Station Crucifixes* may be used to gain the indulgences when one is legitimately hindered from making the Way of the Cross.

The image of the Crucified Redeemer must be attached to the cross or at least it must stand out in relief thereon. The indulgences are attached to the image of Christ which must, therefore, be made of strong material (brass, hard wood; but not lead or tin).

The blessing is given *unico signo crucis nihil dicendo.* One can bless several crosses simultaneously, and affix to them also other indulgences, e.g., Papal Indulgences.

One may be hindered from praying the stations by illness or other reasons (e.g., journey).

To gain the indulgences it is necessary to hold the crucifix in one's hand, and meditate on the Passion of Christ while saying twenty *Our Fathers, Hail Marys* and *Glorys*. If due to manual occupation or other good reasons, one is unable to hold the station crucifix in one's hand, he may, according to a decision of the Penitentiary, Nov. 9, 1933, carry it about him in some manner while praying (AAS 25-502). If several persons take part in the common prayers and they cannot each hold a crucifix, at least the one leading the prayers should do so, while the others pray with him, or alternate in praying or merely follow the prayers mentally. — Of the twenty *Our Fathers*, etc., 14 are said in place of visiting the stations, 5 in memory of the five wounds and one for the intention of the Holy Father. — Sick people who can no longer say 20 *Our Fathers*, etc., without great difficulty may gain the indulgence by kissing a crucifix blessed especially for this purpose and held by a priest or other person, or by merely looking upon the crucifix with sentiments of contrition, while saying a short prayer or ejaculation in memory of the Passion and Death of Our Savior (AAS 23-167). If they are so ill that they cannot even say an ejaculatory prayer they can still gain the plenary indulgence by kissing or looking at the crucifix (AAS 23-523). — The confessor may commute the prayers if the provisions of C. 935 (Cf. 782 above) are observed; but the use of a specially blessed crucifix and the pious remembrance of the Passion of Christ are always required. — The crucifix may also be loaned to another or given away (Cf. 777).

791. — VI. Rosary Indulgences.

By reciting the ordinary rosary of five decades, one can gain an indulgence of five years, even though the rosary is not blessed. By the blessing of a competent priest the following indulgences may also be attached to such a rosary; the Crozier, the Dominican and the Apostolic Indulgences. — If the *Crozier Indulgence* is attached one can gain an indulgence of 500 days as often as he says an *Our Father* or *Hail Mary* on the rosary. It is not necessary to have the intention to pray the entire rosary. Neither is a meditation on the mysteries prescribed. — If the *Dominican Indulgences* have been attached to a rosary one may gain an indulgence of 100 days for every *Our Father* or *Hail Mary,* and other indulgences if one prays the rosary over a certain period of time, or in common, or if he belongs to the Confraternity of the Holy Rosary. To gain the indulgence it is necessary to hold the rosary in one's hand and use it while praying and meditating upon the mysteries (when recited in common only one need have a rosary). — The *Apostolic Indulgences* are contained in a list of indulgences which every pope reapproves and promulgates shortly after his coronation. There is a plenary indulgence for the dying included therein (Cf. 784). These indulgences can also be attached to other objects of devotion (e.g., medals) by a blessing. To gain the indulgences one must carry the devotional object with him or keep it in a becoming manner at home.

Members of a family who recite the *Family Rosary* (five decades) each day in the week may gain a plenary indulgence every Saturday, on two other days of the week and on feasts of the Blessed Virgin.

According to a decision of June 14, 1922 the Apostolic Indulgences can be gained *at the same time* with other indulgences affixed to the same object or works (e.g., Apostolic and Crozier Indulgences). — According to a concession of June 12, 1907 the Dominican and Crozier indulgences may be gained simultaneously.

For gaining indulgences attached to the saying of the rosary it is generally prescribed that one *hold the rosary in his hand.* From a decision of the Sacred Penitentiary, Nov. 9, 1933, we learn that one may gain the same indulgences by merely having the blessed rosary about his person provided one is impeded from holding it in the hand because of manual occupation or for some other reasonable cause (AAS 25-502).

792. — VII. Scapular Indulgences.

The conditions for gaining these indulgences are:

a) The first pair of scapulars that one wears must be *blessed* by an authorized priest. — Scapulars that replace the first pair need not be blessed.

b) Investing with the scapular must be done by a priest authorized to do so. — One and the same blessed scapular may be imposed on a number of people successively.

c) The *names* of those invested must be entered in the *Confraternity register* if the reception in a Confraternity takes place with the investment, as is done with the scapular of the Blessed Trinity, the Seven Dolors and Carmelite Scapulars. — Some, however, have the privilege of enrolling people without the obligation of entering their names in the Scapular Confraternity, e.g., the members of the *Unio Cleri pro missionibus.*

Special conditions are required for obtaining the *privilegium sabbatinum* which is connected with the Carmelite scapular; but these conditions can be commuted by a priest with faculties to do so.

d) The scapular *must be worn* in such wise that one part hangs suspended on the breast; the other, on the back. It may be worn over the garment or next to the skin. — If one does not wear the scapular for a length of time, he does not meanwhile gain the indulgences. A temporary laying aside of the scapular is permitted, e.g., in bathing. If one resumes wearing the scapular after neglecting to do so for a long time he gains the indulgences forthwith, no new investment being necessary, unless one has taken the scapular off in contempt.

792. — *A Scapular Medal* may be worn instead of the scapular (with the exception of the Third Order scapular). It is necessary, however, that one have been validly invested with the scapular. — The medal may be carried in any manner desired (e.g., even in the pocket). Apparently one must also carry or wear it at night. If one carries his scapular medal, e.g., on his rosary or in his pocket he could use a different one at night. — The scapular medal must have a picture of Our Lord with His Sacred Heart on one side and one of the Blessed Mother on the other. — Any priest who is authorized to bless a scapular can also bless scapular medals. He does so with a simple sign of the cross which must be repeated as many times as there are scapulars to be replaced by the medal. This also applies for him who can bless the fivefold scapular with one collective formula. A great number of medals can also be blessed simultaneously to be distributed later to those who ask for them, even to those who are to be invested after the medals have been blessed. Unlike scapulars, a scapular medal can be replaced only by another blessed scapular medal.

794.   Chapter III

FORMULARY

Letters to the Bishop

1. *For Mixed-Marriage Dispensation.*

Your Excellency:

John Smith, a Catholic of St. Mary's parish, wishing to contract marriage with Bertha White, baptized in the Lutheran sect (*or* an unbaptized person), humbly begs a dispensation from the impediment of mixed religion (*or* disparity of cult). The reasons are . . .

I herewith enclose the promises which in my judgment were made and signed in all sincerity.

Enclosed find $ . . . . . as alms.

Respectfully,

REV. JAMES BROWN

795. — 2. *For an Impediment Other Than Mixed Religion or Disparity of Cult.*

Your Excellency:

John Smith of St. Mary's parish, and Bertha White of St. John's parish (*or* both of St. John's parish), humbly beg a dispensation from the impediment of . . . in order to contract marriage (*or* in order to have their marriage validated).

The canonical reasons are: . . .

Enclosed please find $ . . . . . as alms.

Respectfully,

REV. JAMES BROWN

796. — 3. *For a "Sanatio in Radice."*

Your Excellency:

John Simth of this parish was civilly married to Bertha White, a non-Catholic, baptized in the Lutheran sect (*or* unbaptized). John Smith is now repentant and wishes to have the marriage validated. The non-Catholic party does not believe in formal promises, nor in the necessity of renewing consent before a priest. However, she is not opposed to the Catholic baptism and education of the children. Both parties love each other sincerely so that there is no danger of a divorce. Therefore, in the name of John Smith, I beg that Your Excellency grant a *sanatio in radice,* thereby removing the impediment of . . . and dispensing from the law concerning the renewal of consent.

Enclosed please find $ . . . . . as alms.

Respectfully,

REV. JAMES BROWN

797. — 4. *For a Dispensation from the Banns.*

Your Excellency:

John Smith of St. Mary's parish, and Bertha White of St. John's parish (*or* both of St. John's parish), humbly pray that Your Excellency grant that a dispensation from the publication (*or* two *or* three) of the banns.

The reason are as follows...

Enclosed please find $.....as alms.

Respectfully,

Rev. James Brown

798. — 5. *Letter Requesting the Mandata after Absolving from a Reserved Censure.*

Reverendissime et Illustrissime Domine:

Titius contraxit excommunicationem Ordinio (Romano Pontifici speciali, ordinario modo) reservatam ob . . . Cum casus urgeret, eum absolvi a censura. Nunc recurrit per me confessarium ad recipienda mandata. Rescriptum benigne dirigatur ad me confessarium Jacobum Brown. (Name and address.)

Omni qua par est reverentia subscribo,

. . . .

Parochus

799. — 6. *Letter Requesting a Dispensation from a Reserved Vow.*

Eminentissime Domine:

Bertha, cum haberet viginti annos, libere et absolute emisit votum perfectae ac perpetuae castitatis (*or* votum ingrediendi in religionem votorum solemnium). Nunc vero, completo vicesimo quinto aetatis anno, in gravi incontinentiae periculo versatur (*or* ob maximas tentationes diffidit se posse continentem agere vitam: *or* iudicio confessarii vocata non est ad vitam regularem). Quamobrem humillime supplicat pro dispensatione voti, ita ut matrimonium contrahere possit.

Responsum dignetur mittere Eminentia Vestra Rev.ma infrascripto confessario.

Jacobus Brown,

(Address and Date)

800. — 7. *Letter Requesting a Dispensation from an Occult Marriage Impediment.*

Eminentia Reverendissima:

Johannes et Bertha, annorum triginta quinque nata, affines in primo gradu aequali lineae collateralis (super quo impedimento in alio libello supplici petitur dispensatio pro foro externo), vivente adhuc prima uxore Johannis adulterium inter se consummarunt et fidem sibi mutuo dederunt de matrimonio ineundo post mortem primae uxoris. Paulo postea prima uxor Johannis diuturno morbo, quo laborabat, mortua est. Matrimonio igitur, quod Johannis et Bertha contrahere volunt, praeter impedimentum affinitatis obstat quoque impedimentum criminis, quod omnio occultum mansit. Ideo oratores humiliter supplicant pro gratia dispensationis super impedimento.

Causae vero sunt: aetas feminae superadulta, bonum corporale et spirituale prolis ex primo Johannis matrimonio ortae, insuper nimia, suspecta periculosa familiaritas nec non cohabitatio sub eodem tecto, denique propositum contrahendi iam propagatam.

Dignetur Eminentia Vestra executionem dispensationis committere confessario ex approbatis ab oratoribus eligendo atque rescriptum dirigere (mediante agente curiae episcopalis N............... in Urbe) ad infrascriptum.

Eminentiae Vestrae humillimum famulum,

JACOBUS BROWN, PAROCHUS

(Address and Date)

N.B. See 682 for the person to whom the petition is to be made. If the rescript is requested from the Holy See the letter should be addressed:

Alla S Penitenzieria Apostolica
Palazzo del S. Offizio,
Roma, Italy
Eminentissime Princeps

ALPHABETICAL INDEX

(References are to Marginal Numbers)

A

ABBOT, not receiving blessing in contravention of Church regulations 442;
administering Confirmation 488;
minister of Ordination 635.

ABNORMAL, mental states 29 ff.

ABORTION, 212 ff;
excommunication 424, 439;
irregularity 647;
recourse 795.

ABSOLUTION formula 533 ff;
in state of mortal sin 453;
changing and interrupting formula 446;
of a penitent ignorant of religious truth 118, 601;
of persons in occasion of sin 607, 608;
of relapsing sinners 609;
of non-Catholics 558;
conditional 605;
obligation of imparting, deferring, refusing 605, 610;
in danger of death, 579;
absolutio complicis 431, 587;
from reserved sins 585;
from censures 427 ff; 553;
from reserved censures 428 ff;
recourse 797;
punishment for absolving without jurisdiction 442.

ABSOLUTION, general 419.

ABSTINENCE, 387 ff.

ABULIA, 30, 36.

ABUSE, of marriage 757 ff;
self 228.

ACCESSION, natural; 269.

ACCIDENT insurance 313.

ACCOMPLICE, absolution 431; 587 ff;
inquiring after name, 586.

ACCUSATION, in confession 563 ff;
general 551.

ACCUSED, denying the accusation 370;
weakening the testimony of witnesses 374;
flight 204, 208.

ACCUSED person, killing of 214.

ACOLYTE, minor order of 632.

ACQUISITIVE PRESCRIPTION 273.

ACT, circumstances of, 41;
confession 566;
influence on morality, 41;
object of confession 566.

ACTIVITY, personal 3.

ACTS, heroic 69;
human 3 ff;
obstacles 15;
legitimate 422;
moral 38 ff;
incomplete, of married persons 752;
indifferent 38;
object of 40;
voluntary 7 ff.

ACTUS HUMANUS 3 ff;
impediments 15 ff.

ADDED condition in contracts 289.

ADJURATION 189.

ADMINISTRATION, public, of secular offices and property, forbidden to clerics 407.

C

recourse before reception 794;
record after reception 801.

CONVICTS, escape 214;
attendance at non-Catholic
services 126.

CO-OPERATION in sins of others
in general 147;
in sins of injustice 350 ff, 360,
361;
in a crime 424;
of representatives 203;
negative 355, 360.

CORPORALS, washing of 169.

CORRECTION, fraternal 142, 376.

COUGHING, and reception of Holy
Communion 502.

COUNCIL, General, appealing to
434, 441.

COUNSEL, in damages 350, 360,
361;
in crime 424.

COURT pronouncement, declaring
acts legally null 247.

CRANIOTOMY 212 ff.

CREDITORS:
paying 363;
agreement concerning debt
366, 367.

CREMATION 422.

CRIME, marriage impediment
704 ff.

CRIMINAL, killing of 214.

CROSS, stations of the 787 ff;
crucifix 790.

CROZIER INDULGENCES 791.

CRUCIFIX on altar 548;
toties-quoties indulgence for
the dying 784.

CRUCIFIXES, Station 790.

CULT, disparity of 701.

CULTUS latriae, duliae, hyper-
duliae 156.

CURETTAGE 213.

CUSTODIAN of commons, negligence in duty 355.

CUSTOM:
creating a right 45;
abolition of 76, 77;
obstacle to freedom 26 ff.

D

DAMAGE, to property of another 333;
co-operating 350 ff;
counseling 351;
restitution 345;
reparation for 137, 378.

DANCES, co-operation in immoral 151.

DANGER of sin 61;
of life exposing oneself to 208.

DAWN, time limit for beginning
of Mass 544.

DEACON, administering Baptism
471;
administering Holy Com-
munion 498;
blessing of Easter candle 774;
burying the dead 774;
ordination 633;
usurping higher functions 648.

DEAD, apparently, conferring
Sacraments on 461;
absolution 557;
Extreme Unction 628.

DEAF and DUMB, confessions of
570;
gaining indulgences 781.

DEATH, civil declaration of former marriage partner 700.

DEATH, danger of, exposing
oneself to 208;
Baptism in 465;
Holy Communion 503;
duty of confession 556;
administering Sacraments 454;

from irregularities 643;
jurisdiction supplied 582.

DUEL, 216;
books on duelling 401;
penalties 217, 437;
restitution 356.

DULIA 156.

DUTIES, conflicting 70.

DUTY of questioning penitent 604;
in matters concerning purity 242.

DYING:
duty of providing with Sacraments 455, 456;
licit administration of the Sacraments 461, 628;
jurisdiction for confessions of 579, 584;
confession, 557;
absolution from censures 428;
from reserved sins 584;
complex 589;
marriage impediments 676, 678;
assisting at marriage of 739;
indulgences for 783, 784.

DYSTOCIA 213.

E

EASTER COMMUNION 63, 396, 501, 510, 516.

ECTOPIC GESTATION 212 ff.

EDITOR, professional secret 380, 384.

EDUCATION 200;
religious education of children 695.

EFFECTS, imputability of, 13 ff.

EFFECTS of the Sacraments 447 ff.

EGGS, blessed, 169.

EGGS, milk seasoning on days of abstinence 389.

EGOTISM 134.

ELECTION, acceptance of 203;
manifestation of a candidate's faults 374.

ELECTORS, duty of restitution 352.

EMBER DAYS 387.

EMBRACING 236.

EMBRYOTOMY 212.

EMINENT DOMAIN of the state 246.

EMPLOYEE, co-operation with sins of employers 152;
excused from Sunday Mass 198.

EMPLOYER 307.

EMPLOYMENT, contract 307.

ENCLOSURE, obligation 413;
penalties for violation 436.

END or motive, influence on morality 42.

ENEMIES, love of 135 ff.

ENGAGED COUPLES, company-keeping 240, 607;
duties arising from engagement 663;
morose delectation 106, 107;
confession 584, 672;
Confirmation 666;
baptismal record 667;
banns 667 ff;
instruction 672.

ENGAGEMENT, prior to marriage 661.

ENTRY, of Baptism in Registry 486;
of Confirmation 490;
of Mass stipends 541;
of marriage 744;
of Sacred Orders 655.

ENVY 109.

EPIDIDYMIS 213.

EPIKEIA, 56.

EPILEPTICS, irregular 646.

LIES, jocose 368;
officious 368.
LIFE, duties regarding one's own
and that of neighbor 207 ff;
shortening of 208.
LIFE INSURANCE 312;
restitution 356.
LIGHT, sanctuary 169, 520.
LISTENING to detraction 376;
to obscene talk 238.
LITANY, on feast of St. Mark
and Rogation Days 158, 159.
LITURGICAL Books, unauthorized
editions 401.
LOAN 297.
LOANS, liability for extraordinary
expenses 295.
LOBOTOMY 209.
LOCKOUT 307.
LOOKS, immodest 237.
LOOTING of private property in
war 219.
LOST OBJECTS, finding 266 ff.
LOTTERIES 342.
LOVE:
of God 133;
of self 134;
of fellowmen and enemies
135 ff.
LOYALTY to country 205;
oath of allegiance 188;
in promises 290.
LUCID INTERVALS, persons with,
and confession 501;
Holy Communion 501.
LUST 109, 222 ff;
books 401.
LYNCHING 214.
LYING 368.

M

MAKE-UP or dress, occasion of
sin to others 145.

MANICHAEANS on property rights
247.
MANUSCRIPTS 411.
MARGARINE on days of abstinence
389.
MARGIN, buying and selling on
310.
MARITAL INTERCOURSE, of tubercular persons 750.
MARK, indelible, in sacraments
447.
MARK, St., litany on feast of
158, 159.
MARKET PRICE 302.
MARRIAGE ACT, obligation of
rendering 754.
MARRIAGE BOND, as impediment
700;
solution of 761;
form of 729;
impediments: See matrimonial
impediments;
indissolubility of 746;
promise of 704.
MARRIED COUPLES, annulling of
vows 182;
right of inheritance 319;
right to epistolary secrets 382;
mutual rights and duties 201,
746 ff;
property rights 250, 251;
vow of chastity 177, 751.
MARRIED PERSONS, property
rights, joint and separate
250 ff.
MARY, Bl. Virgin, veneration
156.
MASOCHISM 243.
MASS 522 ff;
nuptial 741, 743;
applying nuptial and funeral
Mass 537;
attending on Sundays and
Holydays 63, 195;

POLICE OFFICER:
  killing a criminal 214;
  defending others 215.
POLLUTION 228;
  nightly 229;
  desire for 242;
  in marriage 758 ff.
POLYANDRY 746.
POLYGAMY 746.
POOR, working on Sundays 194;
  and fasting 393;
  and abstinence 394;
  legacies in favor of 321;
  making restitution to 362, 364;
  poor creditors 363;
  canonically poor, definition 689.
POOR SOULS, indulgences 777;
  Masses, 526;
  prayer to 157.
POPE:
  power of jurisdiction 47;
  appeal from Pope to General Council 434, 441;
  personal injury to 431;
  falsification of papal documents 434;
  reserved censures 431 ff;
  reserved sins 599;
  papal benediction 785.
PORTER, Minor Order 632.
PORRO'S OPERATION 213.
PORTIUNCULA, indulgence 779, 780, 781, 782.
POSSESSION, notion and division 245;
  forbidden books 400, 403;
  restoring property of another 337 ff;
  title by prescription 274.
POSSESSION by the devil, irregularity 646.

POSTAL REGULATIONS, violating 281.
POST-MORTEM 209.
  and Caesarean operation 213.
POVERTY, vow 411;
  and marriage dispensations 681.
PRAYER 157;
  condition for gaining indulgences 781;
  to the Saints 157;
  daily 157;
  after Holy Mass 459;
  after ordination 653. See also Breviary, Choir service.
PRAYERBOOKS, approbation for 398.
PREACHER, profession of faith 119.
PRECEPT 46;
  of the three theological virtues 117;
  ten commandments 155 ff;
  of the Church 386 ff.
PRECEPT, Mass of 195.
PRECEPT and law 46;
  commanding an act fobidden under pain of censure 424;
  duty of restitution of lawgiver 350.
PREMATURE BIRTH, inducing 213;
  Baptism 477.
PRESCRIPTION 272, 276, 278, 339;
  title to ownership 274.
PRESENTS 291;
  mention of last will and testament 321;
  inducing sin 280;
  given to children 256.
PRESS:
  clerics collaborating 399;
  in bad publications 150, 399;

If you have enjoyed this book, consider making your next selection from among the following . . .

Prices guaranteed through June 30, 1994.

Popular Hist. of Philosophy. *de la Torre* 15.00
Canons & Decrees/Council of Trent. *Documents* 12.50
Revelations of St. Bridget of Sweden 2.50
St. Catherine Labouré of the Miraculous Medal 12.50
The Glories of Mary. *St. Alphonsus* 9.00
St. Therese, The Little Flower. *Beevers* 4.50
Purgatory Explained. (pocket, unabr.) *Fr. Schouppe* 7.50
Prophecy for Today. *Edward Connor* 4.50
What Will Hell Be Like? *St. Alphonsus Liguori* 75
Saint Michael and the Angels. *Approved Sources* 5.50
Modern Saints—Their Lives & Faces. Book I. *Ball* 18.00
Our Lady of Fatima's Peace Plan from Heaven 75
Divine Favors Granted to St. Joseph. *Pere Binet* 4.00
Padre Pio—The Stigmatist. *Fr. Charles Carty* 13.50
Fatima—The Great Sign. *Francis Johnston* 7.00
The Incorruptibles. *Joan Carroll Cruz* 12.00
St. Anthony—The Wonder Worker of Padua 4.00
The Holy Shroud & Four Visions. *Fr. O'Connell* 2.00
St. Martin de Porres. *Giuliana Cavallini* 11.00
The Secret of the Rosary. *St. Louis De Montfort* 3.00
Confession of a Roman Catholic. *Paul Whitcomb* 1.25
The Catholic Church Has the Answer. *Whitcomb* 1.25
The Sinner's Guide. *Ven. Louis of Granada* 12.00
True Devotion to Mary. *St. Louis De Montfort* 7.00
I Wait for You. *Sr. Josefa Menendez* 75
Words of Love. *Menendez, Betrone, etc.* 5.00
Little Lives of the Great Saints. *Murray* 16.50
Prayer—The Key to Salvation. *Fr. M. Müller* 7.00
Sermons on Our Lady. *St. Francis de Sales* 9.00
Sermons of St. Alphonsus Liguori for Every Sunday 16.50
Alexandrina—The Agony and the Glory. *Johnston* 4.00
Life of Blessed Margaret of Castello. *Fr. W. Bonniwell* 6.00
St. Francis of Paola. *Simi and Segreti* 7.00
Bible History of the Old and New Testaments 10.00
Dialogue of St. Catherine of Siena 9.00
Dolorous Passion of Our Lord. *Emmerich* 15.00
Textual Concordance of the Holy Scriptures. H.B. 35.00
Douay-Rheims Bible. *Leatherbound* 35.00

At your Bookdealer or direct from the Publisher.

Prices guaranteed through June 30, 1994.